INTEREST GROUP POLITICS

INTEREST GROUP POLITICS

Seventh Edition

Edited by

Allan J. Cigler
Burdett A. Loomis
University of Kansas

CQ PRESS

A Division of Congressional Quarterly Inc.
Washington, D.C.

CQ Press
1255 22nd St. NW, Suite 400
Washington, DC 20037

Phone: 202-729-1900; toll-free, 1-866-4CQ-PRESS (1-866-427-7737)

Web: www.cqpress.com

Cover design: McGaughy Design, Centreville, VA

⊚ The paper used in this publication exceeds the requirements of the American National Standard for Information Sciences—Permanence of Paper for Printed Library Materials, ANSI Z39.48-1992.

Printed and bound in the United States of America

10   09   08   07   06   1   2   3   4   5

Library of Congress Cataloging-in-Publication Data

Interest group politics / edited by Allan J. Cigler, Burdett A. Loomis. —
7th ed.
     p.   cm.
  Includes bibliographical references and index.
  ISBN-13: 978-1-933116-76-1 (pbk. : alk. paper)
  ISBN-10: 1-933116-76-5 (pbk. : alk. paper)
 1. Pressure groups—United States. I. Cigler, Allan J. II. Loomis,
Burdett A. III. Title.
 JK1118.I565 2007
  322.4'30973—dc22   2006035661

Contents

IV. Conclusion

Preface

Four years ago, when we were preparing the sixth edition of this book, the terrorist attacks of September 11, 2001, were fresh in our minds, as was the defection of Republican senator Jim Jeffords, who had abandoned his GOP colleagues to caucus with Senate Democrats, thus giving them control of the chamber. Although Rep. Tom DeLay was in full bloom as a highly partisan House majority leader, Washington had not grown as polarized as it would soon become under the unified Republican rule of President George W. Bush and the GOP-controlled Congress.

Although the seventh edition of *Interest Group Politics* will not fixate on the growth of polarization in Washington, this condition has changed how organized interests approach both legislative and electoral politics. DeLay may have resigned his leadership post and his congressional seat, and the Republican dominance on Capitol Hill may be reaching an end, but the partisan taste of national politics seems certain to remain. Organized interests have traditionally focused on narrow issues and particular results, practices that have led them to work with legislators and other officials from both political parties. Indeed, parties and interest groups have complementary but different goals. Political parties want to capture the reins of power while groups ordinarily seek particular policy outcomes, be they private goods, such as a tax provision, or public goods, like clean air.

In the world of Majority Leader DeLay, President Bush, and a supporting cast of Republican loyalists, both inside and outside Congress, organized interests and lobbyists have been forced to adapt to a different, more partisan context in the post-2002 period of Republican dominance, even more than was required in the wake of the GOP's 1994 congressional sweep. The implications of the Democrats' 2006 sweep remain to be seen.

In this edition of *Interest Group Politics* various chapters address the contemporary changes in political context; at the same time, our contributors consider a wide range of important interest group issues, from representation to campaign finance to group identity. As always, we have sought to publish articles that combine insights into contemporary interest group politics with solid scholarship and accessible writing styles. And we are again delighted to bring together veteran contributors like Jeffrey M. Berry, Christopher J. Bosso, and Diana Dwyre (among others) with first-rate younger scholars like Michael T. Heaney and Dara Z. Strolovitch.

CQ Press's editorial staff remains the best in the business. Charisse Kiino has ably overseen the entire project, and Dwain Smith and Gwenda Larsen have provided the great production assistance that we've come to expect. Mary Marik has had just the right touch in editing a gaggle of political scientists; and, of course, Brenda Carter's overall direction is integral to the success of *Interest Group Politics*.

As always, we thank Beth Cigler and Michel Loomis for continuing to put up with our increasingly erratic ways. With the birth of Cade Nelson, Al has survived becoming a grandfather, and Bird has survived not becoming one. And we truly value the opportunity to edit this volume, once again.

In sorrow we dedicate this volume to the late Bill Browne, a superb interest group scholar and valued contributor to previous editions of *Interest Group Politics*. We will miss both his good humor and his scholarly insights.

Allan J. Cigler
Burdett A. Loomis

Contributors

Scott Ainsworth is associate professor of political science at the University of Georgia. He has published widely on interest groups and lobbying and is the author of *Analyzing Interest Groups*, a critical assessment of the field. His current research projects include a book manuscript on the politics surrounding abortion-related legislation in the U.S. Congress.

Jeffrey M. Berry is John Richard Skuse, Class of 1941 Professor of Political Science at Tufts University. His books include *A Voice for Nonprofits* (with David Arons, 2003), *The New Liberalism* (1999), and *The Rebirth of Urban Democracy* (with Kent Portney and Ken Thomson, 1993).

Christopher J. Bosso is professor of political science; associate dean of the School of Social Sciences, Urban Affairs, and Public Policy; and director of the Nanotechnology and Society Research Group at Northeastern University. He writes on environmental politics and on the societal impacts of science and technology. Most recently, his book *Environment, Inc.: From Grassroots to Beltway* (2005) won the 2006 Lynton Caldwell Prize for best book in environmental policy and politics from the Science, Technology and Environmental Policy section of the American Political Science Association.

Allan J. Cigler is Chancellor's Club Teaching Professor of Political Science at the University of Kansas. He received his doctorate from Indiana University. His recent research and writing focus on parties, interest groups, and the role of money in campaigns and elections.

M. Margaret Conway is Distinguished Professor Emeritus of political science at the University of Florida. She is a coauthor of *Women and Public Policy*, third ed. (2005) and *Women and Political Participation*, second ed. (2005) and is the author of *Political Participation in the United States*, third ed. (2000).

Marian Currinder is a senior fellow at the Government Affairs Institute at Georgetown University. An American Political Science Association congressional fellow in 2003–2004, she has authored or coauthored several journal articles and book chapters on campaign finance and congressional politics.

Diana Dwyre is professor of political science and department chair at California State University, Chico. She served as the American Political Science Association Steiger congressional fellow in 1998 and has written extensively on campaign finance, political parties, and congressional elections, including *Legislative Labyrinth: Congress and Campaign Finance Reform* (with Victoria Farrar-Myers, 2001).

Erik K. Godwin is a doctoral candidate in political science at the University of North Carolina at Chapel Hill. He previously worked for the EOP Group, a lobbying firm specializing in executive branch influence, and also served as a White House regulatory analyst in the Office of Information and Regulatory Affairs, where he specialized in environmental and energy-related issues.

R. Kenneth Godwin is Marshall Rauch Distinguished Professor of Political Science at the University of North Carolina at Charlotte. His research interests concern developing models of lobbying behavior and the responsiveness of government.

Virginia Gray is Robert Watson Winston Distinguished Professor of Political Science at the University of North Carolina at Chapel Hill. She teaches and conducts research on state politics, public policy, and interest groups. She has published several books and articles on these topics, including *The Population Ecology of Interest Representation* and *Minnesota Politics and Government*, both coauthored.

Joanne Connor Green is associate professor of political science and director of the Institute on Women and Gender at Texas Christian University. Her research interests include the role of gender in elections and the political process, and she is especially interested in studying and encouraging civic engagement. She is currently completing an introductory American government textbook.

John C. Green is distinguished professor of political science and director of the Ray C. Bliss Institute of Applied Politics at the University of Akron as well as a senior fellow at the Pew Forum on Religion and Public Life. He has carried out extensive research on religion and American politics.

James L. Guth is William R. Kenan Jr. Professor of Political Science at Furman University. He has written extensively on the role of religion in American and European politics and is currently studying the impact of religious factors on the public's attitudes toward foreign policy issues.

Michael T. Heaney is assistant professor of political science at the University of Florida. His current research projects examine the interest group politics of the Medicare prescription drug benefit, protests against the U.S.-Iraq war, and the development of the Chicago school of political science.

Ronald J. Hrebenar is professor and chair of the department of political science at the University of Utah. He is author or editor of thirteen books and more than forty articles and book chapters on interest groups, lobbying, political parties, and elections. He was the director of the University of Utah's Hinckley Institute of Politics from 2003 to 2005.

Lyman A. Kellstedt is professor of political science (emeritus) at Wheaton College. He is the coauthor of numerous books and articles in the field of religion and politics, including chapters of earlier editions of *Interest Group Politics*.

Rogan Kersh is associate professor of public service and associate dean of New York University's Wagner School. He has published widely on U.S. politics and institutions, including a chapter in the sixth edition of *Interest Group Politics*. He is currently completing two books, one on interest group lobbying and another (with James Morone) on the politics of obesity.

Burdett A. Loomis is professor of political science at the University of Kansas. A former American Political Science Association congressional fellow and recipient of a Kemper Teaching Award, he has written extensively on legislatures, political careers, interest groups, and policymaking. In 2005, he worked as director of administrative communication for Governor Kathleen Sebelius of Kansas.

David Lowery is a professor in the department of public administration at the University of Leiden in the Netherlands, where he teaches and conducts research on the politics of interest representation, state and local politics, research methods, and bureaucratic politics. His most recent book is *Organized Interests and American Government* (with Holly Brasher, 2003).

Michael Nelson is Fulmer Professor of Political Science at Rhodes College. He has published several books on the American presidency, including *The Elections of 2004* (2005) and *The American Presidency: Origins and Development, 1776–2002* (with Sidney Milkis, 2003). He is coauthor with John Mason of *How the South Joined the Gambling Nation: The Politics of State Policy Innovation* (2007) and *Governing Gambling* (2001).

Anthony J. Nownes is associate professor of political science at the University of Tennessee, Knoxville. His research interests include group formation and maintenance, lobbying, and the evolution of interest group communities. His book, *Total Lobbying: What Lobbyists Want (and How They Try to Get It)*, was published in 2006.

Karen O'Connor is Jonathan N. Helfat Distinguished Professor of Political Science at American University, where she also directs the Women & Politics Institute. She is a coauthor of one of the leading texts on American politics and has written extensively about interest groups and the courts, women and politics, and judicial politics.

Kelly D. Patterson is associate professor of political science at Brigham Young University and director of the Center for the Study of Elections and Democracy. He is coeditor of *Financing the 2004 Election* (2006) and *Dancing without Partners: How Candidates, Parties and Interest Groups Interact in the Presidential Campaign* (2006).

Linda Mancillas Patterson is a graduate student at American University, where she received the 2005 outstanding student award from the Women & Politics Institute. She holds a bachelor's degree from the University of Alabama at Birmingham and while there received the Department of Government's Mary Wollstonecraft Prize and the Women's Studies Award of Excellence. Currently, she is working on her dissertation, which examines the politics of the law-and-order movement.

Valerie Ploumpis is associate director of the Japan Business Federation (Nippon Keidanren) in Washington, D.C., where she manages its advocacy agenda. She has spent her career working for associations of European and Asian foreign investors in the United States. Ms. Ploumpis received her master's degree from Johns Hopkins University's School of Advanced International Studies and a bachelor's degree from Mills College.

Ruben Rodrigues is a student at University of Santa Clara School of Law, where he is concentrating on intellectual property law. He served as a research assistant for the Nanotechnology and Society Research Group at Northeastern University, where he earned his master's degree. Rodrigues earned his bachelor's degree in engineering at the Massachusetts Institute of Technology.

Matthew M. Singer is a PhD candidate at Duke University, where he is studying electoral mobilization and public opinion.

Corwin E. Smidt is professor of political science and director of the Henry Institute for the Study of Christianity and Politics at Calvin College. He is author, editor, or coauthor of ten books, including *Pulpit and Politics* (2004), *Religion as Social Capital* (2003), and *Evangelicalism: The Next Generation* (2002), as well as numerous chapters in edited volumes and articles in scholarly journals. He has also served as executive director of the Religion and Politics section of the American Political Science Association.

Dara Z. Strolovitch is assistant professor of political science at the University of Minnesota. Her work has appeared in the *Journal of Politics, Social Science Quarterly*, the *National Women's Studies Association Review*, and the *American Journal of Sociology*. Her book, *Affirmative Advocacy: Race, Class, and Gender in Interest Group Politics*, will be published in 2007.

Clive S. Thomas is professor of political science at the University of Alaska Southeast. He is the author or editor of ten books, including *Research Guide to U.S. and International Interest Groups* (2004) and *Political Parties and Interest Groups: Shaping Democratic Governance* (2001).

Eric M. Uslaner is professor of government and politics at the University of Maryland, College Park. He is the author of seven books and more than one hundred articles and has received grants from the National Science Foundation, the Russell Sage Foundation, the C. V. Starr Foundation, and the Embassy of Canada. His most recent book is *The Moral Foundations of Trust* (2002), and his new book in preparation is *The Bulging Pocket and the Rule of Law: Corruption, Inequality, and Trust*.

Alixandra B. Yanus is a graduate student at the University of North Carolina at Chapel Hill. She holds a bachelor's degree from American University, where she received the university award for outstanding scholarship at the undergraduate level. Her research interests are in American politics and the courts, especially external influences on judicial decision making.

INTEREST GROUP POLITICS

1

Introduction
The Changing Nature of Interest Group Politics
Burdett A. Loomis and Allan J. Cigler

The original version of this chapter appeared in the first edition (1983) of this book. It sought to convey what we saw as the most important trends in interest group politics from roughly the 1960s on. In subsequent editions we have modified this chapter in modest ways and have used our concluding chapter to consider the continuing evolution of interest group politics. For the most part, our initial generalizations have been true. Organized interests have proliferated over the past twenty years, and the trend toward increased representation of all kinds of interests continues. Despite some opposition, we still view the imbalance of influence that tilts toward moneyed interests as one of the cornerstones of the interest group system.

Some things we failed to anticipate. The almost complete breakdown of national campaign finance laws has been a surprise, as has parties' ability to take advantage of this failure. Although we understood the potential of outside lobbying strategies, we underestimated the extent to which grassroots, grasstops (local elites), public relations, and advocacy advertising would be used to set the policy agenda. Indeed, the intensity of organized interests' focus on agenda setting has been unexpected.

More than ever, however, we remain convinced that our original emphasis—on interest group representation and the overall responsiveness of the political system—is still valid. Government continues to respond to groups that clearly communicate their interests and have the funding to convey their message effectively. Still, representation is not simply a matter of responding to specific interests or citizens. Government must also respond to society's collective needs, and responsiveness to particular interests can reduce overall responsiveness. Indeed, the vibrancy and success of many organized interests contribute to a policymaking process that continues to struggle in formulating palatable solutions to complex societal problems.

From James Madison to Madison Avenue, political interests have played a central role in American politics. But this great continuity in our political experience has been matched by ambivalence from citizens, politicians, and scholars toward interest groups. James Madison's warnings of the dangers of faction echo in the rhetoric of reformers from Populists and Progressives near the turn of the century to the so-called public interest advocates of today.

If organized special interests are nothing new in American politics, can today's group politics nevertheless be seen as having changed fundamentally? Acknowledging that many important, continuing trends exist, we seek to place in perspective a broad series of changes in modern interest group politics. Among the most substantial of these developments are:

- A great proliferation of interest groups since the early 1960s.
- A centralization of group headquarters in Washington, D.C., rather than New York City or elsewhere.
- Major technological developments in information processing that promote more sophisticated, more timely, and more specialized communications strategies, such as grassroots lobbying and the message politics of issue-based campaigns.
- The rise of single-issue groups.
- Changes in campaign finance laws (1971, 1974) and the ensuing growth of political action committees (PACs), and more recently, the sharp increases in soft money contributions to parties and issue advocacy campaign advertisements for individual candidates.
- The increased formal penetration of political and economic interests into the bureaucracy (advisory committees), the presidency (White House group representatives), and the Congress (caucuses of members).
- The continuing decline of political parties' ability to perform key electoral and policy-related activities, despite their capacity to funnel soft money to candidates.
- The increased number, activity, and visibility of public interest groups, such as Common Cause and the Ralph Nader–inspired public interest research organizations.
- The growth of activity and impact of institutions, including corporations, universities, state and local governments, and foreign interests.
- A continuing rise in the amount and sophistication of group activity in state capitals, especially given the devolution of some federal programs and substantial increases in state budgets.

All these developments have antecedents in earlier eras of American political life; there is little that is genuinely new under the interest group sun. Political action committees have replaced (or complemented) other forms of special interest campaign financing. Group-generated mail directed at Congress has been a tactic since at least the early 1900s.[1] Many organizations have long been centered in Washington, members of Congress traditionally have represented local interests, and so on.

Still, the level of group activity, coupled with growing numbers of organized interests, distinguishes contemporary group politics from the politics of earlier eras. Group involvement trends lend credence to the fears of scholars such as political scientist Theodore Lowi and economist Mancur Olson, who have viewed interest-based politics as contributing to governmental stalemate and reduced accountability.[2] If accurate, these analyses point to a fundamentally different role for interest groups than those suggested by Madison and group theorists after him.

Only during the past thirty years, in the wake of Olson's pathbreaking research, have scholars begun to examine realistically why people join and become active in groups.[3] It is by no means self-evident that citizens should naturally become group members—quite the contrary in most cases. We are faced, then, with the paradoxical and complex question of why groups have proliferated when it can be economically unwise for people to join them.

Interest Groups in American Politics

Practical politicians and scholars alike generally agree that interest groups (also known as *factions, organized interests, pressure groups,* and *special interests*) are natural phenomena in a democratic regime—that is, individuals will band together to protect their interests.[4] In Madison's words, "The causes of faction . . . are sown in the nature of man." But controversy continues as to whether groups and group politics are benign or malignant forces in American politics. "By a faction," Madison wrote, "I understand a number of citizens, whether amounting to a majority or minority of the whole, who are united and actuated by some common impulse of passion, or of interest, adverse to the rights of other citizens, or to the permanent and aggregate interests of the community."[5]

Although Madison rejected the remedy of direct controls over factions as "worse than the disease," he saw the need to limit their negative effects by promoting competition among them and by devising an elaborate system of procedural "checks and balances" to reduce the potential power of any single, strong group, whether that interest represented a majority or minority position.

Hostility toward interest groups became more virulent in industrialized America, where the great concentrations of power far outstripped anything Madison might have imagined. After the turn of the century many Progressives railed at various monopolistic "trusts" and intimate connections between interests and corrupt politicians. Later, in 1935, Hugo Black, then a senator (and later a Supreme Court justice), painted a grim picture of group malevolence: "Contrary to tradition, against the public morals, and hostile to good government, the lobby has reached such a position of power that it threatens government itself. Its size, its power, its capacity for evil, its greed, trickery, deception and fraud condemn it to the death it deserves." [6]

Similar suspicions are expressed today, especially in light of the increased role of money in electoral politics. The impact of groups on elections has grown steadily since the adoption of the Federal Election Campaign Act of 1971 and its 1974 amendments—reform legislation originally intended to limit the impact of organized interests. Instead, such interests accelerated their spending on campaigns. Until the 1990s most concerns focused on PACs; indeed, direct PAC contributions to congressional candidates rose from less than $23 million in 1975–1976 to nearly $260 million in the 1999–2000 election cycle. The number of PACs has leveled off at about 4,000, and only a few are major players in electoral politics. Moreover, PACs encourage large numbers of contributors to pool their funds, a tactic that enhances Americans' political participation.

More worrisome over the past decade have been the growing amount and impact of essentially unregulated money from organized interests. "Soft money" contributions to national political parties totaled nearly $600 million in 2000, almost doubling the amount in the 1996 presidential year. Democrats received 98 percent more, and Republicans upped their totals by 81 percent. Even more troublesome may be issue advocacy advertising by organized interests, which does not fall under the expenditure limits and disclosure requirements of the Federal Election Commission. Thus in the 2000 campaign the drug industry group called Citizens for Better Medicare spent more than $40 million on advertisements designed to help congressional allies, both past and prospective.[7] At the time this group and many like it did not need to disclose where their funds came from. Nor was there any limit on the amount of expenditures, as long as they did not "expressly advocate" a preference for a candidate (that is, use the words *vote for* and similar words) or coordinate efforts with a candidate or party committee.

By focusing on "hard money" activity (largely reported contributions to candidates), "The [Federal Election Commission] . . . could no longer restrain most of the financial activity that takes place in modern elections."[8] Such an environment has renewed calls for additional campaign finance reform. So far, however, Congress has resisted changing laws that regulate group activity in national elections, and public cynicism about special interest influence will likely continue.

Pluralism and Liberalism

Despite popular distrust of interest group politics, political scientists and other observers often have viewed groups in a positive light. This perspective draws on Madison's *Federalist* writings, but is tied more closely to the growth of the modern state. Political science scholars such as Arthur Bentley, about 1910, and David Truman, forty years later, placed groups at the heart of politics and policymaking in a complex, large, and increasingly specialized governmental system. The interest group becomes an element of continuity in a changing political world. Truman noted the "multiplicity of co-ordinate or nearly co-ordinate points of access to governmental decisions" and concluded that "the significance of these many points of access and of the complicated texture of relationships among them is great. This diversity assures various ways for interest groups to participate in the formation of policy, and this variety is a flexible, stabilizing element." [9]

Derived from Truman's work and that of other group-oriented scholars is the notion of the pluralist state in which competition among interests, in and out of government, will produce policies roughly responsive to public desires, and no single set of interests will dominate.

> Pluralist theory assumes that within the public arena there will be countervailing centers of power within governmental institutions and among outsiders. Competition is implicit in the notion that groups, as surrogates for individuals, will produce products representing the diversity of opinions that might have been possible in the individual decision days of democratic Athens.[10]

In many ways the pluralist vision of American politics corresponds to the realities of policymaking and the distribution of policy outcomes, but a host of scholars, politicians, and other observers have roundly criticized this perspective. Two broad (although sometimes contradictory) critiques have special merit.

The first argues that some interests habitually lose in the policy process; others habitually win. Without endorsing the contentions of elite theorists that a small number of interests and individuals conspire together to dominate societal policies, one can make a strong case that interests with more resources (money, access, information, and so forth) usually will obtain better results than interests that possess fewer assets and employ them less effectively. The small, cohesive, well-heeled defense industry, for example, does well year in and year out in policymaking; marginal farmers and the urban poor produce a much less successful track record.[11] Based on continuing unequal results, critics of the pluralist model argue that interests are still represented unevenly and unfairly.

The second critique generally agrees that inequality of results remains an important aspect of group politics. But this perspective, most forcefully set out by Theodore Lowi, sees interests as generally succeeding in their goals of influencing government—to the point that government itself, in one form or another, provides a measure of protection to almost all societal interests. Everyone thus retains some vested interest in the structure of government and array of public policies. This does not mean that all interests get exactly what they want from governmental policies; rather, all interests get at least some rewards. From this point of view the tobacco industry surely wishes to see its crop subsidies maintained, but the small farmer and the urban poor also have pet programs, such as guaranteed loans and food stamps.

Lowi has labeled the proliferation of groups and their growing access to government "interest group liberalism." He argues that this phenomenon is pathological for a democratic government:

> Interest group liberal solutions to the problem of power [who will exercise it] provide the system with stability by spreading a *sense* of representation at the expense of genuine flexibility, at the expense of democratic forms, and ultimately at the expense of legitimacy.[12]

Interest group liberalism is pluralism, but it is sponsored pluralism, and the government is the chief sponsor. On the surface, it appears that the *unequal results* and *interest group liberalism* critiques of pluralism are at odds. Reconciliation, however, is relatively straightforward. Lowi does not suggest that all interests are effectively represented. Rather, there exists in many instances only the appearance of representation. Political scientist Murray Edelman pointed out that a single set of policies can provide two related types of rewards: tangible benefits for the few and symbolic reassurances for the many.[13] Such a combination encourages groups to form, become active, and claim success.

The Climate for Group Proliferation

Substantial cleavages among citizens are essential for interest group development. American culture and the constitutional arrangements of the U.S. government have encouraged the emergence of multiple political interests. In the pre-Revolutionary period, sharp conflicts existed between commercial and landed interests, debtor and creditor classes, coastal residents and those in the hinterlands, and citizens with either Tory or Whig political preferences. As the new nation developed, its vastness, characterized by geographical regions varying in climate, economic potential, culture, and tradition, contributed to a great heterogeneity. Open immigration policies further led to a diverse cultural mix with a wide variety of racial, ethnic, and religious backgrounds represented among the populace. Symbolically, the notion of the United States as a "melting pot," emphasizing group assimilation, has received much attention, but a more appropriate image may be a "tossed salad."[14]

The Constitution also contributes to a favorable environment for group development. Guarantees of free speech, association, and the right to petition the government for redress of grievances are basic to group formation. Because political organization often parallels government structure, federalism and the separation of powers—principles embodied in the Constitution—have greatly influenced large numbers of interest groups in the United States.

The decentralized political power structure in the United States allows important decisions to be made at the national, state, or local levels. Within each level of government there are multiple points of access. For example, business-related policies such as taxes are acted on at each level, and interest groups may affect these policies in the legislative, executive, or judicial arenas. In the case of federated organizations such as the U.S. Chamber of Commerce, state and local affiliates often act independently of the national organization. Numerous business organizations thus focus on the varied channels of access.

In addition, the decentralized political parties found in the United States are less unified and disciplined than parties in many other nations. The resulting power vacuum in the decision making process offers great potential for alternative political organizations, such as interest groups, to influence policy. Even in an era of strong legislative parties (mid-1980s on), many opportunities for influence remain.

Finally, American cultural values may encourage group development. As Alexis de Tocqueville observed in the 1830s, values such as individualism and the need for personal achievement underlie the propensity of citizens to join groups. Moreover, the large number of access points—local, state, and national—contributes to Americans' strong sense of political efficacy when compared with that expressed by citizens of other nations.[15] Not only do Americans see themselves as joiners, but they tend to belong to more political groups than do people of other countries.[16]

Theories of Group Development

A climate favorable to group proliferation does little to explain how interest groups organize. Whatever interests are latent in society and however favorable the context for group development may be, groups do not arise spontaneously. Farmers and a landed interest existed long before farm organizations first appeared; laborers and craftsmen were on the job before unions. In a simple society, even though distinct interests exist, there is little need for interest group formation. Farmers have no political or economic reason to organize when they work only for their families. Before the industrial revolution workers were craftsmen, often laboring in small family enterprises. Broad-based political organizations were not needed, although local guilds often existed to train apprentices and protect jobs.

David Truman has suggested that increasing societal complexity, characterized by economic specialization and social differentiation, is fundamental to group proliferation.[17] In addition, technological changes and the increasing interdependence of economic sectors often create new interests and redefine old ones. Robert Salisbury's discussion of American farming is instructive:

> The full-scale commercialization of agriculture, beginning largely with the Civil War, led to the differentiation of farmers into specialized interests, each increasingly different from the next.... The interdependence that accompanied the specialization process meant potential

conflicts of interests or values both across the bargaining encounter and among the competing farmers themselves as each struggled to secure his own position.[18]

Many political scientists assume that an expansion of the interest group universe is a natural consequence of growing societal complexity. According to Truman, however, group formation "tends to occur in waves" and is greater in some periods than in others.[19] Groups organize politically when the existing order is disturbed and certain interests are, in turn, helped or hurt.

It is not surprising, then, that economic interests develop both to improve their position and to protect existing advantages. The National Association of Manufacturers originally was created to further the expansion of business opportunities in foreign trade, but it became a more powerful organization largely in response to the rise of organized labor.[20] Mobilization of business interests since the 1960s often has resulted from threats posed by consumer advocates and environmentalists, as well as requirements imposed by the steadily growing role of the federal government.

Disturbances that trigger group formation need not be strictly economic or technological. Wars, for example, place extreme burdens on society, and lengthy conflicts lead to a growth of groups, whether based on support of (World War II) or opposition to (Vietnam) the conflict. Likewise, broad societal changes may disturb the status quo. The origin of the Ku Klux Klan, for example, was fear that increased numbers of ethnic and racial minorities threatened white, Christian America.

Truman's theory of group proliferation suggests that the interest group universe is inherently unstable. Groups formed from an imbalance of interests in one area induce a subsequent disequilibrium, which acts as a catalyst for individuals to form groups as counterweights to the new perceptions of inequity. Group politics thus is characterized by successive waves of mobilization and countermobilization. The liberalism of one era may prompt the resurgence of conservative groups in the next. Similarly, periods of business domination often are followed by eras of reform group ascendancy. In the 1990s health care reform proposals raised the stakes for almost all segments of society. Interest group politicking reached historic proportions as would-be reformers, the medical community, and business interests sought to influence the direction of change in line with their own preferences. And given the complexity of health care policymaking, the struggles among organized interests will surely continue for years.

Personal Motivations and Group Formation

Central to theories of group proliferation are the pluralist notions that elements of society possess common needs and share a group identity or consciousness, and that these are sufficient conditions for the formation of effective political organizations. Although the perception of common needs may be necessary for political organization, whether it is sufficient for group formation and effectiveness is open to question. Historical evidence documents many instances in which groups have not emerged spontaneously, even when circumstances such as poverty or discrimination would seem, in retrospect, to have required it.

Mancur Olson effectively challenged many pluralist tenets in *The Logic of Collective Action*, first published in 1965. Basing his analysis on a model of the "rational economic man," Olson posited that even individuals who have common interests are not inclined to join organizations that attempt to address their concerns. The major barrier to group participation is the "free rider" problem: "rational" individuals choose not to bear the participation costs (time, membership fees) because they can enjoy the group benefits (such as favorable legislation) without joining. Groups that pursue "collective" benefits, which accrue to all members of a class or segment of society regardless of membership status, will have great difficulty forming and surviving. According to Olson, it would be economically irrational for individual farmers to join a group seeking higher farm prices when benefits from price increases would be enjoyed by all farmers, even those who contribute nothing to the group. Similarly, it would be irrational for an individual environmentalist to become part of organized attempts to reduce air pollution, when all citizens, members of environmental groups or not, would reap the benefits of cleaner air. The free rider problem is especially serious for large groups because the larger the group the less likely an individual will perceive his or her contribution as having any impact on group success.

For Olson, a key to group formation—and especially group survival—was "selective" benefits. These rewards—for example, travel discounts, informative publications, and cheap insurance—go only to members. Organizations in the best positions to offer such benefits are those initially formed for some nonpolitical purpose and that ordinarily provide material benefits to their clientele. In the case of unions, for example, membership may be a condition of employment. For farmers, the American Farm Bureau Federation offers inexpensive insurance, which induces individuals to join even if they disagree with the group's goals. In professional circles, membership in professional societies may be a prerequisite for occupational advancement and opportunity.

Olson's notions have sparked several extensions of the rational man model, and a reasonably coherent body of incentive theory literature now exists.[21] Incentive theorists view individuals as rational decisionmakers interested in making the most of their time and money by choosing to participate in groups that offer benefits greater than or equal to the costs they incur by participation. Three types of benefits are available. Olson, an economist, emphasized *material* benefits—tangible rewards of participation, such as income or services that have monetary value. *Solidary* benefits are the socially derived, intangible rewards created by the act of association, such as fun, camaraderie, status, or prestige. Finally, *expressive* (also known as *purposive*) benefits derive from advancing a particular cause or ideology.[22] Groups formed on both sides of issues such as abortion or gun control illustrate the strength of such expressive incentives.

The examination of group members' motivations, and in particular the focus on nonmaterial incentives, allows for some reconciliation between the traditional group theorists' expectations of group development and the recent rational actor studies, which emphasize barriers to group formation. Nonmaterial incentives, such as fellowship and self-satisfaction, may encourage the proliferation of highly politicized groups and "have the potential for producing a more dynamic group context in which politics, political preferences, and group goals are more centrally determining factors than in material associations, linking political considerations more directly to associational size, structure, and internal processes."[23] Indeed, pure political benefits may attract members, and even collective benefits can prove decisive in inducing individuals to join large groups. Like elected officials, groups may find it possible to take credit for widely approved government actions, such as higher farm prices, stronger environmental regulations, or the protection of Social Security.[24]

Finally, several studies indicate that the free rider problem may not be quite the obstacle to participation that it was once thought to be, especially in an affluent society. Albert Hirschman, for example, has argued that the costs and benefits of group activity are not always clear; in fact, some costs of participation for some individuals, such as time and effort expended, might be regarded as benefits (in terms of personal satisfaction) by others.[25] Other researchers have questioned whether individuals even engage in rational, cost-benefit thinking as they make membership decisions. Michael McCann noted that "there seems to be a general threshold level of involvement below which free rider calculations pose few inhibitions for . . . commitment from moderately affluent citizen supporters."[26] In short, individuals may join and participate in groups for reasons beyond narrow economic self-interest or the availability of selective benefits.[27]

Contemporary Interest Group Politics

Several notable developments mark the modern age of interest group politics. Of primary importance is the large and growing number of active groups and other interests. The data here are sketchy, but one major study found that most current groups came into existence after World War II and that group formation has accelerated substantially since the early 1960s.[28] Also since the 1960s groups have increasingly directed their attention toward the center of power in Washington, D.C., as the scope of federal policymaking has grown, and groups seeking influence have determined to "hunt where the ducks are." As a result the 1960s and 1970s marked an explosion in the number of groups lobbying in Washington.

A second key change is evident in the composition of the interest group universe. Beginning in the late 1950s political participation patterns underwent some significant transformations. Conventional activities such as voting declined, and political parties, the traditional aggregators and articulators of mass interests, became weaker. Yet at all levels of government, evidence of citizen involvement has been apparent, often in the form of new or revived groups. Particularly impressive has been the growth of citizens' groups—those organized around an idea or cause (at times a single issue) with no occupational basis for membership. Fully 30 percent of such groups have formed since 1975, and in 1980 they made up more than one-fifth of all groups represented in Washington.[29]

In fact, a participation revolution occurred in the country as many citizens became active in an increasing number of protest groups, citizens' organizations, and special interest groups. These groups often comprise issue-oriented activists or individuals who seek collective material benefits. The free rider problem has proven not to be an insurmountable barrier to group formation, and many new interest groups do not use selective material benefits to gain support. Still, since the late 1970s, the number of these groups has remained relatively stable, and they are well established in representing consumers, environmentalists, and other public interest organizations.[30]

Third, government itself has profoundly affected the growth and activity of interest groups. Early in this century, workers found organizing difficult because business and industry used government-backed injunctions to prevent strikes. By the 1930s, however, with the prohibition of injunctions in private labor disputes and the rights of collective bargaining established, most governmental actions directly promoted the growth of labor unions. In recent years changes in campaign finance laws have led to an explosion in the number of political action committees, especially among business, industry, and issue-oriented groups. Laws facilitating group formation certainly have contributed to group proliferation, but government policy in a broader sense has been equally responsible.

Fourth, not only has the number of membership groups grown in recent decades, but a similar expansion has occurred in the political activity of many other interests, such as individual corporations, universities, churches, governmental units, foundations, and think tanks.[31] Historically, most of these interests have been satisfied with representation by trade or professional associations. Since the mid-1960s, however, many have chosen to employ their own Washington representatives. Between 1961 and 1982, for example, the number of corporations with Washington offices increased tenfold.[32] The chief beneficiaries of this trend are Washington-based lawyers, lobbyists, and public relations firms. The number of attorneys in the nation's capital, taken as a rough indicator of lobbyist strength, tripled between 1973 and 1983, and the growth of public relations firms was dramatic. The lobbying community of the 1990s is large, increasingly diverse, and part of the expansion of policy domain participation, whether in agriculture, the environment, or industrial development. Political scientist James Thurber has calculated that 91,000 lobbyists and people associated with lobbying were employed in the Washington, D.C., area in the early 1990s.[33] As of 2001, the *Encyclopedia of Associations* listed approximately 22,200 organizations, up more than 50 percent since 1980 and almost 400 percent since 1955.[34] And this number does not include hundreds of corporations and other institutions (such as universities) that are represented in Washington.

The Growth of Government

Although the government prompted the establishment of some agricultural interest groups in the nineteenth century, since the 1930s the federal government has become increasingly active as a spur to group formation. One major New Deal goal was to use government as an agent in balancing the relationship between contending forces in society, particularly industry and labor. One goal was to create greater equality of opportunity, including the "guarantee of identical liberties to all individuals, especially with regard to their pursuit of economic success."[35] For example, the Wagner Act (1935), which established collective bargaining rights, attempted to equalize workers' rights with those of their employers. Some New Deal programs did have real redistributive qualities, but most, even Social Security, sought only to ensure minimum standards of citizen welfare. Workers were clearly better off, but "the kind of redistribution that took priority in the public philosophy of the New Deal was not of wealth, but a redistribution of power."[36]

The expansion of federal programs accelerated between 1960 and 1980; since then, costs have continued to increase, despite resistance to new programs. In what political scientist Hugh Heclo termed an "Age of Improvement," the federal budget has grown rapidly (from nearly $100 billion in 1961 to $2.1 trillion in 2001) and has widened the sweep of federal regulations.[37] Lyndon Johnson's Great Society—a multitude of federal initiatives in education, welfare, health care, civil rights, housing, and urban affairs—created a new array of federal responsibilities and program beneficiaries. The growth of many of these programs has continued, although that growth was slowed markedly by the Reagan and Bush administrations, as well as by the Republican capture of Congress in 1994. In the 1970s the federal government further expanded its activities in consumer affairs, environmental protection, and energy regulation. It also redefined some policies, such as affirmative action, to seek greater equality of results.

Many of the government policies adopted early in the Age of Improvement did not result from interest group activity by potential beneficiaries. Several targeted groups, such as the poor, were not effectively organized during the period of policy development. Initiatives typically came from elected officials responding to a variety of private and public sources, such as task forces of academics and policy professionals.[38]

The proliferation of government activities led to a mushrooming of groups around the affected policy areas. Newly enacted programs provided benefit packages that encouraged interest group formation. Consider group activity in policy toward the aging. The radical Townsend Movement, based on age grievances, received much attention during the 1930s, but organized political activity focused on age-based concerns had virtually no influence in national politics. Social Security legislation won approval without the involvement of age-based interest groups. Four decades later, by 1978, roughly $112 billion (approximately 24 percent of total federal expenditures) went to the elderly population, and it was projected that in fifty years the outlay would amount to 40 percent of the budget.[39] By the early 1990s, however, the elderly population already received one-third of federal outlays, and long-term projections had been revised upward. The existence of such massive benefits has spawned a variety of special interest groups and has encouraged other organizations, often formed for nonpolitical reasons, to redirect their attention to the politics of aging.

Across policy areas two types of groups develop in response to governmental policy initiatives: recipients and service deliverers. In the sector devoted to policies affecting elderly individuals, recipient groups are mass-based organizations concerned with protecting—and if possible expanding—old-age benefits. The largest of these groups—indeed, the largest voluntary association represented in Washington—is the American Association of Retired Persons (AARP).

The AARP is well over twice the size of the AFL-CIO and, after the Roman Catholic Church, is the nation's largest organization. In 1998 it counted 33 million members, an increase of 23 million in twenty years.[40] Approximately half of Americans ages fifty or older, or one-fifth of all voters, belong to the group, in part because membership is cheap—$8 a year. Much of the organization's revenue comes from advertising in its bimonthly magazine, *Modern Maturity*. The organization's headquarters in Washington has its own zip code, a legislative/policy staff of 165; 28 registered, in-house lobbyists; and more than 1,200 staff members in the field. Charles Peters, editor of *Washington Monthly*, claimed that the "AARP is becoming the most dangerous lobby in America," given its vigorous defense of the elderly population's interests.[41] At the same time, because the AARP represents such a wide array of elderly individuals, it is often cautious and slow in its actions.

Federal program growth also has generated substantial growth among service delivery groups. In the health care sector, for example, these range from professional associations of doctors and nurses to hospital groups to the insurance industry to suppliers of drugs and medical equipment. Not only is there enhanced group activity, but hundreds of individual corporations have strengthened their lobbying capacities by opening Washington offices or hiring professional representatives from the capital's many lobbying firms.[42]

Federal government policy toward the aging is probably typical of the tendency to "greatly increase the incentives for groups to form around the differential effects of these policies, each refusing to allow any other group to speak in its name."[43] The complexity of government decision making increases under such conditions, and priorities are hard to set. Particularly troublesome for decisionmakers concerned with national policy is the role played by service delivery groups. In the area of aging, some service groups are largely organizational middlemen concerned with their status as vendors for the elderly population. The trade associations, for example, are most interested in the conditions surrounding the payment of funds to elderly individuals. The major concern of the Gerontological Society, an organization of professionals, is to obtain funds for research on problems of elderly individuals.

Middleman organizations do not usually evaluate government programs according to the criteria used by recipient groups; rather, what is important to them is the relationship between the program and the well-being of their organizations. Because many service delivery groups offer their members vitally important selective material incentives (financial advantages and job opportunities), they are usually far better organized than most recipient groups (the elderly population in this case, the AARP notwithstanding). As a result, service groups sometimes speak for the recipients. This is particularly true when recipient groups represent disadvantaged people, such as poor or mentally ill peoples.

Middleman groups have accounted for a large share of total group growth since 1960, and many of them are state and local government organizations. Since the late 1950s the federal government has grown in expenditures and regulations more than in personnel. Employment in the federal government has risen only 20 percent since 1955, whereas that of states and localities has climbed more than 250 percent. Contemporary federal activism largely involves overseeing and regulating state and local governmental units, which seek funding for a wide range of purposes. The intergovernmental lobby, which includes the National League of Cities, the International City Manager Association, the National Association of Counties, the National Governors' Association, the U.S. Conference of Mayors, and more, has grown to become one of the most important lobbies in Washington. In addition, many local officials, such as transportation or public works directors, are represented by groups, and even single cities and state boards of regents have established Washington offices.

Direct Intervention.   Not only do public policies contribute to group proliferation, but government often directly intervenes in group creation. This is not an entirely new activity. In the early twentieth century officials in the Department of Agriculture encouraged the formation of the American

Farm Bureau Federation, and officials in the Commerce Department did the same for the U.S. Chamber of Commerce. Since the 1960s the federal government has been especially active in providing start-up funds and in sponsoring groups. One study found that government agencies have concentrated on sponsoring organizations of public service professions:

> Federal agencies have an interest in encouraging coordination among the elements of these complex service delivery systems and in improving the diffusion of new ideas and techniques. Groups like the American Public Transit Association or the American Council on Education ... serve as centers of professional development and informal channels for administrative coordination in an otherwise unwieldy governmental system.[44]

Government sponsorship also helps explain the recent rise of citizens' groups. Most federal domestic legislation has included provisions requiring some citizen participation, which has spurred the development of various citizen action groups, including grassroots neighborhood associations, environmental action councils, legal defense coalitions, health care organizations, and senior citizens' groups. Such group sponsorship evolved for two reasons:

> First, there is the ever-present danger that administrative agencies may exceed or abuse their discretionary power. In this sense, the regulators need regulating. Although legislatures have responsibility for doing this ... the administrative bureaucracy has grown too large for them to monitor. Therefore, citizen participation has developed as an alternative means of monitoring government agencies. Second, government agencies are not entirely comfortable with their discretionary power. ... [T]o reduce the potential of unpopular or questionable decisions, agencies frequently use citizen participation as a means for improving, justifying, and developing support for their decisions.[45]

Citizens' groups thus have two sometimes inconsistent missions: to oversee an agency and to act as an advocate for the groups' programs.

Government funding of citizens' groups takes numerous forms. Several federal agencies—including the Federal Trade Commission, Food and Drug Administration, and Environmental Protection Agency—have reimbursed groups for participation in agency proceedings.[46] At other times the government makes available seed money or outright grants. Interest group scholar Jack Walker found that 89 percent of citizens' groups received outside funding in their initial stages of development.[47] Not all the money was from federal sources, but much did come from government grants or contracts. Government can also take away, however, and the Reagan administration made a major effort to "defund" left-leaning interests, especially citizens' groups. But once established, groups have strong instincts for survival. Indeed, the Reagan administration provided an attractive target for many citizens' groups in their recruiting efforts. This dance of defunding took place again, in 1995, after Republicans won control of the House of Representatives.

Citizens' groups, numbering in the thousands, continually confront the free rider problem because they are largely concerned with collective goods and rarely can offer the selective material incentives so important for expanding and maintaining membership. With government funding, however, the development of a stable group membership is not crucial. Many groups are essentially staff organizations with little or no membership base. In the world of interest group politics, resources are often more important than members.

Unintended Intervention.   Government policies contribute to group formation in many unintended ways as well. Policy failures can impel groups to form, as happened with the rise of the American Agriculture Movement in the wake of the Nixon administration's grain export policies. An important factor in the establishment of the Moral Majority was the perceived harassment of church-run schools by government officials. As for abortion, the 1973 Supreme Court decision in *Roe v. Wade* played a major role in the mobilization of antiabortion rights groups. And the 1989 *Webster* decision, which limited the availability of legal abortions, did the same for abortion rights groups. Even the lack of federal funding can play a role. The rise in the incidence of prostate cancer, coupled with a modest budget for research, helped lead to the formation of the National Prostate Cancer Coalition. This group has pressed the government to increase funding on prostate cancer toward levels that are spent on AIDs and breast cancer, given that the three diseases kill about the same number of individuals each year.

Finally, the expansion of government activity often inadvertently contributes to group development and the resulting complexity of politics. The development of the Bass Anglers Sportsman Society (BASS) is a good example. From the late 1940s through the 1960s the Army Corps of Engineers dammed enough southern and midwestern streams to create a host of lakes, thereby providing an inviting habitat for largemouth bass. Anglers arrived in droves to catch their limits, and the fishing industry responded by creating expensive boats filled with specialized and esoteric equipment. The number and affluence of bass aficionados did not escape the attention of Ray Scott, an enterprising soul who began BASS in 1967. In the early 1990s, with its membership approaching 1 million (up from 400,000 in 1982), BASS remained privately organized, offering its members selective benefits such as a slick magazine filled with tips on how to catch their favorite fish, packages of lures and line in return for joining or renewing their memberships, instant information about fishing hot spots, and boat owners' insurance. BASS also provided a number of solidary benefits, such as the camaraderie of fishing with fellow members in specially sanctioned fishing tournaments and the vicarious excitement of fishing with "BASS pros" whose financial livelihood revolved around competitive tournament fishing. The organization is an excellent example of Robert Salisbury's exchange theory approach to interest groups, because it provides benefits to both members and organizers in a "mutually satisfactory exchange." [48]

In fact, *members* may be a misnomer, in that the nominal members have no effective role in group decision making. In 1993 a federal district judge dismissed a $75 million suit filed against Scott by some BASS members. The judge reasoned that the organization was and always had been a for-profit corporation; its "members" thus had no standing to sue.

Although Scott sold the organization to a private corporation in 1986 (the ultimate expression of entrepreneurial success), he remained active in much of its work and wrote a column for the monthly publication, *BassMaster.* Never denying that the organization was anything but a profit-making entity, Scott stated, "Every time I see one of those BASS stickers I get a lump, right in my wallet." [49]

Like most groups BASS did not originate as a political organization, and for the most part it remains an organization for fishermen, with 600,000 members, even in the wake of its 2001 acquisition by the ESPN television network.[50] Yet BASS has entered politics. *BassMaster* has published political commentary, and in 1980, 1988, and 1992 endorsed George Bush for president. It also has called for easing travel restrictions to Cuba, where world-record catches may lurk.

Most groups claim that access is their major goal within the lobbying process, and here BASS has succeeded beyond its wildest dreams. Former president Bush has been a life member of BASS since 1978 and has claimed that *BassMaster* is his favorite magazine. Scott has used his relationship with Bush to lobby for the fishing community in general and BASS in particular. In March 1989 Scott visited the White House and, during a horseshoe match with President Bush, indicated his concern about rumors that the Office of Management and Budget (OMB) planned to limit the disbursement of $100 million in trust funds for fishery management projects. The next morning Bush informed Scott that "all of *our* monies are secure from OMB or anyone else." [51]

BASS increased its political activities by sponsoring Voice of the Environment, which lobbies on water quality issues, and filing class-action lawsuits on behalf of fishermen against environmental polluters. Although the organization can point to a number of conservation and environmental activities, it is distrusted by much of the mainstream environmental movement. BASS's connections to the boating industry often put it at odds with groups seeking to preserve a pristine natural environment or elite angling organizations whose members fish for trout in free-flowing streams rather than for the bass behind federally funded dams.

Indeed, regardless of Scott's entrepreneurial skills, there would probably be no BASS if it were not for the federal government and the Army Corps of Engineers. Fifty years of dam building by the Corps and the U.S.

Bureau of Reclamation have altered the nature of fish populations. Damming of rivers and streams has reduced the quality of fishing for cold-water species such as trout and pike and enhanced the habitat for largemouth bass, a game fish that can tolerate the warmer waters and mud bottoms of man-made lakes. Finally, because many of these lakes are located close to cities, the government has made bass fishing accessible to a large number of anglers.

From angling to air traffic control, the federal government has affected, and sometimes dominated, group formation. But many other forces have contributed to group proliferation, often in concert with increased public sector involvement.

The Decline of Political Parties

In a diverse political culture characterized by divided power, political parties emerged early in our history as instruments to structure conflict and facilitate mass participation. Parties function as intermediaries between the public and formal government institutions, as they reduce and combine citizen demands into a manageable number of issues and enable the system to focus on society's most important problems.

The party performs its mediating function primarily through coalition building—"the process of constructing majorities from the broad sentiments and interests that can be found to bridge the narrower needs and hopes of separate individuals and communities." [52] The New Deal coalition, forged in the 1930s, illustrates how this works. Socioeconomic divisions dominated politics from the 1930s through the 1960s. Less affluent citizens tended to support government provisions for social and economic security and the regulation of private enterprise. Those economically better off usually took the opposite position. The Democratic coalition, by and large, represented disadvantaged urban workers, Catholics, Jews, Italians, Eastern Europeans, and African Americans. On a variety of issues, southerners joined the coalition, along with a smattering of academics and urban liberals. The Republicans were concentrated in the rural and suburban areas outside the South; the party was made up of established ethnic groups, businesspeople, and farmers and was largely Protestant. Party organizations dominated electoral politics through the New Deal period, and interest group influence was felt primarily through the party apparatus.

Patterns of partisan conflict are never permanent, however, and since the 1940s social forces have contributed to the creation of new interests and the redefinition of old ones. This has destroyed the New Deal coalition without putting a new partisan structure in its place and has provided opportunities for the creation of large numbers of political groups—many that are narrowly focused and opposed to the bargaining and compromise patterns of coalition politics. The changes of recent decades reflect the societal transformation that scholars have labeled the "post-industrial society." Postindustrial society is centered on several interrelated developments:

> affluence, advanced technological development, the central importance of knowledge, national communication processes, the growing prominence and independence of the culture, new occupational structures, and with them new life styles and expectations, which is to say new social classes and new centers of power.[53]

At the base is the role of affluence. Between 1947 and 1972 median family income doubled, even after controlling for the effects of inflation. During that same period the percentage of families earning $10,000 and more, in constant dollars, grew from 15 percent to 60 percent of the population.[54] A large proportion of the population began to enjoy substantial discretionary income and moved beyond subsistence.

The consequences of spreading abundance did not reduce conflict, as some observers had predicted.[55] Instead, conflict heightened, because affluence increased dissatisfaction by contributing to a "mentality of demand, a vastly expanded set of expectations concerning what is one's due, a diminished tolerance of conditions less than ideal."[56] By the 1960s the democratizing impact of affluence had become apparent, as an extraordinary number of people enrolled in institutions of higher education. It is not surprising that the government was under tremendous pressure to satisfy expectations, and it too contributed to increasing demands both in rhetoric and through many of its own Age of Improvement initiatives.

With the rise in individual expectations, class divisions and conflicts were drastically transformed. Political parties scholar Walter Dean Burnham noted that the New Deal's class structure changed, and by the late 1960s the industrial class pattern of upper, middle, and working class had been "supplanted by one which is relevant to a system dominated by advanced postindustrial technology." At the top of the new class structure was a "professional-managerial-technical elite . . . closely connected with the university and research centers and significant parts of it have been drawn—both out of ideology and interest—to the federal government's social activism." This growing group tended to be cosmopolitan and more socially permissive than the rest of society. The spread of affluence in postindustrial society was uneven, however, and certain groups were disadvantaged by the changes. At the bottom of the new class structure were those "whose economic functions had been undermined or terminated by the technical revolution of the past generation . . . people, black and white, who tend to be in hard core poverty areas."[57] The focus of President Lyndon B. Johnson's War on Poverty was to be on this class.

The traditional political party system found it difficult to deal effectively with citizens' high expectations and a changing class structure. The economic, ethnic, and ideological positions that had developed during the

New Deal became less relevant to parties, elections, and voter preferences. The strains were particularly evident among working class Democrats. New Deal policies had been particularly beneficial to the white working class, enabling that group to earn incomes and adopt lifestyles that resembled those of the middle class. And although Age of Improvement policies initiated by Democratic politicians often benefited minorities, many white workers viewed these policies as attempts to aid lower class blacks at the expense of whites. By the late 1960s the white working class had taken on trappings of the middle class and conservatism, both economically and culturally.

At the same time, such New Deal divisions as ethnicity also had lost their cutting edge because of social and geographic mobility.

> It does not seem inaccurate to portray the current situation as one in which the basic coalitions and many of the political symbols and relationships, which were developed around one set of political issues and problems, are confronted with new issues and new cleavages for which these traditional relationships and associations are not particularly relevant. Given these conditions, the widespread confusion, frustration, and mistrust are not surprising.[58]

Various conditions led to the party system's inability to *realign*— build coalitions of groups to address new concerns to adapt to changing societal divisions. For example, consider the difficulty of building coalitions around the kinds of issues that have emerged over the past fifteen or twenty years.

Valence issues—general evaluations of the goodness or badness of the times—have become important, especially when related to the cost of living. Yet most such issues do not divide the country politically. Everyone is against inflation and crime. A second set of increasingly important issues are those that are highly emotional, cultural, or moral in character, such as abortion, euthanasia, AIDS, the death penalty, and drug laws. These subjects divide the electorate but elicit intense feelings from only a relatively few citizens. Opinion on such issues often is unrelated to traditional group identifications. Moreover, public opinion is generally disorganized or in disarray—that is, opinions often are unrelated or weakly related to one another on major issues, further retarding efforts to build coalitions.

There is some question about whether parties retain the capacity to shape political debate even on issues that lend themselves to coalition building. Although the decline of political parties began well before the 1960s, the weakening of the party organization has accelerated in the postindustrial age. The emergence of a highly educated electorate, less dependent on party as an electoral cue, has produced a body of citizens that seeks out independent sources of information. Technological developments—such as television, computer-based direct mail, and political polling—have enabled candidates to virtually bypass political parties in their quest for public office.

The rise of political consultants has reduced even further the need for party expertise in running for office. The recruitment function of parties also has been largely lost to the mass media, as journalists now "act out the part of talent scouts, conveying the judgment that some contenders are promising, while dismissing others as of no real talent." [59]

Considerable evidence suggests that parties have adapted to this new political environment, but party organizations no longer dominate the electoral process. In an era of candidate-centered politics, parties are less mobilizers of a diverse electorate than service vendors to ambitious individual candidates. The weakness of political parties has helped to create a vacuum in electoral politics since 1960, and in recent years interest groups have moved aggressively to fill it. Indeed, in the 2000 election many interests bypassed the parties—and even the candidates' organizations—to advertise directly on behalf of particular candidates, all the while articulating their own positions on key issues such as Medicare, drug pricing, term limits, Social Security, and gun control. Simultaneously, organized interests such as labor, environmentalists, antiabortion rights groups, and some corporations have worked closely with parties both by contributing soft money and by implicitly coordinating the corporation's campaign activities with those of the parties.

The Growth of Interest Groups

Although it may be premature to formulate a theory that accounts for growth spurts, we can identify several factors fundamental to group proliferation in contemporary politics.[60] Rapid social and economic changes, powerful catalysts for group formation, have created new interests (for example, the recreation industry) and redefined traditional ones (for example, higher education). The spread of affluence and education, coupled with advanced communication technologies, further contributes to the translation of interests into formal group organizations. Postindustrial changes have generated many new interests, particularly among occupational and professional groups in the scientific and technological arenas. For instance, genetic engineering associations have sprung up in the wake of recent DNA discoveries, to say nothing of the growing clout and sophistication of the computer industry, from Microsoft's Bill Gates on down.

Perhaps more important, postindustrial changes have altered the pattern of conflict in society and created an intensely emotional setting in which groups rise or fall in status. Ascending groups, such as members of the new professional-managerial-technical elite, have both benefited from and supported government activism; they represent the new cultural liberalism—politically cosmopolitan and socially permissive. At the same time, rising expectations and feelings of entitlement have increased pressures on government by aspiring groups and the disadvantaged. The 1960s and early 1970s witnessed wave after wave of group mobilization based on causes ranging from civil rights to women's issues to the environment to consumer protection.

Threat as Motivation.   Abrupt changes and alterations in status, however, threaten many citizens. Middle America, perceiving itself as downwardly mobile, has grown alienated from the social, economic, and cultural dominance of the postindustrial elites, on one hand, and resentful of government attempts to aid minorities and other aspiring groups on the other. The conditions of a modern, technologically based culture also are disturbing to more traditional elements in society. Industrialization and urbanization can uproot people, cutting them loose from familiar life patterns and values and depriving them of meaningful personal associations. Fundamentalist elements feel threatened by various technological advances (such as use of fetal tissue for medical research) as well as by the more general secular liberalism and moral permissiveness of contemporary life. In the 1990s the growth of the Christian Coalition, both nationally and locally, has profoundly affected both electoral and legislative politics by mobilizing citizens and activists. In addition, the growth of bureaucracy, in and out of government, antagonizes everyone at one time or another.

Elites feel postindustrial threats as well. The nuclear arms race and its potential for mass destruction fostered the revived peace movement of the 1980s and its goal of a freeze on nuclear weapons. In addition, the excesses and errors of technology, such as oil spills and toxic waste disposal, have led to group formation among some of the most advantaged and ascending elements of society.

The growth of the animal rights movement since the mid-1980s illustrates interest groups' potential for enhanced participation and influence. Although traditional animal protection organizations such as the Humane Society have existed for decades, the past fifteen years have spawned a host of proanimal offspring, such as People for Ethical Treatment of Animals (PETA), Progressive Animal Welfare Society, Committee to Abolish Sport Hunting, and the Animal Rights Network. Reminiscent of the 1960s, there is even the Animal Liberation Front, an extremist group that engages in direct actions that sometimes include violence.[61] Membership in the organizations that make up the animal rights movement has increased rapidly; founded in 1980, PETA grew from 20,000 members in 1984 to 370,000 by 1994 and 600,000 in 2001. One estimate places the number of animal rights organizations at 400, representing approximately 10 million members.[62]

One major goal of these groups is to stop, or greatly retard, scientific experimentation on animals. Using a mix of protest, lobbying, and litigation, the movement has contributed to the closing of several animal labs, including the Defense Department's Wound Laboratory and a University of Pennsylvania facility involved in research on head injuries. In 1988 Trans-Species, a recent addition to the animal rights movement, forced the Cornell University Medical College to give up a $600,000 grant, which left unfinished a fourteen-year research project in which cats were fed barbiturates.[63]

As the most visible of the animal rights groups, PETA embarked on an intensive campaign in the early 1990s to influence children's attitudes and values toward society's treatment of animals. Using a seven-foot mascot, Chris P. Carrot, to spread its message, PETA organizers have sought to visit public schools throughout the Midwest. Although some of their message is noncontroversial (for example, children should eat their vegetables), they also argue aggressively against consuming meat. Chris P. Carrot thus carries a placard stating, "Eat your veggies, not your friends." More prosaically, PETA produces publications denouncing hunting, trapping, and other practices that abuse animals; PETA's *Kids Can Save Animals* even encourages students to

> call the toll-free numbers of department stores to protest furs and animal-test cosmetics, to call sponsors and object to rodeos, circulate petitions for "violence-free" schools that do not use frog corpses for biology lab, and to boycott zoos and aquariums, and marine parks.[64]

It is not surprising that PETA protests have spawned countermobilizations, as, for example, in the growth of an antianimal rights movement. In the forefront of such actions are organizations that support hunting as a sport. They must contend with a public that has become increasingly hostile to hunting; a 1993 survey reported that 54 percent of Americans were opposed to hunting, with the youngest respondents (ages eighteen to twenty-nine) expressing the most negative sentiments.[65] In addition, farm and medical groups have mobilized against the animal rights movements, and a number of new organizations have been formed. Such groups range from the incurably ill for Animal Research (iiFAR), representing those who hope for medical breakthroughs in biomedical research, to the Foundation for Animal Health, organized by the American Medical Association in hopes of diverting funds away from animal rights groups.

The most visible group in the animal rights countermobilization, Putting People First (PPF), claimed more than 35,000 members and one hundred local chapters within one year of its formation. PPF counted hunting clubs, trapping associations, rodeos, zoos, circuses, veterinary hospitals, kennels and stables, and carriage horse companies among its membership. Taking a page from animal rights' public relations activities, PPF has begun a Hunters for the Hungry campaign that has provided 160,000 pounds of venison to economically disadvantaged families in the South. To PPF, the animal rights movement has declared war on much of America and is "seeking to destroy a way of life—to tell us we can no longer believe in the JudeoChristian principles this country was founded on. They insist every form of life is equal: humans and dogs and slugs and cockroaches." PPF leaders see the organization as speaking for "the average American who eats meat and drinks milk, benefits from medical research, wears leather, wool, and fur, hunts and fishes, and owns a pet and goes to the zoo." [66]

The intensity of conflict between the animal rights advocates and their opponents typifies the deep cultural divisions of the postindustrial era. Similar differences affect many other key issues, from gun control to education (school choice) to immigration policy. Moreover, many of these conflicts do not lend themselves to compromise, whether because of vast policy differences or group leaders' desire to keep "hot" issues alive as a way to increase membership.

Affluent Members and Sponsors.   Although postindustrial conflicts generate the issues for group development, the spread of affluence also systematically contributes to group formation and maintenance. In fact, affluence creates a large potential for "checkbook" membership. Issue-based groups have done especially well. Membership in such groups as PETA and Common Cause might once have been a luxury, but the growth in discretionary income has placed the cost of modest dues within reach of most citizens. For a $15–25 membership fee, people can make an "expressive" statement without incurring other organizational obligations. Increasing education also has been a factor in that "organizations become more numerous as ideas become more important." [67]

Reform groups and citizens' groups depend heavily on the educated white middle class for their membership and financial base. A Common Cause poll, for example, found that members' mean family income was $17,000 above the national average and that 43 percent of members had an advanced degree.[68] Animal rights groups display a similar membership profile, although they are disproportionately composed of college-educated, urban, professional women.[69] Other expressive groups, including those on the political right, have been aided as well by the increased wealth of constituents and the community activism that result from education and occupational advancement.

Groups can overcome the free rider problem by finding a sponsor who will support the organization and reduce its reliance on membership contributions. During the 1960s and 1970s private sources (often foundations) backed groups. Jeffrey Berry's 1977 study of eighty-three public interest organizations found that at least one-third received more than half their funds from private foundations, and one in ten received more than 90 percent of its operating expenses from such sources.[70] Jack Walker's 1981 study of Washington-based interest groups confirmed many of Berry's earlier findings, indicating that foundation support and individual grants provide 30 percent of all citizens' group funding.[71] Such patterns produce many staff organizations with no members, raising major questions about the representativeness of the new interest group universe. Finally, groups themselves can sponsor other groups. The National Council of Senior Citizens (NCSC), for example, was founded by the AFL-CIO, which helped recruit members from the ranks of organized labor and still pays part of NCSC's expenses.

Patrons often are more than just passive sponsors who respond to group requests for funds. In many cases group mobilization comes from the top down, rather than the reverse. The patron—whether an individual such as General Motors' heir Stewart Mott or the peripatetic conservative Richard Mellon Scaife, an institution, another group, or a government entity—may initiate group development, to the point of seeking entrepreneurs and providing a forum for group pronouncements.

Postindustrial affluence and the spread of education also have contributed to group formation and maintenance through the development of a large pool of potential group organizers. This group tends to be young, well educated, and from the middle class, caught up in a movement for change and inspired by ideas or doctrine. The 1960s was a period of opportunity for entrepreneurs, as college enrollments skyrocketed and powerful forces such as civil rights and the antiwar movement contributed to an idea orientation in both education and politics. Communications-based professions—from religion to law to university teaching—attracted social activists, many of whom became involved in forming groups. The government itself became a major source of what James Q. Wilson called "organizing cadres." Government employees of the local Community Action Agencies of the War on Poverty and personnel from Volunteers in Service to America were active in forming voluntary associations, some created to oppose government actions.[72]

Technological Opportunities.   Compounding the effects of the growing number of increasingly active groups are changes in what organizations can do, largely as a result of contemporary technology. On a grand scale, technological change produces new interests, such as cable television and the silicon chip industry, which organize to protect themselves as interests historically have done. Beyond this communications breakthroughs make group politics much more visible than in the past. Civil rights activists in the South understood this, as did many protesters against the Vietnam War. Of equal importance, however, is the fact that much of what contemporary interest groups do derives directly from developments in information-related technology. Many group activities, whether fund-raising or grassroots lobbying or sampling members' opinions, rely heavily on computer-based operations that can target and send messages and process the responses.

Although satellite television links and survey research are important tools, the technology of direct mail has had by far the greatest impact on interest group politics. With a minimum initial investment and a reasonably good list of potential contributors, any individual can become a group entrepreneur. These activists literally create organizations, often based on emotion-laden appeals about specific issues, from Sarah Brady's Handgun Control to Randall Terry's Operation Rescue.[73] To the extent that an entrepreneur can attract members and continue to pay the costs of direct mail, he or she can claim—with substantial legitimacy—to articulate the organization's positions on the issues, positions probably defined initially by the entrepreneur.

In addition to helping entrepreneurs develop organizations that require few (if any) active members, information technology also allows many organizations to exert considerable pressure on elected officials. Washington-based interests are increasingly turning to grassroots techniques to influence legislators. Indeed, after the mid-1980s these tactics had become the norm in many lobbying efforts, to the point that they were sometimes discounted as routine and "manufactured" by groups and consultants.

Communications technology is widely available but expensive. In the health care debate, most mobilized opinion has come from the best-financed interests, such as insurance companies, the drug industry, and the medical profession. Money remains the mother's milk of politics. Indeed, one of the major impacts of technology may be to inflate the costs of political action, whether for candidates engaged in increasingly expensive election campaigns or in public lobbying efforts that employ specifically targeted advertisements and highly sophisticated grassroots efforts.

Group Impact on Policy and Process

Assessing the policy impact of interest group actions has never been an easy task. We may, however, gain some insights by looking at two different levels of analysis: a broad, societal overview and a middle-range search for relatively specific patterns of influence (for example, the role of direct mail or political action committee funding). Considering impact at the level of individual lobbying efforts is also possible, but here even the best work relies heavily on nuance and individualistic explanations.

Although the public often views lobbying and special interest campaigning with distrust, political scientists have not produced much evidence to support this perspective. Academic studies of interest groups have demonstrated few conclusive links between campaign or lobbying efforts and actual patterns of influence. This does not mean that such patterns or individual instances do not exist. Rather, the question of determining impact is exceedingly difficult to answer. The difficulty is, in fact, compounded by groups' claims of impact and decisionmakers' equally vociferous claims of freedom from any outside influence.

The major studies of lobbying in the 1960s generated a most benign view of this activity. Lester Milbrath painted a Boy Scout–like picture of Washington lobbyists, depicting them as patient contributors to policy-making.[74] Rarely stepping over the limits of propriety, lobbyists had only a marginal impact at best. Similarly, Raymond Bauer, Ithiel de Sola Pool, and Lewis Dexter's lengthy analysis of foreign trade policy, published in

1963, found the business community to be largely incapable of influencing Congress in its lobbying attempts.[75] Given the many internal divisions within the private sector over trade matters, this was not an ideal issue to illustrate business cooperation, but the research stood as the central work on lobbying for more than a decade—ironically, in the very period when groups proliferated and became more sophisticated in their tactics. Lewis Dexter, in his 1969 treatment of Washington representatives as an emerging professional group, suggested that lobbyists would play an increasingly important role in complex policymaking, but he provided few details.[76]

The picture of benevolent lobbyists who seek to engender trust and convey information, although accurate in a limited way, does not provide a complete account of the options open to any interest group that seeks to exert influence. Lyndon Johnson's long-term relationship with the Texas-based construction firm of Brown & Root illustrates the depth of some ties between private interests and public officeholders. The Washington representative for Brown & Root claimed that he never went to Capitol Hill for any legislative help because "people would resent political influence."[77] But Johnson, first as a representative and later as a senator, systematically dealt directly with the top management (the Brown family) and aided the firm by passing along crucial information and watching over key government-sponsored construction projects.

> [The link between Johnson and Brown & Root] was, indeed, a partnership, the campaign contributions, the congressional look-out, the contracts, the appropriations, the telegrams, the investment advice, the gifts and the hunts and the free airplane rides—it was an alliance of mutual reinforcement between a politician and a corporation. If Lyndon was Brown & Root's kept politician, Brown & Root was Lyndon's kept corporation. Whether he concluded that they were public-spirited partners or corrupt ones, "political allies" or cooperating predators, in its dimensions and its implications for the structure of society, their arrangement was a new phenomenon on its way to becoming the new pattern for American society.[78]

Entering the twenty-first century, one could legitimately substitute Sen. Trent Lott's, R-Miss., name for Johnson's and that of defense and shipbuilding giant Northrup Gruman for Brown & Root; the basic set of links were very similar. Any number of events, such as the 1980s savings and loan scandal, show that legislators can be easily approached with unethical and illegal propositions; such access is one price of an open system. In addition, the growth of interest representation has raised long-term questions about the ethics of former government officials acting as lobbyists. Despite some modest reforms, many executive branch officials, members of Congress, and high-level bureaucrats leave office and eventually return to lobby their friends and associates. Access is still important, and its price is often high.

Contemporary Practices

Modern lobbying emphasizes information, often on complex and difficult subjects. Determining actual influence is, as one lobbyist noted, "like finding a black cat in the coal bin at midnight," but we can make some assessments about the impact of group proliferation and increased activity.[79]

First, more groups are engaged in more forms of lobbying than ever before—both classic forms, such as offering legislative testimony, and newer forms, such as mounting computer-based direct mail campaigns to stir up grassroots support.[80] As the number of new groups rises and existing groups become more active, the pressure on decisionmakers—especially legislators—mounts at a corresponding rate. Thus a second general point can be made: Congressional reforms that opened up the legislative process during the 1970s have provided a much larger number of access points for today's lobbyists. Most committee (and subcommittee) sessions, including the markups at which legislation is written, remain open to the public, as do many conference committee meetings. More roll call votes are taken, and congressional floor action is televised. Thus interests can monitor individual members of Congress as never before. This does nothing, however, to facilitate disinterested decision making or foster graceful compromises on most issues.

In fact, monitoring the legions of Washington policy actors has become the central activity of many groups. As Robert Salisbury has observed, "Before [organized interests] can advocate a policy, they must determine what position they wish to embrace. Before they do this, they must find out not only what technical policy analysis can tell them but what relevant others, inside and outside the government, are thinking and planning." [81] Given the volume of policymaking, just keeping up can be a major undertaking.

The government itself has encouraged many interests to organize and articulate their demands. The rise of group activity thus leads us to another level of analysis: the impact of contemporary interest group politics on society. Harking back to Lowi's description of interest group liberalism, we see the eventual result to be an immobilized society, trapped by its willingness to allow interests to help fashion self-serving policies that embody no firm criteria of success or failure. For example, even in the midst of the savings and loan debacle, the government continued to offer guarantees to various sectors, based not on future promise but on past bargains and continuing pressures.

The notion advanced by Olson that some such group-related stagnation affects all stable democracies makes the prognosis all the more serious. In summary form, Olson argued that the longer societies are politically stable, the more interest groups they develop; the more interest groups they develop, the worse they work economically.[82] The United Automobile Workers' protectionist leanings, the American Medical Association's fight against intervention by the Federal Trade Commission into physicians' business affairs, and the insurance industry's successful prevention of FTC investigations all illustrate the possible link between self-centered group action and poor economic performance—that is, higher automobile prices, doctors' fees, and insurance premiums for no better product or service.

In particular, the politics of Social Security demonstrate the difficulties posed by a highly mobilized, highly representative set of interests. Virtually everyone agrees that the Social Security system requires serious reform; at the same time, many groups of elderly citizens (with the AARP among the most moderate) have resisted changes that might reduce their benefits over time. Moreover, many groups outside the traditional Social Security policy community have argued for the system's privatization, either partial or total. The system will have to be modified to maintain its viability, but groups will continue to frame the debate in ways that benefit their interests, perhaps at the expense of the general good.

Conclusion

The ultimate consequences of the growing number of organized interests, their expanding activities in Washington and in state capitals, and the growth of citizens' groups remain unclear. From one perspective, such changes have made politics more representative than ever. Although most occupation-based groups traditionally have been well organized in American politics, many other interests have not been. Population groupings such as African Americans, Hispanics, and women have mobilized since the 1950s and 1960s; animals and the unborn are well represented in the interest group arena, as is the broader "public interest," however defined.

Broadening the base of interest group participation may have opened the political process, thus curbing the influence of special interests. For example, agricultural policymaking in the postwar era was largely the prerogative of a tight "iron triangle" composed of congressional committee members from farm states, government officials representing the agriculture bureaucracy, and major agriculture groups such as the American Farm Bureau. Activity in the 1970s by consumer and environmental interest groups changed agricultural politics, making it more visible and lengthening the agenda to consider such questions as how farm subsidies affect consumer purchasing power and how fertilizers, herbicides, and pesticides affect public health.

From another perspective, more interest groups and more openness do not necessarily mean better policies or ones that genuinely represent the national interest. Government may be unable to process demands effectively, and openness may result in complexity. Moreover, the content of demands may be ambiguous and priorities difficult to set.

Finally, elected leaders may find it practically impossible to build the kinds of political coalitions necessary to govern effectively, especially in an era of partisan parity and the unrelenting demands of the permanent campaign, which requires continual fund-raising from organized interests.

This second perspective suggests that the American constitutional system is extraordinarily susceptible to the excesses of minority faction—in an ironic way a potential victim of the Madisonian solution of dealing with the tyranny of the majority. Decentralized government, especially one that wields considerable power, provides no adequate controls over the excessive demands of interest group politics. Decisionmakers feel obliged to respond to many of these demands, and "the cumulative effect of this pressure has been the relentless and extraordinary rise of government spending and inflationary deficits, as well as the frustration of efforts to enact effective national policies on most major issues." [83]

In sum, the problem of contemporary interest group politics is one of representation. For particular interests, especially those that are well defined and adequately funded, the government is responsive to the issues of their greatest concern. But representation is not just a matter of responding to specific interests or citizens; the government also must respond to the collective needs of a society, and here the success of individual interests reduces the possibility of overall responsiveness. The very vibrancy and success of contemporary groups contribute to a society that finds it increasingly difficult to formulate solutions to complex policy questions.

Notes

1. Kay Lehman Schlozman and John T. Tierney, "More of the Same: Washington Pressure Group Activity in a Decade of Change," *Journal of Politics* 45 (May 1983): 351–377. For an earlier era, see Margaret S. Thompson, *The Spider's Web* (Ithaca: Cornell University, 1985).

2. Theodore J. Lowi, *The End of Liberalism*, 2d ed. (New York: Norton, 1979); Mancur Olson, *The Rise and Decline of Nations* (New Haven, Conn.: Yale University, 1982).

3. Mancur Olson, *The Logic of Collective Action* (Cambridge, Mass.: Harvard University, 1971); Robert Salisbury, "An Exchange Theory of Interest Groups," *Midwest Journal of Political Science* 13 (February 1969): 1–32; and Terry M. Moe, *The Organization of Interests* (Chicago: University of Chicago, 1980).

4. David Truman's widely used definition of interest groups is "any group that, on the basis of one or more shared attitudes, makes certain claims upon other groups in the society for the establishment, maintenance, or enhancement of forms of behavior that are implied by the shared attitudes." Truman, *The Governmental Process*, 2d ed. (New York: Knopf, 1971).

5. James Madison, "Federalist 10," in *The Federalist Papers*, 2d ed., ed. Roy P. Fairfield (Baltimore: Johns Hopkins University, 1981), 16.

6. L. Harmon Ziegler and Wayne Peak, *Interest Groups in American Society*, 2d ed. (Englewood Cliffs, N.J.: Prentice-Hall, 1972), 35.

7. Michael Trister, "The Rise and Reform of Stealth PACs," *The American Prospect*, 11 (September 24, 2000), 32–35.

8. Anthony Corrado, "Financing the 2000 Elections," in *The Election of 2000*, ed. Gerald Pomper (New York: Chatham House, 2001), x.

9. Truman, *Governmental Process*, 519.
10. Carole Greenwald, *Group Power* (New York: Praeger, 1977), 305.
11. Leslie Wayne, "800-Pound Guests at the Pentagon," *New York Times*, March 15, 1998, section 5, 3.
12. Lowi, *End of Liberalism*, 62.
13. Murray Edelman, *The Politics of Symbolic Action* (Chicago: Markham, 1971).
14. Theodore J. Lowi, *Incomplete Conquest: Governing America* (New York: Holt, Rinehart & Winston, 1976), 47.
15. Gabriel Almond and Sidney Verba, *The Civic Culture* (Boston: Little, Brown, 1963), chs. 8 and 10.
16. Ibid., 246–247.
17. Truman, *Governmental Process*, 57.
18. Salisbury, "Exchange Theory of Interest Groups," 3–4.
19. Truman, *Governmental Process*, 59.
20. James Q. Wilson, *Political Organizations* (New York: Basic Books, 1973), 154.
21. Major works include Olson, *The Logic of Collective Action;* Peter Clark and James Q. Wilson, "Incentive Systems: A Theory of Organizations," *Administrative Science Quarterly* 6 (September 1961): 126–166; Wilson, *Political Organizations;* Terry Moe, "A Calculus of Group Membership," *American Journal of Political Science* 24 (November 1980): 593–632; and Moe, *Organization of Interests.* The notion of group organizers as political entrepreneurs is best represented by Salisbury, "Exchange Theory of Interest Groups," 1–15.
22. See Clark and Wilson, "Incentive Systems," 129–166; and Wilson, *Political Organizations*, 30–51. In recent years researchers have preferred the term *expressive* to *purposive*, because, as Salisbury notes, *purposive* includes what we call collective material benefits. *Material, solidary,* and *expressive* would seem to be mutually exclusive conceptual categories. See Salisbury, "Exchange Theory of Interest Groups," 16–17.
23. Moe, *Organization of Interests*, 144.
24. John Mark Hansen, "The Political Economy of Group Membership," *American Political Science Review* 79 (March 1985): 79–96.
25. Albert O. Hirschman, *Shifting Involvements* (Princeton: Princeton University, 1982).
26. Michael W. McCann, "Public Interest Liberalism and the Modern Regulatory State," *Polity* 21 (Winter 1988): 385.
27. See, for example, R. Kenneth Godwin and R. C. Mitchell, "Rational Models, Collective Goods, and Non-Electoral Political Behavior," *Western Political Quarterly* 35 (June 1982): 161–180; and Larry Rothenberg, "Choosing among Public Interest Groups: Membership, Activism and Retention in Political Organizations," *American Political Science Review* 82 (December 1988): 1129–1152.
28. Jack L. Walker, "The Origins and Maintenance of Interest Groups in America," *American Political Science Review* 77 (June 1983): 390–406; for a conservative critique of this trend, see James T. Bennett and Thomas Di Lorenzo, *Destroying Democracy* (Washington, D.C.: Cato Institute, 1986). See also many of the articles in Mark P. Petracca, ed., *The Politics of Interests* (Boulder, Colo.: Westview, 1992).
29. Walker, "Origins and Maintenance of Interest Groups," 16.
30. Robert H. Salisbury, "Interest Representation and the Dominance of Institutions," *American Political Science Review* 78 (March 1984): 64–77.
31. See Jeffery Berry, *The New Liberalism: The Power of Citizen Groups* (Washington, D.C.: Brookings Institution, 1999).
32. Gregory Colgate, ed., *National Trade and Professional Associations of the United States, 1982* (Washington, D.C.: Columbia Books, 1984).
33. Cited in Kevin Phillips, *Arrogant Capital* (Boston: Back Bay/Little, Brown, 1995), 43.
34. *Encyclopedia of Associations,* http://www.library.dialog.com/bluesheets/html/bl0114.html, December 5, 2001.

35. Samuel H. Beer, "In Search of a New Public Philosophy," in *The New American Political System*, ed. Anthony King (Washington, D.C.: American Enterprise Institute, 1978), 12.
36. Ibid., 10.
37. Hugh Heclo, "Issue Networks and the Executive Establishment," in King, *New American Political System*, 89.
38. Beer, "In Search of a New Public Philosophy," 16.
39. Allan J. Cigler and Cheryl Swanson, "Politics and Older Americans," in *The Dynamics of Aging*, ed. Forrest J. Berghorn, Donna E. Schafer, and Associates (Boulder, Colo.: Westview, 1981), 171.
40. The AARP offers free memberships to spouses, which artificially enlarges its ranks, but it remains—by any count—a huge group.
41. See John Tierney's articles, "Old Money, New Power," *New York Times Magazine*, October 23, 1988, 17; and "The Big Gray Money Machine," *Newsweek*, August 15, 1988, 47.
42. Tierney, "Old Money, New Power."
43. Heclo, "Issue Networks and the Executive Establishment," 96.
44. Walker, "Origins and Maintenance of Interest Groups," 401.
45. Stuart Langton, "Citizen Participation in America: Current Reflections on the State of the Art," in *Citizen Participation in America*, ed. Stuart Langton (Lexington, Mass.: Lexington Books, 1978), 7.
46. Ibid., 4.
47. Walker, "Origins and Maintenance of Interest Groups," 398.
48. Salisbury, "Exchange Theory of Interest Groups," 25.
49. Quoted in Ted Williams, "River Retrieval," *Fly Rod and Reel* 15 (January–February 1994): 17.
50. The April 2001 ESPN purchase both enhances and limits the potential political clout of BASS. It loses much of its independent political identity, but might well benefit from its position within the ABC-Disney corporate family.
51. Ray Scott, "Presidential Promises," *BassMaster*, May 1989, 7 (emphasis added).
52. David S. Broder, "Introduction," in *Emerging Coalitions in American Politics*, ed. Seymour Martin Lipset (San Francisco: Institute for Contemporary Studies, 1978), 3.
53. Everett Carll Ladd Jr. with Charles D. Hadley, *Transformations of the American Party System*, 2d ed. (New York: Norton, 1978), 182.
54. Ibid., 196.
55. See, for example, Daniel Bell, *The End of Ideology* (New York: Free Press, 1960).
56. Ladd and Hadley, *Transformations of the American Party System*, 203.
57. For all three quotes in this paragraph, Walter Dean Burnham, *Critical Elections and the Mainsprings of American Politics* (New York: Norton, 1970), 139.
58. Richard E. Dawson, *Public Opinion and Contemporary Disarray* (New York: Harper and Row, 1973), 194.
59. Everett Carll Ladd, *Where Have All the Voters Gone?* 2d ed. (New York: Norton, 1982).
60. But see Virginia Gray and David Lowery, *The Population Ecology of Interest Representation* (Ann Arbor: University of Michigan, 1996).
61. Kevin Kasowski, "Showdown on the Hunting Ground," *Outdoor America* 51 (Winter 1986): 9.
62. Lauristan R. King and Kimberly Stephens, "Politics and the Animal Rights Movement" (paper presented at the annual meeting of the Southern Political Science Association, Tampa, Fla., November 7–9, 1991).
63. Sara Lyall, "Scientist Gives up Grant to Do Research on Cats," *New York Times*, November 21, 1988, A12.

64. John Balzar, quoted in Kit Harrison, "Animal 'Rightists' Target Children," *Sports Afield* 211 (June 1994): 12.
65. "Americans Divided on Animal Rights," *Los Angeles Times*, December 17, 1993, B3. This national survey of 1,612 adults also found that 50 percent opposed the wearing of fur.
66. Phil McCombs, "Attack of the Omnivore," *Washington Post*, March 27, 1992, B1, B4.
67. Wilson, *Political Organizations*, 201.
68. Andrew S. McFarland, *Common Cause* (Chatham, N.J.: Chatham House, 1984), 48–49.
69. King and Stephens, "Politics and the Animal Rights Movement," 15.
70. Jeffrey M. Berry, *Lobbying for the People* (Princeton: Princeton University, 1977), 72.
71. Walker, "Origins and Maintenance of Interest Groups," 400.
72. Wilson, *Political Organizations*, 203.
73. Sarah Brady, wife of former White House press secretary James Brady, organized Handgun Control after her husband was wounded in John Hinckley's 1981 attack on Ronald Reagan. Randall Terry formed Operation Rescue, which seeks to shut down abortion clinics through direct action (for example, blocking entrances), after concluding that other antiabortion rights groups were not effective in halting abortions.
74. Lester Milbrath, *The Washington Lobbyists* (Chicago: Rand-McNally, 1963).
75. Raymond Bauer, Ithiel de Sola Pool, and Lewis Dexter, *American Business and Public Policy* (New York: Atherton, 1963).
76. Lewis A. Dexter, *How Organizations Are Represented in Washington* (Indianapolis: Bobbs-Merrill, 1969), ch. 9.
77. See Ronnie Dugger, *The Politician* (New York: Norton, 1982), 273; and Robert A. Caro, *The Years of Lyndon Johnson: The Path to Power* (New York: Knopf, 1982) and *The Years of Lyndon Johnson: Means of Ascent* (New York: Knopf 1990).
78. Dugger, *Politician*, 286.
79. Quoted in Burdett A. Loomis, "A New Era: Groups and the Grass Roots," in *Interest Group Politics*, 2d ed., ed. Allan J. Cigler and Burdett A. Loomis (Washington, D.C.: CQ Press, 1983), 184.
80. Schlozman and Tierney, "Washington Pressure Group Activity," 18.
81. Robert H. Salisbury, "The Paradox of Interest Groups in Washington—More Groups and Less Clout," in *The New American Political System*, 2d ed., ed. Anthony King (Washington, D.C.: American Enterprise Institute, 1990), 225–226.
82. For an expansion of this argument, see Jonathan Rauch, *Demosclerosis* (New York: New York Times Books, 1994).
83. Everett Carll Ladd, "How to Tame the Special Interest Groups," *Fortune*, October 1980, 6.

I. GROUP ORGANIZATION

2

Targeting Success
The Enduring Power of the NRA
Kelly D. Patterson and Matthew M. Singer

Perhaps no single American interest group is regarded with either greater affection or greater disdain than the National Rifle Association (NRA). Founded more than a century ago, the NRA in the past three decades has evolved into a high-profile advocate for the rights of gun owners, opposing any attempt to compromise what the group leaders argue is the unrestricted right to bear arms as found in the Second Amendment to the U.S. Constitution. The NRA has been largely successful in its policy goals despite the fact that public opinion over the period has supported much stricter gun controls, especially after the Columbine shootings in 1999.

In this chapter, Kelly D. Patterson and Matthew M. Singer examine the origin, development, and activities of the group from an organizational perspective. Over the past thirty years, the NRA has gone through a metamorphosis from mainly an organization for sportspersons into a comprehensive political organization with a cadre of Washington lobbyists, a well-funded political action committee (PAC), a legal foundation, and grassroots political connections in every congressional district. The NRA is currently one of the largest membership groups in Washington, with a full- and part-time staff of over 500, more than 4 million members, and a budget of $200 million.

Despite the success and size of the NRA, the evolution of the group has caused internal stress. Membership fluctuations have caused financial hardship, and the organization has been beset with factional difficulties because it must satisfy two types of members: the Second Amendment fundamentalists who resist any attempt to regulate firearms or ammunition and the shooters who join for sporting and shooting activities. The latter do not see some restrictions on the right to bear arms as unreasonable. The challenge for the NRA, according to Patterson and Singer, "will be to maintain its commitment to a goal that generates enthusiasm (and contributions) from among its members while not alienating the moderate elements that enlarge its membership base."

Single-interest groups capable of promoting one issue over a variety of issues have become a prominent fixture in American politics. These groups condense the emotional aspects of a given issue and vividly connect that issue to the life of the individual.[1] For a variety of reasons, the number of these groups has increased dramatically in America, and the effects of their proliferation can be seen throughout American politics.[2] Their power has been amplified by their aggressive tactics in competitive congressional campaigns and their presence in battleground states in presidential elections.[3] Few single-interest groups have enjoyed the success and notoriety of the National Rifle Association (NRA).

The NRA defines what it means to be a condensational interest group. Its stated goal and national reputation revolve around its ability to promote and protect the rights of gun owners. Its ability to focus on the achievement of its goal seems to be the envy of other interest groups. Very few single-interest groups are as large, complex, and powerful as the NRA. The magnitude of its operation, the size of its budget, and the intensity of its ideological commitment make the NRA a formidable force. It participates in thousands of elections in one form or another in any given electoral cycle and raises millions of dollars to disburse to candidates who are committed to its goals.

Normally success does not come without a price. Organizations that grow powerful and win political battles can become difficult to manage and create bitter enemies. The NRA is no exception. In the past two decades the NRA has suffered attacks from presidents (Republican and Democratic), struggled through financial difficulties, and waged internecine battles that have fractured the organization. It has survived a public and presidential onslaught in the wake of Columbine and other school shootings. The NRA has thrived through these difficulties; in May 2001, *Fortune* magazine named the NRA the most powerful lobby in America.[4] In another poll taken in March of 2005, 73 members of the House of Representatives identified the NRA as the most powerful lobbying group on Capitol Hill.[5] However, in November 2005 when 169 members of Congress were asked which lobby their party would "buck more often if the group weren't so powerful," the NRA was the most frequent response among Republicans and the second most frequent response among Democrats.[6] Today, the NRA seems to have achieved many of its most important goals, including a repeal of the ban on assault rifles, and enjoys continuing success in the electoral arena.

How has the NRA arrived at this point? Are these challenges and successes inevitable in any single-interest group that grows to the size and prominence of the NRA? In this chapter we look at the history and development of the NRA. We focus on the organization's leadership, growth in membership, and campaign activities. We begin with a brief discussion of its history and the rise of its organization and influence. In the next section we look at why individuals join the NRA and the benefits that it provides to its members. We argue that a combination of environmental and organizational factors have led to its growth in membership. Finally, we examine the NRA's participation in numerous campaign activities. These activities receive additional scrutiny in light of the Bipartisan Campaign Reform Act (BCRA) that altered the ways that interest groups participate in political campaigns. We conclude that the NRA, like most large enterprises, faces numerous trade-offs as it expends resources in pursuit of multiple, often conflicting, goals contained in its charter.

History and Purpose

David Truman theorized that groups form to meet the needs of individuals in an increasingly complex society. This *disturbance* theory contends that groups form in response to changes in society and the economy.[7] Disturbances such as war, recessions, and depressions stimulate the creation of groups whose purpose is to restore the balance in society. In the wake of the Civil War, Union officers sought to find a remedy for the poor marksmanship and rifle skills exhibited by the Union throughout the conflict. The original charter of the NRA stated: "The object for which [this organization] is formed is the improvement of its members in marksmanship, and to promote the introduction of the system of accuracy drill and rifle practice as part of the military drill of the National Guard of this and other states, and for those purposes to provide a suitable range or ranges in the vicinity of the City of New York."[8] Through proper training and facilities, the NRA hoped to avert another poor performance by U.S. soldiers.

The organization grew slowly until Congress passed the Militia Act of 1903. This act authorized creation of a national board for the promotion of rifle practice. One of the first acts of the board was the sale of surplus weapons and ammunition to rifle clubs around the United States. The sale of these weapons created potential members who could fuel the organization's growth.[9] Through the first half of the twentieth century the NRA grew modestly. It had fewer than 300,000 members in the 1950s and was concerned primarily with serving the shooting and sporting needs of its members, as identified in the original charter.[10]

Although Truman's theory may explain the origin of groups, it does not explain how groups evolve over time, prosper, or fail altogether. Robert Salisbury posited that groups prosper if the leadership makes a profit and the group provides a proper mix of incentives to its members.[11] This appears to be what the NRA has done. Over time, it built on the mandate in the original charter to adjust to the changing political climate. Where it once provided only a range of material incentives to its members (access to ranges and gun training, for example), it gradually began to play an active role in efforts by the federal government to regulate firearms. In the 1930s Congress passed three main gun control acts. The Uniform Firearms Act of 1930 forbade the delivery of pistols to "convicts, drug addicts, habitual drunkards, incompetents, and minors under the age of 18." Karl T. Frederick, then president of the NRA, served as a special consultant in the framing of this act. The NRA also supported the National Firearms Act of 1934, which taxed and required registration of such firearms as machine guns, sawed-off rifles, and sawed-off shotguns although some controversy occurred over Congress's definition of a machine gun. Finally, the NRA supported the Federal Firearms Act of 1938, which imposed regulations on interstate and foreign commerce in firearms and pistol ammunition and restricted the use of sawed-off shotguns and machine guns.[12] In all of these attempts at regulation, the NRA worked as an insider and supported some restrictions on gun ownership.

The crucial moment for the organization came in 1968, when, in response to the assassinations of Martin Luther King Jr. and Robert F. Kennedy, Congress passed the Gun Control Act of 1968. The Gun Control Act prohibited unlicensed persons from buying, selling, or otherwise transferring rifles, shotguns, handguns, or ammunition outside of their home states or in any form of interstate commerce. Viewing these regulations as serious infringements on Second Amendment rights, the NRA opposed the act, but, as a group of hunters and gun owners interested mainly in sport, it was ill prepared for the rough-and-tumble world of politics. According to Neal Knox, the NRA's former first vice president, "the leadership lacked a taste for [politics]. They considered lobbying beneath them."[13] The NRA had fewer than a million members at the time, and it was unable to prevent passage of the act. To succeed in the future, the NRA needed to provide ideological, or what are often called purposive, incentives to its members. In this case the incentive came to be defined primarily around the constitutional right to keep and bear arms.

The expansion of the incentives offered by the NRA was reflected by changes made to the charter in July of 1977. The certificate of amendment to this charter states that one of the purposes of the NRA is "generally to encourage the lawful ownership and use of small arms by citizens of good repute; and to educate, promote, and further the right of the individual of good repute to keep and bear arms as a common law and constitutional right both of the individual citizen and of the collective militia." The grafting of this additional purpose into the original goal of educating citizens and promoting firearm safety places the organization in a precarious position. Although the NRA can continue to try to fulfill its original purpose, the addition of a new mission can alter the mix of members in the group, making it easier for conflicts to occur. What happens when the portion of the membership dedicated to hunting and sport disagree with the single-minded pursuit of Second Amendment freedoms? Over the past two decades the NRA has faced just such a dilemma.

Membership Has Its Privileges

The NRA is a full-service interest group. It attracts and retains a large and faithful membership through a range of benefits and plans. It services that membership with a gleaming building in Fairfax, Virginia, and a full- and part-time staff of over 500 individuals. The NRA appeals to two types of gun owners: sportspersons, including both hunters and competitive shooters; and Second Amendment fundamentalists.[14] Tanya Metaksa, former director of the NRA's Institute for Legislative Action (ILA), explained that the NRA changed in the late 1970s from a small, tightly knit group of people who were interested in target shooting and supporting the military to a group that began to include members with more diverse interests.[15] To entice these various groups of gun owners to join the NRA, the organization offers a range of benefits that can be categorized into three types: material, solidary, and purposive.[16]

Material incentives involve actual goods, such as assistance with work or other financial opportunities. The NRA has cultivated a relationship with police departments by offering police training sessions that include Police and Security Firearm Training and Law Enforcement Instructor Certification, and it provides as much as $25,000 in life insurance to the families of NRA-member police officers killed feloniously in the line of duty. The NRA also sponsors and trains shooters going to the Olympics and funds research on the causes of violent crime. It is fair to say that large numbers of individuals are connected to the organization through the kinds of opportunities the NRA makes available to any individual who can make a living working with or studying a firearm. The NRA also offers selective benefits that appeal to all of its members. These benefits include gun loss insurance (ArmsCare coverage in the amount of $1,000); accidental death insurance (in the amount of $10,000); and car rental, hotel, and airline discounts.

Numerous opportunities exist for members to develop relationships with each other. These **solidary incentives** can make an otherwise large group seem more like a community, thereby providing the members with a social outlet. The NRA is composed of over 10,000 state associations and local clubs.[17] To better serve its members, the NRA provides specialized benefits to its different membership groups. For the sportspersons, the NRA offers such activities as safety and training programs and recreational and competitive shooting. Every year, more than 700,000 Americans learn from 46,000 NRA certified instructors the safe way to own and use firearms. Safety and training programs include comprehensive clinics for hunters, home firearms safety courses, beginner-to-advanced training for hunters and shooters, hobbyist and gunsmithing classes for gun collectors and designers, and an "Eddie Eagle" gun safety education course for youth. For recreational and competitive shooting, the NRA's Competitions Division sanctions over 12,000 shooting tournaments each year and sponsors more than fifty national shooting championships.

For its general membership, the Friends of the NRA is a grassroots fund-raising organization that hosts periodic dinners and auctions to raise money for local activities in support of NRA goals. The annual NRA national convention allows members the chance to mingle, view exhibits featuring the latest in gun technology, and attend speeches by NRA leaders and government officials. Over 60,000 members attended the 2005 convention in Houston, Texas.[18] Finally, the NRA publishes several different magazines—including *American Hunter, American Rifleman, America's 1st Freedom, Woman's Outlook, Shooting Sports USA,* and *NRA InSights*—for its different membership groups.[19]

The NRA also provides **purposive benefits.** A purposive benefit is the ideological satisfaction an individual receives from seeing the accomplishment of the group's goals. Citizens concerned with Second Amendment rights join the NRA because they expect the organization to protect their rights to own guns. In its pursuit of this goal, the organization has attained a reputation for effectiveness and influence matched by few single-interest groups.

The dedication of the organization and its membership to its purposive goals has earned the NRA a rather dubious reputation. Critics characterize the stance of the organization as fanatical and uncompromising. They "resist any gun controls on the fear that it will lead inexorably to confiscation of all guns owned by private citizens."[20] Some contend that the tactics and goals of the NRA have placed it out of step with its rank-and-file membership. Former president George Bush, for example, resigned his membership in 1995 when an NRA fund-raising letter referred to federal agents as "jack-booted government thugs."[21]

Public Opinion about the NRA

It is the single-minded pursuit of its goal that allows the NRA to withstand a public opinion environment that seems to be hostile toward its all-or-nothing approach. Dependable and long-term trend data about Americans' preferences for stricter gun control are not available, but the data that do exist tend to reveal widespread support for some kind of regulation of firearms.[22] The National Opinion Research Center/General Social Survey (NORC/GSS) indicates that since 1972 more than 70 percent of citizens have said that they would favor a law that would require a person to obtain a police permit before the purchase of a gun.[23] Since 2000, support levels for this measure have been higher than 80 percent.[24] Similar, if not higher, levels of support have been expressed for waiting periods before the purchase of a gun and for laws that would register all guns that are purchased.[25]

Although a majority of Americans favor stricter gun laws, recent polls show that support for increased restrictions on gun ownership is moderating. Since 1990, Gallup has periodically asked if people believe laws covering the sale of firearms should be made more strict, made less strict, or kept as they are. In the early 1990s, over 70 percent of Americans consistently felt that gun laws needed to be tougher. By 2004, however, that percentage had declined to 54 percent.[26] Thus, while there is still majority support for increased restrictions on gun ownership, that percentage has dropped dramatically. Polls reveal a gender gap on the issue: 72 percent of women would make gun laws more strict, but only 52 percent of men feel the same way.[27] Republicans and Democrats also differ in their attitudes on this question. Democrats generally favor more restrictions and are less likely to own firearms.[28]

It is no surprise that NRA members have very different opinions about gun control measures than the general population. In a poll of Utah voters in 1998, 44 percent of NRA members said that there should be no restrictions on gun ownership; only 11 percent of voters who did not belong to the NRA had the same opinion.[29] That same poll showed 42 percent of voters who do not belong to the NRA believe that gun control laws reduce violent crime, but only 12 percent of NRA members believe that tougher gun control legislation would have that effect.[30] Results from a more recent election show the same division. In a poll of Utah voters in 2002, 29 percent of NRA members thought the state's gun laws were too strict, but only 6 percent of voters who did not belong to the NRA had the same opinion.[31] Conversely, 59 percent of voters who did not belong to the NRA strongly agreed that concealed weapons should be banned; only 21 percent of NRA members strongly agreed. Among NRA members polled, 35 percent strongly disagreed with banning concealed weapons, and only 8 percent of nonmembers strongly disagreed.[32]

Because of the public's willingness to support gun control measures and the divergence in views between members of the NRA and the general public, the NRA's standing in public opinion polls has fluctuated. In 1989, 58 percent of the people asked said that they had a "very favorable" or "mostly favorable" opinion of the NRA. By 2000, only 51 percent evaluated the NRA favorably.[33] By the spring of 2006, however, that number had increased to 60 percent.[34] There is a large difference in how owners of guns and non-owners of guns evaluate the NRA: 71 percent of gun owners evaluate the NRA favorably, but only 36 percent of those who do not own guns have favorable evaluations of the organization.[35]

The NRA has also increasingly seen itself at the center of controversies that it did not create. In 1995, the bombing of the federal building in Okalahoma City came only a week after the release of the NRA's fundraising letter describing federal agents as "jack-booted government thugs" and as Nazi storm troopers. Membership subsequently declined as mainstream gun owners grew concerned that the organization had become too antigovernment and ideologically extreme.[36] It took several years and changes in the organization's leadership for the organization to project a more positive image.[37]

The NRA's largest challenge came in the wake of the Columbine school shooting. On April 20, 1999, in the worst school shooting in U.S. history, two students at Columbine High School in Littleton, Colorado, killed

12 of their fellow students and a teacher before they committed suicide. An additional 23 students were injured. The NRA's 1999 convention was scheduled to be held in nearby Denver during the first week in May. Denver's mayor, Wellington Webb, asked the NRA to cancel the convention.[38] The NRA scaled back its convention to one day and canceled a gun show, but it refused to cancel the convention completely. Eight thousand protesters, including students and parents from Columbine, marched in protest of the convention. Only 2,500 NRA members attended the meeting.

Charlton Heston, president of the NRA, asked the audience during his keynote address to have a moment of silence for the victims, and he praised the police officers involved in rescuing the students as "heroes who risked their lives to rescue the students of Columbine from evil, mindless executioners."[39] However, he defiantly explained the organization's decision to not cancel the convention:

> We will not be silent or be told, "Do not come here, you are not welcome in your own land...." What saddens me most [about Webb's request] is how that suggests complicity. It implies that 80 million honest gun owners are somehow to blame, that we don't care as much as they, or that we don't deserve to be as shocked and horrified as every other soul in America mourning for the people of Littleton.... We cannot, we must not let tragedy lay waste to the most rare, hard-won right in history.[40]

The public response to the shooting was an increase in public pressure for additional restrictions on the selling of guns. Polls taken the week after the Columbine shootings showed a 9 percent increase in the number of Americans who considered tougher gun laws the best way to prevent violence.[41] The day after the shooting, the Colorado legislature postponed action on three gun bills that would have reduced restrictions on concealed weapons, an action that more than a dozen state legislatures soon followed.[42] That same week, the U.S. Senate passed a gun control bill that restricted gun sales at gun shows and pawnshops, with Vice President Al Gore casting the deciding vote. Following the Senate vote, Senator Tom Daschle, then minority leader, said, "What you just saw was the [National Rifle Association] losing its grip on the U.S. Senate."[43]

Following the shootings, President Clinton proposed a waiting period for all gun purchases and making parents responsible for some gun crimes committed by their children.[44] He also hosted a meeting on youth violence that included most major gun producers but did not include the NRA. Gun manufacturers, breaking with the NRA, agreed to support increased restrictions on gun ownership. Industry experts agreed that the NRA's constituency was becoming increasingly divided by the public controversy.[45]

The NRA's Republican Party allies in the U.S. House of Representatives passed a much more restricted gun control measure than the Senate did. The NRA spent over $3 million lobbying to prevent the Senate bill from being enacted by the House; much of this money was spent on mailings to its members encouraging them to contact their representatives.[46] Clinton pressured the House to act on the Senate bill by reminding them of Columbine and other school shootings.[47] Despite this pressure, which included an explicit reference in the 2000 State of the Union address about how Columbine demonstrated the need for increased gun control, a compromise bill was never presented by the conference committee to the full Congress.

Growth of the NRA

Despite these challenges, or perhaps because of them, the NRA has experienced phenomenal growth over the past twenty years, and especially since 1999. Although membership fell to 2.8 million in May 1999 following Columbine, one year later its membership had grown to 3.7 million. By the end of 2000, membership had reached 4.2 million, an all-time high. While membership levels declined following the 2000 election, they steadily grew during the 2001–2006 period until they surpassed the 2000 peak. Heading into the 2006 Congressional elections, the NRA boasted a membership of almost 4.4 million.[48]

Various theories seek to account for the growth or decline in the membership of interest groups. Some theories emphasize the benefits that members receive for the dues that they pay.[49] If members receive ample material benefits for their dues, membership figures should remain stable and perhaps even increase. Other theories emphasize the policy environment in which the group operates. If the policy environment is hostile toward the goals of the organization, the threats should stimulate a growth in membership.[50] Single-interest groups routinely trumpet, if not exaggerate, the consequences of particular initiatives or policies in order to appeal for new membership and rally the faithful. Finally, some theories emphasize the economics of group membership. Recessions or increases in dues adversely affect membership because of the damage done to a member's or potential member's disposable income. When individuals have money to spend, they can spend it on interest groups; when economic difficulties arrive, such expenditures become hard to justify. We examine each of these theories below.

The NRA as an ideological organization faces three problems in relation to membership dues. First, demand for ideological benefits is highly *income elastic*, meaning that small fluctuations in members' income will result in large changes in how much individuals want what interest groups provide. If the economy is doing well and people are making more money, they feel more able to back up their ideological beliefs through membership in ideological organizations. Second, demand for ideological benefits will be very *price elastic*, meaning that the organization will be sensitive to

Figure 2.1.   NRA Membership, 1977–2006

Membership (in millions)

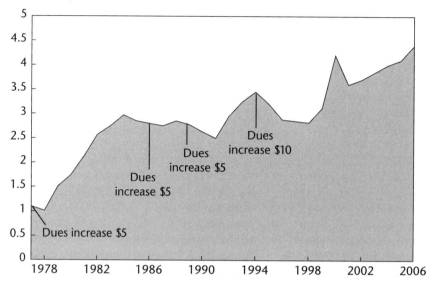

Sources: For membership data from 1977 to 1996 and from 2001 to 2006, see Membership Division of the NRA. For 1997, see "NRA Chief Overcomes Criticism from Ranks," *Lubbock Avalanche Journal*, February 12, 1997. For 1998, see Michael Janofsky, "Enthusiastic NRA Gives Mandate to Charlton Heston," *New York Times*, June 8, 1998, sec. A. For 1999, see Nancy Kletecka, "NRA Banquet Draws Large Crowd," *Southwest Daily Times*, February 8, 2000. For 2000, see "General Information," National Rifle Association, Institute for Legislative Action.

the level of dues. Third, demand for ideological benefits is *sensitive to changes in fashion.* When it is fashionable to belong to the NRA, membership will flourish. When members are viewed as extremists or radicals, it becomes unfashionable to belong to the NRA. Under such circumstances, recruiting and retaining members becomes difficult.[51]

Which theory best accounts for fluctuations and growth in the membership of the NRA? Since 1977 membership in the NRA has more than quadrupled (Figure 2.1). Such growth has occurred despite increases in dues and cutbacks in the benefits offered to members. Before 1977 a one-year membership in the NRA cost $10. Dues have steadily increased to the current level of $35 for a one-year membership (Table 2.1). In 1981 a membership in the NRA fetched a year's subscription to *American Rifleman*, $300 in firearms insurance, $10,000 accidental death and dismemberment insurance, $300,000 worth of shooter's liability insurance, and an NRA cap.[52] The NRA has altered the benefit package through the years, eventually reducing and finally dropping the shooter's liability insurance (Table 2.2). The group still offers $10,000 in personal accident insurance,

Table 2.1.   NRA Membership Dues (in dollars)

Membership period	Before 1977	Oct. 31, 1977	April 1, 1986	July 1, 1989	July 1, 1994	Jan.1, 2006
One year	10.00	15.00	20.00	25.00	35.00	35.00
Two years	19.00	27.50	n.a.	n.a.	n.a.	60.00
Three years	27.00	40.00	55.00	68.00	90.00	85.00
Five years	42.50	60.00	85.00	100.00	140.00	125.00
Lifetime	200.00	300.00	500.00	500.00	750.00	750.00

Sources: American Rifleman, 1977, 1986, 1989, 1994, and 2006.

the magazine subscription, and the NRA cap, but it has replaced the hunter's liability insurance with $1,000 worth of ArmsCare firearms insurance. Membership also includes various discounts and benefits, such as a prescription drug plan and hotel and rental car discounts.

Figure 2.1 shows that membership decreased following each dues increase, and some NRA officials in the past attributed part of the decline in membership to the increase in dues. In 1991, Acting Executive Vice President Gary Anderson said, "a $5 rise in annual dues to $25 in July of 1989 had a major effect on membership."[53] Dues and benefits have remained constant since 1994, but membership has fluctuated greatly from 1994 to 2006.

Another theory contends that membership fluctuates according to the threats experienced by the group.[54] The NRA, like other single-interest groups, is an organization that relies on people's expectations of certain political benefits. People have a notion of what the benefits provided by the NRA are worth to them. They also have an idea of the likelihood that those benefits will not be provided if they do not cooperate through membership in the organization. When threats to gun ownership occur, individuals begin to discover that they may not receive the benefits provided by the NRA. Individuals who may have been disposed to a free ride are motivated to join the organization. This argument maintains that people's risk attitudes change when the threat becomes too great. Normally risk averse, people are slow to invest their money in any ideological organization such as the NRA. Faced with such large potential risks as the regulation of firearms, people become risk seeking as the potential costs of inaction increase.[55] In other words, threats increase awareness of the collective benefits of group membership. From this perspective, leaders of ideological interest groups tend to emphasize threats over prospects in their campaigns for membership.[56]

There does seem to be some indirect evidence for this position. The current executive vice president, Wayne LaPierre, claimed that the growth in membership during the 1990s could be traced to the hostility of the

Table 2.2.   NRA Membership Benefits, 1981–2006

Year	Benefits
1981	Subscription to *American Rifleman* or *American Hunter* $300 of firearms insurance $10,000 of accidental death and dismemberment insurance $300,000–$1,000,000 of shooter's liability insurance NRA cap
1983	Subscription to *American Rifleman* or *American Hunter* $300 of firearms insurance $10,000 of accidental death and dismemberment insurance $100,000 of shooter's liability insurance NRA cap
1985	Subscription to *American Rifleman* or *American Hunter* $300 of firearms insurance $100,000 of hunting liability insurance $10,000 of accidental death and dismemberment insurance Pocket Pal (three-inch lockback knife) or NRA cap
1987	Year subscription to *American Rifleman* or *American Hunter* $600 of gun theft insurance $10,000 of accidental death and dismemberment insurance Discounts on Hertz car rentals NRA window decal NRA cap *Sportsman's Bonus Book* with discounts and rebates
1989	Subscription to *American Rifleman* or *American Hunter* $600 of gun theft insurance $10,000 of accidental death and dismemberment insurance Discounts on Hertz car rentals NRA window decal NRA cap
1991	Subscription to *American Rifleman* or *American Hunter* $600 of gun theft insurance $10,000 of accidental death and dismemberment insurance Law enforcement insurance benefits for officers NRA window decal NRA cap
1997	Subscription to *American Rifleman* or *American Hunter* $10,000 of personal accident insurance $1,000 of ArmsCare firearms insurance No-annual-fee NRA VISA card 40 percent discount on interstate moves of household goods NRA window decal NRA cap

Table 2.2.   NRA Membership Benefits, 1981–2006 *(continued)*

Year	Benefits
2006	Subscription to *American Rifleman* or *American Hunter*
	$10,000 of personal accident insurance
	$1,000 of ArmsCare firearms insurance
	No-annual-fee NRA VISA card
	Custom NRA checks
	Relocation cash bonus equal to 0.40 percent of sale price and/ or purchase price
	50 percent discount on interstate moves of household goods
	Discounts on hotels, rental cars, mobile phones, prescription drugs, laser vision correction
	NRA window decal
	NRA cap

Sources: American Rifleman, 1981, 1983, 1985, 1987, 1989, 1991, 1997, 2006.

Clinton administration toward gun owners. LaPierre stated, "People respond when there's a threat. I think Clinton is mobilizing gun owners at record rates."[57] In 1999, former U.S. representative Gerald B. H. Solomon predicted that the increase in pressure for increased gun control after Columbine would increase mobilization by NRA-sympathetic individuals. "This [challenge] is a rallying cause.... [NRA members] rally together just like the Serbs support Milosevic, because they think their country is being attacked."[58] A recent study also suggests that membership in the NRA increases during periods in which the organization receives negative press coverage.[59]

Highly visible and controversial pieces of gun control legislation, such as the Brady Bill, seem to have the capacity to mobilize members who will most likely view the act as a threat. Some argue that, in the wake of the Brady Bill, membership in the NRA increased dramatically.[60] After the passage of the Gun Control Act of 1968 and the Omnibus Crime Control and Safe Streets Act of 1968, the NRA began its metamorphosis from a mainly sporting organization into a politically motivated giant. Leaders first looked at the failures of the organization's past and hoped to make up for lost ground in their efforts to reverse components of the congressional acts of the late 1960s. A large percentage of bills presented to Congress during the 1970s dealt with the repeal of different aspects of the Gun Control Act of 1968. From 1977 to 1984 the membership of the NRA steadily increased from 1,059,682 to 2,924,488 (Figure 2.1).[61] During this time, around 200 bills were presented to Congress that dealt with the issue of gun control.[62]

During the period 1984–1991, growth in membership stagnated and hovered near the 2,700,000 mark, reaching a low of 2,516,908 in 1991 (Figure 2.1). During these same years, approximately one hundred bills that attempted to repeal various aspects of gun control legislation were presented to each Congress. The focus of Congress and of the country no longer seemed to revolve around gun control issues. The lack of some external threat, shown by the decline in the number of bills providing for the regulation of firearms and the presence of Republicans in the White House, probably contributed to the stall in membership growth.

Beginning with the Brady Bill in 1990, the number of gun control bills before Congress began to increase. Gun control once again became a hot topic in Washington and around the nation. With this increase in gun control bills and the election of a pro–gun control president in 1992, the membership of the NRA soared. Increasing from its low of 2,516,908 in 1991, membership reached 3,454,430 in 1994 (Figure 2.1). The NRA also began to use its monthly magazines—*American Rifleman* and *American Hunter*—to campaign more actively against certain pieces of legislation. The NRA's political renaissance during the run-up to the congressional elections of 1994 convinced members to renew their memberships and also attracted new members. The NRA campaigned actively for Republican candidates for Congress, with great success. The victory brought an unexpected cost, however; with the gun control threat reduced, membership dropped from 3.4 million in 1994 to 2.8 million in 1995.

Just as the perceived victory of 1994 coincided with the decrease in membership, the increase in membership at the end of the decade coincided with an increase in threats, both perceived and real, to the interests of the NRA's key constituencies. In the 1997–1998 Congress, 128 bills were introduced that would have regulated the sale or use of firearms; from 1999 to 2000, 158 bills were introduced.[63] For gun owners, the great perceived threat was the potential for the licensing of handguns. An NRA opponent concluded after the 2000 campaign that for gun owners "licensing equals registration; registration equals confiscation."[64] Perhaps the existence of both a sympathetic White House and Congress since 2000 can explain why membership seems to have leveled off. Chuck Cunningham, federal affairs director of the NRA, senses that the drop in membership following the 2000 election was due to the belief among individuals that they did not need to be members because the legislative and presidential threats to Second Amendment rights would not be very great during the George W. Bush administration.[65]

These fluctuations in membership seriously affect the budget of the NRA because its largest source of revenue is membership dues. The NRA gains its revenues from five main sources: membership dues (55 percent), contributions (15 percent), advertising in its magazines (9 percent), interest and dividends (9 percent), and other sources (13 percent).[66] Increased emphasis on membership drives and fund-raising activities prior to the 2000 elections left the NRA with an operating budget of over $168 million.[67] These membership drives are not cheap, and the NRA has invested heavily in membership drives. The NRA spends on fund raising almost $1 for every $2 that it raises through fund raising; about 46 percent of the funds it raises through fund raising pay for fund-raising activities.[68] The NRA also attracts members through brief promotions with certain manufacturers of hunting and shooting equipment. Since 2001, the NRA has redoubled its membership recruitment efforts by both extending promotional ties with companies and by emphasizing the threats posed by the 2004 and 2006 electoral campaigns.

Organization: Problems and Possibilities

Organizational structures of interest groups can be categorized from the simple and centralized to the complex and federated.[69] The type of structure determines everything from the length of time it takes the organization to make a decision to the kind of input enjoyed by rank-and-file membership. Organizations that allow for input from rank-and-file members are more susceptible to challenges from members and key constituencies within the group, but groups with a more complex decision-making structure generally receive more communications from rank-and-file members and actually solicit the expression of opinions.[70]

Although the NRA is often criticized for responding to the more radical elements among its members, it is in part the responsiveness of the decision-making structure that keeps the members so loyal to the organization and its goals. Members influence the organization and the candidates it supports through a variety of means. Leaders encourage members to communicate to the national office. The leadership of the NRA feels a particular need to listen to the members because so much of the money that goes to the candidates and sustains the organization comes from the dues the members pay. Therefore, the national office solicits advice about which candidates to support, polls the membership, and informs members about campaign activities. The willingness of an organization to listen to its members contributes to the organization's well-being; members will be less likely to continue to contribute to organizations that are not responsive.[71]

Interaction between leaders and members also enhances the NRA's effectiveness. When candidates for office know that the national organization listens to the rank-and-file members, the candidates become more responsive to members in their state or district. For this reason, the ILA, the NRA's lobbying organization, oversees the Political Victory Fund, the organization's PAC.[72] When the NRA talks to an elected official about a particular policy, it wants this individual to understand that the members in the district or state can influence that candidate's electoral fortunes.[73] The NRA uses this strategy of combining lobbying and campaign activities at both the state and federal levels.

The NRA is governed by a board of directors that consists of seventy-five NRA members who are elected by mail ballot by the members of the association, each of whom is entitled to vote. All but one director serves for a term of three years; the director elected at the annual meeting of members serves only a one-year term. The right to hold the office of director is limited to NRA lifetime members who have attained an age of eighteen years and are U.S. citizens. The terms of office of one-third of the board expire each year.[74]

Part of the success of the NRA can be attributed to the stability in major leadership positions. The NRA is a multimillion-dollar enterprise with operations throughout the United States. It is not easy to find talented individuals who are capable of managing such far-flung enterprises. The executive vice president is the most powerful office in the organization because it oversees the day-to-day operations of the NRA. Only five individuals have served in this position during the past twenty years, and two of those served for only one year.[75] This post is currently held by Wayne LaPierre, who has held the office since 1992. Before 1992, he served for six years as executive director of the ILA, the lobbying wing that oversees the Political Victory Fund of the NRA. This pattern of upward movement within the leadership is certainly not uncommon. Gary L. Anderson served as executive director of operations before moving into the office of executive vice president. J. Warren Cassidy, like LaPierre, served as executive director of the ILA before becoming executive vice president.

Representation and Political Influence

NRA electoral support goes only to those candidates who support the NRA's objective: staunch defense of the Second Amendment. Who is deemed faithful to this objective depends in part on the assessment of the local members. The NRA recruits election volunteer coordinators who assess the candidates in each congressional district and pass along their findings to the national office. Members are also free to lobby the national office on behalf of particular candidates. Disagreements between the national office and the rank-and-file members sometimes arise over who should receive electoral support. Because most of the money that the NRA gives to candidates comes from solicitation of its members through the mail, the organization tolerates these disagreements.

Giving money to candidates is only one way in which the NRA gets involved in campaigns. The NRA has developed five distinct levels of involvement.[76] First, it grades candidates and publishes those grades in *American Rifleman*. Candidates for Congress can receive grades ranging from an A to an F. Candidates who most actively help the NRA to achieve its goals receive an A. Individuals who actively oppose the NRA receive an F. The important dimension of the grade is activity. Candidates who lead the charge for NRA principles receive the higher grades. Those individuals openly opposed get failing grades. Some candidates vote for the positions of the NRA but do not lead on the issues. These are the C candidates.

In 2004, the NRA concentrated many of its efforts in those races where an A candidate faced an F or even a C.[77]

Endorsement of a candidate is the second level of involvement. Only faithful allies of the NRA receive its endorsement. An endorsement is better than a good grade because of the signal it sends to local members. Longtime friends of the NRA receive the endorsement of the national organization even when local members may vehemently oppose it. The national organization believes that loyalty should be rewarded, even if the incumbent or candidate may not be popular in the local areas. The endorsed candidates for office in each district are printed on the cover of the November edition of *American Rifleman* along with contact information for the local grassroots coordinator. Endorsed candidates also receive a letter from the NRA outlining the reasons for the group's endorsement; candidates can distribute this letter to their constituents.

The next three levels of involvement pertain to material support. At the third level, the NRA contributes money to the candidate. Some PACs, hoping to gain access after the election, give only to incumbents. Other PACs, seeking to turn the tide in a close race, carefully target their donations.[78] The NRA's wealth means it can do both. It contributes to loyal incumbents who have long fought the organization's battles, and it targets its contributions to those close races in which a contribution can make a difference. The NRA does not just throw money at candidates. It rarely gives the full legal amount to any candidate and it gives only to those candidates who ask.[79] In 2004 the NRA concentrated its efforts on competitive contests and states and gave little to loyal incumbents.

At the fourth level, the NRA uses in-kind contributions, such as fundraising and meet-and-greet events, to help the candidate. The national office involves local members in many of these functions to drive home the point that the candidate should be aware of the NRA rank and file.

Finally, the NRA uses independent expenditures to help its candidates. These kinds of expenditures run the gamut from radio and television ads to telephone banks. Once again, many of these independent expenditures rely on the work of the local members. In *American Rifleman* in 1996, Tanya Metaksa urged local members to help local candidates in that year's election by "making the phone calls, stuffing the envelopes, canvassing the neighborhoods."[80]

Using the local members at these various levels of involvement maximizes the effectiveness of the NRA. It harnesses the members' ideological zeal and translates it into a language candidates for any office can understand: campaign resources. Jim Wilkinson, a spokesperson for the National Republican Congressional Committee, said that one reason they like working with the NRA is that it "does a great job of educating their members, especially in the battleground congressional districts."[81]

From 1977 to 2004, the NRA spent more than $35 million during elections to support or oppose presidential and congressional candidates.

Figure 2.2.   NRA Contributions to Campaigns for National
Office, 1978–2004

Millions of dollars

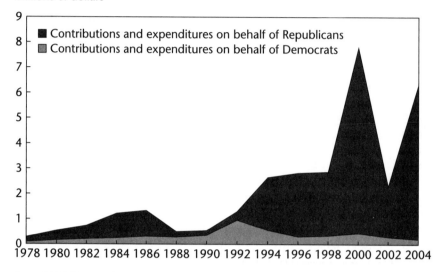

Source: "PAC Financial Summaries (End of Cycle)," Federal Election Commission,
http://www.fec.gov/finance/disclosure/ftpsum.shtml.

Over this time, the NRA has preferred to give to Republican candidates
(Figure 2.2). Expenditures and contributions on behalf of Republican
candidates over this period totaled more than $31.2 million, whereas
Democrats received slightly more than $4.8 million (Tables 2.3 and 2.4).
The NRA has long preferred Republicans, and this preference has
deepened over time. In 1978, 75 percent of NRA expenditures and contributions were to Republican candidates; by 2004, 97 percent went to
Republicans. In 2004, the NRA continued its preference for Republican
candidates, giving them about $6 million; it gave Democratic candidates
only $205,207.

The 1996 presidential campaign stands out as a glaring failure among
the NRA's successes. The NRA was faced with two candidates for whom it
had little or no enthusiasm. While the NRA leadership made several statements urging members to work to defeat Clinton, it refused to endorse his
main opponent, Republican Bob Dole. The NRA believed that Dole had
not been as faithful a supporter as he could have been. The actions of the
NRA in this election serve as an example of how far some single-interest
groups will go to preserve their ideological purity. Rather than compromise
its principles, the NRA worked to defeat President Clinton but did not fully
rally the faithful for former senator Dole. This preserved the NRA's principle of not supporting any candidate who did not enthusiastically protect the

Table 2.3. NRA Contributions and Expenditures on Behalf of Republicans, 1978–2004 (in dollars)

Year	Contributions	Expenditures	Total
1978	272,035	15,745	287,780
1980	336,035	201,190	537,225
1982	540,207	193,761	733,968
1984	500,215	721,287	1,221,502
1986	643,740	693,030	1,336,770
1988	488,487	4,370	492,857
1990	456,285	81,222	537,507
1992	1,098,354	202,969	1,301,323
1994	1,442,519	1,205,189	2,647,708
1996	1,288,371	1,537,580	2,825,951
1998	1,249,911	1,618,860	2,868,771
2000	1,213,844	6,578,476	7,792,320
2002	1,174,081	1,117,994	2,292,075
2004	1,031,753	5,286,822	6,318,575
Total	11,735,837	19,458,495	31,194,332

Source: "PAC Financial Summaries (End of Cycle)," Federal Election Commission, http://www.fec.gov/finance/disclosure/ftpsum.shtml.

Table 2.4. NRA Contributions and Expenditures on Behalf of Democrats, 1978–2004 (in dollars)

Year	Contributions	Expenditures	Total
1978	93,626	2,284	95,910
1980	98,268	63,796	162,064
1982	170,695	38,589	209,284
1984	200,109	49,442	249,551
1986	254,824	60,790	315,614
1988	284,269	0	284,269
1990	293,208	61,898	355,106
1992	632,642	329,861	962,503
1994	410,519	152,626	563,145
1996	262,600	44,572	307,172
1998	283,750	58,188	341,938
2000	472,000	19,362	491,362
2002	183,800	107,960	291,760
2004	183,746	21,461	205,207
Total	3,824,056	1,010,829	4,834,885

Source: "PAC Financial Summaries (End of Cycle)," Federal Election Commission, http://www.fec.gov/finance/disclosure/ftpsum.shtml.

Second Amendment, but it produced what members perceived as a less than optimal electoral outcome.

The NRA faced a very different environment in 2000. Both candidates for the Democratic Party's presidential nomination made gun control a central issue of their campaigns. Key NRA supporters in the House and Senate were also vulnerable, which created the possibility of a Congress and a president that would support increased gun control. Gun opponents also sensed the opportunity. The organization Handgun Control, Inc., spent over ten times more on candidate contributions and issue advocacy in 2000 than it had in 1996.

It is not surprising that the NRA approached the 2000 election with unprecedented vigor. LaPierre and ILA head, James Jay Baker, called the 2000 election "the most important election in the history of the Second Amendment. We're telling people, if they value the freedom to own a firearm, this is the election you'd better get out and vote."[82] The NRA endorsed George W. Bush and encouraged all its members to work for his election.[83]

The NRA didn't just talk about the election's importance; it put its money where its mouth was. The NRA spent over $16.8 million in the 2000 election, more than double any previous election cycle.[84] Of this, only $1.58 million was given directly to candidates.[85] Most of the NRA's spending in candidate races (over $6.5 million) was as independent expenditures on behalf of candidates, including over $2.2 million in support of George W. Bush.

The 2004 presidential election was another election in which the NRA showed its political strength by endorsing one candidate and spending significant time and resources denouncing another. When the NRA officially endorsed President Bush in October 2004, it promised to spend $20 million supporting him and had already spent about $1 million opposing President Bush's challenger, John Kerry.[86] Even before President Bush received the NRA endorsement, he and his running mate were already attempting to paint Kerry as an anti–gun rights senator who had a twenty-year voting record to prove it. At the NRA's 133d national convention, Vice President Dick Cheney stated that John Kerry's approach to the Second Amendment was to "regulate, regulate, and then regulate some more."[87] Kerry's campaign responded by informing voters that Kerry had hunted since the age of twelve and had been a gun owner who had consistently supported the Second Amendment.[88]

To further demonstrate his support for gun ownership, Kerry hunted in several battleground states during the course of his campaign and even printed brochures of himself holding a shotgun; in Ohio, where the race would be one of the closest in the nation, his brochure stated, "John Kerry will defend Ohio." Also in Ohio, he was shown dressed in camouflage and walking out of a cornfield holding a 12-gauge shotgun and a dead goose.[89] The Bush campaign responded to Kerry's hunting trip with pictures of its own: a white poodle wearing a Kerry-style sweater with an inscription: "That dog don't hunt." In addition, NRA officials in a city close to the location Kerry was hunting reminded voters, "You can stage duck hunting photo-ops, but you can't hide from your 20-year anti-gun, anti-hunting record."[90]

In addition to the controversy over Kerry's hunting excursions, the assault weapons ban was a point of contention in the 2004 election. When the ban died on September 13, 2004, Kerry responded by outlining a $5 billion anticrime package and stating that Bush sided with "powerful and well-connected friends in the gun lobby" by not pushing the legislation, which banned nineteen types of semiautomatic assault weapons and ammunition clips with ten rounds or more.[91] Furthermore, Kerry said that President Bush was not responsive to the public, two-thirds of which he said supported renewing the ban.[92] Although the bill died, President Bush had said that he would sign the legislation renewing the ban if it arrived on his desk.[93]

The NRA does not limit its political activities to presidential races. It knows that campaigns for Congress, and even local races, matter a great deal for the success of its organization. In the North Carolina and Colorado senatorial races in 2004, the NRA spent considerable money on the ground war. In both states the NRA sponsored newspaper bags the week before the election. The Colorado bags read, "Vote for Freedom First; Pete Coors for Senate."[94] It used the same tactic in Missouri to support President Bush. The NRA sent a number of direct mailers in Ohio, Missouri, Colorado, and North Carolina. For Republican candidate Richard Burr in North Carolina, the NRA sponsored a rally at a big NASCAR race. The NRA was one of the most involved interest groups in both the Colorado and North Carolina elections. One of Burr's advisers said that the NRA, together with the National Association of Realtors, did "tons of work; everyone else was secondary."[95] It appears that the NRA spent money on the war for the airwaves primarily for presidential battleground states, and it mostly stayed away from television in the races for the Senate. The one exception was in the race for the U.S. Senate in South Dakota, where the NRA aired four unique television spots. The NRA was active in the contest to dominate the airwaves in Ohio and Missouri, but it was neither one of the bigger players nor one of the most prominent.[96] In Ohio, it produced a number of mailers and print advertisements in support of President Bush. Overall, a survey of campaign activity of political parties, interest groups, and candidates reveals that the NRA was only the thirty-seventh-highest group for mail volume. Among groups active in the 2004 election cycle, the NRA ranked twelfth nationally in mail volume.[97]

The political mail from the 2004 election provides some insight into the individuals targeted by the NRA. Recipients of NRA mail were much more likely to be NRA members than those who did not receive its mailings

(45 percent vs. 9 percent). Also, recipients of NRA mail were much more likely to live in Senate battleground states (48 percent vs. 30 percent), self-identify with the religious right (49 percent vs. 16 percent), have a college education (42 percent vs. 22 percent), and be married (93 percent vs. 74 percent). The NRA's mail reached people who were actually more trusting of the government to do what is right than the national sample, which is surprising given the NRA's habit of employing at times very antigovernment rhetoric. Seventy-seven percent of NRA mail recipients believe that most of the time they can trust the government in Washington to do what is right; nationally, only 36 percent feel the same way, while 56 percent trust the government only some of the time.

Although some of these differences may be attributable to the small number of NRA mail pieces in the survey, the results still indicate that the NRA focused most of its mail efforts on competitive Senate races among potential voters who are more likely to support their agenda. It also concentrated its efforts on the presidential battlegrounds, but in those states its efforts were not as prominent. In the competitive North Carolina Senate race, one of the Republican candidate's advisers said that the NRA was one of the campaign's strongest and most influential supporters, and "everyone else was secondary."[98] The NRA played an important, leading role in some senate races, but in presidential battleground states it appears that efforts of other groups overshadowed the NRA's work.

Conclusion

The NRA is clearly one of the most powerful single-interest groups in the United States. Its influence is the result of a sustained and deliberate attempt to attract and retain a large and enthusiastic membership base. The NRA offers a variety of incentives to individuals and expends large sums of money to recruit new members and satisfy current members. These incentives range from social benefits consumed mainly by sportspersons to ideological satisfaction enjoyed largely by hard-core proponents of Second Amendment liberties.

The NRA has enjoyed remarkable success in recent years, but the large membership and perceived power of the NRA do not mean that all is well within the group. Most complex organizations face trade-offs as they seek to allocate resources among various goals. In the case of the NRA, it must satisfy two distinct types of members: those who resist any attempt to regulate firearms or ammunition and those who join for the sporting and shooting activities. The latter are much less politicized and do not see some restrictions on the right to bear arms as unreasonable.

These two groups often contend for the heart and soul of the organization. Conflicts between the two factions have frequently been expressed openly during the process of electing leaders at the annual conventions.[99] Remarkably, moderates have often prevailed in these conflicts, reflecting their staying power within the organization despite its recent success in ideological politics. Such a tension will continue to exist so long as the NRA instantiates these two goals within its charter and the federated structure of the organization allows all members access to the decision-making processes in the national office.

Single-interest groups can fall prey to their own success. NRA membership and fund raising declined in the wake of the Republican revolution in 1994. To remain a vibrant and influential organization, the NRA will have to maintain its commitment to a goal that generates enthusiasm (and contributions) from its members while it takes care not to alienate the moderate elements that enlarge its membership base. Although NRA leaders have said, "if one word describes the state of the NRA today, it is unity,"[100] the combination of divergent constituencies and the NRA's responsive organization always leaves the potential for further disagreements and conflicts. Only time will tell how the NRA will respond to these challenges.

A final challenge facing the NRA is to avoid gaining the reputation of a strictly partisan organization. Most of the NRA's recent political spending has been for Republican candidates, causing the comment that "the NRA, which used to be a fairly bipartisan lobby, has become just another fundamentally GOP constituency group with lots of money."[101]

Like all successful interest groups, the NRA has a knack for promoting its issues. In the wake of Hurricane Katrina, local and federal law enforcement officials began confiscating all guns in the disaster area, no matter who had them. Even though the practice stopped after the NRA and other pro-gun groups challenged its legality, the NRA has still seized upon the issue as a "manageable controversy" that it can exploit to mobilize its base and increase membership. The NRA even sent camera crews to the area to document stories of gun confiscations and of residents using firearms to protect themselves during the breakdown of civil order. It plans on using the footage to attack pro–gun control politicians and to recruit new members. Wayne LaPierre said, "This will probably mint money for us" and draw in new members and more donations because gun rights activists will see what happened as a threat.[102] Even though the gun confiscations after Katrina probably missed the attention of most Americans, the NRA knows its members and target audience were paying attention. It has developed a strong and stable organizational structure to identify and exploit events and issues that will serve to advance its agenda. It is clear that the NRA knows what it needs to do to survive and even prosper.

Notes

The authors would like to thank those who assisted with this chapter, including Chuck Cunningham, political director of the NRA; Tanya Metaksa, former executive director of the Institute for Legislative Action, for her interview; Bernie Hoerr, director of the membership programs in the membership division of the NRA, for providing membership data; and Edward J. Land Jr., secretary of the NRA, for providing information about NRA charters. Carter Swift and Elizabeth Pipkin provided research for previous editions of this chapter. Baxter Oliphant, Paul Russell, Brandon Wilson, Lindsay Nielson, and Nisha Riggs assisted in the research for this edition. Some data used in this chapter were gathered with funds provided by the Pew Charitable Trusts. We would also like to thank the Brigham Young University College of Family, Home, and Social Sciences for providing the resources that made this research possible.

1. Hershey refers to these kinds of groups as *condensational*. She contrasts their tactics with the tactics of groups she labels *referential*. Condensational groups symbolize the issue differently than referential groups: condensational groups personalize the issues to enhance their emotional impact, and referential groups speak of the objective elements of the issue, appealing more to reason than to emotions. Marjorie Randon Hershey, "Direct Action and the Abortion Issue: The Political Participation of Single-Issue Groups," in *Interest Group Politics*, 2d ed., ed. Allan J. Cigler and Burdett A. Loomis (Washington, D.C.: CQ Press, 1986).

2. For a discussion of the reasons for the growth in the number of interest groups, see Jeffrey M. Berry, "Citizen Groups and the Changing Nature of Interest Group Politics," *Annals of American Academy* 528 (July 1993): 30–41.

3. For a discussion of the different groups involved in these kinds of elections, see David B. Magleby, J. Quin Monson, and Kelly D. Patterson, eds., *Dancing without Partners: How Candidates, Parties, and Interest Groups Interact in the New Campaign Finance Environment* (Provo, Utah: Brigham Young University, Center for the Study of Elections and Democracy, 2005) and David B. Magleby, J. Quin Monson, and Kelly D. Patterson, *Electing Congress: New Rules for an Old Game* (Englewood Cliffs, N.J.: Prentice Hall, 2007).

4. Jeffrey H. Birnbaum, "Fat and Happy in D.C.," *Fortune*, May 28, 2001, 94–103.

5. Richard E. Cohen and Peter Bell, "Congressional Insiders Poll," *National Journal*, March 5, 2005.

6. Bara Vaida and Peter Bell, "Biting the Hands ...," *National Journal*, November 12, 2005, 3524–3525.

7. David Truman, *The Governmental Process*, 2d ed. (New York: Knopf, 1971).

8. Quoted in James B. Trefethen, *Americans and Their Guns: The National Rifle Association Story through Nearly a Century of Service to the Nation* (Harrisburg, Pa.: Stackpole Books, 1967), 10.

9. This also seems to be an example of what Graham K. Wilson refers to as encouragement of the growth of interest groups by their proximity to institutions such as political parties and the state. Wilson has argued that the NRA is an example of a group that exists because of early policies by the government that gave it a boost. Graham K. Wilson, *Interest Groups* (Oxford: Blackwell, 1990). A similar argument is made by Burdett A. Loomis and Allan J. Cigler, "The Changing Nature of Interest Group Politics," in *Interest Group Politics*, 2d ed., ed. Cigler and Loomis.

10. For an excellent discussion of the history of the NRA, see Robert Spitzer, *The Politics of Gun Control* (Chatham, N.J.: Chatham House, 1995), 99–115. For a history of the foundation of the NRA, see Trefethen, *Americans and Their Guns*.

11. Robert H. Salisbury, "An Exchange Theory of Interest Groups," *Midwest Journal of Political Science* 13 (February 1969): 1–32.

12. Alan C. Webber, "Where the NRA Stands on Gun Legislation," *American Rifleman*, March 1968, 22–23.

13. Michael Powell, "Call to Arms," *Washington Post Magazine*, August 6, 2000, 8.

14. David Brock, "Wayne's World: In May the NRA Will Decide Whether It Wants to Be a Modern Political Organization or an 'Extremist' Group Sprung from a Liberal's Worst Nightmare," *American Spectator*, May 1997, 38.

15. Quoted in Charles Madigan and David Jackson, "NRA in the Cross Hairs: Lobby Battles Foes, Itself," *Chicago Tribune*, August 3, 1995, sec. N.
16. Peter B. Clark and James Q. Wilson, "Incentive Systems: A Theory of Organizations," *Administrative Science Quarterly* 6 (September 1961): 129–166.
17. Institute for Legislative Action, "General Information," 2001, http://www.nraila.org/research/19991123-generalinfo-001.shtml.
18. National Rifle Association, "City Council Drives Freedom and NRA Out of Columbus," July 18, 2005, http://www.nraila.org/News/Read/Releases.aspx?ID=6143; "NRA Convention Was a Bonanza, In a Few Places," *Kansas City Star*, May 29, 2001, sec. D.
19. *American Rifleman* is for general members, *American Hunter* for hunters, *America's 1st Freedom* for those interested in Second Amendment issues, *Shooting Sports USA* for competitive shooters, and *NRA InSights* for junior members.
20. Brock, "Wayne's World," 38.
21. Scott Shepard, "National Convention; NRA's Message: 'The Gun Lobby Is People,'" *Atlanta Constitution*, May 19, 1995, sec. A.
22. John T. Young et al., "Trends: Guns," *Public Opinion Quarterly* 60 (Winter): 634–649.
23. Ibid., 643.
24. National Opinion Research Center, "General Social Surveys, 1972–2004," http://sda.berkeley.edu/archive.htm.
25. Young et al., "Trends: Guns," 642.
26. Gallup Organization, "Americans Softening on Tougher Gun Laws?" November 30, 2004, http://poll.gallup.com/content/default.aspx?ci=14185&pg=1.
27. Ibid.
28. Joseph Carroll, "Gun Ownership Higher among Republicans Than Democrats: Republican Gun Owners Also More Likely to Hunt," *Gallup Brain*, February 16, 2006; Frank Newport, "Americans Not Convinced That Stricter Enforcement of Current Gun Control Laws Is Sufficient to Curb Gun Violence: Democrats More Likely Than Republicans to Feel New Laws Are Necessary," *Gallup Brain*, January 20, 2000.
29. Data were collected in the 1998 KBYU/Utah Colleges Exit Poll. This exit poll is designed and conducted by students and faculty at Brigham Young University. In the 1998 poll, 930 Utah voters were asked whether they belonged to the NRA as well as their opinions on several gun-related issues.
30. Ibid.
31. Data were collected in the 2002 KBYU/Utah Colleges Exit Poll. This exit poll is designed and conducted by students and faculty at Brigham Young University. In the 2002 poll, 1,007 Utah voters were asked whether they belonged to the NRA as well as their opinions on several gun-related issues.
32. Ibid.
33. Newport, "Americans Not Convinced That Stricter Enforcement of Current Gun Control Laws Is Sufficient to Curb Gun Violence."
34. Lydia Saad, "NRA Viewed Favorably by Most Americans: Majority of Americans Favor Arming Pilots, But Not School Officials," *Gallup Brain*, April 15, 2006, http://institution.gallup.com/content/default.aspx?ci=15868>.
35. Gallup Organization, "Majority of Americans Have Favorable Opinion of the National Rifle Association," May 19, 2000, www.gallup.com/poll/releases/pr000519.asp.
36. Matthew Kauffman, "Can Heston Be a Silver Bullet for the NRA? As President, Actor Gives Group Chance to Cure Ailing Image," *Hartford Courant*, June 14, 1998, sec. A.
37. Ibid.
38. "8000 Protest NRA Convention in Denver," CNN.com, May 1, 1999, http://www5.cnn.com/US/9905/01/nra.protest.02/.

39. Charlton Heston, "Opening Remarks to Members," May 1, 1999, http://www.nrahq.org/transcripts/denver_open.asp.
40. "Heston, NRA Take Stand at Denver Convention," *St. Louis Post Dispatch*, May 2, 1999, sec. A; Charlton Heston, "President's Column," *American Rifleman*, November/December 2000, 16.
41. Associated Press, "Gun Control Bolstered: Americans Want Tougher Gun Laws, Poll Says," *Newsday New York*, May 6, 1999, sec. A.
42. Dan Luzador, "Politicians Distance Themselves from Guns: Concealed Weapons Measures Just Too Hot," *Denver Rocky Mountain News*, May 6, 1999; David Olinger, "Tide Turing on Gun Control," *Denver Post*, May 17, 1999.
43. Ibid.
44. Lorraine Woellert, "Gun Control: Even after Littleton, the NRA Will Keep It at Bay," *Business Week*, May 10, 1999, 47.
45. James Dao, "After Littleton, Gun Industry Sees Wider Gap with the NRA," *New York Times*, May 25, 1999, sec. A.
46. "Inside Washington for August 14, 1999," *National Journal*, August 14, 1999, 2343.
47. "Clinton Slams House on Guns," CNN.com, June 9, 1999, http://www.cnn.com/ALLPOLITICS/stories/1999/06/09/gun.control/.
48. For membership data from 1977 to 1996 and from 2001 to 2006, see Membership Division of the NRA. For 1997, see "NRA Chief Overcomes Criticism from Ranks," *Lubbock Avalanche Journal*, February 12, 1997. For 1998, see Michael Janofsky, "Enthusiastic NRA Gives Mandate to Charlton Heston," *New York Times*, June 8, 1998, sec. A. For 1999, see Nancy Kletecka, "NRA Banquet Draws Large Crowd," *Southwest Daily Times*, February 8, 2000. For 2000, see "General Information," National Rifle Association, Institute for Legislative Action.
49. Salisbury, "An Exchange Theory of Interest Groups."
50. Truman, *The Governmental Process*.
51. John Mark Hansen, "Political Economy of Group Membership," *American Political Science Review* 79 (March 1985): 79–96.
52. The shooter's liability insurance started at $300,000 and was set to increase $100,000 for each year of membership. The insurance was capped at $1,000,000.
53. Steven Holmes, "Rifle Lobby Torn by Dissidents and Capitol Defectors," *New York Times*, March 27, 1991, sec. A.
54. Truman, *The Governmental Process*.
55. Hansen, "Political Economy of Group Membership," 81.
56. Ibid.
57. Peter H. Stone, "Showing Holes: The Once-Mighty NRA Is Wounded, but Still Dangerous," *Mother Jones*, January 1, 1994, 39.
58. James Dao and Don Van Natta, "NRA Is Using Adversity to Its Advantage," *New York Times*, June 12, 1999, sec. A.
59. Brian A. Patrick, *The National Rifle Association and the Media: The Motivating Force of Negative Coverage* (New York: Peter Lang, 2002).
60. Charles Mahtesian, "Firepower," *Governing Magazine*, August 1995, 16.
61. Bernie Hoerr, director of membership programs in the Membership Division of the NRA, provided membership figures.
62. We determined the number of bills relating to gun control by using the *Thomas Bill Summaries and Status, Previous Congresses, Index*. The index includes a brief discussion of the subject of the bill, the bill number, and its sponsor. Any bill listed that mentioned any issue relating to the regulation or deregulation of firearms was included in this analysis.
63. Results of search in the THOMAS database under the Congressional Research Service subject term *firearm control* in the 105th and 106th Congresses.
64. Jonathan Weisman, "For Pro-Bush Interest Groups, It's Wish List Time," *USA Today*, December 15, 2000, sec. A.

65. Chuck Cunningham, interview by David B. Magleby and Kristina Gale, Washington, D.C., November 5, 2004.
66. J. Warren Cassidy, "Here We Stand," *American Rifleman*, January 1991, 7.
67. Powell, "Call to Arms."
68. "National Rifle Association," BBB Wise Giving Alliance, January 2006, http://charityreports.give.org/Public/Report.aspx?CharityID=1420.
69. Philip A. Mundo, *Interest Groups: Cases and Characteristics* (Chicago: Nelson-Hall, 1992).
70. Ibid.
71. Anthony Nownes and Allan J. Cigler, "Public Interest Groups and the Road to Survival," *Polity* 27 (Spring 1995): 379–404.
72. Kelly Patterson, "Political Firepower: The National Rifle Association," in *After the Revolution: PACs and Lobbies in the Republican Congress*, ed. Robert Biersack, Paul Herrnson, and Clyde Wilcox (Boston: Allyn and Bacon, 1998).
73. Tanya Metaksa, interview by Kelly D. Patterson, Washington, D.C., July 18, 1996.
74. E. G. Bell Jr., ed., "Exercise Your Rights: Assist in the Nomination of Directors," *American Rifleman*, July 1995, 56–57.
75. Harlon B. Carter served from 1977 to 1984, G. Ray Arnett served in 1985, J. Warren Cassidy served from 1986 to 1990, Gary L. Anderson served in 1991, and Wayne LaPierre has served since 1992.
76. For a full discussion of how the NRA makes its decisions to allocate these resources see Patterson, "Political Firepower."
77. Chuck Cunningham, interview by David B. Magleby and Kristina Gale, Washington, D.C., November 5, 2004.
78. Paul S. Herrnson, *Congressional Elections: Campaigning at Home and in Washington* (Washington, D.C.: CQ Press, 1995), 109–110.
79. Tanya Metaksa, interview by Kelly D. Patterson, Washington, D.C., July 18, 1996.
80. Tanya Metaksa, "Memorandum: Election of Pro-Gun Candidates," *American Rifleman*, September 1996, 33.
81. Quoted in Peter H. Stone, "In the NRA's Sights," *National Journal*, July 22, 2000, 2366.
82. "Gun Lobby Targets Gore, Democrats," CNN.com, May 23, 2000, http://archives.cnn.com/2000/US/05/23/nra.politics/index.html.
83. See Heston, "President's Column."
84. "Top 50 PAC's—Disbursements, 1999–2000," http://www.fec.gov/press/press2001/053101pacfund/pacdis00.htm, July 2006; Juliet Eilperin, "A Pivotal Election Finds NRA's Wallet Open," *Washington Post*, November 1, 2000, sec. A.
85. "Top 50 PAC's—Contributions to Candidates, 1999–2000," http://www.fec.gov/press/press2001/053101pacfund/paccnt00.htm, July 2006.
86. Sharon Theimer, "National Rifle Association Endorses Bush for President," Associated Press, October 13, 2004.
87. Dan Nephin, "Cheney Portrays Kerry as a Threat to Gun Owners," Associated Press, April 17, 2004.
88. Sharon Theimer, "NRA Ads Focus on Kerry Gun Rights Record," Associated Press, September 8, 2004.
89. Nedra Pickler, "Kerry Goes Hunting as Part of His Push for Social Conservatives," Associated Press, October 21, 2004.
90. "NRA to Take On John Kerry at Press Conference in Youngstown, OH, Oct. 21," NRA News Release, October 20, 2004.
91. Edward Epstein, "Kerry Sets Forth Anti-Crime Plan; He Blames Bush for Demise of Assault Weapon Ban," *San Francisco Chronicle*, September 14, 2004.
92. Stephen Dinan, "Kerry Hits Bush for Lapse of Gun Ban," *Washington Times*, September 14, 2004.
93. James Dao, "N.R.A. Opens an All-Out Drive for Bush and Its Views," *New York Times*, April 16, 2004.

94. Kyle Saunders and Robert Duffy, "The Colorado U.S. Senate Race," in *Dancing without Partners*, 189.

95. Steven Greene and Eric Heberlig, "The Southern Ticket-Splitter Shall Rise Again: The 2004 North Carolina Senate Campaign," in *Dancing without Partners*, 217.

96. Stephen T. Mockabee et al., "The Battle for Ohio: The 2004 Presidential Campaign," in *Dancing without Partners*, 152.

97. To evaluate the nonbroadcast aspects of the NRA's efforts, the 2004 Campaign Communications Survey (CCS) was used. The CCS was conducted by the Center for the Study of Elections and Democracy (CSED) at Brigham Young University and consists of a mixed-mode mail and telephone survey of registered voters nationwide with an oversample in Florida and Ohio. Respondents were asked to complete a questionnaire booklet that included space to note all political contacts (mail, e-mail, phone calls, and in-person contacts) they had during the three weeks leading up to election day. Respondents collected and sent in their political mail, permitting content analysis of the mail pieces they received. Data about campaign activities summarized in this and the following paragraphs all come from the CCS.

98. Greene and Heberlig, "The Southern Ticket-Splitter Shall Rise Again," in *Dancing without Partners*, 217.

99. Kelly D. Patterson and Matthew M. Singer, "The National Rifle Association in the Face of the Clinton Challenge," in *Interest Group Politics*, 6th ed., ed. Allan J. Cigler and Burdett A. Loomis (Washington, D.C.: CQ Press, 2002).

100. Wayne R. LaPierre, "Standing Guard," *American Rifleman*, February 2001.

101. Larry Sabato, quoted in Peter H. Stone, "In the NRA's Sights."

102. Brian Friel, "NRA's Cry: 'Remember New Orleans,'" *National Journal*, November 19, 2005, 3648–3649.

3

Politics of Tribal Recognition
Casinos, Culture, and Controversy
Michael Nelson

Over the past twenty years, Indian tribes have become major players within American interest group politics, largely because of their favored legal status in developing gaming operations, especially large, lucrative casinos. With court decisions and legislation in the 1980s, the interest group politics of American Indians has moved away from the traditional bureaucratic focus (the Bureau of Indian Affairs in the Interior Department) to encompass Congress, state legislatures, the financing of political campaigns, and the hiring of high-profile contract lobbyists to make the tribes' case at the highest levels. Indeed, at the center of the scandals associated with lobbyist Jack Abramoff are large contributions and substantial fees that Abramoff and others solicited from various tribes.

Given the tremendous potential benefits that Indian tribes may obtain through their casino operations, the question of what constitutes a tribe has become of overarching importance. Official recognition by the government has always been important, but gambling's pot-of-gold lure has vastly increased the stakes. In this chapter, Michael Nelson explores the politicized process of gaining recognition as a tribe. With a careful review of the context and two case studies, Nelson opens up a set of political issues that reflect back on the heart of interest group politics; he examines the questions: (1) What *is* an interest? and (2) How do interests get what they want? And the results of the latter question often depend on how the former is answered by the legislatures, the bureaucracy, and the courts.

On January 20, 2003, Chief Quiet Hawk and his band of Golden Hill Paugussetts were told that they were not an Indian tribe, at least not in the eyes of the federal government.[1] Aurene M. Martin, the assistant secretary of the interior for Indian affairs, announced that the Connecticut-based group had failed to show it meets several of the criteria for tribal recognition that the Interior Department's Bureau of Indian Affairs (BIA) established in 1978 and has used ever since. One of the group's failings, Martin said, was that the Golden Hill tribe it claimed descent from ceased to exist in 1823. Another was that the individuals calling themselves the Golden Hill Paugussetts had not demonstrated that they are descended from that or any other Indian tribe.[2]

Reactions to the decision varied considerably. The ranks of the disappointed included not just Quiet Hawk's group of Paugussett wannabes but also the city of Bridgeport, Connecticut. Bridgeport's mayor and council had been counting on the Paugussett group's being recognized as a tribe because recognition would open the door for it to open a casino on tribal land, and Bridgeport wanted part of the action.[3] The demand for casino gambling in lower New England is great. Situated midway between New York City and Boston, southeastern Connecticut already has two large and extremely profitable Indian casinos, Foxwoods and the Mohegan Sun. Economically depressed Bridgeport, full of abandoned downtown acreage, had already agreed to cede 200 acres to the Paugussetts so the tribe could open what Quiet Hawk promised would be the "world's largest casino."[4]

Thomas Wilmot, a wealthy Rochester, New York, developer and a major financial supporter of the Democratic Party, was not happy with the BIA's decision either. In exchange for the right to develop and manage the Paugussetts' planned casino in Bridgeport, he had spent approximately $4 million to help fund their bid for federal recognition.[5] Wilmot had been hoping to follow the path blazed by other non-Indian developers of Indian casinos, such as the investor group headed by South African casino magnate Sol Kerzner that by 2003 had made an estimated $800 million from its relationship with the Mohegan tribe's Mohegan Sun casino.[6]

Disappointment was not the only reaction to Secretary Martin's announcement. Relieved but anxious was the state of Connecticut, notably the Democratic attorney general, Richard Blumenthal, a fierce opponent of tribal casino expansion, and Jeff Benedict, who headed the anti-casino citizens' group, Connecticut Alliance Against Casino Expansion (CAACE). January 2003 marked the third time the Department of the Interior (DOI) had said no to the Paugussetts; the department had also refused to recognize them as an authentic Indian tribe in 1995 and, after an appeal, in 1996. Soon after those earlier rejections, President Bill Clinton appointed Kevin Gover, a Democratic lawyer-lobbyist and Clinton fund-raiser who had represented the Paugussetts in their early recognition efforts, as assistant secretary for Indian affairs. The BIA reopened the case in 1999 (something it had never done after reaching a final determination), but four years later another rejection was announced by Gover's George W. Bush–appointed successor, Aurene Martin.[7] Even that determination, however, was only a "proposed preliminary finding"—hence, the anxiety that tempered the relief felt by Connecticut and CAACE. Happily for them and unhappily for the Paugussetts, Martin rejected one appeal in April 2004, and her boss, Secretary of the Interior Gale Norton, rejected another in March 2005.

Although disappointment and relief prevailed in Connecticut, some actually celebrated Interior's rejection of the Paugussett group's bid for federal recognition as a tribe, at least for a while. No one was happier than the Historic Eastern Pequots and The Donald. The Historic Eastern Pequots are a Connecticut group that had received a proposed preliminary finding from Interior in favor of federal recognition as a tribe in July 2002, seven months before the Paugussetts' bid was rejected. The Pequots, eager to open their own casino, and casino magnate Donald Trump, who had bankrolled much of their multimillion-dollar recognition campaign in hopes of being hired to build and manage the new facility, were more than happy not to have the competition that a Paugussett casino would bring. Unfortunately for Trump, the Pequots eventually tossed him aside once they became convinced they did not need him.[8] Unfortunately for the Pequots, their initial recognition was overturned on appeal in response to an ardent campaign by Attorney General Blumenthal, CAACE leader Benedict, a host of local governments in Connecticut, and several members of Connecticut's congressional delegation.

As the experience of the Golden Hill Paugussetts illustrates, the process by which the federal government decides whether a group deserves recognition as a legitimate, historic American Indian tribe has become an arena for group politics. The recognition process was created by the federal government in 1978, well before the legalization of Indian casino gambling in the late 1980s made tribal recognition as economically desirable and politically controversial as it has become. The process assigned to civil servants in the BIA's Office of Federal Acknowledgement the main responsibility for sorting through documents, artifacts, and other evidence in order to decide whether claimants bidding for federal recognition really are authentic members of a tribe whose continuous existence reaches deep into American history.[9] As Kay Davis, a former BIA employee, recalled, "Before Indian gaming, it was a very nice little process. People would come in and bring their stuff. We could sit down and talk to them. We didn't have all the big lawyers, the big backers."[10] The recent politicization of the recognition process is reflected in the involvement not just of groups of self-identified Indians seeking official status as tribes but also of investor groups, citizens' groups, state and local governments, and even other tribes.

This chapter begins by surveying what the stakes are in bids for tribal recognition. Although tribes have more to gain from being recognized by the

federal government than the right to open gambling halls, the recent legalization of Indian gambling has dramatically increased the benefits of recognition. Twenty years ago no Indian casinos existed, and the money tribes
made from bingo was negligible, around $212 million in 1988. Today approx-
imately 400 tribally owned casinos or high-stakes bingo halls are spread
across nearly thirty states. Together, tribes earn an estimated $20 billion
annually from gambling, a figure that has risen substantially every year.[11]

After assessing what is at stake in bids for tribal recognition, the chapter describes the process the BIA developed in 1978 to evaluate petitions
for recognition and assesses how that process operates today. The chapter
provides two case studies, one of a group whose campaign for recognition
was, like the Golden Hill Paugussetts', unsuccessful and one of a group
whose campaign is almost certain to succeed. Interest group politics infuses
these case studies in two ways. First, the politics of tribal recognition is, in
a sense, the politics of group formation. What tribal claimants seek from the
federal government is recognition that they are who they say they are. Second, pluralist politics, in which competing groups mobilize resources in an
effort to influence important government decisions, prevails even when (as
in the tribal recognition process) those decisions are meant to lie outside the
realm of politics.

The Stakes

Whether measured in cultural, economic, or political terms, the stakes
are high for groups seeking to be recognized as Indian tribes by the federal
government. Some of the benefits that accompany recognition predate the
recent rise of casino gambling. Legitimate members of historically authentic tribes gain the satisfaction of having their cultural identity as descendants of America's only indigenous people affirmed. They also gain the
economic opportunity to claim a share of the roughly $11 billion the federal
government spends each year on health care, education, housing, and other
social programs for Indians.[12] These two reasons alone go a long way toward
explaining why all but 22—less than 4 percent—of the 563 tribes currently
recognized by the federal government secured their recognition before the
first roulette wheel was spun in the first Indian casino.[13]

Another reason for seeking federal recognition spans the pre-casino
and casino eras: the sovereign status that tribes enjoy on reservation land.
Tribal sovereignty is a difficult legal concept to grasp.[14] As an attribute of
self-governing states, sovereignty in the United States largely inheres in the
federal and state governments. But, as Chief Justice John Marshall ruled in
the 1831 case of *Cherokee Nation v. Georgia*, the legal relationship between
the federal government and American Indian tribes concerning sovereignty
is "unlike that of any other two people in history."[15]

On the one hand, Marshall wrote in *Cherokee*, a tribe is sovereign in the
same way the federal and state governments are sovereign: it is a "distinct

political society ... capable of managing its own affairs and governing itself."[16] On the other hand, a tribe is to the federal government like "a ward to his guardian"—that is, the relationship is one of fiduciary trust in which the federal government is empowered to make decisions for the tribe with the understanding that those decisions will be in the tribe's best interest. In that sense, Marshall wrote in the related 1832 case of *Worcester v. Georgia*, tribes are "domestic dependent nations."[17]

One effect of tribal sovereignty, Marshall added in his *Worcester* ruling, is that a tribe is free from interference by the government of the state whose land surrounds it. Thus, he wrote, "the laws of Georgia can have no force" on Cherokee land.[18] Or, as the Supreme Court said more recently in the 1980 case of *Washington v. Confederated Colville Tribes*, unless the federal government chooses, in its role as guardian, to allow states to apply their laws to activities on Indian reservations, "tribal sovereignty is dependent on, and subordinate to, only the Federal Government, not the States."[19]

For many years, the federal government served as an incompetent guardian at best, a venal one at worst; it did one heinous thing after another to Native Americans. The government's ill treatment of Indian tribes ranged from stripping them of their historic lands in the interests of white settlers, railroad companies, and developers to instituting policies verging on outright extermination. The effects of this abuse continue to be felt. Native Americans suffer some of the highest rates of poverty, addiction, unemployment, poor health, and incarceration of any group in the United States.[20]

Politically, however, attempts by American Indians to expand tribal influence began to bear fruit in the late 1960s and early 1970s. The activist American Indian Movement, the litigation-focused Native American Rights Fund, and other groups formed to seek a greater measure of self-determination in tribal political and economic affairs. Popular movies such as *Little Big Man* and *Dances with Wolves* and bestselling books like Vine Deloria Jr.'s *Custer Died for Your Sins*[21] and Dee Brown's *Bury My Heart at Wounded Knee*[22] broadened public support for Native American causes.

Responding positively to these developments were several Republican presidents promoting a "new federalism" that would devolve power from Washington to subnational units of government as well as a number of Democratic congresses that sympathized with the cause of ethnic and racial minorities. In 1975, for example, the Democratic Congress passed and the Republican president Gerald R. Ford signed the Indian Self-Determination and Education Assistance Act, which gave tribal governments considerable discretion over how federal programs would be administered on their reservations. During the 1980s, the Reagan administration concentrated its efforts on economic self-determination for American Indian tribes, partly out of concern for the Indians' well being and partly in the hope that flourishing tribal economies would reduce tribes' dependence on federal assistance, which the administration severely reduced in 1981.

One form of enterprise by federally recognized tribes that the Reagan administration favored was gambling.[23] In the late 1970s, the Seminole tribe in Florida had opened a bingo hall offering higher-stakes games than the state of Florida permitted in nontribal bingo halls. When a federal appeals court rejected the state's efforts to shut down the Seminole facility in 1981,[24] tribes in Wisconsin, California, and other states opened high-stakes bingo halls of their own. Three federal departments—Interior, Housing and Urban Development, and Health and Human Services—provided loans and other financial assistance to help tribes build gambling facilities that could attract customers from surrounding areas. By 1985, about 100 tribes sponsored bingo games, some with jackpots as high as $100,000.

Several state governments, alarmed that much more extensive gambling facilities were operating within their borders than they had authorized by law, elected to fight these efforts. Constitutionally, however, Chief Justice Marshall's decisions from the early 1830s left them on weak ground. Although the relationship between federal and tribal sovereignty is complex, the relationship between state and tribal sovereignty is not. State governments have no intrinsic power over tribes—that is, none that the federal government does not specifically assign to them. Far from wanting to help the states stifle tribal gambling, the federal government was encouraging such enterprises.

Nonetheless, in 1980 the state of California, citing Public Law 280, a federal statute enacted in 1953 that empowers the states to enforce their criminal laws on tribal land, tried to shut down two bingo parlors and a card room operated by the Cabazon and Morongo bands of Mission Indians on their reservations near Palm Springs. In a 1987 6–3 decision that crossed ideological lines (it placed conservative Chief Justice William Rehnquist and liberal Justice William Brennan on the tribes' side and liberal Justice John Paul Stevens and conservative Justice Antonin Scalia on the state's), the Court ruled in favor of the tribes in the case of *California v. Cabazon Band of Mission Indians*.[25] In essence, the majority held that, unless a state consistently treats gambling as either a crime or a violation of its constitution, it cannot forbid gambling on tribal lands. Because California offered a cornucopia of legal gambling—not just bingo and card rooms but also a lottery and pari-mutuel betting on horse races—the Cabazons' gambling operations stood on solid, sovereign constitutional ground.

Responding to concerns expressed by many state governments, Congress quickly (and overwhelmingly: by a 323–84 vote in the House of Representatives and by a voice vote in the Senate) passed the Indian Gaming Regulatory Act (IGRA) of 1988. IGRA was an effort to rein in some of the extreme possibilities raised by *Cabazon*. To be sure, Congress was not about to allow state and local governments to tax tribal gambling operations on tribal land, which would contradict the Supreme Court's oft-affirmed doctrine of tribal sovereignty. But, while sounding the all clear for bingo, IGRA did say that a tribe could operate a "Class III" gambling facility (that is, a casino) against a state government's will only if its reservation was in a state whose own laws allowed Class III gambling. IGRA also stated that, before opening a casino, the tribe must negotiate a compact with the state government covering matters such as the terms of tribal-state criminal justice cooperation and standards for the operation of gambling facilities. Only an entire tribe could own a gambling facility, IGRA further specified, not just a group of enterprising tribal members. And, of course, the only tribes IGRA allowed to do so were those that had secured federal recognition.[26]

These restrictions on tribal gambling turned out to be less imposing in practice than Congress and the states had hoped. Take the provision of the act stating that a federally recognized tribe can operate a casino on reservation land only in a "state that permits such gaming for any purpose by any person": The federal Second Circuit Court of Appeals interpreted the provision to mean that Connecticut, whose laws permitted charitable organizations to hold occasional "Las Vegas Night" fundraising events, also had to allow tribes to own full-scale, round-the-clock casinos.[27] That's how the Mashantucket Pequots, with their reservation situated in the midst of the densely populated Northeast, were able to translate federal recognition in 1983 into the Foxwoods Resort Casino in 1992.[28] Within a few years, Foxwoods had become the most financially successful casino in the world.[29]

To be sure, for the majority of Indian tribes, *Cabazon* was of limited practical benefit. Running a profitable gambling operation requires the proximity of a "feeder market"—that is, a densely populated and nearby metropolitan area or tourism center to provide potential customers. That leaves out nearly all of the 232 federally recognized tribes whose reservations are in Alaska, where only three tribes have found it financially worthwhile to open gambling facilities. Nor, given the federal government's long history of driving Indians onto exactly those lands that white people did not want, was the right to offer high-stakes gambling of much use to many of the tribes in the Great Plains and Rocky Mountain regions of the lower forty-eight states. Although half of the nation's Indians live in five sparsely populated states—Montana, Nevada, North Dakota, Oklahoma, and South Dakota—their share of total tribal casino revenues is only around 3 percent.[30] For more fortunately situated tribes, however, *Cabazon* was like a license to print money. Indeed, forty tribal casinos—around one-tenth of all tribal gambling facilities—each earn more than $100 million per year, totaling around two-thirds of all the money made by American Indian tribes from gambling.[31]

The Process

The Mashantucket Pequots' success in translating federal recognition into a wildly profitable casino stimulated other groups to launch recognition campaigns of their own. From 1993 to 2000, the seven-year period after the Foxwoods Resort Casino began operating, ninety-four groups petitioned BIA for federal recognition as Indian tribes, the sharpest spike in recognition bids ever. (In the seven years prior to Foxwoods's opening, only twenty-two petitions—fewer than one-fourth as many—had been filed.)[32] Currently about 230 groups are waiting in line at various stages of the recognition process.[33] More than fifty of these groups are in California, a rich and populous state that decided in 2000 to grant Indian tribes the exclusive right to own casinos within its borders.[34]

Standing alongside some of these petitioning groups—especially those located near lucrative feeder markets—are developers and other investors who expect to make money from tribes that secure federal recognition. Although IGRA restricts the right to own a tribal casino to the tribe's government, it allows that government to negotiate a seven-year contract with an outside investor to develop and manage the casino in return for as much as 30 percent of the casino's net revenues. To get on the ground floor with recognition-seeking tribal groups, investors put up millions of dollars ($10 million is not unusual)[35] to pay the salaries and expenses of tribal chiefs and council members and to hire small armies of genealogists, anthropologists, historians, lawyers, lobbyists, and public relations firms to build a documentary record that will persuade the BIA to recommend recognition. It's a high-risk investment—Thomas Wilmot lost several million dollars when the Golden Hill Paugussetts were denied recognition—but a bargain if the group is recognized as a tribe. Indeed, for some developers, the seven-year, 30 percent casino management contract is less lucrative than other ventures not restricted by IGRA, such as consulting fees and the hotels, restaurants, and golf courses that often accompany the construction of tribal casinos.

What is the process by which the federal government decides whether a petitioning group is an authentic American Indian tribe? There is a fast track—Congress can recognize a tribe by law, as it did the Mashantucket Pequots of Foxwoods fame. But the politics of congressional recognition has become increasingly perilous. Connecticut, for example, is a roiling sea of irate town governments and citizens' groups, nearly all of them angry about the traffic, congestion, air and water pollution, crime, and other gambling-related social problems brought, they charge, by tribal casinos. Far from encouraging Congress to recognize more tribes, Connecticut's state government and congressional delegation have campaigned in Washington to make tribal recognition harder to obtain.[36] In California, Alabama, Texas, and elsewhere, the politics of federal recognition sometimes has pitted established tribes against would-be tribes.[37] The established tribes do not want Congress to recognize potential new competitors for the already crowded casino market. As a way of securing their political influence, tribes have become major donors to both major political parties and their candidates.[38]

Because the political risks attached to recognizing tribes by legislation are so great, Congress much prefers to defer tribal recognition decisions to the BIA's administrative procedures, which the bureau developed in 1978 and has occasionally tinkered with since then. BIA procedures describe both the criteria that define a group as a legitimate Indian tribe and the process for determining whether a petitioner meets these criteria. Of the seven criteria for federal recognition, some are mere formalities, like providing the BIA with a copy of the group's current governing document.[39] But three criteria are especially hard to satisfy: community continuity, political continuity, and genealogical authenticity. To prove to the BIA that it is a tribe, a petitioning group must show that it "comprises a distinct community and has existed as a community from historical times until the present" (community continuity); that it "has maintained political influence over its members as an autonomous entity," again "from historical times until the present" (political continuity); and that its current membership "consists of individuals who descend from a historical Indian tribe" or "tribes," if two or more tribes were combined some time in the past (genealogical continuity). "From historical times" in this context means all the way back to the first record of the tribe's existence.

None of these three criteria is easy to meet. Most tribes do not have neat stacks of documentary records filed away over the centuries; until recently, written records have not been at the core of most Native Americans' governing traditions. That explains the expense involved for petitioning groups and their financial backers. Experts must be hired to pore over old newspapers, court records, letters, diaries, artifacts, paintings, photographs, and other strands of historical, anthropological, and genealogical evidence. Even if such evidence exists, it usually is hard to find and difficult to interpret.

Compounding the problem is the BIA's unwillingness to specify how much is enough when it comes to meeting these criteria. How long a gap in the record is consistent with historical continuity? The BIA will not say, and its decisions on different petitioning groups have been erratic. For example, in one case the BIA staff said that, based on previous rulings, a seventy-year gap was too long, but the assistant secretary for Indian affairs said it was fine.[40] What percentage of the petitioner's membership must be proven descendants of the original tribe? The BIA says that it need not be 100 percent, but it will not go beyond that, not even with a quantifying term like "most" or "some." In one case, just when the BIA staff thought it had established that 48 percent was not enough, the assistant secretary for Indian affairs said it was.[41]

The process for recognition is even more problematic than the criteria. The hub of the BIA's recognition process is its Office of Federal Acknowledgement (OFA), a small, overworked group of government historians, genealogists, and anthropologists. Small in this case means tiny: since 1993, when the line of groups petitioning for recognition as tribes suddenly got long and the complexity of their well-financed petitions (some of them reaching 100,000 pages) began to grow exponentially, the OFA's staff has shrunk from seventeen to eleven: three historians, three anthropologists, three genealogists, a secretary, and the director.

To make matters worse, as petitions from groups like the Golden Hill Paugussetts have drawn more opposition from state and local governments and citizens' groups with their own battalions of hired scholarly guns, OFA professionals spend an increasing amount of their time on activities that distract them from evaluating the merits of petitions. When, as now happens routinely, opponents of a bid for tribal recognition lodge Freedom of Information Act requests or petitioning groups file suit in federal court to speed up the recognition process, it is the professionally credentialed OFA staff members who must find and copy the documents. "Never did I imagine," said OFA head R. Lee Fleming, "that I would become a glorified Kinko's operator."[42]

The OFA is supposed to take two years to evaluate a petition once a group has submitted its best evidence that it meets Interior's criteria for federal recognition as a tribe. In 2001, Fleming told the congressionally chartered Government Accountability Office that his staff might need fifteen years just to complete the petitions currently before it.[43] And even when the BIA does finish evaluating a petition, the recognition process is far from over. The DOI's assistant secretary for Indian affairs may overturn a negative recommendation and grant federal recognition, as Clinton appointee Kevin Gover did four times before he left office on January 3, 2001, and as his successor, Michael J. Anderson, did twice during the final few hours of the Clinton presidency. (The incoming Bush administration immediately froze Anderson's decisions.)

To make matters more complicated, whether positive or negative, the assistant secretary's decision is not final. Instead, it is a "proposed preliminary finding" that is published in the *Federal Register* pending a 180-day period of comment and additional evidence. Then, after another four months (the petitioner has sixty days to respond when the comment period is over, and the assistant secretary, advised by the OFA, has another sixty days or longer to decide once again), the "final determination" is issued. And even final determinations are not final. A disappointed petitioner or, if the petitioner wins federal recognition as a tribe, disappointed opponents can request the DOI's Board of Indian Appeals to order the assistant secretary to issue a "reconsidered final determination." No matter which side prevails, the loser may then head for federal court under the judicial review provision of the Federal Administrative Procedure Act.

In sum, the process by which the federal government decides whether to recognize an American Indian tribe is long, complicated, expensive, unpredictable, and—even though it was created for the purpose of removing recognition decisions from the realm of politics—riddled with opportunities for groups of all kinds to pursue their interests through political means. As illustrated in the following two case studies, groups of all kinds have chosen to do so.

Case Studies of the Politics of Tribal Recognition

General discussions of what the stakes are when a group petitions the federal government for recognition as an American Indian tribe and of what the process is by which the government evaluates such petitions are essential to understanding the politics of tribal recognition. But how does the process play out in particular cases? The remainder of the chapter consists of two case studies of recent campaigns for tribal recognition. The first is of the Schaghticoke (pronounced SCAT-a-coke) Tribal Nation, a group that tried and failed to be recognized as a tribe. The second is of the Mashpee Wampanoag (WOMP-a-nawg) tribe, a group that tried and is almost certain to succeed.

Schaghticoke Tribal Nation

In 1981, three years after the BIA created the modern process for evaluating petitions for tribal recognition, a roughly 300-member group claiming to be the Schaghticoke Tribal Nation let the BIA know that it intended to submit such a petition. Theirs was a serious claim: for many years the Schaghticokes had owned a reservation in western Connecticut's Litchfield County whose legal basis reached back to an agreement with the colony of Connecticut in the mid-1700s. But the group lacked the means to compile the extensive historical, anthropological, and genealogical record needed to satisfy the BIA's standards of evidence concerning community continuity, political continuity, and genealogical authenticity—that is, to prove that its members were true descendants of a tribe that had functioned continuously for centuries.

The Schaghticokes' prospects brightened after the Mashantucket Pequots opened Foxwoods in 1993. Not long afterward, Fred DeLuca, founder of the Subway restaurant chain, offered to fund the Schaghticokes' recognition campaign in exchange for a promise of $1 billion if the group was recognized and opened a profitable casino.[44] From the mid-1990s to the mid-2000s, DeLuca spent an estimated $14 million to subsidize the salaries and expenses of a small army of historians, genealogists, and other experts who were hired to find and compile persuasive documentation to support the Schaghticokes' claim.[45] In May 2001, midway through this ten-year period, the Schaghticokes secured a federal court order requiring the BIA to issue a proposed preliminary finding by August 2002.[46] Although the bureau always has a backlog of petitions to consider, groups with access to high-priced legal representation can sometimes use the courts to get theirs moved to the front of the line.

With a decision by the BIA imminent, the Schaghticokes did not rely entirely on experts and lawyers to make their case. Knowing that federal recognition requires the assent of the assistant secretary of the interior for Indian affairs, a presidential appointee, they hired Republican lobbyist Paul Manafort to advance their cause in Washington. After

George W. Bush's election as president in 2000, Manafort had assisted the president-elect's transition team, in part by recommending who should be appointed to lead the BIA. Manafort sent his lobbying firm's prospectus to groups petitioning to be recognized as tribes, claiming, "We believe that based on our superior political contacts we could win all necessary approvals in a time between 8 and 16 months."[47] The Schaghticokes took him up on the offer.

For all their efforts, money, and influence, the Schaghticokes received disappointing news on December 5, 2002. Speaking for the BIA, Assistant Secretary Aurene Martin issued a preliminary proposed finding that the group had failed to prove political continuity and community continuity—two crucial but hard-to-satisfy requirements for federal recognition—for substantial portions of the nineteenth century and twentieth century, respectively. Learning from Martin's finding which gaps in the record they needed to fill in order to prove their connection with the historical Schaghticoke tribe, the Schaghticoke Tribal Nation spent the next six months gathering and submitting evidence that they hoped would persuade her and the BIA to reverse this finding. On January 29, 2004, Martin announced that the Schaghticokes' new evidence was persuasive and issued a final determination in favor of recognition.

As the Schaghticokes rejoiced, much of the rest of Connecticut went ballistic.[48] Governor John Rowland, a Republican, and Attorney General Richard Blumenthal, a Democrat, announced that they would appeal the BIA's final determination to the Interior Board of Indian Appeals (IBIA) and, if that did not work, to the federal courts.[49] Claiming that Martin's decision to recognize the Schaghticokes was the product of the "power and political influence" of the group's "friends in positions of power," Blumenthal hired his own battery of historians and other experts to rebut the Schaghticokes' case for recognition.[50] He mobilized thirteen local governments and the Housatonic Valley Council of Elected Officials to join his appeal to the IBIA. Connecticut's two Democratic senators, Christopher Dodd and Joseph Lieberman, also denounced the decision, and three of the state's Republican members of the House of Representatives, Nancy Johnson, Christopher Shays, and Rob Simmons, introduced a bill to rescind federal recognition of the Schaghticokes. Townspeople from Kent, Connecticut, the site of the Schaghticokes' reservation, formed a group called Town Action to Save Kent (TASK) and hired the prominent Republican Washington lobbying firm of Barbour, Griffith and Rogers to persuade Congress and the BIA to overturn recognition.[51] Jeff Benedict, representing the Connecticut Alliance Against Casino Expansion (CAACE), helped rouse public pressure against the Schaghticokes in speeches and newspaper articles around the state as well as on CAACE's Web site. In every case, the Schaghticokes' opponents were less anti-Indian than anti-casino.

Further fuel was added to the fire on March 12, 2004, when the *Hartford Courant* published an article revealing the contents of the January 12,

2004, memo from the BIA staff to Assistant Secretary Martin that formed the basis of her proposed preliminary finding.[52] The memo told Martin that if she made her decision "based on the [bureau's] regulations and existing precedent," she would have to deny recognition to the Schaghticokes because they had been unable to supply sufficient evidence of political continuity. On the other hand, if she ignored precedent and relied instead on the fact that since colonial times the state of Connecticut had a "continual state relationship with a [Schaghticoke] reservation," she could grant recognition. Adopting the latter approach would mean substituting a state's long-standing legal judgment about a tribe for the BIA's own standards, something the BIA had never done and that the bureau's 1978 procedures did not seem to allow. Nevertheless, Martin bought the argument and used the state's historic standards rather than current BIA standards.

Publication of the memo by the *Courant* lent powerful ammunition to those who saw politics rather than law behind the decision by the BIA and Martin. Blumenthal said, "It's almost like a road map for committing robbery ... these are the regulations you have to disregard."[53] "The BIA doesn't need us to say they are breaking the rules," charged CAACE's Benedict. "They have said it themselves."[54] On April 1, 2004, the entire Connecticut congressional delegation met with Secretary of the Interior Gale Norton to complain that the decision to grant federal recognition to the Schaghticokes had been improperly reached and to threaten legislative intervention if it was not overturned.

Meanwhile, Blumenthal's hired experts discovered that the BIA had made a major error in advising Martin that the Schaghticokes had supplied the missing evidence to satisfy the bureau's requirement for community continuity. The evidence the Schaghticokes submitted and the BIA relied on involved historic rates of marriage among tribal members, which were said to exceed 50 percent. In truth, each marriage had been counted twice, reducing the true intratribal marriage rate for certain historical periods to around 20 percent, well below any standard that the BIA had ever found acceptable as proof of a tribe's community continuity. The BIA acknowledged its mistake.[55] Although in this instance the charge was incompetence rather than political favoritism, it was no less damaging to the Schaghticokes' case.

On May 12, 2005, the IBIA accepted Blumenthal's arguments and reversed the BIA's final determination in favor of the Schaghticokes. The appeals board emphasized that, according to the bureau's own procedures, a state government's recognition of a tribe was "not reliable" evidence on which to base a decision to grant federal recognition. The board's decision sent the Schaghticokes' petition back to the BIA for further review.[56] Belatedly, in September 2005, the Schaghticokes launched a media campaign in Connecticut, airing radio and television ads on stations around the state to defend their legitimacy as a tribe and to attack unnamed "elected officials and hired lobbyists" for holding "secret meetings" to plot unfairly against them.[57] It was a classic case of too little, too late. On October 12,

2005, having reconsidered its pro-Schaghticoke final determination in light of the IBIA reversal, the BIA issued a "reconsidered final determination" denying recognition.

Mashpee Wampanoag Tribe

The story of the Mashpee Wampanoag Tribe of Cape Cod, Massachusetts, resembles the Schaghticokes' story in several important ways. Both groups decided to seek federal recognition soon after the BIA introduced its recognition process in 1978. Both found wealthy investors willing to bankroll their campaigns to demonstrate their authenticity as American Indian tribes. Both the Schaghticokes and the Mashpees grew frustrated with the BIA's glacial pace and sued in federal court in hopes of moving to the front of the bureau's line of claimants for federal recognition. Both groups hired well-known and expensive lobbyists to promote their cause in Washington. Both received favorable preliminary proposed findings from the BIA—but there the resemblance ends. The Schaghticokes' bid for federal recognition ultimately was rejected. The Mashpees' bid seems certain to succeed.

The Mashpee Wampanoags, who number around 1,500 members, and the roughly 1,100-member Aquinnah Wampanoags, a tribe on the nearby island of Martha's Vineyard, are the remnants of one of the most storied Indian tribes in American history: the Wampanoag tribe whose members sustained the Pilgrims through their first winter in Massachusetts in 1621.[58] In the late 1970s both the Mashpees and the Aquinnahs, by then long divided from each other, made separate legal claims to large tracts of densely populated land on Cape Cod and Martha's Vineyard, respectively. To resolve the lawsuits, Congress offered both tribes smaller amounts of choice acreage along with federal recognition, which, even in the era before tribal casinos, conferred sovereignty and eligibility for several federal aid programs. The Aquinnahs took the deal, received 500 acres of prime real estate, and in 1987 were officially recognized by Congress as a historic Indian tribe. The Mashpees refused to settle, lost in court, and ended up with nothing more than the rocky 160-acre reservation between Falmouth and Barnstable that they began with.[59]

In 1980, one year after losing their lawsuit, the Mashpees informed the BIA that they intended to seek federal recognition through the bureau's recently developed procedures. The group filed a poorly documented petition in 1990 and, when the BIA rejected the filing as too incomplete to consider,[60] set about finding a wealthy investor who could help them hire the team of experts needed to make an effective argument for recognition. They found Herbert J. Strather, a major casino developer in Detroit. With his financial assistance, the Mashpees assembled a strong and persuasive petition. They filed it with the BIA in 1996 and took their place at the end of the bureau's long and slow-moving line of recognition-seeking claimants.

In 2001, frustrated that nothing was happening with their petition (and nothing seemed likely to for another ten years or more), the Strather-funded Mashpees filed suit against the BIA in federal district court in the District of Columbia. Although Judge James Robertson ruled in the Mashpees' favor, ordering the bureau to evaluate their case for federal recognition immediately, the BIA won a reversal of his decision from the U.S. Court of Appeals for the District of Columbia Circuit. The appeals court ruled in August 2003 that the BIA must be allowed to work through its pile of applications for tribal recognition on a first-filed, first-evaluated basis.[61]

Convinced by the court's decision that continuing to rely on a purely legal strategy would not cause the BIA to act promptly on their petition, the Mashpees turned to politics. Within weeks of losing in court, they hired Greenberg Traurig, the Republican-dominated lobbying firm of Washington power broker Jack Abramoff.[62] "Sometimes," said Chief Vernon Lopez, "it's necessary to go out of your way to get some of the things you need."[63] Strather paid $50,000 to Greenberg Traurig lobbyists Kevin A. Ring and Michael D. Smith to secure their services. The strategy the lobbyists developed was to rouse support for the Mashpees among members of Congress, who in turn would put pressure on the BIA and its parent organization, the Interior Department. With both elected branches of government controlled by Republicans, the strategy had much to recommend it: Republican lobbyists working with Republican members of Congress to influence a Republican-led DOI seemed like a winning formula, especially since it was lubricated by cash and supplemented by a new lawsuit filed by the Mashpees in federal court.

Advised by Greenberg Traurig, Strather and six members of the Mashpee group donated $14,000 to a political action committee (PAC) created by Rep. Richard Pombo. Pombo, a California Republican, chaired the House Committee on Resources, which had jurisdiction over most Indian issues. (Abramoff himself donated another $5,000 to Pombo's PAC.[64]) Other recipients of Mashpee or Abramoff campaign contributions were California Republican House member John Doolittle and Democratic senator Byron Dorgan of North Dakota, the ranking minority member of the Senate Committee on Indian Affairs.[65] At the suggestion of Abramoff lobbyists Ring and Smith, Strather also donated $50,000 to Americans for Tax Reform, a conservative group whose leader, Grover Norquist, is famously well connected to virtually the entire Republican community in Washington.[66]

Taken as a whole, these investments bore fruit. In September 2003 Representative Pombo met with Secretary of the Interior Gale Norton and R. Lee Freeman, head of the BIA's Office of Federal Acknowledgement, and urged them to consider the Mashpees' case promptly.[67] Representative Doolittle wrote to Norton in October complaining that the Mashpees "have been forced to wait too long to receive an answer to their petition for recognition."[68] Later that month, Senator Dorgan was able to insert a provision into the DOI's fiscal year 2004 budget bill stipulating that the BIA must "complete its review of the Mashpee petition as expeditiously as possible."[69] In 2004, Pombo and William Delahunt, a Democratic representative whose district includes Cape Cod and who also received Mashpee money, jointly sponsored a bill to force the BIA to speed up the recognition process for the Mashpees and several other tribes. A few months later, members of the Mashpee group donated another $20,000 to Pombo's PAC.[70]

None of these efforts was by itself successful. Pombo and Delahunt's bill cleared the House Committee on Resources but went no further. Secretary Norton did not order the BIA to put the Mashpees' petition on the top of its pile. Nevertheless, the Mashpees got what they wanted. When they returned to federal district court in February 2005, the DOI, which had beaten them the first time, now chose not to fight. Instead, the DOI settled the case by agreeing to begin evaluating the Mashpees' petition for federal recognition on October 1, 2005, issue a proposed preliminary finding by March 31, 2006, and make a final determination exactly one year later.[71] The preliminary finding, announced right on schedule, favored the Mashpees' bid for recognition in every way.

Ironically, the immediate consequence of the Mashpees' good news was to put a damper on an ongoing campaign to legalize a new commercial form of gambling in Massachusetts. On April 5, 2006, four days after the Mashpees received preliminary recognition, the Massachusetts House of Representatives voted 100–55 to reject a bill to allow slot machines at the state's four dog and horse tracks, even though the state Senate had passed the bill overwhelmingly the previous fall and the vote in the House had been expected to be close.[72] As in several other states, declining revenues at the Massachusetts racetracks had led each track to seek permission from the legislature to become a "racino," a portmanteau for a facility that combines racing with casino-style gambling.[73] Republican governor Mitt Romney campaigned against the bill, arguing that under the terms of the federal Indian Gaming Regulatory Act, any decision by the state government to legalize slot machines would require it to allow the state's federally recognized tribes to open full-blown casinos. Romney's veto threat killed the racino bill and with it, at least for the foreseeable future, Strather's and the Mashpees' hopes of opening a casino even after the tribe received federal recognition.[74]

Conclusion

Why does the preliminary decision to recognize the Mashpees seem certain to stand even though the Schaghticokes' positive preliminary BIA finding was overturned? The answer lies at the heart of the politics of tribal recognition: no group in Massachusetts is mounting an anti-Schaghticokes-style campaign to undo the Mashpees' recognition. Connecticut's laws were such that allowing the federal government to recognize the Schaghticokes as a tribe meant opening the door to another enormous Indian casino in a state that has two such facilities and does not want any more. Massachusetts law forbids casino-style gambling of any kind, thereby closing the door to a Mashpee casino for the foreseeable future. As a result, the sort of grassroots citizens' groups that formed to fight the Schaghticokes in Connecticut did not form to fight the Mashpees in Massachusetts. Because those groups were so active in Connecticut, the Schaghticokes faced intense opposition from nearly all of the state's elected local, state, and federal officials. In contrast, the Mashpees were able to cultivate the support of political leaders with campaign contributions and by other means, and those leaders were free to respond favorably because they were not facing countervailing pressure from grassroots groups of voters. The day the Schaghticokes received a positive preliminary finding from the BIA, Connecticut's leaders took to the barricades against them. The day the Mashpees received their good news, Massachusetts political leaders such as Representative Delahunt and Sen. Edward M. Kennedy spoke only to offer congratulations.[75]

Like all groups that recently have sought federal recognition as historic American Indian tribes, the Mashpees and the Schaghticokes consistently said that their primary motive was not to enter the gambling business. "This is not about gaming," said Mashpee tribal chairman Glenn Marshall on the day his group received the BIA's positive proposed preliminary finding. "This is about recognition. Right now, my focus is on health, housing, and education."[76] Voicing a similar statement, Chief Richard Velky of the Schaghticoke Tribal Nation said that his group sought recognition "to protect our land from further encroachment and to insure that our culture and tribal identity are preserved for our children, our grandchildren, and indeed for all future generations of the Schaghticoke Indian people."[77] Indeed, both groups took their first steps toward recognition in the pre–Indian gambling era, when the only benefits at stake were cultural recognition, sovereignty, and access to certain federal assistance programs.

Nonetheless, as with other recognition-seeking tribes, the possibility of opening a casino on sovereign reservation land has been an attractive one to both the Schaghticokes and the Mashpees. (Even as the Mashpees were denying any firm plans for a casino, they were paying a Boston lobbying firm $120,000 per year to make their case in the state capitol.[78]) And casinos constitute the only plausible explanation of why outside investors like Detroit casino developer Herbert Strather, for the Mashpees, and Fred DeLuca, for the Schaghticokes, chose to pay for the two groups' recognition campaigns.

The centrality of casino gambling in modern considerations of tribal recognition has placed group politics at the center of a process that was designed to be nonpolitical. During the 1970s Congress encouraged the BIA to develop administrative procedures for deciding which groups of claimants deserved federal recognition as authentic Indian tribes because it thought these claims were best left to experts like the genealogists, historians, and anthropologists who staff the bureau's Office of Federal Acknowledgement.

Little did anyone know that the legalization of tribal casino gambling in the late 1980s would take a process that had been depoliticized and repoliticize it as a major arena of group politics at all levels of the federal system and in all branches of the federal government.

Notes

1. The Golden Hills Paugussetts' experience with the tribal recognition process is recounted in Michael Nelson, "The Quest to Be Called a Tribe: The Lure of Casinos Has Raised the Stakes for Federal Recognition," *Legal Affairs*, September–October 2003, 56–58.
2. Jim Adams, "Federal Government Denies Golden Hill Paugussetts," *Indian Country Today*, January 29, 2003.
3. "Another Tribe Denied in Connecticut," *National Gaming Summary*, January 27, 2003, 1, 4.
4. David M. Herszenhorn, "Indian Bureau Rejects Bid for Group's Status as Tribe," *New York Times*, January 22, 2003; "Bridgeport, Tribe Agree to Casino Plan," Associated Press State and Local Wire, January 21, 2003.
5. Rick Green, "Indian Backers Take High Risks," *Hartford Courant*, December 1, 2002.
6. Donald L. Bartlett and James B. Steele, "Look Who's Cashing In on Indian Casinos," *Time*, December 8, 2002.
7. Sean P. Murphy, "Indians Given a Parting Boost," *Boston Globe*, March 25, 2001.
8. Rick Green, "Angry Trump Plays the Lawsuit Card," *Hartford Courant*, May 29, 2003.
9. Until 2003 the Office of Federal Acknowledgement was called the Branch of Acknowledgement and Research.
10. Sean P. Murphy, "Tribal Gamble: The Lure and Peril of Indian Gaming," *Boston Globe*, December 10, 2000.
11. Kevin Peterson, "48 States Raking in Gambling Proceeds," http://www.stateline.org, May 25, 2006, http://archive.stateline.org/html/2006/05/25/214_42.html.
12. Peter Katel, "American Indians," *CQ Researcher*, April 28, 2006, 364.
13. Before 1978, tribal recognition by the federal government was a somewhat haphazard process. Although the term *recognition* was not used until recently, recognition in fact often came about during the eighteenth and nineteenth centuries when the government negotiated a treaty or other agreement with a tribe. In 1934 Congress passed the Indian Reorganization Act in an effort to help tribes strengthen their governments. In providing assistance to a tribe, the Department of the Interior, which was charged with implementing the act, was in effect granting it federal recognition. Other tribes were recognized by acts of Congress.
14. For a fuller discussion of tribal sovereignty, see Steven Andrew Light and Kathryn R. L. Rand, *Indian Gaming and Tribal Sovereignty: The Casino Compromise* (Lawrence: University Press of Kansas, 2005).
15. *Cherokee Nation v. Georgia*, 30 U.S. (5 Pet.) 1 (1831).
16. Ibid.
17. *Worcester v. Georgia*, 30 U.S. 515 (1832).
18. Ibid.
19. *Washington v. Confederated Colville Tribes*, 447 U.S. 134, 154 (1980).
20. Katel, "American Indians," 363–364.
21. Vine Deloria Jr., *Custer Died for Your Sins: An Indian Manifesto* (New York: Macmillan, 1969).
22. Dee Alexander Brown, *Bury My Heart at Wounded Knee: An Indian History of the American West* (New York: Holt, Rinehart and Winston, 1970).

23. For a fuller discussion of Indian gambling, see John Mason and Michael Nelson, *Governing Gambling: Politics and Policy in State, Tribe, and Nation* (Washington, D.C.: Century Foundation/Brookings Institution, 2001), chap. 4.

24. The ruling by the Fifth Circuit Court of Appeals was in the case of *Seminole Tribe of Florida v. Butterworth*, 658 F.2d 310 (1981).

25. *California v. Cabazon Band of Mission Indians*, 480 U.S. 202 (1987).

26. IGRA entitles only an "Indian tribe"—that is, a tribe that "is recognized as eligible ... for the special programs and services provided by the United States to Indians because of their status as Indians, and is recognized as possessing powers of self-government"—to operate gambling facilities. 25 U.S.C. §§2703(5), 2710.

27. Kim Isaac Eisler, *Revenge of the Pequots: How a Small Native American Tribe Created the World's Largest Casino* (New York: Simon and Schuster, 2000), 130.

28. See Michael Nelson, "From Rez to Riches," *American Prospect*, May 21, 2001, 43–45.

29. Light and Rand, *Indian Gaming and Tribal Sovereignty*, 12.

30. Donald L. Bartlett and James B. Steele, "Dirty Dealing: Indian Casinos Are Making Millions for Their Investors and Providing Little to the Poor," *Time*, December 8, 2002.

31. Ibid., 11.

32. Murphy, "Tribal Gamble."

33. "Testimony of R. Lee Fleming, Director, Office of Federal Acknowledgement, for the Hearing before the Committee on Indian Affairs, United States Senate, on the Federal Acknowledgement Process," May 11, 2005, http://www.doi.gov/ocl/2005/FedAcknowledgement.htm.

34. David DeVoss, "California Gambling," *Weekly Standard*, September 15, 2003, 18.

35. Rick Green, "Indian Backers Take High Risks," *Hartford Courant*, December 1, 2002.

36. Nelson, "Quest to Be Called a Tribe."

37. See, for example, Michael Nelson and John Mason, *How the South Joined the Gambling Nation: The Politics of State Policy Innovation* (Baton Rouge: Louisiana State University Press, forthcoming 2007).

38. See, for example, Donald L. Bartlett and James B. Steele, "Playing the Political Slots," *Time*, December 18, 2002; Matthew Continetti, *The K Street Gang: The Rise and Fall of the Republican Machine* (New York: Doubleday, 2006), chap. 6; and Mason and Nelson, *Governing Gambling*, chap. 4.

39. Three other criteria that seldom pose a problem for petitioning groups are: they "must have been an American Indian entity on a substantially continuous basis since 1900"; the membership "must be comprised primarily of people who are not members of an existing acknowledged North American Indian tribe"; and "[t]he tribe must not be the subject of congressional legislation that has terminated or forbidden a federal relationship." Mason and Nelson, *Governing Gambling*, chap. 4.

40. *Indian Issues: Improvements Needed in Tribal Recognition Process* (Washington, D.C.: U.S. General Accounting Office, November 2001), 12–14.

41. Ibid., 12.

42. Bill McAllister, "Tribal Recognition Hot Issue for Interior," *Denver Post*, June 16, 2002.

43. *Indian Issues: Improvements Needed in Tribal Recognition Process*, 3.

44. Rick Green, "A Tribal CEO Stakes His Claim," *Hartford Courant*, June 27, 2005.

45. Rick Green, "Investors Evaluating Bets on Tribal Recognition," *Hartford Courant*, October 17, 2005.

46. "Judge Sets Timeline for Schaghticoke Recognition Process," Associated Press State and Local Wire, May 9, 2001.

47. Jason Lee Stoerts, "Tribal Loyalties," *National Review*, August 8, 2005, 39–41.

48. As with the Golden Hill Paugussetts, the city of Bridgeport was an exception: it hoped the Schaghticokes might locate a new casino there. Avi Salzman, "Another

Tribe and a New Round of Questions," *New York Times*, February 15, 2004. The Black and Latino Caucus of the Connecticut General Assembly also supported the Schaghticokes in hopes that an urban casino might provide jobs for some of the caucus members' constituents. Jim Adams, "Connecticut Mud-Fight Splatters Leader of Bureau of Indian Affairs," *Indian Country Today*, May 19, 2004.

49. When Rowland resigned in an unrelated scandal, his successor as governor, Republican M. Jodi Rell, replaced him in the ranks of leading opponents of recognition for the Schaghticokes.

50. Lolita C. Baldor, "BIA Grants Recognition to Schaghticoke Tribe," Associated Press State and Local Wire, January 29, 2004.

51. Rick Green, "Two Tribes Are Down to the Wire on Recognition," *Hartford Courant*, October 10, 2005.

52. Rick Green, "Indian Bureau Bent Rules," *Hartford Courant*, March 12, 2004.

53. "Report: Bureau of Indian Affairs Knew Approved Tribe Did Not Meet Recognition Rules," Associated Press State and Local Wire, March 12, 2004.

54. Green, "Indian Bureau Bent Rules."

55. Susan Haigh, "Blumenthal Says BIA Error Should Reverse Schaghticoke Recognition," Associated Press State and Local Wire, December 9, 2004.

56. Rick Green and Jesse Hamilton, "No Doubts: Indians Lose," *Hartford Courant*, October 13, 2005.

57. Rick Green, "Schaghticoke Ads Push Issue of Recognition," *Hartford Courant*, September 10, 2005.

58. The Wampanoags' story is told in Nathaniel Philbrick, *Mayflower: A Story of Courage, Community, and War* (New York: Viking, 2006).

59. Sean P. Murphy, "Choices Divide Wampanoag Tribal Bands," *Boston Globe*, August 21, 2004.

60. Theo Emery, "Tribe to Argue Again in Federal Court for Recognition Timeline," Associated Press State and Local Wire, February 13, 2005.

61. Lolita C. Baldor, "Judge Slams BIA for Tribal Recognition Delays," Associated Press State and Local Wire, February 14, 2005.

62. The Mashpees got a bargain. From 2001 to 2004, Abramoff milked six tribes for a total of $66 million for political services that were worth much less. Continetti, *The K Street Gang*, chap. 6.

63. Richard A. Serrano and Judy Pasternak, "FBI Follows Money in Tribe's Beltway Success," *Los Angeles Times*, December 24, 2005.

64. Michael Kranish, "Mashpee Tribe Got Abramoff Boost," *Boston Globe*, December 21, 2005.

65. Erica Werner, "Congressman Interceded for Tribes That Were Abramoff Clients," Associated Press State and Local Wire, January 30, 2006; and John Solomon and Sharon Theimer, "Dorgan Used Lobbyist's Skybox, Helped Client," Associated Press State and Local Wire, December 1, 2005.

66. Kranish, "Mashpee Tribe Got Abramoff Boost."

67. Serrano and Pasternak, "FBI Follows Money in Tribe's Beltway Success."

68. Werner, "Congressman Interceded for Tribes That Were Abramoff Clients."

69. Solomon and Theimer, "Dorgan Used Lobbyist's Skybox, Helped Client."

70. Serrano and Pasternak, "FBI Follows Money in Tribe's Beltway Success."

71. Raja Mishra, "US to Act Quickly on Tribe's Recognition Bid," *Boston Globe*, July 27, 2005.

72. John Laidler, "Legislators Appear Split over Slots," *Boston Globe*, April 2, 2006.

73. Racinos, a recent development in commercial gambling, may be found in eight states, most of them in the northeast. Kim Masters Evans, *Gambling: What's at Stake?* (Detroit: Thomason Gale, 2005), 32.

74. David Kibbe, "Tribe Plans Resort Casino If Massachusetts Passes Slots Bill," *Cape Cod Times*, February 27, 2006.

75. Andrew Miga, "Tribe Granted Preliminary Recognition," Associated Press State and Local Wire, April 1, 2006.

76. Megan Tench and Michael Kranish, "Mashpees Near Federal Recognition," *Boston Globe*, April 1, 2006.

77. "Prepared Testimony of Richard L. Velky, Chief, Schaghticoke Tribal Nation, to the Senate Committee on Indian Affairs," May 11, 2005, http://www.senate.gov/~scia/2005hrgs/051105hrg/velky.pdf#search=%22%22Richard%20L.%20Velky%2C%20Chief%2C%20Schaghticoke%20Tribal%20Nation%22%22.

78. Scott Helman, "US Ruling on Tribe May Affect Slots Vote," *Boston Globe*, March 25, 2006.

4

A More Level Playing Field or a New Mobilization of Bias?

Interest Groups and Advocacy for the Disadvantaged

Dara Z. Strolovitch

Over the course of the twentieth century, more and more segments of American society came to be represented by interest groups. Although the mid-century version of pluralism, developed by David Truman and Robert Dahl among others, painted a reasonably rosy picture of the broad representation of interests throughout society, in fact many groups (African Americans, the poor, and gays and lesbians, among others) received either spotty, ineffective, or nonexistent representation from organized interests. This changed in the 1960s and afterward, when increasing numbers of groups formed, often reacting to governmental policies such as the war on poverty rather than rising up to seek policy change. Scholars of interest groups have paid substantial attention to group formation and the overall representativeness of the universe of groups but have often assumed that formal organization meant that all members of a group were represented equally. But such an assumption may well be unwarranted, especially when group members face multiple disadvantages in acting effectively in American political life.

In this chapter, Dara Strolovitch examines the basic question of how well the least well off are represented. Using survey materials from a unique study, she focuses on those subgroups that are disadvantaged even within traditionally weaker groups. Thus, she finds that issues affecting poor women are addressed less frequently by women's organizations than are those that reflect the interests of the dominant majority within these groups. Ironically, the very existence of many groups that represent disadvantaged populations within the United States may reinforce biases against these populations, even as they seek to rectify past injustices. In sum, Strolovitch paints a nuanced picture of representation by and within groups advocating for disadvantaged populations. For groups such as poor women, gay and lesbian people of color, and female members of unions, the barriers to effective representation are formidable, even within groups that seek to represent their interests.

How well do interest groups represent the disadvantaged? Among the most long-standing and fundamental disagreements about interest groups are issues of whether such political organizations alleviate or exacerbate inequalities in American politics and public policy.[1] Many of the scholars who first considered these questions were quite sanguine about the role of pressure groups in the United States. In the 1950s and 1960s, "pluralists" such as David Truman and Robert Dahl[2] saw power as broadly diffused, and they expressed optimism that advocacy organizations would form to represent societal groups when their interests were at stake in the policy process.[3] Viewing "pressure groups … to be the essence of politics," they were confident that these organizations could protect and advance the interests of the groups across the board.[4] Thus, no one interest would win or lose all of the time.

In spite of this optimism, marginalized groups such as women, racial minorities, and low-income people had few formal political organizations representing their interests in national politics before the 1960s.[5] Critics such as E. E. Schattschneider argued that interest groups exacerbated rather than eased inequalities in political access.[6] Through the process that Schattschneider termed the "mobilization of bias," the concerns of weak groups were "organized out" of politics by elites who manipulated the agenda toward their own interests.[7] As a consequence, he asserted, the interests of weak groups were not merely opposed but were actually excluded from the political agenda. "The flaw in the pluralist heaven," he wrote, "is that the heavenly chorus sings with a strong upper-class accent." He estimated that approximately 90 percent of the population could not access what he called "the pressure system," the informal but extensive system of organizations mobilized to influence national politics.[8]

True as it was when he wrote it, Schattschneider's well-known rejoinder to the optimism of pluralists like Truman and Dahl was soon challenged by the social movements of the 1950s, 1960s, and 1970s. These movements mobilized historically marginalized and excluded groups, in particular women, racial minorities, and low-income people, and spawned hundreds of new organizations.[9] More than 700 organizations, the majority of which were formed after 1960, now represent these groups at the national level.

With their claims of giving voice to the previously voiceless, these organizations and their explosive growth brought with them the promise of a new era in which the interest group system would ensure that everyone would be represented in national policy debates.[10] This chapter examines the extent to which this promise has been fulfilled. Two main questions arise about organizations that represent women, racial minorities, and low-income people in national politics: How do these organizations compare with those that represent more powerful groups? To what degree and in what ways do organizations claiming to speak for marginalized groups address the particular challenges of advocating for disadvantaged subgroups within their own marginalized constituencies?

Legal scholar and critical race theorist Kimberlé Crenshaw has termed the multiply disadvantaged subgroups of marginalized groups such as women, racial minorities, and low-income people "intersectionally marginalized."[11] Recognizing that inequities persist *between* marginalized and dominant groups, an intersectional approach stresses the overlapping inequalities *within* groups and the resulting unevenness in their gains since the 1960s. Examples of intersectionally marginalized groups include gay men of color, discriminated against on both race and sexuality, and low-income women, disadvantaged by both economics and gender.

To examine how well interest groups represent the disadvantaged, this study uses data collected for the 2000 Survey of National Economic and Social Justice Organizations (SNESJO), a survey of 286 organizations that represent women, racial minorities, and low-income people in national politics (see Table 4.1).[12]

Table 4.1. Distribution of National Advocacy Organizations (Nationally and in Sample), by Organization Type

Organization type	Organizations in the United States		Sample	
	Number	Percent	Number	Percent
Asian Pacific American	32	4.5	13	4.5
Black or African American	40	5.5	20	7.0
Latino or Hispanic	43	6.3	16	5.6
Native American or American Indian	35	5.3	13	4.5
Civil rights—general	70	10.1	33	11.4
Immigrants' rights	8	1.1	6	2.1
Labor	175	24.6	42	14.7
Economic justice	153	21.0	66	23.1
Public interest	21	3.0	11	3.8
Women's rights and feminism[a]	137	18.6	66	23.1
Total	714	100	286	100

Sources: The database of organizations was compiled by the author on the basis of information in the following print and online directories: the Electra Pages, electrapages.com; *Encyclopedia of Associations* (Detroit: Gale Research, 2000); Leadership Conference on Civil Rights, lccr.org; the *National Directory of Asian Pacific American Organizations* (Washington, D.C.: Organization of Chinese Americans, 1999); *National Directory of Hispanic Organizations* (Washington, D.C.: Congressional Hispanic Caucus, Inc., 1999); *Public Interest Profiles* (Washington, D.C.: Foundation for Public Affairs, 1999); *Washington Information Directory* (Washington, D.C.: CQ Press, 1998); *Washington Representatives* (Washington, D.C.: Columbia Books, 1999); *Who's Who in Washington Nonprofit Groups* (Washington, D.C.: Congressional Quarterly, 1995); and *Women of Color Organizations and Projects National Directory* (Berkeley, Calif.: Women of Color Resource Center, 1998).

[a]Includes women-of-color, reproductive-rights, and women's health organizations.

To determine the priorities and activities of advocacy organizations, survey respondents were asked about their activities on four different types of issues within a four-part policy typology:

- **Universal issues** that, at least in theory, are likely to affect the population as a whole, regardless of race, gender, sexual orientation, disability, class, or any other identity;
- **Majority issues** that are likely to affect an organization's constituents relatively equally;
- **Disadvantaged-subgroup issues** that are likely to affect an organization's constituents who are disadvantaged economically, socially, or politically compared with the broader constituency; and
- **Advantaged-subgroup issues** that also are likely to affect a subgroup of an organization's constituents but one that is relatively strong or advantaged compared with the broader constituency (see Table 4.2).

Respondents from women's organizations were asked, for example, about violence against women as a majority issue because all women are, theoretically, equally likely to be victims of gender-based violence. These respondents were asked about affirmative action in higher education as an advantaged-subgroup issue because this issue affects primarily college-bound or college-educated women, a relatively advantaged subgroup of all women. Finally, they were asked about welfare reform, a disadvantaged-subgroup issue, as it intersects gender and poverty and affects low-income women, a disadvantaged subgroup of all women.

The survey data that I present below show that interest groups are an important source of advocacy and representation for marginalized groups. But the data also suggest that these organizations trail in numbers and resources those organizations that represent more powerful groups. In addition, the data show that women's, racial-minority, and economic-justice organizations advocate more extensively when it comes to majority and advantaged-subgroup issues than they do in the case of issues affecting disadvantaged subgroups of their broader constituencies. Finally, the survey evidence demonstrates that organizations target the courts more often on behalf of advantaged subgroups of their constituents than they do on behalf of disadvantaged subgroups.

Marginalized Groups and Electoral Representation

Groups such as women, racial minorities, and low-income people have historically been and continue to be severely underrepresented within American politics. Although the situation has improved somewhat over the past several decades with the election of record numbers of women and racial minorities, members of these and other marginalized groups continue to make up only a small percentage of elected and appointed officials when

Table 4.2. Specific Policy Issues Used in SNESJO Questions, by Organization Type and Issue Category

Organization type	Majority issue	Advantaged-subgroup issue	Disadvantaged-subgroup issue	Universal issue
Asian Pacific American	Hate crime	Affirmative action in government contracting	Violence against women	Social Security
Black or African American	Racial profiling	Affirmative action in higher education	Welfare	Social Security
Latino or Hispanic	Census undercount	Affirmative action in higher education	Welfare	Social Security
Native American or American Indian	Tribal sovereignty	Affirmative action in higher education	Violence against women	Social Security
Civil rights—general	Hate crime	Affirmative action in higher education	Discrimination against lesbian, gay, bisexual, and transgender people	Social Security
Immigrants' rights	Green-card backlog	Availability of H1B visas	Denial of benefits to immigrants	Social Security
Labor	Minimum wage	White-collar unionization	Job discrimination against women and minorities	Social Security
Economic justice	Welfare	Minimum wage	Public funding for abortion	Social Security
Public interest	Campaign finance reform	Internet privacy	Environmental racism	Social Security
Reproductive rights and women's health	Late-term abortion	Abortion coverage by insurance and health maintenance organizations	Public funding for abortion	Social Security
Women's rights and feminism[a]	Violence against women	Affirmative action in higher education	Welfare	Social Security

Sources: Issues were selected by the author on the basis of information from *Congressional Quarterly* (Washington, D.C.: CQ Press, 1990, 1993, 1996, and 1999); *New York Times,* "Supreme Court Roundup" (1990–2000); *Congressional Record* (Washington, D.C.: Government Printing Office, 1990–2000); and *Federal Register* (Washington, D.C.: Government Printing Office, 1990–2000).

[a]Includes women-of-color organizations.

compared with their shares of the general population. For example, while women constitute approximately 51 percent of the American population, they hold only 15 percent of the 435 seats in the House of Representatives and only 14 percent of the 100 seats in the Senate. Similarly, while African Americans make up approximately 13 percent of the population, they hold only 9 percent of House seats and a mere 1 percent of Senate seats. Numbers are similarly low for other marginalized groups including Asian Americans; Latinos; Native Americans; low-income people; and lesbian, gay, bisexual, and transgender (LGBT) people.[13]

In addition to the dearth of elected representatives from marginalized groups, other features of the American electoral system further compromise equitable representation for these populations. Geographically based congressional districts, for example, make difficult the election of representatives of groups whose members do not live in residentially distinct areas.[14] Women, for example, share many interests but are not concentrated geographically in particular congressional districts. In addition, the winner-take-all elections that are used to elect members of the U.S. Congress are biased against electoral successes for candidates from minority parties that often represent the interests of racial and ethnic minorities in proportional representation systems, such as those found in many European countries.[15]

Thus, despite record numbers of women and minorities in Congress and other elected offices, it remains difficult for these representatives to have a major impact on formulating or passing legislation that would benefit these groups.[16] Moreover, salient groupings that help to define political interests and preferences, such as those based on race, ethnicity, class, citizenship, and gender, are not static, mutually exclusive categories. Instead, these groups are defined by contingent, dynamic, and intersecting interests. Because individuals belong to many intersecting and overlapping groups, an individual's interests typically exist along more than one dimension. A predominantly Latino electoral district might elect a Latino member of Congress, but this does not guarantee that this representative will attend to the concerns of Latina women, low-income Latinos, or gay and lesbian Latinos. Geographically based elections are thus ill equipped to transmit the multifaceted interests and preferences of groups whose identities and interests are intersectionally constituted.

With their ability to transcend geographic boundaries and advocate for groups of people with shared interests but inadequate formal representation in Congress, interest groups would seem well positioned to compensate for these low levels of formal representation for members of marginalized populations such as women, racial minorities, and low-income people.[17] As Scott Ainsworth writes, while elected representatives have a geographic basis for representing their constituents, interest groups "focus on functional divisions" that are often spread across the entire country.[18] So, for example, an African American member of Congress from New York represents African Americans in a specific congressional district. Although the representative might try to act as a surrogate or a virtual representative for African Americans nationwide, each representative's primary responsibility is to constituents in the district.[19] African American interest groups such as the National Association for the Advancement of Colored People (NAACP), on the other hand, represent African Americans from states and districts all over the country.

Indeed, interest groups have historically been a crucial conduit for the articulation and representation of the interests of the disadvantaged in U.S. politics. For many years, these organizations were the sole political voice afforded groups such as southern blacks and women of all races, who were denied formal voting rights until well into the twentieth century. Long before women won the right to vote in 1920, for example, organizations such as the National American Woman Suffrage Association (formed in 1890) and the National Woman's Party (formed in 1913) mobilized women and lobbied legislators on their behalf, providing some insider access for the mass movements with which they were associated. Similarly, the NAACP (formed in 1909) provided political and legal representation for African Americans in the South who, after a brief period of voting following Reconstruction and the passage of the Fifteenth Amendment in 1870, were largely disenfranchised and denied formal representation until the passage and enforcement of the Voting Rights Act of 1965.

Continuity and Change in the Pluralist Heaven

Although interest groups were often the only voice for these populations, the groups were nonetheless comparatively weak and greatly outnumbered and out-resourced by corporate, business, and professional organizations. The social movements and policy changes of the 1960s changed all that, and there are currently well over forty African American organizations, over thirty Asian Pacific American organizations, and well over one hundred women's organizations representing these populations at the national level. Organizations such as the Leadership Conference on Civil Rights (LCCR), the National Organization for Women (NOW), the Center for Law and Social Policy (CLASP), the National Council of La Raza (NCLR), and the National Asian Pacific American Law Center (NAPALC) have become a significant and visible presence in Washington politics, providing an institutionalized voice to and compensatory representation for the concerns of formerly excluded groups that still have insufficient formal representation in national politics.[20]

These groups' ties to mass movements and their claims to represent marginalized groups caused many to hope that these new organizations would realize the pluralists' promise of a more level representational playing field for groups that were underserved by electoral politics.[21] The extent to which this promise has been fulfilled has been the source of much debate. First, concerns persist about the biases and inequalities in the broader pressure group system.[22] Organizations that represent disadvantaged groups continue to make up only a small portion of the broader interest group universe that counts over 17,000 national organizations and that encompasses organizations representing corporate, business, professional, ideologically conservative, and foreign policy interests.[23] In addition, the growth in the number of organizations representing marginalized groups has produced new concerns about the biases within the universe of organizations that claim to speak on behalf of marginalized populations.

A More Level Playing Field?

The explosion in the number of feminist, civil rights, and economic-justice organizations has brought with it unprecedented levels of representation for women, racial minorities, and low-income people. Indeed, although these groups have suffered a historically compromised position in the American polity, the organizations that currently speak for them bear a striking resemblance to more traditionally powerful lobby groups.

In fact, based only on a list of addresses, it is impossible to distinguish antipoverty organizations from business lobbies, civil rights organizations from professional organizations, and feminist groups from Christian conservative organizations. A majority (61.4 percent) of the organizations surveyed in the SNESJO are located in the greater Washington, D.C., area (Washington, Maryland, and Virginia); and many are in or near "Gucci Gulch," the K Street corridor that is home to some of the most powerful lobbying firms and interest groups in the country. Organizations such as NOW, the NAACP, and the American Federation of Labor–Congress of Industrial Organizations (AFL-CIO) trace their origins to outsider movements that were once considered radical by mainstream political actors. Their geographical proximity to mainstream lobbyists signifies the extent to which many of these organizations have now become political insiders that lobby members of Congress and command the attention of cabinet members and committee chairs.

Although many of the organizations that advocate for marginalized groups resemble political insiders, it is no surprise that they remain outmoneyed by organizations of other, more traditional interests. In addition, they have fewer resources and fewer of the organizational and political tools than do other interests such as business and professional organizations. Fewer than one-third (31.8 percent) of the organizations surveyed in the SNESJO employ a legal staff compared with three-quarters of the organizations in a broader 1986 study of interest groups.[24] Only one-quarter of the organizations in the SNESJO employ lobbyists, and only one-fifth have political action committees (PACs). Kay Schlozman and John Tierney, in contrast, found that 54 percent of the organizations in their 1986 study had PACs, and Kollman in his 1998 research noted that 64 percent of organizations sponsored them.[25]

In addition to these continuing disparities, the growth in the number of social and economic-justice organizations has been outpaced by the growth of business and professional groups—the same organizations that dominated the interest group universe in the years before the mass mobilizations of the 1960s and 1970s and the increase in the number of organizations representing marginalized groups.[26]

In 1986, Schlozman and Tierney reported that corporations made up 45.7 percent of all organizations having a Washington representation, trade and business associations made up 17.9 percent, and professional associations made up 6.9 percent—a total of more than 70 percent of all such organizations. Unions, however, made up less than 2 percent of all organizations having Washington representation; citizens' groups, 4.1 percent; civil rights and racial-minority groups, only 1.3 percent; and organizations concerned with social welfare and the poor, a mere 0.6 percent of organizations in Washington, D.C.

More recent data show that, while the terrain has changed, vast inequalities remain. Drawing on data collected by Kay Lehman Schlozman, Sidney Verba, and Henry Brady as part of the Project on Political Equality, Schlozman and Traci Burch show that of the nearly 12,000 organizations listed in the 2001 edition of the *Washington Representatives* directory, 35 percent represent corporations, 13 percent represent trade and other business associations, and 7 percent represent occupational groups.[27] Less than 5 percent are public interest groups, and less than 4 percent are identity-based organizations representing groups such as women, racial minorities, and LGBT people. Only 1 percent of the organizations listed are labor unions, and only a fraction of 1 percent of the organizations listed in the directory are social welfare organizations or organizations that represent poor and low-income people—a proportion that remains almost identical to the proportion of these organizations fifteen years previously.

In spite of the impressive growth in the number organizations representing disadvantaged groups, interest group politics remains dominated by organizations that represent traditionally powerful groups. While there are more organizations representing women, racial minority, and low-income people than ever before, the representational playing field remains, at best, uneven.

A New Mobilization of Bias?

Although organizations representing marginalized groups remain disadvantaged relative to traditional interests, there is broad agreement that the increase in the number of these organizations has helped these populations in significant ways. For several decades, for example, organizations like the NAACP and NOW (and their associated legal defense funds) have played a central role in legal and legislative efforts to end de jure racial and sex-based discrimination and to increase resources and opportunities for the underrepresented. In spite of these organizations' potential, a great deal of work suggests that the representation provided by these groups replicates the elite bias that was lamented by Schattschneider.[28] Although Schattschneider was concerned primarily with biases toward wealthy and powerful interests within the broader pressure group system, new misgivings have surfaced about biases within the organizations that claim to remedy the inequities resulting from such biases. Has the increased representation provided by organizations representing women, racial minorities, and low-income people benefited advantaged segments of these groups more than it has benefited disadvantaged segments?

Comparing the levels of attention devoted by the organizations to different policy issues allows for an assessment of their advocacy on behalf of disadvantaged subgroups. This is done through data obtained from a series of questions from the SNESJO that asked respondents to gauge how active, on a scale of one to five, their organization had been on each of four designated policy issues. As noted earlier, issues were selected so that each issue corresponded to one of the four categories within the issue typology described earlier. Each organization was therefore asked about its activities as they related to one majority issue, one advantaged-subgroup issue, one disadvantaged-subgroup issue, and one universal issue. While the majority, advantaged-subgroup, and disadvantaged-subgroup issues vary by organization type, the same universal issue—Social Security—was used for all groups.

Examining the average levels of activity by issue type, as well the proportion of organizations that are "very active" and "not active" on each, allows us to see the variation in activity level by issue type (see Figures 4.1 and 4.2). Measured in terms of both the percentage and the mean, organizations are most active on the majority issue (true for 81 percent of organizations), and next most active on the advantaged-subgroup issue (true for 76 percent of organizations), followed by the disadvantaged-subgroup issue (true for 57 percent of organizations). The universal issue comes in last (37 percent of organizations are active).

Thus, for the women's organizations in the SNESJO, 86 percent are active on the issue of violence against women, the majority issue, and almost as many—79.5 percent—are active on the advantaged-subgroup issue of affirmative action in higher education. A smaller proportion of women's organizations—only 60.5 percent—are active on the disadvantaged-subgroup issue of welfare reform. Notably, however, the proportions of women affected by the advantaged-subgroup issue and the disadvantaged-subgroup issue are relatively similar. Let us assume that among the women who are most likely to benefit from affirmative action in higher education are those who eventually obtain college degrees, while the women who are most likely to be affected by welfare reform are those who live below the poverty line. According to the 2002 Current Population Survey, the proportions of women falling into each of these categories are roughly the same. Approximately 17.5 percent of women over the age of twenty-five have college degrees, while about 12.6 percent of all women live below the poverty line, as do 26.5 percent of female-headed households and 22.9 percent of women

Figure 4.1.   Activity Levels—Very Active or Not Active—of
Organizations Surveyed, by Issue Type

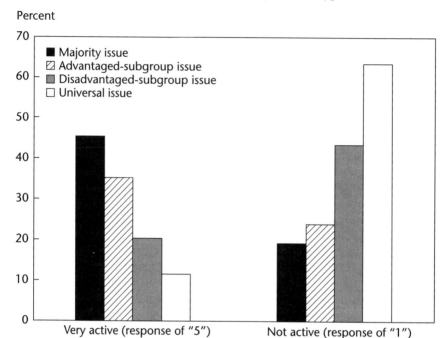

Percent

Sources: Survey of National Economic and Social Justice Organizations (SNESJO); see Dara Z. Strolovitch, *Affirmative Advocacy: Race, Class, and Gender in Interest Group Politics* (Chicago: University of Chicago Press, forthcoming), and Dara Z. Strolovitch, "Do Interest Groups Represent the Disadvantaged? Advocacy at the Intersections of Race, Class, and Gender," *Journal of Politics* 68 (4) (2006): 893–908.

Note: Organization officers were asked, "Please tell me, on a scale of one to five, where one is not active, and five is very active, how active has your organization been on each of the following policy issues in the past ten years?" The four columns on the left reflect the percentage of respondents giving the answer "five." The four columns on the right reflect the percentage of respondents giving the answer "one."

living alone.[29] Thus, while welfare reform affects a small but disadvantaged subgroup of women, affirmative action in higher education affects a small but relatively advantaged subgroup. The disparity in levels of attention to these two issues provides evidence that organizations do indeed provide somewhat more representation for advantaged subgroups than they do for disadvantaged subgroups, and that the proportion of organizations active on each issue is not simply a function of the potential impact of each one.

Although the attention devoted to issues affecting intersectionally disadvantaged subgroups is an important measure of the representation afforded to them by advocacy organizations, these are not the only relevant

Figure 4.2.   Mean Activity Levels of Organizations Surveyed, by Issue Type

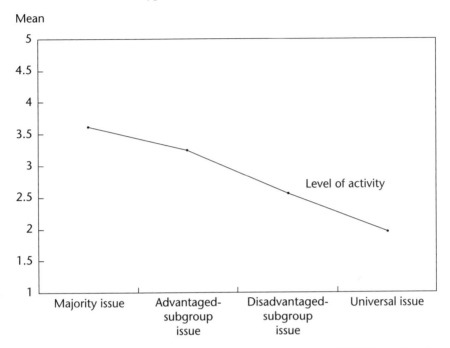

Sources: Survey of National Economic and Social Justice Organizations (SNESJO); see Dara Z. Strolovitch, *Affirmative Advocacy: Race, Class, and Gender in Interest Group Politics* (Chicago: University of Chicago Press, forthcoming), and Dara Z. Strolovitch, "Do Interest Groups Represent the Disadvantaged? Advocacy at the Intersections of Race, Class, and Gender," *Journal of Politics* 68 (4) (2006): 893–908.

Note: Data reflect the mean response to the question, "Please tell me, on a scale of one to five, where one is not active, and five is very active, how active has your organization been on each of the following policy issues in the past ten years?"

components of representation. Also important are the kinds of representational activities that are used and the institutions targeted by organizations as they pursue the interests of their constituents.

Targeting Institutions

Interest groups use a host of tactics aimed at many institutions as they represent their constituents and pursue their policy goals. For example, when they target Congress, they can lobby legislators directly, organize letter-writing campaigns among their constituents, testify at committee hearings, or provide policy makers with information and research. Advocacy organizations can also attempt to influence the executive branch by lobbying the president and presidential advisers regarding pending legislation, or by providing agencies with comments and testimony about proposed regulations. Organizations can also target the courts by filing amicus curiae briefs or bringing test cases and class action suits to represent their constituents.

Organizations' choices about tactics and institutional targets depend on many factors, including their general preferences for one institution over another, the political party in control of each branch, and whether there are preexisting opportunities to address an issue in a given branch.[30] In addition to these influences on their decisions, it is important to consider whether organizations' choices about which political branch to target—legislative, judicial, or executive—vary on the basis of the issue type or the status of the affected group. Here the focus is on the circumstances under which organizations representing marginalized groups target the courts.

Using the courts is significant because the judiciary is the branch of the federal government that is most explicitly (though not exclusively) charged with protecting rights and with checking the powers and actions of the majoritarian, electorally based, legislative and executive branches. As a consequence, the courts are often called on to protect unpopular minorities from the tyranny of majority rule, and organizations representing marginalized groups have often targeted the judicial branch when they have been unsuccessful in the legislative and executive branches.[31] For example, the landmark Supreme Court case *Brown v. Board of Education of Topeka* (1954) was part of an ongoing strategy by the NAACP Legal Defense Fund to bring test cases to the Supreme Court to overturn the separate-but-equal *Plessy v. Ferguson* decision (1896) and make real the equal protection guarantees of the Fourteenth Amendment to the Constitution.[32] As legal scholar Jeffrey Rosen observes:

> In the 50 years since *Brown v. Board of Education*, Americans have imagined that the justices could protect vulnerable minorities from the excesses of democratic politics. From affirmative action to school prayer and presidential elections, the court has enthusiastically accepted the invitation to answer the divisive political questions that politicians are unable to resolve.[33]

The past several decades have yielded significant court victories for marginalized groups,[34] but some worry that organizations that represent these groups may have come to rely too heavily on court-based strategies.[35] Critics argue that the same insulation from the will of the majority that allows judges to rule on behalf of unpopular minorities also lays the basis for portrayals of their decisions in such cases as undemocratic, antimajoritarian, and therefore illegitimate.[36] As such, they see court rulings on behalf of disadvantaged groups that are not in line with public sentiment as potentially elitist and possibly stimulating backlash that ultimately leads to setbacks in the very policy areas the groups have sought to advance.[37]

Others worry that the high financial costs of lawsuits take resources away from other goals such as mass mobilization.[38] Given the potentially significant payoffs of court-based tactics, as well as their monetary and political costs, who stands to benefit?

Figure 4.3 shows the responses to a SNESJO question that asks respondents to select the federal-level political institution (legislative, executive, or judicial branch) that is the most frequent target of their efforts on each of the four policy issues designated for their organization.[39] These data reveal that the percentage of organizations targeting the courts is quite low regardless of the issue type in question. However, the data also show that rates of court use vary markedly by issue type, and that there is a clear progression in the extent of this activity that increases steadily as we move

Figure 4.3. Branch of Government Targeted by Organizations Surveyed, by Policy Type

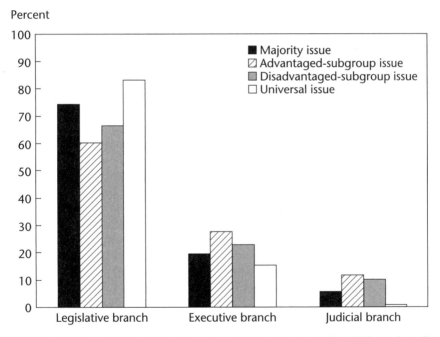

Sources: Survey of National Economic and Social Justice Organizations (SNESJO); see Dara Z. Strolovitch, *Affirmative Advocacy: Race, Class, and Gender in Interest Group Politics* (Chicago: University of Chicago Press, forthcoming), and Dara Z. Strolovitch, "Do Interest Groups Represent the Disadvantaged? Advocacy at the Intersections of Race, Class, and Gender," *Journal of Politics* 68 (4) (2006): 893–908.

Note: Organization officers were asked, "Which of the following political institutions is the most important target of your efforts in trying to influence policy on [the issue in question]?" Data in the columns reflect the percentage of respondents selecting that branch for the policy issue in question. The question was posed so that respondents had to select only one of the institutions.

from universal issues on the low end to advantaged-subgroup issues on the high end. While the legislative branch is the most frequent target of activity for all issues, organizations target the courts approximately twice as often when it comes to issues affecting advantaged or disadvantaged subgroups than they do when it comes to majority issues.

Thus, while only 1 percent of organizations reported that they target the courts the most when pursuing the universal issue, 6 percent of organizations claim that the court is the most important target of their activities when it comes to majority issues, 10 percent target the courts for disadvantaged-subgroup issues, and almost 12 percent claim that the court is the most important target of their activities on the advantaged-subgroup issues. As such, court tactics are most prevalent when it comes to advantaged-subgroup issues. Even though organizations still direct the bulk of their efforts at Congress when it comes to these issues, legislative activity constitutes a far smaller proportion of their activity and judicial activity a far greater proportion of their activity for advantaged-subgroup issues than for the other issue types.

The pattern in these results is notable for three reasons. First, given scholarly concern and popular rhetoric about the use of courts by organizations representing the disadvantaged, we might expect that the organizations in this study would rely heavily on litigation. However, the SNESJO data show that the opposite is true. Instead, in keeping with previous research, the data show that Congress is by far the most frequent target of organizations' advocacy activities and the courts are targeted least often.[40] Compared with their targeting of other branches, advocacy organizations representing marginalized groups do not rely heavily on the courts to advocate for social change or to protect minority rights.

Second, while organizations continue to target the three branches in the same order regardless of the policy type in question, the extent to which they target each institution varies noticeably by issue type. As such, it is the circumstances under which organizations target the courts, rather than particularly high levels of judicial targeting, that are remarkable. In particular, organizations reserve court tactics for policy issues that affect a subgroup of their constituents, suggesting that officers at organizations reserve such tactics for issues that will be more difficult to pursue if they are subjected to majority preferences. In this way, they use the courts as the framers of the Constitution intended—to protect the rights of the minority from the tyranny of the majority.

Finally, while organizations focus their use of the courts on issues that affect subgroups, they are substantially more likely to use the politically and financially expensive courts on behalf of advantaged subgroups of their constituencies than they are on behalf of disadvantaged subgroups. As such, these findings reveal that the disproportionately high levels of activity on behalf of advantaged groups discussed earlier are matched by a disproportionately heavy use of court activity on their behalf as well. Although the differences are not immense, they show clearly that organizations devote a disproportionately large share of their limited judicial targeting to issues that benefit those constituents who are already the best off.

Conclusion

The mobilization of new interests and the formation of new advocacy organizations have led to many changes in the interest group universe since E. E. Schattschneider proffered his gloomy critique of the "pluralist heaven." As James Q. Wilson observes in the introduction to the revised version of his 1974 classic, *Political Organizations*, "Since roughly 1970 we have entered a new era. Groups once excluded are now included. Pluralism that once was a distant promise is now a baffling reality."[41] Indeed, many organizations (and increasing numbers of elected representatives) now advocate in the policy process on behalf of once-excluded groups such as women, racial minorities, and low-income people. Still, the evidence presented here suggests that the nature and extent of this advocacy is extremely uneven.

First, the substantial increase in the number of organizations representing marginalized groups has been outpaced by the growth of organizations representing powerful interests such as business. Although the terrain of representation has improved, it is still not a level playing field. In addition, organizations are less active on issues affecting disadvantaged subgroups of the marginalized populations that they represent than they are when it comes to majority or advantaged-subgroup issues. They compensate somewhat for these low levels of activity by making relatively generous use of court tactics, but, here too, they devote the bulk of their court resources to advantaged subgroups.

Interest groups go a long way to supplement the political voice of marginalized groups such as women, racial minorities, and low-income people in national politics. Indeed, through their litigation and lobbying efforts, these organizations have played crucial roles in advances ranging from school desegregation to family and medical leave. But the evidence suggests that interest group politics reinforce as much as they rectify the biases against marginalized groups—and intersectionally disadvantaged subgroups of those groups—that are present in the broader political environment. Moreover, the relative power of organizations that speak for marginalized groups remains far less than that of the multitude of other organizations that represent more advantaged constituencies. As long as organizations representing marginalized groups remain outnumbered and out-resourced by organizations representing more powerful interests, and as long as women's organizations, for example, continue to expend more energy and resources on issues such as affirmative action in higher education than they do on issues such as welfare reform, this picture is unlikely to change.

Notes

1. Frank R. Baumgartner and Bryan D. Jones, *Agendas and Instability in American Politics* (Chicago: University of Chicago Press, 1993).
2. David Truman, *The Governmental Process* (New York: Knopf, 1951); Robert A. Dahl, *Pluralist Democracy in the United States* (Chicago: Rand McNally, 1967).
3. See also Arthur F. Bentley, *The Process of Government* (Chicago: University of Chicago Press, 1908); E. Pendleton Herring, *Group Representation before Congress* (Baltimore: Johns Hopkins University Press, 1929); Earl Latham, *The Group Basis of Politics* (Ithaca, N.Y.: Cornell University Press, 1952).
4. James Q. Wilson, *Political Organizations* (1974; repr., Princeton: Princeton University Press, 1995), 3.
5. I interchange the terms "advocacy organization," "interest group," and "social movement organization."
6. In addition to Schattschneider's critiques of pluralist assumptions, such ideas were also roundly critiqued by rational-choice theorists, most notably Mancur Olson, *The Logic of Collective Action: Public Goods and the Theory of Groups* (Cambridge: Harvard University Press, 1965), who argued that the goals pursued by interest groups were almost always "public goods," equally available to everyone regardless of whether they participate in the efforts to obtain them. A "rational actor," therefore, would decline the costs of participation unless selective incentives were made available only to participants. Subsequent research has found many conditions under which such "collective action problems" can be overcome. See, for example, Jeffrey M. Berry, *Lobbying for the People* (Princeton: Princeton University Press, 1977); Allan J. Cigler and John Mark Hansen, "Group Formation through Protest: The American Agriculture Movement," in *Interest Group Politics*, ed. Allan J. Cigler and Burdett A. Loomis (Washington, D.C.: CQ Press, 1983), 84–109; John Mark Hansen, "The Political Economy of Group Membership," *American Political Science Review* 79 (1985): 79–96; Andrew McFarland, *Common Cause* (Chatham, N.J.: Chatham House, 1984); Terry M. Moe, "Toward a Broader View of Interest Groups," *Journal of Politics* 43 (1981): 531–543; Lawrence S. Rothenberg, *Linking Citizens to Government* (New York: Cambridge University Press, 1992); and Wilson, *Political Organizations*. Nonetheless, the inevitability of organization is no longer taken for granted.
7. E. E. Schattschneider, *The Semisovereign People* (New York: Holt, Rinehart and Winston, 1960).
8. Ibid., 35. See also Robert Michels, *Political Parties* (New York: Free Press, 1911); C. Wright Mills, *The Power Elite* (New York: Oxford University Press, 1956); Charles Lindblom, *The Intelligence of Democracy* (New York: Free Press, 1963); Theodore Lowi, *The End of Liberalism*, 2d ed. (New York: Norton, 1969).
9. Berry, *Lobbying for the People;* Anne Costain, *Inviting Women's Rebellion: A Political Process Interpretation of the Women's Movement* (Baltimore: Johns Hopkins University Press, 1992); Rodney E. Hero, *Latinos and the U.S. Political System: Two-Tiered Pluralism* (Philadelphia: Temple University Press, 1992); Douglas R. Imig, *Poverty and Power: The Political Representation of Poor Americans* (Lincoln: University of Nebraska Press, 1996); Alvin M. Josephy Jr., Joane Nagel, and Troy Johnson, *Red Power: The American Indian's Fight for Freedom* (Lincoln: University of Nebraska Press, 1999); Doug McAdam, *Political Process and the Development of Black Insurgency, 1930–1970* (Chicago: University of Chicago Press, 1982); Debra Minkoff, *Organizing for Equality: The Evolution of Women's and Racial-Ethnic Organizations in America, 1955–1985* (New Brunswick, N.J.: Rutgers University Press, 1995); Aldon Morris, *The Origins of the Civil Rights Movement: Black Communities Organizing for Change* (New York: Free Press, 1984); Dianne Pinderhughes, "Black Interest Groups and the 1982 Extension of the Voting Rights Act," in *Blacks and the American Political System*, ed. Huey L. Perry (Gainesville: University Press of Florida, 1995); Frances Fox Piven and Richard A. Cloward, *Poor People's Movements: Why They Succeed, How They*

Fail (New York: Vintage Books, 1977); Kay Lehman Schlozman, "What Accent the Heavenly Chorus? Political Equality and the American Pressure System," *Journal of Politics* 46 (1984): 1006–1032; Robert C. Smith, *We Have No Leaders: African Americans in the Post-Civil Rights Era* (Albany: State University of New York Press, 1996); Rodolpho D. Torres and George Katsiaficas, eds. *Latino Social Movements: Historical and Theoretical Perspectives* (New York: Routledge, 1999).

10. In their recent work on the political development of interest groups in the United States, Daniel Tichenor and Richard Harris note that the sources from which data about political organizations are typically collected—surveys, interviews, and directories of organizations—can tell us little about organizations that closed their doors before the 1950s. They argue that most political science work has therefore ignored the "robust set of organized interests engaged in Progressive Era political life" (see Daniel Tichenor and Richard Harris, "Organized Interests and American Political Development," *Political Science Quarterly* 117 [2002–2003]: 593).

11. Kimberlé Crenshaw, "Demarginalizing the Intersection of Race and Gender," *University of Chicago Legal Forum* 139 (1989): 139–167.

12. This study uses data that I collected in using the Survey of National Economic and Social Justice Organizations (SNESJO), a survey of 286 national women's, civil rights, racial-minority, and economic-justice organizations that are active in domestic policy issues. Organizations included in the survey either maintain a Washington, D.C., office or play a leadership role in the national policy activities of the movements of which they are a part. See Debra Minkoff, "Producing Social Capital: National Social Movements and Civil Society," *American Behavioral Scientist* 40 (1997): 606–619; Debra Minkoff and Jon Agnone, "Protest Potential in the U.S. Social Movement Sector" (paper presented at the American Sociological Association, Atlanta, 2003). Telephone interviews were conducted in 2000 by Zogby International. Interviews were completed with officers of 286 organizations out of a universe of 714 organizations (for a 40 percent response rate). The survey includes both organizations with individual members as well as organizations that do not have a mass base. I compiled a database of organizations using information from published directories of organizations, media sources, and movement publications. These sources were also used to collect preliminary data about the groups in order to test for nonresponse and other types of bias in the resulting data. The questions in the SNESJO focused on organizations' activities on public policy issues of the 1990s that have had significant implications for the rights and resources for marginalized groups such as women, racial minorities, immigrants, LGBT people, and low-income people. To contextualize these activities and facilitate comparisons with existing work, the SNESJO replicates key questions from earlier surveys (Berry, *Lobbying for the People;* John P. Heinz et al., *The Hollow Core: Private Interests in National Policy Making* [Cambridge: Harvard University Press, 1993]; Ken Kollman, *Outside Lobbying* [Princeton: Princeton University Press, 1998]; Edward O. Laumann and David Knoke, *The Organizational State: Social Choice in National Policy Domains* [Madison: University of Wisconsin Press, 1987]; Kay Lehman Schlozman and John Tierney, *Organized Interests and American Democracy* [New York: Harper & Row, 1986]; Jack L. Walker, *Mobilizing Interest Groups in America: Patrons, Professions, and Social Movements* [Ann Arbor: University of Michigan Press, 1991], including questions about internal factors such as organizations' resources, activities, and ideology as well as measures of external factors such as the effects of shifts in partisan control of political institutions. The SNESJO addressed only domestic policy issues, and, in order to assess the type of representation provided by organizations, issues were further limited to ones that could be pursued at the national level and through all three branches—legislative, executive, and judicial—of the federal government. Using a two-step method, I also stipulated that the policy issues must have been on the national political "agenda" during the period covered by the study (that is, issues had to involve pending court cases being heard by the Supreme

Court, pending legislation being debated in Congress, or pending policy being set in an executive branch department or agency). To select appropriate questions, I compiled a list of issues from the *Congressional Quarterly* for 1990, 1993, 1996, and 1999, and another from the "Supreme Court Roundup" (a regular feature in the *New York Times*) for 1990–2000. After selecting all issues that were potentially relevant to the groups in the survey, I then searched the 1990–2000 volumes of the *Congressional Record* and of the *Federal Register* to confirm that the issues were on the agendas in the legislative and executive branches as well, noting how many times each issue had been mentioned in each of these sources. I repeated this "reverse" search for each "Supreme Court Roundup." I then selected four policy issues for each organization type—one majority issue, one advantaged-subgroup issue, and one disadvantaged-subgroup issue, and a universal issue. The same universal issue—Social Security—was used for all groups, serving as a control issue. The results of the survey compare closely with previous studies, and data on criterion variables such as location, number of employees, and year founded do not differ significantly from the data on these measures that I collected from publicly available sources for the universe of organizations as a whole in the course of compiling the master list of organizations. Two publications about SNESJO are forthcoming: Dara Z. Strolovitch, *Affirmative Advocacy: Race, Class, and Gender in Interest Group Politics* (Chicago: University of Chicago Press), and Dara Z. Strolovitch, "Do Interest Groups Represent the Disadvantaged? Advocacy at the Intersections of Race, Class, and Gender," *Journal of Politics* 68 (4) (2006): 893–908.

13. "Women in Elective Office 2006," Center for American Women and Politics, Eagleton Institute of Politics, Rutgers, State University of New Jersey, New Brunswick, N.J., May 2006, http://www.cawp.rutgers.edu/Facts/Officeholders/elective.pdf.

14. David Canon, *Race, Redistricting, and Representation: The Unintended Consequences of Black-Majority Districts* (Chicago: University of Chicago Press, 1999); Joshua Cohen and Joel Rogers, "Secondary Associations and Democratic Governance," *Politics and Society* 20 (1992): 393–472; Lani Guinier, *The Tyranny of the Majority* (New York: Free Press, 1994); Andrew Rehfeld, *The Concept of Constituency: Political Representation, Democratic Legitimacy, and Institutional Design* (New York: Cambridge University Press, 2005); Mark E. Warren, *Democracy and Association* (Princeton: Princeton University Press, 2001); Mark E. Warren, "Informal Representation: Who Speaks for Whom?" *Democracy and Society* 1 (2004): 8–15.

15. Guinier, *Tyranny of the Majority;* Iris M. Young, "Social Groups in Associative Democracy," *Politics and Society* 20 (1992): 529–534.

16. Guinier, *Tyranny of the Majority;* Carol Swain, *Black Faces, Black Interests* (Cambridge: Harvard University Press, 1993); Michele Swers, *The Difference Women Make: The Policy Impact of Women in Congress* (Chicago: University of Chicago Press, 2002).

17. Craig Jenkins, "Nonprofit Organizations and Policy Advocacy," in *The Nonprofit Sector: A Research Handbook*, ed. W.W. Powell (New Haven: Yale University Press, 1987), 296–318; Rogan Kersh, "State Autonomy and Civil Society: The Lobbyist Connection," *Critical Review* 14 (2001): 237–258; Rehfeld, *Concept of Constituency: Political Representation, Democratic Legitimacy, and Institutional Design;* Warren, "Informal Representation: Who Speaks for Whom?"

18. Scott Ainsworth, *Analyzing Interest Groups: Group Influence on People and Policies* (New York: Norton, 2002), 69.

19. Edmund Burke, "Letter to Sir Hercules Langriche," in *The Works of the Right Honorable Edmund Burke,* vol. 3 (1792; repr., Boston: Little Brown, 1889); Richard F. Fenno, *Going Home: Black Representatives and Their Constituents* (Chicago: University of Chicago Press, 2003); Claudine Gay, "The Effect of Black Congressional Representation on Political Participation," *American Political Science Review* 95 (2001): 589–602; Gay, "Spirals of Trust: The Effect of Descriptive Representation on the Relationship between Citizens and Their Government," *American Journal of Polit-*

ical Science 46 (2002): 717–732; Jane J. Mansbridge, "Rethinking Representation," *American Political Science Review* 97 (2003): 515–528; Hanna Fenichel Pitkin, *The Concept of Representation* (Berkeley: University of California Press, 1967).

20. Janet K. Boles, "Form Follows Function: The Evolution of Feminist Strategies," *Annals of the American Academy of Political Science and Sociology* 51 (1991): 38–49.

21. Baumgartner and Jones, *Agendas and Instability in American Politics;* Berry, *Lobbying for the People.*

22. Lucig H. Danielian and Benjamin I. Page, "The Heavenly Chorus: Interest Group Voices on TV News," *American Journal of Political Science* 38 (1994): 1056–1078; Schlozman, "What Accent the Heavenly Chorus? Political Equality and the American Pressure System."

23. Frank R. Baumgartner and Beth L. Leech, *Basic Interests: The Importance of Groups in Politics and in Political Science* (Princeton: Princeton University Press, 1998); Virginia Gray and David Lowery, *The Population Ecology of Interest Representation* (Ann Arbor: University of Michigan Press, 1996); Kay Lehman Schlozman and Traci Burch, "Political Voice in an Age of Inequality," in *America at Risk: The Great Dangers,* ed. Robert F. Faulkner and Susan Shell, forthcoming; Daniel Tichenor and Richard Harris, "Organized Interests and American Political Development," *Political Science Quarterly* 117 (2002–2003): 587–612.

24. Schlozman and Tierney's question was slightly broader, asking whether the group has "lawyers on staff." In addition, their study encompassed a sampling of all organized interests, including corporations, trade associations, unions, professional associations, civil rights groups, and citizens' groups.

25. Schlozman and Tierney, *Organized Interests and American Democracy;* Kollman, *Outside Lobbying.*

26. Baumgartner and Leech, *Basic Interests;* Jeffrey Berry, *The Interest Group Society,* 2d ed. (New York: Harper Collins, 1989); Schlozman, "What Accent the Heavenly Chorus? Political Equality and the American Pressure System"; Schlozman and Burch, "Political Voice in an Age of Inequality"; Schlozman and Tierney, *Organized Interests and American Democracy;* Walker, *Mobilizing Interest Groups in America: Patrons, Professions, and Social Movements.*

27. Schlozman and Burch, "Political Voice in an Age of Inequality."

28. Jeffrey Berry, *The New Liberalism* (Washington, D.C.: Brookings Institution Press, 1999); Cathy J. Cohen, *The Boundaries of Blackness* (Chicago: University of Chicago Press, 1999); Kollman, *Outside Lobbying;* Sharon Kurtz, *Workplace Justice: Organizing Multi-Identity Movements* (Minneapolis: University of Minnesota Press, 2002); Piven and Cloward, *Poor People's Movements: Why They Succeed, How They Fail;* Schlozman, "What Accent the Heavenly Chorus? Political Equality and the American Pressure System"; Theda Skocpol, *Diminished Democracy* (Norman: University of Oklahoma Press, 2003); Roberta Spalter-Roth and Ronnee Schreiber, "Outside Issues and Insider Tactics: Strategic Tensions in the Women's Policy Network During the 1980s," in *Feminist Organizations: Harvest of the New Women's Movement,* ed. Myra Marx Ferree and Patricia Yancey Martin (Philadelphia: Temple University Press, 1995), 105–127.

29. "Educational Attainment in the United States: March 2002," http://www.census.gov/ population/www/socdemo/education/ppl-169.html.

30. Baumgartner and Jones, *Agendas and Instability in American Politics;* Thomas G. Hansford, "Lobbying Strategies, Venue Selection, and Organized Interest Involvement at the U.S. Supreme Court," *American Politics Research* 32 (2004): 170–197; John W. Kingdon, *Agendas, Alternatives, and Public Policies* (New York: Harper Collins, 1995); Kollman, *Outside Lobbying;* McAdam, *Political Process and the Development of Black Insurgency, 1930–1970;* David S. Meyer and Debra Minkoff, "Conceptualizing Political Opportunity," *Social Forces* 82 (2004): 1457–1492; Schlozman and Tierney, *Organized Interests and American Democracy;* Walker, *Mobilizing Interest Groups in America.*

31. Lucius Barker, "Third Parties in Litigation: A Systematic View of Judicial Educa-
tion," *Journal of Politics* 29 (1967): 49–69; Alexander M. Bickel, *The Least Dangerous
Branch: The Supreme Court at the Bar of Politics*, 2d ed. (New Haven: Yale University
Press, 1986); Richard C. Cortner, "Strategies and Tactics of Litigants in Constitu-
tional Cases," *Journal of Public Law* 17 (1968): 287–307; Ronald Dworkin, *Taking
Rights Seriously* (Cambridge: Harvard University Press, 1977); Dworkin, *Freedom's
Law: The Moral Reading of the American Constitution* (Cambridge: Harvard University
Press, 1986); Joel F. Handler, *Social Movements and the Legal System: A Theory of Law,
Reform and Social Change* (New York: Academic Press, 1978); David Manwaring,
Render unto Caesar: The Flag Salute Controversy (Chicago: University of Chicago
Press, 1962); Michael W. McCann, *Taking Reform Seriously: Perspectives on Public
Interest Liberalism* (Ithaca: Cornell University Press, 1986); McCann, "Social Move-
ments and the Mobilization of Law," in *Social Movements and American Political
Institutions*, ed. Anne N. Costain and Andrew S. McFarland (Lanham, Md.: Row-
man and Littlefield, 1998), 201–215; Karen O'Connor and Lee Epstein, "Sex and
the Supreme Court: An Analysis of Support for Gender-Based Claims," *Social Sci-
ence Quarterly* 64 (1983): 327–331; Frank J. Sorauf, *The Wall of Separation: The Con-
stitutional Politics of Church and State* (Princeton: Princeton University Press, 1976);
Clement E. Vose, "Litigation as a Form of Pressure Group Activity," *Annals of the
American Academy of Political and Social Science* 319 (1958): 20–31; Clement E. Vose,
Caucasians Only (Berkeley: University of California Press, 1959); Steven L. Wasby,
"How Planned Is 'Planned' Litigation?" *American Bar Foundation Research Journal*
(Winter 1984): 83–138.
32. Mark V. Tushnet, *The NAACP's Legal Strategy against Segregated Education,
1925–1950* (Chapel Hill: University of North Carolina Press, 1987); Wasby, "How
Planned Is 'Planned' Litigation?"
33. Jeffrey Rosen, "Courting Disaster," *New York Times Magazine*, December 5, 2004, 29.
34. Lawrence Baum, *The Supreme Court*, 7th ed. (Washington, D.C.: CQ Press, 2001).
35. Derrick A. Bell Jr., "Serving Two Masters: Integration Ideals and Client Interests
in School Desegregation Litigation," *Yale Law Journal* 85 (1976): 470; Alan David
Freeman, "Legitimating Racial Discrimination through Antidiscrimination Law:
A Critical Review of Supreme Court Doctrine," *Minnesota Law Review* 62 (1978):
1049; Ran Hirschl, *Towards Juristocracy: The Origins and Consequences of the New Con-
stitutionalism* (Cambridge: Harvard University Press, 2004]; Stuart A. Scheingold,
The Politics of Rights: Lawyers, Public Policy, and Political Change [Ann Arbor: University of Michigan Press, 1974]; Mark V. Tushnet, "Critical Legal Studies: A Political History," *Yale Law Journal* 100 (1991): 1515.
36. John Hart Ely, *Democracy and Distrust: A Theory of Judicial Review* (Cambridge: Harvard
University Press, 1980); Gerald N. Rosenberg, *The Hollow Hope: Can Courts Bring
about Social Change?* (Chicago: University of Chicago Press, 1991); Jeremy Waldron,
Law and Disagreement (New York: Oxford University Press, 2001).
37. Rosenberg, *The Hollow Hope: Can Courts Bring about Social Change?*
38. Scott L. Cummings and Ingrid V. Eagly, "A Critical Reflection on Law and Organizing," *UCLA Law Review* 48 (2001): 443. See also Richard Abel, "Lawyers and
the Power to Change," *Law & Policy* 7 (1985): 1–18; Lucie White, "To Learn and
Teach: Lessons from Direction on Lawyering and Power," *Wisconsin Law Review*
43 (1988): 699.
39. The question that they were asked was, "Which of the following political institutions is the most important target of your efforts in trying to influence policy on [the
issue in question]?" Answers of the president and White House offices and the executive agencies were combined into an "executive branch" category. Note that the
question was posed so that respondents had to select only one of the institutions
rather than rank them.

40. Hansford, "Lobbying Strategies, Venue Selection, and Organized Interest Involvement at the U.S. Supreme Court"; Kim Lane Scheppele and Jack L. Walker Jr., "The Litigation Strategies of Interest Groups," in *Mobilizing Interest Groups in America*, ed. Jack Walker (Ann Arbor: University of Michigan Press, 1991), 157–183; Schlozman and Tierney, *Organized Interests and American Democracy*.

41. Wilson, *Political Organizations*, xxii.

5

Big-Money Donors to Environmental Groups
What They Give and What They Get
Anthony J. Nownes and Allan J. Cigler

Public interest groups, those seeking collective political goods, are a central feature of the contemporary interest group universe. Especially prominent are groups that seek to affect public policy on a range of environmental and conservation issues. Many of these groups first came into existence in the 1960s and 1970s and have remained viable, initially surprising many interest group theorists who believed that such groups would have difficulty maintaining an organization owing to the inherent problem of sustaining a membership base when few tangible benefits could be offered to supporters.

Later research has found early scholarly efforts may have overemphasized the importance of having a membership base for both group mobilization and organizational maintenance. Financial resources, from whatever the source, are the most critical factor. Much of the growth and survival of environmental groups has been shown to be top-down rather than bottom-up, as group entrepreneurs prospect for patrons or sponsors who are willing to contribute large amounts of money to the organization. Typical patrons are foundations, corporations, the federal government, and wealthy individual donors. Individual donors—consistent in their giving patterns yet largely unconcerned with the specifics of how their contributions are used—are the most preferred of all donors.

In this chapter, Anthony J. Nownes and Allan J. Cigler, using the results of an in-depth survey of individuals who gave large sums of money to a sample of environmental groups, explore the backgrounds and motivations of large-money donors, their contributions to the organization beyond money, and how money translates into access with group leaders and staff. The authors conclude that large donors are a group development director's "delight," offering financial resources and contributing in other ways to the group's mission, without appearing to intrude upon group decision making.

The expansion of the public interest sector in the 1960s and 1970s was a genuine surprise to those who had been studying interest groups. The tremendous growth in the number and impact of such groups appeared to challenge the prevailing paradigm on group formation and survival.[1] Interest group scholars had been apprehensive that social and political interests representing broad constituencies would have great difficulty organizing and surviving as permanent actors in the political process. The expansion of the public interest sector was generally viewed with enthusiasm, especially by those with a pluralist perspective, who were convinced that public interest groups could act as beneficial "countervailing forces" in American politics, protecting citizens from the excesses of wealthy economic interests.[2]

At the very time the public interest sector was beginning to expand, many political scientists had come to embrace a theory of group development, first put forth by economist Mancur Olson, that suggested that it was unlikely that groups seeking collective benefits could form viable organizations.[3] Such groups would have to face the formidable obstacle of the free-rider problem—the powerful tendency of "rational" individuals to choose not to bear the costs of group involvement (for example, time and dues) because they could enjoy the fruits of the group's efforts even if they were not members. Why, for example, would a person interested in improvements in the environment join an environmental group when personal benefit from possible group successes in providing the collective good (in this case a better environment) could be gained without participating in or helping fund the organization as a member? The tendency to free ride is heightened further by an efficacy problem—the widespread belief that one person cannot make a difference, especially in a large organization.

The empirical reality of a rapidly expanding public interest group universe, coupled with a widely accepted interest group theory that suggested that group proliferation in the sector was unlikely to occur, sparked a resurgence of research interest in the collective action problem. In general, the resulting body of accumulated literature strongly suggests that while the free-rider problem does exist, it may not be as delimiting for the development of groups pursuing collective goods as Olson suggested.[4]

Olson did not totally preclude the possibility that unorganized constituencies could overcome the free-rider problem. One solution, mainly prevalent among unions and professional associations, is coercion. Another is the provision of selective benefits—benefits that accrue only to people who contribute to the attainment of the collective good. Material benefits (that is, goods or services with monetary value) can be especially effective in inducing membership in certain kinds of organizations. But neither of these solutions is particularly effective in overcoming the free-rider problem for public interest groups, especially initially. Such groups are typically composed of autonomous individuals, and the material goods or services they provide are not usually extensive or unique enough to attract members.

Subsequent research, frequently using Olson's basic incentive theory as a starting point, expanded the range of potential motives involved in group participation and the variety of ways individuals might weigh various factors in any cost-benefit decision to join or not join a group. As an economist, Olson was most concerned with material benefits such as income or services that have monetary value. Other scholars have expanded the list of incentives. For example, solidary incentives—the socially derived, intangible rewards created by the act of association—are significant, as are expressive or purposive rewards derived by advancing a particular cause or ideology.[5] Some have argued that, especially in the case of public interest groups, individuals will join organizations even though it is "not rational" in an economic sense; intangible factors such as notions of fairness, rightness, duty, and moral obligations override economic calculations in some individuals and cause them not to free ride.[6] In addition, some individuals "care about the rightness of their actions, regardless of individual or collective practical effect."[7]

Others have argued that the key to group formation and survival is the group entrepreneur, an individual who invests personal resources to get the group up and running by creating a package of membership incentives, often a unique combination of material, solidary, and expressive benefits, to make membership in the group attractive.[8] Group mobilization and maintenance are thus conceived as an exchange involving leaders offering incentives to members in return for support.

The massive proliferation of public interest groups since the 1960s suggests that incentive notions focusing on bottom-up group formation involving entrepreneurs seeking and attracting members may tell only part of the story, perhaps not even the most important part. Much of the growth and survival of public interest groups is top-down, having less to do with the ability of group entrepreneurs to recruit members than their abilities to bypass or substantially reduce the free-rider problem by locating a patron or sponsor for the organization.[9] While both are important, the most organizationally crucial exchange may be between group organizers and patrons rather than group organizers and potential members.

Patrons such as private foundations, corporations, government entities, and wealthy individuals, political scientist Jack Walker has argued, are the driving forces behind public interest group development.[10] Many groups (especially citizen groups), according to Walker's research, receive seed money from patrons at inception and continue to rely on it.[11] Political scientist Jeffrey Berry's study of public interest groups in the 1970s found that at least one-third of such groups received more than half of their funds from patron sources, while one in ten received over 90 percent of their operating funds from patrons.[12] Walker's study in the early 1980s revealed that foundation support and large individual grants provided 30 percent of all citizen group funding. Studies conducted in the 1990s by Anthony Nownes and his colleagues show similar results.[13] For environmental and conservation groups in particular, even mass-member organizations, large individual contributions often exceed membership dues. Having resources, whatever the source, is the key to both group mobilization and survival.

In this chapter, we examine the orientations and motivations of a particular class of public interest group patrons—individuals who contribute large sums of money to a key sector of the public interest group universe: groups that focus on the environment. Little is known about individuals who give large sums of money to such groups, especially from the perspective of the donors themselves. Who are these donors? What motivates them to support the groups they do rather than others? How do groups solicit individual contributions? And as a result of their giving, do individual patrons have special access to group leaders? Overall, we find that besides the personally satisfying act of giving to a politically favored group, for some patrons giving is an entrée to broader group involvement and likely influence. But for many others, donating money is often the only role they play in group activity.

Large-Money Individual Donors: Background

The impact of patron money on public interest groups, including environmental groups, is not without controversy. If we accept the assumption that money leads to influence and that patrons are not neutral actors, the potential for patrons to affect group agendas, priorities, and activities is real. For example, there is some evidence that patronage can be intrusive and distort public interest representation by channeling funds to mainstream, professional organizations rather than newer, more activist groups. Group choices over types of political influence strategies (for example, whether to protest or to engage in mainstream lobbying) may be conditioned by patrons' money. The danger of co-optation (or appearing to look co-opted), which could discredit the group, is ever present. Attempts by oil and waste management companies to offer various types of support to a number of environmental groups in the hopes of decreasing criticism have been quite common—corporate money is typically bottom-line oriented. In short, outside money can compromise the role of public interest representation as a countervailing force.[14]

But all classes of patrons are not alike, and individual large donors appear to be the least problematic from the perspective of group fund-raisers.[15] While foundations are primarily motivated to help like-minded political advocates, foundation funding may be fickle and trendy, not the kind of money that lends itself to a stable financial base for a group.[16] Moreover, foundation funds may be project specific, subtly channeling group activity in certain directions. Corporate patron funds usually come with fewer strings attached, but environmental groups are particularly suspicious of such money, fearing that taking money from a certain company or corporate sector will alienate group members and other supporters.[17] Government grants can be the most problematic of all for environmental groups because they typically come with demanding accountability and report requirements. Moreover, the government grant process may be lengthy and laden with excessive paperwork.[18] More important, environmental groups typically challenge government policy, and cooperating with government might be viewed with suspicion by group supporters.

From the point of view of environmental group fund-raisers, large individual donors seem to pose no such problems and be the most undemanding of all patrons. Individuals seldom give money with onerous or specific strings attached, and there are usually no reports to be filed. Many individual donors are apparently longtime group members who know and trust the groups to which they contribute; they are largely unconcerned with accountability. They may be group patrons, but their support is not really "outside" money compared with other forms of patronage. Individuals are more stable in their giving patterns than other classes of patrons. Group entrepreneurs may be especially appreciative of donations from individuals because they can now pursue their own pet projects using discretionary money that does not have to be defended even to the membership.

There is little doubt that individual large-donor support is an important and probably growing proportion of revenue for public interest groups generally. As early as 1980, large individual gifts made up a higher proportion of citizen group income than did membership dues, over 17 percent.[19] For contemporary environmental groups, the proportions may be even greater, although it depends upon the group in question. Political scientist Christopher Bosso's recent study of environmental groups suggests that membership dues to most environmental groups do not even cover the cost of recruitment.[20] He argues that "annual dues are a development loss leader, the cost of building a base of regular contributors who in time may be convinced to go higher on the 'pyramid of support'—where the real money is."[21] In short, from a financial perspective, the role of membership dues is to attract members who may later be convinced to become large group donors, the most desirable of all patrons.

Data and Methodology

To learn more about large-money donors to nationally active environmental citizen groups, we conducted a mail survey. Because Internal Revenue Service rules enable nonprofits to shield data about specific donors and their financial contributions, we were forced to improvise in designing our sample. First, we chose ten environmental groups, largely on the basis of the availability of information about their donors. We also selected them to maximize the diversity of sample groups. As Table 5.1 indicates, the groups (which remain anonymous because of our promise to those surveyed) are indeed a diverse lot—they differ across many dimensions including size and ideology. Second, we obtained the 2005 annual

Table 5.1.   Sample Groups and Their Characteristics

Group no.	Yearly income (millions of dollars)[a]	Membership[b]	Ideology[c]	No. of surveys received
1.	1–10	10,000–50,000	2	5
2.	21–30	100,000–500,000	2	10
3.	1–10	unavailable	2	4
4.	21–30	100,000–500,000	2	23
5.	over 30	over 1,000,000	3	7
6.	1–10	10,000–50,000	1	1
7.	11–20	500,000–1,000,000	2	18
8.	less than 1	unavailable	unavailable	0
9.	11–20	51,000–100,000	4	20
10.	11–20	10,000–50,000	1	12

Sources: Authors' data; also see note c below.

[a]Yearly income comes from each group's 2005 annual report, except in the case of Group no. 6, for which the figure is taken from the 2004 annual report.
[b]Membership comes from each group's Web site (all sites accessed on July 11, 2006).
[c]Ideology (1–6, 1 = "radical left"; 6 = "free market right") comes from Capital Research Center, a conservative think tank, www.greenwatch.org/gw/default.asp.

report for each group (except for group no. 6, for which we obtained the 2004 annual report). Every annual report listed the names of "large-money individual donors" (as identified by each group, in most cases those contributing at least $1,000 in the last year), along with the amount (not an exact amount, but a range) each individual contributed during the 2004 fiscal year (in the case of group no. 6, FY 2003).

Next, we randomly selected several hundred names from these lists and sought to obtain each individual's address from the Yahoo "People Search" Web site (located at http://people.yahoo.com/).[22] Ultimately we obtained contact information for 354 large donors. Finally, we sent each of our identified large donors a copy of our survey instrument, which comprised mainly close-ended questions but also a few that invited an open-ended response. Respondents were promised complete anonymity. After two rounds of mailings, we received one hundred responses. Sixty-seven surveys were returned as undeliverable (most because of incorrect addresses). Thus, our final response rate was 34.8 percent, quite reasonable given the sensitive nature of a number of our survey questions.

Clearly we cannot pretend that our sample of donors is representative of the population of large donors to environmental groups, or even to our sample groups. All of this notwithstanding, we believe our data set is appropriate for reaching some tentative conclusions about the motivations and orientations of large-money donors and the manner in which such donors relate to the groups they support.

Findings

What are large donors to environmental groups like? Why do they choose to give the large sums of money they do? What motivates them to support the environmental organizations they do? In this section, we will address these and other questions.

Profile of Large-Money Donors to Environmental Groups

While some research is available that examines the backgrounds of public interest group members, little information singles out donors who contribute relatively large sums of money to such groups. A profile of our survey respondents who contributed large sums of money to our sample of environmental groups is presented in Table 5.2.

Table 5.2.   What Are Large Donors Like?

A. Personal characteristics	
1. Median age (in years)	62
2. Female (percent)	56
3. White (percent)	99
4. College degree (percent)	93
5. Advanced degree (percent)	61
6. Married (percent)	69
7. Employed full time (percent)	37
8. People in donor's household (average number)	2
9. Children living at home (percent)	19
10. Years spent in present community (average number)	27
11. Religious affiliation	
a. Protestant (percent)	52
b. Catholic (percent)	6
c. Jewish (percent)	7
d. No religion (percent)	28
e. Other (percent)	6
B. Financial information	
1. Net worth (median)	$3,200,000
2. Annual income (median)	$190,000
C. Political and social involvement	
1. "Very interested" in national affairs (percent)[a]	88
2. "Very interested" in local affairs (percent)[a]	58
3. "Very interested" in state affairs (percent)[a]	60
4. Voted in 2004 presidential election (percent)	95
5. Initiated contact with federal elected official (percent)[b]	69
6. Initiated contact with local elected official (percent)[b]	58
7. Initiated contact with state elected official (percent)[b]	56
8. Contributed money to PAC, candidate, or party (percent)	79
9. "Virtually never" attend religious services (percent)[c]	41
10. Belong to other type of group (percent)[d]	95
11. Democratic party identification (7-point scale) (percent)	62

Table 5.2.   What Are Large Donors Like? *(continued)*

D. Group and giving information	
1. First contribution (average amount)	$2,225
2. Last donation was matched (percent)	2
3. Number of large contributions made (average)	11
4. Belong to the group they support (percent)	94

Source: Authors' data.

Notes: N = 100 (Ns may vary across survey items owing to missing data).

[a]Percentages in C1–C3 are based on responses to the following survey item: "How interested are you in each of the following—not at all interested, somewhat interested, or very interested?"
[b]Percentages in C5–C7 are based on responses to the following survey item: "There is a variety of ways that people can get involved in politics. How about you, have you engaged in any of the following activities in the past 24 months?" Answer options were "Yes" and "No."
[c]Percentage is based on responses to the following survey item: "Approximately how often would you say you attend religious (church or worship) services—more than once per week, once per week, once or twice a month, several times a year, once or twice a year, or virtually never?"
[d]Percentage based on responses to the following survey item: "Many large contributors to environmental and conservation organizations are active in other types of organizations as well. Here is a list of various types of organizations. Could you tell us whether or not you are involved in some way in each type?" Answer options were: "Fraternal group," "Service club," "Veteran's group," "Political club," "Labor union," "Sports group," "Youth group," "Hobby or garden club," "School fraternity or sorority," "Nationality group," "School service group," "Farm organization," "Literary, art, or discussion group," "Professional or academic association/society," "Church-affiliated group," "Health group," or "Any other group."

In a variety of ways, our respondents look a lot like what other researchers have found when they have examined contributors to charities, political candidates, and parties, although large donors are even more homogeneous in terms of their backgrounds and demographic characteristics.[23] Our respondents are disproportionately white (99 percent), very well educated (93 percent with a college degree and 61 percent with an advanced degree), married (69 percent), and rooted in their communities (the average time lived in their present community is twenty-seven years). Fifty-six percent of our donors are female.

As a group, large-money environmental group contributors are especially distinctive for their relative affluence, their stage in the life cycle, and their ongoing involvement in political affairs. Not unexpectedly, they are well-off financially. The median respondent has a net worth of over $3 million and an annual income of $190,000. Only slightly more than one-third of our respondents are currently employed full time; most are retired (median age of 62) and no longer have children living at home.

It is not surprising, of course, that relatively wealthy individuals who have left the workforce are disproportionately represented among large donors to environmental groups. But what this means for the future of large-donor giving to environmental groups is less clear; especially difficult is untangling life-cycle from generational effects. For example, could it be that the relatively senior makeup of our responding donors is a proxy for when their generation became interested in environmental issues—in the late 1960s and 1970s—when environmental issues were high on the political agenda? Future generations of senior citizens, even those well-off financially, simply may not have the level of commitment to environmental issues as do many of the current generation. Although it is obviously logical that big-money donors are drawn disproportionately from the ranks of the financially well-off, older citizens, the pool of such givers may shrink in the future.

As a group, our respondents are plainly attentive to politics at all levels. Ninety-five percent voted in the last presidential election, and 88 percent consider themselves "very interested" in national affairs, with 58 and 60 percent attentive to local and state affairs, respectively. Apparently many are not simply passive political observers either. More than two-thirds indicated that they had contacted an elected federal official over the past two years, while 58 percent said they had initiated contact with a local elected official, and 56 percent said they had initiated contact with a state elected official. Sixty-two percent of respondents indicated that they either lean Democrat or are Democratic Party identifiers.

The data presented in Table 5.2 also indicate that all but 6 percent of respondents are members of the group to which they donate. Eighty-four percent of our respondents have contributed more than once to the group, and the average number of total contributions is eleven. Approximately 12 percent of our respondents have made more than twenty large contributions, and over 75 percent have made five or more large contributions (not shown). In all, the data suggest that once a supporter crosses the threshold and becomes a large donor, giving becomes a habit.

Large-Donor Motivations

The potential range of explanations for why people become important group benefactors is broad and often unique to each individual donor. In our survey we attempted to isolate the central motivations of large donors in two ways. First, we asked a series of structured, close-ended questions directed at having respondents prioritize their motivations for giving. Second, we asked respondents to comment on the specific circumstances or unique events that led to their first large contributions.

Table 5.3 presents our findings concerning the relative impact of various motivations underlying our respondents' decisions to make large donations to environmental groups. Purposive and expressive (or extrarational) motivations head the list of reasons for giving. The top reason cited by large donors is "the advancement of social and environmental justice," while "empathy with animals and other living things" ranks third. Many respondents also clearly feel they gain "intrinsic rewards from supporting an organization whose goals" they support. However, the second

Table 5.3.   Why Do Large Donors Give?

Reason for giving	Score[a] (average)
1. The advancement of social and environmental justice	2.63
2. My strong interest in preserving outdoor recreational opportunities	2.51
3. Empathy with animals and other living things	2.41
4. Gaining intrinsic rewards from supporting an organization whose goals I support	2.26
5. Fulfilling my civic duty	1.72
6. The chance to learn more about politics and government	1.62
7. Tax advantages	1.51
8. Adherence to social norms (i.e., giving is expected of me)	1.41
9. Excitement	1.24
10. Enhanced self-esteem	1.23
11. The opportunity to honor a friend or loved one	1.22
12. Gaining respect from people I admire	1.14
13. I did not want to say no to someone who asked	1.09
14. The chance to further my job or career	1.01

Source: Authors' data.

Notes: $N = 95$ (*N*s may vary across survey items owing to missing data).
Table is based on responses to the following survey item: "People contribute to environmental and conservation organizations for a variety of reasons. How about you? Please tell us if each of the following reasons was not at all important, somewhat important, or very important in your decision to contribute to [specific group]."

[a]Score is an average based on the following coding of responses: 1 = "not at all important," 2 = "somewhat important," 3 = "very important."

most widely cited reason for giving—"my strong interest in preserving outdoor recreational opportunities"—can be considered both a purposive and a material benefit (a potential tangible benefit from personally engaging in such recreation). The chance to fulfill "my civic duty," and the tax benefit that comes with contributing to a charitable organization are both attractive to a number of donors. Overall, supporting a worthy cause for selfless reasons appears to dominate large-donor motivations for giving.

The open-ended responses we solicited suggest a range of motivations for first-time gifts. In many cases, a specific incident, event, or circumstance triggered the initial decision to give. Some donors indicated their contribution was made in memory of a loved one with a strong interest in the environment. But more typical was an environmental or political issue or event that triggered interest. For example, one respondent wrote: "I made a one-time contribution to [the group I support] in response to a particular case of sulfide mining in the upper peninsula of Michigan." Another donor was motivated to contribute when the group she supports "championed the cause to stop the governor of Alaska from selling hunting licenses to kill wolves from planes." A few respondents indicated that their initial large contribution came in response to a change in presidential administrations that they believed would have negative environmental consequences.

Giving a large donation to a group that one believes in can also be an alternative for those who find it difficult to be more personally involved in a group. One respondent wrote to us: "I am a military spouse and often the only level of commitment can be monetary, because of moving every one to three years. I will be more involved when we retire and settle down somewhere, most likely on the local level.…"

But, as the results of our closed-ended question indicate, purposive and intangible reasons dominate respondent thinking about the reasons behind their initial donations. As one respondent noted: "I believe that preserving natural space is important. I live in a city and enjoy all that that entails, but wish to keep the city 'in the city.' Places to get away to and that preserve habitats need to be secured for people and the creatures that live there."

How Does a Donor Choose Which Group to Support?

There are literally hundreds of environmental and conservation groups in the United States. Some are broad-based organizations that tackle a range of environmental concerns and have a national focus—for example, the Audubon Society and the Sierra Club—while others are more locally or regionally based. Some are extremely narrow, representing, in some cases, a particular mammal or bird or species of fish. In sum, individual donors have a myriad of choices in deciding which group or groups to support.

We asked our respondents what kinds of criteria they use to evaluate groups and how they came to choose which to support. Table 5.4 summarizes the results of our query.

What most attracts large donors to specific organizations is apparent from Table 5.4. "The specific cause the organization supports" is considered "very important" by virtually all respondents, with "the organization's approach to solving environmental/conservation problems" a close second. The organization's reputation, expertise, and level of professionalism are important considerations as well.

No doubt a large part of organizational attraction is how well a group can create and perpetuate a positive image that conveys success. Some of the open-ended comments we received are revealing. One respondent wrote: "I feel that [the group I support] is the strongest organization with concerns [about] the environment. I appreciate reading about their activities." Another, commenting on the same organization, wrote: "The [group I support] does very much good work by seeing that federal and state governments follow the law! … [sic] as well as help educate the public." Phys-

Table 5.4.   How Does a Large Donor Choose Which Specific Organization to Support?

Factor	Score[a] (average)
1. The specific cause the organization supports	2.95
2. The organization's approach to solving environmental/ conservation problems	2.89
3. The level of the organization's expertise	2.83
4. The organization's reputation	2.76
5. The level of professionalism of the organization's management	2.75
6. Being certain my money is being spent appropriately	2.73
7. The efficiency with which the organization achieves its goals	2.62
8. Being allowed to determine how much I will donate	2.38
9. The organization's substantial need for my contribution	2.25
10. Not being asked for money too often	2.18
11. The organization's prompt responses to my questions and concerns	2.13
12. The politeness and courteousness of organizational leaders and staff members	2.06
13. The feeling that I am safe in my transactions with the organization	1.97
14. Being informed about how precisely my contribution is being used	1.87
15. Knowing that the organization cares about its large donors	1.79
16. The organization's approach to soliciting my contribution	1.77
17. Being thanked for my gift	1.74
18. The timely nature of the organization's communications with me	1.73
19. Being recognized as an important part of the organization	1.60
20. Being asked for appropriate sums of money	1.51
21. The individual attention I receive from group staff and leaders	1.32
22. The organization's individually tailored benefit package	1.15

Source: Authors' data.

Notes: $N = 97$ (*N*s may vary across survey items owing to missing data).
Table based on responses to the following survey item: "There are many environmental and conservation organizations in the United States. When choosing which specific organization(s) to support, donors may consider many factors. Please indicate how important each of the following factors was in helping you decide to support [the group you support]—not at all important, somewhat important, or very important."

[a]Score is an average based on the following coding of responses: 1 = "not at all important," 2 = "somewhat important," 3 = "very important."

ical group presence can be important to conveying a desired image as well. One respondent, who noted that he usually contributes just $100 a year, indicated he rewarded his group with his first $1,000 contribution because he "liked their store-front public outreach efforts" on the Pacific coast. "Other [groups]," he said, "should do the same thing."

But having a high profile is not the only way to create a favorable image. Small, narrower groups have some advantages with large donors who prefer more specialized organizations. One respondent, for example, wrote: "[My group's] strength is the niche they hold with their scientific base. Many environmental groups blend together and seem redundant."

Perhaps the most obvious feature of our findings is the relative lack of importance respondents place on their relationship with the organization itself in affecting which group(s) financially to support. Table 5.4 is anchored by interaction criteria—that is, criteria that involve how a group interacts with its large donors. Initially, it appears, donors are relatively unconcerned about individual attention, individualized benefit packages, recognition, and being kept informed about how specifically their contributions are spent. Sometimes donors do get irritated, however, if they are left with the feeling that all the organization wants is their money. As one respondent noted: "I have never had much attention from the organization (which is okay) except one call to remind me I had *not* sent in an annual check, from the head of it. I sent the check, but it annoyed me."

Donors appear to care a bit more about the accessibility of group leaders and staff. But overall, despite a voluminous literature suggesting that large donors are mercurial people who must be courted and flattered, our data suggest that large donors are more attracted by a group's goals, how well it operates, and its political achievements than they are by how well the group treats them personally.[24]

What Donors Value Once They Have Contributed

Often the decision about which group to support is made with relatively little information at hand and is based primarily on a perceived association of the group with some generalized public good such as advancing environmental causes. Once they have donated, however, contributors learn organizationally specific information that, as Lawrence S. Rothenberg observed in his study of Common Cause members, "is best gained experientially."[25] Donors form impressions about the group's political successes and its efficiency as an organization, learn of some of the specific tangible material benefits the group provides large donors, and possibly develop a sense of the potential social benefits of interacting with group leaders and staff. They may also find that their special status as large contributors opens wider doors for participation and influence in the group.

To learn more about the benefits that large donors value, we asked respondents a number of close-ended questions. We were especially interested in the relationship between large donors and the group decision-makers and staff, and whether or not large donors have special access and input into group decisions by virtue of their contributions.

Our first question was comprehensive: we asked respondents to rank (from "not important" to "very important") a variety of potential benefits donors might receive. The findings are presented in Table 5.5.

Table 5.5.   What Benefits Do Large Donors Value?

Benefit	Score[a] (average)
1. Advocacy of important values, ideas, or policies	2.79
2. Representation of my opinions before government	2.61
3. Information on pending legislation and government policy	2.34
4. Magazine(s), newsletter(s), or other publication(s) or informational service(s)	2.06
5. The opportunity to participate in public affairs	1.88
6. The opportunity to take part in public education programs	1.56
7. Special access to key group decision-makers	1.53
8. The opportunity to socialize with group leaders and/or board members	1.45
9. Organized trips or tours	1.43
10. Meetings and/or conferences	1.40
11. The opportunity to socialize with other members and large donors	1.37
12. Contacts with professional colleagues	1.34
13. Information and advice telephone lines	1.23
14. Special recognition of my gift(s) in group publications or at special events	1.21
15. Discounts on consumer goods	1.16
16. Free or discounted entry to particular places	1.15
17. Awards	1.11
18. Discounts on insurance	1.06
19. Organizational credit card	1.05

Source: Authors' data.

Notes: N = 96 (*N*s may vary across survey items owing to missing data).
Table based on responses to the following survey item: "There is a variety of benefits and activities that may attract large donors to support an environmental or conservation organization. Some benefits and activities may be more important to large donors like you than others. Using the scale below, please indicate how important each of the following benefits and activities is to you as a large donor—not at all important, somewhat important, or very important. If [specific group] does not provide the benefit or activity, please choose the 'organization does not provide' answer."

[a]Score is an average based on the following coding of responses: 1 = "not at all important," 2 = "somewhat important," 3 = "very important." "Organization does not provide" responses were not included in analysis.

Purposive and expressive factors stand out as the most valued benefits. A group's "advocacy of important values, ideas, or policies," and "representation of my opinions before government" are the two highest-ranked benefits. The ability of a group to keep respondents informed about government activity is highly valued as well, especially through publications and other informational services. Some of the material benefits of group membership, such as discounts on consumer goods or organizational credit cards, which have been shown to be important in attracting rank-and-file members to some public interest groups, are largely unimportant to large donors to environmental organizations. It is important to note that one does not have to be a large donor to receive such benefits.

At least some large donors value what they believe is "special access" to key group decision makers as well as the opportunity to socialize with group leaders or board members. The potential access by moneyed interests is one of the more controversial issues surrounding patronage for citizen groups generally and environmental groups in particular, raising the question of whether such groups get co-opted because of their relationships with patrons. Although it is impossible to address the co-optation question directly with our data, our findings can speak to the question of whether large donors have the ear of the people who run the organizations they support. We have already noted that at least some large donors place some value on their perceived special access to group officials. We now turn to examining the access issue in greater detail.

Large Donors and Access to Decision Makers

How frequently do large donors interact with group personnel? Results from our survey bearing on this question are presented in Table 5.6. Generally speaking, most large donors never interact or seldom interact with group leaders or staff. The data show that most respondents do not even interact with other large donors or rank-and-file members. But there are a

Table 5.6.   How Often Do Large Donors Communicate with Other Group Actors?

| | Frequency of contact[a] | | | | |
Group actor(s)	Never	1–2 times per year or less	3–6 times per year	7–12 times per year	Once a month or more
1. President	64	18	13	2	3
2. Other officers	73	11	13	1	1
3. Staff	56	24	12	2	6
4. Other large donors	83	8	5	3	1
5. Members	77	8	5	3	6
6. Board members	76	6	13	2	3

Source: Authors' data.

Notes: N = 98 (Ns may vary across survey items owing to missing data).
Table is based on responses to the following survey item: "How often do you communicate with each of the following groups or individuals about organizational matters—never, 1–2 times per year or less, 3–6 times per year, 7–12 times per year, about once per month, or more than once per month?"

[a]Numbers are percentages.

number of donors who do interact frequently, especially with group officers and staff. For example, 36 percent of respondents indicated some communication with the group's president at least once a year, while 44 percent indicated they had some communication with the group's staff.

What factors account for certain large donors disproportionately interacting with group leaders or staff? What are the characteristics of the most involved large donors? To shed some light on these questions, we constructed three OLS regression statistical models.[26] The results of these analyses are presented in Table 5.7. In the first model the dependent variable is *frequency of contact with group president/executive director*, considered by respondents to be the most influential person in the group. The variable was coded on a six-point scale: 1=never, 2=1–2 times a year or less, 3=3–6

Table 5.7.   OLS Regression Results: Large Donors and Access to Group Leaders and Staff

Variable	Model 1[a] Frequency of contact with group president/ executive director B	(SE)	Model 2[b] Frequency of contact with group staff B	(SE)	Model 3[c] Importance of access to group leaders as benefit B	(SE)
Constant	.583	(.651)	1.447	(.946)	1.218	(.514)**
Age	.002	(.009)	−.004	(.013)	−.003	(.007)
Marital status	.193	(.232)	.028	(.337)	.114	(.198)
Employment status	.030	(.243)	−.191	(.353)	.245	(.197)
Gender	−.234	(.246)	−.512	(.357)	.132	(.199)
Amount given	.435	(.073)***	.489	(.106)***	.134	(.059)**
	$R^2 = .403$ $N = 71$		$R^2 = .284$ $N = 71$		$R^2 = .125$ $N = 63$	

Source: Authors' data.

Notes: Table entries are unstandardized regression coefficients, with standard errors in parentheses.

[a]In model 1, the dependent variable is *frequency of contact with group president/executive director* (1 = never, 2 = 1–2 times per year or less, 3 = 3–6 times per year, 4 = 7–12 times per year, 5 = about once a month, 6 = more than once a month).
[b]In model 2, the dependent variable is *frequency of contact with group staff members* (1 = never, 2 = 1–2 times per year or less, 3 = 3–6 times per year, 4 = 7–12 times per year, 5 = about once a month, 6 = more than once a month).
[c]In model 3, the dependent variable is *importance of access to group leaders as benefit* (1 = not at all important, 2 = somewhat important, 3 = very important). For coding of independent variables, see text.
**$p < .05$ (two-tailed)
***$p < .001$ (two-tailed)

times a year, 4=7–12 times a year, 5=about once a month, 6=more than once a month. The variable is less than ideal for use as a dependent variable in OLS regression (since responses are not normally distributed), but it is adequate for illustrative purposes. Our independent variable of interest is *amount given in last year*, a categorical indicator coded as follows: 1=$1,000–$2,499; 2=$2,500–$4,999; 3=$5,000–$9,999; 4=$10,000–$24,999; 5=$25,000–$49,999; 6=$50,000–$99,999; 7=$100,000 and above. As control variables, we included *age* (continuous); *marital status* (0=not married, 1=married); *employment status* (0=not employed full time, 1=employed full time); and *gender* (0=male, 1=female).

The results indicate that there is a strong positive association between the amount a donor gives and the frequency of contact between the donor and the key decision maker for the group. The same relationship holds in the second model (this time the dependent variable is *frequency of contact with group staff*, which is coded the same as the previous dependent variable). In other words, the amount a respondent gives is positively related to the frequency with which the respondent interacts with group staff. The final model examines the relationship between the self-reported value of access to group leaders as a benefit and the amount given by the donor. Again the relationship is positive.

These findings cannot prove that more money means more access for big donors. First of all, we do not know whether the largest of large donors are *given* more access by dint of their giving or if they *demand* more access than other donors. Similarly, we do not know for certain whether the largest large donors give more *because* they value access more than other donors or if they are *given* more access and thus appreciate this benefit more than other donors. In the end, however, our statistical results show the following:

- Higher levels of giving are associated with higher levels of contact with group leaders, and
- Higher levels of giving are associated with greater appreciation of access to group leaders.

We explored the relationship between large donors and group decision makers in a number of other ways as well. For example, we asked our respondents the following question: "If you were dissatisfied with a decision that [the group to which you donate] made concerning a key issue, what would be your most likely reaction?" Our results suggest that large donors are not content to go along to get along. Only 19 percent said they would "not voice [their] dissatisfaction and would go along with the decision." Fifty-seven percent said they would "voice [their] dissatisfaction, but probably would go along with the decision" nevertheless, while 11 percent said they would "try to get the decision reversed." Another 14 percent said they would "withdraw from the organization."

When asked what they would do if the group they support contin-ued to make decisions with which they disagreed, our respondents answered as follows: 5 percent said they would "not voice [their] dissat-isfaction," while 20 percent said they "probably would go along with the decisions." Fifteen percent said they would "try to get the decisions reversed," but fully 66 percent said they would "withdraw from the orga-nization."

Among our respondents there was no correlation between the size of the last gift and the donor's personal propensity to opt to withdraw. But there is an association between the number of gifts a donor has provided and the donor's propensity to use the withdrawal option. We conducted a number of statistical tests to find out if there was a relationship between the number of large gifts a respondent had given and how the respondent would react if the group made a decision the respondent did not agree with, and our results did not produce any statistically significant findings. However, the correlation between the *number of large contributions* variable (continuous) and the *what you would do if the group continued to make decisions with which you disagreed* variable (1 = "not voice dissatisfaction," 2 = "voice dissatisfaction," 3 = "try to get the decisions reversed," 4 = "withdraw") is negative ($r=-.518$, $p=.000$).[27] It seems reasonable to conclude that the more extensive the relationship between the group and the donor, the less likely the donor is to raise objections or quit. Donors may grumble, but walking away from a group with which they have a long-term investment is very difficult.

Besides Giving, What Other Activities Engage Large Donors?

Table 5.8 shows that large donors are active in some ways and inac-tive in others. On the one hand, a majority of respondents do not report doing any specific thing for the group. Apparently, while all large donors give a lot, many do not do a lot. On the other hand, it appears that the largest givers do the most. To determine who does the most, we constructed a variable called *involvement*, which adds up respondents' responses to all the items (except item no. 21) found in Table 5.8 (for each item a respon-dent is given a score of 1 if the respondent did not engage in that activity, and a score of 2 if the respondent did engage in that activity; the scale thusly runs from 20 to 40). There is a significant positive relationship between our *number of large contributions* variable and *involvement* ($r=.468$, $p=.001$). There is also a significant relationship between *involvement* and *amount given in last year* ($r=.434$, $p=.000$), and between *involvement* and *years since first large contribution* (continuous), ($r=.452$, $p=.001$). In all, these findings suggest that giving money is not a substitute for doing other things. In fact, level of involvement increases *pari passu* with large giving. Groups that attract and recruit large donors are also attracting and recruiting active members.

Table 5.8.   What Do Large Donors Do Other Than
Contribute Money?

Activity	Percent[a]
1. Contacted a government official on behalf of the organization	45.0
2. Tried to recruit new members/donors	39.0
3. Attended conference or workshop	29.0
4. Given time for special projects	25.0
5. Served on a committee	22.0
6. Represented the organization to other organizations or to the general public	20.0
7. Provided consulting/expertise to the organization free of charge	18.0
8. Served on the organization's board of directors	18.0
9. Held a meeting at my home	17.0
10. Wrote to newspaper or magazine on behalf of the organization	17.0
11. Solicited donations	16.0
12. Helped to organize meetings	15.0
13. Served as an officer of the organization	15.0
14. Served as a volunteer lobbyist	11.0
15. Gave or lent equipment or supplies	7.5
16. Helped with office work	7.5
17. Provided special services to other members/donors	5.0
18. Volunteered as staff	5.0
19. Picketed or demonstrated	4.0
20. Provided transportation on behalf of the organization	4.0
21. Other (did something else)	63.0

Source: Authors' data.

Notes: $N = 95$ (Ns may vary across survey items owing to missing data).
Table based on responses to following survey item: "Individuals can be involved in organizations in a variety of ways. Below you will see a list of several ways that individuals participate in and help the organizations they support. Please indicate whether or not you have engaged in each of the following activities for [name of specific group]."

[a]Column number is percentage of respondents who report engaging in row activity.

Conclusion

It is easy to see why large donors are crucially important to environmental public interest groups. These donors provide valuable monetary resources to the groups they support, and they do this in a largely unobtrusive manner. Many large donors also contribute broadly to group efforts in a variety of nonmonetary ways. In this chapter, drawing upon our survey of one hundred large donors to environmental groups, we have attempted to paint a broad portrait of large contributors to environmental public interest groups. In this section, rather than simply summarizing our findings, we will close with a number of observations about the large donors we surveyed and their importance to the groups they support.

First, large donors may be an endangered (or at least a threatened) species. Our data show that large donors to environmental groups are, to be blunt, old. If, as Robert Putnam and others have argued, this generation of the elderly is uniquely participatory, environmental groups may face a financial crisis when the current generation of large donors passes on.[28] To survive in the very competitive world of environmental political advocacy, groups are going to have to find ways to attract the next generation of financially comfortable elderly.

Second, until the profile of large donors (and members, for that matter) changes, environmental groups will remain open to the charge that they are skewed toward the interests of affluent, well-educated, white people. Entire swaths of the public—including nonwhites, the poor, and the young—are virtually absent from the large-donor pool. Many others, including unmarried, full-time workers, and people with children living at home are vastly underrepresented. None of this is surprising (least of all the fact that the poor are underrepresented here), and surely environmental groups themselves are not to blame for the lack of diversity among their large donors. But until environmental groups find a way to reach out to and attract affluent people of color, younger people, and others who are traditionally underrepresented, they remain open to the charge that they are essentially elitist organizations.

Third, there is absolutely no question that large donors to environmental organizations give primarily for purposive reasons. Although it would be foolish to discount the gravity of the free-rider problem, it is clear from our data that large donors are not rational in any strict economic sense. No matter how we try to twist and bend the notion of rationality, the fact remains that large donors give because they value the collective political benefits that environmental groups seek.

Fourth, the way that groups treat their large donors is much less important than the work the groups do. Our data suggest that large donors simply are not very interested in the service they get from the groups they support. Rather, the typical donor chooses which group to support (as well as whether or not to continue supporting the group) largely on the bases of the cause the group supports, how the group approaches environmental problems, and how effective the group is. Generally, large donors do not much care how they are treated by the groups they support. They place little value on being recognized or thanked or coddled. The best way to attract and retain large donors is for the group to be successful in its pursuance of environmental public goods.

Fifth, large donors are a development director's delight. Most large donors are repeat donors, many engage in activities in addition to giving, and virtually all are strongly committed to the groups they support. Moreover, and perhaps even more important for group staff, large donors are hardly gadflies. Very few large donors contact group leaders and staff members on a regular basis, and most appear content to have only sporadic contact with the people who run and belong to the groups they support.

Sixth, it may indeed be the case that the largest of large donors have special access to the people who run environmental groups. While we cannot conclude on the basis of our data that exceptionally large donors exert disproportionate influence over group leaders, the data suggest that these donors value and receive access to group leaders more often than other donors do. To us, this indicates that the question of patron influence over group decisions remains an open and important one.

Finally, we wish to note that large donors are singularly valuable citizens in a civic sense. In an era of declining social capital, large donors provide a surfeit of money for organizations that represent individual citizens rather than large institutions. Moreover, these citizens are deeply rooted in their communities, they take a somewhat active role in the groups they support, and they appear to care deeply about the larger world around them and the creatures that inhabit it. They engage in a wide variety of other activities that we tend to associate with the public-regarding democratic citizen—they vote, they keep up with current affairs at all levels of government, and they communicate with their elected officials. None of this is the least bit bad.

Notes

1. On the "advocacy explosion" see Mark P. Petracca, "The Rediscovery of Interest Group Politics," in *The Politics of Interests: Interest Groups Transformed*, ed. Mark P. Petracca (Boulder: Westview Press, 1992), 13–18; Jack L. Walker, "The Origins and Maintenance of Interest Groups in America," *American Political Science Review* 77 (1983): 394–397. On the proliferation of public interest groups, see Jeffrey M. Berry, *Lobbying for the People: The Political Behavior of Public Interest Groups* (Princeton: Princeton University Press, 1977), chap. 1.
2. For a good discussion on the concept of countervailing power, see Andrew S. McFarland, "Interest Groups and the Policymaking Process: Sources of Countervailing Power in America," in *The Politics of Interests*, 58–79.
3. See Mancur Olson, *The Logic of Collective Action: Public Goods and the Theory of Groups* (Cambridge: Harvard University Press, 1965).
4. For an excellent review of the literature on how groups overcome the barriers to formation and survival, see Frank R. Baumgartner and Beth L. Leech, *Basic Interests: The Importance of Groups in Politics and in Political Science* (Princeton: Princeton University Press, 1998), chap. 4.
5. On solidary incentives, see James Q. Wilson, *Political Organizations* (Princeton: Princeton University Press, 1995), chap. 3. On expressive benefits, see Robert H. Salisbury, "An Exchange Theory of Interest Groups," *Midwest Journal of Political Science* 13 (1969): 15–22.
6. For a brief summary of this literature, see Baumgartner and Leech, *Basic Interests*, 73–74.
7. Jack H. Nagel, *Participation* (Englewood Cliffs, N.J.: Prentice Hall, 1987), 33–34.
8. See especially Salisbury, "An Exchange Theory of Interest Groups."
9. See especially Walker, "The Origins and Maintenance of Interest Groups in America." See also Baumgartner and Leech, *Basic Interests*, 74–77.
10. Walker, "The Origins and Maintenance of Interest Groups in America," 398–401. See also Jack L. Walker Jr., *Mobilizing Interest Groups in America: Patrons, Professions,*

and Social Movements (Ann Arbor: University of Michigan Press, 1991), especially chap. 5.

11. Walker, *Mobilizing Interest Groups in America*, chap. 5.

12. Berry, *Lobbying for the People*, chap. 3.

13. See, for example, Allan J. Cigler and Anthony J. Nownes, "Public Interest Entrepreneurs and Group Patrons," in *Interest Group Politics*, 4th ed., ed. Allan J. Cigler and Burdett A. Loomis (Washington, D.C.: CQ Press, 1995), 77–99; Anthony J. Nownes and Allan J. Cigler, "Public Interest Groups and the Road to Survival," *Polity* 27 (1995): 379–404.

14. On co-optation and other threats associated with patronage, see J. Craig Jenkins and Craig M. Eckert, "Channeling Black Insurgency: Elite Patronage and Professional Social Movement Organizations in the Development of the Black Movement," *American Sociological Review* 51 (1986): 812–829; Doug McAdam, *Political Process and the Development of Black Insurgency, 1930–1970* (Chicago: University of Chicago Press, 1982), especially chap. 2; Ronald G. Shaiko, *Voices and Echoes for the Environment: Public Interest Representation in the 1990s and Beyond* (New York: Columbia University Press, 1999), especially 185–190.

15. See Nownes and Cigler, "Public Interest Groups and the Road to Survival," 388–393.

16. Ibid., 393–395.

17. Shaiko, *Voices and Echoes for the Environment*, 109.

18. Cigler and Nownes, "Public Interest Entrepreneurs and Group Patrons," 93–94.

19. See Walker, "The Origins and Maintenance of Interest Groups in America," 400.

20. Christopher J. Bosso, *Environment Inc.: From Grassroots to Beltway* (Lawrence: University Press of Kansas, 2005), 111.

21. Ibid.

22. We did this primarily during the summer of 2005.

23. On the characteristics associated with voluntarism and other forms of civic engagement, see Sidney Verba, Kay Lehman Schlozman, and Henry E. Brady, *Voice and Equality: Civic Voluntarism in American Politics* (Cambridge: Harvard University Press, 1995).

24. See, for example, Kent E. Dove, Alan M. Spears, and Thomas W. Herbert, *Conducting a Successful Major Gifts and Planned Giving Program: A Comprehensive Guide and Resource* (San Francisco: Jossey-Bass, 2002); Adrian Sargeant and Elaine Jay, *Building Donor Loyalty: The Fundraiser's Guide to Increasing Lifetime Value* (San Francisco: Jossey-Bass, 2004).

25. Lawrence S. Rothenberg, "Organizational Maintenance and the Retention Decision in Groups," *American Political Science Review* 82 (1988): 1133.

26. OLS (ordinary least squares) regression is a widely used statistical technique used to account for the variation in a dependent variable based on a linear combination of several independent variables. For a good basic introduction to OLS regression, see Michael S. Lewis-Beck, *Applied Regression: An Introduction*, Sage University Paper Series on Quantitative Applications in the Social Sciences, 07-001 (Beverly Hills, Calif., and London: Sage Publications, Inc., 1980).

27. All correlations reported in this chapter are Pearson's correlation coefficients.

28. See especially Robert D. Putnam, *Bowling Alone: The Collapse and Revival of American Community* (New York: Simon & Schuster, 2000), chaps. 2, 3, and 14 in particular.

6

Interest Organization Communities
Their Assembly and Consequences
David Lowery and Virginia Gray

Scholars have made impressive theoretical and empirical contributions to our understanding of how and under what conditions individual organized interests are formed. They have typically focused at the micro level on the motivations of potential members and the role of group entrepreneurs and patrons in finding the resources necessary for a group to become a viable entity. Much less attention has been paid to broadly understanding populations of organized interests *as populations*, addressing such questions as why a particular configuration of organized interests exists at a specific point in time. In the end, this has major implications for policy making and the structure of representative bias in the political system.

In this chapter, David Lowery and Virginia Gray present the broad outlines of a *population ecology* theory to account for how particular interest organized communities arise and how they change over time. In particular, Lowery and Gray concentrate on two traits of organized interests as populations: first, the *density* of interest communities—how crowded they are—and, second, the *diversity* of such communities—the balance of different types of interest organizations, reflecting potential bias. They demonstrate with empirical evidence that the population ecology perspective has great promise for understanding both the mobilization and influence processes of organized interests.

In the conclusion, the authors discuss the broader implications of their work, noting that "the density and diversity of communities of interest organizations can matter, but do not always do so." The biggest challenge for those who study the structure of interest organization communities is to identify the circumstances under which such traits have an important impact on the policy process.

Social scientists have long studied the politics of interest representation, but we have only recently begun to study populations of organized interests as *populations*.[1] In part, this failure was due to a lack of good data on interest organization populations. We will see that valid censuses of the organizations that lobby state and national governments became available only recently. An even more telling reason for our collective inattention to interest organization populations was the sense that nothing especially interesting happened at the population level of analysis as compared with the activities of individual organizations.

This does not mean that the interest organization community was unimportant. Scholars, politicians, and pundits have long looked askance at large numbers of lobbying organizations descending on capitols in the pursuit of exercising private interest though public policy. They were especially concerned about the perceived imbalance of who was at the table since it was clear—even without good data on interest organization communities—that they were dominated by business interests. Rather, it was assumed that populations were assembled in a simple additive manner by summing up the successful mobilization events of individual interest organizations.

In short, all of the interesting stuff seemed to happen at the level of the individual interest organization. The population of interest organizations into which new organizations entered did not feed back to alter the life chances of individual organizations. Moreover, our theories of lobbying strategies were largely influenced by examining the relationship between individual interest organizations and public officials. We did not often stop to think how the presence of potentially allied and opposed interests altered the tactical and strategic behavior of lobbying efforts and their prospects for success. Again, while interest organization populations were clearly viewed as important, they were also viewed, if somewhat paradoxically, as not especially interesting.

The last decade has seen significant change in this assessment of populations of organized interests. Theories of populations of organized interests as populations stand between theories about the mobilization of individual interest organizations and theories about lobbying. The structure of interest communities feeds back to influence the mobilization process and then may influence how interest organizations lobby. More important, the processes by which interest communities are assembled involve much more than simply adding up mobilization events. Rather, processes that give rise to mobilization events of individual organized interests provide only the raw material for populations of interest organizations. That raw material is then sculpted by processes uniquely operating at the community level.

The new theories that seek to explain how interest communities are assembled are somewhat abstract, in part because we all find it easier to think in terms of individual members or groups, individual entrepreneurs who found new organizations, and individual lobbyists encountering a public official. The payoff for this abstractness is significant, however, if it points to contextual forces that we might not otherwise have considered, although they may significantly influence how individual members, entrepreneurs, and lobbyists behave.

In reviewing this new body of theory and evidence, we focus on two key traits of interest communities—interest system density and diversity. After briefly describing each trait, we explore the theories that purport to account for variations in density and diversity and the evidence used to assess the veracity of these theories. We conclude by considering the implications of population density and diversity for understanding both mobilization and influence processes that are the topics of other chapters in this volume.

Interest Community Density

The first trait that is used to describe interest communities is their density, or how crowded they are. How many organized interests lobby governments in the United States? The usual answer offered by pundits and reformers is "too damn many!" Indeed, every decade for the last century or more has produced claims that lobbying communities have exploded in size and threatened to overwhelm the political process.

Such claims are problematic in several respects. Perhaps most important, many observers of the Washington interest community view its sheer size and presumed growth as evidence of undue political influence. The accumulation of undue influence resulting from seemingly ever larger interest systems is further assumed by some—most prominently Mancur Olson in his 1982 book, *The Rise and Decline of Nations*—to have grave consequences for public policy and economic growth.[2] We will return to this important and contentious claim in the conclusion.

Before we consider the effectiveness of lobbying, we note that assertions of undue influence were, at least until recently, based on either informal impressions[3] or very indirect ways of measuring the number of organizations engaged in lobbying: through directories of professional and trade associations[4] or the number of political action committees (PACs) engaged in campaign finance activity.[5] Such indirect sources gave widely different answers to the simple question of how many organizations were engaged in lobbying. Most associations are not active politically at any given time, which leads to significantly inflated estimates of interest system density. And most organized interests do not sponsor PACs, which led to rather significant underestimates of the size of lobbying populations. More valid counts of the number of organizations engaged in lobbying were developed only after the adoption of lobby registration laws. While the states adopted such laws by the mid-1970s, the national government adopted meaningful registration rules with the Lobbying Disclosure Act of 1995.[6]

Lobby registration reports indicate that lobbying communities are indeed crowded, although not nearly so much as some have asserted. As seen in Figure 6.1, national lobby registrations more than doubled in number to reach 16,873 registrations in the first three years following adoption of the Lobbying Disclosure Act. With some variation, the Washington lobbying population was stable until 2003, after which registrations increased significantly to 20,000 or so organized interests.

In contrast, far fewer organizations engage in campaign finance activity. As seen in Figure 6.2, the number of PACS registered with the Federal Election Commission increased sharply during the late 1970s and early 1980s. PAC registration was first required by the Federal Election Campaign Act of 1974, which became operational with the congressional races of 1978. But, since then, the number of PACs active in federal campaign activities has been quite static with roughly 3,000 *connected* PACs, linked to other organizations such as firms or trade associations that often also lobby, and 1,000 or so nonconnected or freestanding PACs. Although complete data on state lobby registrations has been available only for some years, the data indicate that the number of organized interests active in the states nearly doubled in number during the 1980s to reach a total of 29,352.[7] The pace of growth then slowed so that 36,961 organizations were registered to lobby in the states in 1999, the last year for which we have complete data.

Figure 6.1.   National Lobby Registrations, 1996–2005

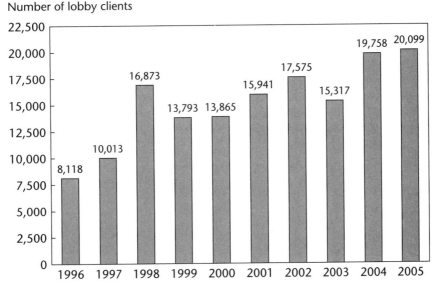

Number of lobby clients

Source: Senate Office of Public Records, personal comunication, April 19, 2006.

Figure 6.2.   National Political Action Committee (PAC) Registrations, 1977–2005

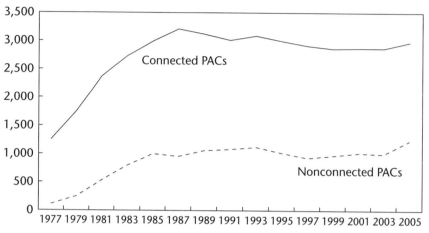

Number of PAC registrations

Source: "FEC Issues Semi-Annual Federal PAC Count," Federal Election Commission, Press Office, http://www.fec.gov/press/press2006/20060223.paccount.html.

Are these numbers large? It depends, of course, on what we compare them with. When compared with the numbers of public officials being lobbied, such numbers must indeed appear daunting. For just one policy area—health care—there are nearly thirteen lobbyists per member of Congress.[8] But from the perspective of the number of organizations that could engage in lobbying, these numbers are quite small. Manufacturing firms are, with health care organizations, among the best represented in state and national lobbying. But less than one-half of 1 percent of California's nearly 50,000 manufacturing firms, for example, registered to lobby the California legislature in 1997, and the California Manufacturing Association had fewer than 900 members. In short, while many organizations lobby, most do not.

If it is very difficult to specify in any absolute sense whether lobbying communities are too large or too small, there is no question that they vary over both time and across governments. As we have seen, national and state lobby registrations have at times grown rapidly while at other times only slowly. In a few cases, these changes are incredibly sharp. Florida's population of organized interests boomed from 1,604 registrations in 1982 to over 3,000 in 1990, only to fall to under 2,000 registrations in 1995.[9] Such variation is equally large when we compare the size of lobbying populations across states. Some have relatively few lobbying registrations by organizations while others have many. In 1999, for example, only 72 organizations registered to lobby the Wyoming legislature, the same year in which 2,272 organizations registered in California. It is this variation in densities that is the central focus of research on the assembling of interest communities.

Why are some interest communities more crowded than others? Why and how does the density of interest communities change over time? How we answer these questions is important for a number of reasons. Most important, we have already seen that at least some scholars assume that large numbers of lobbying organizations alone constitute evidence of significant undue influence. But whether large and growing interest communities matter in terms of economic and political outcomes depends in large part on how we answer questions about how interest populations are assembled. That is, scholars have developed three quite different explanations of the growth and density of interest communities. More to the point, some of these accounts provide a far more benign assessment of large and growing interest systems than others. And variation in the densities of interest communities over time and across governments is the critical tool scholars use to assess the veracity of the three explanations.

Two of the three most prominent explanations of the growth of interest communities are firmly rooted in explanations of the mobilization of individual interest organizations. In his 1951 book, *The Governmental Process*, David Truman argued that interest groups form when like-minded individuals come together to address shared or common problems.[10] In this view, mobilization or the formation of interest groups is a natural and spontaneous response as citizens seek solutions to *disturbances* in their lives through public policy. To Truman, then, the size of the interest community was limited only by the number and intensity of disturbances giving rise to the mobilization of new interest groups. If interest communities are becoming ever more crowded, then that is merely the result of a society that is growing increasingly complex. With greater social and economic complexity, the number and intensity of disturbances at least potentially amenable to public policy solutions grow. Importantly, Truman gave no special attention to interest communities per se. In his view, all of the interesting action occurs at the level of individual interest groups and how they are mobilized. The interest community is generated merely through the accumulation of these mobilization events. And the size of this community changes with the frequency of disturbances giving rise to the mobilization or demobilization of individual interest organizations.

Mancur Olson's explanation of the density of interest systems is also firmly rooted in his understanding of how individual interest organizations are created. In his 1965 book, *The Logic of Collective Action*, Olson rejected Truman's argument that mobilization was natural.[11] Instead, he argued that we all have incentives to *free ride*, or to let others address policy issues of concern to us by participating in interest groups. We would benefit from the actions of the groups even without exerting ourselves so long as others did so. But if we all make such calculations, then no one will make the effort to form organizations to address shared problems.

Thus, shared problems are not enough to ensure mobilization. Indeed, in Olson's view, only certain kinds of interest organizations are likely to form. The first are very small groups in which free riding is readily observed and thereby inhibited, especially small groups with large stakes in public policy. Thus, Olson implied that automobile companies will far more readily organize to prevent the adoption of clean air regulations than will citizens concerned about environmental quality. Second, however, even larger groups can overcome incentives to free ride by providing *selective benefits* for joining a group. Unlike the collective benefit arising from a public policy solution to a shared disturbance, a selective benefit is received only through membership in the group. Thus, while those concerned with air quality will benefit from pollution regulations whether or not they participate in an environmental group, they cannot receive the environmental organization's magazine or its discounts on hiking trips unless they actually join.

Although effective, the use of selective benefits to overcome collective action problems arising from free riding may come at a cost. That is, membership in such organizations may be no longer linked to a policy issue or shared disturbance, but may be based instead on receipt of the selective benefit. Thus, any lobbying the organization undertakes is merely a *by-product* of the provision of selective benefits, not in the pursuit of *collective benefits* associated with addressing shared problems.

How then, in Olson's view, are interest populations constructed? In one respect, Olson's account of interest organization density is similar to Truman's. That is, interest communities were formed merely through the summation of mobilization events. Nothing special happened at the population level. As organized interests discovered solutions to collective action problems, the interest community would grow larger. Small groups with large stakes in public policy might organize more readily. But over time, even large groups would join the interest community based on provision of selective benefits.

At this point, Olson's analysis of interest communities departed sharply from Truman's with Olson's assertion that interest groups rarely die once having overcome free riding. Indeed, Olson concluded: "Organizations with selective incentives in stable societies normally survive indefinitely."[12] While we will see that this assumption was not valid, it is also quite consistent with Olson's analysis of mobilization. That is, if members join organizations largely for selective benefits, they will remain members even after the policy disturbance initially justifying the group's formation is solved. More to the point, if interest organizations do not die, the potential supply of selective benefits is limited only by the creativity of interest organization entrepreneurs, and then the growth of interest populations is unconstrained. Interest communities will always grow, even until the costs they impose on society through the adoption of policies of special benefit to themselves cause economies to slow and even collapse, a process Olson labeled the *institutional sclerosis* hypothesis.

While sharply disagreeing with each other, scholars became increasingly dissatisfied with both of these mobilization-based accounts of the construction of interest communities. Just as Olson's analysis of collective action sharply undermined Truman's assumption that mobilization was natural and inevitable, research on individual motivations for joining interest organizations increasingly showed that Olson's analysis of free riding was at least overstated.[13] Much of this research is more appropriately considered in the chapters on the mobilization of individual interest organizations presented in this volume. But these findings have important implications for explaining the density of interest communities by their suggestion that the process by which individual mobilization events are summed to form interest communities is far more complex than either Olson and Truman thought. Just as important, examination of actual populations of interest organizations suggests that something more than just a simple process of accumulation was occurring. As observed earlier, many organized interests die, sometimes at alarming rates that reach as high as 50 percent over a decade. In short, something more seemed to be occurring with populations of organized interests than could be accounted for by examining only the manner in which individual organizations are mobilized.

The *population ecology* explanation arose from this dissatisfaction. The most important characteristic of this account of interest community density is its assumption that populations are more than a simple accumulation of mobilization events. These are clearly important. As organizations form, they become the raw material from which interest communities are sculpted. Something unique happens at the population level that does the sculpting.

Before we examine these population-level processes, however, it is worth noting that this explanation is to at least some extent agnostic about whether Truman's or Olson's view of the mobilization of individual interest organizations is more valid. One version of the model, we will see, borrows insights from Truman's analysis. But the explanatory processes highlighted by the population ecology approach should operate equally well whether mobilization occurs as described by Olson or by Truman. But rather than starting with mobilization, the population ecology approach highlights the role of environmental resources in constraining the size of organizational populations.[14] That is, organizations are assumed to be dependent upon resources in the environment for their survival. Thus, the relative abundance of these resources largely determines the *carrying capacity* of the political system for organized interests, or how many organizations can survive. In this contest for survival, critically, the most telling kind of competition is among similar organized interests or those that are dependent upon the same kinds of environmental resources.

We can make these assumptions more concrete by examining two different kinds of population ecology analyses of organized interests. The first are time series studies of a single type of organization. Although quite typical of sociological studies of the density of nonpolitical organizations such as publishers and breweries, this kind of analysis has been applied only rarely to interest organizations.[15] A recent example is a study by Anthony Nownes of the formation of gay and lesbian organizations.[16] As seen in the solid line in Figure 6.3, the number of gay and lesbian organizations operating within the United States varied considerably over three distinct periods.

The first was a period of very slow growth from 1950 to 1970. A population ecology perspective suggests that few gay and lesbian political organizations could survive during this time period owing to a lack of resources available in the environment. The critical resources for advocacy groups of this type include members and the dues they contribute. While it is unlikely that the proportion of the population who were gay or lesbian was smaller then, it is also true that lobbying for homosexual rights was not considered an acceptable form of political activity during the 1950s and 1960s. As a result, few potential supporters of gay and lesbian advocacy groups were willing to publicly identify themselves as homosexuals by becoming members. With few members and the resources they provide, the environment could

Figure 6.3.　Density and Number of Foundings of American Homosexual Rights Organizations, 1950–1998

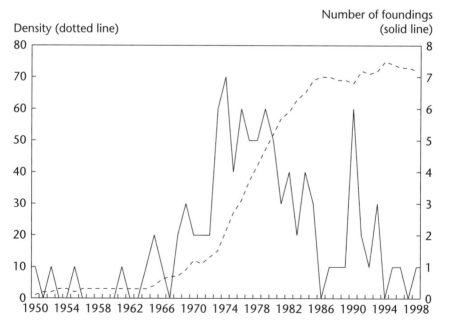

Source: Anthony Nownes, "The Population Ecology of Interest Group Formation: Mobilizing for Gay and Lesbian Rights in the United States, 1950–1998," *British Journal of Political Science* 28 (2004): 49–76.

support only a few generalist advocacy groups. In the language of population ecology, this is a period of legitimation, during which few organizations are founded, as seen in the jagged line in Figure 6.3, and many of those that are founded fail to survive for very long.[17]

The second period is one of rapid growth after a given type of organization has become part of the accepted landscape of advocacy organizations. As more potential members were willing to join and contribute to gay and lesbian advocacy groups, a formerly spare resource environment was transformed into one that was rich. As a result many new organizations were founded and a far smaller proportion failed. Importantly, such growth episodes are also periods of rapid specialization. Nownes's example shows that after 1970 or so there were enough potential members willing to join gay and lesbian organizations so that more specialized groups could be mobilized to focus on narrower concerns of the homosexual community.

After the mid-1980s, we see a third period of density dependence, during which the rapid growth of the gay and lesbian interest community leveled off as fewer new organizations were founded and existing organizations again experienced higher rates of disbanding. Quite simply, the resources of the new, richer environment had been largely exploited by the new advocacy groups founded after 1970. With many specialized gay and lesbian organizations, potential members and sponsors had plenty of choices about which organizations to support. But the marginal value of joining a fourth or fifth such group after one already supported two or three was no longer sufficient to support a growing population. The resource environment had reached its carrying capacity.

Time series studies of this type are invaluable for looking across the development of a population of organized interests. When we reexamine Figures 6.1 and 6.2 on the growth of national lobbying and PAC registrations and consider the growth rate of state lobby registrations by organizations in the 1980s and 1990s, for example, we see a period of rapid growth followed by a period of stability or density dependence. But these kinds of studies are also limited in that they look at environmental resources only indirectly. In the case of gay and lesbian advocacy groups, for example, we can only indirectly see the effects of environmental resources given additional knowledge about the recent history of the politics of homosexuality in the United States. We cannot examine directly how actual variations in numbers of potential members of these groups or the size of the political agenda of interest to them influenced group founding and disbanding rates. What, for example, explains the boom-and-bust cycle of the Florida interest system discussed earlier or the rapid growth of the number of national lobby registrations in 2004 and 2005? But a related body of research by Virginia Gray and David Lowery focusing on cross-state variations in the sizes of interest communities allows us to more directly examine the impact of competition among similar organizations for scarce resources.

Gray and Lowery's energy-stability-area (ESA) model of interest system density is used to examine variations in both the overall size of state interest communities and among a number of more specialized subcategories or guilds of interests, such as organizations of health care professionals.[18] The ESA model has two key variables representing the availability of resources in the environment needed to support interest organizations.[19] The first is labeled the area term of the model and is interpreted as the potential number of constituents in the interest domain that might be represented by an interest organization. The main effect of this variable is expected to be positive so that we should observe more mobilized organizations in states with more potential constituents. Thus, as seen in Figure 6.4, large states with many citizens and large economies tend to support many more interest organizations of all types. For example, all states will have some organizations representing health care professionals. These organizations will tend to have more members in larger states.

But larger states will also have many more organizations representing more specialized interests. Many of these additional organizations will be more specialized groups representing the interests of, for example, pediatricians rather than doctors in general. But this relationship is also expected to be progressively less positive so that growth rates decline as numbers of

Figure 6.4.   Density Dependence of State Interest Communities, 1997

Lobby registrations by organizations

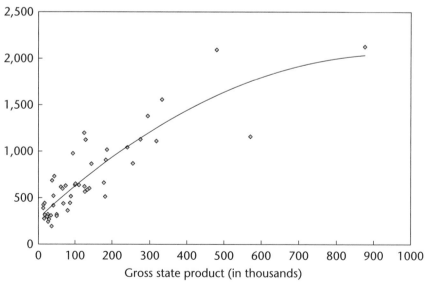

Gross state product (in thousands)

Source: Authors' calculations.

potential constituents increase. This reflects density dependence or crowding within the community as more and more nominally similar organizations
competitively exclude each other from ever finer and more precise representation of interests and the resources needed to maintain the organizations. At some point, quite simply, there will be a declining marginal return
from ever more fine-grained representation. As a result, the birth rates of
organizations decline and the death rates of older organizations increase as
interest communities become crowded.[20]

The second term of the ESA model is energy, which refers to the policy issues of concern to organizations and the level of uncertainty about
their solution used to stimulate mobilization. These are typically measured by the size of political agenda in a given policy area and level of
party competition, respectively.[21] As issues of concern to health professionals, for example, become more prominent on state policy agendas, organizations supporting or opposing proposed policies will have additional
resources with which to mobilize potential members and sponsors. The
same is true with party competition. If the out-party is threatening to
become the in-party, both supporters and opponents of status quo policies have reason to mobilize in support of their positions. Thus, the
energy term of the model reflects well Truman's notion in *The Governmental Process* that policy disturbances promote mobilization rather than
Olson's view of lobbying as merely a by-product of the provision of selective incentives.

Politics and policy—or rather political and policy uncertainty—matter
in the population ecology explanation. In terms of the state organized interests in Figure 6.4, states' populations falling above the density dependent
response function are typically those with more competitive party systems,
or more active policy agendas, or both. Many of those falling below the line
have less active policy agendas, or less competitive political party systems,
or both. In contrast with the latter, the political and policy resource environments of the former are richer, allowing them to support more interest
organizations than might otherwise survive.

Political and policy energy help to account for our difficult cases of the
Florida boom-and-bust pattern of population growth and the rapid growth
of federal lobby registrations in 2004 and 2005. In Florida's case, there was
a sharp increase in policy energy during the 1980s, when a significant fiscal crisis placed nearly every tax and spending issue a state might consider
on the table at one time. When the crisis was solved, or at least addressed,
Florida's policy environment could no longer support such a large population of organized interests. Similarly, although 2004 and 2005 were periods
of Republican control of all of the major institutions of the national government, the perceived willingness of GOP lawmakers to consider the
proposals of business interests was viewed by many as an injection of policy energy into the political system that encouraged such organizations to
descend on Washington in ever greater numbers.

Interest Community Diversity

Density is not the only trait of populations that interests us. We are also interested in the balance of different types of interest organizations or the diversity of interest communities. If, for example, business interests are thought to be too well represented in Washington and in state capitols, that influence might in part be mitigated by better representation by citizens' groups or organizations representing social interests.[22] But, unlike density, interest communities can be diverse with respect to any number of traits of interest organizations. Among many possible definitions of diversity, scholars have examined, for example, the relative balance of institutions—such as firms, cities, universities—lobbying on their own relative to associations (in which institutions are members, such as trade associations) and the membership groups that individuals join, like the National Rifle Association.[23] Still, most studies of diversity address the balance of the substantive interests represented by organizations.

There is little question that business interests overwhelmingly dominate interest communities. As seen in Figure 6.5, organizations representing other governments, labor unions, nonprofit groups, ideological groups, and education interests constituted only about one-third of the Washington lobbying community in 2004. Business interests provided the remaining two-thirds of registrations. If anything, as seen in Figure 6.6, state interest communities are even more dominated by business interests. Education, social (civil rights, environmental, good-government, religion, tax, and women's groups), welfare, and local government organizations made up less than one-fifth of state lobbying communities in 1999, a balance that has not changed very much over time.[24] Business interests have always been well represented, but some business interests are better represented in terms of lobbying organizations than others. Among the states, we find a variety of combinations of organizations representing different substantive interests.[25] As with interest system density, this variation can help us to test competing theories about the origins of diversity and bias in interest communities.

Why are some interest communities more diverse than others? Why are some kinds of interests represented by more interest organizations than others? Or, even more specifically, why are business interests so heavily represented while social and other interests are relatively less well represented in terms of numbers of lobby registrations? Answers to these questions are unlikely to be independent of theories of the density of interest systems. That is, the diversity of an interest community concerns the *relative densities* of different kinds of interest organizations. Thus, if we can explain why we tend to find more manufacturing or environmental interest organizations lobbying at different times and before different governments, we should be able to explain why we tend to find more manufacturing than environmental organizations lobbying.

In short, explanations of the diversity of interest communities must be logical extensions of one or more of our explanations of interest system

Figure 6.5.   Substantive Diversity of the Washington Lobbying
Community, 2004

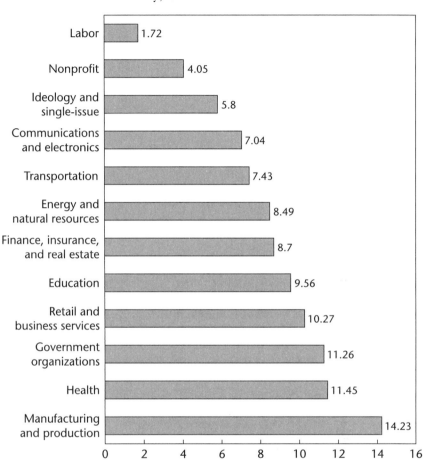

Labor 1.72
Nonprofit 4.05
Ideology and single-issue 5.8
Communications and electronics 7.04
Transportation 7.43
Energy and natural resources 8.49
Finance, insurance, and real estate 8.7
Education 9.56
Retail and business services 10.27
Government organizations 11.26
Health 11.45
Manufacturing and production 14.23

Percent of registrations

Source: Center for Responsive Politics, database of spending for lobbying,
http://www.opensecrets.org/lobbyists/list_indus.asp, April 29, 2006.

density. Importantly, the three explanations share one common idea. That
is, none of our three explanations suggests that interests in society are represented through lobbying organizations in an unbiased manner. Indeed,
no one has yet been able to define what an unbiased interest community
would look like. Still, the three explanations differ sharply in pointing to
quite different sources of bias.

Our first explanation of interest system density was provided by
David Truman,[26] who argued that interest organizations form when citizens
spontaneously come together in response to disturbances that might be

Figure 6.6.   Substantive Diversity of State Lobbying
Communities, 1999

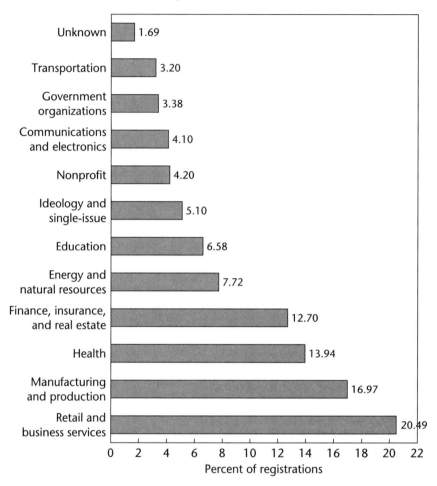

Source: Authors' calculations.

addressed through public policy. This explanation of density points to two
processes that might account for variations in the diversity of interest systems. The first is simply that patterns of disturbances are unlikely to be
equally spread over all of the issues that citizens might be concerned about.
Some problems arise only once, such as the 1977 treaty between the United
States and Panama in which the United States relinquished control of the
Panama Canal. Such issues then disappear from policy agendas as problems
are solved via public policy or are mitigated in other ways. Other disturbances are very cyclical in nature. Levels of inflation and unemployment

associated with the business cycle, for example, are at times very prominent and other times of less immediate concern. And attention to still other issues—civil rights, defense spending, or even lobbying reform—wax and wane depending on events in society and how crowded the policy agenda is.

If, as Truman suggested, policy disturbances are the foundation of organizational mobilization, then the relative balance of lobbying organizations we observe should reflect or be biased in a manner reflecting policy agendas. If business interests are heavily represented in interest communities relative to other kinds of interests, it is because there are so many issues on policy agendas of concern to business interests. And if there are many more religious organizations lobbying today than in the past, it is because we now have many more issues of concern to religious citizens that might be addressed through public policy action.

While variations in the prominence of issues is the most important process Truman used in accounting for the diversity of interest communities, he also drew special attention to a very special kind of disturbance. The key to this process is Truman's assumption that proponents of competing interests respond to each other. That is, Truman assumed that the lobbying efforts of supporters of one side of an issue could constitute a disturbance for competing interests that would then lead to their countermobilization. Thus, mobilization might proceed in waves as competing interests mobilize in response to each other.[27] Geoffrey Layman's analysis in his 2001 book *The Great Divide* of the ongoing culture war in the United States points to just such a wave pattern.[28] Layman argues that interest organizations representing the religious right, such as the Moral Majority Coalition and the Christian Coalition of America, mobilized largely in response to the successes during the 1960s and 1970s of socially liberal interest organizations. The activities of religious right organizations, in turn, led to the mobilization of new liberal organizations such as People for the American Way. The diversity of the interest community concerned about cultural issues thus changed as the actions of one set of interest organizations constituted a disturbance for others, thereby stimulating competing lobbying efforts.

The second explanation of diversity is in large part based on Olson's analysis of the collective action problem and how it influences mobilization rates. Before we consider how Olson's analysis of free riding is now used to explain variations in the diversity of interest communities, it is worth noting an earlier and related explanation emphasizing wealth and power.

Fears about the power of large business interests has been a recurring theme in American politics since at least the Gilded Age of the 1890s. In his 1960 book, *The Semisovereign People*, E. E. Schattschneider brought renewed academic attention to these fears in response to the positive view of organized interests offered by Truman.[29] Schattschneider did not provide a detailed explanation of the sources of business power, however; he focused instead on the comparative overrepresentation of business interests. He basically assumed that business interests had both a clearer understanding of their self-interest and a greater capacity to organize than did common citizens. The clarity of understanding arises, presumably, from the very significant stakes large business organizations have in public policy. Organizational ability, Schattschneider implied, arises largely from the wealth that is used to support lobbying. The relative cost of hiring a lobbyist is, after all, likely to be far smaller for a huge chemical company than it is for the citizens living in a neighboring community where chemical wastes might be dumped.

Olson's analysis of interest organization mobilization added an interesting complication to this understanding of interest system diversity or bias. That is, the problem of free riding applies to all types of interest organizations, including large businesses concerned about public policy. Yet, Olson suggested, it applies more forcefully to some types of interests than to others, and at least some of this variation goes back to the kinds of variables cited by Schattschneider. That is, business interests are likely to have a well-developed sense of self-interest that might be employed to discount incentives to free ride simply because their stakes in public policy decisions are often so large. Indeed, these stakes can be so large that a large institution might well lobby on its own even when it forgoes collective lobbying with other companies concerned about the issue.[30] And if some level of organizational capacity or resources are needed to overcome incentives to free ride in the pursuit of collective benefits by subsidizing the provision of selective benefits, then large, wealthy business interests should find it easier to mobilize than those concerned about other kinds of interests.

Among the factors noted by Schattschneider, Olson drew special attention to the number of organizations that might lobby collectively. Olson noted simply that when numbers are small, such as when the big-three automobile companies still dominated the market in cars and trucks, each company's share of the collective good of policies favorable to the industry as a whole was quite large. Thus, as numbers of potential members fall, it is easier to overcome problems of collective action. While Olson largely applied his theory to understand why business interests are overrepresented before government in comparison with social groups, other scholars were quick to note that it applied equally as well to variations in representation across different sectors of business activity. Business sectors with few firms, such as steel companies, should be better represented relative to those with many, such as grocery stores.[31] Today, this combined Schattschneider-Olson explanation is perhaps the most prominent account of the diversity of interest communities.[32]

There are, however, some good reasons to believe that neither the Truman nor the Schattschneider-Olson explanation provides a complete account of the diversity of interest communities. Most important, the explanations we employ at different levels of analysis must be, if not fully integrated into a single explanation, at least consistent with each other. That is, if we find that the collective action explanation provides an incomplete account of why individuals join interest organizations or how patterns of mobilization of separate organized interests combined to determine the density of a portion of the interest community, then it is unlikely that it will explain why some interest communities are more diverse than others. Explanations at the first level of analysis of individual joining become the necessary building blocks at the next levels of analysis, the understanding of density and then the diversity of interest communities.

More to the point, we have already seen that there are good reasons to go beyond Truman and Olson in understanding the density of interest systems. We have argued that a population ecology model better accounts for variations in density. This explanation emphasized the importance of numbers of potential members and sponsors of organizations and the political and policy energy available to mobilize support in determining the numbers of organized interests that can survive in a given time and place. These variables are, of course, related to those noted by Truman and Olson. Political and policy energy are certainly related to the patterns of policy disturbance discussed by Truman. And numbers of potential constituents matter a great deal in both the population ecology model of density and Olson's analysis of mobilization based on propensities to free ride. So, is there a distinctive population ecology model of interest system diversity? And, if so, does it differ from the Truman and Olson models?

The answer to both questions is yes, but it is not a simple answer. The definition of diversity provided by the population ecology approach is, however, quite straightforward. The diversity of the interest community is defined simply as a summation of the densities of different subsets or guilds of interest organizations found in any one place or time. But once we move beyond this definition, things become a bit more complex. This complexity arises from a unique feature of the population ecology model of density—its attention not just to individual interest organizations, but to the number of similar organizations that are already in the interest community. That is, the impact of political and policy energy and the number of potential constituents change as interest systems become larger. As interest communities become more crowded, density dependence sets in so that birth rates of new organizations decline and death rates of older organizations rise.

Just as important, this responsiveness of interest organizations to both the supply of potential members and sponsors and political and policy energy varies markedly across different types of interest organizations. Some types of organizations are more sensitive to changes in number of constituents and political and policy energy than others. Thus, the populations of some types of organized interests are more density dependent than others. In this interpretation, then, the diversity of the interest community is simply a summation of the densities of different subsets of lobby organizations found in a place or time. But that level of diversity changes in complex ways as the interest community becomes more crowded and the several guilds of organized interests respond differently to both the increased availability of resources needed for survival and the enhanced levels of competition for resources.

We can illustrate this with the model presented in Figure 6.7. The figure outlines the density dependent response paths of the size of two interest guilds in the fifty states. The model assumes that the fifty states are identical in all respects except economic size, as measured by gross state product (GSP). That is, each state's economy is split evenly between only two types of economic activity—a manufacturing sector and an agriculture sector. Thus, the interest organization communities of all of the states will have only two guilds representing, respectively, manufacturing and agriculture interests. The solid and dashed lines in the figure chart the responsiveness of the number of lobbying organizations in each guild to changes in GSP. Thus, the points on the two lines indicate the number of interest organizations of each type a state is expected to support on its lobby registration rolls at a given economic size.

The key implication of the figure is that the diversity of the lobbying communities will differ markedly as economies grow. In an economy sized at GSP-1, agriculture organizations dominate the interest community with twenty-three (62.16 percent) lobby registrations. Manufacturing, by con-

Figure 6.7.   The Changing Diversity of a Simple
Interest Community

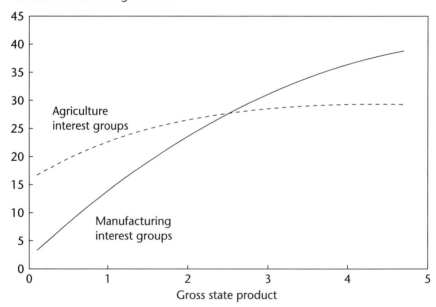

Number of interest organizations

Gross state product

Source: Authors' calculations.

trast, is represented by only fourteen (37.84 percent) organizations. This pattern is reversed, however, when state economies grow to GSP-4. Manufacturing interests are now the largest guild in the interest community, with thirty-six (57.14 percent) organizations. And the agriculture sector is represented by only twenty-seven (42.86 percent) organizations. The point of our simple model is that as long as the steepness and density dependence of the response functions of different interest guilds vary, the diversity of the interest community will change as the economies of states become larger.

At one level, then, the diversity of interest communities requires no special explanation beyond that provided by a population ecology account of the density of different interest guilds. Diversity is determined by a simple summation of the levels of density of different types of interest organizations.

But at another level, this account begs the question of why different types of interest organizations have different responses to environmental resources and levels of competition for those resources. Why is the manufacturing sector response function in Figure 6.7 steeper and less density dependent than that of the agriculture sector? Lowery, Gray, and Fellowes[33] tested a number of candidate answers to this question by examining the density response functions of seventeen subsets of interest organizations in the American states. Contrary to Olson's analysis, they found little evidence that guilds with larger numbers of firms grew more slowly than those with fewer. And, contrary to Schattschneider, they found no evidence that the wealth of the sector[34] influenced its rate of growth in response to changes in environmental resources. In a separate analysis,[35] Virginia Gray and her colleagues found that, contrary to Truman's wave hypothesis, different guilds were not very responsive to each other. Increases in the density of one did not seem, over the short term, to trigger increases in another.

Instead, differences in the responsiveness of the different guilds to changes in resources arise from differences in the economies of scale of different types of economic activity. The number of firms engaged in some types of economic activity grows slowly even as economies and populations become larger. For example, smaller states often have the same number of utilities, cities, and school districts as larger states, even if each individually is smaller in the former. As economies become larger, the number of interest organizations representing these sectors grows slowly. Other types of economic activity—manufacturing, banking, and health care, especially—are highly sensitive to changes in the size of the economy and the population. As economies grow, the number of organized interests representing these sectors grows as well. Thus, as economies grow, an interest community will have relatively fewer organizations representing cities and utilities and relatively more representing manufacturing and health care interests. The diversity of the interest community will change not because of the wealth or power of different guilds or difference in their levels of free riding, but because differences in the economies of scale of interest representation are closely related to economies of scale of economic activity.

Finally, and of special interest given discussions about bias in interest systems against organizations representing social interests, these guilds tend to fall somewhere between interest guilds that are highly responsive to changes in the environmental resources needed for survival and those that are only weakly responsive. Thus, the number of lobbying organizations representing social interests found in interest communities tends to decline relative to fast growers like banking interests and those representing health care interests and to increase relative to the slow growers like cities, utilities, and school districts.

Implications

In this chapter, we have discussed how interest communities are assembled. In doing so, we examined new theories of populations of organized interests as populations, emphasizing the traits of density and diversity. The population ecology theory of interest system density suggests that the size of the interest community is determined by much more than a simple adding up of successful mobilization events. The size of interest systems is at least in part self-limiting through a process of density dependence that sets the carrying capacity of political systems for organized interests. The population ecology theory of interest system diversity suggests that bias in the interest community is more than an expression of power and influence of big business. Rather, bias is determined through how economies of scale of different economic activities are translated into economies of scale of interest representation.

In the end, though, some might ask whether and how the population traits of density and diversity really matter, especially in terms of the mobilization of individual organizations and in terms of both lobbying strategy and lobbying effectiveness. This question can be addressed on several levels. A first and most direct response is simply that the construction of interest communities should still be interesting even if it has little immediate impact on the mobilization of individual organizations or on lobbying behavior. Who is at the policy table is an important issue in its own right, and that is precisely the issue that a population-level focus addresses.

At the same time, however, many studies of mobilization or influence need not be attentive to the community-level traits of density or diversity. When scholars examine how a specific interest organization is formed, maintains itself, or adopts particular lobbying tactics, such as Lawrence Rothenberg's study of Common Cause,[36] the characteristics of the population within which they work are constants. This does not mean that they are unimportant, only that they can reasonably be ignored for purposes of saying something about a specific organization.

But when we compare organizations in different places or the same organization at different times, the structure of the interest community *might* be important. That is, the contexts in which the organizations we compare may differ sufficiently that the context—the density and diversity of the interest community—must itself be part of explanations we develop.

Importantly, we have deliberately indicated that the population traits of density and diversity might matter when we compare organizations across time and space. Whether they do or not depends, of course, on the weight of empirical findings on their importance for specific behaviors. To date the strongest evidence that the density of interest communities matters concerns the mobilization of individual interest organizations. Many institutions and membership-based groups that might lobby do not do so. And many organizations that lobby at one time either withdraw from lobbying activity or disband as organizations. In part, we have seen the density of the interest community itself influences the difficulty of initially mobilizing and then maintaining interest organizations.

There is also some evidence, although this topic has been only rarely studied to date, that density influences the choice of lobbying tactics. Organized interests are more likely to use multiple lobbying tactics when community crowding makes it difficult to attract the attention of political officials.[37] The need to maintain a unique organizational identity when interest communities are crowded with similar organizations clearly influences how organizations ally with each other against other organizations with competing preferences for public policy.[38] It is clear, then, that population-level traits can matter.

Still, most scholars who are attentive to the structure of the interest community are concerned about how density and diversity influence lobbying outcomes, and it is on this topic that our evidence is most ambiguous. In part, our confusion about this issue reflects the discipline's confusion over the effectiveness of lobbying in general. Some scholars argue that lobbying is almost always successful and that policy can be readily purchased by those representing private interests.[39] Some scholars also assume that the density and diversity of interest communities constitute evidence of relative purchasing power.[40] Other scholars argue nearly the opposite, suggesting that organizations engage in lobbying only when they cannot achieve their purposes through other means or engage in lobbying for purposes other than the narrow pursuit of public policy, such as stimulating joining in order to survive as an organization.[41] In this sense, lobbying may be a sign of weakness rather than strength[42] or may be unrelated to actual influence.

Even when many interest organizations are united in their efforts to change public policy, numbers are sometimes no guarantee of success. Mark Smith's analysis of business lobbying in Washington in his 2000 book, *American Business and Political Power*, found that business was least effective when it was united, in large part because the issues on which the business community is united tend to be those the public cares about and opposes, such as environmental issues.[43] Politicians are loath to ignore the aroused public, even in the face of a united business community.

Empirical studies of specific policy issues fall on both sides of this great divide, with evidence on population density and diversity generating quite mixed results. Virginia Gray and her colleagues, for example, report that the density and diversity of lobbying communities had little impact on the initial adoption of state laws providing assistance to seniors and the poor in purchasing prescription drugs. But they also found that once the public spotlight was off the issue after the adoption of these laws, the density and diversity of state lobbying communities significantly influenced whether and how the laws were later revised.[44] So, the density and diversity of communities of interest organizations can matter, but do not always do so. Better identification of when and how they do so is perhaps the most important challenge now facing those who study the structure of interest organization communities.

Notes

1. For the most part, we use the term *organized interests* rather than the more conventional terms *interest groups* or *pressure groups*. Quite simply, most organizations that lobby today are not groups in the sense of having members. Rather, they are freestanding institutions—firms, governments, cities, universities, other types of institutions.
2. Mancur Olson Jr., *The Rise and Decline of Nations* (New Haven: Yale University Press, 1982).
3. See, for example, Robert Salisbury, "Interest Representation: The Dominance of Institutions," *American Political Science Review* 81 (1984): 64–76.
4. Kay Lehman Schlozman and John Tierney, *Organized Interests and American Democracy* (New York: Harper and Row, 1984).
5. Kevin B. Grier, Michael C. Munger, and Brian E. Roberts, "The Determinants of Industry Political Activity, 1978–1986," *American Political Science Review* 88 (1994): 911–926.
6. State laws vary somewhat, but these variations, with one exception, do not seem to influence the number of organizations registered to lobby. The one exception is the requirement in some states that state government agencies register to lobby. We exclude these from the state counts to follow. For a discussion of state lobby registration rules, see David Lowery and Virginia Gray, "How Some Rules Just Don't Matter: The Regulation of Lobbyists," *Public Choice* 91 (1997): 139–147. For a discussion of the Lobbying Disclosure Act of 1995, see Frank R. Baumgartner and Beth L. Leech, "Interest Niches and Policy Bandwagons: Patterns of Interest Group Involvement in National Politics," *Journal of Politics* 63 (2001): 1191–1213. For a discussion of PACs, see Frank J. Sorauf, *Inside Campaign Finance* (Boulder: Westview Press, 1992).
7. Virginia Gray and David Lowery, *The Population Ecology of Interest Representation* (Ann Arbor: University of Michigan Press, 1996).
8. Maureen Glabman, "Lobbyists That the Founders Just Never Dreamed of," *Managed Care*, August 2002, http://www.managedcaremag.com/archives/0208/0208.lobbying.html.
9. Holly Brasher, David Lowery, and Virginia Gray, "State Lobby Registration Data: The Anomalous Case of Florida (and Minnesota too!)," *Legislative Studies* 24 (1999): 303–314.
10. David Truman, *The Governmental Process* (New York: Knopf, 1951).
11. Mancur Olson Jr., *The Logic of Collective Action* (Cambridge: Harvard University Press, 1965).

12. Olson, *Rise and Decline of Nations*, 40.
13. Olson's model has attracted plenty of criticism at the individual level over the years. Scholars have shown that organizations with members are quite adept at overcoming barriers to collective action; see Robert Salisbury, "An Exchange Theory of Interest Groups," *Midwest Journal of Political Science* 13 (1969): 1–32; Jack L. Walker Jr., *Mobilizing Interest Groups in America: Patrons, Professionals, and Social Movements* (Ann Arbor: University of Michigan Press, 1991); Steven J. Rosenstone and John Mark Hansen, *Mobilization, Participation, and Democracy in America* (New York: Macmillan, 1993). Research has also shown that citizens have a range of membership incentives—and varied interpretations of those incentives—that mitigate both free riding and the by-product consequences of the use of narrowly material selective incentives; see Terry M. Moe, *The Organization of Interests* (Chicago: University of Chicago Press, 1980); John Mark Hansen, "The Political Economy of Group Membership," *American Political Science Review* 79 (1985): 79–96.
14. Some of the key works in the larger sociological literature on organizational environments include Howard E. Aldrich and Jeffrey Pfeffer, "Environments of Organizations," *Annual Review of Sociology* 2 (1976): 79–105; Michael T. Hannan and John Freeman, *Organizational Ecology* (Cambridge: Harvard University Press, 1989); Jeffrey Pfeffer and Gerald R. Salancik, *The External Control of Organizations* (New York: Harper and Row, 1978).
15. Howard E. Aldrich and Udo Staber, "Organizing Business Interests: Patterns of Trade Association Foundings, Transformations, and Deaths," in *Ecological Models of Organizations*, ed. Glenn R. Carroll (Cambridge, Mass.: Ballinger, 1978), 111–126; Michael T. Hannan and John Freeman, "The Ecology of Organizational Mortality: American Labor Unions, 1836–1985," *American Journal of Sociology* 94 (1988): 25–52.
16. Anthony Nownes, "The Population Ecology of Interest Group Formation: Mobilizing for Gay and Lesbian Rights in the United States, 1950–1998," *British Journal of Political Science* 28 (2004): 49–76.
17. The analysis of death rates of these organizations is provided in Anthony Nownes and Daniel Lipinski, "The Population Ecology of Interest Death Formation: Mobilizing for Gay and Lesbian Rights in the United States, 1945–1998," *British Journal of Political Science* 29 (2005): 303–319.
18. Gray and Lowery, *The Population Ecology of Interest Representation*.
19. The stability term of the model draws on Olson's insight that interest communities must be largely reconstructed from scratch after profound changes in political regimes, such as after devastating wars. But while Olson viewed such processes as occurring over a century or so, ESA empirical analyses have found that interest systems reach equilibrium or their carrying capacity for interest organizations far more quickly. Thus, while the stability term of the model remains of theoretical interest, it has not had empirical import in models of interest communities in stable Western democracies.
20. Virginia Gray and David Lowery, "The Expression of Density Dependence in State Communities of Organized Interests," *American Politics Quarterly* 29 (2001): 374–391; David Lowery, Virginia Gray, and James Monogan, "The Construction of Interest Communities: Distinguishing Bottom-Up and Top-Down Models" (paper presented at the annual meeting of the Midwest Political Science Association, Chicago, April 2006).
21. Virginia Gray et al., "Understanding the Demand-Side of Lobbying: Interest System Energy in the American States," *American Politics Research* 33 (2005): 404–434.
22. Jeffrey Berry, *The New Liberalism* (Washington, D.C.: Brookings Institution Press, 1999).
23. Salisbury, "Interest Representation"; David Lowery and Virginia Gray, "The Dominance of Institutions in Interest Representation: A Test of Seven Explanations," *American Journal of Political Science* 42 (1998): 231–255.

24. Schlozman and Tierney, *Organized Interests and American Democracy;* Gray and Lowery, *The Population Ecology of Interest Representation*, 102–103.
25. Ibid., 100.
26. Truman, *The Governmental Process.*
27. Ibid., 59.
28. Geoffrey Layman, *The Great Divide* (New York: Columbia University Press, 2001).
29. E. E. Schattschneider, *The Semisovereign People* (New York: Holt, Rinehart, and Winston, 1960).
30. Salisbury, "Interest Representation," 64–76.
31. Empirical work on this hypothesis is quite controversial, but for a good example of such research, see Grier, Munger, and Roberts, "The Determinants of Industry Political Activity, 1978–1986."
32. This combined Schattschneider-Olson interpretation of bias is especially well presented by Schlozman and Tierney in their 1986 book, *Organized Interests and American Democracy.*
33. David Lowery, Virginia Gray, and Matthew Fellowes, "Sisyphus Meets the Borg: Economic Scale and the Inequalities in Interest Representation," *Journal of Theoretical Politics* 17 (2005): 41–74.
34. Wealth was measured by the average gross state product (GSP) in the sector per firm in the sector.
35. Virginia Gray et al., "Reconsidering the Countermobilization Hypothesis: Health Policy Lobbying in the American States," *Political Behavior* 27 (2005): 99–132; see also John P. Heinz et al., *The Hollow Core* (Cambridge: Harvard University Press, 1993). Heinz and his colleagues essentially argue that policy proponents and opponents are only dimly aware of each other's activities. These short-term results differ, however, from Layman's finding of decades-long interaction between liberal and conservative organizations discussed earlier.
36. Lawrence Rothenberg, *Linking Citizens to Government* (New York: Cambridge University Press, 1992).
37. Virginia Gray and David Lowery, "Reconceptualizing PAC Formation: It's Not a Collective Action Problem, and It May Be an Arms Race," *American Politics Quarterly* 25 (1997): 319–346.
38. Marie Hojnacki, "Interest Groups' Decisions to Join Alliances or Work Alone," *American Journal of Political Science* 41 (1997): 61–87.
39. Fred S. McChesney, *Money for Nothing: Politicians, Rent Extraction, and Political Extortion* (Cambridge: Harvard University Press, 1997).
40. Schlozman and Tierney, *Organized Interests and American Democracy.*
41. David Lowery, "Why Do Organizations Lobby?" *Polity*, forthcoming.
42. Heinz et al., *The Hollow Core.*
43. Mark Smith, *American Business and Political Power* (Chicago: University of Chicago Press, 2000); see also Arthur T. Denzau and Michael C. Munger, "Legislators and Interest Groups: How Unorganized Interests Get Represented," *American Political Science Review* 80 (1986): 89–106.
44. Virginia Gray, David Lowery, and Erik K. Godwin, "Public Preferences and Organized Interests in Health Policy: State Pharmacy Assistance Programs as Innovations," *Journal of Health Politics, Policy, and Law* 32 (2007).

II. GROUPS IN THE ELECTORAL PROCESS

7

Getting the Spirit?
Religious and Partisan Mobilization in the 2004 Elections

James L. Guth, Lyman A. Kellstedt, John C. Green, and Corwin E. Smidt

Recent decades have witnessed the growth of activity among religious interests in elections, contributing to the increasing ascendance of culture and moral issues on the nation's campaign and policy agendas. Religious activists on the political right believe that government action is needed to reverse what they believe is a nationwide moral decline. Christian right mobilization, in particular, has been widely credited for reenergizing the Republican Party, helping it gain control of both houses of Congress in 1994 and the presidency in 2000. Religious activists of a liberal persuasion have increased their electioneering activities as well, typically to counteract the perceived influence of the religious right, usually with a Democratic Party preference.

In this chapter, James L. Guth and his colleagues examine the tactics and targets of religious interest groups in the 2004 election, focusing on efforts to bring sympathizers to the polls. With so few undecided voters among the electorate in 2004, most political observers felt that the key to the election hinged on the abilities of the parties and their allied interests to get their supporters to the polls. Using the results of a nationwide random poll of 4,000 adults, the authors find that religious contacting was extensive and played an important role in 2004. Their evidence suggests that religious contacts had little impact on vote choice but had a major impact on increased turnout, produced more interest in the campaign, and induced greater activism. Generally speaking, religious-group efforts aided Republicans more than Democrats.

The authors speculate that religious activities during campaigns are now part of the "institutionalized routines of many religious interests." Such groups will continue to "shape the contours of the electoral process," both cooperating and competing with parties and other interest groups.

Religious Groups and Electoral Politics:
Targets and Techniques

Since the late 1970s religious conservatives have experimented with a variety of electoral tactics to mobilize religious constituencies. Early groups such as the Moral Majority sought to activate pastors, who would in turn motivate their flocks by "registering, informing, and endorsing." When the limitations of this tactic became evident, new groups such as the Christian Coalition recruited laity to place voter guides in churches, persuade fellow parishioners to vote for favored candidates, and move sympathizers to the polls. Other groups specialized in conventional political techniques such as direct mail, phone calls, faxes, and, by the late 1990s, email and Web-based contacts.

In 2004 groups making up the Christian right pulled out almost every weapon in their historic arsenal. Jerry Falwell and others solicited clergy leadership, whether through registration drives in churches, placement of voter guides, or candidate endorsements. The Christian Coalition distributed voter guides, albeit less extensively than in the past, but other groups filled that gap, including Focus on the Family, the Family Research Council, the Traditional Values Coalition, and Concerned Women for America. These organizations also utilized many conventional mobilization strategies, from fax blasts to telephone banks. The Southern Baptist Convention (SBC), the nation's largest Protestant body, rolled out a massive voter registration campaign, "iVoteValues," in cooperation with Baptist churches, Focus on the Family, and the Family Research Council. A host of other groups such as Redeem the Vote, Let Freedom Ring, Vote the Rock, Pastors for Bush, and Reclaim America registered voters and provided electoral guidance for conservative Christians.[1]

The Christian right was not the only religious force active in 2004. Liberal groups such as Americans United for Separation of Church and State (AU), People for the American Way, and The Interfaith Alliance (TIA) tried to neutralize the Christian right's so-called politicizing of religion and threats to separation of church and state. AU, in particular, revived its quadrennial legal campaign against churches that "abused" their tax-exempt status by engaging in partisan politics. AU filed complaints with the Internal Revenue Service (IRS) alleging several violations in 2004, primarily in Evangelical churches, but also in Roman Catholic and African American Protestant venues. In some areas, religious liberals even monitored Evangelical and Catholic services for candidate endorsements or other prohibited actions by clergy or laity. Although Christian conservatives reacted angrily, they also worked to keep supporters within IRS guidelines. The AU campaign may have deterred some congregational politicking, but voter guides still appeared, and many clergy found ways to convey candidate preferences to parishioners.[2]

Some liberal religious groups went beyond hampering the Christian right to mobilizing "progressive" religious forces. TIA, led by clergy from many traditions, prepared materials to help citizens make electoral decisions. These focused not so much on candidates as on basic values and appropriate religious action. In most instances, however, those values were much more Democratic than Republican. Similarly, Jim Wallis of Sojourners, a rising star of the religious left, sponsored full-page newspaper ads proclaiming, "God is not a Republican." After conceding "Or a Democrat, either," the document directly attacked the Christian right's "religious" support of President George W. Bush's policies, arguing that peace, poverty, and the environment were "moral issues."[3] Such religious left activities were much more visible than in past elections, but they did not match the scope or coordination of those by the Christian right.

A similar ideological confrontation emerged among Catholics. Some conservative bishops and laity demanded stronger church action against politicians—mostly Democrats—whose actions ignored the church's anti-abortion stance. When Catholic John Kerry won the Democratic nomination, his pro-choice record led several bishops to suggest that he might be denied the Eucharist if he appeared at Mass in their dioceses, giving rise to what journalists quickly dubbed "the wafer watch." Although moderate bishops counseled a pastoral approach to erring politicians, this controversy set the stage for vigorous campaign politics within the Catholic community.

After an embarrassing brush with electoral politics in 1976, the United States Conference of Catholic Bishops (USCCB) has usually confined itself to issuing a wide-ranging, nonpartisan review of issues and providing information to parish leaders on legally permissible electoral activities. But when the USCCB updated and reissued *Faithful Citizenship* in 2004, conservative Catholics were dismayed. They saw paramount issues such as abortion, euthanasia, stem cell research, cloning, and same-sex marriage being treated no differently than, say, the minimum wage. A lay organization, Catholic Answers Action, responded with its "Voter's Guide for Serious Catholics," which stressed the "five non-negotiables." A clear attack on many Catholic Democrats, including Kerry, this guide was quickly adopted by some conservative bishops and priests for their dioceses and parishes and circulated by organizations such as Priests for Life. Some bishops banned the guide, however, often on legal grounds that it clearly favored the GOP and was unlikely to pass muster with the IRS or because they felt it did not capture the full range of Catholic moral concern.

Indeed, several state bishops' conferences wrote their own guides, reflecting the varying political coloration of each body. Where excluded from parish distribution, Catholic Answers Action countered by leafleting cars in church lots the Sunday before the election and placing full-page newspaper ads. On the other side, the Catholic Action Network for Social Justice, Call to Action, Pax Christi, a coalition of religious orders, and Catholic social service organizations offered materials quite critical of Bush policies and sympathetic to Kerry. Thus, the war of the voter guides made unprecedented amounts of material available to Catholics in 2004.[4]

Meanwhile, the political parties did not rely entirely on religious allies to activate friendly religious communities. The Republican strategy was certainly best developed. Driven by the assessment by Karl Rove, senior adviser to President Bush, that four million Evangelicals (and presumptive Bush supporters) failed to vote in 2000, the GOP concentrated on religious traditionalists. The Bush campaign consulted regularly with Christian right and conservative Catholic leaders but often went its own way, organizing local Evangelical and Catholic teams to activate sympathetic parishioners. This independent effort sparked controversy when the Bush campaign requested church directories from friendly congregations for purposes of voter registration and contact. This move was criticized even by the president's strongest religious allies, such as Richard Land of the Southern Baptist Convention. The campaign also held special functions for Catholics during the GOP national convention as well as meetings for Hispanic Protestant pastors and Orthodox rabbis.[5]

Perhaps the most innovative GOP initiative was among African Americans. Ever since the civil rights era of the 1960s, the politics in African American Protestant churches had favored the Democrats. In 2004, however, the GOP sought to make inroads, paying solicitous attention to traditionalist pastors anxious about same-sex marriage and attracted by Bush's faith-based social programs. Signs of GOP progress prompted renewed Democratic attention, as both Senator Kerry and Senator Edwards spent most Sundays in African American Protestant churches. They were joined in October by former vice president Al Gore, who "sprinted across six pulpits" in a single Sunday. The assault culminated, as in 2000, with Bill Clinton's conference call to hundreds of African American Protestant ministers.[6]

The Democrats also tried to reclaim some religious territory among white Protestants and Catholics, as Senators Kerry and Edwards infused their rhetoric with religious language. But religious outreach units created by the Kerry campaign and the Democratic National Committee (DNC) foundered on controversies over personnel. The DNC Web site briefly offered a special voter guide for church distribution, but it was quickly withdrawn under hostile fire. Indeed, secular activists, a key element of the Democratic base, objected to the very idea of religious mobilization. During the campaign, groups such as Catholics for Kerry wooed particular constituencies, but the scope of their activity was modest.[7]

By all accounts, then, political action in religious venues took many forms in 2004. After the election, politicians, journalists, and some scholars attributed Bush's victory to the effectiveness of Christian right and GOP appeals to voters concerned with moral values. Although other observers were skeptical, the role of religious activism clearly merits further attention.[8]

Exactly how pervasive was religious mobilization in 2004? Which techniques reached the largest audiences? Which religious communities received the most campaign contacts? And, of course, how effective were these efforts in generating votes? For our own assessment, we turn to the

Fourth National Survey of Religion and Politics.[9] In this survey we asked about six religious contacts: clergy encouragement to register and vote, political discussions with friends in church, direct contact by religious or moral-concerns groups, voter guides in churches, registration drives in churches, and clergy endorsement of candidates. Because we asked identical or very similar questions in 1996 and 2004, we can also assess changes in religious contacting over time (for ease of presentation, these data are discussed in the text and not presented in tables).[10]

Religious Traditions and Theological Factions

To simplify our inquiry, we focused on the four largest Christian traditions in the United States: white Evangelical Protestants, white Mainline Protestants, African American Protestants, and white Roman Catholics.[11] These communities account for more than two-thirds of the 2004 electorate and were the targets of political mobilization by both sides. As ethnocultural historians have argued, these traditions supply critical building blocs for party coalitions, changing with partisan strategies and programs. At the end of the twentieth century, Evangelicals were a strong GOP constituency, having moved away from their Democratic leanings at mid-century. African American Protestants, on the other hand, anchored the Democratic coalition, reflecting the enduring effects of the civil rights movement. Meanwhile, Mainline Protestants and white Catholics, once the respective backbones of the GOP and the Democratic Party, were increasingly divided, with no dominant partisan preference.[12]

As religious traditions shifted partisan loyalties, vital crosscutting changes occurred within each tradition. In sociologist James Hunter's vivid depiction, religious communities were torn by "culture wars," battles over abortion, gay rights, and other social issues produced by theological divisions. Mainliners, Roman Catholics, and even Evangelicals have split into competing theological factions, with "orthodox" believers aligning with the GOP, and "progressives" with the Democrats.[13]

We combine "ethnocultural" and "culture wars" perspectives to pinpoint mobilization targets in 2004. To classify voters, we first put them to a *religious tradition* (Evangelical, Mainline, African American Protestant, or Roman Catholic) on the basis of denominational affiliation. Then we assigned those in the three white Christian traditions to a *theological faction*, on the bases of religious belief, behavior, and affiliation with religious movements:

- **Traditionalists** are orthodox in belief, involved in traditional religious practices, and often identify with conservative religious movements.
- **Centrists** are less orthodox on historic tenets of their faith, less engaged in traditional practices, and usually not identified with religious movements.

- **Modernists** adopt heterodox beliefs, seldom participate in traditional practices, and often identify with theologically liberal movements.[14]

We also include smaller Christian communities in some analyses, such as Hispanic Protestants and Catholics, both important electoral constituencies. As with African American Protestants, we do not divide them into theological factions in the tables as their numbers are small, even in our large sample, although we sometimes report results from such divisions in the text. Given their even smaller numbers, Jews, Muslims, Hindus, Buddhists, and others are combined in a "non-Christian" category; and several small Christian traditions are combined in a category called "other Christian." Finally, Americans with no religious commitments or only nominal ones—a growing Democratic constituency—are classified as "seculars."[15]

Contours of Religious Contacting in 2004

In Table 7.1 we list the proportion of the public as a whole, in each religious tradition, and in each theological faction reporting contacts. First, note that only a minority of the general public received any single form of communication: one-third heard a religious leader urge them to vote, about one in four discussed the election with a friend in church, roughly one in seven was contacted by a religious or moral-concerns interest group, but fewer than one in ten found a voter guide in church and even fewer reported that their church registered voters or that congregational leaders endorsed a candidate.

Naturally, contacts were more numerous among regular worshipers, perhaps providing a better gauge of the absolute frequency of church-based activities. Compared with 1996 and 2000, discussion in church and clerical admonitions to vote increased slightly, and religious interest group contacts grew considerably, but voter guides were less numerous than in 2000 and much less so than in 1996. Clergy endorsements actually doubled from 2000 to 2004, but from only 3 percent to 6 percent, returning to the 1996 level (data not shown).

The extent and nature of contacts varied substantially by religious group. Overall, the most common form of contact was clergy encouraging parishioners to register and vote. Not only do pastors often regard such admonitions as part of their role, but in 2004 many groups encouraged this activity, recognizing the potential electoral impact. If Evangelical or Catholic traditionalists swarmed to the polls, Bush might benefit; if African American Protestant pastors galvanized their churches, Kerry could gain. In fact, around one-half of both African American Protestants and Evangelicals reported such urgings, as did two-fifths of white and Hispanic Catholics, and well over one-third of Hispanic Protestants. Even the diverse non-Christian and other-Christian categories reported significant clerical encouragement. Not surprisingly, secular citizens experienced few such contacts.

Table 7.1. Frequency of Religious Contacts, by Religious Group, 2004

	Clergy urged vote	Discussed in church	Interest group contact	Voter guides in church	Registered in church	Clergy endorsed candidate	At least one contact
General public	32	23	15	9	7	6	50
Regular attendees	52	35	22	13	11	9	73
Religious tradition							
Evangelical	45	36	22	11	9	7	65
Theological faction							
Traditionalists	61	50	31	17	13	9	83
Centrists	31	24	13	6	5	5	51
Modernists	26	21	15	4	2	3	44
Mainline	28	24	12	4	5	4	48
Traditionalists	42	34	14	6	5	5	64
Centrists	24	23	12	2	5	3	46
Modernists	20	16	11	5	4	3	38
Roman Catholic	40	19	19	10	7	11	59
Traditionalists	55	28	22	13	11	12	75
Centrists	39	15	17	10	6	13	60
Modernists	24	17	18	7	3	8	44
African American Protestants	49	29	19	21	15	7	69
Hispanic Catholic	38	27	11	27	10	7	71
Hispanic Protestant	36	33	15	6	14	10	63
Non-Christians	28	30	15	4	5	6	47
Other Christians	23	20	10	7	5	2	38
Seculars	5	5	8	3	1	1	15

Source: National Survey of Religion and Politics, University of Akron and Pew Forum on Religion & Public Life, 2004.

Furthermore, among Evangelicals, Mainliners, and white Catholics, traditionalists received many more clergy reminders than did centrists or modernists. Indeed, in all three communities traditionalists were twice as likely to hear a call to vote as were modernists. There were, moreover, some interesting departures from 2000: although Mainline and African American Protestants reported the same level of clerical urgings, white Catholics received slightly more, and Evangelical numbers jumped from 35 percent to 45 percent. All three Evangelical factions reported an increase, confirming the pervasive efforts to mobilize them in 2004. On the other hand, levels for Mainline and Catholic factions merely matched those in 2000.

Political discussion in church was the next most common contact, with Evangelicals most involved, followed closely by Hispanic and then African American Protestants. Indeed, the past three presidential elections have witnessed a progressive politicization of Evangelical churches as discussion participants grew from 28 percent in 1996 to 30 percent in 2000 and 36 percent in 2004. Among the large traditionalist faction, discussions rose from 41 percent in 1996 to 47 percent in 2000 to 50 percent in 2004. African American Protestants fell back slightly from 32 percent in 2000 to 29 percent in 2004, but they still exceeded the 26 percent for 1996.

Mainliners rebounded from a low discussion level of only 18 percent in 2000, back to the 24 percent reported in 1996. As among Evangelicals, the increase was concentrated among traditionalists, who jumped from 22 percent in 2000 to 34 percent in 2004 (but who were still short of their 39 percent in 1996). Centrists also increased their political discussion slightly (from 17 to 23 percent), but modernists lost ground, from 19 to 16 percent. As in the past, white Catholics talked least with fellow parishioners, with only 19 percent reporting church conversations, slightly above the 15 percent for both 1996 and 2000.

But for the first time in our surveys Catholic traditionalists were much more likely to talk about politics than their centrist and modernist co-parishioners. Indeed, the modest overall Catholic increase was due entirely to the growth in traditionalist discussions from 15 percent in 2000 to 28 percent in 2004. Still, that is far below the activity of their Evangelical and Mainline counterparts. Why Catholics engage in less political discussion in church remains a puzzle—especially given campaign controversies over Senator Kerry's status as a Catholic and the role of church leaders.[16]

On the whole, then, church political discussion was dominated by traditionalists. Even among Hispanics, traditionalists were much more engaged in such conversations (53 percent for Catholics, 47 percent for Protestants). Political discussions in religious settings are clearly an important part of campaign strategies, though rather hard to assess using survey techniques. Christian right groups have long encouraged such electoral proselytizing and, if 2004 is any example, party officials may be following suit. Both have recognized the critical nature of two-step political communications, building on the informal exchanges that shape political attitudes of religious communities, especially conservative ones.[17]

The third most frequent type of political contact in 2004 was direct communications from Christian right and moral-concerns interest groups. Although some persisted with tested techniques such as voter guides, most clearly shifted emphasis in 2004 to direct contacts through phone banks, door-to-door canvassing, mail, faxes, e-mail, and Web sites. Indeed, such contacts doubled in 2004, reaching 15 percent of potential voters (and about one-quarter of regular churchgoers), up from only 7 percent in 2000. Evangelicals, Catholics, and African American Protestants led the way. Once again, traditionalist Evangelicals received far more contacts than any other faction, followed at a distance by Catholic traditionalists. Note that Catholic centrists and modernists enjoyed a small but clear advantage over their Evangelical and Mainline counterparts. The data thus confirm what campaign news coverage suggested: an escalation of direct religious group contact in 2004.

Press accounts have often highlighted the use of voter guides to communicate with religious voters. These have a long tradition and have been deployed by pro-life groups since the 1970s.[18] In 2004, as we have seen, Christian right groups made similar efforts, and various Catholic sources produced competing guides. How many citizens actually found election information at their sanctuary? As Table 7.1 shows, only 9 percent reported candidate information at church, down markedly from the 13 percent reported in 2000 and 15 percent in 1996. As in the past, availability varied by tradition and theological faction. Interestingly, Hispanic Catholics and African American Protestants reported the most voter guides, ahead of Evangelical and Catholic traditionalists, usually the targets of media attention. Over the past three elections, however, guide usage has dropped dramatically in the larger traditions, from 21 to 11 percent among Evangelicals, from 13 to 4 percent among Mainline Protestants, and from 18 to 10 percent among white Catholics. Among Evangelical traditionalists, the drop was from 31 to 17 percent, and among Catholic traditionalists, from 29 to 13 percent. Only among African American Protestants has usage remained fairly constant.

There are several reasons for the decline. The Christian Coalition had fallen on hard times by 2004, reducing its ability to generate and distribute these materials. Second, the Christian Coalition and its allies focused on a few key electoral states rather than the entire country. Third, the highly publicized campaigns in 2000 and 2004 by Americans United arguably had some deterrent effect, as did rumblings from the IRS. Fourth, some groups concluded that guides only created controversy and did not serve the purpose intended. Even those produced in 2004 were often distributed directly to voters rather than through church bulletins or tables in narthexes—a practice "so 1980ish," as one campaign activist put it.

Journalistic accounts suggest that registration drives in church were much more fashionable in 2004, but Table 7.1 shows that only 7 percent of the public (and 11 percent of regular worshipers) reported such activities. African American and Hispanic Protestant churches were most active, followed by Hispanic Catholic and Evangelical congregations. Again, Evangelical and Catholic traditionalists were slightly more likely to report registration efforts, but on the whole, churches did not register voters on a large scale although there was significant activity in some. Of course, much registration activity among religious people went on outside of churches, such as Focus on the Family's effort to sign up its own members, only half of whom had been registered previously.

Finally, perhaps in response to interest group blandishments of clergy, there was a small revival in explicit candidate endorsements by pastors. Although Christian right enthusiasm for this tactic had waned by 1996, in 2004 a few groups still urged ministers to tell parishioners how they should vote, reportedly a custom in African American Protestant congregations as well. Despite some highly publicized cases, however, endorsements remained very rare, with every theological faction except for traditionalist and centrist Catholics scoring in single digits. (When members of either faction heard a priest endorse a candidate, it was almost always a Republican candidate.) In other religious groups, clerical endorsement was even rarer: only 9 percent of Evangelical traditionalists reported a pastoral endorsement (again, almost always of a Republican). Even among African American Protestants only 7 percent reported an endorsement, but unlike previous years, these were evenly divided between parties, perhaps reflecting the Bush campaign's wooing of conservative African American clergy.

Obviously, factors that always constrain pastoral endorsements still held in 2004. Most clergy either adhered to old adages against explicitly mixing religion and partisan choices, wanted to avoid congregation disharmony, or feared review of their tax-exempt status by the IRS, which was reportedly on alert in 2004. Keep in mind that, although explicit endorsements were still quite rare, many clergy found subtle (and not so subtle) ways inside and outside of religious services to convey their preferences.[19]

What can we conclude, then, about religious activity in 2004? Clergy encouragement of voting and political discussion in church continued at a fairly high level or even increased, but it varied by tradition, with Evangelical and African American Protestants still leading the way. Interest group contacts clearly increased, but voter guides were even less evident than in 2000, especially among Evangelicals; voter guides held their ground only among Hispanic Catholics and African American Protestants. Voter registration drives were most common among religious minorities, but they reached only a small segment of the religious public. Finally, explicit clergy endorsements revived slightly but remained uncommon.

Overall, then, religious contacting was fairly extensive. As the last column in Table 7.1 shows, one-half of all citizens and almost three-quarters of regular churchgoers received at least one religious communication. Interestingly, Hispanic Catholics led the way, with African American Protestants coming in next, followed by Evangelicals, Hispanic Protestants, white Catholics, and Mainline Protestants. In each group, religious contacts were slightly more numerous than in 2000. And in the large white Christian communities, traditionalists received the most religious contacts. Although we need to be cautious because of their small numbers, African American Protestants, Hispanic Catholics, and Hispanic Protestants showed the same tendency, with over 80 percent of traditionalists in each group reporting at least one contact. On the other side, modernists got fewer such cues; indeed, their totals are quite similar across traditions. Not surprisingly, centrists in each tradition fell between traditionalists and modernists.

While not all contacts bristled with partisanship, those that did were Republican. The direction of contacts (whether from a moral-concerns interest group, friend in church, or pastor) favored the GOP by a five-to-two margin, slightly higher than in 2000. This varied by technique, with a bigger Republican edge (three-to-one) in interest group contacts, and a narrower (two-to-one) advantage in church conversations and clergy endorsements. The ratios also differed by faction: among traditionalist Evangelicals, interest group contacts and conversion attempts by friends in church each favored the GOP by over ten-to-one. Even the rare pulpit endorsements endorsed Republicans by six-to-one. Overall, then, Evangelical traditionalists received more than eight Republican messages for each Democratic one. Mainline and Catholic traditionalists experienced a more modest GOP preponderance (about four-to-one). Among centrists and modernists in all three white traditions, the imbalance was much smaller, but none saw Democratic contacts outnumber Republican ones. Only for African American Protestants did figures run the other way, but by a much smaller margin than in 2000, as the GOP targeted sympathetic religious conservatives. Our queries do not capture the amorphous partisan impact of friendly conversations or subtle clerical cues.

The role of religious contacts must be put in broader perspective. Religious interests are significant allies (and sometimes competitors) of party committees, candidate organizations, and other interest groups. As Table 7.2 shows, religious messages stack up quite favorably with those from Republican party and candidate organizations, Democratic party and candidate organizations, liberal organizations such as America Coming Together, labor unions and environmental groups, and conservative organizations such as the Club for Growth, gun owners, and business groups. And among traditionalists, especially Evangelicals, religious contacts often outnumbered such secular ones.[20]

Religious contacts are often targeted differently than partisan and interest group contacts. Table 7.2 does reveal the imprint of Karl Rove's celebrated outreach to religious conservatives: Evangelical traditionalists reported by far the most Republican Party and candidate contacts, followed at some distance by Catholic traditionalists. Among Mainliners, Republicans had less success (or perhaps less interest) in targeting messages to

Table 7.2. Religious and Secular Sources of Contact (percent of group receiving at least one such contact)

		Religious contacts	Republican Party	Democratic Party	Liberal groups	Conservative groups
General public		50	37	37	22	15
Religious tradition	Theological faction					
Evangelical		65	45	35	18	18
	Traditionalists	83	54	37	20	20
	Centrists	51	40	34	16	13
	Modernists	44	28	29	10	23
Mainline		48	44	40	21	18
	Traditionalists	64	43	36	19	23
	Centrists	46	44	40	17	11
	Modernists	38	45	44	27	22
Roman Catholic		59	43	41	27	16
	Traditionalists	75	48	33	19	20
	Centrists	60	45	47	33	15
	Modernists	44	36	37	23	13
African American Protestants		69	17	31	26	13
Hispanic Catholic		71	19	24	16	14
Hispanic Protestant		63	23	27	11	8
Non-Christians		28	32	47	30	11
Other Christians		23	27	30	14	13
Seculars		5	36	41	28	14

Source: National Survey of Religion and Politics, University of Akron and Pew Forum on Religion & Public Life, 2004.

traditionalists, perhaps because centrists and modernists were approached with economic and foreign policy appeals. GOP contacts were also infrequent among religious minorities, suggesting that the party was depending on Hispanic and African American religious allies to make its case.

For their part, Democrats reached some sympathetic religious communities, such as Mainline modernists and Catholic centrists, two critical swing groups, but they also outperformed the GOP among seculars as well as among non-Christian faiths, both Democratic constituencies. And, although they did not send as many messages to African American and Hispanic Protestants, with assistance from liberal interest groups they still outdid the GOP.

Many factors affect which voters received all these political contacts. Using multivariate analysis, we explored factors that predicted reception of messages from the five sources in Table 7.2. Across the entire sample political contacts were most numerous among highly educated, wealthy, and older citizens. After that the patterns diverge: religious communications went overwhelmingly to those deeply involved in religious life. After church attendance, reliance on religious information sources, and attitudes toward religion in public life are taken into account, only Evangelical traditionalists received additional religious contacts. Surprisingly, residence in a state with a 2004 referendum on same-sex marriage did not produce more religious contacts.[21]

Party communications, naturally, focused on partisans: the Republican Party and the Republican candidates wooed strong Republicans—and especially strong conservatives—and Democrats contacted their own partisans. This tendency largely accounts for religious differences in Table 7.2: each party targeted its strongest constituencies. The only independent religious bias of party efforts is that the GOP contacted Evangelical traditionalists even more frequently than their strong Republican partisanship and conservative ideology would predict, while Democrats contacted Mainline modernists at a higher rate as well. Both parties, naturally enough, concentrated on the closely contested battleground states; indeed, residence there was the strongest single predictor of party communications. Finally, the likelihood of conservative and liberal group contacts was influenced almost exclusively by strong ideological commitments and, for liberal groups, higher education and residence in a battleground state (data not shown).

Impact of Religious Contacting

How did all this contacting affect potential voters? Assessing such influence has always been risky, but Table 7.3 provides a first cut at the potential influence of religious contacting, reporting bivariate data on presidential choice, turnout rates, and citizen activism in the four largest religious traditions.[22]

Table 7.3. Impact of Religious Contacts on Presidential Choice, Voter Turnout, and Activism (bivariate data)

	Evangelical			Mainline Protestant			White Catholic			African American Protestant		
Groupings	Bush[a]	Voted[b]	Active[c]	Bush[a]	Voted[b]	Active[c]	Bush[a]	Voted[b]	Active[c]	Bush[a]	Voted[b]	Active[c]
N =	408	648	648	268	393	393	279	393	393	128	254	254
All	79	63	28	53	68	32	56	67	30	17	50	20
Theological subgroup												
Traditionalist	88	71	33	65	78	30[ns]	74	78	28[ns]	—	—	—
Centrist	71	56	23	49	71	28	52	69	33	—	—	—
Modernist	57	55	28	44	56	38	39	55	27	—	—	—
Religious contacts												
High	84	77	49	54[ns]	96	62	43[ns]	75	49	14	55[ns]	31
Some	81	66	28	48	77	41	57	77	33	26	50	14
None	70	51	14	58	57	19	61	53	20	7	47	18
Republican contacts												
High	86	85	51	65	85	49	53[ns]	79	43	25	96	36
Some	79	72	31	52	78	38	60	67	34	41	71	34
None	73	51	18	48	58	23	55	64	25	11	44	17

Right group contacts												
High	98	82	78	72	78	44	36[ns]	99[ns]	83	49	99	34
Some	83	81	44	73	82	50	53	69	41	23	75	48
None	77	59	22	48	66	28	57	67	27	14	45	16
Democratic contacts												
High	66	85	51	43	78	53	36	78	46	24[ns]	74	44
Some	78	77	34	43	74	39	52	66	37	16	59	14
None	83	54	22	61	63	23	65	65	23	17	45	19
Left group contacts												
High	79[ns]	75	51	43[ns]	86	66	45	89	65	30[ns]	99	56
Some	75	79	43	47	85	49	42	74	50	21	55	32
None	80	60	25	56	64	26	62	64	22	14	46	13

Source: National Survey of Religion and Politics, University of Akron and Pew Forum on Religion & Public Life, 2004.

[a]Mean Republican vote for president
[b]Percentage turning out to the polls
[c]Percentage engaging in two or more political activities other than voting in 2004
[ns]Not significant at $p < .10$

As the table shows, Bush carried Evangelicals overwhelmingly, white Catholics by a comfortable margin, and white Mainliners by a thin edge. He also doubled his meager 2000 vote among African American Protestants. The turnout pattern was different, with Mainliners and Catholics voting a little more frequently than Evangelicals, who were still slightly above the national average and well ahead of their 2000 performance—just as Karl Rove hoped. African American Protestant turnout, on the other hand, slumped from 2000 and was well below the national figure. The 2004 campaign also produced considerable activism: almost one-third of Mainliners were quite active, followed by Catholics and Evangelicals a couple of percentage points back, and by African American Protestants at some distance.

Vote choice, turnout, and activism all varied by theological faction. First, religious traditionalists were very likely to vote for Bush and modernists for Kerry. More ominously for the Democrats, traditionalists voted, but modernists were the least likely to go to the polls. Activism varied by religious community: among Evangelicals, traditionalists were most active, joined by Mainline modernists and Catholic centrists. As this pattern hints, among Evangelicals, Bush supporters dominated activism; among Mainliners, it was Kerry backers; and among Catholics, Kerry activists had only a slight edge. Among African American Protestants (and other groups not shown on Table 7.3), Kerry activists swamped Bush enthusiasts, in both number and activity.

Did contacts have a role in producing these results? Certainly the bivariate data often suggest considerable impact. Among Evangelicals, for example, religious, GOP, and conservative interest group contacts all seem to favor Bush, while Democratic and (perhaps) liberal group contacts suppress his total. Among Mainliners, all the partisan and ideological contacts appear to push voters in the directions we expect, but religious contacts have a mixed impact. Among Catholics, all kinds of contacts seem to favor the Democrats, a strange result; as is the result for African American Protestants, where all contacts appear to help Bush although many of the results are not statistically significant.

As expected, virtually all communications stimulate turnout, although the impact of religious contacts seems largest in the three white traditions. The picture is even sharper for activism: all political contacts are associated with significantly increased involvement within each religious group. (This same pattern appears in Hispanic religious communities, among non-Christians, and among seculars.) We might surmise, then, that contacting has some influence on vote choice, more on turnout, and a great deal on activism.

Establishing the actual impact of political communications is more complicated. Voters' decisions for a particular candidate, to go to the polls, or to become active are shaped by myriad influences, including partisanship and ideology; political interest and knowledge; and personal traits such as income, education, age, and gender. For example, blandishments to vote for a candidate may reach only those already favorably disposed by partisanship and ideology, leading to the erroneous conclusion that the contacts produced the result. Similarly, reminders to vote inundate those already likely to do so because of political interest, previous involvement, or strong partisanship. Such factors must be held constant before we can conclude that religious, partisan, or interest group messages had an independent effect.

To sort out all these factors, we ran a series of multivariate analyses on vote choice, turnout, and political activism. We incorporated religious variables; the various contacts (religious and secular); partisanship and ideology; psychological engagement (political interest and knowledge); and social traits such as education, income, gender, and age. If religious or other contacts have an independent impact even when all other variables are taken into account, we can be confident of our findings.

Did contacting influence voters' choice of candidate in 2004? Our analysis suggests that it did not (data not shown). Not surprisingly, vote choice was dominated by partisanship and ideology, with strong GOP and conservative preferences outweighing their Democratic counterparts. Beyond that, only a few factors mattered: religious traditionalists were more likely to choose Bush while African American Protestants and non-Christian groups leaned toward Kerry. Interestingly, income, education, gender, and age added no significant explanatory power. None of the contacts influenced vote choice, although religious and liberal interest group contacts came closest ($p < .25$), in the expected directions. Whether the analysis was applied to the entire electorate, or to specific religious communities, the answer was the same. Clearly, contacts either went primarily to the political faithful or, when they did not, failed to change minds.[23]

Contacting had more impact on turnout. Table 7.4 reports on several multivariate analyses focusing on the mass public, the four largest religious traditions, and seculars. We have included the contacting measures; other factors that normally influence turnout, such as higher education, income, age, gender; psychological engagement (political interest and knowledge); and strength of partisanship and ideology. Finally, we included both religious traditionalism, to determine whether citizens' religious beliefs encouraged or discouraged turnout, and attendance at religious services on election weekend, to allow us to gauge the effect of religious contacts beyond the general stimulus produced by the social interaction there. As the dependent variable is dichotomous, we used logistic regression for the analysis. Positive coefficients indicate variables stimulating turnout, negative ones identify those suppressing it. As we have kept the full (and varying) range of scores for our independent predictors, we cannot compare the size of coefficients to indicate their relative power.

For the whole sample, psychological engagement had a significant effect, while better-educated, wealthier, and older citizens were also more likely to vote—as are women, when everything else is taken into account. Republicans of every level of commitment outvoted their Democratic

Table 7.4. Impact of Religious Contacts and Other Factors on Turnout in 2004
(logistic regression coefficients)

Groups	All respondents	Evangelical Protestants	Mainline Protestants	White Catholics	African American Protestants	Seculars
N =	2730	648	393	416	254	517
Religious traditionalism	-.006	-.190	.094	.213	-1.156[c]	.106
Attended election week	.406[b]	.556[a]	1.099[b]	-.140	-.087	1.586
Contacts						
Religious sources	.133	-.069	.578[a]	.430	-.095	-.124
Republican Party	.247[b]	.096	.375	.405	1.248[a]	.240
Conservative group	.153	.211	-.252	-.828	.906	.622
Democratic Party	.152	.472[a]	-.170	-.192	.010	.217
Liberal group	.179	-.025	.402	.474	-.221	.313
Party and ideology						
Strong GOP	.626[c]	.862[c]	.428[b]	.842[c]	.317	.833[c]
Strong conservative	.107	.092	.095	.315	.113	-.021
Strong Democrat	.411[c]	.661[c]	.306[a]	.394[a]	.235	.550[a]
Strong liberal	.145[a]	.240	.144	.369	-.151	.308[a]
Psychological engagement	.735[c]	.872[c]	.604[c]	1.320[c]	.890[c]	.577[c]
Social and demographics						
Education	.668[c]	.714[c]	.574[c]	1.045[c]	.393[a]	.705[c]
Income	.148[c]	.144[b]	.110	.063	.510[c]	.194[b]
Female	.289[b]	.433	.106	.381	.831[a]	.196
Age	.024[c]	.022[b]	.015	.036[c]	.012	.029[c]
Adj. R squared	.559	.595	.505	.655	.608	.596

Source: National Survey of Religion and Politics, University of Akron and Pew Forum on Religion & Public Life, 2004.

[a] $p < .05$
[b] $p < .01$
[c] $p < .001$

counterparts, although strong liberal ideology provided a little help for the latter. As we anticipated, church attendance just before election day also stimulated voting, but beyond that, religious contacting did not spur turnout. In fact, although all types of contact have coefficients in the right direction, only Republican messages bolstered the chances of voting once other factors were accounted for.

The story varies slightly within major religious communities. Psychological engagement and education were important for most groups, but the impact of other demographic variables differed. Republican partisanship encouraged turnout among Evangelicals, Catholics, and seculars but was weaker among Mainliners and African American Protestants, not quite reaching statistical significance among the latter. Democratic Party identification was less effective among the general public. Strong liberal identification was a significant force only among seculars. Finally, religious traditionalism was an insignificant factor—except for African American Protestants, for whom it was a deterrent to voting.[24]

The impact of church attendance the week prior to the election was notable in the large Evangelical community, more so among Mainline Protestants, and, surprisingly, evident even among seculars and nominals (few attended during election week, but those who did were much more likely to vote). Among Catholics and African American Protestants, however, presence at worship did not create additional incentives to vote. Religious contacts fostered higher turnout only among Mainliners and white Catholics (whose coefficient just misses statistical significance). Other contacts had only sporadic independent impact: interestingly, Democratic contacts moved more Evangelicals to the polls, and GOP contacts stimulated African American Protestant voting. But other contacts were ineffective in stimulating turnout, and their coefficients sometimes even move in the wrong direction. Indeed, only among seculars do most run in the right direction, but even here none significantly boosted the chances of voting.

All this is surprising, given the historic emphasis by interest groups and parties on contacting voters, as well as the emphasis on direct contact as a stimulus to voting found in experimental studies. A little further analysis suggests that contacting has an important, but less direct, impact on voter turnout than assumed in our model. Perhaps contacting increases political attention during the campaign, thereby increasing the likelihood that a citizen will go to the polls. Our political engagement variable uses one item tapped in our spring survey, before the campaign, asking how often the respondent talked about politics, and items tapping political knowledge, asked in the postelection survey and presumably not much influenced by the campaign.

If we add a variable to the equation about how closely the respondent followed the election campaign, we not only increase considerably our ability to predict voting, but we also discover an indirect effect of religious contacting: both regular church attendance (not just on election Sunday) and religious contacts increased citizens' attention to the campaign, even when their base level of psychological engagement is in the equation. In other words, religious contacts encouraged more attention to the campaign than would be expected on the basis of long-term political interest and knowledge. This was especially true for Evangelical Protestants and also true for Mainliners and Catholics. Interestingly, only church attendance had such an impact among African American Protestants. None of the party or interest group contact measures had any similar effect, either in the sample or in specific religious communities. Only among secular voters did all nonreligious contacts increase attention to the campaign. This finding strongly suggests that some of the impact of religious contacting seen in Table 7.3 is produced by increasing the political interest and attention of those contacted, an effect often abetted by regular church attendance.

If this argument is correct, we should find that contacting also stimulates other political activity. We calculated an activism scale based on six political activities: attending a political meeting, working for a candidate, donating money, attending a protest or demonstration, contacting a public official, or trying to persuade someone to vote for a candidate. Table 7.5 shows that religious and other political contacts explain part of that activism.

Across the entire sample, the following factors fostered activism: psychological engagement, strong partisanship (but only liberal ideology), higher education, and income. Religious traditionalism had a mild negative effect. Among the contacts, liberal interest groups had the largest impact, followed by religious sources, with Democratic and conservative group communications further behind but still significant. Only Republican contacts had no independent impact. Although psychological engagement universally encouraged activism, the rest of the picture is quite distinct for each religious community: Evangelicals were activated by religious contacts, strong Republican partisanship, and conservative interest groups—just the effect sought by Karl Rove. Note that for Evangelicals these factors obliterate the usual strong effects of education and income.

Mainline activism was fostered by education and strong Democratic loyalties and was discouraged by religious traditionalism, but religious contacts and liberal interest groups also stimulated activism in that theologically and politically divided community. A similar picture appears among white Catholics, although strength of ideology mattered more than partisanship for them. Once again, however, religious and liberal group contacting dominated, with the latter having a larger impact, perhaps reflecting the frequency of labor union and liberal ideological contacts among Catholics. As in the Evangelical case, Catholic activism in 2004 was not influenced by education and income.

African American Protestants exhibit a unique profile. For them, theological traditionalism was a major deterrent to activism, but regular church attendance worked powerfully in the other direction. Beyond those religious influences, only liberal interest group contact and personal income

Table 7.5. Impact of Religious Contacts and Other Factors on Political Activism (OLS regressions, standardized coefficients)

Groups	All respondents	Evangelical Protestants	Mainline Protestants	White Catholics	African American Protestants	Seculars
N=	2730	648	393	416	254	517
Religious traditionalism	-.061[b]	-.026	-.095[a]	-.016	-.194[b]	-.021
Usual church attendance	-.004	-.035	-.060	-.091	.278[c]	.008
Contacts						
Religious sources	.132[c]	.170[c]	.221[c]	.147[b]	-.030	.023
Republican Party	.035	.088[a]	.074	.018	-.045	-.032
Conservative group	.042[a]	.162[c]	.024	.054	-.116	-.006
Democratic Party	.090[c]	.053	.007	.043	-.021	.255[c]
Liberal group	.181[c]	.042	.158[c]	.231[c]	.279[c]	.155[c]
Party and ideology						
Strong Republican	.088[c]	.169[c]	.057	.023	-.013	.092[a]
Strong conservative	.006	-.014	.014	.109[a]	-.064	-.060
Strong Democrat	.065[c]	.037	.129[a]	.010	-.009	.160[c]
Strong liberal	.101[c]	.056	.048	.113[a]	.034	.150[c]
Psychological engagement	.279[c]	.260[c]	.259[c]	.333[c]	.110	.251[c]
Social and demographics						
Education	.071[c]	.066	.128[a]	.053	-.013	.123[b]
Income	.045[a]	.040	-.020	-.021	.296[c]	-.008
Female	.041[a]	.100[b]	.039	-.027	-.098	.044
Age	.002	.004	.016	-.004	.031	.079[a]
Adj. R squared	.306	.297	.292	.275	.173	.426

Source: National Survey of Religion and Politics, University of Akron and Pew Forum on Religion & Public Life, 2004.

[a] p <.05
[b] p <.01
[c] p <.001

(but not education) predicted activism. Finally, among seculars the story was simple: strong Democratic and liberal identifications bolstered by Democratic and liberal interest group contacts spurred activism, as did higher education and age.

Conclusions

Thus, religious contacting played an important role in 2004. The number of communications increased from previous presidential years, reaching many religious citizens, especially traditionalists, and compared quite favorably with those from secular sources. Religious contacts did not have a major impact on vote choice, but they certainly increased turnout, produced more interest in the campaign, and, especially, induced greater activism. And we can say with a few qualifications that religious group efforts generally favored the Republicans. What is the future for religious campaign activities?

First, we can be confident that they will continue, especially on the part of religious conservatives, if only because such tactics are now part of the institutionalized routines of many religious interest groups. If the past two presidential elections are any indication, religious liberals will also intensify their efforts to duplicate the strategies of the Christian right, thereby providing assistance to Democratic candidates.

Second, the specific techniques used by religious interest groups will continue to evolve with experience, changing technology, and new target audiences. For example, the oft-noted influence of the Democratic "blogosphere" during the 2004 election may well be duplicated by conservative religious counterparts, already credited with revolutionizing the internal politics of the Southern Baptist Convention, a vital linchpin in the Christian right.[25]

Finally, both political parties will seek to enhance their own capacities to appeal to religious citizens. In 2004 the White House and GOP clearly had the edge, but the Democratic Party is seeking to improve its own communication capacities with religious constituencies. Although neither the liberal religious groups nor the Democrats are likely to match the formidable machinery of Christian conservatives and the GOP, even modest improvements might have a crucial impact in a close race.

All in all, religious interest groups will continue to shape the contours of the electoral process, albeit in ever-changing ways, both cooperating and competing with the political parties and other interest groups.

Notes

1. For examples of Christian right activities, see Bob Louis, "Falwell Answers Critics by Offering Political Seminar," Associated Press, August 6, 2004; David D. Kirkpatrick, "Churches See an Election Role and Spread the Word on Bush," *New York Times*, August 9, 2004, sec. A; and Michael Foust, "iVoteValues Effort Registers 1,000s of Voters," *Baptist Courier*, November 18, 2004, 7.

2. The AU complaint is discussed in Rob Boston, "Church Service or Campaign Commercial?" *Church and State*, September 2004, 8–9; and Bill Broadway, "In Election Season, IRS Sits in Judgment," *Washington Post*, October 9, 2004, sec. B. The IRS commissioner later reported "a disturbing amount" of legally suspect political activity in churches; see David D. Kirkpatrick, "Pastors' Get-Out-the-Vote Training Could Test Tax Rules," *New York Times*, March 21, 2006, sec. A. Perhaps our 2004 survey of Southern Baptist pastors provides some notion of this activity from the perspective of pastors. Voter guides appeared in half their congregations, identical to the 2000 number. Forty-seven percent reported praying publicly for a candidate and over half reported endorsing a candidate in public, but very few did so from the pulpit. The use of guides, public prayers, and candidate endorsements were all most common among strong Republicans—half of all SBC pastors.

3. For Interfaith Alliance materials, consult the group's Web site, http://www.interfaithalliance.org/site/pp.asp?c=8dJIIWMCE&b=836427. For the Sojourners ad, see "God Is Not a Republican," *New York Times*, August 30, 2004, 17.

4. United States Conference of Catholic Bishops, *Faithful Citizenship: Civic Responsibility for a New Millennium and USCCB General Counsel Guidelines for Catholic Organizations* (Washington, D.C.: USCCB, 2004). For the voter guide issue, see Mindy Sink, "At Mass, Politics Squeezes into the Pews," *New York Times*, May 17, 2004, sec. A; Dennis Coday, "Election Guide Fever," *National Catholic Reporter*, September 24, 2004, 8; David D. Kirkpatrick and Laurie Goodstein, "Groups of Bishops Using Influence to Oppose Kerry," *New York Times*, October 12, 2004, sec. A; and Kathleen D. Mylott, "Bishops and Campaign 2004," *National Catholic Register*, January 2–8, 2005, 2.

5. For the GOP campaign, see Alan Cooperman, "Churchgoers Get Direction From Bush Campaign," *Washington Post*, July 1, 2004, sec. A; David D. Kirkpatrick and Michael Slackman, "Republicans Try to Expand Appeal to Religious Voters," *New York Times*, September 3, 2004, 11; Alan Cooperman and Thomas Edsall, "Evangelicals Say They Led Charge for the GOP," *Washington Post*, November 8, 2004, sec. A; and Keith Peters, "Grass-Roots Efforts Made a Difference in Vote 2004," *National Catholic Register*, November 11–December 4, 2004, 3.

6. David D. Kirkpatrick, "Black Pastors Backing Bush Are Rarities, but Not Alone," *New York Times*, October 5, 2004, sec. A, and Jim Dwyer and Jodi Wilgoren, "Gore and Kerry Unite in Search for Black Votes," *New York Times*, October 25, 2004, sec. A.

7. Julia Duin, "Kerry Advisers Tell Hopeful to 'Keep Cool' on Religion," *Washington Times*, June 18, 2004, 1; Matea Gold, "Democrats Are Trying to Make a Leap of Faith," *Los Angeles Times*, August 8, 2004, 1; "Democrats' Religious Director Quits," *National Catholic Register*, August 15–21, 2004, 2; "Kerry Church Vote Pitch Criticized," Associated Press, October 9, 2004; and David M. Halbfinger and David E. Sanger, "Kerry's Latest Attacks on Bush Borrow a Page from Scripture," *New York Times*, October 25, 2004, sec. A.

8. Katherine Q. Seelye, "Moral Values Cited as a Defining Issue of the Election," *New York Times*, November 4, 2004, 4. For more on religious voting patterns, see James L. Guth et al., "Religious Influences in the 2004 Presidential Election," *Presidential Studies Quarterly* 36 (June 2006): 223–242.

9. We surveyed a random sample of 4,000 adult Americans between February and April 2004. After the election, 2,730 of the original respondents were reinterviewed. The final data were weighted to match the demographic characteristics of the U.S. adult population. The survey was conducted by the Survey Research Center at the University of Akron, and cosponsored by the Pew Forum on Religion & Public Life, with additional support for the postelection portion from the Paul B. Henry Institute for the Study of Christianity and Politics at Calvin College and the William R. Kenan Jr. Endowment at Furman University.

10. For the 1996 and 2000 analyses, see James L. Guth et al., "Thunder on the Right? Religious Interest Group Mobilization in the 1996 Election," in *Interest Group Politics*, 5th ed., ed. Allan J. Cigler and Burdett A. Loomis (Washington, D.C.: CQ Press, 1998), 169–192; and James L. Guth et al., "A Distant Thunder? Religious Mobilization in the 2000 Elections," in *Interest Group Politics*, 6th ed., ed. Allan J. Cigler and Burdett A. Loomis (Washington, D.C.: CQ Press, 2002), 161–184.

11. For the concept of religious tradition, see David C. Leege and Lyman A. Kellstedt, eds., *Rediscovering the Religious Factor in American Politics* (Armonk: M.E. Sharpe, 1993); and John C. Green et al., *Religion and the Culture Wars* (Lanham, Md.: Rowman and Littlefield, 1996), chaps. 10, 13–14.

12. For the historic role of religious traditions in American party coalitions, see Mark Noll, ed., *Religion and American Politics: From the Colonial Period to the 1980s* (Oxford: Oxford University Press, 1990). For the contemporary situation, see Geoffrey C. Layman, *The Great Divide: Religious and Cultural Conflict in American Party Politics* (New York: Columbia University Press, 2001).

13. For the culture-wars thesis, see James D. Hunter's *Culture Wars: The Struggle to Define America* (New York: Basic Books, 1991).

14. For more detailed discussion, see Guth et al., "Religious Influences."

15. We do not expect numerous religious contacts among seculars, but we are interested in how parties and other interest groups may approach this group.

16. Perhaps Catholic churches lack the free time built into the schedules of African American Protestant, Evangelical, and even Mainline churches. Some scholars also suggest that Catholicism's historic de-emphasis of the laity may have depoliticizing effects. Or perhaps the larger size of the typical Catholic parish inhibits discussion. For observations on the impact of Protestant and Catholic churches on parishioner politics, see Sidney Verba, Kay Schlozman, and Henry E. Brady, *Voice and Equality: Civic Voluntarism in American Politics* (Cambridge: Harvard University Press, 1995), 320–330. For a valuable corrective and extension, see Paul A. Djupe and J. Tobin Grant, "Religious Institutions and Political Participation in America," *Journal for the Scientific Study of Religion* 40 (June 2001): 303–314.

17. The classic discussion of the two-step flow of communications is Elihu Katz and Paul F. Lazerfeld, *Personal Influence* (Glencoe, Ill.: Free Press, 1955). For political effects of membership, see Kenneth D. Wald, Dennis E. Owen, and Samuel S. Hill Jr., "Churches as Political Communities," *American Political Science Review* 82 (June 1988): 531–548.

18. For the early voter guides, see Marjorie Hershey and Darrell M. West, "Single-Issue Politics: Prolife Groups and the 1980 Senate Campaign," in *Interest Group Politics*, ed. Allan J. Cigler and Burdett A. Loomis (Washington, D.C.: CQ Press, 1983), 31–59.

19. Journalists seemed to find more such endorsements than our survey did: Robert D. McFadden, "On the Final Sunday, Sermons Pulse with the Power of Spiritual Suggestion," *New York Times*, November 1, 2004, sec. A; Josh Getlin, "Pulpits Ring with Election Messages," *Los Angeles Times*, November 1, 2004, 1.

20. For a provocative treatment of political mobilization in contemporary America, see Steven E. Schier, *By Invitation Only: The Rise of Exclusive Politics in the United States* (Pittsburgh: University of Pittsburgh Press, 2000).

21. Further analysis shows that one type of contact—from religious and moral-concerns groups—was much higher in such states, but other types were often less numerous.

22. For easy illustration, we define high activity as undertaking two political actions beyond voting. For the analysis in Table 7.5 we use the full scale.

23. Indeed, contacts did not even affect party attachments: although many voters shifted their party identification somewhat during the campaign, political contacts played no role in that change (data not shown).

24. This comports with previous studies of the African American church; see Fredrick C. Harris, *Something Within: Religion in African-American Political Activism*

(New York: Oxford University Press, 1999); Henry E. Brady, Sidney Verba, and Kay Lehman Schlozman, "Tilting Conservative: Religious Involvement, Political Issue Positions, and Political Participation in America" (presented at the annual meeting of the American Political Science Association, Washington, D.C., August 30–September 2, 2005).

25. K. Daniel Glover, "The Rise of Blogs," *National Journal,* January 21, 2006, 30–35. For bloggers' impact on the SBC, see John Pierce, "SBC Messengers Pick CP Supporter Frank Page as President," *Baptists Today,* July 2006, 15.

8

Interest Group Money in Elections

Marian Currinder, Joanne Connor Green,
and M. Margaret Conway

Federal election politics today rely on high-tech information gathering and timely communication with the electorate—all of which cost money. Candidates and parties seeking funds have found organized interests willing to contribute to those who share their policy views. Campaign spending by interest groups has escalated in recent years, and federal campaign finance laws have been largely ineffective in limiting the role of special-interest money in campaigns.

In this chapter, Marian Currinder, Joanne Connor Green, and M. Margaret Conway—documenting some of the most significant trends—examine the role of interest group money in federal elections. The authors focus on the rise of political action committees (PACs) as potent political forces, with PACs contributing both "hard" money directly to candidates and spending "soft" money to influence electoral outcomes. Although hard-money contributions have increased during each election cycle, the most spectacular increases (up more than 500 percent from 1991 to 2000) have been in soft money, a situation that ended in 2002 with reform in federal campaign legislation. Prior to 2002, soft money could be contributed in unlimited amounts, and six-figure contributions by companies, interest groups, and individuals were not unusual. It is difficult to assess how effective the 2002 reforms will be, but changes are certainly under way.

Finally, the authors examine some additional criticisms of campaign finance laws, evaluate the potential of suggested reforms, and highlight the increase in the amount of funds raised and spent outside the limits of federal law. The authors doubt that the recently enacted campaign finance reforms will be effective in achieving their goal of limiting the influence of group money in elections. At this point, it seems that group money is simply channeled into activities that remain outside of federal legal scrutiny.

In a democratic government, how do we help citizens communicate their policy preferences fairly and effectively? And how do we ensure that political parties and candidates can communicate their policy views to the electorate and mobilize supporters? Voting in elections and lobbying elected officials are two ways that citizens can articulate their preferences. Because of the key role of elections in democratic political systems, the electoral structure must prevent undue influence from any one set of groups or interests. And parties and candidates must have enough money to communicate and mobilize properly.

Running for office is expensive. In the early years of the republic, candidates tended to be part of the local elite and usually funded their own campaigns. Thus, when George Washington ran for office in 1757, he followed a standard electoral practice of that time and used his own money to purchase liquor for potential voters. Two decades later future president James Madison lost reelection to the Virginia legislature when he refused to follow that custom.[1]

After 1824 the creation of political parties that included regular citizens led to other methods of funding campaigns. Elected officials and parties used patronage (appointment of supporters) to fill nonelective public offices, with the understanding that a certain percentage of all officeholders' salaries would be contributed to the party to help fund the next campaign. Government contracts were also distributed on the basis of past and promised future support of the governing party, with the contract recipient expected to contribute to the officeholders and the party that granted the contract.

Objections to what the public viewed as political corruption led to federal and state laws limiting the use of patronage and preferments. The Civil Service Reform Act of 1883 and subsequent laws limited patronage first at the federal level and then in any state program receiving federal funding. One consequence was increased dependence on prominent business leaders and interest groups to fund campaigns. The Tillman Act, enacted in 1907 after a congressional investigation revealed large contributions from insurance companies to officeholders and candidates over several elections, prohibited corporations and national banks from contributing part of their income directly to candidates for federal office.

In the 1920s people began calling for new federal legislation after a Pennsylvania senatorial contest exceeded federal spending limits, Congress investigated candidate and party spending practices, and the Supreme Court ruled that limits on expenditures by federal candidates in primary elections were illegal. Demands for campaign finance reform increased during the 1924 Teapot Dome scandal, in which the secretary of the interior granted oil drilling rights on federal lands to a private company while receiving illegal contributions of $400,000. In response, Congress in 1925 enacted the Corrupt Practices Act. The act continued the ban on campaign contributions from banks and corporations, strengthened reporting requirements for campaign contributions and expenditures by federal candidates and party organizations, and raised the limit on how much could be spent in a campaign to a maximum of $5,000 for House of Representatives candidates and $25,000 for Senate candidates unless state law set lower limits. Enforcement was weak, however, and candidates' reports (filed with the Office of the Clerk of the U.S. House) were hard to access and were retained for only two years.[2]

Federal legislation to limit the influence of labor unions in federal elections, enacted temporarily by the Smith-Connally Act of 1943 and then permanently by the Taft-Hartley Act of 1947, prohibited union contributions to federal-level political organizations and candidates and expenditures from union dues on behalf of candidates for national office. The unions responded by creating political action committees (PACs), to which members donated money to support political candidates. The unions' desire to have political action committees legitimized by federal law was a major force behind the Federal Election Campaign Act (FECA) of 1971.

Federal Regulations After 1971

The Bipartisan Campaign Reform Act (BCRA) of 2002, the Federal Election Campaign Act of 1971 and its amendments of 1974, 1976, and 1979, and the Revenue Act of 1971 govern campaign finance primarily at the federal level. Also important are several court decisions interpreting federal laws as well as regulations and advisory opinions of the Federal Election Commission (FEC), which administers and enforces federal campaign finance laws. These laws have created several mechanisms for individuals and groups in order to fund federal campaigns.

To limit undue influence, individuals and most organizations are restricted in the amount of money they can give directly to a candidate or a political party in any year or two-year election cycle. These direct contributions are referred to as federal contributions, or "hard" money, as they pertain to the hard limit outlined in the statutes. The contribution limits for an individual are $2,000 per election to a candidate for federal office, $25,000 per year to the national political party committees, and $5,000 per election to a campaign committee. An individual may contribute no more than $95,000 in hard money in any one year to FEC-regulated PACs, national party organizations, and candidates for federal office.

Federal campaign finance laws give multicandidate committees—those contributing to five or more candidates for federal office—an advantage, whether they are independent or affiliated. A multicandidate committee (usually called a PAC) may give no more than $5,000 per candidate per election. Thus, a PAC may give a candidate up to $5,000 for a primary election, $5,000 for a runoff primary election if one is required, and $5,000 for a general election contest. There is no limit on how much a PAC may spend on *independent expenditures*—campaign efforts that are not coordinated in any way with the candidate, representatives of the candidate, or the candidate's campaign committee. Because PACs are able to raise and funnel large amounts to campaigns for federal office and to spend unlimited amounts of money in independent expenditures, the number of PACs has grown. Public concern about their influence on members of Congress has grown as well.

The 1974, FECA amendments permitted government contractors to establish PACs, thus greatly expanding the universe of businesses and labor unions eligible to use this form of political expression. The FEC's decision in April 1975 to permit corporations and labor unions to use their treasury funds to create PACs and to administer their activities, including soliciting funds from employees and stockholders, facilitated the establishment and operation of more PACs.[3] Authorization of the use of payroll deductions to channel funds to PACs was another boost.

Supreme Court decisions also stimulated the creation of PACs and PAC activities. In 1976, in *Buckley v. Valeo*, the Supreme Court indicated that the 1974 FECA amendments did not limit the number of local or regional PACs that unions or corporations and their subsidiaries could establish.[4] That decision also clarified the right of PACs to make independent expenditures on behalf of a candidate. The use of *issue advocacy*, in which a group or individual communicates about issues, is not regulated and need not be reported to the FEC. *Buckley* permits unlimited spending on issue advocacy so long as the ads do not explicitly advocate election or defeat of a candidate. Words such as "vote for, support, vote against" and "defeat" attached to a candidate's name are not permitted.[5] The Supreme Court made a clear distinction between discussing issues and candidates and advocating electoral victory or defeat.[6] PACs now prefer issue advocacy ads to independent expenditures on behalf of a candidate (independent expenditures are reported to the FEC, but issue advocacy ads are not).

In 1976 further amendments to FECA restricted labor union and corporation PAC contributions to one contribution in the amount of $5,000 per candidate per election, regardless of the number of PACs created by a corporation's divisions or subsidiaries or a labor union's locals. The process of clarifying what is permissible continues, with the FEC and other interested parties proposing amendments to laws and FEC advisory opinions.

FECA was amended again in 1979 to allow state and local parties to use unregulated soft money for grassroots activities tied to federal elections. Soft money was not subject to FECA regulations because it was to be raised and spent on party-building activities. And because soft money could be raised in unlimited amounts, it was particularly appealing to the parties. Shortly thereafter, the national party organizations sought and received permission to establish their own soft-money accounts. About two decades later, the soft-money loophole became the most controversial provision in the campaign finance law.

Congress approved its next major campaign finance overhaul in 2002, with the passage of the Bipartisan Campaign Reform Act. The BCRA's main objectives were to ban the national parties and congressional campaign committees from raising and spending soft money and to regulate preelection issue advertising by independent groups. The act also doubled the hard-money contribution limits for individuals, from $1,000 to $2,000 per candidate, per election. New limits were placed on individual contributions to the national, state, and local party committees as well. In any two-year election cycle, individuals are subject to an aggregate contribution limit of $95,000, of which no more than $37,500 can be given to candidates and no more than $57,500 can be given to all national party committees and PACs.

BCRA prohibits members of Congress, federal officials, and federal candidates from raising soft money for national, state, and local party organizations. They can, however, raise up to $20,000 for groups that are classified as 527 and 501(c) organizations, which are regulated by the Internal Revenue Service and can engage in federal election activities as long as they do not specifically advocate for the election or defeat of a candidate. These organizations—particularly the 527s—proved to be quite influential in financing the 2004 elections. These groups are not regulated by the FEC and can raise and spend soft money with few restrictions. With the passage of the BCRA, the soft-money loophole consequently became the "527 loophole."

The new law defines *electioneering communication* as broadcast, cable, or satellite advertisements that clearly refer to a federal candidate during the period within sixty days of a general election and thirty days of a primary election. The national, state, and local party organizations may spend hard money only on electioneering communications that attack or promote a federal candidate. Corporations and unions can engage in targeted electioneering communication, but only through their PACs.

Almost as soon as the BCRA became law, its constitutionality was challenged on First Amendment grounds (*McConnell v. FEC*). The U.S. District Court for the District of Columbia struck down the law's ban on soft money but upheld its restrictions on electioneering communications. The court issued a stay of its ruling, which kept the BCRA in effect as enacted while the law was under appeal at the Supreme Court. On December 10, 2003, the Supreme Court, in a 5–4 decision, upheld the constitutionality of the BCRA's key provisions. The BCRA's restrictions on soft money and on electioneering communications were thus validated.[7]

PACs

Although PACs existed before 1974, their numbers were limited and most were affiliated with labor unions. The first notable effect of changed laws and the FEC's interpretation of the laws was explosive growth in the number of corporate PACs (Table 8.1). Although labor union and corporate PACs have multiplied significantly, most do not raise and contribute large amounts of money. During the 2003–2004 campaign cycle, only 109 corporate PACs, out of the 1,756 registered, spent more than $500,000. In

Table 8.1. Number and Type of Political Action Committees, Selected Years from 1974 to 2006

Year	Corporate	Labor	Trade, membership, health	Independent	Cooperative	Corporation without stock	Total
1974	89	201	318				608
1976	433	224	489				1,146
1978	785	217	453	162	12	24	1,653
1980	1,206	297	576	374	42	56	2,551
1982	1,469	380	649	723	47	103	3,371
1984	1,682	394	698	1,053	52	130	4,009
1986	1,906	417	789	1,270	57	157	4,596
1988	2,008	401	848	1,345	61	169	4,832
1990	1,972	372	801	1,321	60	151	4,677
1992	1,930	372	835	1,376	61	153	4,727
1994	1,875	371	852	1,318	56	149	4,621
1996	1,836	358	896	1,259	45	134	4,528
1998	1,821	353	921	1,326	45	133	4,599
2000	1,548	318	844	972	38	115	3,835
2002	1,508	316	891	1,019	41	116	3,891
2004	1,538	310	884	999	35	102	3,868
2006	1,622	290	925	1,233	37	103	4,210

Source: Federal Election Commission, press release, February 23, 2006, http://www.fec.gov/press/press2006/20060223paccount.html.

Notes: For 1974 and 1976 the data for trade, membership, and health PACs include independent, cooperative, and corporation-without-stock PACs. On November 24, 1975, the FEC issued its "SUNPAC" advisory opinion. On May 11, 1976, FECA (Public Law 94-283) was enacted. All data are from the end of the year indicated from 1974 through 1998. Data for 2000 to 2006 are as of January 1 of the stated year.

fact 21 percent of all corporate PACs made no contributions to candidates in the 2004 election. Together thirty-six corporate PACs spent some $31.8 million. Fifty-seven of the 327 registered labor union PACs each spent $500,000 or more, and thirty-three contributed at least $500,000 to candidates. The fifty wealthiest labor PACs spent a remarkable $159.2 million. These PAC expenditures represent a dramatic increase from previous years. Corporate PACs raised $4.7 million more in 2004 than they did in 2002, while labor PACs raised $2.4 million more in 2004 than in 2002. In 2004, corporate PACs contributed $1.6 million more to candidates in 2004 than in 2002, but labor PACs contributed $1.8 million less.[8]

One basic distinction among PACs is between independent and affiliated PACs.

Affiliated PACs

Labor unions; corporations; cooperatives; and trade, health, and professional organizations create affiliated PACs. Each PAC is a separate, segregated fund that collects money to contribute to political campaigns, to use in independent expenditures for or against a candidate, or to sponsor campaign ads supporting or opposing a policy. Affiliated PACs get their funds from donations from individuals associated with the sponsoring organization. Corporations and labor unions are not allowed to make direct campaign contributions to their PACs from their treasuries, but they can use treasury funds to establish and administer a PAC and to communicate with people associated with the organization. For example, an affiliated corporate PAC may contact the corporation's employees or shareholders, and an affiliated labor union PAC may contact labor union members for such activities as communicating candidate endorsements or supporting voter registration drives.

The number of affiliated PACs has increased substantially since the 1970s. The largest increase occurred in corporate PACs, which jumped from 89 in 1974 to 1,622 in 2006, an increase of 1,822 percent (see Table 8.1). In contrast, PACs affiliated with trade associations, membership organizations, or health-related organizations grew more modestly, increasing from 318 in 1974 to 925 in 2006 (290 percent). PACs sponsored by labor unions increased from 201 in 1974 to 290 in 2006 (144 percent). 2006 marks the first year since 1980 that the number of registered labor PACs has dropped below 300.[9]

Independent PACs

After clarification of federal campaign finance law in 1976, independent (also called nonconnected) PACs were created. The number of independent PACs increased from 162 in 1978 to 1,233 in 2006, an increase of 761 percent. Officially independent of any organization, independent PACs include leadership PACs and issue, ideological, and type-of-candidate PACs.

Leadership PACs. Some federal politicians head leadership PACs independent of those politicians' individual campaign committees. Like other

PACs, leadership PACs receive donations from individuals and groups and then contribute to political candidates. Politicians can give candidates up to $1,000 per election out of their personal campaign committees and up to $5,000 per election out of their leadership PACs. Politicians with leadership PACs thus can give $12,000 to candidates facing primary and general elections; politicians without leadership PACs can give only $2,000. The number of leadership PACs registered with the FEC has grown considerably over the past two decades, as has the amount of money these PACs raise and contribute. In 1978 fewer than 10 leadership PACs contributed a total of $62,485; during the 2004 election cycle, 231 leadership PACs gave $27.9 million (73 percent of which was given to Republican candidates).[10]

Most leadership PACs are connected to members of Congress. Members typically use their leadership PAC funds to support both personal and party goals. Funds are used to pay for travel, political consultants, overhead, and other activities that may indirectly benefit the member's political fortunes. Leadership PAC funds also support party-building and party-maintenance activities. By contributing money to incumbent colleagues, promising nonincumbent candidates, and party campaign committees, members with leadership PACs assist in party efforts to gain or maintain majority status.

Members interested in keeping or securing formal leadership posts are more likely to give heavily to their colleagues across the board. Rep. Nancy Pelosi, D-Calif., who was vying to be the Democrats' whip in the 107th Congress (2001–2003), gave more leadership PAC money to her colleagues than any other member of Congress during the 2000 election cycle. In the subsequent Democratic House caucus election to replace Whip David Bonior, D-Mich., Pelosi defeated Rep. Steny Hoyer, D-Md., by twenty-three votes.[11] Pelosi then went on to become House minority leader when Rep. Richard Gephardt, D-Mo., retired to enter the 2004 Democratic presidential primaries. In 2003–2004, Pelosi contributed $624,500 out of her leadership PAC to colleagues and candidates for office. Steny Hoyer, who became minority whip when Pelosi became minority leader, contributed $792,500 in leadership PAC funds during the 2004 election cycle.

Even when there is little or no competition in leaders' home districts, most leaders are able to consistently raise millions of dollars. The ability to attract huge amounts of campaign money allows leaders to help other candidates and foster colleague support and loyalty. During the 2003–2004 election cycle, Speaker of the House J. Dennis Hastert, R-Ill., contributed $841,500, former House majority leader Tom DeLay, R-Texas, contributed $980,278, and House majority whip Roy Blunt, R-Mo., contributed $712,039. Rep. John Boehner, R-Ohio, who replaced Tom DeLay as majority leader in 2006, contributed $715,847. Tom DeLay contributed more money out of his leadership PAC in 2003–2004 than any other member of the House and Senate.[12] Other members may contribute on a more selective basis and give to candidates who can help them achieve their specific leadership goals. Committee and subcommittee chairpersons who face leadership challenges may give to members of their own panels to secure their support.

Issue, Ideological, and Type-of-Candidate PACs.   During the past decade, there has been a dramatic increase in another category of independent PACs—those that support a particular ideology, type of candidate, or issue. Examples include the Americans for a Republican Majority, the Campaign for Working Families, the Human Rights Campaign Fund Political Action Committee, and EMILY's List. EMILY's List is the most successful of the PACs supporting female candidates. The name is an acronym derived from "Early Money Is Like Yeast"—it makes the dough rise. Founded in 1985 by Ellen Malcolm to fund Democratic, pro-choice female candidates, the PAC has raised great sums of money. Its endorsed candidates have high rates of electoral success, in part because EMILY's List is careful in its choice of whom to endorse. Perhaps not unexpectedly, EMILY's List has been criticized for not endorsing more candidates who might have lower probabilities of electoral success.

Supporters of EMILY's List are expected to contribute $100 per year to the organization and to make at least two $100 contributions to female candidates for Congress or for statewide office who have been endorsed by EMILY's List. The contribution checks are made out to the candidate's campaign fund and mailed to EMILY's List headquarters, which bundles together the checks for each candidate and forwards them to the candidate. This practice, known as "bundling," is widely used by PACs. Therefore, when PACs practice bundling, the amount of money contributed to a candidate by a political action committee may significantly underrepresent the hard-money contributions stimulated by the PACs' activities.

In 1986, EMILY's List raised more than $350,000 for two Senate candidates. In 1990, PAC members, using the bundling technique, donated $1.5 million to fourteen candidates. During the 2003–2004 election cycle, EMILY's List bundled $10.7 million for women candidates, receiving that money from more than 100,000 EMILY's List members. According to reports filed with the FEC, EMILY's List spent $34 million during the 2003–2004 election cycle (up from $22.8 million in the 2001–2002 cycle), thus ranking third among PACs in total receipts and expenditures. A substantial part of that was spent to educate and mobilize women voters in states where EMILY's List had endorsed Democratic female candidates seeking election as governor, U.S. senator, or U.S. representative or as candidates for state and local offices.[13]

Funneling and Bundling

PACs are very creative in allocating resources. One strategy is bundling, when PACs collect checks made out to particular candidates and then send each candidate the checks all at once. Another type of bundling is hosting a fund-raiser for a candidate. These fund-raisers bring together groups interested in the politician's future. One example is the insurance industry's meet-and-greet event for congressional challenger Greg Walden in 1998. The event took place at an exclusive French restaurant near Capitol Hill. Another example is the breakfast sponsored by Florida citrus growers for Rep. Dan Miller, R-Fla., the week after Walden's fund-raiser. The list of such events is long.[14]

Many PACs bundle contributions from supporters, presenting individual contributions en masse to candidates. In 2003–2004, a large amount of money was presented in bundles from a variety of sources. Some groups, like EMILY's List, gave money only to candidates from one party; others donated to candidates from both parties. Morgan Stanley, for example, bundled nearly $600,000 to the reelection campaign of President Bush. MBNA bundled money for both Democratic and Republican candidates for both the House and the Senate. EMILY's List supports only Democratic women who are pro-choice; the Club for Growth supports only Republican candidates who support lower taxes and limited governmental expenditures. Although the groups clearly have different agendas, they are successful in employing the bundling technique to augment support they can provide to candidates.[15]

In addition to bundling money, PACs also funnel money by giving money to other PACs or to the political parties, from which they also can receive money. A few PACs have begun steering other PACs' contributions. These *lead PACs* analyze elections and candidates and provide information to other PACs with similar goals.[16] The Business Industry Political Action Committee (BIPAC), for example, studies candidates' records and electoral prospects and serves as a cue for other probusiness PACs and corporations. When BIPAC announces its support for a candidate, it is attesting to the candidate's probusiness credentials. BIPAC's Web page states that, for every $1 BIPAC contributes to a candidate, $92 has been tracked to come from the business community.[17] PACs also give money to other PACs with similar policy agendas.

By examining the PACs that spent the most money in the 2000 election cycle (the Political Victory Fund of the National Rifle Association [NRA] and EMILY's List), we can see different patterns in resource allocation. The NRA Political Victory Fund spent $16.8 million in the 1999–2000 election cycle. Of this, $6.46 million was independent expenditures and $1.78 million was donated to candidates, party organizations, and other PACs. The group spent more than $2 million on behalf of George W. Bush and more than $500,000 on behalf of John Ashcroft (then a Republican senator and Senate candidate in Missouri who, after losing the election, was appointed attorney general in the George W. Bush administration). The PAC donated $97,350 to Republican Party committees (both state and local) and $10,150 to Democratic Party organizations. It donated varying amounts to 284 candidates of both parties in 2000. Additionally, $115,300 went to other PACs.

EMILY's List expenditures were very different.[18] This PAC disbursed $14.7 million in hard money in 2000, contributing almost $1.6 million to candidates, parties, and other PACs. Unlike the NRA's Political Victory Fund, which spent $6.46 million on independent expenditures, EMILY's List allocated only $21,478 to independent expenditures. EMILY's List targeted direct contributions to only thirty-four candidates, all of them Democratic women who support abortion rights. Furthermore, EMILY's List donated more money to the Democratic Party committees ($150,000) than the NRA's PAC gave to both parties ($107,500). EMILY's List transferred less than the NRA Political Victory Fund to other PACs ($26,000 compared with $115,300) but spent more than $6.7 million in nonfederal soft-money expenditures; the NRA's PAC spent none. EMILY's List typically engages in issue advocacy, spending more than $3 million in twenty-six targeted states in 1998 on 8 million direct mailings and 2 million telephone calls to 3.4 million women.[19]

Patterns of PAC Contributions

During the 2003–2004 election cycle, PACs operating at the federal level raised $915.7 million (up 34 percent over 2002) and spent $842.9 million, up 28 percent over 2001–2002. Of the funds spent, $310.5 million went to candidates for federal office (up 10 percent from 2001–2002), 79 percent went to incumbents, 7 percent went to candidates challenging incumbents, and the rest went to candidates for open seats. PACs' overwhelming financial support for incumbent members of Congress is one reason why they are rarely defeated in their bids for reelection.

Representatives are more dependent on PAC contributions than are senators. In the 2003–2004 election cycle, PACs spent almost $310 million on congressional races. House candidates received $231.4 million from PACs, while Senate candidates received $76.1 million. Republican candidates received $176 million, an increase of 21 percent from the previous cycle, while Democrats received $134.3 million—2 percent less than in 2002.[20]

PAC Decision Making

Influences on PAC decisions regarding campaign contributions include:

- Goals of the PAC.
- Expectations of contributors.
- Official positions of decision makers.
- Location (Washington, D.C., location compared with other locations).

- Strategy of the PAC.
- Competitive position of the PAC.[21]

Interest groups have several strategies available to them, and the impact of these strategies may be difficult for outside observers to assess.[22]

An organization may follow a *maintaining strategy* to preserve access to certain legislators, or it may follow an *expanding strategy* to gain access to additional legislators. These legislators would not normally be receptive to the PAC's interests because of the demographic characteristics of the legislators' constituencies. The results of the limited research on this topic suggest that PACs generally emphasize a maintaining strategy, with only one-third of contributions representing an expanding strategy.[23] Individual PACs also tend to be more responsive to the needs of vulnerable representatives and senators who have befriended the PAC's interests.[24]

PAC decision-making patterns vary. If the PAC has staff based in Washington, that staff tends to play a greater role in deciding who gets contributions and how much they get. Contributions are also more likely to occur through a Washington-based fund-raising event.[25] PACs whose local affiliates raise most of the PAC's money tend to follow the more parochial concerns of the local groups. But these tendencies may not be the most rational allocation strategies. PACs should allocate funds either to strengthen or broaden access or to replace opponents, but parochialism may require that an already supportive member of Congress receives substantial locally raised funds.[26] The degree of parochialism appears to vary by type of PAC—for example, defense-interest PACs are more locally oriented than labor-interest PACs.[27]

Partisanship and ideology also may influence PAC decision making— for example, defense PACs tend to be less ideological in their contribution decisions than labor, oil, and auto PACs.[28] Business PACs vary in the extent to which they pursue a partisan support strategy; usually this is associated with the vulnerability of a political party's incumbents. When political tides appear to be favoring Republicans, business PACs may contribute more to Republican challengers than when the political climate is less favorable.

Incumbents' voting records may be another major factor in contribution decisions. An incumbent who voted against legislation that a PAC considered vitally important would be unlikely to receive a campaign contribution. But there are exceptions. Some PACs will contribute to candidates who oppose them in the hope of minimizing the intensity or frequency of the opposition. F. L. Davis found this factor to be statistically significant; R. L. Hall and F. W. Wayman also suggest some PACs attempt to minimize the opposition.[29] One study of PACs affiliated with Fortune 500 companies found voting records on key legislation to be the second most frequently cited criterion in making contribution decisions; the most frequently cited was the candidate's attitude toward business.[30] NARAL Pro-Choice America (a national pro-choice organization) usually gives money to Democratic candidates, but it has given money to pro-choice Republicans. Likewise, the NRA usually contributes money to Republican candidates, but it will also contribute money to Democratic candidates who advocate gun rights. The National Association of Realtors (which contributed over $4 million in 2004 to candidates for Congress) contributes nearly equal amounts to Democrats and Republicans but will contribute only to those who support its policy agenda.[31]

Some research suggests that corporate PACs' decisions about whether and to whom to contribute are also influenced by the size of the company's federal contracts, the company's size, and whether the federal government regulates the company's business.[32] The jurisdictions of committees on which incumbent members serve influence contribution decisions by both corporate and labor PACs,[33] but some research indicates committee jurisdiction is more relevant in decisions regarding House incumbents than Senate incumbents.[34] Some PACs also must be concerned about competition for supporters. Contributions that would leave the PAC open to criticism and thus endanger future support from donors must be avoided. Independent PACs that raise funds through mass mail solicitations must be particularly wary.[35]

Another factor that affects PAC contributions is concern about influence with key holders of power. If PAC Y gives to a member of Congress and PAC X does not, will that affect PAC X's access to that member? Although some PACs act as though it would, others could pursue a different strategy: giving to the challenger, with the hope that the incumbent might become more attentive. The effectiveness of that strategy would be limited by the extent to which the PAC's preferred policy outcomes conflict with the strength of a contrary ideology held by a member of Congress or by the intensity of support for a different policy position in that member's constituency.

Independent Expenditures

Remember that independent expenditures are expenditures made by individuals, organized interests, and party committees to support or oppose candidates for federal office, but they are in no way coordinated with candidates' campaigns. The first widely documented use of independent spending was in 1980 when the National Conservative Political Action Committee (NCPAC) spent more than $1 million to defeat several Democratic senators. Democrats who supported the 1978 Panama Canal Treaty were targeted specifically and subject to negative advertising. Four of the targeted senators lost their bids for reelection, allowing NCPAC to claim credit for helping the Republicans secure a Senate majority for the first time since 1954. Other PACs followed suit and independently spent millions of dollars during the 1982 and 1984 elections to support or oppose candidates for federal office.[36]

Since the 1980 elections, the amount of independent spending related to federal elections has varied considerably. In 1990, independent expenditures in House races were just under $2 million. Two years later independent expenditures in House races totaled more than $4 million. In 1994 this figure dropped to $2.1 million, then jumped to $4.8 million in 1996. By 2000, independent spending on House races came in at just less than $8 million. In 2004, PAC independent expenditures totaled $6.4 million in House races and $7.5 million in Senate races. PACs devoted the majority of their independent expenditures in 2004 to the presidential race, where they spent $43.5 million.[37]

Why is independent spending erratic from one election to the next? Because it can backfire. Political advertisements bought with independent money tend to be more negative and thus can work against the candidate the ad supports. In 1982 NCPAC ran 1,000 "attack" television ads against Sen. John Melcher, D-Mont. Melcher responded by running an ad accusing NCPAC of coming from outside the state and trying to influence the Montana vote. Being the subject of attack ads helped Sen. Paul Sarbanes, D-Md., raise money nationwide for his 1982 campaign. Both senators were reelected.[38]

Another way for groups to advocate the election or defeat of a federal candidate is through internal communications. Labor unions, membership organizations, and other associations can spend unlimited amounts on communicating political messages to their members. Only communications that directly endorse a candidate must be disclosed to the FEC, so it is difficult to determine exactly how much groups spend communicating with their members. David Magleby reports that in 2000 groups dedicated $10.2 million to internal communications, more than half of which was spent (mostly by labor unions) advocating for the election of presidential candidate Al Gore. For groups with large membership bases, internal communications can be particularly effective. The U.S. Chamber of Commerce, for example, joined forces in 2000 with local and state chambers of commerce—a move that provided access to 3 million businesses for internal communications. Much of the $15 million in expenditures the chamber reported for 2000 was for member communications.[39] Internal communications play an increasingly important role in political campaigns mainly because they come from trusted sources and can reach large numbers of potential voters.

Another relatively recent trend in interest group spending is to endow academic chairs at universities in honor of members of Congress or, even more prestigious, name an institute after a politician. The law allows interest groups to make tax-deductible donations, which often garner attention. One example is the Trent Lott Institute at the University of Mississippi (the alma mater of Senator Lott, R-Miss.), to which MCI WorldCom was a large donor. MCI has a large vested interest in telecommunications legislation. Following MCI's contribution to the institute, Senator Lott (majority leader at the time) named an MCI representative to a commission that was considering the question of taxing the Internet.[40]

Favoring contributors is not limited to members of Congress; the executive branch has a long tradition of rewarding political supporters with appointed positions. Ambassadorships are perhaps the most notorious rewards for loyal service. In his first year in office, former president Bill Clinton named five $100,000-plus Democratic donors to ambassadorships. Of President George W. Bush's ambassadors, 38 percent (fourteen of thirty-seven) donated more than $100,000 to the Republican Party or to Republican candidates. President Bush also named three of his top fund-raisers to cabinet secretary posts: Tom Ridge to Homeland Security, Elaine Chao to Labor, and Don Evans to Commerce. In fact, Bush appointed one-third of his 2000 campaign's top fund-raisers or their spouses to agency positions, advisory committees, or ambassadorships.[41]

These strategies have triggered concern among scholars, journalists, and many political leaders about the role of PACs in federal campaign funding. PACs may have enormous influence, affecting who is viewed as a viable candidate, the outcomes of elections, and access to policy making. Because PACs have become a major source of campaign funds for congressional candidates, an inability to obtain PAC support may mean a candidate cannot afford to run an effective campaign. If elected, the successful candidate must be ever mindful of campaign funding sources, both past and future. The escalating costs of congressional and senatorial campaigns force incumbent legislators to be watchful of how policy positions and votes might affect their campaign fund raising.

Soft Money

Soft money, also referred to as nonfederal money, falls beyond FECA's statutory limitations and is thus very controversial. Although the money is officially raised to support party building, there is no denying that the expenditures affect individual candidacies and campaigns. Reform advocates had long expressed concern over the soft-money loophole in campaign finance law, and in 1996 they finally found a receptive audience. Lawmakers and regulators alike were astounded by the extensive use of soft money in the 1996 presidential race between Bill Clinton and Bob Dole. During the 1992 election, the parties raised a combined total of $86.1 million in soft money; by 1996, that figure had tripled to $262 million. Soft money provided the parties with a way to pay for issue advertising, which was increasingly perceived as an effective way to promote party candidates and agendas. Court decisions had allowed these ads to be financed with soft money as long as they steered clear of language that urged voters to vote for or against a candidate.

This precedent was established when the U.S. District Court in the western district of Virginia ruled that interest groups could spend soft money on issue advocacy so long as they did not violate the *Buckley* standard (which mandates that the ads must not explicitly try to influence voting).[42] In the case that established the soft-money precedent, the Christian Action Coalition ran ads two weeks before the 1992 presidential election; the ads negatively and forcefully opposed Democratic candidate Bill Clinton's "militant" stance on homosexual rights. The court ruled that the ads were advocating an issue position, not explicitly trying to defeat Clinton's candidacy.

Four years later, in *Colorado Republican Federal Campaign Committee v. FEC* (1996), the Supreme Court ruled that political parties were allowed to spend money on behalf of candidates without using hard money.[43] That same year the FEC charged the Christian Coalition with violating federal law by using issue ads to benefit the Republican Party and its candidates. The case was dismissed. The Court ruled that advocacy was considered illegal only when a group substantially negotiates with the candidate or party. This ruling opened the door to the growing use of soft money to fund issue advocacy.[44] The clear pattern in federal court decisions is to apply a very strict standard for issue advocacy, in which the ads must unambiguously and explicitly urge voters to vote for or against a candidate to be considered a coordinated expense.[45]

As a direct consequence of these rulings, the use of soft money for issue advocacy in elections grew at an incredible rate. In 1996 organized labor engaged in interest group election advocacy in forty-four congressional elections. Business groups countered with issue advocacy.[46] The groups targeted their support on the basis of candidates' issue stances. Steve Forbes, a candidate for the Republican presidential nomination, established Americans for Hope, Growth, and Opportunity in 1997 to generate grassroots support for his flat tax and school choice proposals. The PAC raised more than $13 million to spend on issue advocacy. In 1998 PACs began to allocate their resources more strategically, targeting districts with very competitive races.[47]

The surge in soft-money fund raising and issue advertising forced regulators to rethink their ability to control campaign spending. Candidates were increasingly relying on party soft-money expenditures to supplement their campaigns, and parties were increasingly relying on candidates to help them raise soft money. Candidates, parties, and interest groups could claim that they were acting within the law because FECA provided no guidelines for regulating these nonfederal funds. Despite repeated requests from reform advocates for tighter regulations, the FEC failed to issue new guidelines; as a result, soft-money fund raising continued to grow at unprecedented rates. During the 2000 elections, the parties raised a combined total of $495 million in soft money (42 percent of total party receipts in 2000).

As candidates and parties became increasingly reliant on soft money, more and more independent groups began to climb aboard the soft-money bandwagon. Many of these groups spend soft money on television and radio advertisements for or against candidates. In addition, groups generated grassroots support by contacting individuals directly and using phone banks and direct mail to mobilize voters.[48] For example, the AFL-CIO spent between $18 million and $19 million on issue advocacy in 1998 to defeat Republican candidates. The group mailed 9.5 million pieces of direct mail, made 5.5 million telephone calls, and spent a reported $5 million on television and radio issue advocacy.[49] The Business Roundtable, an organization of large U.S. companies, spent a reported $5 million to generate opposition to the Patients' Bill of Rights, managed-care reforms, and environmental regulations in 1998.[50] U.S. Term Limits spent $11.6 million to build support for term limits in 1998.[51] More recently, in the 2004 elections, a number of pro–Democratic Party 527 groups used sophisticated technology to collect information about voters' issue positions. They then shared this information with Democratic candidates who used it to target voters.

In 2004, issue advocacy spending by independent groups was most evident on television. America Coming Together, a pro-Democratic 527 group, raised more than $125 million; and the Media Fund, another pro-Democratic 527, raised $50 million to spend on broadcast advertising. Two pro-Republican 527 groups, Progress for America and Swift Boat Veterans for Truth, raised $50 million and $7 million, respectively. Overall spending by advocacy groups during the 2004 elections came in at just over $435 million.

Some PACs also spend money on campaign services, similar to what political parties offer, by providing extensive in-kind contributions. Paul Herrnson reports that some PACs provide polling, media, and research services to candidates.[52] Some PACs are even providing campaign consultants. The National Committee for an Effective Congress provided Democrats in a few marginal districts advice on voter mobilization and targeting. Issue PACs sometimes train workers and lend them to candidates. The Human Rights Campaign holds campaign-training seminars to train volunteers and then sends the volunteers out to work for specific candidates.[53] The National Association of Realtors' PAC, the American Medical Association's PAC, and the AFL-CIO's PAC often give polling data to candidates.[54]

Interest groups are also funding parties' national conventions. Over 140 largely corporate contributors gave at least $100,000 to the national political party conventions in 2004. According to the Campaign Finance Institute, donations in the amount of $35 million—or more—were received by the two convention committees (21 donations by the Republican and 14 donations by the Democrats).[55] According to the Center for Responsive Politics, three corporations gave $1 million to each party's convention. The American International Group donated $2 million for the Democratic convention (and $500,000 to the Republicans).[56] Groups do not stop their expenditures with direct contributions; they also provide services and host fund-raisers. For example, AT&T was the "official long-distance service provider" at the Democratic national convention. In addition to installing new phone lines, AT&T handed out free calling cards. At the Republican national convention, where AT&T was the "official wireless service provider," company representatives handed out 500 free cell phones to Republican officials.[57]

Such activities were not unique to the 2004 conventions. For example, at the 2000 Republican convention, then-House whip Tom DeLay raised $1 million to lavish Republican House members with chauffeured cars, concierge services, hospitality lounges, and lush parties.[58] One corporate party at the Republican national convention cost $500,000; three others cost $400,000. At the Democratic convention, the NRA, Philip Morris Corporation, and UST Inc. sponsored a party for "Blue Dog" Democrats (an organization of conservative Democrats in Congress) at the Santa Monica Pier amusement park; it featured musical entertainment by Patty Loveless, food, and rides. Bristol-Myers Squibb Company and Merck and Co. (both drug makers) were gold sponsors of a $400,000-plus party, "Mardi Gras Goes Hollywood," given by Sen. John Breaux, D-La.[59] Corporate sponsors of these parties have or will have policy concerns before Congress.[60]

In addition to funding party conventions, interest groups are increasingly funding presidential inaugurations. President Bush's second inauguration represented an additional opportunity for individuals and groups to show their support. The inaugural committee capped contributions at $250,000, and more than 50 individuals or groups gave this amount, earning them the title of underwriters. More than 90 sponsors gave $100,000. United Parcel Service, for example, donated $250,000.[61] Over 200 large donations, largely from corporations, raised more than $25 million to offset the cost of the celebration. Some scholars and journalists are concerned that these contributions to the conventions and inauguration are designed to bypass federal law and that they raise ethical concerns. Others state that contributions provide groups and corporations ways to express their civic pride and patriotism.

In 1998 the amount of soft money raised by both parties declined (Table 8.2). More interest groups in 1998 spent money on issue advocacy than on soft-money contributions. Hard-money contributions remained high because they are considered important in influencing individual races. Record amounts of soft and hard money were raised in the 2000 election cycle. In fact, the two major political parties raised a total of $495 million in soft money in 1999–2000. In 2002, the last election cycle in which the parties could raise and spend soft money, Republicans and Democrats raised a combined total of $496.1 million in soft money and $658.8 in hard money. But the ban on party soft money did not mean less money in the bank for the parties: between January 2003 and October 2004, the national party committees raised a combined total of more than $1 billion and spent about $875 million. Incredibly, the hard-money totals for 2004 were greater than the combined hard- and soft-money totals raised in any previous campaign.[62]

Table 8.2.   Political Party Hard- and Soft-Money Contributions, 1991–2004 (in millions of dollars)

Election cycles	Hard money	Soft money[a]
1991–1992	445	86.1
1993–1994	384.7	101.6
1995–1996	438.1	162.1
1997–1998	445	224.4
1999–2000	741	495.1
2001–2002	658.8	496.1
2003–2004	784.8	—[b]

Sources: Federal Election Commission, January 12, 2001, http://fecweb1.fec.gov/press/011201party funds.htm; "Party Financial Activity Summarized for the 2004 Election Cycle," Federal Election Commission, March 14, 2005, http://www.fec.gov/press/press2005/20050302party/Party2004 final.html.

[a]Includes only national party soft money.
[b]Soft money was prohibited in the 2003–2004 election cycle.

Relations between Political Parties and Interest Groups

The relationship between parties and PACs is complex. On one hand, parties see PACs as competing with them for scarce resources—campaign dollars. The parties have reacted with concern to the large amounts interest groups spend on issue advocacy. Parties appeal to donors by claiming the need to offset interest group expenditures.[63] On the other hand, parties often see PACs as allies to help advance party causes. For example, Americans for Tax Reform (which has ties to the former chair of the Republican National Committee, Haley Barbour) received $4.6 million from the Republican National Committee during the 1996 election to articulate the Republican tax reform policies. The Democratic National Committee donated several hundred thousand dollars to the Rainbow Coalition and the A. Philip Randolph Institute to generate interest among supporters for the committee's policy agenda.[64] Interest groups contributed $495 million in soft money to federally registered party organizations in 2000 ($245.2 million to Democrats and $249.8 million to Republicans).[65]

In the mid-1990s several Republican leaders invoked an aggressive, and sometimes hostile, relationship with PACs and lobbyists as retribution for what the leaders felt were unfairly high contributions from PACs to Democrats when that party was in power. In 1994, House whip Tom Delay refused to meet with any lobbyists who didn't contribute money to Republicans. His hardball approach was termed the "K Street strategy" (many large lobbying firms have their offices on K Street in Washington, D.C.).[66] The K Street project was an aggressive program designed to induce corporations and interest groups to hire Republican-oriented lobbyists, to support Republican-endorsed legislation, and to increase contributions to Republican candidates for Congress. In 1998 Republican leaders in the House refused to meet with lobbyists from the Electronic Industries Alliance after a Democrat took the helm of the organization. John Linder (then chair of the National Republican Congressional Committee) confirmed to *Roll Call* (a newspaper on Capitol Hill) that GOP leaders were blocking legislation important to the Electronic Industries Alliance.[67] Linder also reported that the leadership was not pleased that the National Association of Home Builders (a large and powerful organization) had hired a Democrat as its chief executive. After scandals in 2005–2006, Republican leaders stated they would abandon this strategy.

Interest Groups, Lobbyists, and Campaign Finance

Interest groups play a significant role in congressional campaign fund raising. Controversy exists as to whether their fund-raising activities are designed to reward members of Congress for past support, to induce future support, or to enhance future access. Relationships between some members of Congress and lobbyists have resulted in scandals, criminal charges, and even criminal convictions of both members of Congress and lobbyists. In extreme cases, members have been forced to resign not only from their leadership positions but also from Congress. One of the most recent, and now most notorious, lobbying scandals involves Jack Abramoff, whose close associations with several members of Congress and congressional staff members led to conspiracy, fraud, and tax evasion convictions. Abramoff was closely associated with former House majority leader Tom DeLay and his K Street project.[68] Although scandals such as those involving Abramoff and DeLay are for the most part atypical, public scrutiny compelled Congress to draft new laws regulating lobbying practices and campaign finance.[69]

Despite these recent attempts to reform lobbying practices on Capitol Hill, lobbyists continue to play a major role in raising money for congressional reelection campaigns. One business lobbyist kept every invitation he received to congressional fund-raising events in January 2006. He received more than sixty and sent checks to most members of Congress who solicited funds despite never having asked more than half of them for assistance on legislation benefiting his clients.[70] In addition to hosting the usual receptions where checks are expected from those who attend, members of Congress extract contributions from lobbyists in a number of ways. Rep. Michael G. Oxley, R-Ohio, chairman of the Financial Services Committee, formed a book club. Each month a junior member of the committee would select a book on finance and distribute copies to lobbyists. The price of admission to the club was a financial contribution to that month's featured junior committee member. Because membership in the book club provided lobbyists face time with Oxley, lobbyists felt compelled to attend the club's meetings. One lobbyist, perhaps speaking for the majority, commented "I've never read one of the books. Are you kidding me? Read? I went to law school."[71]

Another unique plan for extracting campaign funds from lobbyists was recently organized by Rep. Joe Barton, R-Texas, chairman of the Energy and Commerce Committee. Lobbyists were invited to ride along on an eight-hour train trip from Fort Worth to San Antonio at a cost of $2,000 per lobbyist and $5,000 per PAC. The day before the Senate debated a major asbestos bill, lobbyists for both sides of that issue were invited to a birthday party for Sen. Arlen Specter, R-Pa., chairman of the Judiciary Committee. Individuals were charged $500 to attend, and PACs were charged $1,000. Senator Specter stated that no special group had been targeted in the invitation list.[72]

Members of Congress justify such fund-raising efforts by pointing to the ever increasing costs of campaigns although few members of the House run for reelection in highly contested districts. In 2004, only 8 percent of incumbents (thirty-seven House members) faced a close contest for reelection.[73] By raising substantial campaign funds, incumbents discourage challengers and thus reduce the probability of serious threats to their reelection. Even some conservative lobbyists suggest that the answer to the campaign finance crisis is federal funding of congressional campaigns.[74]

In addition to raising money for lawmakers, interest group representatives also provide perks to members of Congress and their staffs. In recent years such perks have included luxury fact-finding trips, jobs for spouses and family members, golf outings to resorts in the United States and Europe, and fund-raising parties for members of Congress in Washington and at the national party conventions. One of Abramoff's more controversial lobbying tactics was to secure funding for members of Congress to take so-called fact-finding tours to European capitals and golf resorts in the United States and Europe.

Funding for these types of activities is sometimes funneled through nonprofit organizations. For example, the Ripon Education Fund, an independent but Republican-affiliated nonprofit, provided trips for twenty members of Congress to London in 2003. Accompanying the congressional group were more than one hundred registered lobbyists.[75]

Some lobbyists have in effect assumed another role—directing fund-raising efforts for members of Congress. Gregg Hartley, former top aide to Rep. Roy Blunt and a lobbyist for a number of large corporations, recently served as director of Blunt's fund-raising efforts. Bruce Gates, who assisted Rep. John Boehner in his efforts to be elected House majority leader in 2006, is a lobbyist for private clients. William Oldaker, a lobbyist for a number of health care clients, leads fund-raising efforts for two dozen Democratic members of Congress. The role those lobbyists play in fund raising is not unusual. In 2006, seventy-one members of Congress listed lobbyists as treasurers of their reelection committees, in contrast with just fifteen lobbyists serving as treasurers of lawmakers' campaign committees in 1998.[76]

In January, 2006, when lobbyist Jack Abramoff pleaded guilty to conspiracy to commit bribery, his sentencing agreement required him to provide evidence about members of Congress who had accepted perks from him or his clients. Abramoff pointed to actions members had taken, such as killing legislative proposals opposed by contributors, inserting special provisions to benefit contributors' interests in legislation, and earmarking appropriations or including special tax provisions to benefit campaign contributors.[77] The various ways in which lobbyists and members of Congress interact can present the appearance—and, in some cases, the reality—of corruption.

Criticisms of FECA and the BCRA

Criticisms of FECA and its implementation in the 1990s and 2000 are numerous. Reform proponents argued that large sums benefited candidates and parties in ways that evaded legal limits. The soft-money loophole was seen as particularly corrupting to the American political system, as it gave undue influence to wealthy individuals, corporations, labor unions, and organized groups (social, economic, and ideological) able to raise large sums of money.

The amount of soft money collected by both the Democratic and Republican Parties' federal-level campaign committees increased enormously between the 1991–1992 and 2001–2002 election cycles—$86.1 million compared with $496.1 million (see Table 8.2). As a proportion of the total amounts (both hard and soft money) received by the national party committees, soft money increased from 17 percent to 43 percent. This sharp increase helped fuel passage of the 2002 BCRA, which prohibits the national party organizations from raising and spending soft money.

The BCRA also places restrictions on preelection issue advertising, but it does not prevent interest groups from funding issue advocacy ads designed to support or oppose a candidate or party. An additional problem is that the identity of an ad's sponsors has been easy to conceal, especially if the group is registered in a state such as Virginia, which facilitates nondisclosure of a group's sponsors and contributors. Some of these groups have registered under Section 527 of the Internal Revenue Code, which allows them to engage in election activities without being subject to federal campaign finance rules and disclosure requirements. Congress enacted a law in 2000 requiring disclosure through filings with the Internal Revenue Service, but this has done little to curb spending by 527 committees.[78]

Another criticism of campaign finance laws is that the limits on the size of campaign contributions originally created by the 1974 FECA were not automatically adjusted for inflation. FECA limited individuals to $1,000 per candidate, per election and limited PACs to $5,000 per candidate, per election. The BCRA doubled the individual contribution limit to $2,000, per candidate, per election but left unchanged the limits placed on PACs. Although doubling the individual contribution limit was significant, critics contend that the limit is still too low. Campaign costs have increased at a rate exceeding the consumer inflation rate, primarily because of increased use of the mass media and the high rate of inflation in such costs. Also, the law favors wealthy candidates, as any candidate can spend unlimited amounts of personal money on campaigning. The BCRA contains a millionaire opponent's provision, which allows candidates who face self-financed millionaires to accept contributions over the legal limits. Even so, wealthy candidates have a tremendous advantage over their challengers.

Related to that is the time legislators must allocate to raising money for reelection. House incumbents raised an average of $1.1 million during the 2003–2004 election cycle, which translates into approximately $11,000 per week over the 104 weeks of the two-year term. Time spent fund raising significantly reduces the time incumbents can devote to their legislative and constituency service obligations. Further increasing the size of contributions allowed from an individual or a PAC might alleviate this pressure. The time demands of Senate campaign fund raising are much larger, even if spread over six years. Senate incumbents in 2004 raised an average of $8.6 million, with campaigns in large states such as California, Florida, New York, and Texas costing much more.[79] This enormous need for campaign funds gives an advantage to interest groups that have PACs and further advantages to those that bundle contributions from individuals.

Additional Campaign Finance Reform

Almost as soon as Congress passed and President Bush signed the BCRA of 2002 into law, calls for more reform began. The BCRA put an end to the system that for years allowed the parties to raise and spend millions in unregulated soft money, but the new system is far from perfect. Most criticism is directed at the loophole that allows 527 groups to raise and spend soft money in the same way the parties did before the BCRA became law.

Proposals for Reform

The BCRA's sponsors, Sen. John McCain, R-Ariz., Sen. Russell Feingold, D-Wis., Rep. Christopher Shays, R-Conn., and Rep. Martin T. Meehan, D-Mass., claim that the law's intent was not to reduce the amount of money spent on federal elections but to stop federal officeholders and the parties from soliciting unregulated soft money. Even so, they have acknowledged that more reform is needed. In 2004, the BCRA's sponsors proposed legislation prohibiting 527 groups from raising and spending soft money on federal campaigns.[80] Although this bill was unsuccessful, the House in 2006 passed legislation that would bring 527 groups under the same federal contribution guidelines as PACs. Debate over the Republican-backed bill became fiercely partisan, as Democrats benefited disproportionately from 527 spending in the 2004 elections and fear that regulations restricting 527 spending would hurt them in upcoming elections. The Senate has yet to take action, but the bill is thought to face slim odds against Democratic opposition.[81] Anticipating a showdown with Senate Democrats, House Republicans inserted language regulating 527s into their lobbying reform bill. This would put senators who oppose further regulation of 527s in the potential position of having to vote against a broad lobbying reform bill (in an election year, no less).[82]

Some, including FEC member Ellen Weintraub, believe that the focus on 527 organizations is misguided. Tightening restrictions on these groups, they argue, will result in a huge transfer of resources to other nonprofit, tax-exempt groups. This option is appealing because 527 organizations must disclose information about contributions and expenditures while other organizations, including 501(c) groups, do not. In fact more politically oriented groups are now choosing to organize under Section 501(c) of the tax code rather than under Section 527.[83]

Other critics—including the BCRA's sponsors—maintain that the FEC has repeatedly failed to enforce the law and should be replaced with a tougher, more independent agency. The FEC's failure to regulate 527 groups as they do other organizations whose primary purpose is to influence federal campaigns is particularly contentious.

Other recent reform proposals center on better disclosure laws. An editorial in the *New York Times* challenged senators to give up their current practice of filing paper campaign finance reports and begin to file electronically. The editorial points out that members of the House, along with other federal candidates, party committees, and PACs, would make their campaign finance reports available to the public much more quickly by filing electronically.[84]

Criticisms of Reform Proposals

Reform proposals face a variety of criticisms. One is that some proposals violate the U.S. Constitution's First Amendment protections of free speech. The Supreme Court has consistently limited states and Congress from enacting campaign finance laws that infringe on an individual's or group's political expression, as expression is equated with free speech. In *Buckley v. Valeo* the Supreme Court clearly distinguished between campaign contributions and independent expenditures. Contributions are defined as money given directly to a party, a candidate, or a PAC, which then have complete control over how the money is used. An independent expenditure is money spent directly by a person or an entity to influence an election, and those who spend funds in this category can exercise full control over how their funds are spent.

Federal law can regulate and limit direct contributions (hard money) and coordinated expenditures (expenditures made on behalf of candidates), but not independent expenditures. The Court's rationale was that expenditures are forms of political expression that show whom donors support and why. As such, independent expenditures are strictly protected as a form of free speech. In contrast, the government can regulate contributions because contributions have the potential for corruption or quid pro quo (exchanging contributions for votes, for example). The government does not have as compelling an interest in limiting independent expenditures because the potential for corruption is smaller and the benefit for communication of political beliefs (free speech) is great.[85]

In December 2003, the Supreme Court invalidated the BCRA's provisions requiring that parties choose between making independent or coordinated expenditures on behalf of candidates and prohibiting persons aged seventeen or younger from making campaign contributions. Both provisions were interpreted as violations of free speech. Free speech challenges to the BCRA's restrictions on preelection issue advertising have been heard in lower courts but have yet to reach the Supreme Court.

Another aspect of the *Buckley* decision is equality. Many believe it is important to equalize the relative effects of election financing and political expression by both individuals and groups. The Court, however, ruled that any attempt to influence the relative voices of some is not permissible under the First Amendment. Hence any plan to maximize the voice of one group in relation to others appears to be unconstitutional.

The second criticism of many reform proposals is that federal regulation of some aspects of campaign finance violates the Constitution's establishment of a federal system, which provides that regulation of elections be left primarily to the states. But Article 1, Section 4 of the Constitution permits Congress to enact laws that affect all aspects of congressional elections, except the manner in which senators are elected, which can be changed only by constitutional amendment.

Another criticism is that the ban on soft money cripples the ability of federal-level political party organizations to influence the federal government's policy agenda. But the extent to which party organizations today play such a role is debatable. Party fund raising in the 2004 elections challenged this assumption. Remarkably, the hard-money totals for both parties were greater than the combined hard- and soft-money totals they had raised in any previous election.[86] A record number of Americans contributed to the parties and to federal candidates in 2004, in part because of party-sponsored outreach efforts. The parties' efforts in voter registration and get-out-the-vote drives have been important in mobilizing potential voters.[87]

For now, the ban on soft-money fund raising does not appear to have hindered parties' ability to finance such efforts. One interesting finding is that in 2004 PACs reported spending a total of $144.5 million in nonfederal funds (soft money), up from $26.4 million in 2002 (see Table 8.3).[88]

Table 8.3.   PAC Nonfederal Spending (Soft Money) in Two-Year
Election Cycles, 1992–2004 (millions of dollars)

Year	Nonfederal spending
1992	8.3
1994	9.3
1996	10.7
1998	15.8
2000	24.2
2002	26.4
2004	144.5

Source: "PAC Activity Increases for 2004 Elections," Federal Election Commission, press release, April 13, 2005, http://www.fec.gov/press/press2005/20050412pac/PACFinal2004.html.

Democratic and Democratic-leaning groups reported the largest soft-money expenditures, with America Coming Together spending a remarkable $116.9 million (EMILY's List reported the second-highest level, with $8.1 million). It is too soon to see whether this trend increases, but if it does it raises new areas of concern because the BCRA does nothing to address or regulate soft-money expenditures by interest groups.

One last consideration is an examination of what the reform proposals can't address: the self-financing of campaigns. The Supreme Court ruled (in *Buckley*) that self-financing is a form of individual free speech and was absolutely protected. In 2004, candidates spent more than $133.3 million on their own candidacies. Twenty-three candidates for the Senate and the House each spent more than $1 million to self-finance their campaigns.[89] Rather than promote equality of influence, we are creating a millionaires' club in Congress. All these concerns mean we must be cautious in revising our system of campaign finance. Any proposals to limit access by a multitude of potential candidates must be resisted.

Conclusion

Efforts to regulate and limit the role of interest groups in campaign finance have met with limited success. The group most affected by the laws—members of Congress—must enact them. Both personal and partisan concerns make change difficult, as was evident in the inability of the House and Senate to agree on a campaign finance reform bill in the first session of the 107th Congress (2001). As public sentiment in support of campaign finance reform grew, however, partisan conflicts diminished, resulting in the successful passage of the Bipartisan Campaign Reform Act in the second session of the 107th Congress (2002). As with all reform, the passage of time is necessary before we can fully assess the consequences of the changes.

Notes

1. George Thayer, *Who Shakes the Money Tree?* (New York: Simon and Schuster, 1973), 25.
2. Robert K. Goidel, Donald A. Gross, and Todd G. Shields, *Money Matters* (Lanham, Md.: Rowman and Littlefield, 1999), 24; Frank J. Sorauf, *Money in American Elections* (Glenview, Ill.: Scott, Foresman, 1988), 30; Thayer, *Who Shakes the Money Tree?* 62–65.
3. See Edwin Epstein, "Emergence of Political Action Committees," in *Political Finance,* ed. Herbert Alexander (Beverly Hills, Calif.: Sage, 1979), 159–179.
4. *Buckley v. Valeo,* 424 U.S. 1 (1976).
5. *FEC v. Massachusetts Citizens for Life,* 479 U.S. 238 (1986).
6. Anthony Corrado et al., *Campaign Finance Reform: A Sourcebook* (Washington, D.C.: Brookings Institution, 1997).
7. Joseph E. Cantor, "Campaign Financing," Issue Brief for Congress no. IB87020 (Washington, D.C.: Congressional Research Service, July 16, 2004), Summary, http://fpc.state.gov/documents/organization/34816.pdf.
8. "PAC Activity Increases for 2004 Elections," Federal Election Commission, press release, April 13, 2005, http://www.fec.gov/press/press2005/20050412pac/PACFinal2004.html.
9. Ibid.
10. Center for Responsive Politics, http://www.opensecrets.org/pacs/industry.asp?txt=Q03&cycle=2004; Ross K. Baker, *The New Fat Cats* (New York: Priority Press Publications, 1989); Clyde Wilcox, "Member to Member Giving," in *Money, Elections, and Democracy,* ed. Margaret Latus Nugent and John R. Johannes (Boulder, Colo.: Westview, 1990).
11. Juliet Eilperin, "Democrats Pick Pelosi as House Whip," *Washington Post,* October 11, 2001, sec. A.
12. "Leadership PACs: PAC Contributions to Federal Candidates, 2003–2004," Center for Responsive Politics, May 16, 2005, http://www.opensecrets.org/pacs/industry.asp?txt=Q03&cycle=2004.
13. "Where We Come From," EMILY's List, http://www.emilyslist.org/about/where-from.html; http://www.opensecrets.org/pacs/lookup2.asp?strid=C00193433&cycle=2004.
14. For a good discussion of this phenomenon, see Elizabeth Drew, "Money Culture," in *Principles and Practice of American Politics,* ed. Samuel Kernell and Steven S. Smith (Washington, D.C.: CQ Press, 2000), 718–740.
15. "Big Picture: 2004 Cycle," Center for Responsive Politics, http://www.opensecrets.org/bigpicture/bundles.asp?cycle=2004&type=H.
16. Paul S. Herrnson, "Money Maze: Financing Congressional Elections," in *Congress Reconsidered,* 7th ed., ed. Lawrence C. Dodd and Bruce I. Oppenheimer (Washington, D.C.: CQ Press, 2001), 103.
17. "About BIPAC," BIPAC, http://www.bipac.org/about/about.asp.
18. All data obtained from the FEC, http://www.fec.gov.
19. Herrnson, "Money Maze," 117.
20. "PAC Activity Increases for 2004 Elections."
21. Theodore J. Eismeier and Philip H. Pollock III, "An Organizational Analysis of Political Action Committees," *Political Behavior* 7, no. 2 (1985): 192–216.
22. Richard A. Smith, "Interest Group Influence in the U.S. Congress," *Legislative Studies Quarterly* 20 (February 1995): 89–139.
23. John R. Wright, "PAC Contributions, Lobbying, and Representation," *Journal of Politics* 51 (August 1989): 713–729.
24. J. David Gopoian, "What Makes PACs Tick? An Analysis of the Allocation Patterns of Economic Interest Groups," *American Journal of Political Science* 28 (May 1984): 259–281.

25. Larry J. Sabato, *PAC Power: Inside the World of Political Action Committees* (New York: Norton, 1985), 42–43.
26. John R. Wright, "PACs, Contributions, and Roll Calls: An Organizational Perspective," *American Political Science Review* 79 (June 1985): 400–414.
27. Gopoian, "What Makes PACs Tick?" 279.
28. Ibid., 271.
29. See F. L. Davis, "Sophistication in Corporate PAC Contributions: Demobilizing the Opposition," *American Politics Quarterly* 20 (October 1992): 381–410; R. L. Hall and F. W. Wayman, "Buying Time: Moneyed Interests and the Mobilization of Bias in Congressional Committees," *American Political Science Review* 84 (September 1990): 797–820.
30. Ann B. Matasar, *Corporate PACs and Federal Campaign Financing Laws* (New York: Quorum, 1986), 58, Table 13.
31. See, for example, Mark J. Rozell, Clyde Wilcox, and David Madland, *Interest Groups in American Campaigns: The New Face of Electioneering* (Washington: CQ Press, 2006), 101–102.
32. R. B. Grierand and M. C. Munger, "Committee Assignments, Constituent Preferences, and Campaign Contributions," *Economic Inquiry* 29 (January 1991): 24–43.
33. J. W. Endersby and M. C. Munger, "Impact of Legislator Attributes on Union PAC Campaign Contributions," *Journal of Labor Research* 13 (Winter 1992): 79–97; M. C. Munger, "A Simple Test of the Thesis That Committee Jurisdictions Shape Corporate PAC Contributions," *Public Choice* 62 (1989): 181–186.
34. K. B. Grier, M. C. Munger, and G. M. Torrent, "Allocation Patterns of PAC Monies: The U.S. Senate," *Public Choice* 67 (1990): 111–128.
35. Eismeier and Pollock, "Organizational Analysis," 207–208.
36. Goidel, Gross, and Shields, *Money Matters*.
37. "Independent Expenditures by PACs during 1999–2000," May 31, 2001, http://www.fec.gov/press/press2001/053101pacfund/pacie00.htm; "2003–2004 Summary of PAC Independent Expenditures," http://www.fec.gov/press/press2005/20050412pac/indepexp.pdf.
38. David B. Magleby, "Interest Group Election Ads," in *Outside Money: Soft Money and Issue Advocacy in the 1998 Congressional Elections*, ed. David B. Magleby (Lanham, Md.: Rowman and Littlefield, 2000).
39. Ibid.
40. Drew, "Money Culture," 728.
41. Center for Responsive Politics, http://www.opensecrets.org/bush/ambassadors/index.asp; "A Third of Top Bush Fund-Raisers for 2000 Given Appointments," Associated Press, November 19, 2004.
42. *FEC v. Christian Action Coalition*, 894 F. Supp. 946 (W.D. Va., 1995).
43. *Colorado Republican Federal Campaign Committee v. FEC*, 116 Sup. Ct. 2309 (1996).
44. Marianne Holt, "Surge of Party Money in Competitive 1998 Congressional Elections," in *Outside Money*, ed. David Magleby, 25.
45. Corrado et al., *Campaign Finance Reform*, 235.
46. See Magleby, "Interest Group Election Ads," in *Outside Money*, ed. David Magleby, for a good discussion of this phenomenon.
47. Ibid.
48. Ibid.
49. Herrnson, "Money Maze," 116; see Allan J. Cigler, "1998 Kansas Third Congressional District Race," in *Outside Money*, ed. David Magleby, 77–92, for a good discussion of specific tactics employed in one such district.
50. Drew, "Money Culture," 739.
51. Herrnson, "Money Maze," 116.
52. Ibid., 103.

53. Mark Rozell and Clyde Wilcox, *Interest Groups in American Campaigns* (Washington, D.C.: CQ Press, 1999).

54. Herrnson, "Money Maze," 111; Rozell and Wilcox, *Interest Groups in American Campaigns.*

55. "IRS Stalls on Re-Examination of Policy as the Parties Begin Soliciting Host City Bids for 2008," Campaign Finance Institute, February 22, 2006, http://www.cfinst.org/pr/022206.html.

56. "Donor Double Take at the Conventions," Center of Responsive Politics, http://www.opensecrets.org/newsletter/ce72/02double.asp.

57. Ibid.

58. Dana Milbank, "On the Outside Looking In as Tom DeLay Whips Up Some Fundraisers," *Washington Post*, August 2, 2000, sec. C.

59. Ruth Marcus and Juliet Eilperin, "Party's Targets among Sponsors of Social Events," *Washington Post*, August 17, 2000, sec. A.

60. Mike Allen, "For Some, Party Was Just Too Grand," *Washington Post*, August 4, 2000, sec. A.

61. "The Usual Suspects, Part II," Capital Eye, http://www.capitaleye.org/inside.asp?ID=152.

62. "Party Financing Continues to Grow," Federal Election Commission, press release, October 25, 2004.

63. Magleby, ed., *Outside Money.*

64. Herrnson, "Money Maze," 105.

65. "Political Parties," Center for Responsive Politics, www.opensecrets.org/parties/index.asp.

66. Drew, "Money Culture," 724.

67. Ibid., 735.

68. DeLay was forced to resign first from his leadership position and then from the House of Representatives after several fund-raising scandals unfolded; DeLay claimed his chances for reelection were reduced by the scandal.

69. Jeffery H. Birnbaum and Dan Balz, "Case Bringing New Scrutiny to a System and a Profession," *Washington Post*, January 4, 2006, sec. A. At the time of publication of this book, no law has been enacted although both houses of Congress are debating the issue.

70. Richard S. Dunham and Eamon Javers, "Shakedown on K Street," *Business Week*, February 20, 2006, 34.

71. Ibid.

72. Ibid., 36.

73. "Elections," *CQ Almanac Plus 2004* (108th Congress, 2d Session), Vol. 60 (Washington, D.C.: CQ Press, 2004), 17–18, sec. 18.

74. Dunham and Javers, "Shakedown on K Street," 36.

75. Thomas B. Edsall, "Lobbyists Help Fund Ripon Society Travel," *Washington Post*, January 23, 2006, sec. A.

76. Brody Mullins, "Growing Role for Lobbyists: Raising Funds for Lawmakers," *Wall Street Journal*, January 27, 2006, sec. A.

77. Jeffrey Birnbaum and Dan Balz, "Case Bringing New Scrutiny to a System and a Profession," *Washington Post*, January 6, 2006, sec. A; Susan Schmidt and James V. Grimaldi, "Abramoff Pleads Guilty to 3 Counts," *Washington Post*, January 4, 2006, sec. A.

78. Public Law 106-230, 106th Cong., 2d sess. (July 1, 2000).

79. "Big Picture: 2004 Cycle."

80. Helen Dewar, "Bill Would Curb '527' Spending; No Action Expected before Elections," *Washington Post*, September 23, 2004, sec. A.

81. Tory Newmyer, "Fate of 527 Bill Still Uncertain," *Roll Call*, April 17, 2006.

82. As of this writing, the Senate had not yet taken up either of the House bills.

83. Thomas Edsall, "'527' Legislation Would Affect Democrats More," *Washington Post*, March 28, 2006, sec. A.

84. "Beware of What's Sold as Reform," *New York Times*, March 8, 2006.

85. See Corrado et al., *Campaign Finance Reform*, 61–63, for a clear discussion of this topic.

86. "Party Fundraising Continues to Grow," Federal Election Commission, press release, October 25, 2004.

87. M. Margaret Conway, "Political Mobilization in America," in *The State of Democracy in America*, ed. William Crotty (Washington, D.C.: Georgetown University Press, 2001); M. Margaret Conway, "Political Participation in the 2000 Election," in *America's Choice*, ed. William Crotty (Boulder, Colo.: Westview, 2001).

88. "PAC Activity Increases for 2004 Elections."

89. "Congressional Candidates Spend $1.16 Billion during 2003–2004," Federal Election Commission, press release, June 9, 2005, http://www.fec.gov/press/press2005/20050609candidate/20050609candidate.html.

9

527s
The New Bad Guys of Campaign Finance
Diana Dwyre

The American system of private funding of elections poses a dilemma of having to choose between two fundamental values in conflict, the freedom to express political views and political equality. The unequal distribution of resources potentially enables financially advantaged individuals and organized interests to support their preferences in a manner that greatly distorts the one-person-one-vote notion that underlies political equality, a central democratic principle. Campaign reform efforts in recent decades have been directed primarily toward decreasing the role of well-financed interests in elections and informing the public of all campaign transactions. Unfortunately, many organized interests have learned to defy the intent of the campaign finance laws; organized interests with resources have continued to have a potent effect on election outcomes.

In this chapter, Diana Dwyre traces the development and recent impact of 527 committees, nonprofit organized interests designed to influence elections. Such organizations can collect unlimited sums of money from contributors; in contrast, contributions to parties, individual candidates, and political action committees (PACs) are limited by campaign finance law. Although some 527s existed prior to the 2004 elections, the most recent presidential election witnessed a tremendous proliferation of such groups and their extensive involvement in both grassroots voter mobilization efforts and issue advocacy advertising during the campaign, activities traditionally conducted by the political parties and PACs. Roughly two-thirds of 527 activity in 2004 was conducted by new groups formed to influence the presidential election. The groups were typically created to circumvent the intentions of the Bipartisan Campaign Reform Act of 2002 that banned contributions of soft money to the national parties and greatly restricted issue advocacy electioneering by organized interests. Such groups were clearly partisan in orientation although they were officially forbidden by law to coordinate their activities with the respective parties.

In her conclusion, Dwyre raises a series of questions about the future impact of 527 committees upon our representative democracy. She believes that the surge in 527 activity has diminished the control that candidates and parties have had over the issues discussed in the campaigns and, therefore, has potentially reduced electoral accountability.

Political action committees, characterized as the powerful moneyed special interests, were once the bad guys of campaign finance. Then political parties became the object of scorn because of the massive amounts of unlimited and unregulated soft money they raised and spent. Now that party soft money is banned, section 527 groups are the new bad guys of campaign finance.

A section 527 committee is a tax-exempt, private political organization that is created to engage in political activities. These political groups are organized under section 527 of the U.S. tax code, which defines them, what information they must disclose, and what penalties might apply if the regulations are not followed. Section 527 groups enjoy exemption from income and gift taxes except for investment income. A section 527 political organization is a political party, association, fund, or other organization formed and operated primarily for the purpose of "influencing or attempting to influence the selection, nomination, election or appointment of any individual to any Federal, State, or local public office or office in a political organization, or the election of Presidential or Vice-Presidential electors."[1] Since their primary purpose is to influence elections, 527 groups are different from some other groups, such as section 501(c)(3) and 501(c)(4) nonprofit groups that may not work to influence elections as their primary purpose and whose contributors must sometimes pay the federal gift tax.

The legal definition of section 527 groups does not reveal how they have been used and why they have become the subject of new campaign finance reform efforts. After a brief review of some campaign finance bad guys of the past, I consider why these nonprofit groups have become the *new* bad guys.

Campaign Finance Bad Guys of the Past

During the era of big party bosses, the corrupt party machines and their special-interest corporate benefactors were the bad guys. Party bosses controlled the nomination of candidates who would carry the water for the big corporate backers that financed the parties' campaign efforts. Parties provided patronage to loyal partisans who voted for machine candidates in return. This system worked well to keep the machine politicians in power and to serve the corporate interests that financed their campaigns via the party machines, but it was hardly a model of representative democracy. Party loyalty was based not on ideology but on a quid pro quo of electoral support in exchange for patronage. Much of Congress, many state legislatures, and a number of statehouses and city halls across the country were controlled by party bosses beholden to big corporate interests.

Progressive reforms in the early 1900s aimed to shut down the corrupt machines. The 1907 Tillman Act banned direct campaign contributions by corporations and national banks. Introduction of the primary election in various states took the power of nomination away from the party bosses and gave it to ordinary citizens. Civil service reform eliminated much of the patronage that fueled the party electoral machine. These changes weakened the links among the party machines, their loyal voters, and their corporate sponsors. Although special-interest influence has never vanished, the power of the party machines declined and thus so did this particular system of corruption.

Campaign finance emerged as a salient issue again in the 1970s, motivated in part by the Watergate scandal and some significant turnover in Congress. In the wake of Watergate, the 1974 amendments to the 1971 Federal Election Campaign Act (FECA) aimed primarily to restrain the influence of wealthy individuals—"fat cats" such as W. Clement Stone, the insurance executive who in 1968 had given $2.8 million in contributions, mostly to Richard Nixon's presidential campaign.[2] The individual-contributor fat cats were the bad guys, and they were the focus of the reforms. However, "Congress apparently overlooked the incentive for collective action it was creating with PAC [political action committee] limits five times greater than those placed on individuals," $5,000 per election for PACs and $1,000 per election for individuals.[3] These contribution limits applied to each election, so that a PAC could give a total of $10,000 to a congressional candidate, $5,000 for the primary election, and $5,000 for the general election. Not surprisingly, these generous rules of operation contributed to a proliferation of PACs: the number of PACs registered with the Federal Election Commission (FEC) went from 608 in 1974, to 2,551 in 1980, to 4,172 in 1990.[4]

PACs then became the new bad guys of campaign finance for they were seen as channels of undue influence by moneyed special interests. As PAC influence grew, PACs also diminished the role of the more majoritarian political parties. The number of dollars that flowed from PACs to congressional candidates suggested a great deal of special-interest influence. Moreover, since PACs give overwhelmingly to incumbents, their significant role in the financing of elections contributed to a sharp decline in electoral competition in the 1980s, especially in races for the House of Representatives, and thus to calls for campaign finance reforms to rein in the power and influence of PACs, particularly corporate PACs.[5]

As the undesirability of PACs and their potential for corrupting influence grew, the parties' reputations improved. Some saw parties as the only campaign finance players motivated to allocate campaign funds in a manner that would promote rather than decrease electoral competition, a necessary ingredient for legitimate elections in a representative democracy.[6] That is, parties are more likely than PACs and individual contributors to direct resources to nonincumbent candidates because the parties are primarily motivated to attain or maintain majority status and thus are more inclined to support challengers who might help a party gain the majority or further secure its majority status by winning more seats. By the 1990s, the parties were raising record amounts of money and increasingly distributing it to nonincumbents, as competition for control of the House and the Senate became more intense. During this time, the GOP took control of the House in 1994 for the first time in forty years. Control of the Senate remained close and switched from one party to the other more than once.

Then the parties became the bad guys, for they became the new channels through which huge sums of special-interest money were directed in the form of unlimited and largely unregulated "soft" money (that is, nonfederal money). Recognizing the parties' unique role in supporting grassroots voter mobilization efforts, Congress in 1979 amended the FECA to allow parties to spend unlimited amounts of federal money (in other words, "hard" money raised under the contribution limits established in the 1974 FECA amendments) on certain grassroots activities that promote voter participation. In 1978, however, the FEC issued Advisory Opinion 1978-10 that permitted the use of corporate and union money to pay for a portion of voter drives conducted in connection with a federal election. Combined, Congress's and the FEC's campaign finance changes allowed the parties to collect unlimited amounts of soft money from previously prohibited sources (corporations and unions) and to use it to help pay for their voter mobilization activities.

The national parties did not take long to find ways to take advantage of this new source of campaign funds. The parties spent an estimated $19.1 million in soft money during the 1980 election cycle, $15.1 million by the Republicans and $4 million by the Democrats.[7] By the 2000 election cycle, both national parties had figured out how to raise and spend tremendous amounts of soft money in ways that helped federal candidates. The vehicle of choice was the issue advocacy ad. These ads did not expressly advocate the election or defeat of a candidate and therefore did not count as a contribution to a candidate, but they made it clear who deserved the voters' support. Soft money, which was usually raised in very large amounts from a few sources, allowed the Democrats to reach parity with their historically better-funded GOP rivals. In the 1999–2000 election cycle, the national party committees raised $495.1 million in soft money, with the Democrats raising $245.4 million and the Republicans taking in $249.9 million.[8]

Federal officeholders raised much of this soft money for their parties, creating a clear and disturbing connection between big money and lawmakers that implied at least the possibility of quid pro quo activities. The call for reform that cut off this potential avenue for corruption grew after the 2000 election as the number and magnitude of scandals that involved soft money grew.[9] Passage of the Bipartisan Campaign Reform Act (BCRA, also known as the McCain-Feingold law) in 2002 banned these unlimited soft-money contributions to federal political parties and forbade federal officeholders and party officials from raising soft money. It was an effort to get soft money out of federal elections and to break the connection between lawmakers and big-money contributors.

Section 527 Groups: The New Bad Guys

Many reform advocates worried that at least some of those who had contributed large sums of soft money to the parties were likely to find other outlets to satisfy their desire to influence federal elections.[10] They argued that, as one avenue for influence was closed, big spenders were likely to seek others. The most likely channel for such large sums of interested money was the section 527 group—the tax-exempt organizations that may accept unlimited contributions, even from corporations and unions, spend unlimited amounts of money on voter mobilization and issue advocacy advertising, and operate with little regulation or oversight. Before we examine whether 527s have become the new channel for soft money, a bit of background on their history and evolution is called for.

Section 527 political organizations have been around for many years, but they were not noticed much until the 2000 election. Congress added section 527 to the Internal Revenue Code in 1974 to provide political organizations exemption from federal income and gift taxes. It was assumed that such political entities were already registering and reporting their contributions and expenditures to the FEC or to state agencies, so Congress did not create any registration or disclosure rules for section 527 political organizations. They were required only to file a (confidential) tax return with the Internal Revenue Service (IRS).[11] It was not until 2000, after 527 groups ran a series of ads with no paper trail to identify their source, that section 527 groups were required to disclose their activities.

Section 527 groups are political organizations that engage in activities intended to influence the outcome of federal elections, but they are not subject to FECA limitations and disclosure requirements as long as they do not "expressly advocate" the election or defeat of a federal candidate and do not coordinate with a candidate.[12] Before passage of the BCRA in 2002, express advocacy was narrowly defined as those communications during elections that used the so-called magic words "vote for," "vote against," "support," or "defeat," which were mentioned in a footnote of the Supreme Court's decision in *Buckley v. Valeo* (1976). Yet political parties and other political organizations had figured out how to influence elections without the magic words by using issue advocacy advertising. Issue ads supposedly discuss an issue, but when such ads are broadcast close to election day and feature a candidate for office, they quite clearly inform voters about whom they should vote for or, more often, vote against, without using the magic words. This nonexpress advocacy electioneering is not difficult to do, as the following example illustrates.

The 2000 Election

Just days before the 2000 Super Tuesday presidential primary, a 527 group with no past and no track record, Republicans for Clean Air, ran television ads critical of the environmental record of Sen. John McCain, R-Ariz., and supportive of the record of the Republican governor of Texas, George W. Bush. The ad, which ran in New York (and elsewhere), said:

[*Comment on screen: Paid for by Republicans for Clean Air*]

ANNOUNCER: Last year, John McCain voted against solar and renewable energy. That means more use of coal-burning plants that pollute our air.

New York Republicans care about clear air. So does Governor Bush. He led one of the first states in America to clamp down on old coal-burning electric power plants.

Bush clean air laws will reduce air pollution by more than a quarter million tons a year. That's like taking five million cars off the road.

Governor Bush: Leading so each day dawns brighter.[13]

Because these groups were not required to disclose their activities, their officers, or their contributors, the political media scrambled to find out who was behind the Republicans for Clean Air ad. The day before Super Tuesday, it was reported that the mystery group was the creation of Dallas businessman and friend of George W. Bush, Sam Wyly, and his family, who spent about $2.5 million on the ad campaign.[14]

A number of other groups with equally vague and euphemistic names operated during the 2000 election; examples include:

- Americans for Equality, established by the NAACP,
- Republican Majority Issues Committee, established by Tom DeLay, who was then a powerful Republican member of the House of Representatives from Texas,
- Business Leaders for Sensible Priorities, led by Ben Cohen, founder of Ben & Jerry's ice cream, to advocate for less spending on weapons and more on education.[15]

The secrecy surrounding these 527 groups led critics to dub them "stealth PACs" during the 2000 election, and Congress acted in the midst of the election to impose reporting obligations on 527 groups. During debate on the bill in the House, Rep. Greg Ganske, R-Iowa, noted that "these stealthy political action committees could be getting money from the communist Chinese, Columbian drug lords, the Mafia, who knows."[16]

On July 1, 2000, President Clinton signed Public Law 106-230, which required 527 groups to notify the IRS within twenty-four hours of organizing and to disclose periodically to the IRS their contributions and expenditures: that is, the names and addresses of those who contribute $200 or more per year, with their occupation and employer if the contributor is an individual; and the names and addresses of any person receiving expenditures of $500 or more per year.[17] An amendment passed on November 2, 2002, exempted state political organizations from these expanded disclosure requirements if they focused only on state-level elections and disclosed their contributions and expenditures to state agencies.

The goal was to bring 527 group activities out into the open, and the new law closely resembled the reporting requirements for federal political committees that report to the FEC. The new disclosure requirements withstood legal challenge, with the U.S. Court of Appeals for the Eleventh Circuit unanimously asserting that the disclosure requirements were constitutional because the requirements were the condition of receiving a government-subsidized tax exemption. The court invited any organization not wishing to disclose this information to forgo the tax exemption, and it noted that "the fact that the organization might then engage in somewhat less speech because of stricter financial constraints does not create a constitutionally mandated right to a tax subsidy."[18]

There were many problems with the IRS Web-based disclosure system, making it difficult to track 527 contributions and expenditures effectively. The database was not searchable and required that a user open the more than 14,800 files to find who contributed and what expenditures were made from 527s. Moreover, there was lax enforcement of disclosure violations. For example, Public Citizen, a campaign finance watchdog group, found in April 2002 that occupation and employer information was missing for 67 percent of all itemized individual contributors, and that some 527s failed to file reports at all.[19] Also in 2000 Congress mandated (Public Law 106-230) that the IRS improve its public disclosure system by the end of June 2003, and the IRS has improved it. Yet this fix did not end calls for more regulation of section 527 groups.

The BCRA (the McCain-Feingold law) became law in 2002, but it did not take effect until the 2003–2004 election cycle. While organized interests such as 527 groups must comply with the BCRA ban on electioneering "broadcast communications" that are aired thirty days before a primary and sixty days before a general election and paid for with soft money, much of what such groups do during elections remained unchanged. Indeed, get-out-the-vote (GOTV) activities and phone, mail, e-mail, and Internet voter contact are not considered "broadcast communications" under the BCRA.[20]

The new campaign finance law also banned unlimited soft-money contributions to national political parties, and many observers speculated that the party soft-money ban would motivate big soft-money donors to direct their dollars to the loosely regulated section 527 organizations. Their activities during the pre-BCRA 2002 election and the post-BCRA 2004 election reveal the flexibility of these groups as vehicles for influencing elections and some reasons why there is increased pressure to limit their activities.

The 2002 Election

One scholarly account of the 2002 election was entitled *The Last Hurrah? Soft Money and Issue Advocacy in the 2002 Congressional Elections* because 2002 was the last election in which the parties could legally raise and spend soft money before the McCain-Feingold law took affect.[21] Three of the four congressional campaign committees raised record amounts of soft money in the 2002–2003 election cycle.[22] Indeed, most of the unregulated and unlimited soft money continued to flow to the parties, so there was little 527 group activity in 2002. However, the actions of the FEC and the reactions of the parties provide some insight into the potential of 527 groups to become increasingly significant in the world of federal campaign finance.

In July 2002 the FEC issued some of the implementation rules for the new BCRA. One rule permitted creation of independent nonprofit partisan groups that would not be considered party committees and therefore would not be subject to the party soft-money ban in the BCRA. In the final weeks before election day 2002, operatives close to both parties established a number of these nonparty partisan groups as section 527 organizations. They were dubbed shadow parties and quasi parties by some critics who pointed out that unlimited soft money could be filtered through these partisan 527s even if the official party committees could no longer raise and spend soft money.[23] Indeed, former party officials established some of these new partisan 527s. For instance, a former Democratic Congressional Campaign Committee political director organized the Democratic Senate Majority Political Action Committee, and Bill Paxon, a former Republican member of the House who had chaired the National Republican Congressional Committee set up and ran the Leadership Forum.[24]

Some groups with no clear party ties were active in 2002. The Arkansas Senate race that year featured a Boston-based section 527 group, the Reform Voter Project (RVP), which spent nearly $700,000 to defeat the incumbent Republican senator, Tim Hutchinson, who had "voted against the McCain-Feingold campaign finance reform and because he did favors for special interest contributors."[25] The RVP was established during the 2002 election "to turn up the heat on politicians who voted against common-sense campaign finance reform."[26] Their ads against Hutchinson on issues such as Social Security and the minimum wage helped Democrat Mark Pryor defeat the incumbent. A Pryor campaign strategist said he had not heard of the RVP until the group began to run ads in July,[27] suggesting that there was no illegal coordination between the 527 and the Pryor campaign. The RVP reported spending roughly $1.4 million in 2002 on various activities in ten states.[28] Ironically, the RVP used section 527 of the tax code, an organizational vehicle some consider a soft-money loophole, to curb special-interest influence in elections by opposing candidates who had voted against campaign finance reform. Overall, section 527 organizations raised an estimated $151 million for the 2002–2003 election cycle,[29] a mere preview of what was to come in 2004.

The 2004 Election

The 2004 election, the first federal election under the new BCRA rules, featured more reasons for many in and outside of Congress to call for further regulation of section 527 organizations. The sheer magnitude of fund raising and spending by 527 groups was reason for concern for some, particularly because many of the 527 groups active in the 2004 election were brand new organizations. During the 2003–2004 election cycle, federal 527 groups raised an estimated $426 million,[30] up from $151 million for the pre-BCRA 2002 election (the first election for which reliable data are available).[31] Approximately two-thirds of 527 activity in 2004 was conducted by new groups formed to influence the presidential election.[32] There were far more Democratic-oriented 527 groups that far outspent Republican-leaning 527s in 2004: the Democratic groups spent about $320 million; and the GOP groups spent an estimated $109 million.[33] Table 9.1 lists the top ten 527 spenders of each partisan persuasion in 2004.

Table 9.1.   Spending by Top Federal 527 Organizations Active in the 2004 Election

Section 527 committee	Expenditures (dollars)
Democratic-leaning groups	
America Coming Together	78,040,480
Joint Victory Campaign 2004[a]	72,588,053
Media Fund	57,694,580
Service Employees International Union Political Fund	46,726,713
AFSCME Special Account	22,332,587
MoveOn.org Voter Fund	21,346,380
New Democratic Network—Nonfederal Account	12,524,063
Citizens for a Strong Senate	10,228,515
1199 SEIU Nonfederal Committee	8,115,937
EMILY's List Nonfederal	8,100,752
Republican-leaning groups	
Progress for America Voter Fund	35,631,378
Swift Boat Vets and POWs for Truth	22,565,360
College Republican National Committee	17,260,655
Club for Growth	9,629,742
Club for Growth.net	4,039,892
National Federation of Republican Women	3,462,507
November Fund	3,124,718
National Association of Realtors	2,989,377
California Republican National Convention Delegation	1,612,595
Republican Leadership Coalition, Inc.	1,440,479

Source: Campaign Finance Institute, "527 Group Fundraising Grew More Slowly in First Quarter of 2006 than 2004," news release, May 19, 2006, http://www.cfinst.org/pr/051906.html, Table 2.

[a]Joint Victory Campaign 2004 served as the fund-raising arm for America Coming Together (ACT) and the Media Fund; therefore it transferred most of its funds to ACT and the Media Fund.

Perhaps the best known and most controversial 527 group in 2004 was formed to defeat the Democratic Party nominee for president, John Kerry. The Swift Boat Veterans for Truth (later renamed the Swift Boat Veterans and POWs for Truth) was a group of almost 200 Vietnam swift boat veterans offended by Kerry's focus on his service in Vietnam and by his antiwar activities after returning from the war. The swift boat veterans' organization spent $22.6 million on issue ads and mailings in 2004.[34] The swift boat ads accused John Kerry of lying about his record in Vietnam, for which he received several military medals. The first swift boat ad, "Any Questions," was dramatic and raised serious questions about Kerry's character:

JOHN EDWARDS [from a speech used in Kerry's "Three Minutes" ad]: If you have any question about what John Kerry's made of, just spend three minutes with the men who served with him thirty years ago....

[*Comment on screen: Here's what those men think about John Kerry.*]

AL FRENCH: I served with John Kerry.

BOB ELDER: I served with John Kerry.

[*On screen: www.swiftvets.com*]

GEORGE ELLIOT: John Kerry has not been honest about what happened in Vietnam.

[*On screen: George Elliot; Lieutenant Commander; 2 Bronze Stars*]

AL FRENCH: He is lying about his record.

[*On screen: Al French; Ensign; 2 Bronze Stars*]

LEWIS LETSON: I know John Kerry is lying about his first Purple Heart, because I treated him for that injury.

[*On screen: Lewis Letson; Medical Officer; Lieutenant Commander*]

VAN ODELL: John Kerry lied to get his Bronze Star. I know, I was there—I saw what happened.

[*On screen: Van Odell; Gunners Mate 2nd Class*]

JACK CHENOWETH: His account of what happened and what actually happened are the difference between night and day.

[*On screen: Jack Chenoweth; Lieutenant J.G.; Navy Commendation Medal*]

ROY HOFFMAN: John Kerry has not been honest.

[*On screen: Roy Hoffman; Rear Admiral; Distinguished Service Medal; Silver Star*]

ADRIAN LONSDALE: And he lacks the capacity to lead.

[*On screen: Adrian Lonsdale; Commander; Legion of Merit; Bronze Star*]

LARRY THURLOW: When the chips were down, you could not count on John Kerry.

[*On screen: Larry Thurlow; Lieutenant J.G.; Bronze Star*]

BOB ELDER: John Kerry is no war hero.

[*On screen: Bob Elder; Lieutenant; Bronze Star*]

GRANT HIBBARD: He betrayed all his shipmates. He lied before the Senate.

[*On screen: Grant Hibbard; Lieutenant Commander; 2 Bronze Stars*]

SHELTON WHITE: John Kerry betrayed the men and women he served with in Vietnam.

[*On screen: Sheldon White; Lieutenant; 2 Bronze Stars*]

JOE PONDER: He dishonored his country. He most certainly did.

[*On screen: Joe Ponder; Gunners Mate 3rd Class; Purple Heart*]

BOB HILDRETH: I served with John Kerry. John Kerry cannot be trusted.

[*On screen: Bob Hildreth; Lieutenant; Bronze Star, Purple Heart*]

ANNOUNCER [VOICE OVER]: Swift Boat Veterans for Truth is responsible for the content of this advertisement.

[*On screen: Paid for by Swift Boat Veterans for Truth and Not Authorized by Any Candidate or Candidate's Committee. www.SwiftVets.com. Swift Boat Veterans For Truth Is Responsible for the Content of This Advertisement*].[35]

The "Any Questions" ad was run briefly in only three battleground states—Iowa, Ohio, and West Virginia—beginning August 5, 2004. Normally such a small media buy would not have much impact on a presidential race. However, this ad was discussed and rebroadcast, in whole or in part, first on cable news shows and then by more mainstream television, giving the allegations made by the swift boat veterans tremendous exposure nationwide.[36] The allegations were investigated by a number of news outlets and others, and most concluded that they were not supported by the facts.[37] But that did not seem to matter. The damage had been done, and, to make matters worse, the Kerry campaign did not respond quickly or adequately to the charges owing in part to his lack of funds (after a presidential candidate officially becomes the party's nominee, and if that candidate chooses to participate in the public funding system, he can no longer spend money that he has raised privately).[38]

The Kerry campaign filed a complaint with the FEC charging that the swift boat veterans were illegally coordinating their activities with the Bush campaign. The Bush campaign denied the charge. The swift boat veterans made another small ad buy in the same states for a new ad, "Sellout," that accused Kerry of selling out his fellow soldiers by testifying before the Senate in 1971 about crimes committed by U.S. military personnel in Vietnam. This second round of ads received some free media as well, and any bump Kerry received from the Democratic convention seemed to have evaporated by the end of August.[39]

Another Republican-leaning 527 group, Progress for America Voter Fund, spent $35.6 million in 2004 in support of President Bush's reelection. The group sent out millions of pieces of mail and thousands of e-mails to voters.[40] Progress for America ran nine ads during the election, with a particularly powerful and influential one called "Ashley's Story" that aired two weeks before election day. The ad was about a young girl, Ashley, whose mother died in the World Trade Center on September 11, 2001. The ad told the story of how President Bush spontaneously stopped to talk with and hug Ashley at a campaign event in Ohio, a battleground state that contributed significantly to the Bush victory. Ashley says to the camera, "He's the most powerful man in the world and all he wants to do is make sure I'm safe, that I'm OK."[41] The ad was further distributed via the Internet and e-mail, reaching millions more voters directly. The Ashley ad effectively portrayed Bush as a compassionate and emotional though strong leader, while Kerry was often seen as distant and cold.[42]

Democratic-leaning 527 organizations also hit the airwaves in 2004. Harold Ickes, who had served as deputy chief of staff for President Clinton, founded the pro-Democratic Media Fund for the 2004 presidential election to run ads attacking the Bush administration's policies. The Media Fund spent $57.7 million in the 2004 election cycle, most of it for television advertising time beginning in March 2004.[43] The Media Fund worked with other 527s, such as the AFL-CIO and MoveOn.org, to help keep Kerry a viable candidate during months of heavy spending by the Bush campaign. After the election, Media Fund president Eric Smith commented that "one of the pitfalls of not being able to coordinate [with the candidate's campaign is that] ... you may not always be able to do what the campaign wants you to do."[44] He noted that the GOP 527 media groups started later in the year and thus had the advantage of months of Bush campaign advertising and therefore more cues about what the campaign wanted.[45] That 527 organizations may not coordinate with the parties or candidate campaigns potentially reduces their effectiveness, but this is one aspect of 527 regulation that breaks the potentially corrupt link between big-money contributors and officeholders.

Congress intended to break this link by banning party soft money with the passage of the BCRA.

Democratic-leaning 527 groups focused much of their attention on GOTV grassroots efforts. America Coming Together (ACT) was the largest effort to mobilize Democratic voters in 2004. It spent an estimated $78 million in 2004, more than any other 527 committee, primarily on GOTV efforts.[46] ACT employed as many as 5,000 paid organizers and canvassers to register new voters, contact them throughout the campaign, and get them out to vote; it used about 17,000 volunteers on election day.[47] ACT reported that its workers made 16 million phone calls in the last weeks of the election, sent 23 million pieces of mail, and distributed 11 million flyers.[48]

The Democratic-leaning groups, ACT and the Media Fund, became the subject of some controversy because of the source of some of their funds. International financier George Soros and Progressive Car Insurance chairman Peter Lewis each contributed $20 million to get the anti-Bush 527s off the ground.[49] Soros ended up giving $24 million to 527s to defeat George Bush in 2004, far more than the $208,000 he had given in soft money to the parties in 2000 and 2002.[50] So controversial was Soros's giving that it backfired somewhat and helped his opponents raise more money. GOP election lawyer Ben Ginsberg noted after the election, "George Soros was absolutely the best fundraising tool the Republican 527s had going because he had given so much money in such a way and he was so dogmatic in his views."[51] Also active on behalf of the Democrats were groups such as MoveOn.org and labor unions. Unions spent an estimated $94 million in 527 activity during the 2004 election cycle, up from about $55 million in the 2002 cycle and more than the $36 million in soft money that labor unions used to give to Democratic party committees.[52]

Are 527s the New Soft-Money Conduits?

Some reformers in Congress and many in the campaign finance reform interest group community worried that once the national parties were banned from raising and spending soft money, section 527 groups would become the new vehicle for wealthy individuals, groups, corporations, and unions to pour soft money into federal elections. Indeed, in an effort to cut off this possible conduit for soft money, Congress included in the BCRA a provision that bans national and state party committees and their agents from raising soft money for section 527 organizations.[53]

A recent analysis by Weissman and Hassan shows that all of the now-banned party soft money did not find its way to 527 groups in 2004:

> [P]ost-BCRA *levels* of giving are not simply explained by the "hydraulic theory" that money, like water, inevitably finds it way around an obstacle. *Most* former individual soft-money donors have not given large donations to 527s. But for those who did in 2004, one may say that a river of party soft money has turned into an ocean of 527 money.[54]

Those individuals who gave $200,000 or more to federal 527s in 2004 generally had given far less soft money to parties in the 2000 and 2002 election cycles. George Soros, for example, gave $24 million to 527 groups in 2004 but only $208,000 in soft money to Democratic party committees in 2000 and 2002. Bob Perry of Perry Homes gave $8.1 million to 527s in 2004 but only $140,000 in soft money to GOP party committees in the two previous elections.[55] Even the big soft-money givers to the parties in the past gave far more soft money to 527s in 2004: "... 73 former soft-money donors provided $157 million to 527s—three times the combined amount they had given to parties in 2000 and 2002 and [to] 527s in 2002 ... a vast escalation in their total donations."[56] Almost half of the money contributed to 527s in 2004 (about $194 million) came from a mere 77 individuals.[57] Individual contributions to 527s accounted for most of the increase in fund raising by 527 groups, jumping from $37 million in 2002 to $256 million in 2004.[58] So, many former soft-money donors to parties did not gravitate to 527s, but those who did significantly increased their contributions.

The 527 money from individuals appeared more ideologically focused than motivated by access to lawmakers or party officials, suggesting a new and different motivation for giving soft money.[59] Indeed, a number of 527 groups were active for the first time in 2004, some of them not likely to be heard from again. Of the top federal 527 groups listed in Table 9.1 above, five of the top ten pro-Democratic and five of the top ten pro-Republican groups were "first timers." For example, Swift Boat Veterans and POWs for Truth formed specifically to defeat presidential candidate John Kerry, and it has not been active since the election. Weissman and Hassan call these short-lived groups "drive-by" 527s.[60]

One of the major changes in soft-money giving was that corporations did not contribute nearly as much soft money to 527 groups in 2004 as they had given to the parties in previous elections. Under the pre-BCRA campaign finance regime, there were reports that some business donors felt they had been subjected to a party "shakedown" for soft money, and corporations probably were relieved to give less soft money now that the parties no longer had this leverage over them.[61] Corporate givers were also reluctant to give, in part because their lawyers advised against giving to 527s until there was more certainty about the legality of doing so.[62] Business donations to section 527 groups declined from $32 million in 2002 to $30 million in 2004, falling far short of the $216 million in soft money that business interests had given to the national parties in 2002.[63] Because corporations had given more soft money to Republican party committees in the past, this reluctance to give to 527s hurt the GOP-leaning groups.

Labor unions, on the other hand, did not hesitate to give to and form their own 527 organizations. Labor union contributions to 527s increased from $55 million in 2002 to $94 million in 2004, far more than the $36 million in soft money that the labor unions gave to Democratic Party committees in 2002.[64] Most of labor's increased 527 activity was conducted by two unions, Service Employees International Union (SEIU) and American Federation of State, County, and Municipal Employees (AFSCME), which accounted for $73.2 million of the $94.4 million in union donations to federal 527s in 2004.[65] Most of this union activity was in the form of cash and in-kind contributions to Democratic-leaning 527s.

Section 527 groups have not become merely a new conduit for soft money previously given to parties. Many former soft-money contributors to the political parties did not give to 527 groups in 2004. The increase in soft-money activity in 2004 came from a smaller donor base than the former party soft-money givers. Section 527 groups are certainly a vehicle of choice for those who want to give or spend unlimited amounts of money on federal elections, but they cannot do so unnoticed because their activities now must be disclosed. One of the goals of the BCRA was to separate federal officeholders from big-money givers, and that has happened to some extent. How section 527 and other nonprofit groups are used in the future will determine whether the BCRA cure might not have produced some more undesirable consequences.

527s and Democracy

Some argue that to best achieve the goals of our representative democracy we should take all of the money out of elections by instituting a publicly funded campaign finance system. This could level the playing field between incumbents and challengers as well as stop the money chase in which candidates must engage to be serious contenders for federal office. Public funding is also expected to eliminate lawmakers' reliance on special-interest money and reduce special-interest group influence over policy making. The goals of such a reform are to increase the level of competition in elections, which would enhance the legitimacy of the mechanism by which the people rule, and to temper the influence of those in society with the most resources so that less privileged and less powerful voices might also be heard.

The ban on party soft money may have accomplished one of these goals. One of the BCRA's chief sponsors, Sen. Russell Feingold, D-Wis., said, "The point was to break the connection between the officeholder and the money."[66] It is now not possible for any individual, group, corporation, or labor union to give huge amounts of soft money to officeholders or political parties. This should significantly weaken the direct connection between big money and policy makers and presumably the potential for quid pro quo exchanges of policy for money.

Political scientist Sidney Milkis argues, however, that the BCRA actually will strengthen the link between interest groups and candidates, much like E. E. Schattschneider had asserted many years before:

> ... the BCRA will weaken *party politics* and strengthen *pressure group* politics. Nonfederal funds [soft money] have served as an important incentive for candidates and interest groups to cooperate with political

parties; consequently, these funds have strengthened political parties as intermediary organizations between public officials and special interests. By banning nonfederal funds, the BCRA will encourage interest groups to exert influence directly on candidates and public policy.[67]

Journalist Jonathan Rauch disagrees, noting that the BCRA took care of the direct means of corruption and undue influence by banning party soft money. Rauch asserts that it is "hard to see why giving $1 million to an independent group, such as the Sierra Club or the National Rifle Association, would corrupt anyone. After all, private groups are in no position to offer legislative favors or shake down constituents."[68] Of particular concern to Rauch and others is the effect further restrictions on 527 groups would have on freedom of expression in federal elections, as more campaign speech is brought under hard-money fund raising and spending limits.

The fact that some of this big money is now raised and spent by outside groups, such as section 527 committees, may present other concerns. For example, many of the new 527 groups are partisan groups doing much of what parties have traditionally done in elections, particularly voter contact and mobilization. America Coming Together and Progress for America acted as shadow parties that were responsible for much of the GOTV activity in 2004; ACT, especially, was trying to make up for years of poor organizing by the Democratic Party apparatus. Leaders of these partisan 527s were former party operatives, many of whom left their party jobs to establish the new 527s and are likely to return to party work in the future. The 527s operate just as the parties did when they spent soft money on issue ads, that is, they are unable to coordinate with candidates' campaigns. However, 527 groups do not have the same concern that parties and candidates do about being held responsible for their messages. Kerry campaign pollster Mark Mellman put it this way after the 2004 election:

> What we saw in some of the 527 advertising—I'll use Swift Boats as an example here—is a set of accusations that were made that the Bush campaign said today they would never have made because they were, in their view, not factual and it would have rebounded to discredit George Bush. You have a situation here where people are free to say things, have free speech, but no one is held responsible for the consequences of that speech.[69]

The surge in 527 activity diminished the control that candidates and parties had over the issues discussed in the campaigns and therefore reduced the potential for electoral accountability.

Scholars also have pointed out that, compared with interest groups, parties are more likely to distribute resources in a manner that promotes competition, that is, parties may provide resources to challengers instead of incumbents.[70] Others note that even with soft money at the parties' disposal, levels of party competition did not increase because parties focused their resources on a small number of highly competitive races.[71] Yet, parties still direct a larger share of their resources to nonincumbents than interest groups do. Short of complete public funding, which is unlikely to happen, it is difficult to take an approach to campaign finance that does not raise some concerns about competition, influence, and accountability.

What Lies Ahead?

The McCain-Feingold reformers had not anticipated that banning party soft money would result in such increased activity by 527 committees that it circumvented the intent of the BCRA. The 527 groups conducted many of the same kind of GOTV and issue advocacy advertising that the parties had. In fact, the parties had never been able to attract the kind of soft-money contributions that billionaires George Soros and Peter Lewis gave to 527 organizations in 2003 and 2004. Much of this pitched activity was doubtless due to the passion on both sides of the presidential race and, in the case of Soros and Lewis, the intense desire to defeat George Bush. The political environment also was highly polarized, contributing to the intensity of electoral activity. Will we see as much 527 activity in the 2006 midterm elections, during the 2008 presidential election, and beyond?

Whether section 527 groups remain the vehicle of choice for interested citizens and groups to influence elections depends in part on whether Congress and the FEC change the laws and regulations that govern 527 organizations. Reform advocates, arguing that 527s should be brought under the same hard-money regulations as parties and PACs for their election-related activities, continue to push for further regulation of 527s. However, the fact that efforts of many 527 groups were seen as quite effective suggests that the same types of activities are likely to be continued. ACT chief executive officer Steve Rosenthal noted the group's success at a postelection forum: "Overall, the Kerry vote totals were about 10 percent higher than Al Gore [in 2000] nationwide. In the states that we were in, the turnout was about 20 percent higher than Gore."[72] Indeed, many congressional Democrats are now opposed to further regulation of 527 committees, no doubt owing in part to the success of pro-Democratic 527s in 2004. Many advocacy groups (for example, Sierra Club) also oppose any further restrictions for they would like to continue to operate as 527s.

The FEC is dealing slowly with 527-related cases from the 2004 election. In June 2006, the agency refused to follow a federal judge's advice to issue uniform rules for 527s, and it continues to deal with 527 complaints case by case.[73] Therefore, unless Congress acts, 527 electoral activity is likely to continue in future elections. FEC chairman Michael E. Toner, a Republican, noted after his fellow commissioners failed to issue new 527 rules that "... no one should be surprised if 527 soft-money spending in '06 and '08 becomes one of the driving forces in determining which candidates are elected."[74] The Swift Boat Veterans and POWs for Truth, ACT, and the

Media Fund have disbanded, however, for they were driven by the special circumstances and passions of the 2004 election.

Without a continuing policy or electoral goal, such groups have little reason to remain active, and it is difficult to sustain such election-focused and ideologically driven groups from election to election. Labor unions and other groups with a more permanent status are likely to continue to be quite active in future elections. Absent the influx of funds from billionaires like Soros and Lewis and without the extreme passion and polarization that characterized the 2004 election, overall 527 activity may not reach these levels again in the near future. If the Democrats choose Hillary Clinton as their presidential nominee in 2008, however, we *are* likely to see similarly high levels of polarization and intensity and therefore probably record levels of 527 activity.

Notes

1. Internal Revenue Service, "Exemption Requirements—Political Organizations," 2002, http://www.irs.gov/charities/political/article/0,,id=96350,00.html, May 23, 2005.
2. Frank J. Sorauf, "Political Action Committees" in *Campaign Finance Reform: A Sourcebook*, eds. Anthony Corrado et al. (Washington, D.C.: Brookings Institution Press, 1997), 123.
3. Ibid.
4. Ibid., 140.
5. See, for example, Gary Jacobson, *Money in Congressional Elections* (New Haven: Yale University Press, 1980); Elizabeth Drew, *Money and Politics: The New Road to Corruption* (New York: Macmillan, 1983); and Philip M. Stern, *Still the Best Congress Money Can Buy* (Washington, D.C: Regnery Gateway, 1992).
6. See, for example, Paul S. Herrnson, *Congressional Elections: Campaigning at Home and in Washington*, 2d ed. (Washington, D.C.: CQ Press, 1998), 237–245.
7. Anthony Corrado, "Soft Money," in *Campaign Finance Reform*, 172–173.
8. Federal Election Commission, "FEC Reports Increase in Party Fundraising for 2000," news release, May 15, 2001, 1.
9. See, for example, Allan J. Cigler, "Enron, a Perceived Crisis in Public Confidence, and the Bipartisan Campaign Reform Act of 2002," in *Review of Policy Research* 21, no. 2 (2004): 233–252.
10. For example, see the report by Public Citizen, a good-government group organized by Ralph Nader as "an independent voice for citizens in the halls of power," entitled *Déjà vu Soft Money: Outlawed Contributions Likely to Flow to Shadowy 527 Groups that Skirt Flawed Disclosure System*, April 5, 2002, at http://www.citizen.org/congress/campaign/issues/nonprofit/articles.cfm?ID=7372.
11. Brookings Institution, "Recent Developments in Campaign Finance Regulation: Section 527 Organizations," February 28, 2001, at http://www.brook.edu/gs/cf/headlines/527_intro.htm.
12. Anthony Corrado, "Money and Politics: A History of Federal Campaign Finance Law" in *The New Campaign Finance Sourcebook*, eds. Anthony Corrado et al. (Washington, D.C.: Brookings Institution Press, 2005), 34.
13. "GOP Enviro Ad Mystery Solved," *National Journal's Ad Spotlight*, March 7, 2000, http://www.nationaljournal.com.
14. Diana Dwyre, "Campaigning outside the Law: Interest Group Issue Advocacy," in *Interest Group Politics*, 6th ed., eds. Allan J. Cigler and Burdett A. Loomis (Washington, D.C.: CQ Press, 2002), 150–151.

15. Ibid., 154.
16. Eric Schmitt, "House Rejects Bill Requiring Donor Disclosure," *New York Times*, June 10, 2000, sec. A.
17. *U.S. Code* 26, sec. 527(j).
18. *Mobile Republican Assembly v. United States*, No. 02-16283 (Eleventh Circuit, December 24, 2003), as quoted in Trevor Potter, "Campaign Finance Disclosure Laws," in *The New Campaign Finance Sourcebook*, 128–129.
19. Public Citizen, *Déjà vu Soft Money*.
20. Allan J. Cigler, "Interest Groups and the Financing of the 2004 Elections," in *Financing the 2004 Election*, ed. David Magleby (Washington, D.C.: Brookings Institution Press, 2006).
21. David B. Magleby and J. Quin Monson, eds., *The Last Hurrah? Soft Money and Issue Advocacy in the 2002 Congressional Elections* (Washington, D.C.: Brookings Institution Press, 2004).
22. Ibid., 45–46.
23. See Amy Keller, "McCain Takes Aim at 'Shadow' Groups," *Roll Call*, November 18, 2002. The term "shadow Democratic party" was first coined by GOP critics, but it was soon used by the media. See "*Washington Post* Again Labeled Progressive Groups with Political 'Foes' Term," June 7, 2005, http://mediamatters.org/items/20040514004.
24. Diana Dwyre and Robin Kolodny, "National Political Parties after BCRA," in *Life after Reform*, ed. Michael J. Malbin (Lanham, Md.: Rowman and Littlefield, 2003), 87.
25. Reform Voter Project, "Reform Voter Project: Holding Politicians Accountable," www.reformvoter.org/2002/index.html.
26. Ibid.
27. David B. Magleby and Jonathan W. Tanner, "Interest-Group Electioneering in the 2002 Congressional Elections," in *The Last Hurrah? Soft Money and Issue Advocacy in the 2002 Congressional Elections*, ed. David B. Magleby and J. Quin Monson (Washington, D.C.: Brookings Institution Press, 2004), 80–81.
28. Reform Voter Project, "Reform Voter Project: Holding Politicians Accountable."
29. Steve Weissman and Ruth Hassan, "BCRA and the 527 Groups," in *The Election after Reform*, ed. Michael J. Malbin (Lanham, Md.: Rowman and Littlefield, 2006), 81.
30. Campaign Finance Institute, "527 Group Fundraising Grew More Slowly in First Quarter of 2006 than 2004," news release, May 19, 2006, www.CampaignFinanceInstitute.org.
31. Weissman and Hassan, "BCRA and the 527 Groups," in *The Election after Reform*, 81.
32. Corrado, "The Future of Campaign Finance: Congress, the FEC, and the Courts" (presentation at the Brookings Institution, Washington, D.C., October 20, 2005), quotation from transcript pages 6–7, www.brookings.edu/comm/events/20051020campaign.htm.
33. Campaign Finance Institute, "527 Group Fundraising Grew More Slowly in First Quarter of 2006 than 2004," Table 2.
34. Ibid.
35. Jennifer Koons, "Veterans Question Kerry's War Record," NationalJournal.com, August 5, 2004, http://nationaljournal.com/members/adspotlight/2004/08/0805 sbvft1.htm.
36. Institute of Politics, John F. Kennedy School of Government, Harvard University, *Campaign for President: The Managers Look at 2004* (Lanham, Md.: Rowman and Littlefield, 2006), 215.
37. Paul R. Abramson, John H. Aldrich, and David Rohde, *Change and Continuity in the 2004 Elections* (Washington, D.C.: CQ Press, 2006), 39; also see, for example, *Detroit Free Press*, August 21, 2004, sec. A.
38. See discussion of this funding issue in Abramson, Aldrich, and Rohde, *Change and Continuity in the 2004 Elections*, chap. 1 and page 39.

39. Ibid., 39.
40. Glen Justice, "Advocacy Groups Reflect on Their Role in the Elections," *New York Times*, November 5, 2004, sec. A.
41. Meg Kinnard and Jennifer Koons, "Both Sides Seek to Appeal to Security Moms," NationalJournal.com, October 19, 2004, http://nationaljournal.com/members/adspotlight/2004/10/1019wh1.htm#.
42. Allan J. Cigler, "Interest Groups and the Financing of the 2004 Elections," in *Financing the 2004 Election*.
43. Campaign Finance Institute, "527 Group Fundraising Grew More Slowly in First Quarter of 2006 than 2004," Table 2; and Institute of Politics, *Campaign for President*, 221.
44. Institute of Politics, *Campaign for President*, 222.
45. Ibid., 222–223.
46. Campaign Finance Institute, "527 Group Fundraising Grew More Slowly in First Quarter of 2006 than 2004," Table 2.
47. Institute of Politics, *Campaign for President*, 230.
48. Justice, "Advocacy Groups Reflect on Their Role in the Elections."
49. Weissman and Hassan, "BCRA and the 527 Groups," in *The Election after Reform*, 86.
50. Ibid., Table 5.2.
51. Institute of Politics, *Campaign for President: The Managers Look at 2004*, 212.
52. Anthony Corrado, "The Future of Campaign Finance: Congress, the FEC, and the Courts," quotation from transcript page 7, www.brookings.edu/comm/events/20051020campaign.htm.
53. Corrado, "Money and Politics: A History of Federal Campaign Finance Law," in *The New Campaign Finance Sourcebook*, 39.
54. Weissman and Hassan, "BCRA and the 527 Groups," in *The Election after Reform*, 96–97. Italics in original.
55. Ibid., 94–96, Table 5.2.
56. Ibid., 93.
57. Corrado, "The Future of Campaign Finance," quotation from transcript page 7, www.brookings.edu/comm/events/20051020campaign.htm.
58. Weissman and Hassan, "BCRA and the 527 Groups," in *The Election after Reform*, 90–91.
59. Matt Bai, "Wiring the Vast Left-Wing Conspiracy," *New York Times Magazine*, July 24, 2004, 30; and comments by Eric Smith, president of the Media Fund, in Institute of Politics, *Campaign for President*, 238.
60. Weissman and Hassan, "BCRA and the 527 Groups," in *The Election after Reform*, 83.
61. Dwyre and Kolodny, "National Political Parties after BCRA," in *Life after Reform*, 98.
62. Jeanne Cummings, "Companies Pare Political Donations," *Wall Street Journal*, June 7, 2004, sec. A; Thomas B. Edsall, "Republican Soft Money Groups Find Business Reluctant to Give," *Washington Post*, June 7, 2004; and Institute of Politics, *Campaign for President*, 211.
63. Weissman and Hassan, "BCRA and the 527 Groups," in *The Election after Reform*, 90.
64. Ibid.
65. Ibid., 109.
66. Eliza Newlin Carney, Peter H. Stone, and James A. Barnes, "New Rules of the Game," *National Journal*, December 20, 2003, 3802.
67. Sidney M. Milkis, "Parties versus Interest Groups," in *Inside the Campaign Finance Battle: Court Testimony on the New Reforms*, ed. Anthony Corrado, Thomas E. Mann, and Trevor Potter (Washington, D.C.: Brookings Institution Press, 2003), 45. Italics in original.
68. Jonathan Rauch, "Here's a New Campaign Finance Reform Plan: Just Stop," *National Journal*, May 7, 2005, http//:nationaljournal.com/pubs/nj/index.htm.
69. Institute of Politics, *Campaign for President*, 240.

70. Milkis, "Parties versus Interest Groups" in *Inside the Campaign Finance Battle*, 45; Herrnson, *Congressional Elections: Campaigning at Home and in Washington*, 245.
71. Jonathan S. Krasno and Frank Sorauf, "Why Soft Money Has Not Strengthened Parties," in *Inside the Campaign Finance Battle*.
72. Institute of Politics, *Campaign for President*, 230–231.
73. Kate Phillips, "Election Panel Won't Issue Donation Rules," *New York Times*, June 1, 2006, sec. A.
74. Ibid.

III. GROUPS IN THE POLICY PROCESS

10

Nonprofit Organizations as Interest Groups
The Politics of Passivity
Jeffrey M. Berry

When Americans think about interest groups, they usually do not consider a host of organizations that are part of their daily lives—the Red Cross, community shelters, arts organizations, and literally thousands upon thousands of others. But nonprofit organizations do constitute one large segment of the interest group universe, even if most of us think of them more as service providers than political actors. Indeed, most nonprofits do play major roles in providing services to various constituencies—the poor, those without health insurance, the arts community, and so on. But nonprofits also play political roles, albeit not as obviously or aggressively as other interest groups. Still, within a pluralistic society, nonprofits often constitute the most steadfast groups that represent the relatively powerless among us. As former Senate majority leader and 1996 Republican presidential candidate Bob Dole put it, in his usual pithy manner, "There aren't any poor PACs or food stamp PACs or nutrition PACs...."

In this chapter, Jeffrey M. Berry, who has written extensively on nonprofit organizations, explores the reasons behind their relative passivity when it comes to entering the political fray. Using evidence from an extensive survey of nonprofits, Berry documents how their leaders are both ignorant of the laws governing their groups' potential activities and reluctant to engage in perfectly legal and acceptable political actions. Berry sees the passivity of nonprofits as doing a disservice for the least powerful elements of American society as they compete within a group environment where powerful interests are almost always effectively represented (if not ultimately successful in achieving their goals). Berry's work also expands our notion of what an organized interest is, in that nonprofits do make up a major and growing portion of groups that provide representation within our system of government.

Many believe that American democracy suffers from a combination of pathologies that are working to weaken the vitality of our way of life. At the heart of this illness appears to be a spreading cancer of apathy: various measures show that over time we are participating less in community life and government affairs. But a committee appointed by the American Political Science Association recently reported that many barriers make participation more difficult than it needs to be. These scholars concluded, "faulty design may either fail to draw citizens into politics or place excessive demands on them."[1] Beyond the cultural influences that discourage Americans from civic engagement, or at least make us apathetic, are obstacles produced by public policy. In short, participation is regulated in many different ways, and government can make it easier or harder, more accessible or less accessible, if it so chooses.

One barrier to participation is the law on public charities. As an inducement to donate to worthy causes, Congress enacted a law in 1917 granting a tax deduction to those who contribute to qualifying nonprofit organizations. There are twenty-seven different kinds of nonprofits under American law, but only one type, those that come under section 501(c)(3) of the tax code, can offer tax deductions to donors.[2] All other types of nonprofits are exempt from federal income taxes, although that is only a modest benefit as such organizations are not in the business of making a profit.[3] Tax deductibility is highly prized, as it provides a powerful incentive for individuals to contribute or to contribute more than one would otherwise be inclined to. For someone with a marginal tax rate of 35 percent, a $1,000 contribution to the American Heart Association actually costs just $650.

The tax benefit comes at the expense of other taxpayers. Because the government still needs to fund the same number of aircraft carriers, reimburse hospitals for the same volume of Medicaid charges, and maintain every other program it finances, all taxpayers must make up for the charitable deductions with higher tax payments. In effect, all taxpayers subsidize the deduction offered to donors to 501(c)(3) nonprofits. This taxpayer subsidy of charitable deductions justifies government regulation of nonprofit expenditures.

Therein lies the rub. As will be detailed below, the government has erected some significant obstacles to the participation of nonprofits in the public policy-making process. The limit on both direct legislative lobbying and grassroots mobilization by 501(c)(3)s is particularly troublesome. The poor, the working poor, immigrants, the disabled, and other marginalized constituencies do not form interest groups on their own. Yet all who use social services depend on nonprofits to represent them. Indeed, half of all nonprofits large enough to file a tax return with the federal government are either human-services providers or health care organizations (see Figure 10.1). The impact of charity law, however, is to strongly discourage nonprofits from representing their clients and constituents in the governmental process.

Figure 10.1. Nonprofit Organizations in the United States, by Type of Organization, 2000

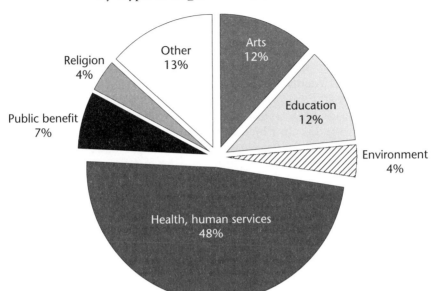

Source: Strengthening Nonprofit Advocacy Project, survey carried out in 2000 of nonprofits filing Internal Revenue Service Form 990.

Note: Data derived from 583 nonprofit organizations.

This problem of how poor people are represented is viewed here through the prism of interest group politics. An array of both barriers and easements regulates the participation of various types of interest groups in the political process. What is striking is that nonprofits are far more restricted in the policy-making process than business, labor, or professional associations.

In its examination of the political behavior of nonprofits, this study draws on data from the Strengthening Nonprofit Advocacy Project, which included a random sample survey of nonprofits from around the country, follow-up interviews with some of the executive directors who filled out the questionnaire, and focus groups with panels of nonprofit executive directors and board members.[4] The analysis of nonprofits is here organized into five sections. The first considers the changing role of nonprofits in America, emphasizing in particular the revolution in welfare policy. Second, the law on public charities is described, and the practical implications of the statute's ambiguity are discussed at length. The next section reports on research measuring the actual impact of the law on the attitudes of the executive directors of nonprofits and on the political behavior of these organizations. Fourth, attention turns to the continuing efforts of conservatives to intimidate liberal nonprofits through proposals to further restrict nonprofits' participation in the policy-making process. The final section outlines a strategy for overcoming the political weakness of nonprofits.

Growth Industry

The role of nonprofits within the American political system has changed dramatically. Between the mid-1960s—the beginning of the Great Society programs—and 2003, the number of nonprofits registered with the federal government rose eightfold, from roughly 100,000 to 800,000 organizations. In 2004, the last year for which statistics are available, 65,000 new nonprofits registered under 501(c)(3) with the Internal Revenue Service (IRS).[5] As a point of comparison, in recent years the number of nonprofits has increased at a rate of roughly two and a half times that of businesses.[6] All the more remarkable is that this growth developed during a period when civic engagement declined in many worrisome ways.[7] Whether the surge of nonprofits reflects something of a replacement effect, where participation has shifted from some traditional kinds of organizations, is unclear.

An enormous range of organizations has emerged to provide services to those in need. Such nonprofits include Safe Space, a New York City organization that runs group homes for foster children; La Clínica del Pueblo, a community health center in Washington, D.C., which operates largely in Spanish for its neighborhood's Latino population; the Jewish Association for Residential Care, which provides independent living services in the Detroit area for those with developmental disabilities; and Family Place, a Dallas shelter for battered women. These nonprofits and thousands more form the nation's safety net.

Multiple causes have contributed to the sharply rising number of nonprofits, but one of the most important is the transformation of the American welfare system. A quiet revolution in welfare began with the Kennedy administration's decision in 1962 to expand social services in the hopes of reducing dependency. The ultimate hope was rehabilitation: giving individuals the skills and support they needed to leave welfare altogether. Thus began a movement that led national policy away from income maintenance— providing clients with a check or voucher—and toward social services. Gradually, more and more programs began to offer job training, educational opportunities, and support services designed to help the disadvantaged achieve a better life. This trend culminated with the passage of welfare reform in 1996—the law intended, in President Clinton's words, "to end welfare as we know it." Among its many provisions is a lifetime restriction limiting a family to no more than five years of income assistance.

The relationship between the emphasis on social services and the growth of nonprofits is easy enough to decipher. Providing services to the welfare population is far more labor intensive than providing recipients with a monthly check.[8] When the Transitional Work Corporation in

Philadelphia enrolls welfare recipients into one of its job programs, it must hire highly skilled personnel to provide the relevant training. An office of the Department of Labor could easily employ the exact same kind of people who work for the Transitional Work Corporation and assign them the same kind of job with the same kind of clients. Instead, the government understandably regards this nonprofit as a far superior alternative. If the government offered a comparable program by itself, it would have to pay 100 percent of all costs. In contrast, a nonprofit will typically raise a good deal of its income from private donors. The Transitional Work Corporation, for example, receives funding from the Anne E. Casey Foundation, the Joyce Foundation, and the Pew Charitable Trusts in addition to its grants from government.[9]

Because the poor, disadvantaged, and politically marginalized do not generally organize on their own, the vast expansion of the nonprofit world would seemingly hold out the promise of broader representation in the policy-making process. This sector is composed of capable, resourceful, and respected organizations that could act as a forceful and articulate voice for their clients and constituents. Unfortunately, as we shall see, the nonprofit sector is instead a muted, timid constellation of organizations. In representing the poor, weak, and disadvantaged, the political voice of nonprofits is but a whisper.

Nonprofits' Unique Barrier

Although the basic rationale for government regulation of the taxpayer subsidy to nonprofits is entirely justifiable, the substance of that regulation is a far more difficult issue.[10] One of the rules governing nonprofits is that they are prohibited from engaging in partisan activity—making campaign contributions or endorsing candidates, for example. This is not controversial as few would argue that taxpayer-subsidized dollars should go to candidates running for office. Another of the restrictions involves lobbying and grassroots mobilization of clients or constituents. It is this policy, enforced by the IRS, that has proved to be problematic.

The origins of the lobbying restriction on nonprofits go back to 1919 when the Department of the Treasury issued regulations to accompany the law passed two years earlier creating the tax deduction for charitable organizations. The statute specifies that nonprofits qualifying for 501(c)(3) status must be working for "religious, charitable, scientific, testing for public safety, literary, or educational purposes." Trying to ensure that the taxpayer subsidy was not extended to the wrong kind of organizations, the Treasury Department issued a regulation declaring that tax-deductible status could not be extended to those organizations "formed to disseminate controversial or partisan propaganda."[11] In 1934 Congress added teeth to the regulation and wrote into law a provision that tax deductibility could not be granted or maintained by a nonprofit where a "substantial part" of that organization's activities "is carrying on propaganda, or otherwise attempting, to influence legislation."[12]

Rather than just being content with articulating a policy that lobbying and grassroots mobilization must remain within limits, American law still today categorizes such activities by nonprofits as propaganda. This term seems more descriptive of the rhetoric of a dictatorship than of behavior by community-based organizations providing services to the disadvantaged. If it was just some antiquated wording, little should be made of this definition. Unfortunately, the spirit and meaning conveyed by that term still reflect the view of the IRS.

Ambiguity

The harshness of the law is compounded by its maddening ambiguity. The law on public charities permits lobbying, but a nonprofit's lobbying cannot be "substantial." One might expect that the IRS would have defined this term so that nonprofits would know how much lobbying and grassroots mobilization they can do without running afoul of the law. This is no small matter since the ultimate penalty for violating the law is the loss of tax deductibility, which for most nonprofits is equivalent to the death penalty. To lose tax deductibility is to lose a significant percentage of funding that comes from individuals and virtually all that may come in the form of foundation grants. At the same time, many nonprofits have a need to talk frequently with officials from government, and nonprofit officials often interpret this limitation as a barrier.

Surprisingly, the IRS has steadfastly refused to define what "substantial" means, and it has never issued a specific set of guidelines to help nonprofits understand the lobbying provision of the law. Repeated requests have been made to the IRS by nonprofits, asking it to distinguish a substantial amount of lobbying from that which is insubstantial. Over the years the IRS has not budged, and its responses as to what falls below the substantial threshold are much too vague to be helpful. Interest groups of all types badger administrative agencies for clarity as to the meaning of ambiguous laws or regulations and, often, receive new regulations or instructional documents as a result. For many years there was no obvious reason why the IRS refused to offer an operational definition of the "substantial" standard. Only in recent years has a real obstacle emerged for the IRS if, unlikely as it might seem, the agency would now like to define the term. Republicans in Congress have made it clear that they do not want more lobbying by nonprofits as they consider that sector overwhelmingly liberal. The IRS has no interest in generating a conflict with conservative legislators, particularly since liberal legislators have never pushed for a standard to clarify the lobbying provision.

As to what constitutes "lobbying," IRS statements and legal interpretations have been more helpful.[13] The law indicates that lobbying refers only to the lobbying of a legislative body: Congress, state legislatures, and city councils. This includes direct lobbying of legislators or their staffs by nonprofit representatives as well as grassroots campaigns in which a 501(c)(3) works to activate its members, clients, or constituents by asking them to contact legislators about a specific bill. An important ambiguity here—some say loophole—is that "educating" legislators and their staffs is considered to be distinct from lobbying and, thus, not restricted by 501(c)(3). This, of course, is a useful fiction because nonprofits educate legislators so as to influence them; and to try to influence is to lobby. Political scientists regard the law's application to only legislative bodies as particularly illogical. In the case of nonprofits, why is unlimited lobbying of an administrative agency or filing a court suit permissible while legislative lobbying must be harshly restricted?

Enforcement

The law on public charities is complex, ambiguous, and administered by a bureaucracy that lacks the resources to oversee the nonprofit sector. Not surprisingly, enforcement of the law is erratic at best. Yet nonprofits are strongly influenced by the belief that the IRS is monitoring them and is ready to take action should they violate the lobbying provisions of 501(c)(3). The Tax Exempt and Government Entities Division (TE/GE Division) of the IRS has responsibility for approximately 1.6 million nonprofits of all types, including, as mentioned above, the nation's 800,000 501(c)(3)s.[14] However, the agency has only 290 auditors to monitor and investigate problems at all these nonprofits.[15]

As we interviewed the executive directors of nonprofits and conducted our focus groups with panels of executive directors and members of boards of directors, it became evident that many nonprofit leaders do believe that the IRS is looking over their shoulders. Few have any idea that the TE/GE Division is seriously underfunded and understaffed, to the point of being incapable of systematically overseeing public charities. Despite the feebleness of this bureau of the IRS, the fear is real and is derived from a number of sources. For example, leaders take note of the occasional high-profile audit of a nonprofit that has allegedly violated the law. Also, they may receive guidance from lawyers and accountants who have little understanding of the law and advise their nonprofit clients to play it safe by not getting involved in lobbying. Executive directors are sensitive to signals from their boards of directors, which, if they don't truly understand the law, may similarly advise caution.

The IRS's 1966 controversial revocation of the Sierra Club's tax-deductible status for its overt lobbying on a government proposal to build two dams on the Colorado River generated an unwarranted but powerful legacy of a vigilant, aggressive IRS.[16] Other nonprofits have occasionally been punished for violating the lobbying provision of section 501(c)(3), but there is no count of such actions because the IRS does not issue public documents or explanations of its actions when it audits nonprofits.

Hostility toward nonprofits can come from sources other than the IRS, thus creating a more general climate of fear that leads to excessive caution by officials of nonprofits. For 501(c)(3)s, the major sources of concern beyond the IRS are the administrative agencies—federal, state, and local—that distribute grants in a given nonprofit's policy area. For non-health-related public charities, government funding amounts to about 20 percent of annual income. Our survey showed that for human-services providers the figure grows to about 33 percent. Even though there is no restriction against the lobbying of administrative agencies, nonprofits receiving grants—or hoping to win grants in the future—will often be tempered in making any public criticism of an agency that may fund them. Not only is there a worry about hurting grant prospects, but an additional concern is that an angry agency can file a complaint with the IRS's TE/GE Division, alleging lobbying beyond the substantial threshold and possibly catalyzing an audit of the nonprofit's lobbying endeavors.

Impact

The basic effects of government regulation on nonprofits have been described in general terms. The Strengthening Nonprofit Advocacy Project provided an opportunity to test the basic supposition that nonprofits are actively discouraged from participating in public policy making. The random sample of 501(c)(3)s was drawn from the universe of the 220,000 nonprofits that filed a tax return with the IRS for 1998;[17] their executive directors filled out the project's questionnaire.

Ignorance

To assess the impact of the nation's tax law on the behavior of nonprofits, the questionnaire probed along a number of dimensions. One simple but highly telling approach was to ask executive directors what they knew about charity law. Respondents answered a short true-or-false quiz on 501(c)(3) rules; the results of the quiz can be found in Table 10.1. In a word, the executive directors did miserably. Their knowledge of 501(c)(3) provisions is spotty at best. Since the answer for each question was presented as either yes or no, simply guessing would yield a score, on average, of 50 percent correct. On only three of the eight questions did the executive directors of nonprofits do appreciably better than if they had flipped a coin and guessed heads or tails. On two questions they scored below 50 percent—worse than if they had flipped a coin.

In fairness, a few of the questions were difficult. The question the executive directors scored the lowest on—whether it is permissible to lobby if part of the organization's funding came from government—requires some

Table 10.1.   Results of True-or-False Questions on
Understanding of Charity Law, Asked of Executive
Directors of Nonprofit Organizations

Can your organization:	Correct answer	Percentage answering correctly
Use government funds to lobby Congress?	No	93
Endorse a candidate for elected office?	No	84
Talk to elected public officials about public policy matters?	Yes	80
Support or oppose federal regulations?	Yes	62
Take a policy position without reference to a specific bill under current regulations?	Yes	61
Support or oppose federal legislation under current IRS regulations?	Yes	54
Sponsor a forum or candidate debate for elected office?	Yes	45
Lobby if part of your budget comes from federal funds?	Yes	32

Source: Strengthening Nonprofit Advocacy Project, survey carried out in 2000 of nonprofits filing Internal Revenue Service Form 990.

Note: This set of questions began with the following statement: "There is a good deal of confusion about whether various activities by nonprofits relating to the policymaking process are permissible. Based on your understanding, can your organization: …"

subtlety in understanding the law. It's typically impermissible to use government funds to lobby Congress, but there is no prohibition against lobbying if other funds are used to pay for any expenses associated with lobbying. At the same time, it's not rocket science to understand this difference. Even more disturbing is that only a bit more than half (54 percent) of nonprofit executive directors know that their organization has the right to take a public stand on a bill before Congress. In other words close to half the executive directors of this nation's nonprofits believe their organization lacks rights guaranteed by the First Amendment.

Despite this level of ignorance about the law, one might quickly leap to the executive directors' defense by pointing out that running a nonprofit is a demanding job. Nonprofit directors typically contend with insufficient budgets, growing demands for services, staffing shortages, and far too many responsibilities in running their organizations. After managing the operations of their nonprofit, monitoring its finances, supervising the staff, and directing fund raising, spending time on advocacy is surely seen by many executive directors as a time-consuming luxury they cannot afford. In this vein, ignorance of 501(c)(3) regulations becomes one of the excuses not to engage in advocacy. It is also the case that some nonprofits have little reason to lobby as they may not be heavily affected by public policy.

Still, too many nonprofits have every reason to lobby legislators, and they choose not to do it. Every nonprofit leader, at the very least, should understand what the law says. If directors mistakenly believe that they do not even have the right to take a stand on legislation, their constituents will never be represented and their interests will never be sufficiently taken into account by members of Congress or state legislators. Understanding that you have the right to lobby is certainly the first step toward doing it.

Avoidance

Demonstrating that executive directors are relatively ignorant of the legal standards relating to nonprofit lobbying does not directly prove that those executives or their organizations are inactive. It's possible that executive directors ignore what the law says because they believe lobbying is so vital to their clients or to constituents' interests that they are willing to risk the consequences. Alternatively, they may believe that there is little chance of being caught by the IRS for violating 501(c)(3) regulations and have little hesitation in lobbying when they think it will do some good. And some 501(c)(3)s may create an affiliated organization that is not tax deductible and use it for lobbying purposes.[18]

The survey was again used to determine whether beliefs about the law actually influenced the behavior of nonprofits. Only one such test will be detailed here, but all our statistical tests as well as the data from the interviews and focus groups point in the same direction: 501(c)(3) status deters participation. As part of the questionnaire, the executive directors were asked about nine different tactics that can be used to try to influence policy makers. For each tactic, such as testifying before a legislative body or encouraging their members to write, call, or email policymakers, respondents scored their own organization as to the level of utilization. The question used a five-point scale, with zero representing "never" and, at the other end, four representing "ongoing interaction."

Before assessing what these scores mean, an initial question must be addressed: "compared with what?" How are we to know whether participation scores are relatively higher or lower than we might expect? To provide a point of comparison, we conducted a similar survey of "H electors." A bit of background will be helpful. The H election is a little-understood part of the tax code that actually allows nonprofits to escape the ambiguity of the substantial lobbying standard. In 1976, legislation included an option for 501(c)(3)s that gives nonprofits an expenditure ceiling on lobbying expenses. In stark contrast to the ambiguity of the substantial standard, the

H election is quite explicit. The 1976 law created a sliding scale specifying the amount that can be spent on both direct lobbying and grassroots lobbying. Spending limits depend on the size of the annual income of the nonprofit. For example, a small nonprofit with an income under $500,000 can spend up to 20 percent of its budget on direct lobbying and another 5 percent on grassroots lobbying. These percentages decline with increasing annual income, but they are generous at all levels.[19] What's more, the H election defines lobbying more precisely than the conventional definitions under 501(c)(3) and excludes many expenses (research on legislation, for example) that could be reasonably assessed as lobbying expenses. The bottom line is that few nonprofits would ever reach the lobbying expense limits set for H electors.

Despite the obvious advantage of not having to guess whether their lobbying crosses the substantial threshold, few nonprofits have chosen to become 501(c)(3) H electors. Many, if not most, executive directors appear unaware of the option. Some know about it but worry that taking the H election would signal the IRS to conduct an audit of the organization because of its ostensible political activity. There's no evidence that H electors are singled out for an auditing of lobbying expenses by the IRS, but this belief persists. In truth there's absolutely no disadvantage in taking the H election, and selecting it does not affect tax deductibility in any way. Nevertheless, only 2.4 percent of all 501(c)(3)s are H electors, which reflects not only ignorance of the option or misinformation about it, but also the IRS's lack of interest in promoting the H election. When a newly formed nonprofit applies to the IRS for tax-deductible status, there is no option for the H election on the application form. By default a new nonprofit is subject to the ambiguous substantial standard. Consequently, assuming a nonprofit actually knows about the H election, it has to obtain tax form 5768 and fill it out.

Since H electors self select their unusual status, they do not constitute a true control group. Rather, they allow us to view a set of 501(c)(3)s that is largely unencumbered by the lobbying restrictions that almost all other (97.6 percent) nonprofits contend with. From the H electors' responses to the quiz on the lobbying law (which is not shown in Table 10.1), we know that they are far more knowledgeable about the law on public charities and, as we see in Table 10.2, they are far more active and aggressive in their advocacy efforts. Because the H electors do self select, their overall greater level of advocacy in comparison with the conventional nonprofits means little. We would expect that organizations that seek out the protection of the H election to be more politically active. The more relevant comparison divides the nine tactics into two groups. One set of tactics is more legislative in orientation and more aggressive in the approach to government. The second set of tactics is more cooperative in nature and more attuned to the administrative process. The averages are computed from the means on the five-point scale.

Table 10.2.   Results of Questions on Tactics of Advocacy, Asked
of Executive Directors of Nonprofit Organizations

Tactics	Frequency, mean scores	
	H electors	Conventional nonprofits
More legislative, more aggressive		
Testifying at hearings	2.2	.7
Lobbying on a bill or policy	2.5	.9
Encouraging members to write, call, fax, email	2.6	1.2
Releasing research reports to the media, public, or policy makers	1.9	.8
Average	**2.3**	**.9**
More administrative, less aggressive		
Meeting with government officials	2.8	1.4
Working in a planning or advisory group	2.7	1.4
Responding to requests for information	2.5	1.5
Discussing grants with government officials	1.7	1.3
Socializing with government officials	1.8	1.4
Average	**2.3**	**1.4**

Source: Jeffrey M. Berry, with David F. Arons, *A Voice for Nonprofits* (Washington, D.C.: Brookings Institution Press, 2003), 101.

Notes: This set of questions began with the following statement: "A variety of means of communicating and interacting with those in government are listed below. Please use the scale on the right to indicate how frequently, if at all, your organization engages in these activities. (By 'your organization' we mean the executive director, other staff, volunteers, or members of the board.) In this scale, '0' means never, '1' is relatively infrequent interaction, and '4' is ongoing interaction." The averages are the mean of the aggregate scores for each tactic, not the mean of all responses. For the H electors, 320 responded; for conventional nonprofits, 583 responded. The aggregate responses to each tactic are a tiny bit smaller.

Recall that 501(c)(3) status applies only to legislative lobbying and not at all to the lobbying of administrative agencies. Here the comparison is telling. The H electors have identical aggregate scores for both sets of tactics; they lobby legislators and their staffs at the same rate they lobby administrators and their staffs. From what we know from the literature on lobbying, this makes perfect sense. Interest groups that want to maximize their influence in the policy-making process have to be prepared to lobby wherever it is most appropriate for the issue at hand.[20]

For the conventional nonprofits, the pattern is quite different. Unlike the H electors, there is considerable difference between the use of the cluster of tactics that are legislative in nature and are more overtly aggressive and those that are more administrative and less aggressive. The aggregate rate for the administrative tactics is more than 50 percent higher than that of the legislatively focused cluster.

Moreover, we also found that the H electors do not appear to be different from the conventional nonprofits in the policy areas they choose, nor in the level of financial support they receive from government.[21] The impact of 501(c)(3) on conventional nonprofits is unequivocal: The law on public charities strongly discourages nonprofits from representing their clients and constituents in the legislative process.

Mobilizing Constituents

The analysis so far has focused on the political behavior of organizations. The survey did, however, yield some data on the mobilization of followers. Because such a large percentage of nonprofits work with poor and disadvantaged clients, one might expect that the potential for activating their constituents is relatively low. One of the most persistent findings about political behavior is that political activity correlates strongly with social class. Thus, for those nonprofits primarily serving a low-income population, there is ample reason to use strategies oriented toward lobbying by professionals representing constituents rather than trying to directly mobilize clients or followers.

This is a critical distinction. Representing clients through lobbyists and mobilizing clients directly share the identical goal of seeking to change public policy. Nevertheless, they are two very different lobbying strategies. Some lobbyists, such as those representing corporations, make only limited use of their clients and are quite effective in influencing government. Still, although the participation of members, followers, or clients is not absolutely necessary to achieve influence, such mobilization unquestionably helps organizational representatives in their efforts to influence policy makers.

A low-income constituency, although it may be more difficult to engage, is not impossible to activate. Being poor does not mean one is apathetic. Nor does it mean that one does not understand the elemental connection between public policy and the current availability and quality of services. There is clearly far more potential for enlisting nonprofit clients and supporters than the current levels of such lobbying documented by our survey. A finer-grained analysis of the advocacy of nonprofits indicates that regulatory restrictions artificially limit the mobilization of nonprofit followers. One of the tactics of influence asked about in the survey was the degree to which an organization encouraged "members to write, call, fax, or email policy makers." In Table 10.2 we see that conventional nonprofits indicate a very low level of usage, an average of only 1.2 on this zero-to-four scale. By comparison, H-electing nonprofits score 2.6. Because H electors have been shown to be roughly similar in their organizational dimensions to conventional nonprofits, the large difference in the scores for grassroots mobilization points toward the perceived restrictions in 501(c)(3) regulations and not the nature of the constituency as the real culprit.

For the poor and disadvantaged, the negative consequences of 501(c)(3) provisions extend beyond the diminished political prowess of sympathetic nonprofits. Part of the process of mobilizing constituents at any income level is to educate them about issues and about the governmental process. This teaching opportunity is lost when nonprofits shy away from involving their followers. Moreover, individual participation can lead to a greater sense of political efficacy, critical for those who are not active in other realms of civil society.[22] This, too, is lost.

Intimidation

The impact of ignorance and misinformation about the law on public charities is probably far greater than these data can reveal. As commonly understood, the message of 501(c)(3) is not simply "don't lobby legislators," but something more pointed and insidious: "nonprofits should be nonpolitical." And if organizations are supposed to be nonpolitical and uninvolved in public policy making, then the type of people nonprofits hire and the way responsibilities of the professionals on the staff are defined will be different from the way they would be in an organization that defines public policy advocacy as part of its mission. In the end, the socialization process that defines the appropriate role of a nonprofit works to create organizations that are nonpolitical in both their structure and outlook.

Nonprofit leaders' misconceptions about the law come not only from their ignorance and failure to learn what it actually says but also from the actions of the IRS, agency administrators, and legislators. The Sierra Club case, which sent an enormously powerful signal to all 501(c)(3)s, was the beginning of what has become periodic harassment of nonprofits. Following that episode, the Nixon administration held up requests for 501(c)(3) status from nonprofits that it regarded as political opponents.[23] A court suit forced the administration to back down. During the Reagan administration, the Office of Management and Budget proposed new guidelines that would have forbidden nonprofits receiving federal grants from engaging in any kind of lobbying, legislative or otherwise. A nonprofit that wanted to try to influence government would have had to start a completely separate organization to handle advocacy, while the core 501(c)(3) organization with tax-deductible status would remain removed from any lobbying.[24] This proposal also failed, as the White House retreated because of adverse publicity.

Congressional Republicans initiated another round in this ongoing fight after they captured the House of Representatives in 1994. With Newt Gingrich taking over as Speaker of the House and effectively as head of the party, new, bold initiatives sprang forth from Republicans in Congress. One popular objective was to try to find a way of disempowering politically active nonprofits. What enrages conservatives is that many nonprofits receive federal grants and then, allegedly, use that money to lobby the government for liberal policies. Conservative firebrand Grover Norquist, the head of Americans for Tax Reform and a close ally of Gingrich, said, "We will hunt [these liberal groups] down one by one and extinguish their funding sources."[25]

Many House Republicans coalesced around legislation introduced by Rep. Ernest Istook, R-Okla. The Istook amendment took many forms, but in its most antagonistic version it expanded the range of tactics qualifying as lobbying under 501(c)(3) and then restricted any advocacy under this broader definition to no more than 5 percent of an organization's budget. The bill received serious consideration in the House of Representatives and catalyzed a fierce counterattack by nonprofits around the country. As legislators began to hear from local nonprofit leaders back in their districts, support for the legislation cooled and the proposal eventually died.

Like the Sierra Club case in the 1960s, however, this episode had a lingering impact. Representative Istook's attack reverberated throughout the nonprofit grapevine; 501(c)(3) organizations found it easy to believe that the federal government monitored them closely and disapproved of those nonprofits that engage in advocacy. Our interviews confirmed that executive directors were aware of the legislation, and many were nervous about adopting an advocacy role because of the government's apparent hostility toward nonprofit involvement in the policy-making process. Representative Istook ostensibly lost the battle but surely gained ground in the war by frightening those nonprofits uncertain of their rights under the law.

The attack on nonprofits has continued in the George W. Bush years. In many ways, the administration has tried to stop nonprofits from speaking out on various issues:

- Advocates for Youth, a nonprofit that works to promote effective policies on preventing teenage pregnancy, sexually transmitted diseases, and HIV/AIDS, was subjected to three audits in eight months by the Centers for Disease Control and Prevention. An internal government memo leaked to the *Washington Post* described the organization as an "ardent opponent" of the administration's policies.[26]
- The IRS initiated an investigation of the National Association for the Advancement of Colored People because its board chairman, Julian Bond, tacitly endorsed Democrat John Kerry at the civil rights organization's annual convention in 2004 (nonprofits with 501(c)(3) status may not endorse candidates). The only specific action that Bond called for, however, was expanding voter registration drives. Voter registration drives are perfectly legal under charity law. The real "violation" seemed to be the blistering criticism of Bush in Bond's speech.[27]
- After the Bush administration introduced a bill in 2003 to alter the Head Start program, some local Head Start directors publicly

criticized the legislation. The U.S. Department of Health and Human Services tried to stop the advocacy by sending a letter to all Head Start grantees telling them that they could not lobby against the bill because they receive federal funds. This letter was categorically inaccurate. As noted in the discussion of our survey, the law permits federal grantees to lobby as long as no government funds are used.[28]

- The Individuals with Disabilities Education Act (IDEA) funds approximately one hundred parent centers around the country; these centers provide a range of services and education for families with disabled children. A bill introduced by Rep. Michael N. Castle, R-Del., proposed amending IDEA by banning grants to parent centers that did any kind of "federal relations." Negative fallout from the proposal led Representative Castle to drop this provision, but it may have accomplished its goal by ominously threatening the centers.[29]

Many more examples could be offered but the pattern should be sufficiently clear. Since the Nixon years, Republicans in Congress and Republican administrations have continually gone after nonprofits, trying to intimidate them with proposed legislation, regulatory directives, and IRS audits.

The Republican antagonism is grounded in two strongly held beliefs, one philosophical and the other partisan. The philosophical argument is that interest group politics should emanate from people who organize on their own and promote their causes with their own resources. Government grants, therefore, should not be used to support, even indirectly, any kind of advocacy by nonprofits. To do so would be to favor one sector with taxpayer dollars over all others. This position conveniently overlooks market failure—that the most disadvantaged in society do not have the resources to form organizations to act on their behalf. Nor does it recognize all the ways in which government facilitates lobbying by other interest group sectors.

The second belief is that nonprofit advocacy provides direct political support for liberals and Democrats. In this view, Democrats use the rules of government to support themselves when they are in power and, thus, Republicans are justified in doing the same. Republicans are certainly correct in their assessment of the political views of those nonprofits that do become engaged in advocacy. Most 501(c)(3) nonprofits support a large and active government, and in this sense they are classic liberals. Conversely, nonprofits stand in the way of minimal government, the most basic pillar of conservative philosophy. Not surprisingly, many nonprofit advocates also favor the kinds of programs—family planning, abortion, strong business regulation, national health insurance, and consumer protection—that conservatives dislike. The Republicans' logic is unassailable: by weakening nonprofit advocacy, conservatives will reduce liberal advocacy.

Overcoming Political Weakness

For all the services that nonprofits provide to working Americans, to the poor, and to the disadvantaged, the political party that ostensibly represents these same interests has not been terribly energetic in trying to protect these organizations from the Republicans' attacks. Democrats in Congress have certainly opposed the policy proposals aimed at silencing nonprofits; but protecting 501(c)(3)s has not been a priority, and there has been little effort in trying to push through policies that would help to empower the sector.

The Democrats' lackluster record in this regard reflects in large part the broader political weakness of the nonprofit sector. The feebleness of nonprofits may seem counterintuitive. In any American city, nonprofits constitute a major element of the civic fabric of the community. Nonprofits are highly respected institutions and, collectively, their boards of directors represent a who's who of any city. They engage huge numbers of volunteers, and their donors surely comprise a large segment of a community's leadership.

At the same time, the very breadth of the sector weakens it. The categorization of all the kinds of organizations that qualify under 501(c)(3) provisions into one grouping greatly exaggerates the commonality among the constituent parts. Community health centers, arts councils, hospices, meals-on-wheels, and animal rights groups share little in common beyond their legal status. The collective action problem among the full range of organizations that constitutes this sector is enormous. Some national organizations, such as Independent Sector and the National Council of Nonprofit Associations, work on behalf of all nonprofits; many statewide associations of nonprofits do the same. Unfortunately these peak associations have yet to develop a working alliance that has proved to be politically influential.

Trade associations of nonprofits in separate fields, often organized on a statewide basis, have greater political sophistication than the typical 501(c)(3). These organizations, like a statewide association of mental retardation centers, could, along with the national nonprofit leadership groups and statewide associations of nonprofits, provide the nucleus of a stronger, empowered nonprofit sector. These organizations have existed for years, and their weakness in promoting the broad nonprofit sector is hardly encouraging.[30]

Beyond the weakness of their leadership organizations, substantial as it is, lies another significant hurdle for nonprofits in overcoming the barrier to advocacy. Lobbying by nonprofits is not broadly seen as a means of enabling democracy or balancing other, more powerful interest groups. The democratic process falls short when significant constituencies with obvious interests before government are inactive and their voices just a murmur. In contrast with private sector lobbies, nonprofits are celebrated in America as embodying the compassion and generosity of our culture. The extensive voluntarism that is part and parcel of the nonprofit sector is similarly praised.

Despite the many virtues of nonprofits, this widespread admiration does not extend to appreciation of their efforts to raise the voice of their clients and constituents in the policy-making process.

Perversely, charity law considers nonprofits a danger to democracy and regards their advocacy as potentially propagandistic. Although this line of argument is not used against nonprofits in public debate, the guiding philosophy of the law does influence the IRS and stands as one important reason why the agency refuses to help nonprofits navigate the lobbying restriction in 501(c)(3). After all, the IRS took fourteen years to write the regulations that put into effect the provision in the 1976 tax law that created the H election alternative.

Conservatives continue to attack nonprofit lobbying, arguing that these organizations are simply another set of selfish interest groups. As long as the debate focuses on lobbying by nonprofits and the grants they receive from government, the conservatives will maintain a strong political position. Those who believe that nonprofits should be involved in public policy making and who believe that it is important for 501(c)(3)s to mobilize their clients and supporters so that they participate should try to shift the terms of this argument. In the best of all possible worlds, discussion of nonprofit advocacy should focus on representation, inclusion, and civic engagement. In these contexts, emphasis should be placed on the disadvantaged who cannot otherwise participate, whose voice will not be heard unless nonprofits work to amplify it. Arguments about advocacy should be connected to the appealing, sympathetic clienteles of nonprofits, such as frail elderly, the disabled, battered women, developmentally challenged children, and single working mothers. These constituencies must come to life, vividly drawn, to move discussion away from abstract principles about lobbying and toward a message about letting all Americans participate.

A sensitivity to the way rhetoric is used and how to design messages about nonprofits is just a first step. More important is organizing. Because trade associations have done a poor job educating and mobilizing rank-and-file nonprofits, thought should be given to shifting organization downward to the local level and to the creation of nonprofit councils.[31] These should be small, elite-driven organizations rather than a formal coalition of nonprofits from the area. Trying to organize a large coalition of local nonprofits is expensive, and most nonprofits will not want to pay dues to join.

The main purpose of a nonprofit council should be to make legislators understand that they are being closely monitored by a cadre of nonprofit leaders. Such a council, composed of a cross section of assorted nonprofit executive directors and board members, could easily command periodic meetings with local, state, and federal legislators. If a council regularly met with its member of the U.S. House of Representatives, it would be difficult for that legislator—no matter how conservative—to explain to presidents of banks, chief officers of hospitals, and ministers why a vote for something like the Istook amendment would be acceptable. When such elites say, "You're trying to shut up my organization, and this will make it more difficult for the United Way and homeless shelters and the local council of churches," it changes the calculus of such a vote in Congress or the state legislature.

To ensure that a nonprofit council is not viewed as hostile to legislators, it should include some friends and campaign contributors. At the same time, this council must be prepared to play a little hardball, an approach uncharacteristic of the nonprofit sector. But this leadership council would not have to formally organize and would not need 501(c)(3) status as it needs little funding. It could be housed in someone's business, with the little clerical assistance necessary provided by an assistant of one of the board members. One tool it could use would be the familiar legislative tactic of a report card, which would be distributed to an extensive mailing list of local nonprofits that, provided the report card is nonpartisan in nature, could then reprint and distribute the card. Whatever the tactical approach, the essential point is for the council to be obviously engaged in oversight of legislators.

The federal government and individual states and cities depend on nonprofits to administer the welfare state. As government is now structured, it cannot function without nonprofits to provide social services. Nonprofits have adapted well to the needs of government, mixing government funds and charitable contributions that they solicit in order to provide services to those in need.[32] But nonprofits need to adapt themselves further to become more effective voices for those who have no other advocate before government. These organizations need to define advocacy as part of their mission and stop pretending that the regulatory limits on their participation form a legal barrier to active involvement in public policy making. The law permits nonprofits to be advocates, but, unfortunately, too many nonprofit leaders believe otherwise.

Notes

1. Stephen Macedo et al., *Democracy at Risk* (Washington, D.C.: Brookings Institution Press, 2005), 160.
2. Lester M. Salamon, *America's Nonprofit Sector*, 2d ed. (New York: Foundation Center, 1999), 8.
3. Following colloquial practice, I will use the term *nonprofit* to refer exclusively to those organizations with 501(c)(3) tax-deductible status.
4. Jeffrey M. Berry, with David F. Arons, *A Voice for Nonprofits* (Washington, D.C.: Brookings Institution Press, 2003).
5. "Tax-Exempt Organizations Registered with the IRS," *Chronicle of Philanthropy*, September 1, 2005, 37.
6. Murray S. Weitzman, Nadine T. Jalandoni, Linda M. Lampkin, and Thomas H. Pollak, *The New Nonprofit Almanac and Desk Reference* (New York: Jossey-Bass, 2002), 12.
7. Robert D. Putnam, *Bowling Alone* (New York: Simon & Schuster, 2000); and Theda Skocpol, *Diminished Democracy* (Norman: University of Oklahoma Press, 2003).
8. See Richard P. Nathan et al., "The 'Nonprofitization Movement' as a Form of Devolution," in *Capacity for Change? The Nonprofit World in the Age of Devolution*,

Dwight F. Burlingame et al. (Indianapolis: Center on Philanthropy at Indiana University, 1996), 33.

9. See the Web site, www.transitionalwork.org, for information about the Transitional Work Corporation.

10. Evelyn Brody and Joseph J. Cordes, "Tax Treatment of Nonprofit Organizations: A Two-Edged Sword?" in *Nonprofits and Government: Collaboration and Conflict*, ed. Elizabeth T. Boris and C. Eugene Steuerle (Washington, D.C.: Urban Institute, 1999); Miriam Galston, "Lobbying and the Public Interest: Rethinking the Internal Revenue Code's Treatment of Legislative Activities," *Texas Law Review* 71 (1993): 1269–1354; and Henry Hansmann, "Economic Theories of Nonprofit Organizations," in *The Nonprofit Sector*, ed. Walter W. Powell (New Haven: Yale University Press, 1987).

11. Janne G. Gallagher, "Charities, Lobbying, and Political Activity" (background paper prepared for the Nonprofit Sector Strategy Group, Aspen Institute, October 19, 1998), 1.

12. Revenue Act of 1934, 48 Stat. 760, sec. 517. For a detailed history of the evolution of the basic law on nonprofits and the subsequent amendments and regulations, see Judith E. Kindell and John Francis Reilly, "P. Lobbying Issues," http://www.irs.gov/pub/irs-utl/topic-p.pdf.

13. Bruce R. Hopkins, *Charity, Advocacy, and the Law* (New York: Wiley, 1992); and Bob Smucker, *The Nonprofit Lobbying Guide*, 2d ed. (Washington, D.C.: Independent Sector, 1999).

14. The record keeping is such that some cease to exist before they are eventually purged from IRS lists. IRS rules require 501(c)(3)s with a yearly income of at least $5,000 to register with the agency. Nonprofits with a yearly income of at least $25,000 must file a yearly tax return, and those returns are a matter of public record.

15. Brad Wolverton, "IRS Asks Organizations Seeking Charity Status to Supply More Details," *Chronicle of Philanthropy*, January 6, 2005, http://philanthropy.com/premium/articles/v17/i06/06002701.htm.

16. Ironically, the Sierra Club had a separate 501(c)(3) foundation and used it to receive tax-deductible donations after the revocation. Not only was it not hurt by the revocation, it actually profited as the ensuring controversy over the IRS's action created both publicity and sympathy for the organization, leading to a gain in membership.

17. The survey does not include churches as they are not required to file a tax return with the IRS, and nonprofit tax returns constitute the universe from which we sampled. Other kinds of faith-based organizations are included as it is only congregations that are not required to file a return. Universities and hospitals were removed from the samples that were drawn because they are egregious statistical outliers and would have skewed any statistical analysis of the nonprofit world. An overview of the survey methodology and the full set of findings for the study can be found in Berry, with Arons, *A Voice for Nonprofits*. A more detailed description of the survey methodology is available in Jeffrey M. Berry, David F. Arons, Gary D. Bass, Matthew F. Carter, and Kent E. Portney, *Surveying Nonprofits: A Methods Handbook* (Washington, D.C.: Aspen Institute, 2003).

18. Nonprofits that are dedicated advocacy organizations can qualify under section 501(c)(4), a misleadingly labeled category for "social welfare" organizations. These nonprofits can lobby without limit although they are subject to restrictions on partisan activity. Some 501(c)(3)s have affiliated 501(c)(4)s that allow them to conduct their lobbying through the (c)(4) without concern for IRS limits while still being able to raise tax-deductible donations through the (c)(3). This requires separate boards of directors and some strict accounting so that there is no commingling of funds, which must be raised separately. The use of affiliated 501(c)(4)s is not growing in

popularity as the number of organizations registering as social welfare nonprofits has not increased significantly in recent years, while the number of 501(c)(3)s pushes ever higher.

19. Smucker, *The Nonprofit Lobbying Guide*, 55.
20. See, generally, Jeffrey M. Berry and Clyde Wilcox, *The Interest Group Society*, 4th ed. (New York: Longman, 2006).
21. Berry, with Arons, *A Voice for Nonprofits*, 60–64.
22. Joe Soss, "Lessons of Welfare: Policy Design, Political Learning, and Political Action," *American Political Science Review* 93 (1999): 363–380.
23. Richard Corrigan, "Public Interest Law Firms Win Battle with IRS over Exemptions, Deductions," *National Journal*, November 21, 1970, 2541–2549.
24. Gary D. Bass, Shannon Ferguson, and David Plocher, *Living with A-122: A Handbook for Nonprofit Organizations* (Washington, D.C.: OMB Watch, 1984).
25. Jeff Shear, "The Ax Files," *National Journal*, April 15, 1995, 925.
26. James Wagoner, "Charities Should Disagree with Government," *Chronicle of Philanthropy*, October 28, 2004, 69.
27. Jeffrey M. Berry, "Who Will Get Caught in the IRS's Sights?" *Washington Post*, November 21, 2004, sec. B.
28. Gary D. Bass, Kay Guinane, and Ryan Turner, *An Attack on Nonprofit Speech: Death by a Thousand Cuts* (Washington, D.C.: OMB Watch, 2003), 2–4.
29. Ibid.
30. Alan J. Abramson and Rachel McCarthy, "Infrastructure Organizations," in *The State of Nonprofit America*, ed. Lester M. Salamon (Washington, D.C.: Brookings Institution Press, 2002).
31. Jeffrey M. Berry, "Charities of the World—Unite!" *Chronicle of Philanthropy*, September 2, 2004, 27.
32. Lester M. Salamon, "The Resilient Sector," in *The State of Nonprofit America*.

11

Is Corporate Lobbying Rational or Just a Waste of Money?

Erik K. Godwin, R. Kenneth Godwin, and Scott Ainsworth

Why do businesses lobby legislators? The answer seems simple and obvious—a profit-seeking business should attempt to influence legislation when a particular political decision would yield a financial advantage to the firm. Lobbying is typically an expensive investment for businesses, and this view would seem to require that the benefits of lobbying should exceed the costs; otherwise the business would be losing money by engaging in the activity. Surprisingly, research on the subject is mixed, and, in fact, some of the most recent research suggests that many firms are losing money when they lobby. If this were to be the case, it would appear that much lobbying is irrational, as corporations and businesses spend millions of dollars on an activity that actually decreases their net worth!

In this chapter, Erik K. Godwin, R. Kenneth Godwin, and Scott Ainsworth argue that, although business lobbying can often look chaotic and purposeless, there is an underlying logic and rationality to the enterprise. Contending that lobbying on legislation should be viewed as a two-stage, ongoing activity, they find that the goals and strategies pursued at an early stage in the process often are quite distinct from (and may appear contradictory to) those pursued later. Often the first stage in the lobbying process involves the pursuit of collective goods, which normally involves coalition behavior among business interests to get an item on the political agenda and to have it defined to the coalition's advantage. The second stage in the process typically involves an organized interest acting alone or with just a few others in search of some particular, private good.

In the authors' view, "What appear to be contradictory findings in the literature more often reflect the fact that the studies are examining different stages in the lobbying process." Lobbying money is indeed well spent.

The greatest uncertainty in Washington is not whether you will win or lose a floor vote, but whether your issue will be attended to at all.

Beth L. Leech et al., "Drawing Lobbyists to Washington:
Government Activity and Interest-Group Mobilization,"
Political Research Quarterly, *2005*

There are many more deals and compromises on K Street than on Capitol Hill.

Lobbyist involved in the Jobs for Americans Act

An interesting contradiction appears in the research concerning lobbying. When political scientists take a sample of issues from the *New York Times, CQ Weekly Report,* or lobbying disclosure reports and make a list of all the interests that lobbied on each issue, researchers find that the vast majority of lobbying occurs on very few issues. These issues are characterized by a great deal of media attention and substantial conflict among competing interests. In addition, the number of interested parties who win on the issue and the number who lose are approximately the same.[1] In contrast, when political scientists take a sample of lobbyists and examine their success in achieving their lobbying goals, the researchers find that almost all lobbyists win much more frequently than they lose. The issues the lobbyists talk about receive little media attention and involve very little conflict.[2]

There is an equally remarkable logical contradiction in the lobbying behavior of for-profit corporations. They appear to join lobbying coalitions with great frequency. But, as we explain below, such behavior seems irrational. For example, suppose you are the chief executive officer of Wendy's International, Inc., the restaurant chain, and an issue comes before Congress that affects Wendy's and all other fast-food corporations. Your lobbyists want to know whether they should join the lobbyists from McDonald's, Burger King, Taco Bell, Applebee's, and other restaurant chains that already are lobbying on the issue. Rational-choice theory tells us that the CEO should tell the Wendy's lobbyists not to waste their time and the company's resources joining such a coalition. Instead, the CEO should tell the lobbyists to concentrate on issues that benefit only Wendy's. But corporations don't seem to do this. They appear to act just as irrationally as a person who drives to the polls on election day and casts a ballot despite the knowledge that the probability of getting killed in an auto accident while driving to the polls is much higher than the probability of that single vote actually deciding that election.

In this chapter we explain that, although lobbying by firms can look just as irrational as voting by individuals,[3] that impression is likely to be incorrect. We utilize a model that incorporates multiple policy-making stages and reveals why a lobbyist will have different goals when she[4] moves from one stage of the policy process to the next. We use the 2004 American Jobs Creation Act (hereafter referred to as the "jobs bill") and the Environmental Protection Agency's regulation of perchlorate, a chemical in rocket fuel, to illustrate the two-stage model.

Our approach to studying lobbying is an example of the *exchange model* of lobbying. An organization provides benefits to policy makers and, in exchange, the policy makers make decisions that favor the organization. Organizations use political action committee (PAC) contributions, political support at election time, information, and other resources to convince policy makers to select a particular policy alternative. There need be nothing sinister about the exchange. For example, a lobbyist may point out to a legislator representing the district where her firm is located that a particular policy would keep 500 people who work for the firm from being laid off. The lobbyist might promise the legislator that if the policy passes, her firm will inform the 500 workers that the legislator helped them keep their jobs and will urge the workers to vote for the legislator in the next election. The firm also might show its appreciation by donating $5,000 from its PAC to the legislator's reelection campaign.

If a firm believes that the benefits a legislator will provide are worth the lobbying costs to the firm, then the firm will lobby. Alternatively, if the legislator does not have sufficient sway over the process, is unwilling to use his influence, or wants to charge the firm too much for the service, then the firm elects not to lobby. This seems reasonably straightforward. Why, then, do some scholars maintain that lobbying is irrational? We believe the answer to this question centers around two important ideas: governments supply both private and collective goods, and lobbying is a multistage process.

Collective and Private Goods

A *private good* occurs when the government gives a benefit to a single organization or individual. For example, the government may grant a regulatory waiver to a single chemical plant, provide a tax loophole that benefits only one firm, or award a contract to a single firm to build a highway. A *collective good* benefits many individuals or firms. For example, a cut in the corporate income tax rate benefits almost all firms. A key aspect of a collective good is that once the government provides it to one individual or firm, all similar individuals or firms receive it. While firms lobby for both private and collective goods, the lobbying strategies they use to obtain the two types of goods differ. A hypothetical example may help clarify the difference between lobbying for collective goods and lobbying for private goods.

Pretend that Congress is considering a new law that would require the Environmental Protection Agency (EPA) to impose stricter regulations on a class of agricultural pesticides. Only three corporations—Dow, DuPont, and Monsanto—produce the pesticide. If the new regulation were to apply immediately to all plants that produce the pesticide, this would be extremely expensive for the three corporations. To prevent this, the three corporations form a coalition and lobby Congress to have wording placed in the new law that allows EPA to provide waivers to the plants that currently produce the pesticide. This wording permits EPA to decide how long the existing plants can delay meeting the new regulation. The wording that allows waivers is a collective good because it potentially benefits all three corporations.

Once the bill containing the regulation becomes law, Dow, DuPont, and Monsanto may have different interests. Let's suppose that the plants that produce these chemicals for Dow are significantly older than the production facilities of DuPont and Monsanto. Dow planned to replace its plants over the next five years, but DuPont and Monsanto would like to use their plants for ten more years. Dow may decide to lobby EPA to limit all waivers to five years as this will not impose any new costs on Dow but it will impose substantial costs on DuPont and Monsanto. This would give Dow an advantage over its two competitors. Limiting the waivers to five years is, therefore, a private good for Dow. It is the only firm that benefits from the limitation.

The above hypothetical example illustrates an important situation in lobbying: sometimes a firm finds it necessary to join a coalition and lobby for a collective good in an early stage of the policy process so that it can lobby for a private good at a later stage. As we will see below, sometimes these coalitions involve hundreds of organizations. Once the coalition has achieved the collective good, however, the coalition may break apart as different organizations pursue different private goods. Firms that cooperated in stage 1 of the lobbying process may become competitors in stage 2. Keeping this in mind, let's turn now to the arguments that lobbying is irrational.

Arguments That Firms Act Irrationally

Before we begin our discussion of whether lobbying is rational or irrational, we need a working definition of *rational* as it applies to firms. Based on the assumption that firms attempt to maximize profits, we define *rational lobbying* as any attempt at political influence where the expected benefit is the largest payoff that the firm can receive from expending those resources, taking all other investment opportunities and risk into account. For example, suppose that two firms spend $15,000 each lobbying for a government contract that only one firm will win. If each firm has a fifty-fifty chance of winning the contract and the contract will yield a profit of $60,000, the expected value of the lobbying is $30,000 ($0.50 \times $60,000$). If a $30,000 profit is the best return that the firm could obtain from investing the $15,000, then lobbying for the contract is rational. This is true for the firm that ultimately wins the contract and for the firm that does not. Note that our definition is consistent with the microeconomic interpretation of firm behavior and with the public choice approach to politics. This is important because for the rest of this chapter we assume that profit maximization is the dominant goal of a business. While firms may have other objectives, we do not include them in our model of lobbying.

The political scientists who maintain that firms act irrationally when lobbying make three arguments. First, lobbyists spend their resources on issues where they are unlikely to win and use strategies that are likely to fail. Second, firms often lobby when it is unnecessary because other firms with more at stake in the policy decision will provide the necessary lobbying to achieve the goal. Third, the policy process is so complex and uncertain that it is impossible for firms to choose the lobbying strategy that will maximize profits.

Firms Pick the Wrong Issues and Use the Wrong Strategies

Perhaps the most puzzling aspect of lobbying behavior is that firms seem to spend more money lobbying on issues where they are less likely to win than on issues where they are more likely to win. For decades, political science research has shown that lobbyists are most successful when they lobby on issues that are nonpartisan, narrow in scope, have low visibility to the public, and generate little organized opposition.[5] But organizations do not do this. In their study of lobbying activity in Washington, D.C., Frank Baumgartner and Beth Leech found that most lobbying occurs on just a few issues.[6] Using data from the 1996 lobbying disclosure reports, Baumgartner and Leech examined more than 19,000 lobbying efforts. They found that twenty-six issues accounted for 81 percent of all reported lobbying activity, and more than one hundred organizations lobbied on each of the twenty-six issues. These twenty-six issues were partisan, broad in scope, highly visible to the public, and involved substantial conflict. As Figure 11.1 indicates, more than 1,000 organizations lobbied on some issues.

Lobbyists also appear to use the wrong lobbying strategies. Christine Mahoney and Frank Baumgartner found that firms win more often when they lobby alone than when they lobby as part of a coalition.[7] Similarly, Kenneth Godwin, Edward Lopez, and Barry Seldon have shown that profit-maximizing firms should lobby more often for private goods than for collective goods. But, despite the seeming irrationality of the behavior, firms choose to lobby in coalitions more often than they lobby alone; and they appear to lobby more frequently for collective goods than for private goods.[8]

Firms Should Free Ride More Frequently

Closely related to the arguments that firms are lobbying on the wrong issues and using the wrong strategies is the contention that lobbyists are spending resources unnecessarily. Mancur Olson Jr. showed that if a government policy will benefit large numbers of individuals (if it is a collective good), the rational individual usually will not contribute her resources to lobbying for that good. She will not lobby because she will receive the collective good whether or not she contributes.[9] Social scientists label those who do not contribute to a collective good but receive the benefit as *free riders.* They free ride on the efforts of others.

To see the collective-action problem, pretend for a moment that it is worth $50 to you for the government to prevent oil exploration in the Arctic National Wildlife Refuge (ANWR). If the government does this, it provides a collective good to you and to everyone who shares your policy preference. Is it rational for you to donate $50 to an environmental organization that will use the $50 to lobby against drilling for oil in ANWR? No. If environmental interests prevent drilling in ANWR, you receive the benefit whether or not you donated the $50. But it is highly unlikely that *your* $50 contribution will make any difference in the lobbying effort. Environmental groups will spend hundreds of thousands of dollars lobbying on the issue, and it will not make any difference whether they spend $500,000 or $500,050. Because a $50 contribution will not make a difference, a rational person will free ride on this issue and keep the $50.

Protecting ANWR is a collective good not only for individuals but also for organizations that favor greater environmental protection. Pretend that you are a lobbyist for a hypothetical interest group named the Worldwide Organization for Wildlife Sustainability through Environmental Regulation (WOWSER). WOWSER's membership cares deeply about the ANWR bill, but WOWSER looks at the large number of organizations lobbying on the issue and decides that, even if it spent all of its lobbying resources on the issue, its efforts would not change the policy outcome. For this reason, WOWSER decides to use its lobbying resources to convince the National Park Service to give WOWSER 50 permits to take people on rafting trips on the Colorado River through the Grand Canyon. If WOWSER's lobbyists are successful, WOWSER can use these permits to increase its revenues by promising people who donate $5,000 a "free trip" through the Grand Canyon with other tree-hugging WOWSERs. The permits are private goods for WOWSER because only it is receiving the extra permits. If WOWSER is rational, it will forget about ANWR and use its resources to lobby for the permits.

In his analysis of why individuals and organizations normally will free ride, Olson pointed out that those who have less to gain from a collective good will exploit the efforts of those who have a greater stake in the issue. For example, let's say that it is worth $50 to you to save ANWR from oil exploration, and it is worth $1 million to Bill Gates, the founder of Microsoft. Olson argues that, although it may be rational for Bill Gates to use his resources on this issue, if you are rational you will free ride on his efforts. The same is true for organizations. In our example of the chemical companies, let's say that it is worth $50 million per year to Dow to obtain language in the bill that allows EPA to grant waivers to plants, but that language is worth only $5 million to Monsanto. Olson's analysis indicates that Monsanto is likely to free ride on the efforts of Dow. As Figure 11.1 shows, however, firms do not appear to do this. Surely, when there are 1,000 firms lobbying on an issue, the efforts of one firm are unlikely to change the policy outcome. Firms should be like WOWSER and use their resources to obtain private goods.

Politics Are Too Uncertain to Allow a Maximization Strategy

The third reason that scholars give for the irrationality of lobbying stems from the uncertainty of the lobbying process. David Lowery and Virginia Gray maintain that the decision of whether or not to lobby on an issue can be rational only if an organization is able to compare what the outcome would be if it lobbies with what the outcome would be if it does not lobby.[10] But even huge, technologically sophisticated companies known for their decision-making capabilities cannot estimate accurately the probable impacts of their lobbying on governmental decisions that involve hundreds of decision makers and hundreds of lobbyists. There are just too many factors involved. For this reason, Lowery and Gray argue that models of lobbying based on rational decision making are inappropriate.

As evidence of their position, Lowery and Gray show that past empirical studies found that firms do not free ride when a profit-maximization strategy indicates that they should. Rational models predict that firms usually will free ride when the desired goal is a collective good. But this is not what firms do. Mahoney and Baumgartner contend that a firm's uncertainty over its impact on policy is the reason that firms do not free ride.[11] If an issue will significantly affect a firm's profits, uncertainty forces participation. For example, assume that a proposed tax cut would increase a firm's profit by $100 million. If the firm does not know what the impact of its lobbying will be on the outcome, then the firm must go ahead and lobby, Mahoney and Baumgartner argue. Even a small possibility that the firm's lobbying efforts will make the difference in the policy outcome creates a $100 million gamble. That is too much of a gamble for the firm to free ride.

In summary, lobbying by firms seems irrational because they use the wrong strategies and lobby on the wrong issues. The wrong issues are highly visible collective goods. The wrong strategy is to join a coalition to pursue a collective good when they could free ride. The correct strategy would be to lobby independently for private goods. As Figure 11.1 demonstrates, however, there are many issues on which hundreds of interests lobby. Critics of rational models maintain that in these situations there are far too many lobbyists and decision makers involved for a firm to accurately estimate the impact of its efforts on policy outcomes. In the absence of this information, firms cannot lobby in ways that maximize their profits.

Figure 11.1.   Number of Interest Groups Active across a Sample of Issues, 1996

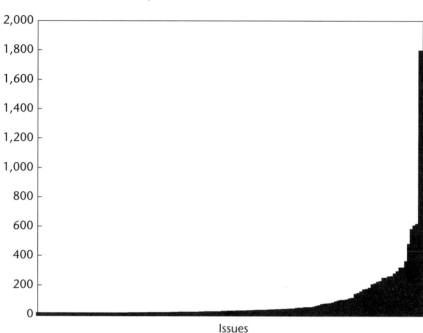

Source: Frank R. Baumgartner and Beth L. Leech, "Interest Niches and Policy Bandwagons: Patterns of Interest Group Involvement in National Politics," *Journal of Politics* 63, no. 4 (November 2001): 1200. Reprinted with permission from Blackwell Publishing.

Note: A list of bills, the number of organizations that lobbied on each bill, and numbers of lobbying reports is available beginning on page 1208 of Baumgartner and Leech, "Interest Niches and Policy Bandwagons."

Multistage Lobbying: Making Sense of Firms' Behavior

The key evidence to support the irrationality arguments is that firms are not free riding when they should and they are forming coalitions when they should not. But what if lobbying is a two-stage process that provides collective goods in the first stage and private goods in the second? If this is the case, how does this affect the irrationality arguments?

To examine this question, we conducted sixty-three interviews with corporate lobbyists during the summer of 2004.[12] We asked each lobbyist to name up to five issues on which she spent substantial time during the previous year and to name up to five issues on which she did not lobby even though the issue had a significant impact on her firm. The respondent then estimated the value of each issue to her firm where the categories were less than $10 million, $10 to $50 million, $50 to $100 million, and more than $100 million. We asked whether a favorable decision on an issue would benefit only her firm, her firm and one or two others, or a large number of firms. We labeled these as "private goods," "intermediate goods," and "collective goods."[13]

For each collective-good issue, we inquired whether the benefits the lobbying firm would gain from a favorable decision were relatively small or relatively large when compared with the benefits that other lobbying firms would receive. We then asked the respondent whether she lobbied on the bill or was a free rider. If she lobbied, we asked whether she worked as part of a coalition or lobbied independently. We requested the lobbyists to take us through each lobbying effort from the beginning to the end and to describe her coalition members (if any).

As indicated above, the critical evidence that lobbying is not rational relates to the fact that firms free ride less frequently than rational models of the lobbying process predict. In particular, Olson's collective-action model predicts that firms that have less to gain from a collective good will free ride on the efforts of firms that will receive greater benefits. Twelve of the sixty-three lobbyists we interviewed spent resources only on private goods and always were free riders when the goods were collective. Thus, the question is not "Does free riding occur?" It clearly does. The appropriate question is "Why do firms not free ride more frequently on those issues where other firms stood to gain considerably more than their firm?" In our interviews, thirty-nine lobbyists indicated that during the previous twelve months they had lobbied for a collective good when their firm was a relatively small beneficiary. The respondents provided several explanations for their participation.

In politics, size matters; and every free rider reduces the likelihood that an issue will reach the agenda. One reason lobbyists gave for not free riding was that doing so would reduce the size of the coalition and thereby lower the probability that policy makers would give their issue serious consideration. And, as the opening quote to this chapter makes clear, the biggest obstacle facing an interest is not winning a vote on the floor of the House of Representatives or the Senate, but getting a committee to give serious consideration to an issue. In any given session of Congress, more than 10,000 bills are introduced. Of those, only 16 percent of bills introduced into the House get consideration by a congressional committee, and only about 10 percent make it to a floor vote.[14] Of those bills that make it to a floor vote, the majority pass both houses of Congress. These figures suggest that if a lobbyist can get her issue on the agenda, prospects are good for ultimate success. If a lobbyist cannot do this, everything else is moot.

Almost always when an interviewee mentioned that lobbying for the collective good might fail if she did not participate, the lobbyist also indicated that the potential benefit to her firm was large. If an issue had a potential benefit of more than $50 million to a firm, more than 90 percent of the lobbyists participated in lobbying for the collective good. This supports the argument of Mahoney and Baumgartner that if the value of a good is sufficiently high for a firm, then uncertainty over the firm's likelihood of affecting the policy outcome forces the firm to lobby. Another interpretation of this evidence is that, although a firm may be uncertain about the exact probability that its lobbying will make a difference, the firm may be able to estimate a minimum probability. For example, if a firm stands to gain $50 million from a collective good and the lobbying effort will cost the firm $20,000, then the firm need only know that its probability of making a difference is greater than 0.0004.[15] Whatever decision calculus was used to incorporate risk remains a question— not a single lobbyist in our interviews mentioned that uncertainty over her impact affected her decision to lobby or to free ride.

A second reason lobbyists gave for participating in a coalition was that they were asked to participate by another firm in the industry or by the industry's trade association. The lobbyist was willing to chip in to the effort because she believed that the group's lobbying efforts were most effective when the group presented a united front to decision makers. These lobbyists also expected other firms would reciprocate in future lobbying endeavors. Many lobbyists work with the same firms on many issues over time. Although another firm might be the major beneficiary today, the lobbyists expect that their firms will benefit on a different issue later. Think of helping a neighbor fix a flat tire. You do not reap any immediate reward from the activity as it is not your car. It is understood, however, that the neighbor will help you in a similar fashion when you need it. If you and your neighbor live there long enough, something is bound to come up. In lobbying, firms live there long enough.

Another important reason firms lobbied at the collective-good stage of the lobbying process was that the firm needed to protect its position for lobbying during the second stage, when it would seek private goods. Seventeen of the fifty-one lobbyists who participated in collective-good lobbying indicated that they lobbied during the early phase of the legislative process because they wanted a private good later in the legislative process. We will see examples of this situation when we discuss the 2004 jobs bill later in this chapter.

A New Model of the Lobbying Process

Our interviews with lobbyists for Fortune 1,000 companies indicated that lobbying often involves multiple stages. In stage 1, interests seek collective goods. In stage 2, they are more likely to seek private goods. Using this information we constructed a two-stage model of the lobbying process.[16]

Two-stage lobbying strategies that involve collective goods and private goods occur frequently. During our interviews we discovered that firms often find themselves lobbying for collective goods early so that they can obtain private goods later. This occurs because if a firm is to obtain private goods it must first get a collective-good issue on the agenda. As we will demonstrate, a model of lobbying that takes into account the different tactics employed during different stages of the lobbying process allows us to make sense of lobbying behavior that previously seemed chaotic and irrational.

Stage 1

The first stage of the lobbying process involves interests forming a coalition that lobbies to get a collective-good issue on the political agenda. To achieve this, the coalition chooses and implements its lobbying strategy. Getting an issue on the agenda is difficult because the coalition is competing with many other interests that also want policy makers to attend to their issues. Agenda setting is so critical that scholars often model it as a separate step in the policy process. In our model, however, the key distinction between stage 1 and stage 2 lobbying is that stage 1 involves collective goods while stage 2 involves private goods or goods that benefit only a few interests.

Agenda Setting. If the coalition cannot convince policy makers to give attention to its collective-good issue, then lobbying stops and there are no opportunities for obtaining private or collective goods in stage 2. As we saw above, more than 10,000 bills are introduced into Congress each year but only a fraction of those receive serious attention. Similarly, interests make thousands of appeals to bureaucratic agencies for action each year, but the agencies have time to deal with only a small portion of these requests. Each bill or appeal to an agency involves costs and benefits to the policy makers who will decide its fate. For example, the Senate Agriculture, Nutrition, and Forestry Committee has jurisdiction over everything from forests to farming to aspects of child health and animal rights. The Sierra Club might want a ban on cutting old-growth trees during the same session that logging companies want additional subsidies. The pet-health lobby may want limits placed on using animals to test the health effects of pesticides while other interests want additional funding for research into better pesticides. The various farm lobbies may be asking for additional agriculture subsidies while other interests want to eliminate the existing subsidies. As legislators have finite time and resources with which to consider issues, only some can receive consideration.

We saw above that, ceteris paribus, larger coalitions have an advantage when it comes to securing a place on the political agenda. Research by Glen Krutz found that a bill is more likely to receive serious consideration if the legislator who sponsored the bill demonstrates substantial effort in support for it.[17] Manifestations of this effort include obtaining multiple cosponsors from both political parties, writing letters to the members of the committees with jurisdiction over the issue, and making a speech on the floor of the legislative chamber explaining the importance of the bill. Lobbyists can help the legislator in these tasks. In our interviews, 76 percent of lobbyists who joined coalitions to support collective goods reported helping draft legislation. These lobbyists also found cosponsors for bills, identified potential legislative allies, and assisted the bill's sponsor in informing other legislators of the issue's importance. In short, lobbyists play an important role in assuring that their issue receives consideration.

Defining the Collective Good.   A second critical part of stage 1 lobbying concerns defining the collective good correctly. It must be defined in a way that benefits coalition members in stage 1 and paves the way for them to obtain additional benefits in stage 2. For example, in the energy bill introduced in 2003, lobbyists for some energy companies wanted a provision in the bill that would provide subsidies for synthetic fuels. The difficulty was that the coalition members did not agree on the definition of synthetic fuels. If the term was limited to coal gasification, the definition reduced the size of the coalition because it eliminated firms that wanted to include other technologies and other sources of the synthetic fuels such as waste plastic. Limiting the definition to coal gasification gave an advantage to companies that owned large coal deposits and had invested in gasification technology. The energy coalition had to decide whether it wanted a larger coalition or a more limited coalition that could provide greater benefits to fewer firms. As we will see in our two case studies, issue definition is an essential part of the lobbying process because it limits the size of a coalition and dictates who will be the winners and the losers in stage 2.

Stage 2

After the firms within the winning coalition have obtained the collective good, they move to secure the best possible private benefits. Sometimes the firms are in direct competition with one another, as was the case in our hypothetical example of chemical firms seeking waivers for their plants that produced pesticides. At other times coalition members seek vastly different private goods. In this second situation we often find pork barrel politics. Each firm in the coalition is willing to support the provision of private goods to other coalition members in return for reciprocal support for the firm's preferred good. In the 2003 energy bill, for example, petroleum interests supported coal gasification and a nuclear waste depository at Yucca Mountain. In return, coal interests supported the repository at Yucca Mountain and drilling in ANWR, and the nuclear interests supported drilling in ANWR and coal gasification.

An important aspect of the decision model is that that definition of the collective good at stage 1 determines the private goods that will be available at stage 2. For this reason, stage 1 is a struggle not only to obtain policymakers' attention, but also to determine who will be allowed to pursue private goods in stage 2. Assume for a moment that you are the lobbyist who is putting together a coalition. Your goals include forming a large enough coalition to get on the political agenda, defining the collective good in a way that benefits your firm and is acceptable to policy makers, and setting up stage 2 so that your firm can effectively pursue private goods.

The first goal dictates that you will invite all firms that will benefit from the collective good. This encourages you to define the collective good as broadly as possible. The second goal, however, limits the coalition membership to firms that are pursuing politically acceptable goals. If the coalition defines the collective good in a way that encourages opposition by other interests, this reduces your chances to obtain the collective good. The third goal presents a different problem. You do not wish to include firms that will compete with you in lobbying for private goods in stage 2. In fact, you would like to define the collective good in a way that benefits you and harms your competitors. Thus, while your first goal—getting on the agenda and winning the collective good—encourages a large coalition, the second and third goals are likely to limit the size of the coalition.

Perhaps an analogy will help. Let's say that you enjoy fishing. You would like to fish in a national forest near your home, but the forest currently is closed to fishing. To get the Forest Service to open the area to fishing, you need to get other fishers to join with you in petitioning the Forest Service. Goal 1 says to get as many people as possible to join your coalition. You want this because the Forest Service is more likely to respond if it believes opening the forest will benefit many people. Goal 2, however, suggests that you exclude those persons who want to catch a species of fish that is sufficiently rare as to put it on the list of threatened species. Goal 2 may also require that the Forest Service grant only a limited number of fishing permits and require that all fishing be "catch and release." In other words, to keep your goal acceptable to the Forest Service, you must limit the collective good. Goal 3 is particularly tricky. You want to limit the competition for the fish in a way that is advantageous to you. If you prefer fly fishing, you may want the Forest Service to limit fishing in the forest to fly fishing only. You might try to convince the Forest Service that fly fishing does less damage to the fish than other forms of fishing. If you are a skillful lobbyist, you will not lobby for the fly-fishing-only provision until after the Forest Service has decided to open the forest to fishing. That way you can maximize your chances of getting on the agenda and then later limit your competition for the fish.

To see how the model applies to the real world of lobbying, we use two case studies. The first is the jobs bill that became law in 2004. The second case is a regulatory action that occurred in 2005. We turn now to those cases.

Case 1: The Jobs Bill

Two bills dominated the legislative calendar during the summer of 2004. One was the American Jobs Creation Act (the jobs bill) and the other was an omnibus energy bill that was introduced in 2003 but remained active in 2004. For reasons we discuss below, these bills can be treated as a single bill. Twenty-four lobbyists whom we interviewed indicated that at least one of the bills had a significant impact on their firms. Of these, eighteen lobbied on the bills and six did not. The bills had all of the characteristics of "irrational lobbying." They were highly partisan and highly visible to the public, and more than 500 organizations lobbied on each bill. Several coalitions formed on the issues, and the goals of firms seemed to change over time.

If ever there existed an ideal case when a firm would be uncertain about whether its lobbying would change a policy outcome, the jobs-energy bill with its shifting coalitions and issue definitions was it. Until very late in the legislative process, there was tremendous uncertainty over what would be included in the bills.

Stage 1

The jobs bill was known to lobbyists as "FSC/ETI." The bill was a response to the European Union's decision to levy an import tax on goods produced in the United States until the United States revoked two tax subsidies, the Foreign Sales Corporation (FSC) and Extraterritorial Income (ETI) provisions. The World Trade Organization (WTO) had ruled that the FSC/ETI tax loopholes were illegal subsidies under the existing WTO agreements, and the WTO allowed the European Union to enact retaliatory tariffs on U.S.-made products until the United States revoked the subsidies. But the revocation of the FSC/ETI subsidies would increase the taxes of U.S. corporations by approximately $77 billion over a ten-year period.

The Bush administration supported the repeal of the FSC/ETI subsidies, but it called for new legislation to provide tax benefits to corporations harmed by the repeal. Three options (or collective-good definitions) emerged as contenders to replace the lost benefits. One option provided domestic manufacturing firms a tax deduction based on the wages paid to employees located in the United States so long as at least 50 percent of the labor costs of the product were paid to U.S. employees. A coalition of manufacturing firms and organized labor supported this option.

The second alternative included tax reductions for all production and service activities in the United States, whether or not they were engaged in manufacturing and whether or not the goods involved were to be exported. The Republican leadership in the House of Representatives (particularly Bill Thomas, chairman of the House Ways and Means Committee), the U.S. Chamber of Commerce, and conservative think tanks such as the Cato Institute and the Heritage Foundation supported this option.

The third option included tax cuts for all corporations and combined these cuts with large sections of the 2003 energy bill that had not passed Congress. This option was supported by firms with large overseas operations, energy companies, and the Republican leadership in the Senate. The White House preferred a tax cut restricted to the industries most affected by the repeal of FSC/ETI, but President George W. Bush did not aggressively campaign for a particular option for fear of alienating one or more business groups.

Stage 1 of the lobbying process was particularly important in the jobs bill as it determined which industries and firms would receive significant tax cuts. Early in the bargaining process a compromise that looked as if it would succeed included a tax cut for manufactured goods, the provision for

50 percent of labor costs going to U.S. workers, and many portions of the 2003 energy bill. These energy provisions contained two highly charged issues: opening up ANWR to oil exploration and finalizing Yucca Mountain as the site for a nuclear waste repository. These two provisions had held up the energy bill during the previous year because of the likelihood that the Democrats would filibuster the bill.

The rationale for attaching the energy provisions to the jobs bill was that this combination would split two major constituencies of the Democratic Party: organized labor and environmentalists. Legislators representing districts and states where organized labor was a powerful constituency would support the combined bill because of the 50 percent American labor provision. Labor believed that such a provision would reduce the outsourcing of manufacturing jobs to foreign countries. The support of these legislators would prevent a Democratic filibuster and allow the ANWR and Yucca Mountain provisions to pass in the Senate.

This coalition of manufacturing, labor, and energy interests did not hold together. High-technology firms required a substantial change in the bill if they were to remain in the coalition. They wanted the 50 percent American labor provision dropped because many of their products would not meet the 50 percent requirement. Manufacturers would still get a tax break for salaries and wages paid to U.S. workers, but there would be no floor on the percentage of the labor that had to be American. Organized labor refused to accept that change. Now the coalition leaders had to make a decision. Did they want to include organized labor or high-tech companies? The coalition, in conjunction with the Republican leadership in Congress, chose to include the high-tech corporations.

By dropping the 50 percent provision, the tax cut would apply to more companies, and the new coalition reflected the Republican Party's desire to reduce all corporate tax rates.[18] The cost of dropping the 50 percent provision was the loss of support from organized labor. Without the Democratic senators who represented states with large concentrations of organized labor, the bill became vulnerable to a Democratic filibuster. This possibility forced a new definition of the collective good and required a new lobbying strategy.

The coalition decided to split the bills once again into a tax cut bill and an energy bill. This made a Democratic filibuster of the jobs bill unlikely, but it also reduced support for the energy bill. To deal with this, the coalition provided the energy interests a fail-safe position. The Senate would decide the energy bill prior to voting on the jobs bill. If the Senate defeated the energy bill, its most important provisions other than ANWR and Yucca Mountain would be inserted in the jobs bill during the House-Senate conference committee. In return for that promise, the energy interests would continue their lobbying efforts on behalf of the jobs bill.[19]

At the end of stage 1, the big winners were manufacturing interests and the energy companies. The big losers were firms engaged in service activities, organized labor, energy companies whose priorities included ANWR or Yucca Mountain, and environmental groups that objected to other aspects of the energy bill.

Stage 2

Once the general outlines of the jobs bill were defined, the second-stage lobbying began. At this point, stage 1 winners worked to ensure that their private goods were part of the final bill. Stage 1 losers attempted to insert provisions in the bill that would lessen their losses. Most important, firms began lobbying for private goods.

When the jobs bill was signed into law, it contained special tax provisions worth more than $131 billion over ten years plus a buyout of tobacco allotments that cost the U.S. treasury an additional $10 billion. The bill included over fifteen pages of special provisions. Among these were that certain architectural, engineering, and banking services were defined as "production" so that they could qualify for the tax cut; bonds issued to build sustainable-design projects (for example, a particular shopping center that included energy-saving technologies) became tax free; professional sports franchises could amortize "intangibles"; timber sales now qualified for capital gains treatment; NASCAR track improvements made before 2008 qualified for special tax treatment; corporate legal costs to fight a claim of unlawful discrimination became tax deductible; gamblers who were not U.S. citizens could delay until April 15 paying federal tax on gambling winnings in casinos operated in the United States rather than having to pay the taxes before leaving the country; the size of firms eligible for small-business tax breaks increased; who could be classified as a family member in family-owned small businesses expanded; defense contractors with multiyear products could delay paying taxes on profits until the completion of the projects; and firms that had accumulated income in foreign tax havens could repatriate that income to the United States and pay a tax rate of 5.25 percent rather than the normal corporate tax rate of 35 percent.

Our interviews with lobbyists active on the jobs and energy bills provided substantial insight into their activities during the maneuverings over these bills.[20] A majority of lobbyists gave two reasons for participating in a lobbying effort that involved hundreds of other lobbyists. First, the bill was extremely important to their firms. Second, their firms wanted a special provision in the bill. In other words, the lobbyists worked to obtain not only the collective goods decided at stage 1 but also to gain a private or intermediate good in stage 2. Not surprisingly, most of the lobbyists who were active on the jobs bill reported lobbying both as part of a coalition and as an independent actor. They lobbied as part of a coalition in stage 1 and lobbied independently in stage 2.

Among the most interesting statements by the lobbyists were those concerning how decisions about the bills were made. As the quote by the

K Street lobbyist at the beginning of the chapter suggests, many lobbyists believed that the decisions and compromises reached in stage 1 were made by lobbyists rather than legislators. The lobbyists who directed the competing coalitions often met with the Republican leadership in Congress, but the initial deals were made by lobbyists.[21]

Our interviews with lobbyists also found evidence of free riding. Six lobbyists whose firms were significantly affected by provisions in the bill chose not to lobby on it. In each case the free rider reported that, although a favorable outcome on the jobs bill was important to her firm, lobbying on the bill was not the best use of her time. For example, a lobbyist for a moderately large banking firm believed that her firm's interests were identical with those of the larger banking corporations. Their lobbying efforts would protect her interests. A particularly interesting example was a lobbyist for one of the energy producers. She reported that she dropped out of the coalition when the energy and jobs bills were split. She decided to free ride on the jobs bill despite the fact that several of the energy provisions benefited her firm and despite requests from energy trade associations that she remain active. The most important issue for her firm was a safe storage site for nuclear waste (Yucca Mountain). When that provision was excluded from the fail-safe agreement between the supporters of the jobs bill and the energy coalition, she saw no reason to participate further in the coalition efforts.

Ultimately, although the Democratic leadership in Congress opposed the final bill, it could not put together a filibuster to stop its acceptance. The bill contained too many private goods in too many districts for the party to gather the necessary number of senators to stop the bill. Similarly, although the cost of the final bill was twice what President Bush had indicated he was willing to accept, he signed the legislation into law as Public Law 108-357.

Case 2: The Regulation of Perchlorate

The two-stage model is equally applicable when lobbying occurs to achieve regulatory outcomes. Firms seek to obtain favorable outcomes by lobbying such regulatory bodies as the Food and Drug Administration, EPA, the Department of Transportation, the Occupational Safety and Health Administration, and the Federal Aviation Authority. To achieve their desired outcomes, firms often join coalitions in stage 1 of the lobbying process and then lobby independently in stage 2. EPA's regulation of the chemical perchlorate illustrates this process.

Perchlorate is a common oxidizer in rocket fuel. It functions as a catalyst that permits combustion in environments that do not supply oxygen. The medical community uses the chemical as a medical tracer because it allows physicians to track the dispersal of medicine throughout the body. Unfortunately, the chemical has two undesirable characteristics. First, it is remarkably persistent in the environment. Large amounts of perchlorate remain in the soil and water as a result of the rocket and defense industries. Second, high exposure to the chemical reduces the ability of the human thyroid to take in iodine. This can cause goiter in adults and developmental disorders in the fetuses of women who have hypothyroidism or an iodide deficiency. The Safe Water Drinking Act (SWDA) requires EPA to determine the safe level of exposure to perchlorate for all at-risk populations.

EPA typically uses scientific studies to determine the allowable level of a chemical. That level becomes the reference dose (RfD) and serves as the baseline for all federal laws regulating the production, use, and cleanup of the chemical. States may apply more stringent standards, but most follow the lead of the federal government. RfD decisions carry substantial financial implications. A change in an RfD can cost companies millions of dollars in manufacturing or cleanup costs. Given the stakes, it is not surprising that firms lobby heavily on RfD decisions. In 2005, EPA put forth a draft policy that changed the perchlorate RfD, and several of the companies that would be harmed by the new policy began a lobbying effort against it. This lobbying effort provides examples of coalition formation to pursue a collective good, free riding, and the breakup of a coalition as the firms moved from cooperation to achieve a collective good to the noncooperative pursuit of private goods.

Stage 1

EPA was required under SWDA to make a determination of risk for perchlorate. The accompanying RfD decision had the potential to adversely affect nine extremely large producers and consumers of the chemical. Initially, all nine firms participated in a joint effort to provide EPA with the scientific information necessary to set the reference dose. This group shared the research costs and cooperated to answer EPA's scientific questions. When EPA issued its draft policy, the nine firms realized that the agency intended to pursue an RfD substantially more stringent than the firms believed was merited by the scientific research. The EPA draft policy set the allowable standard at 1.0 part per billion (ppb) despite scientific evidence that supported a standard that was at least 30 times greater. The 1.0 ppb RfD would cost each of the nine firms more than $50 million.

The perchlorate issue provides an example of how a political entrepreneur can put together a coalition. In this case, a lobbyist saw an opportunity to earn a large fee while simultaneously saving the perchlorate manufacturers and users a great deal of money. The lobbyist, a former regulatory analyst within the White House Office of Management and Budget (OMB), was extremely knowledgeable concerning EPA regulatory rules and procedures. In her OMB position, she routinely had evaluated proposed EPA regulations, and she was intimately familiar with the strategies that organizations harmed by a regulation could employ to prevent its adoption.

The lobbyist approached the nine firms with a major interest in the RfD and offered to form a coalition and coordinate the cooperative lobbying effort. Five of the nine firms agreed to participate while four did not. The lobbyist then designed a lobbying strategy that would produce the collective good of a less stringent perchlorate RfD while allowing firms to pursue additional private goods.

In stage 1, the lobbyist orchestrated a campaign in which government agencies and departments that depended on perchlorate petitioned OMB and the White House to force EPA to adopt an RfD more in line with the scientific evidence. The lobbyist also provided evidence that the costs to society of the proposed 1.0 ppb RfD would greatly exceed the benefits.[22] Ultimately, EPA abandoned its draft policy in favor of a 24.5 ppb threshold. The coalition had achieved its desired collective good.

Why did only five of the firms participate? One reason is that an RfD is almost a perfect collective good. EPA cannot give some firms a standard of 24.5 ppb while demanding that others meet a 1.0 ppb standard. As the same RfD applies to everyone, coalition members in stage 1 could not exclude free riders from enjoying the collective good. With one exception, firms that joined the coalition had a greater stake in the collective good while firms that had a lesser stake decided to free ride. The lobbyist who formed the coalition reported that each of the firms that joined the coalition was prepared, if necessary, to bear the entire cost of lobbying for a less stringent RfD. By joining the coalition, each firm spent fewer resources than it would have if it had lobbied independently. In addition, all five firms previously had worked with the same lobbyist on a similar issue, and all expected that they would lobby together on future issues.

Although free riding accounted for some of the nonparticipation in the coalition, it was not the only reason that firms did not participate. Potential retaliation by EPA against firms that challenged its proposed rule was an important disincentive for firms. Our interviews indicated that one firm (we will call it firm A) did not join the coalition because its profits depended too heavily on government contracts. Firm A concluded that angering EPA might create even greater costs than the adoption of the 1.0 ppb RfD. EPA has extensive latitude in choosing firms to investigate for possible violations of environmental regulations, and government contractors present particularly inviting targets. EPA can delay contracts to a firm until it has investigated potential violations of environmental regulations and the firm has completed the necessary remedial actions. This potential cost dictated that firm A not participate in the coalition.

Stage 2

Obtaining the collective good opened the door for all nine firms to lobby independently for private goods. In this second stage the firms sought different private benefits, and sometimes the firms had competing interests.

For example, one of the members of the coalition (firm B) also was a major government contractor. Many of its contracts included cleaning up sites contaminated by perchlorate. Those contracts allowed firm B to charge cleanup costs plus a guaranteed profit to the government. While firm B did not have the technology to clean up sites to the 1.0 ppb standard, the 24.5 ppb allowed more perchlorate contamination than the firm preferred. To obtain a more stringent standard, firm B lobbied EPA to set a maximum contaminant limit (MCL) for perchlorate. An MCL limits the amount of a chemical allowed in drinking water. On average, EPA sets the MCL of a chemical at 20 percent of the allowable RfD. This would make the effective perchlorate standard close to 5.0 ppb and would generate additional profits for firm B.

Other firms, however, preferred to avoid additional restrictions on perchlorate. In most circumstances, the firm that creates the perchlorate contamination must pay to clean it up. In this situation, firms prefer a high RfD and no MCL. The cost of cleaning a contaminated site to 5.0 ppb can be substantially greater than cleaning a site to the 24.5 ppb level. At the time this book went to press, EPA had not decided whether it would issue an MCL for perchlorate.

The coalition firms also had different regional interests. States on the West Coast and in the Midwest often require stricter limits on a chemical than the federal standard. Southern and southwestern states rarely require stricter standards. Firms operating largely in the West and Midwest wanted the coalition to lobby for a uniform national standard that would prevent stricter state regulation. Firms that operate mainly in the South and Southwest did not want to share the lobbying costs of obtaining a single nationwide standard. As the private interests of the firms in the coalition began to diverge, the coalition broke up and each firm pursued its goals independently.

Discussion

It is easy to see why studies of lobbying reach different conclusions regarding the goals, strategies, and effectiveness of lobbying. Studies examining collective goods in stage 1 observe a crowded, raucous process with shifting coalitions, changing goals, great complexity, and significant uncertainty. Other studies—those looking at private goods in stage 2—may see only one or two organizations lobbying for a specific set of well-defined outcomes. Because the lobbying goals and strategies in stage 1 and stage 2 are so dissimilar, scholars often see confusion and inconsistency in lobbyists' activities. In reality, however, their actions are logical and consistent.

What appear to be contradictory findings in the literature more often reflect the fact that the studies are examining different stages in the lobbying process. For example, three scholars doing case studies of the jobs bill might come to three different conclusions about lobbying. A scholar focusing on stage 1 would see firms joining coalitions that pursue broad collective goods over which there is substantial conflict. The scholar would likely stress coalition formation and issue definition as the key tasks of lobbyists, and he would see substantial irrational behavior because firms that should have been free riders were not.

A scholar focusing on stage 2 might see little coalition activity and observe interested parties pursuing narrow objectives that involve little conflict and provide benefits to only one or a few firms. This scholar would conclude that the firms pursue their goals in a rational manner as they act independently to pursue private goods.

A third scholar, unaware of the multistage nature of lobbying, might follow the bill from its beginning to its end and conclude that firms and their lobbyists act in inconsistent and irrational ways. The researcher might see lobbyists for organized labor supporting oil exploration in ANWR and Yucca Mountain at one moment and then see them working to defeat these same provisions later. This inconsistency of goals appears to violate the requirement of rational models that firms have consistent preferences.

Similarly, if a researcher follows the efforts of the firm B's lobbyist on the perchlorate issue, he might see the lobbyist working for a less strict per-chlorate standard early in the policy process and then lobbying for a more restrictive standard later. This lobbying strategy would appear confused and irrational. As we have seen, however, firm B's actions were consistent with the firm's goals and completely rational.

In conclusion, effective lobbying often involves multiple stages. Collective goods dominate stage 1, where large coalitions often are necessary to get an issue on the political agenda and to define it in a way that is favorable to coalition members. In stage 2, a lobbyist is more likely to lobby for bene-fits that advantage only her firm or a small group of firms. Once we recognize this, not only do we see lobbying as rational, but also we have a much better understanding of the role of interest groups in American politics.

Notes

1. See for example Frank R. Baumgartner and Beth L. Leech, "Interest Niches and Policy Bandwagons: Patterns of Interest Group Involvement in National Politics," *Journal of Politics* 63, no. 4 (November 2001): 1191–1213; and Christine Mahoney and Frank R. Baumgartner, "The Determinants and Effects of Interest-Group Coali-tions" (paper prepared for annual meeting of American Political Science Association, Chicago, September 2–5, 2004).

2. William P. Browne, *Cultivating Congress* (Lawrence: University of Kansas Press, 1995); and R. Kenneth Godwin and Barry J. Seldon, "What Corporations Really Want from Government: The Public Provision of Private Goods," in *Interest Group Politics*, 6th ed., ed. Allan J. Cigler and Burdett A. Loomis (Washington, D.C.: CQ Press, 2002).

3. Voting need not be irrational. You may receive important psychological benefits from doing your duty as a citizen. You may also receive social benefits by telling others that you voted. These psychological and social benefits do not apply, however, to profit-maximizing corporations.

4. In this chapter we use feminine pronouns to refer to lobbyists and use masculine pronouns to refer to other individuals.

5. Theodore J. Lowi, *The End of Liberalism* (New York: Norton, 1969).

6. Federal law requires that all organizations that spend more than $20,000 on lobbying in a six-month period must file a lobbying disclosure report that indicates the issues on which they lobbied.

7. Mahoney and Baumgartner, "The Determinants and Effects of Interest-Group Coalitions."

8. R. Kenneth Godwin, Edward Lopez, and Barry Seldon, "Incorporating Policymaker Costs and Political Competition into Rent-Seeking Games," *Southern Economic Journal* 73 (July 2006): 233–250.

9. Mancur Olson Jr., *The Logic of Collective Action: Public Goods and the Theory of Groups* (Cambridge: Harvard University Press, 1965). A rational firm also will free ride even if its contribution will make a difference in the size of the collective good so long as the marginal benefit to the firm of the increased collective good is less than the cost of the contribution.

10. David Lowery and Virginia Gray, "A Neopluralist Perspective on Research on Organized Interests," *Political Research Quarterly* 57 (2004): 163–175.

11. Mahoney and Baumgartner, "The Determinants and Effects of Interest-Group Coalitions."

12. To obtain the interviews, we chose lobbyists who filed a lobbying disclosure report indicating that they had lobbied for a firm listed by *Fortune* magazine as one the 1,000 largest publicly held companies in the United States. We drew two random samples of lobbyists. The first consisted of lobbyists who were direct employees of the corporation. The second was made up of lobbyists who were not employees of the corporation but were hired by the firm to lobby on a specific issue. When contacting internal lobbyists, we attempted to interview the firm's chief lobbyist. When a firm listed multiple external lobbyists, we randomly selected among those listed. We contacted potential respondents with a short letter indicating that we wished to interview them concerning how they selected their lobbying goals and strategies. We then telephoned their office and requested an appointment lasting 30 to 45 minutes. When we had thirty-three appointments in each category, we stopped the contacting. We made eighty-five calls to obtain the sixty-six appointments. Of the sixty-six appointments, we completed sixty-three interviews.

13. In the pretest, we divided goods into only two categories: (1) the rent benefited only the respondent's firm or (2) the rent benefited multiple firms. The respondents had a strong preference, however, to divide their answers into three categories: (1) only their firm, (2) their firm and one or two others, and (3) many firms. We label the second category "intermediate goods."

14. Glen S. Krutz, "Issues and Institutions: 'Winnowing' in the U.S. Congress," *American Journal of Political Science* 49 (April 2005): 313–326.

15. Even if the firm cannot accurately estimate a minimum value, it does not eliminate the possibility of deciding rationally. The discipline of decision analysis provides decision rules for making decisions under conditions of uncertainty and risk.

16. A formal version of this model was developed by Scott Ainsworth and Kenneth Godwin, "Coalitions and Competition: Corporate Lobbying as a Two-Stage Rent Seeking Game" (paper presented at the annual meeting of the Midwest Political Science Association, Chicago, April 20–23, 2006).

17. Krutz, "Issues and Institutions."

18. The bill still advantaged domestic manufacturing, but it did not exclude products that had less than 50 percent U.S. labor.

19. For public evidence of this agreement, see the policy alert of the United States Combined Heat and Power Association, April 6, 2004, http://uschpa.admgt.com/Alert040604.htm.

20. Interested readers also can search on the Internet for "FSC/ETI" and find numerous policy alerts from trade associations urging their members to support or oppose particular provisions of the bills.

21. A logical question is "Why not include all corporations in the bill?" The Republican Party had pledged that all tax cuts would be "revenue neutral." This meant that a tax cut in one place had to be paid for by a tax increase elsewhere. Although Congress definitely can increase the size of a tax cut by employing various accounting gimmicks to maintain the appearance of revenue neutrality, it cannot increase the size of the cuts indefinitely. A tax cut that included all corporations would have reduced substantially the tax cut to manufacturing companies.

22. The Office of Information and Regulatory Affairs (OIRA) within OMB reviews all proposed regulatory rules that have an impact on the U.S. economy of more than $100 million, and OIRA conducts a benefit-cost analysis of the proposed rule. A proposed rule can become law even if its costs to society exceed the benefits, but the process puts tremendous pressure on agencies to propose regulations that have a net social benefit.

12

Identity Crisis
How Interest Groups Struggle to Define Themselves in Washington
Michael T. Heaney

Interest groups face identity crises when citizens, members, staff, or legislators have a significantly different idea of what the group is about than does its leadership or membership. Issue niche theory asserts that groups modify their identities in response to these crises by narrowing their issue portfolios until they monopolize a specific area of public policy.

Michael T. Heaney argues here that forming narrow issue niches is one, but not the only, strategy available to interest groups as they seek to manipulate their identities. For example, a group can instead attempt to create a broad issue niche in which it claims expertise over an entire domain of public policy like the environment, energy, health care, or transportation. Alternatively, a group can stress its role as the authentic representative of a constituency that is especially important to politicians. Or groups can attempt to modify their brand by changing their name, logo, or appearance. Heaney makes the case for a multidimensional theory of identity in which interest groups combine strategies pertaining to issue niches, representation, and branding to shape how they are understood. This approach broadens our understanding of how organizations act to become effective within the highly competitive context of interest group politics. Effective self-definition is often a recurring challenge on the long road to policy-making success.

AARP is a nonprofit, nonpartisan membership organization for people age 50 and over. AARP is dedicated to enhancing quality of life for all as we age. We lead positive social change and deliver value to members through information, advocacy and service.

AARP mission statement

The AARP basically is an insurance company that offers attractive travel discounts in exchange for payment of a small annual fee. It does not seek opinion from its members. It does not submit its leadership to vote by members. Members have no mechanism for making their views known to spokesmen, other than writing letters to the organization's house organ.

Jayne L. Greene in a 2003 letter to the Washington Post

AARP—formerly known as the American Association of Retired Persons—has become the older American's 800-pound gorilla, known for its sheer size and political muscle.

Steven A. Holmes in a 2001 article in the New York Times

What is the AARP? According to the above statements, AARP is, alternatively, a broadly representative membership organization, a business entity cloaked in nonprofit clothing, or a politically savvy player in Washington. While these perspectives are not necessarily mutually exclusive, they each frame AARP's core identity according to a different motivation: member service, economic self-interest, and political power. Many politicians and policy advocates working in Washington form their own opinions of what AARP is and is not. These opinions affect AARP's ability to forge alliances with other interest groups and to advance its policy agenda on Capitol Hill. AARP can work to change the way others think about it, but the power to do so is not entirely in its own hands. For example, AARP faced an identity crisis in the fall of 2003 when it encountered widespread condemnation for its decision to support a Republican-sponsored Medicare reform bill.[1] Although AARP replied immediately and forcefully to its critics, the implications for its identity may be long lasting.

When the term *identity crisis* is discussed, an interest group like AARP is probably not the first thing that comes to mind. Rather, one might imagine a 40-year-old man who suddenly becomes uncomfortable with the evidence that he has reached middle age or a teenage girl who has lost confidence that she fits in with her friends at school.[2] Nonetheless, organizations do have identities and do experience identity crises, albeit different from those of individuals.[3] An interest group's identity is a complex product of the views of its leadership, employees, members, legislators, lobbyists, media elites, and other influential people who hold an opinion of what the group is about. An interest group faces an identity crisis when public perceptions about what it stands for diverge significantly from how its leadership or membership wants the organization to be viewed.

A group's identity emerges and changes over time, as political actors inside and outside the organization debate its nature and reflect on its role in politics. Sometimes a consensus emerges about who or what a group is. Other times, substantial disagreements pop up, which may trigger an identity crisis. Disagreements often result from a group's visible, but controversial, decisions. For example, when the Pharmaceutical Research and Manufacturers of America (PhRMA) teamed with right-to-life groups to try to stop the importation of Canadian drugs (by arguing that the bill in question would allow the morning-after pill to be imported), even the pharmaceutical industry's strongest congressional supporters became highly critical of its decision to link abortion to a business issue.[4]

For other groups, lack of a clear identity stems from invisibility: they have yet to find a way to stand out in a crowded policy environment.[5] For example, the Council for Government Reform is a group that focuses on a range of conservative causes, with a special emphasis on issues that affect the elderly, but it has trouble communicating its identity to key audiences because other actors in the policy community are not familiar with it.[6] This is a common problem, as witnessed by a recent survey of interest group representatives, roughly half of whom feared that their identities are not well understood on Capitol Hill.[7]

If interest group leaders attempt to achieve their goals in part by manipulating their organization's identity, then understanding this process is necessary to make sense of interest group strategies. Political scientist William P. Browne argues that groups form unique identities by creating narrow, issue-oriented reputations for expertise.[8] According to this *issue niche theory*, a group faced with an identity crisis could solve this problem by narrowing its focus until no other group had an overlapping issue concern. While Browne is surely correct that owning an issue is one way for a group to solidify its identity, this strategy is only one of the available possibilities. *Representation* is one alternative, in which interest groups ground their identities in their ability to facilitate a connection between legislators and a broad constituency. *Branding* is another strategy, in which interest groups manipulate visual and textual elements (such as their names, logos, or Web pages) to modify their images among attentive audiences.

This chapter advances a *multidimensional theory* that recognizes interest group reliance on issue niches, representation, and branding as strategies for building identity and resolving identity crises. Examination of various data suggests that identity is a mechanism that connects interest group behavior from grassroots membership to elite lobbying activities.

Multiple Dimensions of Identity

Issue niche theory assumes that interest groups "cultivate specific and recognizable identities" through "accommodat[ing] one another by concentrating on very narrow issues."[9] According to this view, each group aspires to own an issue—and respects every other group's desire to do the same— to assure stable access to the resources associated with that issue. Groups want policy makers to know that they are the ones that have the necessary expertise on the issue in question. Thus, as the number of interest groups grows over time, issue niches become progressively narrower and policy communities become increasingly fragmented.

Achieving dominant control over an issue is one effective way to establish a clear identity. The long-standing position of the American Civil Liberties Union as the leading defender of First Amendment freedoms is an excellent example of this strategy at work.[10] Still, focusing on a narrow issue may not be the best way to create a desirable identity. First, the era of neutral policy expertise seems to have passed, with virtually all issue analysis presumed to emanate from a biased ideological or partisan point of view.[11] A group must have not only an issue but also a predetermined position on that issue to be recognized and respected. For example, Common Cause is known not only for its expertise on the issue of campaign finance but also for its longtime position favoring more federal regulation of campaign contributions. If issue position, rather than issue narrowness, sets groups apart, then there may be room for several interest groups to work on the same issue, thus diminishing the incentives for groups to specialize too narrowly.

A second problem with groups developing narrow issue expertise is that drawing upon this knowledge may be inconvenient for policy makers. An interest group with a narrow issue niche resembles a boutique in a downtown business district. On occasion, shoppers are willing to make a special trip to find the perfect item they desire, like the diamond ring that will last a lifetime. More often, shoppers demand a wide range of items to fill their market baskets and find that their time is better spent by going to the local Wal-Mart. Similarly, a policy maker may prefer to establish close, trusting relationships with one (or a few) interest groups that provide useful information on many issues; this is more efficient than forming a large number of weaker relationships with many separate groups.[12] The U.S. Chamber of Commerce, for example, is available to comment on virtually any issue—from immigration to telecommunications to tariffs—that matters to business. Communicating regularly with the chamber will likely be more convenient for legislators than consulting with independent issue experts every time a new business concern hits the agenda. If interest group lobbying is a service to members of Congress, legislators will often demand full service and one-stop shopping.[13]

A third problem with the strategy of working on only a narrow issue (or a small number of issues) is that it may be not be the most efficient use of group resources. Advocating on any single issue requires that an interest group set up an office, hire staff to monitor the Washington scene, and acquire experts who are able to analyze and discuss the collected information. All of this requires money. After the necessary infrastructure is in place and the group is working on its niche issue, it may make sense to add a few more issues. A group like the National Right to Life Committee—

which ostensibly occupies an issue niche on abortion—can easily expand its operations to take on stem cell research, euthanasia, Medicare, and the free speech issues of campaign finance reform.

Hiring experts on related issues may make the whole policy team more productive by expanding access to social networks, stimulating intraoffice discussions, and boosting capacity during periods of peak demand on any one issue. Thus, once an interest group has paid the fixed cost of operating on a single issue, it possesses incentives to expand, rather than contract, its issue involvement. This pressure, which economists refer to as *economies of scope*, makes it likely that interest groups will behave in the exact opposite manner from what issue niche theory predicts.[14]

If creating a monopoly over a narrow issue niche is not a good strategy for all interest groups to forge their identities, what are the alternatives? The most important are representation and branding. In a strategy of representation, an interest group asserts that it is the legitimate voice of an important political constituency and that it holds an effective monopoly over connecting its members to legislators.[15] This strategy is conceptually similar to forming an issue niche in its emphasis on exclusive control over something important to legislators. The representation strategy differs from the issue niche approach in that it does not ordinarily make sense to argue that a constituency is narrow. As a rule, the larger and more mobilized the constituency, the more vital it is to reelection-minded politicians.[16]

Achieving status as the authentic representative of a particular constituency must be cultivated deliberately over time, as with issue expertise. Legislators are too wise to recognize just anyone as the voice of their constituents. In his seminal study of how the farm lobby gained and lost influence in Congress during the middle of the twentieth century, John Mark Hansen demonstrates that would-be representatives must establish that they have a competitive advantage over other sources of information and that this advantage recurs over time.[17] Convincing legislators that these conditions are met has become increasingly difficult in recent years because the strong member-participation tradition of associations has largely been replaced by sterile methods of corporate management.[18] Thus, to project a representation-based identity, groups must facilitate direct personal connections between legislators and their organization's grassroots membership. Brokering these connections is likely to increase a group's recognition and influence in the policy process.[19]

Both the issue niche and representation strategies envision identity formation as a process of securing autonomy in an environment where multiple groups compete for scarce resources. From this point of view, the fundamental identity crisis is obscurity: relevant audiences lack information about who or what a group is. The appropriate solution is to offer added information about the group—about its issues or its members—throughout the policy community.

An interest group may also confront an identity crisis if key audiences know a group exists but have the wrong idea (from the standpoint of the group's leadership or membership) about what the group is and does. In this case, the external image of a group—whom it represents, what it works on, what it stands for—is out of alignment with the internal image of the group.

A carefully orchestrated branding strategy may be a solution to an identity crisis rooted in a problematic image.[20] The objective of branding is to either establish an information shortcut between the group and the key elements of its identity or eliminate existing shortcuts that may pose a problem for the group. For example, the Health Industry Manufacturers Association (HIMA) found that it confronted misinformation about who it was and what it did. The words "industry" and "manufacturers" in the organization's name conjured images of heavy equipment and large warehouses. Yet HIMA's member companies manufactured some of the word's most advanced medical equipment, including pacemakers, defibrillators, and magnetic resonance imaging machines. An obvious solution to the problem was to rebrand the organization to highlight these advanced technologies. In line with this strategy, the organization changed its name in 2000 to the Advanced Medical Technology Association, or AdvaMed.[21] Effective branding—such as the change from HIMA to AdvaMed—has the potential to transform the way relevant audiences perceive and react to an organization's identity.

The struggle to define its identity in Washington is one that each interest group undertakes on its own terms. Groups face myriad constraints and opportunities, based on their unique histories, members, budgets, and goals. Thus, it is a mistake to conclude that all groups build their identities uniformly using one strategic approach. The flaw in issue niche theory is not that groups never form issue niches; instead, it is the theory's failure to recognize other paths to establishing a strong identity. Similarly, Virginia Gray and David Lowery are too restrictive in their argument that "exclusive access to members and finances ... may be more critical than securing ... viable issue niches."[22] While Gray and Lowery are no doubt correct when they claim that access to either members or finances is critical to survival, their assertions that this access must be "exclusive" and that survival is the dominant motivation behind identity formation go too far. Identity formation is driven not just by the minimal impulse for survival but also by the desire to climb in the Washington status hierarchy through gaining more recognition, influence, and prestige. Members and finances constitute a part of that equation, but just a part.

The three strategies presented here—issue niche creation, representation, and branding—establish the foundation for multiple dimensions of identity. Interest groups not only possess various options for establishing identities, but they also may elect to build their identities in tandem across multiple dimensions. A group may choose to emphasize both its member base and its issue expertise as, for example, when the Consumer Federation of America simultaneously claims to represent all consumers and to possess expertise on issues like credit card debt, cable regulation, and home ownership. The complex nature of many groups compels them to articulate their identities across multiple dimensions and allows them to reach out broadly to the diverse audiences attentive to what they do.

Which Identities Prevail?

Beyond these scholarly debates over establishing and employing identities, how are we to know which identities actually prevail in the course of practical politics? No study has ever investigated the identities articulated by the full range of Washington interest groups. Browne's research focuses entirely on the agricultural policy domain, and other research on the question is limited to the health policy domain.[23] Gray and Lowery do not examine Washington interest groups at all but instead survey groups operating in six states. To know how interest groups actually create their identities, we need to look at a wide range of groups and how they explain who they are to the public at large.

The research here investigates the identities of all interest groups that maintained their own lobbying operations in Washington between 1998 and 2003. By focusing on interest groups with in-house lobbyists, I exclude the thousands of interest groups that rely only on contract lobbyists to represent their interests. I do not dispute that groups represented exclusively by contract lobbyists are an important part of public policy making, but the focus here is on how groups assert their presence in Washington.[24] Addressing only groups that speak for themselves is a reasonable limitation, which still allows for analyzing a sample representing the major interest groups that influence national policy making. Included here are 1,076 groups across all domains of public policy, from the AARP to the Zionist Organization of America.[25] The majority of these groups hire contract lobbyists to supplement their in-house activities although each is represented by at least one of its own employees.[26]

The identity of these interest groups was ascertained by looking at their public statements about who they are. Public statements provide considerable insight into identity because they are vetted intensively within the organization. Although it is unlikely that these statements are arrived at through a genuinely democratic process, their public posting invites comment and criticism, making it likely that they at least reflect the views of the organization's dominant faction.[27] Because public statements are, by their nature, accessible to diverse audiences, they implicitly reflect groups' efforts to speak simultaneously to different constituencies. Groups may be able to hide their private statements from many audiences (although private statements harbor the risk of eventually becoming public), but statements made on-the-record are certain to follow them for years to come. Groups thus weigh their public statements carefully, which strengthens their validity as a source of data on identity.

For each of the 1,076 groups, concise public statements were sought to convey the nature of the group's identity as presented by the group's leadership.[28] Almost all these groups maintained a Web page (94 percent), which contained a mission statement (52 percent), a mission-like statement (21 percent), or another organizational description (59 percent) that provided basic information about organizational identity.[29] For 1,010 groups (94 percent of the sample), at least one of the three types of public statements of identity was available.

Each public statement was analyzed for the use of any of nine dimensions of identification:

- **Representation** is the claim by an organization that it speaks on behalf of a set of individuals or institutions, whether or not they are official members of the organization. An interest group may represent groups such as the poor, small businesses, or people who want smaller government.
- **Member services** are particular benefits supplied exclusively to members, such as information or educational opportunities.
- An **issue** is a specific policy concern, like food safety or antitrust policy.
- An **issue position** is an explicitly stated policy preference on an issue, like strengthening federal government assurances of food safety or the elimination of antitrust lawsuits.
- **Values** encompass a wide range of socially desirable qualities, like excellence or openness.
- **Ideology** is a consistent and all-encompassing political worldview, like progressivism or conservatism.[30]
- **Organizational tools** are routine operational activities, like advocacy, education, and research.
- **Modes of organization** reflect the different structures of participation and decision making—federations, associations, and grassroots networks—within interest groups.
- **Superlative statements** indicate that a group is the oldest, largest, or most prestigious of a class of organizations.

Group statements could be coded into all, some, or none of these dimensions. Both the mean and the mode number of dimensions are exactly 4.00. The overwhelming majority of group statements (73 percent) have between three and five dimensions. At the minimum, seventeen groups fall into only one of these categories and, at the maximum, four groups fall into eight categories. Table 12.1 reports the percentage of groups using each dimension, an example of the group using it, and the reason the group was assigned to that category.

Table 12.1. Dimensions of Identification

Dimension	Percentage of groups	Exemplar group	Reason
Representation	75.94	American Electronics Association	Represents "all segments of the technology industry."
Member services	20.89	American Institute of Certified Public Accountants	Serves to "provide its members with resources, information, and leadership."
Issue	24.45	American Life League	Works on the issue of abortion.
Issue position	19.51	Americans for Computer Privacy	Advances the right "to encode information without fear of government intrusion."
Values	92.18	United Services Automobile Association	Stands for service, loyalty, honesty, integrity, and financial security.
Ideology	4.46	60-Plus Association	The "conservative" alternative to the AARP.
Organizational tools	86.53	American Phytopathological Society	Performs its work through publications, meetings, symposia, and workshops.
Mode of organization	47.52	National Association of Industrial and Office Properties	Operates through a "grassroots network."
Superlative statement	29.21	National Corn Growers Association	"NCGA is the largest trade organization in the United States representing corn growers."

Source: Public statements by 1,010 interest groups.

Note: Although the total number of groups examined was 1,076, only 94 percent of the sample (1,010 groups) made publicly available at least one of the three types of public statements of identity.

The summary of public statements reveals which dimensions are most and least frequently a part of interest group identities. Fewer than one group in twenty links its identity to an ideological or partisan orientation, largely because of concerns about nonprofit status.[31] Conversely, more than nine of ten groups (92 percent) include some expression of values when explaining who they are, which makes this dimension not very useful in separating groups from each other. Representation is a component of identity for three-fourths of the groups (76 percent), while about one in five (21 percent) stresses particular member services. Issues help define identity for about one-fourth (24 percent) of the groups, with about 20 percent taking an explicit stand on a specific position. Further, most groups (87 percent) enumerated the tools they use to do their work, and almost half (48 percent) noted their organizational modes. Less than 30 percent of groups (29.21 percent) compared themselves favorably with other organized interests.

Dimensions of interest group identity are closely related. For example, a group that does not claim to have members or to represent anyone will not stress member services. Similarly, a group needs to pick an issue before it defines itself on the basis of an issue position. Thus, relationships among these dimensions should illuminate aspects of the strategies behind their use, as illustrated in the matrix of correlations among the identity dimensions (Table 12.2). Each number in this table represents the correlation of the dimension listed in a row with the one listed in the column. A positive number indicates that the dimensions tend to go together, and a negative number implies that the dimensions oppose one another. The presence of an asterisk to the right of the number denotes that the correlation is strong enough to be statistically significant: the relationship between the two dimensions is due to something more than just mere chance.

The correlation matrix reveals a clear division between interest groups that emphasize representation in their identities and those that emphasize issues. Representation correlates positively with member services and mode of organization, which often stresses relations with members; but representation correlates negatively with issues, issue positions, values, and ideology. In contrast, issues correlate positively with issue position, values, and ideology.[32] This pattern strongly suggests that many interest groups strategically choose between an issue-identity orientation and a representation-identity orientation, although some groups do attempt to combine the two. Although the representation-identity orientation is summoned more frequently, the issue-identity orientation is still invoked consistently and coherently. These two strategies dominate the interest group articulation of identity. Some space for branding resides in the use of organizational tools, models, and superlative statements. Indeed, branding is often a way for a group to highlight the representational or issue-oriented aspects of identity.

Table 12.2. Correlation Matrix of Dimensions of Identification

Dimension	Representation	Member services	Issue	Issue position	Values	Ideology	Organizational tools	Mode of organization
Member services	0.2836*							
Issue	-0.2133*	-0.1337*						
Issue position	-0.2023*	-0.1423*	0.8594*					
Values	-0.1036*	-0.0771	0.0285	0.0969*				
Ideology	-0.1703*	-0.0638	0.0893*	0.0996*	0.0450			
Organizational tools	0.0630	0.0672	0.0085	0.0039	0.1011*	0.0008		
Mode of organization	0.1147*	0.0220	0.0017	0.0209	-0.1283*	0.1496*	-0.0072	
Superlative statement	0.0712	0.0288	0.0601	0.0575	-0.0318	0.0513	0.0875*	0.1897*

Source: Public statements by 1,010 interest groups.

Notes: Although the total number of groups examined was 1,076, only 94 percent of the sample (1,010 groups) made publicly available at least one of the three types of public statements of identity.

*Statistical significance at the 0.01 level.

How Groups Use Broad Issue Niches
and Multidimensional Strategies

Analysis of public statements by interest groups provides convincing evidence that many of them use issues in defining their identities, but groups rarely construct the narrow niches predicted by issue niche theory.[33] Instead, their issue foci are usually broad, sometimes encompassing entire policy domains (or more). Beyond addressing whether an interest group asserted an issue-based identity, the research examined which issues were emphasized, including education (five groups), environment (six), health care (thirteen), intellectual property (four), public health (three), reproductive health (five), taxation (five), trade (four), and transportation (four). Occasionally, as predicted by issue niche theory, a group mentions an extremely specific issue—such as the environmental performance of cement kilns—but this is not the norm. When groups define their identities on the basis of issues, they often use position, rather than narrowness, as a means of differentiation from competing groups.

Understanding how issues affect groups' identities can be gleaned by examining the reactions of a key audience: congressional staff members. Congressional staff are the gatekeepers for members of Congress, so what they know (or do not know) about a group may determine whether it gains meaningful access to the member. Eighty-eight congressional staff members (forty-six Republicans and forty-two Democrats) were presented with a series of policy issues and were asked to name the interest groups they associated with the issue. This question directly taps the degree to which congressional staff identify interest groups with specific issues, and their responses to the abortion issue (see Table 12.3) nicely illustrate the opportunities and difficulties posed by issue-based strategies of identification.

In addition to listing whether or not a group was mentioned, Table 12.3 notes whether the group was mentioned first, which indicates the respondent's strength of belief.[34] The responses are divided by party, with Democratic staff members being usually, but not always, proabortion, and Republican staff members being usually, but not always, antiabortion. Interest groups are listed by the frequency with which staff members mention them without prompting.

The results indicate that only a few interest groups have gained wide recognition on the issue of abortion. Three are on the proabortion side—NARAL Pro-Choice America, Planned Parenthood Federation of America (PPFA), and the National Organization for Women (NOW); and three are on the antiabortion side of the issue—the National Right to Life Committee (NRLC), the Christian Coalition of America, and the U.S. Conference of Catholic Bishops. First mentions are common for only three groups: NARAL, NRLC, and PPFA. These results should be distressing to a number of groups that have attempted to build identities exclusively on the abortion issue. Groups like the American Life League and the National

Table 12.3.   Interest Groups with Positions on Abortion, as Identified by Congressional Staff in 2003

Interest group	Democrats		Republicans		All
	First mentions	Total mentions	First mentions	Total mentions	Total mentions
NARAL Pro-Choice America	29	36	15	28	64
National Right to Life Committee	5	26	18	32	58
Planned Parenthood Federation of America	5	27	5	17	44
Christian Coalition of America	1	11	1	10	21
United States Conference of Catholic Bishops	0	7	1	8	15
National Organization for Women	0	1	4	6	7
Concerned Women for America	0	0	0	3	3
National Partnership for Women and Families	0	3	0	0	3
American College of Obstetricians and Gynecologists	0	0	0	2	2

Source: Author interviews with eighty-eight congressional staff members, spring and summer, 2003.

Notes: The question asked was: "In the next part of the interview, I will name an issue, and I would like for you to tell me which interest groups you think of when you think of that issue. The first issue is abortion. Which interest groups do you associate with abortion?"
The following interest groups were mentioned only once: Alan Guttmacher Institute, American Civil Liberties Union, American Life League, Catholics for Free Choice, Democrats for Life, Eagle Forum, EMILY's List, Family Research Council, Georgia Right to Life, National Abortion Federation, Operation Rescue, and the Republican Pro-Choice Coalition.

Abortion Federation are classic issue-niche-based groups, but they receive almost no recognition. Thus, it is possible for groups to sustain identities linked principally to an issue, but only a limited number can do so on any particular issue.

The responses of congressional aides hint at how interest groups build their identities in multiple dimensions. Differences between Democrats and Republicans unpack the role of issue position in shaping identity. Democrats are more likely to think of "their" group, NARAL, and to think of it first when prompted to list groups that address the issue of abortion. Likewise, Republicans are more likely to list "their" group, NRLC, before listing proabortion groups. It is not that each side does not recognize the existence of groups on the other side—Republicans know that NARAL exists and Democrats are aware of NRLC—but the issue position increases familiarity and strengthens identification.

A multidimensional strategy is one way for interest groups to amplify their identities when they are unable to attract attention on the basis of their issues alone. For example, the Republican Pro-Choice Coalition, Catholics for Free Choice, and Democrats for Life are all memorable because they assume positions that are at odds with the social groups they claim to represent (Republicans and Catholics tend to oppose abortion, while Democrats usually support it). The Alan Guttmacher Institute is best known for specializing in the use of an organizational tool: high-quality empirical research (on reproductive health). Concerned Women for America (CWA) and NOW gain recognition for representing women on alternative sides of the political spectrum (CWA is conservative, while NOW is liberal). Thus, although these groups fail in securing identities on the basis of issues alone, they succeed by combining issues with other dimensions. In the case of NOW, for example, a mix of issues, representation, and ideology defines the group in the minds of many observers.

Strengthening Representation

If issues-based identities are usually broad, leaving interest groups with the option of narrowing them in some way, then representation-based identities are the exact opposite. Interest groups start by representing some narrow interest and then try to broaden their representational claims over time. AARP, for example, had its origin in representing retired teachers when the National Retired Teachers Association (NRTA) was founded in 1947. NRTA expanded its mission to represent all the retired by forming American Association of Retired Persons in 1958. Over time, the mission stretched still further, by representing anyone over age fifty willing to pay dues, and this expansion culminated in the organization formally changing its name to just AARP in 1998.[35]

If AARP's leadership had its way, it would claim to represent all older Americans, present and future—in short, almost everyone. Other groups make similar expansive claims to the extent that they can get away with it. The U.S. Chamber of Commerce represents all American businesses, the AFL-CIO fights for all working people, the American Medical Association (AMA) speaks for all doctors, and so on. Legislators and other policy makers are wise enough to be skeptical of these assertions. Many doctors are not members of the AMA, for instance. The presence of such understandable skepticism raises dilemmas for both groups and policy makers. If an interest group did genuinely represent a broad constituency, how would it communicate that fact persuasively? How would policy makers know whether to accept the representational identity, as asserted?

Interviews with congressional aides (described above) generated comments from them on a list of 171 interest groups active on health policy issues.[36] In particular, they were asked to note which groups actively represented constituencies within their district (for House staff) or state (for Senate staff). Table 12.4 reports the top fifteen groups that firmly established these representational connections. The American Hospital Association (AHA) tops the list, followed by AMA, AARP, and the American Cancer Society. Other interests on the list include disease patients and their families, health professionals, unions, insurance companies, and community health centers.

It is tempting to imagine that the ranking reported in Table 12.4 corresponds to a natural ordering of constituencies in health care. We might reason that it makes sense that hospitals are the most widely representative interest because there are hospitals in every district and state. Still, some health constituencies not on the list may be more common than hospitals. Chain drug stores are everywhere, so why is the National

Table 12.4.   Health Groups Identified for Local-Level Representation

Rank	Total mentions	Interest group
1	64	American Hospital Association
2	55	American Medical Association
3	52	AARP
4	49	American Cancer Society
5	44	Blue Cross and Blue Shield Association
5	44	National Breast Cancer Coalition
7	38	Alzheimer's Association
7	38	Juvenile Diabetes Research Foundation International
9	36	American Association of Nurse Anesthetists
9	36	American Heart Association
11	34	American Diabetes Association
11	34	National Association of Community Health Centers
13	33	AFL-CIO
14	31	American College of Obstetricians and Gynecologists
14	31	American Nurses Association

Source: Author interviews with seventy-seven congressional staff members, spring and summer, 2003.

Note: The question asked was: "Please look at the following list of interest groups that work on health policy issues. Who is especially well organized in your district (or state)?" This question was not asked of aides serving primarily as staff to congressional committees, which is why there are eleven fewer data points available in this table than in Table 12.3.

Association of Chain Drug Stores not listed? Similarly, why is the breast cancer lobby recognized, but not organizations for equally devastating cancers of the lung and the prostate? Why obstetricians and not pediatricians? The answer is that an identity for representation depends on the ability of a group's leaders to make themselves intermediaries between members of Congress and their constituents. To better understand how some groups are able to make this connection, lobbyists were interviewed at each of these fifteen interest groups and the national grassroots directors at ten of them.

Every organization with a strong representation-based identity achieves legitimacy according to its own unique style. At the same time, one common element in each of the leading organizations is that they systematically use their organizational structures and tools directly to represent their members. Strong representation demands effective organization. First and foremost, this means coordinating action through a multilayered communication network of e-mail, conference calls, miniconferences, and in-person meetings. Second, organizational members are channeled through a well-structured hierarchy of volunteers. In the National Breast Cancer Coalition, for example, this imperative translates into six levels: (1) board members, (2) field coordinators, (3) team leaders, (4) national action network members, (5) conference participants, and (6) regular members.[37] At the American Heart Association, a similar volunteer hierarchy is complemented by a parallel structure of thirteen scientific councils that address topics like cardiovascular nursing, clinical cardiology, and strokes.[38]

Interest groups with strong representation-based identities stress the importance of making quality contacts with legislators, as opposed to simply making any contact. As Frank J. Purcell, director of federal government affairs at the American Association of Nurse Anesthetists put it: "Technology makes grassroots organization both more capable and more capable to do poorly."[39] To address the issue of representation through quality electronic communications, the American Cancer Society created a formal e-advocacy program and hired a full-time manager of e-advocacy and technology.[40] The Juvenile Diabetes Research Foundation International holds a "children's congress" in Washington every two years, to introduce juvenile diabetes patients to members of Congress, along with its Promise to Remember Me Campaign to facilitate in-district contacts.[41] All these groups strive to maximize the impact of member interactions with legislators by coupling well-trained member-advocates with appropriate lobbyist follow-through with legislative aides.

The struggle to forge a clear representational identity is inextricably bound to other identity elements in the organization. Member services, modes of organization, and organizational tools are all part of projecting an identity as representatives of a politically relevant constituency. The next section examines the final component in the strategic identity formation process: branding.

Marketing Identity

The previous two sections depict the struggle for identity as grounded in substantive polices and actual political concerns. Which issues is the group working on? How is the group connecting legislators and constituents? But groups need not work directly on issues or develop representational ties in order to be perceived as doing so. Conversely, people may think that a group is not doing these things when, in fact, it is. In short, image matters; and organizations shape their images in the modern media age through branding.

Everything that an organization does reflects on its brand. The Web page, logo, stationery, and even the attire and conduct of staff members are all part of the brand. For simplicity, I focus here on the crudest element of a brand: the organization's name. Leaders of interest groups commonly believe that changing an organization's name can have a significant effect on how its identity is perceived. One recent study on the identities of health care interest groups reports:

> Twenty-three percent of the organizations participating in the study indicated that they had made some change in their name in the past 10 years. An additional 5 percent revealed that there was some active consideration of changing their name. About a third (32 percent) of the time, name changes are considered or undertaken because organizational names are confusing. Organizations also change (or consider changing) their names because they have added new issues to their portfolios (33 percent of the time) or because they have added new categories of members (9 percent of the time).[42]

The analysis of public statements by 1,010 interest groups reported in this chapter is roughly consistent with the earlier study. At least 7.03 percent of these groups made a significant change in the organizational name during the six-year period covered by the data (1998–2003). Many of these name changes were the direct result of mergers, but others were the product of a straightforward rebranding strategy. Some changes were subtle, such as the shift of the Metals Service Center Institute into the Steel Service Center Institute in 2002 (originally it was the American Iron, Steel, and Heavy Hardware Association). Perhaps the replacement of "metals" with "steel" conveys greater strength and clarity.

In a slightly more radical change, Zero Population Growth became Population Connection in 2002—an especially interesting modification from the point of view of the theory presented in this chapter. The original name of the group invoked two dimensions of identification: the issue (population) and the issue position (reducing population growth to zero). The new name, in contrast, retains the invocation of issue identification (population) but eliminates the statement of an issue position in favor of an ostensibly neutral point of view. Population Connection still fights to reduce population growth, but the new branding potentially alters the organizational appeal.

Table 12.5.   Examples of Name Changes by Interest Groups

Former name	New name
American Association of Health Plans	America's Health Insurance Plans
American School Food Service Association	School Nutrition Association
American Society for Personnel Administration	Society for Human Resource Management
American Trade Association Executives	American Society of Association Executives
Association of Independent Television Stations	Association of Local Television Stations
Environmental Defense Fund	Environmental Defense
Independent Insurance Agents of America	Independent Insurance Agents & Brokers of America
Industrial Telecommunications Association	Enterprise Wireless Alliance
NOW Legal Defense and Education Fund	Legal Momentum
Sierra Club Legal Defense Fund	Earthjustice
Women's Legal Defense Fund	National Partnership for Women and Families

Source: Public statements by 1,010 interest groups.

Note: Although the total number of groups examined was 1,076, only 94 percent of the sample (1,010 groups) made publicly available at least one of the three types of public statements of identity.

Population Connection sounds less radical and more flexible in its approach to population management problems. Of course, Population Connection's pro-growth opponents can always point to the group's history in disputing the authenticity of its new orientation. Rebranding is a strategic attempt to alter identity, but there is no guarantee that it will achieve that goal.

Examples of recent name changes by interest groups not mentioned elsewhere in this chapter are listed in Table 12.5. In each case, the logic of strategic identity manipulation through branding is apparent. Several of these modifications endeavor to communicate new values, as "nutrition" replaces "food service" and "human resource management" replaces "personnel administration." Some groups attempt to abandon old affiliations, as Legal Momentum breaks from NOW and Earthjustice breaks from the Sierra Club. Although there are many intricate reasons for these varied alterations, the overwhelming evidence indicates that they are rooted in carefully designed branding strategies. These changes illustrate how interest groups turn to branding as a mechanism for amplifying or muting dimensions of group identity.

Conclusion

Where does the multidimensional theory of identity leave AARP in the midst of its identity crisis? How ought AARP appease the enraged seniors burning their hotel discount cards on its doorstep? What should AARP tell Democratic politicians who feel betrayed by its endorsement of the Republican-sponsored Medicare bill? Will AARP be able to woo Republican politicians into the negotiating room when major legislation is on the table? Can AARP depend on brand loyalty from a new generation of fifty-somethings who are more affluent and conservative than the previous cohort?

The easy answer for AARP is to amplify its desired identity using all three strategies: issue niches, representation, and branding. AARP's first major policy endeavor after the Medicare debate was to oppose President George W. Bush's proposal for Social Security reform.[43] This move emphasized AARP's broad niche on seniors' issues and, by opposing the president, highlighted its independence from the political establishment.[44] AARP thus asserted its identity on the dimensions of issue and issue position. On the dimension of representation, AARP attempted to placate members through damage control operations begun immediately after its Medicare announcement as it dispatched its chief executive officer, William D. Novelli, to seniors' forums throughout the country. It continued to rely on its award-winning grassroots advocacy program to connect its members with legislators.[45] With respect to branding, AARP is the KFC of interest group politics. A few million dollars of television advertising were well within AARP's means.

Although AARP was able to quell the Medicare controversy (temporarily, at least), its opponents continue to challenge its identity for assorted reasons. AARP came under fire in 2005, for example, from cultural conservatives who attacked its stance on same-sex partnerships.[46] For groups like AARP, crisis may be inextricably bound to identity.

The more indeterminate crises of identity are confronted every day by thousands of smaller interest groups that seek to increase their influence vis-à-vis policy-making institutions. All groups cannot dedicate millions of dollars to advertising every time they make a controversial decision, and they must make careful strategic choices about how to use their time and resources. Nevertheless, they can choose from various strategies, either alone or, more likely, in a combination. Their choices in their identity struggles are limited neither by issues (as Browne has argued) nor by members and resources (as Gray and Lowery contend). Instead, interest groups craft their identities in a multidimensional space in which they blend elements from several alternatives. At the same time, their choices are necessarily limited: groups' abilities to craft their identities are restrained by the need to appeal to attentive audiences—legislators, the media, and the public, for example—who have a say in how their identities are understood.

Identity serves as a flexible mechanism to pull together myriad aspects of interest group activities, from grassroots organizing to elite lobbying to coalition building. A group's identity affects its ability to win sympathy from the public, dues from members, loyalty from staff, and favors from legislators. Thus, anything a group does to affect how it is viewed by one of these audiences also matters to the others. If a group's membership grows or shrinks considerably, for example, legislators have incentives to give it more or fewer favors. Likewise, if legislators regard the group with higher or lower esteem, members have greater or lesser incentives to contribute to the work of the organization. These responses from varied audiences do not operate seamlessly or automatically, and from time to time they will be significantly out of alignment with each other. When these identity crises surface, interest groups can and do turn to issue niches, representation, and branding as strategies to affect a realignment consistent with their goals.

Notes

The idea for this chapter was originally proposed by William P. Browne, who invited me to write it with him. Bill's untimely death in 2005 sadly made our collaboration impossible. This chapter is dedicated to his memory. Also, I am indebted to Elizabeth Rubenstein of Yale University for outstanding research assistance. Jonathan Ellzey, Cassandra Farley, David Paul, and Daniel A. Smith provided helpful suggestions. This research received generous financial support from the Center for the Study of American Politics at Yale University and the Santa Fe Institute.

1. David Cook, "AARP Chief Admits Losing up to 10,000 members: Senior Group Came under Fire for Backing GOP on Medicare," *Chicago Sun-Times*, December 12, 2003.
2. For the classic discussion of identity from this perspective, see Erik H. Erikson, *Identity: Youth and Crisis* (New York: Norton, 1968).
3. Harrison C. White, *Identity and Control: A Structural Theory of Social Action* (Princeton: Princeton University Press, 1992).
4. Bob Cusack, "Drug Industry Does Battle with an Image Problem: Policymakers Say Drug Makers Must Improve Standing," *The Hill*, September 17, 2003.
5. Robert H. Salisbury, "The Paradox of Interest Groups in Washington: More Groups, Less Clout," in *The New American Political System*, rev. ed., ed. Anthony King (Washington, D.C.: American Enterprise Institute, 1990), 203–229. For a recent analysis of why the Washington policy community has become so crowded, see Beth L. Leech et al., "Drawing Lobbyists to Washington: Government Activity and the Demand for Advocacy," *Political Research Quarterly* 58 (March 2005): 19–30.
6. For more information about the Council for Government Reform, see http://www.govreform.org/.
7. Michael T. Heaney, "Outside the Issue Niche: The Multidimensionality of Interest Group Identity," *American Politics Research* 32 (November 2004): 611–651.
8. William P. Browne, "Organized Interests and Their Issue Niches: A Search for Pluralism in a Policy Domain," *Journal of Politics* 52 (May 1990): 477–509.
9. Ibid., 477.
10. Samuel Walker, *In Defense of American Liberties: A History of the ACLU*, 2d ed. (Carbondale: Southern Illinois University Press, 1999).
11. Andrew Rich, *Think Tanks, Public Policy, and the Politics of Expertise* (New York: Cambridge University Press, 2004). Just because policy expertise is biased does not mean that it cannot be informative. See Kevin M. Esterling, *The Political Economy of Expertise* (Ann Arbor: University of Michigan Press, 2004).
12. Daniel P. Carpenter, Kevin M. Esterling, and David M. J. Lazer, "The Strength of Strong Ties: A Model of Contact-Making in Policy Networks with Evidence from U.S. Health Politics," *Rationality and Society* 15 (October 2003): 411–440.

13. On the concept of interest groups as service bureaus, see Raymond E. Bauer, Ithiel de Sola Pool, and Lewis Anthony Dexter, *American Business and Public Policy: The Politics of Foreign Trade* (New York: Atherton Press, 1963). A more recent perspective on this topic is presented in Richard L. Hall and Alan V. Deardorff, "Lobbying as Legislative Subsidy," *American Political Science Review* 100 (February 2006): 69–84.

14. John C. Panzar and Robert D. Willig, "Economies of Scope," *American Economic Review* 71 (May 1981): 268–272.

15. This perspective on representation is consistent with the definition advanced by Andrew Rehfeld, "Towards a General Theory of Political Representation," *Journal of Politics* 68 (February 2006): 1–21, in that it explains representation "simply by reference to a relevant audience accepting a person as such" (p. 1).

16. David Mayhew, *Congress: The Electoral Connection* (New Haven: Yale University Press, 1974).

17. John Mark Hansen, *Gaining Access: Congress and the Farm Lobby, 1919–1981* (Chicago: University of Chicago Press, 1991).

18. Theda Skocpol, *Diminished Democracy: From Membership to Management in American Civic Life* (Norman: University of Oklahoma Press, 2003).

19. Michael T. Heaney, "Brokering Health Policy: Coalitions, Parties, and Interest Group Influence," *Journal of Health Politics, Policy and Law* 31 (October 2006): 887–944.

20. Helmut Schneider, "Branding in Politics—Manifestations, Relevance and Identity-Oriented Management," *Journal of Political Marketing* 3 (October 2004): 41–67.

21. See AdvaMed's Web site at http://www.advamed.org/.

22. Virginia Gray and David Lowery, "A Niche Theory of Interest Representation," *Journal of Politics* 58 (February 1996): 91–111.

23. Heaney, "Outside the Issue Niche."

24. For an excellent discussion of how interest groups choose between in-house and contract representation, see John M. de Figueiredo and James J. Kim, "When Do Firms Hire Lobbyists? The Organization of Lobbying at the Federal Communications Commission," *Industrial and Corporate Change* 13 (December 2004): 883–900.

25. U.S. Senate Office of Public Records, http://sopr.senate.gov/, January–February 2005.

26. For comparisons of in-house and contract lobbying behavior by corporations, see Holly Brasher and David Lowery, "Corporate Context of Lobbying Activity," *Business and Politics* 8 (April 2006): 1–25.

27. For the seminal analysis of intraorganizational decision making, see David B. Truman, *The Governmental Process: Political Interests and Public Opinion* (New York: Knopf, 1951), chs. 5–7.

28. The searches were conducted under my supervision by my research assistant, Elizabeth Rubenstein, who collected and coded all the information described below.

29. If a Web page was not available, we checked the 2004 print edition of the *Encyclopedia of Associations* for information, although there were only ten cases in which this yielded information not otherwise available on the Web. See Kimberly N. Hunt, *Encyclopedia of Associations: National Organizations of the U.S.* (Detroit: Gale Research Company, 2004).

30. A group that explicitly asserted a position as "nonpartisan" was coded using the ideological dimension. Although these groups claim that they are not affiliated with any specific party, they nonetheless define themselves with reference to an ideological system.

31. Jeffrey M. Berry and David F. Arons, *A Voice for Nonprofits* (Washington, D.C.: Brookings Institution Press, 2003). The strong aversion to ideology and partisanship may be a result of the fact that I analyzed public statements. In private, interest groups may be more willing to identify themselves according to an ideology, though only slightly more so. See Heaney, "Outside the Issue Niche."

32. I considered the possibility that dimensions of identification used by an interest group depend on the type of public statement in question. For example, formal mission statements might tend to contain different dimensions than other kinds of organizational descriptions. To check for this possibility, when the correlations are estimated with mission statements only, the conclusions hold pertaining to representation, member services, issues, and issue positions. However, statistically significant correlations on ideology and values disappear.

33. While many interest group scholars have come to think of niches as inherently narrow, owing largely to Browne's theory, there is nothing in the underlying theory of organizational niches that implies that they must be narrow. A niche is simply a space in which an organizational population experiences favorable conditions under which it can grow. See Michael T. Hannan and John Freeman, *Organizational Ecology* (Cambridge: Harvard University Press, 1989), 95–97.

34. In this case, the group mentioned first is mentioned more swiftly than the groups mentioned second, third, and so on, although this is not a precise measure of response time. An important recent study on this topic is Martin Johnson, "Timepieces: Components of Survey Question Response Latencies," *Political Psychology* 25 (October 2004): 679–702.

35. AARP, *AARP History*, http://www.aarp.org/about_aarp/aarp_overview/a2003-01-13-aarphistory.html, April 28, 2006.

36. Although focusing on health groups may be limiting when attempting to ascertain the broad scope of identities employed by interest groups, evidence from this domain deepens our knowledge of how identity strategies are put into practice. Further, health groups represent the general interest group community well because virtually every sector of society has an interest in health, including employers, labor unions, veterans, manufacturers, the professions, and citizens' groups.

37. Kimberly Love and Sharon Ford Watkins, staff members of the National Breast Cancer Coalition, interview by the author, December 3, 2003.

38. Diane Canova, vice president of advocacy for the American Heart Association, interview by the author, December 10, 2003.

39. Frank J. Purcell, interview by the author, December 3, 2003.

40. Barry Jackson, manager of e-advocacy and technology for the American Cancer Society, interview by the author, December 5, 2003.

41. Lawrence A. Soler, vice president of government relations for the Juvenile Diabetes Research Foundation International, interview by the author, February 24, 2004.

42. Heaney, "Outside the Issue Niche," 626.

43. Merrill Goozner, "Don't Mess With Success: There's Nothing Wrong with Social Security That a Few Changes Can't Fix," *AARP Bulletin*, January 2005.

44. Ben Pershing, "AARP Faces Heat," *Roll Call*, February 16, 2004.

45. Kevin J. Donnellan, "Reaching for the Gold: AARP Seeks to Set the Standard for Grassroots Advocacy," *Public Affairs Review*, 2002, 12–15.

46. Deborah Solomon, "AARP's Antagonist," *New York Times*, March 13, 2005.

13

American Interests in the Balance?
Do Ethnic Groups Dominate Foreign Policy Making?

Eric M. Uslaner

When we think about interest groups in American politics, we ordinarily focus on corporations, trade associations (software manufacturers, for example), professional associations (like lawyers' organizations), or groups that represent particular segments of the population (such as the National Organization for Women). Indeed, most lobbying does address domestic issues ranging from tax policies to Social Security to interstate highways. But many Americans have strong links to countries or interests outside the United States. Cuban expatriates, for example, have long exercised disproportionate influence over Florida politics. Historically, pro-Israel interests have proved especially powerful because of their ability to raise funds for and gain access to elected officials from both parties.

In this chapter, Eric M. Uslaner examines the strength—both absolute and relative—of the Israeli lobby in the context of increasing interest group activity that links American ethnic groups and, on occasion, religious groups to both global interests and to U.S. decision making. Over time, the Israel lobby has faced various challenges, yet it has managed through its lead organization (the American Israel Public Affairs Committee) to retain its position as an extraordinarily powerful lobby. Still, as Uslaner notes, growing population groups in the United States, such as Latinos, will likely change the face of ethnic-based lobbying in the United States as will the long-term policies of operating in a global environment, albeit one that requires national vigilance as well as new economic connections.

When we think of interest group politics, we generally focus on domestic policy. On foreign policy, the entire country is supposed to speak with a single voice. Policy is supposed to reflect a national interest that has its roots in moral principles.

Because the stakes of foreign policy are higher than those of domestic policy—the wrong decision in foreign policy could lead to a nuclear confrontation—we expect foreign policy decisions to be less subject to the whims of group pressure. Instead, we make decisions based on a common interest. Foreign policy should be made on the basis of principles—American principles. Americans should be primarily concerned with domestic issues and put American interests first when looking beyond our borders.

The terrorist attacks on September 11, 2001, raised the foreign policy stakes considerably. For a time after the attacks, the American people spoke with one voice. Confidence in national institutions, especially in the military and in President George W. Bush, reached new peaks. Americans saw themselves and their allies in a struggle for survival and dominance in a hostile world once more. The fall of communism had led many to believe that the twenty-first century would be America's. The terrorist attacks challenged that premise.

It thus became even more critical for foreign policy to be based on a consensus, reflecting the national interest. Since the attacks, the consensus on foreign policy has waned as the United States became immersed in a war in Iraq that strongly divided the country and faced another looming issue in the Middle East—the development of nuclear weapons by the Islamic regime in Iran.

The terrorist attacks and the war in Iraq particularly raised specific questions about the support the United States has long given to Israel. Two prominent academics—John J. Mearsheimer at the University of Chicago and Stephen M. Walt at Harvard—published an essay in the *London Review of Books* (and a longer version on a Harvard Web site) attacking supporters of Israel as partly responsible for the terrorist attacks, for pushing the United States into the war in Iraq, and for promoting military action against Iran. These essays led to a debate over whether American foreign policy in the Middle East was driven more by domestic political pressures or by the nation's strategic interests.[1]

Yet, for all of the heat that these essays generated—ranging from assertions of sloppy scholarship to charges of anti-Semitism[2]—little had changed in the constellation of interest group influence in foreign policy since September 11, 2001, or in the larger issues of foreign policy. Criticism of the pro-Israel lobby was not new, even if in the past it had not been expressed with such vehemence by prominent critics. Mearsheimer and Walt were upset that so little had changed. The war in Iraq raised some of the same questions that the Vietnam conflict raised almost 40 years earlier: What should America's role in the world be? Which actors should have the greatest role in shaping foreign policy?

American Jews have long lobbied successfully on behalf of Israel, and many groups have tried to copy the Jewish model. Irish Americans, Greek Americans, Cuban Americans, Latinos, Armenian Americans, and even Arab Americans followed the lead of the pro-Israel lobby to press support for their own ethnic interests. Yet, only one other ethnic group, Cuban Americans, has achieved anything near the prowess of the pro-Israel lobby.

Pro-Israel groups initially focused on the moral claims that Jews made for Israel. As the Palestinian resistance (the intifada) developed in the 1980s, some leaders criticized Israel's military response to rock throwing by Palestinian youths. Once the pro-Israel forces lost their moral monopoly, they began to act like any other interest group—rewarding their friends and punishing their enemies. They took an increasingly active role in raising money to back candidates for office. The second intifada, which began in October 2000, was even more violent on both sides, and many in the United States became more critical of Israel. The George W. Bush administration nevertheless continued to support Israel, partly for strategic reasons (it did not trust the Palestinian leadership, and Pentagon officials saw Israel as a reliable ally) and partly for political reasons (Bush heavily courted the Jewish vote in the 2004 elections).

Foreign policy interest groups began to look more and more like domestic groups, with one key difference: now it was unclear whether some groups were more loyal to their "mother country" than to the United States. In some cases, especially where constituency groups were weak politically, foreign countries took a direct role in American domestic politics. In the 1996 presidential election, foreign interests allegedly made direct campaign contributions to the reelection campaign of President Bill Clinton. Some of these funds may have even come from the government of China, which was seeking to protect its favored trading status with the United States.

Many people worried that decisions that ought to be made on the basis of moral concerns—What should the role of America be in the world, especially when it is the only superpower?—instead are now made through group conflict and campaign contributions. When does it become illegitimate for Jewish Americans to lobby on behalf of Israel or Cuban Americans against the Castro regime in Cuba or Chinese Americans to take sides between the "two Chinas" (the People's Republic and Taiwan)? If it is acceptable for Chinese Americans to lobby for China, why is it not acceptable for the Chinese to lobby for themselves? If the Chinese (or others) can appropriately exert pressure in Washington, should they be prohibited from influencing who gets sent to Washington?

Here is the dilemma underlying group conflict in American foreign policy. When an ethnic group is united, it can take the high ground. When American Jews were single-minded in their support for Israel and when Cuban Americans were united in their opposition to the Castro regime, both groups could make moral arguments. As divisions grew within both communities, it was more difficult to gain support outside one's own group for the cause. When you cannot be sure everyone is with you, you may feel compelled to use more confrontational strategies to win support.

How legitimate do others view these tactics and how successful can they be? In an April 1997 *New York Times*/CBS News survey, 45 percent of Americans said that they were bothered most by foreign government contributions to "buy influence," compared with 25 percent who were concerned by the influence of American special interest groups and 21 percent who were concerned by the influence of "wealthy people."[3]

Ethnic Groups in Foreign Policy

Mohammed E. Ahrari has suggested four conditions for ethnic group success in foreign policy. First, the group must press for a policy in line with American strategic interests. Second, the group must be assimilated into American society yet retain enough identification with the mother country so that this foreign policy issue motivates people to take some political action. Third, a high level of political activity is required. Fourth, groups should be politically unified.[4] There are other criteria as well. The group's policies should be backed by the larger public. The group should be sufficiently numerous to wield political influence. Finally, the group must be seen as pursuing a legitimate interest.

American Jews are distinctive in their ability to affect foreign policy. They have established the most prominent and best-endowed lobby in Washington by fulfilling each of the conditions for an influential group. In recent years, some conditions have not been met, and the pro-Israel lobby is no longer the dominant force it once was. Its rival in Washington, the pro-Arab lobby, has remained weak because it has failed to meet any of the conditions.

The Israel and Arab Lobbies

The best-organized, best-funded, and most successful of the ethnic lobbies represents the interests of Israel. The most important ethnic lobby on foreign policy is the American Israel Public Affairs Committee (AIPAC). Washington insiders surveyed by *The Hotline*, a Web site linked to *National Journal*, rated AIPAC as the second most powerful lobby in the capital,[5] behind only the feared National Rifle Association. Jews, who dominate the pro-Israel lobby, make up 2.7 percent of the American population. They are strongly motivated and highly organized in support of Israel. Since its inception in 1951, the lobby has rarely lost an important battle. In recent years, Israel's policies have become more controversial in the United States—and within Israel itself. The splits within Israel have been mirrored in the American Jewish community.

Israel receives by far the largest share of American foreign aid, more than $3 billion a year. Only Egypt even approaches the Israeli aid figure.

In 1985 Israel and the United States signed a free-trade pact. Israel benefits from large tax-exempt contributions from the American Jewish community.[6] No other foreign nation is so favored.

AIPAC, founded in 1952, has a staff of more than 200, more than
100,000 members, and an annual budget of $47 million. It operates, with
considerable political acumen, out of offices one block from Capitol Hill:[7]
"In a moment of perceived crisis, it can put a carefully researched, well-
documented statement of its views on the desk of every Senator and Congressman and appropriate committee staff within four hours of a decision
to do so."[8]

AIPAC's lobbying connections are so thorough that one observer
maintained that "a mystique has grown up around the lobby to the point
where it is viewed with admiration, envy, and sometimes, anger."[9] Activists
can readily mobilize the network of Jewish organizations across the country to put pro-Israel pressure on members of Congress in their constituencies, even in areas with small Jewish populations. AIPAC claims to enact
over one hundred pieces of pro-Israel legislation a year, through over 2,000
meetings with members of Congress. At its 2006 conference dinner, the
organization took twenty-seven minutes to read out the roll call of legislators and officials in attendance—including representatives of fifty-seven
embassies (including the ambassadors to the United States from Pakistan
and Oman, neither of which has diplomatic relations with Israel), 25 percent of the members of the House of Representatives, more than half of
the members of the Senate, and twenty Bush administration officials.
Addressing the conference were Secretary of State Condoleezza Rice,
Speaker of the House J. Dennis Hastert, R-Ill., and House minority leader
Nancy Pelosi, D-Calif.

The leaders supported Israel and a congressional resolution—sponsored
by the chairman and ranking minority member of the House Committee
on International Relations, the chief whips of both parties in the House and
the Senate, and the House majority leader at the time, Rep. Tom DeLay,
R-Texas—stating that Israel should make concessions in the Middle East
only after the Palestinians had established an accountable government.[10]
As of the fall of 2006, serving in Congress are eleven Jewish senators (with
two other Jewish members joining them in 2007) and twenty-six Jewish
members of the House, including the majority party whip (Eric Cantor, of
Virginia), the only Jewish Republican in the House. Eight of the twenty-
three Democrats on the House Committee on International Relations,
including the ranking minority member, are Jewish as are three of the eighteen members (from both parties) of the Senate Committee on Foreign
Relations. In the House, both parties have established pro-Israel caucuses,
most of the members of which are not Jewish.

The Arab lobbying effort has been far less successful. No major Arab
organizations operated before 1972, and a Washington presence for Arabs
did not begin until 1978. One analysis concluded, "Most Arab embassies

throw impressive parties, but have little day-to-day contact with Congress, according to lawmakers and aides."[11]

The Arab uprising in the West Bank and Gaza that began in 1987 energized and united the Arab American community. The National Association of Arab Americans now maintains a grassroots network organized according to congressional district, patterned directly after AIPAC.[12] The 1990 Gulf War split Arabs once more, as supporters of Iraqi leader Saddam Hussein did battle with more moderate factions. In 1988, Democratic presidential candidate Michael Dukakis rejected the endorsement of Arab American leaders. Arab Americans joined forces with the National Association for the Advancement of Colored People and La Raza in pressing for an end to discrimination, especially profiling at airports.

After September 11, 2001, as Arab Americans (and Muslims generally) found themselves under suspicion, much of the agenda of Arab American groups shifted to protection of civil liberties although the continuing conflict in the Middle East remained at the center of their agenda. The Israeli-Palestinian conflict became intertwined with the war in Iraq and charges that Syria was supporting terrorism. When the George W. Bush administration proposed selling the rights to manage facilities in six American ports to Dubai Ports World, a firm based in the United Arab Emirates, members of both houses of Congress protested the potential loss of American control of shipping, and the deal was cancelled by the firm. Senator Robert Menendez, D-N.J., withdrew support of an Arab American candidate for local office in New Jersey when the candidate said that he did not consider Palestinian suicide bombers to be comparable with the September 11 terrorists.[13]

There is one Arab American senator, one governor, four members of the House (all but one a Republican), and 17 state legislators (fewer than the number of Jewish legislators in the New York General Assembly alone). In 2006, there were seven Arab American nonincumbent candidates for the House and four for state legislatures. The Arab American members of Congress are all Christians; the first Muslim member of Congress will take office in 2007. Arab Americans do not represent a united front on Middle East issues as the Jewish members do. The most widely respected, Rep. Ray LaHood, R-Ill., is a Lebanese Christian who is a member of the Republican Israel Caucus. The newest member, Rep. Charles Boustany Jr., R-La., writes on his Web site that he is a strong supporter of the administration's war on terror and of the war in Iraq. Only Rep. Nick J. Rahall II, D-W.Va., Rep. Darrell Issa, R-Calif., and Sen. John E. Sununu, R-N.H., regularly express opposition to Israel. The Arab American Institute's 2004 Congressional Scorecard shows little support for its positions within either house of Congress, except from a small number of very liberal Democrats (mostly African Americans).[14]

The roots of the friendship between the United States and Israel include (1) a common biblical heritage (most Arabs are Muslim, an unfamiliar religion to most Americans); (2) a shared European value system

(Islam is often sharply critical of the West's perceived lack of morality); (3) the democratic nature of Israel's political system (most Arab nations are monarchies or dictatorships); (4) Israel's role as an ally of the United States (most Arab countries have been seen as either unreliable friends or as hostile to American interests); and (5) the sympathy Americans extend toward Jews as victims (Arabs are portrayed as terrorists or exploiters of the American economy through their oil weapon).[15]

Jews benefit from a high rate of participation in politics, and Arab Americans are not as great a political force. Jews are among the most generous campaign contributors in American politics: 60 percent of individual contributions to President Clinton's 1992 campaign came from Jewish donors. From 1990 to 2005, pro-Israel groups donated $56.8 million to candidates for federal office and to political parties, compared with $297,000 donated by pro-Arab and pro-Muslim groups. From 2000 to 2004, the fifty members of AIPAC's board donated an average of $72,000 to political campaigns—and one in five was among the top donors to the 2008 presidential campaigns. Jews are substantially more likely to vote, to try to influence others' voting choices, to attend political meetings, to work for a party or a candidate, to write letters to public officials, and to follow the campaign through television, radio, magazines, and newspapers. Also, they are almost four times as likely as other Americans to donate money to candidates for office or to political organizations. In 2000 approximately 90 percent of Jews reported voting for president.[16]

Arab Americans have traditionally not been very active in politics, but following September 11, 2001, Arab American groups have pressed for increasing activism and turnout—not merely to change foreign policy but also to protest hate crimes against Arab Americans and racial and ethnic stereotyping.

Although Arab groups are divided among themselves and have no common frame of reference, American Jews have traditionally been united behind support of Israel. In a 2005 survey of American Jews, 36 percent felt very close to Israel, and 41 percent felt fairly close; 79 percent said that being close to Israel was a very important part of their Jewish identity.[17] An earlier poll (taken in 1982) found that three-quarters of American Jews argue that they should not vote for a candidate who is unfriendly to Israel, and one-third would be willing to contribute money to political candidates who support Israel.[18]

Overall, the pro-Israel lobby before the late 1980s met all of the conditions identified as critical for a group to be successful. Jews were well assimilated, had a high level of political activity, were united in their support of Israel, and had the support of public opinion. Israel was seen as a strategic asset by the American public and particularly by decision makers. Backers of AIPAC and other organizations did not stand to gain from their lobbying; they had to contribute their own money to participate. Although not numerous in comparison with many other groups, American

Jews and other supporters of Israel were concentrated in key states—New York, California, and Pennsylvania—that were important to presidential candidates.

Arab Americans have not met any of the conditions identified as critical to the success of a lobbying group. Americans have generally not seen Arab nations as strategic allies. Many Arab Americans have not been well assimilated into American society and politics; the community is neither homogeneous with respect to Middle East politics nor politically active. American public opinion has never been favorable to the Arab (or Palestinian) cause. The financing of Arab American organizations by Middle Eastern interests and the active pursuit of changes in U.S. policy by economic interests have served to weaken the legitimacy of the Arab American cause.

In 1987, however, the pro-Israel groups began to lose some of their clout. The intifada against Israeli control of the West Bank and Gaza raised international consciousness about the Palestinian cause and led to a lessening of American public support for the Jewish state. The intifada also led to conflicts within the Jewish community as to what Israel ought to do. When Israel and the Palestine Liberation Organization signed peace accords at the White House in September 1993, a deeper schism arose among American (and Israeli) Jews. It is always difficult to deal with former enemies.

The power of the pro-Israel lobby rested on unity within the Jewish community and on achieving widespread support beyond this small group. Yet conflicts over religion and peace led to the fractionalization of the Jewish lobby. AIPAC became increasingly linked to the more hawkish, right-wing government in Israel in the 1980s. An internal power struggle within AIPAC ousted the conservative leadership and restored the liberal tilt to the organization. In turn, the (then) opposition Likud Party in Israel stepped up its efforts to discredit the peace process. When George W. Bush succeeded Bill Clinton and stood more firmly with Israeli hawks, AIPAC shifted to the right once more—even taking positions on American domestic issues such as supporting drilling for oil in the Alaska wilderness. AIPAC and other Jewish organizations that supported Arctic drilling saw their stands as helpful to themselves politically, because the Bush administration placed a high priority on this policy, and as a way to weaken Arab domination of the American oil market.[19]

The pro-Israel forces in Washington were thrilled in 2000 when the Democratic Party nominated as its candidate for vice president Sen. Joseph Lieberman of Connecticut, an Orthodox Jew and strong supporter of Israel. American Jews hoped that the election of the first Jewish vice president would cement American support for Israel at a time when tensions flared in the Middle East. The Democratic ticket barely lost the election. Jewish mobilization did not make the difference in states with the largest Jewish populations: Gore carried New York, New Jersey, California, Connecticut, and Maryland by overwhelming margins, and he barely lost Florida (and the election) to Bush.

Recently Arab Americans have emerged as a more unified and ener-gized bloc than they were in the past. Arab Americans took a much more active role in the 2000 presidential elections, endorsing Republican candi-date George W. Bush. Yet their lobbies still rank far behind the pro-Israel groups in influence. Arab American groups do not have clout comparable with the Israelis mainly because their positions do not garner public sup-port and Arab Americans have not been as active as Jewish Americans in the political arena. Another reason is that Arab American lobbies always seem to be against something—Israel—rather than for something as the pro-Israel groups are.

In 2000 a large number of Muslim groups, fearing that the election of Senator Lieberman as vice president would solidify American support for Israel, banded together to endorse Bush over Gore. They focused on Michigan, a state that was expected to be close and that has the largest con-centration of Arab Americans. Many Arab Americans stood behind Green Party nominee Ralph Nader, a Lebanese American. Positions on the Mid-dle East were the main motivating factor among Arab American voters. Arab Americans gave Bush a 46 percent to 38 percent margin over Gore, with 14 percent going to Nader, far more than his 2 percent of the national vote.[20] Even though Bush won, Arab Americans could hardly claim credit. Bush did not carry any of their target states: Gore won Michigan, and one of two Arab American senators, Spencer Abraham, R-Mich., lost his reelec-tion bid. In California, the entire Democratic ticket, including Senator Dianne Feinstein, won handily.

There are no hard data on Arab American turnout—or even on the division of the vote in 2004—but it is clear that activism has increased sig-nificantly and that the Arab American vote has shifted from Bush to the Democrats in protest over Middle East policies, the war in Iraq, and restric-tions on civil liberties.[21] The Bush campaign made a concerted effort to woo Jewish voters in 2004; Jewish voters who considered Israel to be the most important issue in the election were much more likely to vote for Bush, but they constituted a small share (15 percent) of the Jewish elec-torate in the 2004 election. Jews remained loyal to the Democratic Party, perhaps in part because Kerry's brother had converted to Judaism and was very active and well known in many Jewish organizations, but more so because Jewish voters linked Bush to the Christian right. Jewish voters had strongly negative views of evangelicals, and these attitudes pushed even politically and religiously conservative Jews back to the Democratic Party. In 2004, almost 80 percent of Jews voted for Democrat John Kerry.[22]

The most critical reason why pro-Israel groups are more successful than pro-Arab groups is not the strength of AIPAC, but AIPAC's strategic advantage with the American public. Over time Americans have been considerably more supportive of Israel than of the Palestinians. When Israeli policy has come under criticism, as during the two intifadas, sup-port for Israel over the Palestinians has fallen to about 45 percent. Yet, backing for the Palestinians is consistently lower, at approximately 10 to 20 percent (with the rest favoring either both sides or neither party). When Palestinians or other Arabs are seen as the aggressors, Israel's support rises considerably—usually to around 50–55 percent. When the Islamic party Hamas won the Palestinian elections in 2006, support for Israel rose to 59 percent. Another survey of Americans found that they ranked Israel third in favorability among fourteen nations, behind only England and Canada, and they ranked the Palestinians twelfth, ahead of only North Korea and Iran.[23]

American policy in the Middle East is more favorable to Israel than to the Palestinians because the American public has long taken sides in support of Israel. AIPAC, to be sure, exerts considerable influence, but there is little reason to believe that it can change the direction of policy against the tide of public opinion. It is likely more accurate to say that AIPAC is most successful when public attitudes toward Israel are most favorable and that the pro-Israel lobby is most likely to face difficulties in its agenda when the public is more critical of Israel. This is true of all lobbies, including other ethnic lobbies. The terrorist attacks of September 11, 2001, did not lead to a fundamental shift in American public opinion. If anything, the attacks solidified support for Israel. Right after the attacks, many Americans identified with Israelis as victims of terrorist attacks.

Other Ethnic Interest Groups

No foreign policy interest group, and certainly no ethnic group, has the reputation for influence that the pro-Israel forces have. Even a weakened AIPAC still sets the pace—for two reasons. First, AIPAC is the model for most other successful groups. Second, like the Jewish community, other ethnic groups have been divided over the best course of action for their countries of concern. The ethnic lobby that was poised to capture the role of "king of the Hill" from AIPAC, the Cuban American National Foundation, has been fraught with its own conflicts.

Latinos

Latinos now constitute about 12 percent of all Americans, up from 6.4 percent in 1980. The 2000 census showed that the Latino population in the United States jumped by 60 percent over ten years, so that Hispanics now have the same share of the population as African Americans. The growth was particularly strong in California, where Latinos make up about one-third of all residents, and among Mexican Americans who are by far the biggest immigrant group. The all-Democratic Hispanic Caucus in the House of Representatives grew from five members to twenty members from 1976 to 2006; there are also five Republican Latino members of the House and three Latino senators (two of them Cuban American).

Yet Latinos have little political unity. The largest groups of Latinos are Mexicans and Puerto Ricans, who are relatively poor and likely to back liberal Democratic candidates in elections. The fifth-largest—and best organized—group is Cuban Americans, who are much more affluent and generally support conservative Republicans.[24]

Mexican Americans constitute 60 percent of all Latinos, but many are not American citizens, and even those who are have ambivalent feelings toward Mexico. Until recently Mexican leaders did not encourage intervention on behalf of Mexico by Mexican Americans. Now they do, and they even campaign in the United States.[25]

The next largest group is Puerto Ricans. They too are divided over the status of Puerto Rico: some favor statehood, others want the continuation of Puerto Rico's commonwealth status, and some seek independence. For countries such as El Salvador and Nicaragua, where American policy is more controversial, foreign policy lobbies are dominated by religious organizations, such as the Washington Office on Latin America, that have few ties to the indigenous communities. Such organizations largely focus on human rights issues. Some have influence on Capitol Hill, but their lobbying activities tend to concentrate more on legislators who are already committed to their cause.[26]

Cuban Americans are much better off financially, and they vote heavily for Republican candidates. Cubans represent just 5.3 percent of Latinos in this country, yet they have established the second most potent ethnic lobby in the country, the Cuban American National Foundation (CANF). Cuban Americans are generally strongly anticommunist.

CANF's founder, Jorge Mas Canosa (who died in late 1997), was called "the most significant individual lobbyist in the country."[27] CANF lobbied successfully in 1985 for Radio Marti and in 1990 for TV Marti, direct broadcast stations that aim at Cuba from the United States. In 1996 Mas and the CANF were the major movers in the Helms-Burton Act that tightened the American economic embargo against Cuba. The federal government funds a resettlement program for Cuban refugees that the CANF runs. The CANF has one hundred directors, each of whom contributes $10,000. It claims 50,000 donors. Cuban American political action committees (PACs) contributed $242,000 to political candidates in 2004, with two-thirds going to Republicans.[28]

Yet the CANF may have been too partisan for its own good. The CANF has had close ties to Republicans. In early 1993 it blocked a Cuban American nominee of the Clinton administration for the post of chief policy maker on Latin America. Fearing it might lose influence, the CANF then moved to establish closer relations with Clinton. But good relations with the Clinton administration faded as the Cuban American community faced its biggest crisis in years, perhaps ever. For several months in 1999 and 2000, the dominant issue in both foreign and domestic policy in the United States was what the United States would do with a little boy who survived a harrowing journey on a raft from Cuba, a country ninety miles away from the Florida coast. Six-year-old Elián González and his mother escaped Cuba on a raft. The raft sank, Elián's mother drowned, but the little boy was rescued and taken to American shores. His father, who was divorced from his mother, had stayed behind in Cuba. He wanted his son back. The American government agreed with the father.

So did the American public, which favored returning the boy to his father by 63 percent to 25 percent. Only Latinos in Florida, and especially Cuban Americans there, insisted that the little boy remain in the United States. The Democratic mayor of Miami said that he would hold the Clinton administration responsible for any unrest that occurred when the boy was finally returned to Cuba, and many of the 40,000 Cuban American Democrats changed their party registration to Republican—perhaps handing the White House to Republican George W. Bush, who carried Florida by barely more than 500 votes.[29]

The CANF was patterned after AIPAC, and, ironically, it is currently facing some of the same strains that the pro-Israel lobby has encountered. Like AIPAC, it has gone through an internal power struggle. In 1997, popular singer Gloria Estefan came under sharp attack by CANF supporters when she supported a Miami concert by Cuban musicians.[30] By now, just a quarter of younger Cuban Americans favor banning musical groups from Cuba from coming to the United States.

Cuban Americans, like Jewish Americans, are less united than they once were. Cuban government representatives now can address audiences in Florida without being harassed, and a Spanish language radio station in Miami now airs a talk show with a host who regularly attacks the CANF and other hard-liners. The head of Cambio Cubano even went so far as to meet with Castro in 1995.[31]

A Washington-based group, Ignored Majority, argues:

> Immigrants since the 1980s have shared relatively little political affinity with the original immigrants of the 1960s. These newer waves have been made up of people leaving Cuba largely for economic rather than political reasons. These people now make up more than 50 percent of the Cuban-American community.[32]

More recent immigrants or Cuban Americans born in the United States are less likely to support the trade embargo against Cuba, and they favor establishing a dialogue with the Cuban government and even anticipate diplomatic relations. They are much more supportive of unrestricted travel to Cuba, of permitting Cuban musical groups to perform in Miami, and of repatriating refugees who try to enter the United States by boat or raft. A candidate's position on Cuba is much less important to those born in the United States, and they are much less likely to call themselves Republican (about 40 percent) and more likely to say that they are Democrats (about 30 percent).[33] Bush still carried the Cuban American vote handily, although his support in 2004 dropped by about 10 percent. More telling, in 2004 Cuban Americans were more concerned—by 33 percent to 27 percent—with the war in Iraq than with Cuba.[34]

The conflicts between older and newer immigrants reflect events that have divided the Cuban American community. In 2003, the Bush administration sent back twelve Cuban refugees who hijacked a boat and tried to land in the United States. Former CANF officer, Otto Reich, who received a recess appointment as assistant secretary of state for Latin America when he could not be confirmed by the Senate in 2001, put new restrictions on contact with Cuba. The new policy reduced family visits to Cuba by half and placed strong restrictions on how much money Cuban American visitors could spend on travel or send to relatives in Cuba.

The fragmentation of the Latino community traditionally has limited the unity and effectiveness (especially on foreign policy issues) of the Hispanic Caucus in the House of Representatives. But the immigration issue united Latinos and the Hispanic Caucus. In 1996, when the Republican congressional majority enacted restrictive immigration legislation, Latinos from every nationality and from both parties banded together to protest this legislation. In 2006, facing pressure from conservatives in his party to restrict immigration further, President George W. Bush proposed a policy that would grant a conditional amnesty to some illegal aliens but would also send 6,000 troops to patrol the border with Mexico. Republican conservatives such as Rep. Tom Tancredo of Colorado pressed for stronger legislation that would send illegal aliens back home. In April 2006, immigrant rights groups, led by Latinos, planned protest demonstrations against this legislation in sixty cities, with almost 200,000 expected in Washington, D.C. Even with the strong showing of political organization in these demonstrations, Latino voting rates still were far lower than turnout for other groups. Over two-thirds of Latino immigrants enter the United States illegally; thus, they can march but cannot vote. Because the greatest source of population growth for Latinos is new births, it will be many years before these young people are eligible to vote.[35]

The backlash against Republican immigration proposals in 1996 led to a surge in Latino support for the Democrats in 2004. More than 70 percent of Hispanics voted Democratic for president, and the Latino vote played a big role in delivering California—and five new House seats—into the Democratic column. Yet, the presidential victor, George W. Bush, had a strong record in courting the Latino vote—he speaks Spanish and has a Latino sister-in-law—and in 2004 he courted the Latino vote with considerable success. Exit polls indicated that Bush held Kerry to 50 percent of the Latino vote in Texas and to between 66 and 70 percent in California and Colorado; in New York, Kerry carried almost 80 percent of the Latino vote. How the Republican position on immigration will affect the Latino vote in future elections is a central question.[36]

Greeks, Turks, and Armenians

Few ethnic groups have as determined enemies as Turkish Americans. For many years, Turks had to worry primarily about Greek Americans. Now their main concern is with Armenian Americans. It is no wonder that each of these ethnic lobbies has tried to ally itself with AIPAC.

Greek Americans were long considered second in power to the pro-Israel lobby. The American Hellenic Institute Public Affairs Committee (AHIPAC) is consciously modeled after AIPAC; the two groups have often worked together. AHIPAC lobbied successfully for an arms embargo on Turkey after its 1974 invasion of Cyprus and has pressed for a balance in American foreign aid to the two states. The 2 million Greek Americans are very politically active and loyal to the Democratic Party: in 1988 they raised more than 15 percent of Greek American Michael Dukakis's early campaign funds. In contrast, the Turkish American community of 180,000 is not well organized. Recently it has employed a Washington public relations firm to lobby the government, but it has no ethnic lobby and maintains a low profile. One member of Congress has stated, "I don't have any Turkish restaurants in my district."[37] Greek American influence has waned, as American foreign policy has shifted emphasis from Greece and Turkey to other trouble spots, especially after the fall of the Soviet Union limited the strategic value of both Greece and Turkey to the United States.

Armenian Americans are more recent entries into the ethnic group mix. For many years Armenian Americans did not organize because there was no independent Armenia. When the Soviet Union broke up in 1989, Armenia regained its independence.

Since then, the Armenian American community has become energized on two issues. One is the contested border with Azerbaijan, also formerly part of the Soviet Union. The two countries have fought over the province of Nagorno-Karabakh, an enclave of ethnic Armenians within the boundaries of Azerbaijan. Azerbaijan has imposed an embargo on Armenia, and the United States in turn imposed restrictions on aid to oil-rich Azerbaijan. The Armenian American lobby, the Armenian Assembly of America, with 7,000 members and a budget of $2.5 million, has fought for increased American aid to Armenia and the blocking of assistance to Azerbaijan.

The second issue is condemnation of Turkey for its alleged genocide of 1.5 million Armenians during World War I. Armenian Americans have pressed for a congressional resolution condemning Turkey and have mobilized considerable support in Congress. In 2006, the Public Broadcasting Service aired a documentary on the charges of a Turkish genocide and provided Turkish representatives an opportunity to present their side in a debate. Armenian Americans protested this "even-handedness" in petitions to the network.

Turkish groups have been buffeted by the strong alliances between pro-Israel forces and Turkey's historic antagonists, the Greeks and the

Armenians. But recently Turkey, even though its population is 99 percent Muslim, has forged its own links with American Jews. Turkey and Israel have military links because both fear Syria (a common neighbor), Iraq, and Iran. In 1997 the B'nai B'rith Anti-Defamation League presented Turkish prime minister Mesut Yilmaz with its Distinguished Statesman award. Yilmaz also met with leaders of AIPAC and the American Jewish Committee.[38]

African Americans

African Americans, like Latinos, traditionally have been more concerned with domestic economic issues than with foreign policy concerns. Most African Americans cannot trace their roots to a specific African country. Until the 1960s, black participation in politics was restricted by both law and socioeconomic status. Few African Americans served in Congress, especially on the foreign policy committees, or in the Department of State. African Americans contribute little money to campaigns, and electorally they have been strongly tied to the Democratic Party, thus cutting off lobbying activities to Republican presidents and legislators. African American foreign policy activities increased over the issue of the ending of the apartheid system of racial separation in South Africa.

The South African issue united African Americans. President Ronald Reagan, pushed by the weight of public opinion, a mobilized African American community, and a supportive Congress, ultimately agreed in 1985 to accept sanctions against the South African government. The Congressional Black Caucus has also taken firm stands on sending U.S. troops to Somalia, lifting the ban on Haitian immigrants infected with the AIDS virus, and pushing the United States to restore ousted Haitian president Jean-Bertrand Aristide to office.

Five of the members of the House Committee on International Relations are black, including the ranking minority members on three of the six subcommittees; African Americans increasingly have held key positions on foreign policy in the executive branch, including the current secretary of state (Condoleezza Rice) and her predecessor (Colin Powell).

Immigration from the Caribbean, especially from Haiti, has changed the dynamic of black involvement in foreign policy issues. Haitian immigrants in southern Florida have mobilized politically, winning a majority of seats on the city council and the mayoralty in North Miami. Charging that many refugees from Haiti were turned away, they took strong exception to Cuban American demands that Elián González be allowed to remain in the United States.

Asian Americans

Asian Americans are the second-fastest-growing ethnic group in the United States. Asian Americans now constitute 3.7 percent of the population,[39] but Asian Americans have not been prominent in political life. Because most immigrants have not become citizens, their participation rate is substantially lower than that of other ethnic groups. Only eight Asian Americans serve as members of Congress, six in the House and two in the Senate (both from Hawaii). The first Asian American governor was Gary Locke, D-Wash., who served from 1997 to 2005.

Asian Americans are not united politically. There are tensions between Japanese Americans and Chinese Americans stemming from Japan's occupation of China during World War II. Vietnamese immigrants bear grudges against Cambodians, and Hindus and Moslems from South Asia have long-standing quarrels.[40]

Asian Americans have mostly cast ballots for Republicans, although Japanese Americans are an exception. Many Asian Americans share the GOP's emphasis on family values and anticommunism. In 2000, perhaps upset over the Republicans' restrictive immigration policies, Asian Americans voted for Gore over Bush by a margin of 55 percent to 41 percent.[41]

In 1994, Asian Americans in Congress formed the Congressional Asian Pacific American Caucus, admitting members without regard to race or ethnicity. Only one Asian American member, the nonvoting delegate from American Samoa, serves on a congressional foreign policy committee.

The Indian American population tripled from 1980 to 1997, and Indian Americans have become increasingly involved in politics. Indian Americans have the highest income of any ethnic group in the United States, yet Indian Americans have not been active in politics until recently. There are no Indian American members of Congress—indeed, there is only one Indian American state legislator—but there is a congressional caucus on India and Indian Americans with over one hundred members, mostly Democrats. To combat the growing influence of Indian Americans, Pakistani Americans raised $50,000 for Hillary Rodham Clinton in her 2000 Senate campaign in New York.[42]

Are Ethnic Politics Dangerous?

Mearsheimer and Walt charge that "the United States has a terrorism problem in good part because it is so closely allied with Israel" and "[w]ere it not for the [pro-Israel] Lobby's ability to manipulate the American political system, the relationship between Israel and the United States would be far less intimate than it is today."[43] These assertions are bold. But they are not new. Twenty-five years ago, former senator Charles McC. Mathias Jr., R-Md., worried that ethnic politics might make it difficult for the nation to speak with one voice on foreign policy:

> Factions among us lead the nation toward excessive foreign attachments or animosities. Even if the groups were balanced—if Turkish-Americans equaled Greek-Americans or Arab-Americans equaled Jewish-Americans—the result would not necessarily be a sound, cohesive foreign

policy because the national interest is not simply the sum of our special interest and attachments ... ethnic politics, carried as they often have been to excess, have proven harmful to the national interest.[44]

Pro-Israel groups usually place intense constituency pressure on legislators who make either anti-Israel or pro-Arab statements. Pro-Israel PAC contributions dwarf those of any other ethnic group on foreign policy: in 2002, pro-Israel groups gave $8,427,000 to political candidates; the figure seemingly fell to $6,095,000 in 2004, but the 2002 figure includes donations to state and local parties and the 2004 figure does not. Virtually every senator and most members of the House have received support from pro-Israel PACs. AIPAC spent $820,000 on lobbying in 2005 (it does not endorse candidates for office or donate money to them), and the Zionist Organization of America spent an additional $96,200 to make its case to Congress. Pro-Arab PACs spent just $142,500 on donations in 2004, and no information is available on any lobbying expenditures. The Arab American Institute reported that the Arab American Leadership Council PAC made fifty-three contributions to federal candidates in 2000–2002, but this could not be verified.[45]

Even though ethnic lobbies do not stand to benefit financially from a foreign policy that suits their preferences, many Americans are simply so skeptical of the role of money in politics that they will worry that something is not right. Support for foreign policy initiatives might be seen as open to influence to campaign contributions.

Although 61 percent of Americans believe it is acceptable for American Jews to contribute money to Israel, almost 40 percent of Americans believe that Israel has too much power in America. Americans do not believe that American Jews have too much power, however; most Americans believe that Jews have the "right amount" of power, with just 10 percent saying that Jews have "too much power." In 1984 (the last time the question was asked), 29 percent of Americans said that American Jews were more loyal to Israel than to the United States, and in 1998 60 percent said that Arab Americans are more loyal to Arab countries.[46]

Campaign contributions by another ethnic group, Asian Americans, became a source of contention in the 1996 elections. Where did the money come from—from Asian Americans or from Asians? What did the contributors want? Were the funds donated to promote good government or to buy influence for foreign interests? Asian Americans reportedly gave $10 million or more in 1996, mostly to Democrats and especially to President Clinton. Asian American contributions came under scrutiny when it was revealed after the 1996 elections that at least $1.2 million of the donations to the Democratic National Committee (DNC) were improper. The DNC's chief fund-raiser among Asian Americans, John Huang, appeared to have promised face-to-face meetings with the president for large contributors.[47]

James Riady of the Indonesian conglomerate, Lippo Group, made substantial contributions to the DNC and met with the president in the

Oval Office six times. DNC official Huang was previously U.S. chief of the Lippo Group. Other contributors included Buddhist nuns from a Taiwan-based order who wrote checks for $140,000 at a luncheon with Vice President Al Gore. And it was alleged, though not documented, that the Chinese government tried to funnel contributions to the DNC in 1996.[48]

Conclusion

Americans worry about foreign influence in domestic politics. We have distinguished between campaign contributions and lobbying by foreign agents and governments and donations and pressures from American companies with interests abroad. Our laws reflect this distinction. Could we have drawn the line too sharply?

One test of what constitutes an American interest, though hardly an ethical one, is what works. Perhaps there is no moral resolution to the problem of money in politics but only a recognition that tactics that prove too heavy-handed may backfire. Pro-Israel groups were buffeted by charges that they had inappropriately mixed lobbying with fund raising.

Charges of undue influence seem to have limited the amounts of money ethnic interests give to candidates. Now the key question seems to be how to distribute funds. Pro-Israel groups have long been associated with the Democratic Party because Jews are among the most loyal parts of the Democratic constituency. In 2002 pro-Israel groups gave 75 percent of their contributions to the Democratic party, but this fell to 64 percent in 2004. Pro-Arab groups gave almost 85 percent of their donations to Democrats. Most other ethnic groups also favor the Democrats, with Cuban Americans being the exception.

Pro-Israel and anti-Castro groups depend on the support of public opinion and the moral force of their arguments to prod policy makers to back their causes. Yet, as Cuban American groups have discovered, antipathy to the Cuban regime seems to have peaked. The pro-Israel lobby benefits from the unpopularity of its opposition. Americans now expect the Castro regime to fade away, but they are less sanguine about peace in the Middle East. Foreign policy now resembles domestic policy more than ever. The consensus on what American policy should be has evaporated, and with it went the argument that there was a distinctive moral foundation to our international relations. Interest groups can be of significant importance, but the evidence is simply not compelling enough to argue that interest groups alone can shift foreign policy priorities.

Notes

Support of the General Research Board, University of Maryland—College Park, is gratefully acknowledged. Some of the data employed come from the Inter-University Consortium for Political and Social Research, which has no responsibility for any interpretations herein.

1. John J. Mearsheimer and Stephen M. Walt, "The Israel Lobby," *London Review of Books*, March 23, 2006, http://www.lrb.co.uk/v28/n06/mear01_.html; and Mearsheimer and Walt, "The Israel Lobby and U.S. Foreign Policy," March 2006, http://ksgnotes1. harvard.edu/Research/wpaper.nsf/rwp/RWP06-011/$File/rwp_06_011_walt.pdf.
2. Alan Finder, "An Essay by 2 Professors Creates a Debate about the Influence of a Jewish Lobby," *New York Times*, April 12, 2006, sec. A; and Alan Dershowitz, "Debunking the Newest—and Oldest—Jewish Conspiracy: A Reply to the Mearsheimer-Walt 'Working Paper,'" April 2006, http://www.ksg.harvard.edu/ research/working_papers/dershowitzreply.pdf.
3. Francis X. Clines, "Most Doubt a Resolve to Change Campaign Financing, Poll Finds," *New York Times*, April 8, 1997, sec. A.
4. Mohammed E. Ahrari, "Conclusion," in *Ethnic Groups and Foreign Policy*, ed. Mohammed E. Ahrari (New York: Greenwood Press, 1987), 155–158.
5. See www.nationaljournal.com/pubs/hotline, March 4, 2006.
6. Cheryl A. Rubenberg, "The Middle East Lobbies," *The Link* 17 (January–March 1984): 4.
7. Thomas L. Friedman, "A Pro-Israel Lobby Gives Itself a Headache," *New York Times*, November 8, 1992, E18.
8. Sanford Ungar, "Washington: Jewish and Arab Lobbyists," *Atlantic*, March 1978, 10; Jeffrey Birnbaum, "The Power Player Who Faces Charges for Talking," *Washington Post*, April 21, 2006, sec. A.
9. Ben Bradlee Jr., "Israel's Lobby," *Boston Globe Magazine*, April 29, 1984, 64.
10. American Israel Public Affairs Committee, "AIPAC: About Us, Who We Are," http://www.aipac.org/documents/whoweare.html, May 18, 2006; Birnbaum, "The Power Player Who Faces Charges for Talking"; Dana Milbank, "Amid AIPAC's Big Show, Straight Talk with a Noticeable Silence," *Washington Post*, March 7, 2006, sec. A.
11. Bill Keller, "Supporters of Israel, Arabs Vie for Friends in Congress, at White House," *Congressional Quarterly Weekly Report*, August 25, 1981, 1528.
12. Ibid.; Rubenberg, "The Middle East Lobbies"; Steven L. Spiegel, *The Other Arab-Israeli Conflict* (Chicago: University of Chicago Press, 1985), 8; and David J. Saad and G. Neal Lendenmann, "Arab American Grievances," *Foreign Policy* (Fall 1985): 22.
13. Shawn Zeller, "Arab-Am Voters Down on Dems?" *CQ Weekly*, April 10, 2006, 949.
14. Rep. Charles Boustany Jr., Web site, "War on Terror," issue statement, http:// boustany.house.gov/Legislation.asp?ARTICLE2979=3011; Arab-American Institute, "2004 Congressional Scorecard," http://aai.bluestatedigital.com/page/file/ 3f5da6f62c38b29ed3_v6m6iilaa.pdf/2004_Scorecard.pdf.
15. John W. Spanier and Eric M. Uslaner, *American Foreign Policy Making and the Democratic Dilemmas*, 6th ed. (New York: Macmillan, 1994), chap. 7; Andrew Kohut, *America's Place in the World II* (Washington, D.C.: Pew Research Center for The People and The Press, 1997), 99.
16. Thomas L. Friedman, "Jewish Criticism on Clinton Picks," *New York Times*, January 5, 1993, sec. A; the American National Election Study 2004 and a survey of Jewish citizens by the National Jewish Democratic Council made available to me by the council; Glenn Frankel, "A Beautiful Friendship?" *Washington Post Magazine*, July 16, 2006, 25.
17. American Jewish Committee, "2005 Annual Survey of American Jewish Opinion— Israel," http://www.ajc.org/site/apps/nl/content3.asp?c=ijITI2PHKoG&b=846741&ct =1740367.
18. Susan Pinkus, "Poll Analysis: U.S. and Israeli Jews Have Many Common Views, Some Striking Differences," *Los Angles Times*, April 19, 1998, http://www.latimes.com/ news/custom/timespoll/la-980419jewishpoll-407pa1an,1,7372435.htmlstory?coll =la-util-times_poll; Leon Hadar, "What Israel Means to U.S. Jewry," *Jerusalem Post, International Edition*, June 19–25, 1982, 11.

19. Jason Gitlin, "Drilling for Jewish Energy," *Jerusalem Report*, June 13, 2005, 46.
20. James Zogby, "How Arab Americans Voted and Why," *Middle East Online*, http://www.jordanembassyus.org/121900004.htm, May 31, 2001; John Sherry, "California Muslims Flex Electoral Muscles," *The Hill*, July 12, 2000, http://www.hillnews.com/news/news9.html, July 13, 2001; and Guillaume Debre, "Arab Americans Emerge As Key Voting Bloc," *Christian Science Monitor*, April 4, 2000, http://www.csmonitor.com/durable/2000/04/04/p2s1.htm, May 31, 2001.
21. "Kerry Has Big Lead Among Arab-Americans in Battleground States; Nader Nabs 20 Percent," http://nationaljournal.com/pubs/hotline, March 12, 2004.
22. Eric M. Uslaner and Mark Lichbach, "The Two Front War: Jews, Identity, Liberalism, and Voting," unpublished paper, http://www.bsos.umd.edu/gvpt/uslaner/uslanerlichbachjewishvotingbehavioriii.pdf.
23. "Gallup: Support for Israel Continues to Increase," http://nationaljournal.com/pubs/hotline, March 27, 2006; and "U.S. Voters Say Russia Is Better Friend Than France, Quinnipiac University National Survey Shows," http://www.quinnipiac.edu/x11385.xml?ReleaseID=892, March 15, 2006.
24. Laura Morrow, Lou DiSipio, and Rodolfo de la Garza, *The Latino Vote at Mid-Decade* (Claremont, Calif.: Tomás Rivera Policy Institute, 1996).
25. Pam Belluck, "Mexican Presidential Candidates Campaign in U.S.," *New York Times*, July 1, 2000, sec. A.
26. Bill Keller, "Interest Groups Focus on El Salvador Policy," *Congressional Quarterly Weekly Report*, April 24, 1982, 895–900.
27. John Newhouse, "Socialism or Death," *New Yorker*, April 27, 1992, 77.
28. This and succeeding contribution data come from the Web site of the Center for Responsive Politics, http://www.opensecrets.org.
29. David W. Moore, "Public: Reunion of Elian with Father Should Have Occurred," Gallup Organization Poll Releases, April 25, 2000, http://poll.gallup.com/content/default.aspx?ci=2965&pg=1, May 2, 2000; Andres Viglucci and Diana Marrero, "Poll Reveals Widening Split Over Elian," *Miami Herald*, April 9, 2000; and Katharine Q. Seeyle, "Boy's Case Could Sway Bush-Gore Contest," *New York Times*, March 30, 2000, sec. A.
30. Larry Rohter, "MTV Worker Ousted over Cuba Concert," *New York Times*, June 9, 1994, sec. A; Steven Greenhouse, "U.S. Reportedly Finds That Head of Radio Marti Tried to Dismiss His Critics," *New York Times*, July 27, 1995, sec. A; Guy Gugliotta, "USIA Probes Activist's Role at Radio Marti," *Washington Post*, July 22, 1995, sec. A; Donald P. Baker, "Miami's Cuban American Generations Split over Anti-Castro Rule," *Washington Post*, October 18, 1997, sec. A.
31. Mireya Navarro, "New Tolerance Sprouts among Cuban Exiles," *New York Times*, August 25, 1995, sec. A; Mireya Navarro, "Castro Confers with Exiled Foe," *New York Times*, June 28, 1995, sec. A.
32. Philip Schmidt, "Ignored Majority: The Moderate Cuban American Community," Latin America Working Group Education Fund, Washington, D.C., 2004, http://www.lawg.org/docs/IgnoredMajority.pdf.
33. Ibid., and "2004 FIU Cuba Poll," Florida International University, Institute for Public Opinion Research, http://www.fiu.edu/~ipor/cubapoll/index.html, May 16, 2006.
34. Abby Goodnough, "Hispanic Vote in Florida: Neither a Bloc Nor a Lock," *New York Times*, October 17, 2004, sec. A; author's analysis of 2004 exit polls; and "Poll: U.S. Cubans Less Preoccupied with Castro," *Miami Herald*, May 17, 2006.
35. N.C. Aizenman, "From Latinos' Rally, Hope for a Movement," *Washington Post*, April 9, 2006, sec. A; Roberto Suro, "Latino Power?" *Washington Post*, June 26, 2005, sec. B.
36. Eric Schmitt, "New Census Shows Hispanics Are Even with Blacks in U.S.," *New York Times*, March 8, 2001, sec. A; Eric Schmitt, "Census Shows Big Gain for

Mexican-Americans," *New York Times*, May 10, 2001, sec. A; Steven Greenhouse, "Guess Who's Embracing Immigrants Now," *New York Times*, March 5, 2000, sec. WK.

37. Thomas M. Franck and Edward Weisband, *Foreign Policy by Congress* (New York: Oxford University Press, 1979), 191–193.

38. Ted Clark, "Report on Turkey and Jewish-American Organizations," *Morning Edition*, National Public Radio (December 23, 1997), unofficial transcript.

39. U.S. Census Bureau, "Profiles of General Demographic Characteristics 2000," http://www.census.gov/prod/cen2000/dp1/2kh00.pdf, June 4, 2001.

40. Stanley Karnow, "Apathetic Asian-Americans?" *Washington Post*, November 29, 1992, sec. C; James Sterngold, "For Asian-Americans, Political Power Can Lead to Harsh Scrutiny," *New York Times*, November 3, 1996, sec. A.

41. See "Exit Poll Results: Election 2000," http://www.udel.edu/poscir/road/course/exitpollsindex.html, June 4, 2001.

42. Miles A. Pomper, "Indian-Americans' Numbers, Affluence Are Translating into Political Power," *CQ Weekly*, March 18, 2000, 580–581; Raymond Bonner, "Donating to the First Lady, Hoping the President Notices," *New York Times*, March 14, 2000, sec. A.

43. Mearsheimer and Walt, "The Israel Lobby and U.S. Foreign Policy," 5, 14.

44. Charles McC. Mathias Jr., "Ethnic Groups and Foreign Policy," *Foreign Affairs* 59 (Summer 1981): 981.

45. Center for Responsive Politics, http://www.opensecrets.org, accessed April 10, 2006; and Center for Responsive Politics, http://www.opensecrets.org/lobbyists/induclient.asp?code-Q05&year=2005, May 3, 2006; "Third Election Cycle Where Arab American PAC Hits Goal," Arab American Institute, press release, October 24, 2002, http://www.aaiusa.org/press-room/986/pr102402. This PAC did not show up on the Web site of the Center for Responsive Politics, http://www.opensecrets.org.

46. Marjorie Hyer, "Tolerance Shows in Voter Poll," *Washington Post*, February 13, 1998, sec. E; CBS News, press release, October 23, 1988; questions on Arabs and Jews from the section on polls in Lexis-Nexis Academic Universe, Reference Section, May 31, 2001.

47. Terry M. Neal, "Asian American Donors Feel Stigmatized," *Washington Post*, September 8, 1997, sec. A; Tim Weiner and David E. Sanger, "Democrats Hoped to Raise $7 Million from Asians in U.S.," *New York Times*, December 28, 1996, sec. A; and Michael Weisskopf and Michael Duffy, "The G.O.P.'s Own China Connection," *Time*, May 5, 1997, 45–46.

48. Ruth Marcus, "Oval Office Meeting Set DNC Asian Funds Network in Motion," *Washington Post*, December 29, 1996, sec. A; Terry M. Neal, "Asian American Donors Feel Stigmatized."

14

What Happened to the Japanese Lobby in Washington?

The Decline of the Japan Lobby and the Rise of the New China Lobby

Ronald J. Hrebenar, Valerie Ploumpis, and Clive S. Thomas

Americans have long viewed organized political interests with uneasiness. Although we recognize their inevitability in a free society, we nevertheless tend to suspect their motivations. Especially disquieting have been foreign lobbies, which have tried to influence both domestic and foreign policy in Washington, at times seemingly at the expense of the national interest of the United States. Over the last half century, the lobbying activities on behalf of Japanese interests have periodically commanded exceptional attention, as the United States has striven to compete effectively with one of the nation's chief trade rivals.

In this chapter, Ronald J. Hrebenar, Valerie Ploumpis, and Clive S. Thomas describe the growth and development of the Japan lobby as a political force, starting with its beginnings prior to World War II. In their view, the Japan lobby has been difficult to understand because it has so many facets and actors, ranging from cultural-educational organizations that aim to create favorable public opinion toward the Japanese in the minds of U.S. citizens to professional economic organizations and direct lobbying operations that represent Japanese business interests in the United States. The Japan lobby has been especially successful in cultivating "intellectual America" by making donations and grants to U.S. universities, foundations, and charitable institutions and by magnifying the voices of Americans already favorably oriented toward Japanese culture. In the policy process, much of the success of the Japan lobby has been due to the skillful employment of an "insider" lobby of former U.S. government officials, professional Washington lobbyists, superlawyers, and political consultants whose services the Japan lobby has purchased.

Over the last decade and a half, a variety of factors, chiefly a decreased fear of Japanese industrial competitiveness and the rise of China as the primary economic competitor of the United States, has led to a much diminished Japan lobby presence in Washington. The authors believe the lobby "is not much needed in the current atmosphere of U.S.-Japanese relations and the changed relationship heralded by the events of September 11, 2001." But if needed in the future, it could quickly reappear.

When Michael Crichton's novel, *Rising Sun*, was released as a motion picture in the summer of 1993, there was considerable reaction from Japanese Americans, native Japanese, Asian Americans, and even non-Japanese Americans. On the *New York Times* op-ed page, Roger M. Pang wrote:

> The Asians are the villains.... Mr. Crichton's larger purpose is to present a dark vision of Japan's economic ambitions.... [T]he book portrays the Japanese as hard-edged exploiters of an increasingly vulnerable America.[1]

Pang's comments echo the concerns of many Japanese regarding the stereotypes Americans hold about contemporary Japan, concerns that extend to cultural misunderstandings, economic difficulties, and political confusions. The Japanese government and many individual Japanese are also convinced that Americans simply do not understand enough about Japanese culture to appreciate differences in behavior between the two societies. Many Japanese are also convinced that many Americans, including some of the nation's top political and business leaders, have blamed Japan for the inability of the United States to compete economically in recent years and for American political problems in various parts of the world. Such was the nature of Japanese and American perceptions in the early 1990s. A *New York Times*-CBS News-Tokyo Broadcasting poll of July 6, 1993, supported these conclusions. The poll found that nearly two-thirds of Japanese described their country's relations with the United States as "unfriendly." This was the highest such negative Japanese response to such a question ever surveyed.[2]

Acutely aware of these negative perceptions, Japanese organizations have spent billions of dollars in recent decades to influence American attitudes toward Japan, Japanese culture, Japanese politics, and Japanese business and its practices. In his 1990 book, *Agents of Influence*, Pat Choate dubbed these efforts "the Japan Lobby."[3] Choate's book represents one perspective, in many ways a snapshot, of the nature of Japanese lobbying in the United States. But it is not the only one.

In this chapter we examine the Japan lobby from three perspectives. First, we trace its historical development. Second, we examine the three elements of the lobby: cultural, economic, and political. We then discuss the decline of the lobby in the face of the rise of other elements of the Asian lobby, particularly the new China lobby.

Origins of the Japan Lobby: Its Pre–World War II and Early Postwar Composition

The earliest form of the Japan lobby, as Mindy Kotler has noted, largely comprised American missionaries who served in Japan in the late nineteenth and early twentieth centuries and returned to the United States to plead the case of Japan as a potential Asian, Christian ally. The central thrust of these missionary advocates was the goal of educating Americans about the unique nature of Japan and the creation of an American model to aid Japanese political development. The missionary advocates sought a Christian Japan, urged the end of anti-Japanese immigration laws, and defended Japanese expansionary activities in Asia.[4]

In the years preceding World War II, the Japanese government and a few American corporate interests that did business with Japan lobbied for Japanese interests in the United States. One lawyer, James Lee Kaufman, represented nearly all of the American businesses operating in prewar Japan. Of course, all of this lobbying ceased with the onset of war in 1941.[5] The postwar Japan lobby focused on the threat of communism to Japan and to American interests in the Pacific. American businesspeople sought to rebuild Japan as a potential market for American products.[6] One early organization, the American Council on Japan (ACJ), typified the early pro-Japan American advocacy groups. The ACJ sought to bring Japan into the American security system, and it promoted the role of American business in the reconstruction of Japan. One of its leaders was Harry F. Kern, the foreign editor of *Newsweek*.[7]

Harry Kern capitalized on his two-nation political access by opening his own consulting firm, Foreign Reports, in the mid-1950s. He developed a roster of Japanese clients, to which several Arab companies were added. Soon after, Mike Masaoka, longtime spokesperson of the Japanese American Citizens League in Washington, D.C., established a consulting-lobbying operation for Japanese interests. As a pioneer in representing Japanese trade interests but aware of the negative attitude of many Americans toward Japan, Masaoka defended his work as a "duty to U.S.-Japan relations" and an attempt to "keep Japan on America's side."[8] William Tanaka, a Japanese-American lawyer, opened the first law firm in the District of Columbia to represent Japanese business interests. Kotler designates Tanaka as the first Japanese hired gun because he detached emotional concerns on the part of Americans from the task of representing Japan.

Japan also sought to employ lobbyists who were not of Japanese extraction to represent its interests. One of the first celebrities hired was the 1948 Republican presidential candidate, Thomas E. Dewey, who was enlisted in 1959 to lobby against restrictions on Japanese cotton products. The Japan External Trade Organization (JETRO), a spin-off of the Japanese Ministry of International Trade and Industry (MITI), paid Dewey $500,000 over five years.[9]

The Japanese continued to Americanize their lobbying efforts during the 1950s as various textile conflicts dominated U.S.-Japanese trade discussions. The Japanese established several front organizations to give their effort an American look. Mike Masaoka created the American Textile Importers Association, which was composed entirely of American companies whose interests paralleled those of Japanese textile manufacturers. Washington, D.C., lawyers Nelson Stitt and Noel Hemmendinger founded another front organization, the U.S.-Japan Trade Council, which has played a significant role in Japanese lobbying over the past three decades. Stitt and Hemmendinger were the first of a flood of U.S. government officials who would leave government service to represent Japanese interests.

The U.S.-Japan Trade Council used its annual budget of $300,000, most of which was provided by Japan's Ministry of Foreign Affairs through its Japan Trade Promotion Office in New York City, to produce intellectually respectable and useful information for Washington opinion makers. The Japanese did not admit to controlling the U.S.-Japan Trade Council until the Department of Justice filed suit in 1976. The organization changed its name to the Japan Economic Institute (JEI) and openly acknowledged its funding from the Ministry of Foreign Affairs of Japan.

The next step in the growth of the Japan lobby came with the passage of the 1975 Trade Act, which forced the Japanese (and others) to organize to deal with a more complex U.S. trade policy environment.[10] The Japanese aggressively pursued American trade experts to represent Japan's interests in the wake of the legislation. One of the major U.S. hired guns to sign on with the Japanese was Harald Malmgren, who had served as deputy special trade representative for President Gerald Ford and was one of the drafters of the 1975 Trade Act. Malmgren, one of the first expert lobbyists hired by the Japanese who was not a lawyer, successfully kept tariffs from being imposed on Japanese televisions in 1978. He received $300,000 for his three months of work on the case. Malmgren continued to work for the Japanese on trade issues; later, and before his death in 2002, Malmgren functioned as an information and communication conduit between Japan and the United States.

Since the early 1960s, Japanese interests have hired American advisers to teach them about U.S. politics and how to influence American public policy. One of the most important of these teacher-advisers has been Richard V. Allen, who later served as Richard Nixon's chief foreign policy and national security aide in the 1968 presidential campaign. After a stint on the National Security Council, Allen became deputy assistant to the president for international trade and economic policy. In 1980, Allen was Ronald Reagan's foreign policy and national security adviser during the presidential campaign. During that campaign the *Wall Street Journal* revealed that in 1970 Allen had written to a powerful Japanese political leader criticizing Japanese lobbying efforts and urging the Japanese to create an American-led lobbying machine.[11]

Three Components of the Japan Lobby

The Japan lobby can best be understood by examining its three components: the cultural, economic, and political. The three are often interrelated and harnessed to achieve particular goals, but examining them separately helps in understanding the contemporary role and success (in some cases declining success) of the lobby.

Japan's Cultural Lobby

Japan's cultural lobby consists of several large organizations.[12] These include the Japan Foundation, the Japan-U.S. Friendship Commission, the Japan Society, and the United States–Japan Foundation. Two of these organizations—the two foundations—essentially operate as funding sources for many other, largely U.S. organizations that affect American attitudes toward Japan.

Japan Foundation.   The Japan Foundation—or Kokusai Koryu Kikin— is perhaps the best known of the Japanese cultural organizations in the United States. Founded as a special body of the Japanese Ministry of Foreign Affairs in October 1972, its aims are to deepen other nations' understanding of Japan, to promote better mutual understanding among nations, and to encourage friendship and goodwill.[13] Funded by the Japanese government and the Japanese private sector, its program budget had grown to ¥18 billion by 2004–2005. The Japan Foundation is a worldwide program with more than a dozen overseas offices. It has instituted new programs over the past two decades, such as the Japanese Language Institute (July 1989), the ASEAN Cultural Center (1990), and the Center for Global Partnership (CGP, April 1991). The Japan Foundation has become the core organization of Japan's international cultural exchange activities.

To accomplish its goals, the Japan Foundation promotes Japanese studies abroad by providing grants to organizations and offering financial assistance to researchers. It also supports Japanese-language education overseas (including salary assistance for full-time Japanese-language instructors), student study tours, Japanese speech contests, the translation and publishing of Japanese materials, and the broadcasting of Japanese-language educational television programs. Altogether, as of 2002, the Japan Foundation spends three times as much of its budget in the United States as it does in the second-ranked nation for its expenditures, China.

The Japan Foundation established the CGP for the specific purpose of improving relations between the United States and Japan. Offices were established in Tokyo and New York City. Among the issues the CGP placed on its initial agenda were world economics, disarmament, environment, economic development, and various urban problems such as education and immigration. In fiscal year 2005–2006, the CGP provided financial assistance to dozens of projects in the United States, including:

- Six conferences held at the University of Illinois, Columbia University, the University of Kansas, the Social Science Research

Council, the North American Coordinating Council on Japanese Library Resources, and Washington University in St. Louis;
- Nine Ph.D. fellowships for students at Harvard University, the University of California–Berkeley, the University of Wisconsin–Madison, Princeton, and the University of Illinois;
- Seventeen research fellowships;[14] and
- Seven major library-support programs and three publication-support programs as well as many arts and TV productions, film festivals, exhibitions, and performing arts and Japanese-language programs.

The CGP has also established other significant projects in the general area of improving an understanding of Japan in the United States. It has assisted the Roper Center for Public Opinion Research at the University of Connecticut in the collection of Japanese public opinion polls. It also initiated and financed the establishment of the Japan Documentation Center within the Library of Congress for the purpose of improving U.S. access to the latest information and publications on contemporary Japan. An important part of this new library is a collection of Japanese government publications and published studies by Japanese think tanks.

The CGP is also one of the major remaining funders of research about U.S.-Japanese political and security relations. In the 2005–2006 cycle, the CGP was funding research on bioethics, the U.S.-Japan economic relationship, U.S. military policy in Asia, nuclear weapons and Asia, the Korean problem, and the role of U.S. and Japanese industries in limiting weapons of mass destruction.

Perhaps the most important project of the CGP was the establishment of the Abe Fellowships, named after the late Japanese foreign minister. Abe Fellowships are awarded to academic researchers and specialists who "work to promote political research through mutual exchange between Japanese and U.S. specialists." The program is administered by the CGP, the U.S. Social Science Research Council, and the American Council of Learned Societies. In fiscal year 2005–2006, twelve U.S. and four Japanese scholars were awarded fellowships. The CGP also administers a set of programs for promoting "mutual understanding on the regional and grassroots level." These outreach programs promote public understanding of problems faced by both Japan and the United States and the raising of public awareness on global issues. Programs are targeted at educators, students, and other citizens.

The CGP has also been funding programs to enhance the quality of Japanese culture and education in U.S. school systems in the South and Midwest. On the level of higher education, the CGP made substantial donations to several universities to support the establishment or expansion of Japanese studies centers and programs. In the early 1990s, these included the Center for Japanese Economy and Business at Columbia University, the Center for East Asian Studies at the Monterey Institute of International Studies, the Reischauer Institute of Japanese Studies at Harvard University, the Harvard University Center for International Affairs, the Center for East Asian Studies at the University of Chicago, and programs at Bowling Green State University, the Hoover Institute, San Diego State University, and the University of Hawaii. Despite all these programs—new and old—the Japan Foundation has had to operate in the 2000s with a smaller budget than in the days when the Japanese economy was roaring with double-digit growth rates. Perhaps with the return of the new growth in the Japanese economy, the Japan Foundation will receive additional funds to expand and enrich its programs.

Japan-U.S. Friendship Commission.   Perhaps the most unusual of the Japanese cultural organizations is the Japan-U.S. Friendship Commission (JUSFC), an independent agency of the U.S. government "dedicated to promoting mutual understanding and cooperation between the United States and Japan." The JUSFC is headquartered in Washington, D.C. It administers grant programs in support of Japanese studies in the United States, American studies in Japan, and activities in the arts involving Japanese content. The JUSFC was established by Congress in 1975 to administer a trust fund formed from part of the Japanese government's repayment for U.S. facilities built in Okinawa and later returned to Japan and for postwar American assistance to Japan. Annual income from the fund amounts to about $3 million. JUSFC is administered by a commission of U.S. officials that includes members of the Senate and House, representatives from the Department of State and the Department of Education, and the chairs of both countries' national endowments for the arts and for the humanities.

A major part of JUSFC's budget traditionally has gone into training the next generation of American-Japanese scholars—Americans who will become specialists on various aspects of Japanese studies. To further this goal, programs have been started to provide for graduate student fellowships, graduate school faculty and curriculum development, library support, faculty research, language training, and general programs of public education. In general, the commission has sought to fund very focused, collaborative research projects. Because of budget restrictions, the commission has been focused on American studies in Japan, legislative exchanges, and legislative staff exchanges to Japan.

Japan Society.   The Japan Society of New York uses grants from various foundations and from Japanese and American corporations to expand American understanding of Japan. Founded in 1907, the society is the oldest and largest Japanese cultural advocate in the United States. Despite its role as a cultural bridge between Japan and the United States, the Japan Society also sees itself as a significant force in reducing political and economic stress between the two nations. Cyrus Vance, the society's chairman in 1992, noted in the organization's 1990–1991 report:

> As an organization devoted to enlightened and mutually enriching relations between the United States and Japan, the Japan Society had its work cut out for it this past year.... I sense real urgency about the danger of the negative trend characterizing mutual attitudes. We seem to be drifting rather mindlessly toward thinking of each other in adversarial terms.... This kind of challenge brings out the best in the Japan Society, its members and supporters.

The heart of the Japan Society's effort to promote mutual understanding is a series of programs that provide forums for discussions of the political, economic, business, and social issues that affect the two countries, as well as educational programs that promote cross-cultural understanding. The Japan Society in New York holds more than one hundred discussion meetings, conferences, and exchanges each year to foster better understanding between Japan and the United States. The National Association of Japan-America Societies (NAJAS), with 40 organizations in 32 states, is an umbrella organization that used to have its offices in New York City in the same building as the New York Japan Society, but recently it moved to Washington, D.C., as have many other interest groups in recent years. In 2006, the NAJAS joined with the Japanese Embassy and Nippon Keidanren, an association of large Japanese businesses, to sponsor a series of "speaker caravans" around the United States. NAJAS members across the nation held 800 public affairs programs, 500 corporate programs, and more than 160 cultural programs in recent years.

The Japan Society runs an extensive exchange program with three important subprograms. The U.S.-Japan Leadership Program for a decade sent Americans to Japan to learn about Japanese society. It evolved in 1996 into two new programs: the Local Government and Public Policy Fellowships, and the U.S.-Japan Foundation Media Fellows Program. However, it is the cultural contributions of the Japan Society that are particularly significant. Each year the society hosts hundreds of events to showcase Japanese culture, including Japan's performing arts and films, and dozens of educational and language support programs. In many respects, the Japan Society of New York is a very important part of the city's cultural life.

United States–Japan Foundation. This is another organization based in New York City that seeks to further bilateral cultural relations. It has a greater role to play in policy analysis (globalization, U.S.-Japanese trade relations, and foreign policy topics), and it is especially interested in supporting the work on Japan of young scholars. It also supports various exchange programs. As an indication of the foundation's efforts to raise its visibility in the United States, in 2006 it had several former U.S. presidents on its board of directors.

Another smaller program is primarily designed to facilitate better understanding between Japanese and American legislators and staff. The Japan Center for International Exchange (JCIE/Japan) runs a program that facilitates a congressional staff exchange program. As of 2004, over 130 congressional staff members have traveled to Japan under this program. It particularly seeks out young, up-and-coming future leaders to educate about the U.S.-Japanese relationship and Japan in general.

Japan's Economic Lobby

In its heyday, the Japanese economic lobby was composed of several types of professional organizations that coordinated well to represent Japanese business interests. One part generated a tidal wave of general economic data and specific subsector analyses, another provided think-tank advocacy for Japanese economic policies, and others represented specific industries through trade associations.[15] Located in Washington, D.C., the Japan Economic Institute of America (usually referred to as JEI)—the reconstituted and legitimized successor of the U.S.-Japan Trade Council—was the primary source in the United States for economic and business data on Japan. JEI was a unit of the Japanese Ministry of Foreign Affairs, which largely funded its operations. Those operations included hosting a series of seminars on Japan, with an emphasis on business and trade issues.

JEI's major contribution to the understanding of Japan was in its three publications: the *Japan Economics Report* (weekly); the *Japan-U.S. Business Report* (monthly); and the *Japan Economic Survey* (monthly). JEI also issued periodic reports about Japan that covered Japanese fiscal policy, budgetary process, defense, trade competition, education, banking, foreign affairs, industrial policy, labor, political reform, U.S.-Japan trade relations, health policy, and the status of women. For those seeking detailed and current information on Japan, these publications were among the best in the world. JEI's last president was Arthur Alexander. With a doctorate in economics from the Johns Hopkins University, Alexander came from the RAND Corporation to head JEI's staff of seven. Despite JEI's significant presence in Washington, D.C., it folded in 2001 when the Japanese Ministry of Foreign Affairs cut its funding.

A powerhouse that has had a profound effect on U.S.-Japanese economic relationships is the Institute for International Economics (IIE). Located in Washington, D.C., and headed by C. Fred Bergsten, IIE derived a significant part of its research funding in the 1980s from Japanese sources. The organization is cited frequently in the *New York Times* and the *Washington Post;* and whenever a story is published on U.S. trade problems or Japanese economics, Fred Bergsten is usually cited "to put the issue into proper perspective." Bergsten was also a favorite expert source of Hobart Rowen, who in the 1980s was the chief economics writer for the *Washington Post* and a nationally syndicated columnist. Since the 1990s,

IIE has largely shifted its attention and research agenda to China; China's role in Asia; and China's economic, political, and social relations with the United States.

Amassing and providing information have always been the primary objectives of Japanese lobbying organizations—inside and outside Japan—and the Japan lobby developed a formidable information-gathering network. The Japanese are voracious accumulators and consumers of information of all kinds—political, social, and economic. Consequently, much of the money the Japan lobby spent in the United States was allocated for the collection and interpretation of such information. The Japanese government, in particular, through its fifteen consulates in the United States, is a major collector of all types of hard data and opinion.[16] Complementing the consular operations of the Ministry of Foreign Affairs is the JETRO program of the Ministry of Economics, Trade, and Industry (METI). JETRO not only promotes Japanese business but also conducts so-called soft-side propaganda campaigns that use the provision of information as their vehicle.

Akio Morita, head of Sony Corporation, founded a group that brought together 160 Japanese companies with major investments in the United States. Originally named the Council for Better Investment in the United States, the group was renamed the Council for Better Corporate Citizenship (CBCC) in September 1989.[17] Now led by the powerful Japanese business association Keidanren, CBCC's self-described mission is to work "diligently to promote good relations between Japanese-affiliated companies and various stakeholders, including their respective local communities, as good corporate citizens."

Japan's Political Lobby

During the 1980s and early 1990s, Japan's political lobby hired many of Washington's most powerful residents to represent Japanese interests. These included former U.S. trade representatives, former CIA directors, former White House national security advisers, former chairs of national political party committees, former secretaries of state, and even an occasional cabinet member or two.[18] Choate claimed that by the late 1980s the Japanese were spending at least $100 million a year lobbying in the United States plus "another $300 million each year to shape American public opinion...."[19] In 1993, Japanese interests hired more than 125 American law firms, economic consultants, and public relations firms.[20] The Japan lobby was especially effective in dealing with Congress and congressional staff. The Japanese embassy in Washington, D.C., regularly assigned four staff members to become familiar with congressional staff members and members of Congress.[21]

By any measure, the stakes of the game for the Japanese in their political and, particularly, their economic relations with the United States are enormous. The Japanese-American bilateral economic relationship is perhaps the most important in the world. The two economies have developed a complementary pattern in many sectors, but conflict continues in some sectors, concern over the U.S.-Japanese trade deficit (totaling more than $80 billion a year in favor of Japan) continues, some impediments to U.S. and other imports persist, and restructuring of the U.S.-Japan security relationship continues.

Japan Lobby's Intellectual Initiatives

As suggested earlier, various ministries of the Japanese government, such as the Ministry of Education and the Ministry of Foreign Affairs, have worked to shape American public opinion through various educational programs. These include programs for K–12 schools, media materials for home viewing, cultural events in various communities and higher-education settings, and several programs that bring Americans to Japan. The Ministry of Finance maintained an informal council of economic advisers that included more than one hundred of the world's top trade experts, and fifty-two were American. In the 1990, Chalmers Johnson estimated that more than 80 percent of all programs concerning Japan that operate in the United States are financed by the Japanese. Choate, who believes the 80 percent figure is low, called this tactic "shaping the marketplace of ideas."[22]

Japan has funneled tens of millions of dollars to a relative handful of elite universities to assist in the establishment or expansion of major Japan studies programs or centers. Universities such as Harvard, Yale, the University of California–Berkeley, Washington (in St. Louis), Michigan, and others regularly compete for renewal of existing grants or for new funds from organizations such as the Japan Foundation or Japanese corporate foundations. These corporate foundations include those established by Toyota, Honda, Hitachi, Nissan, Mitsui, and other major Japanese corporations with operations in the United States. Other academics are cultivated through programs of sponsored language study, teaching, and research in Japan. Programs have been established to bring politicians; media personnel; schoolteachers; and federal, state, and local government staff on fact-finding trips to Japan.

The key to understanding the significance of the opinion-influencing efforts is to note that their primary goal is to magnify the voices of Americans who already support Japan. Supporters of Japan are assisted financially and offered forums for presenting pro-Japanese positions. Holstein cites the examples of Peter G. Peterson, Fred Bergsten, and Stephen Bosworth. Peterson, secretary of commerce in the Nixon administration, chaired the Blackstone Group, a New York-based investment bank that was a major player in multibillion-dollar acquisitions in the United States by Sony, Bridgestone, and Mitsubishi. Nikko Securities invested $100 million in

Blackstone and provided another $100 million for a fund Blackstone manages. Peterson also chaired the Council on Foreign Relations and the Institute for International Economics. The latter organization, of which Bergsten is president, received about 10 percent of its budget in the 1980s from Japanese sources, including the U.S.-Japan Foundation, which was chaired by Stephen Bosworth, a former ambassador. Holstein asserts that Peterson, through speeches and articles, supported the position that the United States needs the capital that Japan provides and should not change its policies toward Japanese investment. Peterson, Bergsten, and Bosworth were all supporters of free trade long before their Japanese connections began, but all three have been of great assistance to Japanese efforts to mold public opinion.[23]

Japan Lobby in Comparative Perspective

At its peak, was the Japan lobby very different from the lobbies representing other important nations in Washington? Even the poorest, least-developed nations have spent millions of dollars lobbying Washington. Kenya and Zaire in the early 1990s paid more than $1 million a year to hire the services of Black and Manafort. Other African nations followed their example.[24] Among developed nations, Japan's reported lobbying and related expenditures, although high, were not disproportional to their economic relationship with the United States. The Canadians ($22 million), Germans ($13 million), French ($12.8 million), and Mexicans ($11 million) all had substantial lobbying expenditure reports in 1992.[25] Mitchell found that in terms of numbers of lobbyists the Japanese lobby was outranked by both the British and Canadians.[26]

What Has Happened to the Japan Lobby Since 1990?

Looking back at the chapter about Japanese lobbying in Washington, D.C., that was in the fourth edition of this book, published in 1996, is like viewing the contents of a time capsule. A major change has come over the Japan lobby in the past fifteen years. What is that change and why did it happen? Let us look at the lobby then and now.

U.S.-Japan relations during the early 1990s were dominated by trade and investment conflicts that kept former U.S. trade representatives Charlene Barshefsky (1997–2000), Mickey Kantor (1993–1996), and Carla Hills (1989–1993) crisscrossing the Pacific Ocean and Washington lobbyists hard at work. Members of Congress railed about the lack of a level playing field for American producers. Newspapers across the United States carried stories about Japanese barriers to U.S. steel, textiles, beef, apples, autos and auto parts, semiconductors, supercomputers, pharmaceuticals and medical devices, machine tools, public works tenders, retail distribution, and the like.

During the 1990s every prominent Washington trade lobbyist could converse knowledgeably about "pioneer preferences" for the broadcasting spectrum, the properties of amorphous metal transformers, pre-NAFTA tariffs on television picture tubes, the annual tonnage of exported Washington State red apples, and the value of Japan's flat-glass market. Animated conversations were sparked about such famed trade cases as the Fuji-Kodak dispute, the Betamax-Sony standard, and NTT procurement reciprocity arrangements.

Naturally, this list of irritants between the United States and Japan kept Rolodexes of American lobbyists spinning. Tens of thousands of pages of legal briefs were committed to fighting allegedly discriminatory U.S. customs and maritime transport regulations, "Buy America" provisions, heavy-handed U.S. antidumping and countervailing-duty regulations, patent procedures that allowed for so-called submarine applications to surface, restrictive export controls to third-market purchasers, tariffs on certain products, U.S. trade sanctions that prohibited trading partners from doing business with third countries (the pariah countries of Iran, Libya, Cuba, and Burma), and prohibitions on foreign ownership of American broadcasting.

Just fifteen years ago, most major Japanese companies retained a half dozen registered lobbyists at prominent law firms and plenty of consultants for additional firepower when the need arose. Today, all Washington, D.C., law firms with big trade practices—Akin Gump Strauss Hauer & Feld, LLP; Hogan & Hartson, LLP; Wilkie Farr & Gallagher, LLP; Alston & Bird, LLP; and a handful of others—still have Japanese clients, but their billable hours are a fraction of what they used to be. Actually, the list of paid lobbyists for Japan in the 1980s and early 1990s looked almost like a who's who of the Washington, D.C., establishment. Luminaries such as former secretary of state Henry Kissinger and former CIA director William Colby were just the most well-known of the dozens of powerful Washington insiders who worked for the Japanese. Before the Clinton administration, it seemed that the White House office of the U.S. Trade Representative was a training ground for future lobbyists for Japanese interests.

Think tanks and their prominent staff members too have shifted gears from Japan to China and other hotter targets. Clyde Prestowitz seems to have lost interest in chronicling the threat of the Japanese industrial competitiveness and has turned his focus to China and India and what he calls an "asymmetric global economic structure."[27] In his newest book, *Three Billion New Capitalists: The Great Shift of Wealth and Power to the East,* Prestowitz posits that America's future is "far more fragile and ephemeral than much of the world believes" because of the emerging robust market economies in China, India, and eastern Europe.[28] Similarly, Pat Choate of the famed call-to-arms book, *Agents of Influence,* about the threat of Japanese industrial competitiveness, ran for vice president in 1996 on Ross

Perot's Reform Party ticket and has subsequently moved his focus to intellectual property theft. His most recent book is *Hot Property: The Stealing of Ideas in an Age of Globalization.*[29]

Japan's corporate presence in Washington has slimmed down, too. Many of the Japanese companies that used to have a major presence in Washington, D.C., during the 1980s and 1990s have scaled back dramatically. Most dispatch fewer senior corporate executives from Tokyo, preferring instead to hire Americans locally to fill senior positions; offices have been moved off Washington, D.C.'s prestigious K Street to less impressive addresses; and budgets have been tightened considerably. Some Japanese companies, including Fuji Bank, Nichimen, Tomen, and Mitsubishi Motors, have shut the doors of their Washington offices altogether.

One trade association, awkwardly named the International Electronic Manufacturers and Consumers of America (IEMCA), once managed by Valerie Ploumpis, one of the authors of this chapter, was established in 1987 with the express purpose of inoculating the American subsidiaries of Japanese high-tech companies from protectionist legislation and regulation. At its peak, IEMCA member companies included Sony, Fujitsu, Toshiba, Sharp, Hitachi, and other similar companies. IEMCA's membership began to decline just ten years after its creation, and IEMCA formally closed shop in 2004. Virtually all IEMCA's member companies have gravitated to trade associations with much broader interests and rosters.

To be sure, Washington lobbyists today still represent Japanese clients. But virtually all of the superlobbyists identified in the 1995 version of this chapter as Japan's hired guns have moved on to other interests (notably China) and an entirely different client base.

That lobbyists have moved on to more lucrative and challenging assignments is not surprising. The issues involving Japan today are far less heated; they include, for example, the occasional appropriations bill that may include a narrow antidumping or countervailing-duty case or a patent dispute. Even the current U.S.-Japanese dispute over beef has not generated much new lobbying business. In fact, the decline in lobbying and hiring of lobbyists for Japan and Japanese interests is dramatic. The Center for Public Integrity's list of the top one hundred firms that hire lobbyists finds no Japanese interest listed. Indeed, Daimler-Chrysler, BP Amoco, and Sanofi-Aventis appear to be only firms on this list with partial foreign ownership. On the *National Journal* list of the "Top Five Clients of the Top 15 Lobbying Firms" for the second half of 2005, only Nissan North America appears.[30] The U.S. Department of Justice (DOJ) also monitors foreign lobbyists, including government-sponsored organizations. According to the DOJ, nine of the thirty-seven registrants that represent Japan are offices of JETRO, which describes itself as a government-related organization working to promote mutual trade and investment between Japan and the rest of the world.[31]

Beyond the welcome absence of bilateral trade irritations, geopolitical factors have also lessened, thus reducing the need for Japanese companies to lobby in Washington. Just days after the attacks on the World Trade Center in 2001, Prime Minister Junichiro Koizumi declared Japan to be a strong ally in support of President Bush's war on terrorism. This was followed by the dispatch of Japanese soldiers to Iraq (marking the first time since World War II that Japanese troops were sent to foreign soil; they were withdrawn in June 2006), which went far to win the appreciation of the Bush White House and has probably led to the administration's subsequent disinclination to exert any pressure on Japan for its trade and investment practices. In short, the political heat was off the Japanese!

The most visible trade issue of 2005–2006 centered around the safety of American-produced beef and the Japanese ban on beef imports until the U.S. certified the safety of beef. This beef issue occupied about 40 percent of the time of Japanese trade and congressional experts, but the reality was that the issue was relatively minor. In May 2006, the U.S. and Japanese negotiators working on the beef ban forced an agreement to facilitate an upcoming trip by Prime Minister Koizumi to the White House to discuss mostly security issues. The ban was lifted by the Japanese in June of 2006. These much more important security stakes centered on the North Korean nuclear weapons and war-on-terrorism issues that have cemented the U.S.-Japanese relationship during the past five years.

Besides these factors, other forces were at work to reduce the need for the Japan lobby to be the powerhouse it was in the 1980s. Broader, macroeconomic trends were also working in Japan's favor. The popping of Japan's "bubble economy" in the early 1990s plunged the country into a decade of stagnant growth. In the course of just a few years, American fears of Japanese industrial competitiveness shifted to alarm that Japan would fall into a deflationary economic spiral. Instead, China, with its rampant intellectual-property piracy, cutthroat pricing, and stubborn undervaluation of its currency, quickly replaced Japan as the primary economic threat to the United States.

Benign factors played a role too. Global manufacturing practices in the auto sector over the past ten years have led to coproduction by Japanese and American companies, thereby eliminating most of the sectoral irritations. Now, Hondas, Toyotas, and Nissans are being produced in the United States in large numbers and thus, as home manufactured, are much better protected from political pressures in Washington. In addition, Japan's economic reforms also reduced American economic concerns by consolidating Japanese banks and opening the financial market to foreign service providers, including U.S. insurance companies and banks.

Finally, to some extent, the Japanese government itself played a hand in its own downgraded presence in Washington. The Japanese Ministry of Foreign Affairs cut off all funding for the excellent research group headed by Arthur Alexander, the Japan Economic Institute, in 2001, and no other group has picked up its mission. Japan closed its Kansas City consulate in 2005, and JETRO closed its New York City library in July 2006.

Rise of the New China Lobby; Japan Lobby in the Wings

From the 1940s to the early 1970s, one of the strongest lobbies in Washington, D.C., was the China lobby, that is, the Nationalist China–Taiwan lobby. Led by Madame Chiang Kai-shek and *Time* magazine's publisher, Henry Luce, it dominated congressional and executive branch decision making regarding China. Its power was broken by the Nixon-Kissinger opening of relations with the People's Republic of China (PRC) in 1973. As a result, key parts of the old Nationalist China lobby, such as the Committee of One Million opposed to Communist China in the United Nations, quickly disappeared. Parts of this old lobby survived in various conservative publications and think tanks around Washington. In fact, despite U.S. recognition of the PRC, it was not until more than twenty years later, when the U.S.-PRC trade conflicts became significant in the late 1990s, that a new China lobby—now pro-Beijing instead of pro-Taipei—emerged.

The economic events that brought political pressures on the PRC in U.S. politics during the late 1990s and early 2000s are quite clear. For example, Japanese trade with the United States constituted 43 percent of the U.S. trade deficit in 1994 (the PRC accounted for 20 percent that year), but by 2005 the Japanese share declined to 11 percent and the PRC share rose to 28 percent. In terms of dollars, the U.S.-PRC trade deficit was $202 billion in 2005 compared with the deficit of $86 billion with the Japanese. Americans noted that it seemed that every product they bought was made in China. The Chinese passed Japan as the world's largest holder of foreign currency reserves in early 2006.

U.S. senators attacked Chinese trade and currency policies, and books and articles began to appear in the American media about the "Chinese threat" to America.[32] When articles appeared on the subjects of the rise of China and the Chinese threat to the United States in terms of economic growth, the need on the part of the PRC to develop a powerful new China lobby became clear. As a result, China, like Japan—the nation it replaced as a major foreign lobbying force in Washington—went out and hired an army of powerful lobbyists and researchers to protect its interests. In many respects, the new China lobby resembles the old Japan lobby. It has invested huge amounts of money in corporations and trade associations that seek closer economic ties with China, it has hired many of the super-lobbyists and public relations firms in Washington, and it has also invested heavily in the culture side of lobbying in the United States.

The Japanese lobby has not disappeared forever. If needed in the coming years, it could reappear very quickly. It simply is not much needed in the current atmosphere of U.S.-Japanese relations and the changed relationship heralded by the events of September 11, 2001.

Notes

1. Roger M. Pang, "Rising Sun Is Old Business: Asians Are Still the 'Bad Guys,' " *New York Times*, August 8, 1993.
2. "Sixty-Four Percent of Japanese Say U.S. Relations Are Unfriendly," *New York Times*, July 6, 1993.
3. Pat Choate, *Agents of Influence: How Japan's Lobbyists in the United States Manipulate America's Political and Economic System* (New York: Knopf, 1990).
4. This discussion on the history of the Japan lobby and the role of the U.S.-Japan Economic Institute draws extensively from Mindy Kotler's, "Making Friends: A History of Japan's Lobby in Washington, D.C.," *Venture Japan* 2, no. 2 (1990).
5. For a study of the pre–World War II Japan lobby, see Jonathan G. Utley, "Diplomacy in a Democracy: The United States and Japan, 1937–1941," *World Affairs* 139, no. 2 (Fall 1976): 130–140.
6. The early history of the Japan lobby in the first years after World War II can be found in Howard Schonberger, "The Japan Lobby in American Diplomacy: 1947–1952," *Pacific Historical Review* 46, no. 3 (August 1977): 327–359. For more on this period, see Russell Warren Howe and Sarah Hays Trott, *The Power Peddlers: How Lobbyists Mold America's Foreign Policy* (Garden City, N.Y.: Doubleday, 1977), 29–100.
7. Kotler, "Making Friends," 58. Kotler argues that *Newsweek* was seeking a Japan focus to compete with *Time*, which at the time was focusing on China.
8. Ibid.
9. "Pat Choate vs. Komori Yoshihisa," *Bungeishunju* [in Japanese] 68 (November 1990): 268–278.
10. Kotler, "Making Friends," 59.
11. Choate, *Agents of Influence*, 69.
12. Ron Hrebenar interviewed personnel at the major Japanese cultural foundations and societies in New York City in June 1993. During the same month, he conducted interviews in Washington, D.C., with several staff of the Japanese economic organizations. Hrebenar interviewed these groups in New York City and Washington, D.C., again in February and March 2006.
13. The Japan Foundation Law, Article 1, passed by the Diet on June 1, 1972.
14. Much of the material on the cultural lobby has been obtained from the above noted interviews. Additional information can be obtained by going to these organizations' well-maintained Web sites: Japan Foundation, http://www.jpf.go.jp/; United States–Japan Foundation, http://www.us-jf.org/; Japan Society, http://www.japansociety.org/; and U.S.-Japan-U.S. Friendship Commission, http://www.jusfc.gov/.
15. The U.S.-Japan Trade Council was perhaps the best example of the Japan lobby's use of front groups to promote Japanese interests. Choate notes that after this bad experience, the Japanese joined hundreds of real U.S. trade associations and public interest groups such as the Consumers for World Trade, a Washington, D.C.-based advocate of open-door U.S. trade policies. Other prominent Japanese-dominated trade associations include the International Electronic Manufacturers and Consumers of America, the Pro-Trade Group, and the Japan Automobile Manufacturers Association.
16. Japan has more consulates in the United States than any other nation has ever had. Choate, *Agents of Influence*, 222. This is also the largest number of consulates Japan has in any nation. China has five consulates in the United States; five consulates is also the second-highest number of consulates Japan has in any other nation.
17. William J. Holstein, *The Japanese Power Game: What It Means for America* (New York: Scribner's, 1990), 234.
18. Ibid., 223.
19. Choate, *Agents of Influence*, xviii.

20. *New York Times*, November 2, 1993.
21. Choate, *Agents of Influence*, 75.
22. Ibid., 39. Japanese cultural lobbying must also be placed into a comparative perspective to evaluate the proportionality of Japanese efforts to influence U.S. attitudes regarding Japan. Two other nations have long operated extensive cultural lobbying efforts similar to those of the Japan Foundation. The United Kingdom's British Council and Germany's Goethe Institute are those nations' equivalents of the Japan Foundation. Both have a much longer history than the Japan Foundation, far larger budgets, more extensive organizations, and larger staffs. Choate, *Agents of Influence*, 187, 228. Choate argues that Japan has carefully cultivated its ties with "intellectual America" so as to be able to guide the academic and scholarly side of the policy-making process. Holstein discusses the "surprisingly sophisticated perception game to shape the way Americans think about trade, investment, technology, military relations, and other issues of keen importance to Japan." Holstein, *Japanese Power Game*, 228.
23. Holstein, *Japanese Power Game*, 230.
24. *National Journal*, May 18, 1991, 1189.
25. "Foreigners Find New Ally in U.S. Industry," *New York Times*, November 2, 1993.
26. Neil J. Mitchell, "The Global Polity: Foreign Direct Investment and Political Action Committees" (paper presented at the annual meeting of the Western Political Science Association, San Francisco, March 19–21, 1992).
27. Clyde Prestowitz, *Trading Places: How We Allowed Japan to Take the Lead* (New York: Basic Books, 1988).
28. Clyde Prestowitz, *Three Billion New Capitalists: The Great Shift of Wealth and Power to the East* (New York: Basic Books, 2005).
29. Pat Choate, *Hot Property: The Stealing of Ideas in an Age of Globalization* (New York: Knopf, 2005).
30. "Top Clients of the Top 15 Firms," *National Journal*, March 25, 2006, 33.
31. Information at the JETRO Web site, http://www.jetro.go.jp/en/jetro/activities/.
32. See Ken Bradshaw, "As Trade Deficit Grows, So Do Tensions with China," *New York Times*, March 10, 2006; Joseph Kahn, "Seeking Friends in Senate, China Tries Charm," *New York Times*, March 23, 2006; David Lague, "China Is Told of U.S. Impatience on Trade," *New York Times*, March 30, 2006; Andy Mukherjee, "Labeling China: Manipulator or Misaligner?" *International Herald Tribune*, May 19, 2006; and Doron Levin, "Japan Bashing Out of Style," *International Herald Tribune*, May 23, 2006. One of the better studies of the new China lobby appeared in the late 1990s right after the most-favored-nation status was granted to the PRC after a huge lobbying effort on its behalf; see Robert Dreyfuss, "The New China Lobby," *American Prospect*, January–February 1997, 30–32.

15

Where Have All the Interest Groups Gone?

An Analysis of Interest Group Participation in Presidential Nominations to the Supreme Court of the United States

Karen O'Connor, Alixandra B. Yanus, and Linda Mancillas Patterson

Although interest groups have often worked in support of, or in opposition to, a president's judicial nominations, especially to the Supreme Court, full-blown campaigns to defeat Court nominees came to the fore only in the past twenty years. President Reagan's 1987 naming of Judge Robert Bork of the Federal Circuit Court of Appeals met stiff and successful resistance, to the point that the well-publicized opposition campaign coined the verb "to Bork" a nominee. But Bork's defeat only served as a prelude to the acrimonious battle over President George H.W. Bush's appointment of Clarence Thomas to replace Thurgood Marshall on the Court. The Clinton appointees received less vigorous opposition, in part because they did not set off such fierce ideological battles. Then, for more than a decade, from the mid-1990s through 2005, no vacancies opened on the Court. The conventional wisdom was that a battle royal would break out among organized interests if and when George W. Bush got an opportunity to make a nomination.

This chapter, by Karen O'Connor, Alixandra B. Yanus, and Linda Mancillas Patterson, examines the roles played (and not) by organized interests in the confirmation process that saw John Roberts first nominated for an associate justice position to replace Justice Sandra Day O'Connor and then renominated to serve as chief justice, replacing William Rehnquist after his death. Subsequently, President Bush nominated Harriet Miers to become associate justice and then withdrew that nomination, replacing her with Samuel Alito. Even though the Roberts and Alito choices would almost certainly move the Court to the right, there were few substantial public campaigns; and although both nominees attracted opposition and negative votes, they were confirmed with relative ease. The predictions of another round of Bork-like vitriol did not come to pass. Ironically, as the authors note, the only real interest group success in opposing a judicial candidate came in the conservatives' opposition to Harriet Miers.

As Sherlock Holmes discovered, sometimes it is the dogs that do not bark that are the most significant. In 2005–2006, President Bush's nominations did not stir up sufficient liberal opposition to endanger his choices' confirmations. Only the howls of the conservatives proved central to this season of judicial confirmations.

Interest groups are involved in American politics in various, often-invisible ways. This is especially true within the judicial process. Conventional wisdom for years taught that federal judges, especially the justices of the U.S. Supreme Court, were above the political fray, subject only to an occasional well-planned test case litigation strategy.[1] By the mid- to late 1970s, however, political scientists began to recognize and study the pervasive role of interest groups in every step of the judicial process.

This chapter will examine the role of interest groups in the process of nominating and appointing justices to the Supreme Court. To that end, we first present a short introduction of how a vacancy on the Supreme Court is filled. Next, we offer a historical overview of several Supreme Court appointments that were especially controversial and thus most likely to attract interest group participation.[2] We next turn to President George W. Bush's 2005 nominations to the Supreme Court, filling the vacancies left by the retirement of Associate Justice Sandra Day O'Connor and the death of Chief Justice William H. Rehnquist. The nominations of John G. Roberts Jr., Harriet Ellan Miers, and Samuel A. Alito Jr. are examined to provide both a description of how the most recent appointments unfolded and an exploration of the roles interest groups played in those processes, especially in comparison with judicial nominations of the past.

The Process of Filling Vacancies on the U.S. Supreme Court

The formal process of nominating a justice to the Supreme Court is straightforward. Article II of the Constitution gives the president the power to nominate judges to the federal courts "by and with the advice and consent of the Senate." While the power to nominate is absolute, a wise president generally attempts to nominate only those potential jurists who will be approved by the Senate.

Procedurally, before a president nominates a Supreme Court justice, the Office of the Counsel to the President gathers possible names and conducts extensive background investigations of those individuals. These examinations generally include an analysis of all the written work, speeches, and opinions of the potential nominees if they have served on a lower court. During the Rehnquist Court, all of the justices with the exception of the chief justice had prior judicial experience. On the Roberts Court, all nine justices have served on the federal bench. During this prenomination period, if a vacancy appears imminent, interest groups may already be going on the offensive, "warning" the public about the importance of a possible vacancy or collecting funds in support of or in opposition to potential nominees, or both.

Historically, the American Bar Association (ABA), a professional organization of attorneys, conducts a separate investigation to evaluate and rate the nominee's fitness to serve on the bench.[3] These rankings range from well qualified, to qualified, to not qualified. In 2001, the Bush administration articulated its belief that the ABA was too liberal and, therefore, it would no longer provide it with names of candidates for appointment to any federal judgeships, including the Supreme Court.[4] Instead, President George W. Bush and his advisers have relied heavily on the less formal evaluations of the 25,000-member Federalist Society. The Federalist Society is a conservative organization of law students, lawyers, and judges that was formed in 1982; current Supreme Court justice Antonin Scalia was one of its founders.

Once the president settles on a nominee, the Federal Bureau of Investigation conducts a more formal investigation, interviewing hundreds of people who have had dealings with the nominee. The White House also appoints handlers to assist a nominee with the extensive paperwork involved with the nomination, organizes meetings between the nominee and key senators, and prepares the nominee for public Senate confirmation hearings.

At the next stage of the judicial confirmation process, the nominee appears before the full Senate Judiciary Committee. During these hearings, members of the committee question the nominee on past rulings and other actions of public interest. The committee also usually hears from individuals who provide character references, such as former colleagues, law clerks, or expert lawyers offering their opinions of the nominee's abilities and judicial temperament. Interest group leaders are also selected to testify by the majority and minority members of the committee. At this stage of the process, members of the majority party, who hold a number of committee seats roughly proportional to their representation in the whole Senate, have tremendous power to select potential witnesses and establish the overall tone of the hearings. Most hearings are quite civil, and until recently a plethora of interest groups favoring and objecting to the nomination were given significant time publicly to state their views of the nominee.

When the Judiciary Committee completes its investigation and public hearings, it votes to reject or approve the nominee. At this stage, a nomination may die, the committee can report a favorable recommendation to the full Senate, or it can send the nomination to the Senate with no recommendation. If the nomination is reported to the full Senate, interest groups on both sides continue to try to influence the votes of individual senators, at least on the relatively small number of nominations that prove genuinely controversial. They can also urge a filibuster[5] against the nominee.[6] These orchestrated interest group lobbying efforts then take on more targeted and earnest efforts in the form of e-mail, radio, newspaper, or televised appeals.

After debate in the Senate, a vote is taken. If a simple majority of the senators present vote in favor of the nominee, the nominee is confirmed and quickly sworn into office. Supreme Court justices, like all federal judges, serve until their resignation, retirement, or death. The only way a Supreme Court justice can be removed is through the impeachment process.

The Historical Role of Interest Groups in Judicial Nominations and Confirmations

The Senate has rejected or forced the president to withdraw a judicial nominee only twenty-nine times since 1789.[7] Before 1900, however, about one-quarter of all presidential nominees to the Supreme Court were rejected by the Senate. In 1866, for example, President Andrew Johnson nominated Henry Stanberry, widely regarded as a brilliant lawyer, to a vacancy on the Court. But the Senate's hostility toward President Johnson and his Civil War policies led the Senate to reduce the size of the Supreme Court from ten members to seven, taking away Johnson's opportunity to fill any vacancies on the Court. Congress fixed the size of the Court at nine in 1869. From then until 1916, no nominations attracted widespread attention or the kind of interest group involvement that highlighted the nomination of the first Jewish justice, Louis D. Brandeis.[8]

The Louis D. Brandeis Nomination

In 1916, President Woodrow Wilson nominated Louis D. Brandeis to serve on the Supreme Court. Brandeis, a progressive, liberal, Jewish lawyer, was known widely for his work on behalf of progressive causes and as pro bono counsel for the National Consumers' League (NCL). This interest group was formed in the late 1800s to lobby for maximum hour and work safety laws for women and children. As counsel for the NCL, Brandeis became famous for his use of what came to be called the Brandeis brief in *Muller v. Oregon* (1908). *Muller* was a challenge to the constitutionality of an NCL-supported law enacted by the Oregon legislature. The act banned women from working more than eight hours a day. With virtually no law on his side, Brandeis instructed women in the NCL to scour the New York Public Library to find studies that might support his claim that women workers needed special protection from the state to maintain their health and child-bearing abilities.[9] The brief he ultimately filed contained only three pages of legal argument and over one hundred pages of statistical information, albeit crude, drawn from European studies that supported his contention.[10] In 1908, the Supreme Court accepted Brandeis's arguments in full and marked the Court's first major use of nonlegal information from interest groups.

Although Brandeis delivered a victory for the NCL in *Muller*, his progressive politics led to the wrath of many in the business community, who viewed employer-employee relations to be within the sole purview of employers and not the government's responsibility. Thus, when Brandeis was nominated to serve on the Court, powerful business interests immediately organized to stop his nomination. They were joined by a number of other groups, including the Boston Brahmins, an informal group of ultrarich, conservative, Protestant New Englanders who were driven by their anti-Semitism and dislike for Brandeis's progressive positions on social and economic issues.[11] Even the president of Harvard University circulated an anti-Brandeis petition among Boston corporate lawyers and Harvard faculty members. Brandeis was also opposed by seven past presidents of the ABA, including former U.S. president and Supreme Court chief justice William Howard Taft.

Echoing a form of interest group participation that was to become common, an ex-president of Harvard and nine Harvard law professors answered these protests with a letter in support of Brandeis. Labor unions, which supported Brandeis's earlier work in *Muller* and other cases, also lobbied in his favor.[12]

Brandeis's nomination hearings lasted nearly four months. Although Brandeis himself never testified before the Senate or its Judiciary Committee, he did meet with some senators and had several distinguished friends and interest groups advocate on his behalf. Ultimately, the Judiciary Committee voted, 10–8, along strict party lines in support of his nomination. The Democratically controlled Senate then approved his nomination by a 47–22 vote.

It would be quite some time before another Supreme Court nomination attracted this kind of widespread public attention. Interest group participation, however, never completely disappeared from the nomination process. In 1930, for example, interest groups including the National Association for the Advancement of Colored People (NAACP) lobbied successfully to block the nomination of Judge John Parker because of his controversial views on race. And, in 1946, the ABA formally created a committee to evaluate nominees and to give the ABA a more formal role in the nomination process. Other interest groups also involved themselves in particularly controversial nominations such as Richard M. Nixon's appointments in 1969 of Clement Haynsworth Jr. and in 1970 of G. Harrold Carswell.[13] But, it was the nomination of Judge Robert H. Bork that changed the nature of Supreme Court nomination politics.

The Robert H. Bork Nomination

In June 1987, Associate Justice Lewis Powell announced his retirement from the Court. President Ronald Reagan then nominated Judge Robert H. Bork of the U.S. Court of Appeals to fill the vacancy. Bork was a renowned legal theorist and a vocal critic of the Supreme Court's ruling in the famous abortion case *Roe v. Wade* (1973). Thus, within an hour of the announcement, Senator Edward M. Kennedy, D-Mass., took to the floor of the Senate, declaring: "Robert Bork's America is a land in which women would be forced into back-alley abortions, blacks would sit at segregated lunch counters, rogue police could break down citizens' doors in midnight raids, schoolchildren could not be taught about evolution, writers and artists could be censored at the whim of government."[14] Kennedy's remarks immediately got the attention of interest group representatives, establishing the hostile tone that was to become the hallmark of the Bork confirmation hearings.

Moreover, the timing of Bork's nomination, which was announced just before the Senate recessed for the summer, gave interest groups an unprecedented amount of time to launch a unified attack on the nominee. A wide array of liberal interest groups opposed Bork's nomination for the reasons articulated by Senator Kennedy. Simultaneously, a coalition of conservative, religious, and criminal justice groups mobilized in his favor.[15] Both sides focused their initial efforts on grassroots mobilization, asking their members and sympathizers to contact their representatives and senators. Across the South, black churches sponsored "Bork Sundays," during which hundreds of handwritten letters and notes opposing the nomination filled collection plates. Grassroots mobilization resulted in "hundreds of thousands of letters and phone calls" pouring into the offices of members of Congress.[16] In an unusual move, both the American Civil Liberties Union (ACLU) and the AFL-CIO, an umbrella association representing millions of unionized workers, formally announced their opposition to the Bork nomination.[17] In addition, several groups, including the National Abortion Rights Action League (NARAL) and People for the American Way (PFAW), sponsored numerous television, radio, and newspaper ads that opposed the nomination.[18]

Supporting Bork, Dan Casey, the executive director of the American Conservative Union (ACU), claimed that the ACU "led the charge for Bork at the 'grassroots.'"[19] Its efforts included mailings to its 60,000 members, urging their support of Bork as well as asking for contributions to help the group with its fight. The ACU also produced pro-Bork ads that aired on television in the key states of Arizona, Louisiana, and Alabama, where sitting senators appeared undecided on the nominee. Other conservative groups such as the Christian Voice and the Moral Majority lobbied for Bork, but ACU director Casey asserted that all of the conservative groups were hampered by a lack of funds, and he blamed the White House for its failure to help groups boost Bork's cause.[20]

Judge Bork's confirmation hearings before the Senate Judiciary Committee were unusually candid. He gave detailed answers to committee members, which provided additional fodder for liberal opponents who, along with his conservative supporters, were allowed to testify in record numbers. Sixty-eight conservative and eighteen liberal groups testified (Table 15.1).

Even though the Judiciary Committee voted 9–5 to reject Bork's nomination, the full Senate took the unusual step of voting on his nomination, defeating it by a 58–42 vote, the widest rejection ever of a Supreme Court nominee.[21] Bork's defeat shocked many conservative interest groups,

Table 15.1.   Interest Groups Appearing in Selected Senate
Judiciary Committee Hearings, 1976–2005

		Interest groups	
Nominee	Year	Liberal	Conservative
Stevens	1976	2	3
Scalia	1986	5	7
Bork	1987	18	68
Kennedy	1987	12	14
Souter	1990	13	8
Thomas	1991	30	46
Ginsburg	1993	6	5
Breyer	1994	8	3
Roberts	2005	5	4
Alito	2005	2	1

Source: Adapted from Karen O'Connor, "Lobbying the Justices or Lobbying for Justice? The Role of Organized Interests in the Judicial Process," in *The Interest Group Connection,* 2d ed., ed. Paul S. Herrnson, Ronald G. Shaiko, and Clyde Wilcox (Washington, D.C.: CQ Press, 2005), 324; updated and revised by the authors.

which vowed that they would never let this happen to another one of their Supreme Court nominees.[22]

The Clarence Thomas Nomination

In 1991, Associate Justice Thurgood Marshall, the first African American to sit on the Court, announced his retirement. President George H.W. Bush quickly nominated another African American, Judge Clarence Thomas of the U.S. Court of Appeals for the District of Columbia Circuit, to fill the vacancy. Fifteen months earlier, despite Thomas's limited legal experience, President Bush had named him to fill Judge Bork's seat on that federal appellate court.

Major controversy erupted slowly over Thomas's nomination, with traditional civil rights coalitions conflicted about opposing a black nominee. First, the ABA evaluated Thomas only as qualified, with two members of the committee rating him as not qualified. Both liberals and conservatives then began to form coalitions. The pro-Thomas coalition was led by five major players: the Family Research Council, Coalitions for America,[23] Concerned Women for America, the Christian Coalition, and the Traditional Values Coalition. The anti-Thomas forces were orchestrated primarily by the Leadership Conference on Civil Rights, the Alliance for Justice, NARAL, and PFAW.[24] They were joined by senior citizens groups and women's rights groups, including the National Organization for Women (NOW).[25]

As the Thomas nomination proceeded, the nation was shocked when National Public Radio journalist Nina Totenberg went on the air to announce that a then-anonymous woman had told Democratic staff members of the Senate Judiciary Committee that she had been sexually harassed by Thomas. The alleged harassment had begun when he was her supervisor at the Equal Employment Opportunity Commission, the federal agency charged with enforcing civil rights laws. Two liberal interest groups, the Alliance for Justice and PFAW, were instrumental in bringing law professor Anita Hill, the complainant, to the attention of committee staff.[26] Hill's blockbuster allegations immediately altered the scope and nature of the hearings, which the Senate decided to continue, calling Hill to testify.

Following these accusations, all major television networks immediately took the unprecedented step of televising the Judiciary Committee's hearings from gavel to gavel. The nation was captivated as Hill recounted her experiences with Clarence Thomas and detailed her allegations of sexual harassment. Upon the conclusion of her testimony, Thomas returned to the committee to complain vigorously that he had been the object of a "high-tech lynching for uppity blacks."[27]

Perhaps because they had learned from the Bork nomination, conservative groups were quick to defend Thomas in the public arena. In the days following Anita Hill's testimony, these groups sponsored several television ads that attacked the character of two Democratic senators on the Judiciary Committee. They also filled senators' offices with more than two million pieces of direct mail supporting the Thomas nomination and testified before the Judiciary Committee on Thomas's behalf in near record numbers. Interest groups were also joined by private individuals and law professors, who either supported or attacked the truthfulness of both Hill and Thomas.

Ultimately, in a highly unusual move, the Senate Judiciary Committee made no recommendation to the full Senate. The Senate then voted 52–48 to confirm Thomas. Several conservative southern Democrats, fearing retribution at the polls from African Americans, crossed party lines to support Thomas.

The Role and Impact of Interest Groups in the Era Following the Bork and Thomas Nominations

In 1990, in the wake of the swirl of political controversy and media attention to the Bork nomination, the *Northwestern University Law Review* published papers from a symposium analyzing the role of interest groups in judicial nominations. At the center of that symposium was a piece by judicial scholar and law professor Martin Shapiro that argued that "interest groups play a small role in the appointment process and ought not to be of great interest to students of the Supreme Court."[28] He posited that, according to the exchange theory of interest groups, groups must have something to give to governmental actors in exchange for their support.[29] Shapiro claimed that pinpointing exactly what—if anything—groups gave to governmental actors in judicial nominations was nearly impossible.

Another line of research, however, offers a suggestion about what interest groups may provide. Donald R. Matthews and James A. Stimson's work, for example, concluded that members fear casting a single wrong vote and look to a variety of sources, including interest groups, to make sure that they do not cast a fatal vote on a matter of high salience to their districts.[30] Although their work concerned only House members, the salience of many judicial nominations is apparent, and some southern Democratic senators, such as Wyche Fowler of Georgia, lost their reelection bids by casting the "wrong" vote on a Supreme Court nominee.

More recently, more specific works on the role of interest groups in Supreme Court nominations also take issue with Shapiro. Gregory A. Caldeira and John R. Wright, for example, conclude that interest groups play three roles "as they attempt to mold senators' perceptions of the direction, intensity, and electoral implications of constituency opinion."[31]

These roles include:

- **Disseminating policy information** to constituents in the hopes of moving public opinion in the interest group's favor. These actions can include purchasing ads in the print media, creating and running advertisements on television or radio, using targeted mailings, and disseminating fact sheets about the nominee. Today it would also include spreading information to constituents and group members via the Internet and creating Web pages containing information about the nominee.
- **Organizing constituents** to call, mail, fax, or otherwise contact their senators or other key senators. The volume of communications is one critical indicator a senator can use to gauge the actual interest of his or her constituents in the nomination.
- **Providing information directly to senators** about the policy and electoral consequences of their votes. To that end, interest groups try to gain invitations to appear before the Senate Judiciary Committee to testify about their position on a nominee; they also meet with key committee staffers and file prepared statements in support or opposition of potential judges and justices. These actions often are closely coordinated among like-minded groups and are designed to fit into overall themes that groups or coalitions of groups are communicating to the public as well as to lawmakers.

Caldeira and Wright argue that, after accounting for all three types of participation, the reported number of interest groups testifying at the Bork hearings, for example, "represented only a pale reflection of the extraordinary effort" actually spent by liberal interest groups, in particular, to defeat that nomination.[32] By using two surveys of interest groups conducted between 1989 and 1992, the authors concluded that interest group participation in the nominations of Robert H. Bork, David Souter,[33] and Clarence Thomas had a statistically significant impact in the outcome of each nomination, even after controlling for variables such as political party, ideology, constituents, and campaign contributions. Of particular importance was interest groups' ability to engage in the costly grassroots activities to generate support or opposition to the nomination.[34]

Still, some political scientists contend that interest groups today are now "missing in action" from federal judicial nominations.[35] They maintain that Bork's nomination was a rare "watershed" for interest group activity. And, although interest groups' activities even produced a new verb—"to bork"—no nominees have been borked since.[36]

Some of the variation in interest group participation across time may result from the important role that the chair of the Judiciary Committee plays in allowing interest groups to participate in a formal way. For example, when Senator Edward M. Kennedy chaired the committee, he was much more amenable to inviting interest groups to have their say. In contrast, Senator Orrin Hatch, R-Utah, was reluctant to allow interest groups to testify one way or another. His successor, Senator Arlen Specter, R-Pa., who presided over the Roberts and Alito hearings, holds a similar stance. Specter has stated that "we do not need outsiders to tell us how to conduct our business."[37] Beliefs such as Specter's necessarily lead to fewer opportunities for interest groups to express their views on the record. But, that does not mean that interest groups do not participate actively in the process. Instead, it means that they must participate in different ways, as was the case during the two most recent vacancies to occur on the Supreme Court.

Role of Interest Groups in Nominations Made by George W. Bush

On July 1, 2005, Associate Justice Sandra Day O'Connor, a twenty-four-year veteran of the bench, surprised some Court observers by announcing her retirement. O'Connor's retirement marked the end of an unprecedented ten-year period when there had been no vacancies on the Supreme Court—the most recent two justices appointed to the Court, Ruth Bader Ginsburg and Stephen Breyer, had been appointed by President Bill Clinton in 1993 and 1994, respectively.

Although many Court watchers had expected the more than ten-year drought of Supreme Court nominees to come to an end during President Bush's term, most observers expected that Chief Justice William H. Rehnquist, who was suffering from life-threatening thyroid cancer, would be the first member of the Court to depart. So many observers expected that Rehnquist's remaining time on the Court would be limited that, following his announcement of his illness in late 2004, the White House began to prepare a list of jurists who would be excellent candidates to replace him.

President Bush drew from this list to fill O'Connor's seat and nominated Judge John G. Roberts Jr. of the U.S. Court of Appeals for the District of Columbia. Judge Roberts exemplifies the Bush administration's preparations for a vacancy—his first interview with Attorney General Alberto Gonzales regarding a potential nomination to the Supreme Court took place on April 1, 2005, three months before Justice O'Connor announced her retirement. A second interview with several top administration staff members occurred in early May. This group included Counsel to the President, Harriet Miers, who in that position was charged with vetting all possible nominees. On May 23, Miers interviewed Roberts again and followed up with another interview on July 8, after Justice O'Connor announced her retirement.[38]

Immediately after Roberts's nomination, conservative interest groups clamored to endorse the nominee. The American Center for Law and Justice (ACLJ), best known as the litigating arm of the Christian Coalition, pledged to spend nearly a million dollars to support his confirmation. Progress for America (PFA) pledged to spend as much as $18 million to ensure that the conservative Roberts was approved by the Senate. Liberal groups, on the other hand, were reluctant to enter the fray so quickly. NARAL Pro-Choice America simply urged its members to ask their senators to question Roberts about *Roe v. Wade* (1973). At the same time, the Alliance for Justice waited to oppose the nominee until it learned more about him.

The course of Roberts's nomination was altered on September 3, 2005, when Chief Justice Rehnquist died after thirty-three years on the bench. Two days later, President Bush announced that he was withdrawing Roberts's appointment to O'Connor's seat and nominating Roberts to be chief justice.

Less than one month after Roberts was nominated for chief justice, on October 3, 2005, President Bush nominated Harriet Miers to replace Justice O'Connor. Liberal groups largely laid low in the wake of Miers's nomination. Women's rights groups were relieved that O'Connor was replaced with another woman, and that Meirs's record was not as clearly conservative as other recent Bush appointments to the federal bench. Many conservative groups, however, were outraged that she was not "conservative enough." As news of Miers's ambivalent positions on abortion and the right to privacy were revealed, Concerned Women for America called for her name to be withdrawn;[39] other groups launched new Web sites, including WithdrawMiers.org and BetterJustice.org. The latter highlighted a television ad that began: "Even the best leaders make mistakes," referring to President Bush.[40] Fidelis, a pro-life Roman Catholic interest group, announced that the "nomination was beyond repair."[41] After more and more conservative groups announced their objections to Miers's philosophy and qualifications, she withdrew her name from consideration on October 27, 2005. It took President George W. Bush only a few days to nominate Judge Samuel A. Alito Jr. of the U.S. Court of Appeals for the Third Circuit to replace her.

Again, PFA was the first conservative group to begin a full-blown campaign for Alito. As with its ads for Roberts, PFA's ads for Alito urged that Alito be given a "fair up or down vote" by the Senate. Other conservative and religious groups soon joined the chorus. So important was one of these groups, Focus on the Family, that after Alito's confirmation the new justice actually sent a note to Dr. James Dobson, its president, "to express ... heartfelt thanks to you and the entire staff ... for your support during the past few challenging months."[42] Liberal groups responded rather quickly to the Alito nomination. PFAW, for example, launched an anti-Alito Web site, SaveTheCourt.org, and a coalition of liberal groups calling themselves IndependentCourt.org began to air a number of television and radio ads.

Mobilizing Interest Group Activity

As demonstrated above, interest groups, like the White House, recognize that a new member of the Court can have a critical impact on the Court's decisions. Thus, many interest groups attempt to mobilize support or opposition for each nominee. The tactics used by these groups represent strategic decisions because these actors often have limited human and financial resources and must decide which tactics will best serve their objectives.

Here we consider in greater detail how groups used a number of strategies and tactics during the Roberts, Miers, and Alito nominations. Although groups may lobby individual senators, prepare representatives of other groups for testimony before the Judiciary Committee, conduct polls to boost awareness of the nominee, hold marches and rallies, or appear on radio or cable news to disseminate their messages, we limit our analysis to the following tactics: (1) testifying before the Senate Judiciary Committee; (2) formal position taking; (3) advertising; and (4) mass mailings. We also examine interest groups' (5) increasing use of technology—including e-mails, Web sites, and blogs—to complement the aforementioned traditional strategies.

Testifying Before the Senate Judiciary Committee

Testifying before the Senate Judiciary Committee is the most formal strategy pursued by interest group representatives discussed here. Because it represents an opportunity for groups to express their opinions to the people who have the power to accept or reject a Supreme Court nominee, testimony long has been a popular tactic for groups with enough national prestige to garner an invitation from the committee.

During the Roberts and Alito nominations, interest group participation in the Senate Judiciary Committee's hearings was limited. As shown in Table 15.1, only nine groups—five liberal and four conservative—participated in the Roberts hearings. Numbers were even lower during the Alito hearings, when only three groups testified before the committee. These numbers represented a huge decline from many earlier Supreme Court Judiciary Committee hearings; the three groups participating in the Alito nomination were the smallest number of groups to testify in a Supreme Court nomination hearing in the last thirty years.[43] The lack of formal participation, however, cannot be taken as an indicator of an absence of interest groups' desire to testify. Instead, the small number may reflect the successful efforts of Senator Specter and other Republicans on the committee to assure that hearings appeared less controversial by refusing to allow interest groups to participate.[44]

Lawyers' professional associations played the most prominent role during the Roberts and Alito hearings. The ABA and the National Bar Association, a group that represents African American lawyers, were the only two groups to take part in both the Roberts and Alito hearings. A variety of civil rights groups, including the Planned Parenthood Federation of America, the National Women's Law Center, the Mexican American Legal Defense and Education Fund, and the NAACP Legal Defense Fund participated in one of the two hearings. Only one business group, the National Association of Manufacturers, and one think tank, the Hudson Institute, participated in any capacity; both supported Roberts.

Position Taking

Taking a position on a judicial nominee is one of the most low cost and potentially high-visibility actions a group may take. Such actions serve to mobilize members, can help generate contributions to support the effort, and fulfill members' expectations. Understandably, a large number of groups announced formal positions on Roberts, Miers, and Alito.

Leading conservative groups such as PFA wasted little time endorsing John Roberts, doing so on July 21, 2005; and many other groups soon followed suit. Dr. James Dobson of Focus on the Family and Tony Perkins of the Family Research Council, for example, held a conference call with more than 200 reporters nationwide announcing their support of Roberts.[45] Dobson praised Roberts as a jurist "who will interpret the Constitution and not try to legislate from the bench."[46] These early endorsers gained later support from broadly based business groups such as the National Association of Manufacturers and the U.S. Chamber of Commerce.

Liberal groups, however, were more confounded about what to do with the Roberts nomination. Although Roberts was, by most estimates, a rather conservative judge, he was not the ideologue that many liberal groups had hoped to be able to oppose with vigor. Moreover, Roberts's scarce paper trail on the U.S. Court of Appeals for the District of Columbia made it difficult for liberal groups to gather significant ammunition against his nomination. Moreover, the Bush administration continued to drag its feet on producing Roberts's legal work from when he was an adviser to President Reagan. For these reasons, many liberal groups, including the National Bar Association and Alliance for Justice, were slow to commit themselves to a formal position, choosing instead to issue tentative reports on Roberts' judicial record in late July and early August and reserve formal judgment until closer to the nomination hearing.

The first broad-based liberal interest group to oppose Roberts was the 75,000-member PFAW, which announced its position more than a month after Roberts's initial nomination. In announcing the group's opposition, President Ralph Neas noted that PFAW's "review of John Roberts' record and the tens of thousands of pages of documents" the Bush administration eventually made public proved that Roberts would "endanger much of the progress made by the nation in civil rights over the past half-century. If John Roberts replaces Sandra Day O'Connor, the balance of the court will shift to the right for decades to come."[47] Still, the group's uncertainty was evident when it coupled its announcement with a refusal to say whether it would launch the kind of aggressive attack it had mounted eighteen years earlier over the Bork nomination.[48]

Soon after PFAW's announcement, other liberal groups such as the Leadership Conference on Civil Rights and the Alliance for Justice also announced their opposition. They joined PFAW and several other liberal groups that had announced their stance on the nominee earlier in the summer, including MoveOn.org, NARAL Pro-Choice America, the National Abortion Federation, and NOW, as the core of the opposition to Roberts.

Following President Bush's nomination of Harriet Miers, conservative groups were once again quick to take a formal position. While some groups, including PFA and the American Center for Law and Justice, expressed a willingness to support anyone selected by President Bush, many other conservative groups quickly declared their opposition to Miers. They viewed her as underqualified and, more important, not the conservative ideologue they had hoped to see fill Justice O'Connor's crucial swing seat on the Supreme Court. As noted earlier, liberal response to the Miers nomination was quite limited. Because Miers had almost no public record, groups such as NARAL Pro-Choice America took no official stance, and many believed that she was the best that they could expect.

The response time of the liberal groups changed dramatically when Bush nominated Samuel Alito to replace Miers's withdrawn nomination. Several key liberal groups, including PFAW and the Alliance for Justice announced their opposition to the Alito nomination within hours,[49] and other liberal groups, such as MoveOn.org and NARAL Pro-Choice America, quickly followed suit. There were, however, several stragglers in the liberal coalition, as some groups, including the National Urban League, chose to wait until after the holidays and the New Year to make their opposition official.

The conservative response to Alito was similar to the Roberts nomination. Prominent groups such as the Family Research Council and PFA were quick to express their support for the nominee. Conservative women's groups, including Concerned Women for America, mobilized and organized a press conference, entitled "Women for Alito," at the National Press Club. "We feel called once again as women to stand in opposition to the shrill radical women's organizations set to destroy Judge Alito ... and frankly any other nominee President Bush introduces," proclaimed Connie Mackey of the Family Research Council. She was joined at the podium by Women for Faith and Family's Mary Ellen Bork, wife of Robert H. Bork, who urged conservative women's groups not to let what happened to her husband happen to Judge Alito.[50]

Advertising

Advertising is a common tool in presidential and legislative elections. Thus, it should be no surprise that interest groups also use television and radio advertising to support or oppose judicial nominations. Although interest groups have advertised on television and radio for the past twenty years, the growth of cable news has increased the number of strategic opportunities for interest groups to reach particular audiences. In fact, nearly all of the ads for or against the Bush nominees were aired on cable news programs, which have audiences who are far more engaged in political affairs than most Americans.

Advertising in support of and in opposition to the Bush nominees began even before Justice O'Connor officially resigned from the Court. For example, PFA, a group that has consistently aired ads supporting the Bush administration's actions on a variety of fronts, launched a $250,000 advertising campaign in June 2005. This campaign emphasized the importance of a fair up or down vote for all judicial nominees.

MoveOn.org, a group that was begun during the impeachment of President Bill Clinton that uses Internet petitions and a Web site to raise large sums of money in very short periods of time, was the first liberal group to respond to the PFA ad. MoveOn.org responded on the day of Justice O'Connor's resignation with an ad that urged Americans to fight for a moderate jurist who would protect Americans' privacy. This $280,000 ad aired on cable news and in Maine, Nebraska, South Carolina, and Virginia.[51] MoveOn.org was later joined on the liberal side of the aisle by PFAW, which, a week after O'Connor's resignation, sponsored a national ad encouraging President Bush to nominate a judge who would protect Americans' fundamental freedoms.

The apparent ad battle slowed when President Bush selected John Roberts Jr. as his nominee. Although close to $2 million was spent on advertising in support of or in opposition to the Roberts nomination, two weeks after Bush announced his nominee, only two ads had hit the airwaves. One of these initial ads, produced by PFA, aired on cable news and during Sunday morning news talk shows and called Roberts "brilliant" and listed a number of the accolades he had accumulated throughout his judicial career. PFA followed this ad with one defending Roberts's right not to answer questions relating to issues such as abortion that could come before the Supreme Court.

The only other major conservative ad to hit the airwaves during the Roberts confirmation process was sponsored by the National Right to Life Committee. It aired in eight cities in Illinois. The ad targeted Senator Richard J. Durbin, D-Ill., who was once pro-life but now professes to be pro-choice. The ad attacked him for opposing the Roberts nomination because of Roberts's apparent pro-life stance on the abortion issue.

Although liberal groups did not run many ads during the Roberts nomination, one group sponsored what was perhaps the most talked about advertisement of the three Bush nominations. Created and paid for by NARAL Pro-Choice America, this ad accused Roberts of having ties to violent antiabortion protesters and being someone "whose ideology leads him to excuse violence against other Americans."[52] The ad generated an immediate uproar that forced NARAL to pull much of its targeted two-week, $500,000 ad buys. It also prompted PFA to launch a response ad that called NARAL "desperate" and accused it of "taking the low road."[53]

The relatively quiet advertising battle during the Roberts campaign carried over to the failed Miers nomination, with spending totaling just over $750,000. It is interesting that the Miers ads were sponsored by conservative groups with different views of her nomination. PFA once again led off with the first ad, which called Miers a trailblazer and encouraged senators to give her a fair up or down vote. In contrast, three weeks later, an ad sponsored by Americans for Better Justice ran only on the conservative FOX News Channel and featured sound bites from conservative ideologues such as Robert H. Bork and Rush Limbaugh, both of whom were critical of Miers's nomination. This ad ended by encouraging viewers to urge Bush to withdraw the nomination. Eventually, however, Miers opted to remove herself from consideration, paving the way for President Bush to nominate Judge Samuel A. Alito Jr.

Despite the relatively low levels of advertising during the Roberts and Miers nominations, forecasters expected that the Alito nomination would eclipse the spending and airwave activity that had occurred during the Bork nomination.[54] While more ads were aired about the Alito nomination than the Roberts or Miers nominations, interest groups still underperformed analysts' initial expectations.

Conservative groups once again accounted for the majority of spending and were led by PFA. The group sponsored a number of ads on cable news and in states such as Louisiana, North Dakota, and South Dakota, which Republicans carried in 2004 and whose Democratic senators faced reelection in 2006. All followed a similar format, attacking Alito's critics for their opposition and featuring an assortment of Alito defenders—professors, colleagues, and former clerks—who defended his judicial integrity. PFA also paid for former Alito clerks as well as conservative law professors to go to Arkansas, where they joined members of the Arkansas Family Council Action Committee on the steps of the state capitol to announce a ten-day, thirty-six-city tour in support of the nominee.

PFA's efforts to target potentially vulnerable senators were aided by the Coalition for a Fair Judiciary, which focused on senators in North and South Dakota, and the Family Research Council, which targeted senators in Nebraska. Each of these ads emphasized Alito's judicial experience and qualifications and accused liberals of being extremists out of touch with mainstream America.

In addition to their television ad buys, the Family Research Council also paid for several radio advertisements, which aired in South Dakota, Louisiana, and Arkansas and focused largely on issues of religious expression. A similar advertisement sponsored by the Committee for Justice hit airwaves in Colorado, Wisconsin, and West Virginia.

Liberal groups were once again less active on the airwaves than their conservative counterparts. Although PFAW was the first liberal group to purchase air time, the most active entity during the Alito nominations was a coalition of more than fifty groups that came together under the name of IndependentCourt.org. This coalition put together four different ads that aired on cable news and in several of the states targeted by conservative groups, including Arkansas and Maine. Its ads emphasized several of Alito's controversial lower court decisions, and they criticized his positions on a number of issues, including criminal law, abortion, and discrimination.

At first glance, the decision of interest groups to spend less on advertising than many analysts predicted is puzzling. It may be explained in part by a strategic decision not to spend money on a nonsalient issue; polls showed that Americans were not as tuned in to these nominations as they had been for Bork and Thomas. Furthermore, both Roberts and Alito had impeccable legal credentials, which made it difficult to arouse public dissent. And, the Alito nomination process ended up occurring over the holidays, a time when many Americans' attentions are focused elsewhere. While groups could use their members' intensity to raise funds, given the apparent inevitability of both nominees' confirmation, it made little sense for liberals to spend scarce resources on a losing campaign. In contrast, major advertising campaigns, especially targeted ones, made sense for conservatives who used the nominations as opportunities to mobilize and expand their base as they geared up to the 2006 midterm elections.

One final explanation may flow from the senators who were making their decisions on whether to confirm these nominees. During both the Roberts and Alito nominations, senators on both sides of the aisle expressed grave concerns about the tenor of the ads, and they tried to make it clear that they were not affecting their decisions. Senator Patrick Leahy, D-Vt., the ranking minority member of the Senate Judiciary Committee, was a particularly emphatic critic. In one interview before the Roberts nomination hearings, Leahy commented that interest groups were "wasting their money on ads." He asserted that outside lobbying groups "whether on the right or on the left, have become, for me anyway, basically irrelevant."[55]

Mass Mailings

Groups on both sides of the Roberts, Miers, and Alito nominations were just as quick to use the nominations as a reason to contact their members as in past Supreme Court nominations. Many of the mailings contained detachable postcards for members to send to their senators, suggested language for letters or phone numbers to call to voice an opinion on a particular nominee, or included petitions for members to sign. Nearly all of the mass mailings also contained urgent messages for funds to support a group's battle for or against the various nominees. These fundraising messages are particularly important because groups raise a large amount of their financial support during these kinds of high-visibility campaigns.

Even before Justice O'Connor retired, one conservative interest group, Concerned Women for America (CWA), was urging its members to write letters to the editor and to encourage President Bush to hold firm in nominating a "pro-Constitution nominee."[56] In November 2005, CWA told its membership that thanks to their involvement and gifts, CWA was able to play a vital role in the confirmation of John Roberts as chief justice. At its Capitol Hill headquarters, CWA staff and volunteers distributed T-shirts, stickers, pens, signs, and water bottles in support of the Roberts effort.[57] After Judge Alito's Senate confirmation, CWA informed its members that they had helped launch a nationwide coalition of profamily groups that included the Eagle Forum, the Teen Pact and Abstinence Clearinghouse, the Family Research Council, and Women of Faith and Family.[58]

Liberal groups also used mailings to mobilize their members before the Roberts nomination. For example, NARAL Pro-Choice America's president, Nancy Keenan, sent a letter to supporters noting that "[Justice O'Connor's] departure presents an opportunity to reshape the Court significantly as she has been the crucial swing-vote to protect many freedoms, including the health exception guaranteeing a woman's right to an abortion if her life or health is in danger."[59] Other groups followed with mass mailings after nominations were announced. During the Roberts nomination, for example, the Center for Reproductive Rights, a pro-choice litigating group, sent "Dear Friend" letters that noted the need for Judge Roberts to explain his views on reproductive rights to the Senate. It warned members to be ready for a potentially costly, state-by-state battle to protect abortion rights if Roberts was appointed to the Court.

Technology

The Roberts, Miers, and Alito nominations were the first nominations to the Supreme Court since 1994. In the more than ten years between those nominations and President Bush's appointments, the technological landscape changed dramatically. The Internet, e-mail, and blogs were just a few of the major innovations that occurred between 1994 and 2005.

A body of research has documented the growth of technology as a tool in electoral campaigns.[60] From candidate Web sites to the massive e-mail lists pioneered by former presidential candidate Howard Dean, interactivity has been a landmark of recent electoral campaigns. Interest groups, too, have used technology to their advantage during elections. Some groups, including MoveOn.org and PFA, have used the Internet as a fund-raising tool. Others have posted advertisements and reports on their Web sites, and still others have established blogs to follow electoral campaigns. Here we explore how groups translated technology into a tool to promote their points of view on the Roberts, Miers, and Alito nominations.

Web Sites.   The gateway to using the Internet to support or oppose judicial nominees is a Web site. All of the interest groups engaged in the battles over Roberts, Miers, and Alito had their own sites, and many groups launched additional ad hoc sites in support of or in opposition to the nominees. These sites and the groups' own home pages were updated regularly with information supporting or opposing nominees almost instantaneously following the announcement of each nominee. In one notable example, PFA took remarkably short amounts of time to update its Web site regarding Bush's nominees. It took the group just seven minutes to announce its support of Roberts online, eleven minutes for Harriet Miers, and thirty-nine minutes to update its Web page to announce its support of Alito.[61]

PFA also formed twenty ad hoc state coalitions, each with its own Web site, in an attempt to highlight the local relevance of each nomination.[62] While many groups posted their on-air political advertisements on their Web sites, PFA went one step further, allowing visitors to download their television ads onto iPods for more portable viewing.[63]

On the liberal side of the aisle, MoveOn.org used its Web site to organize a petition drive against the Roberts nomination that accused him of being anti-environment, anti-civil rights, and pro-life, three issues of substantial concern to its members. It also posted a similar petition targeted against Alito's nomination.

As the respective nomination proceedings unfolded, groups also tried to attract the public to their Web sites to read analyses of the nominees' paper trails. Their sites also included interactive features that allowed visitors to e-mail members of Congress in support of or in opposition to a nominee. Perhaps most important, these sites allowed browsers to make online contributions, a key factor to the survival of any interest group.

Some groups also reached beyond their own home pages to contact tech-savvy individuals. PFA, for example, spent $60,000 to buy ads on state and national news Web sites. Experts estimated that this ad buy allowed PFA to reach over 16 million potential supporters.[64]

E-mails.   Most interest groups have lists of members and addresses of contributors assembled and ready to use. For these groups, sending their supporters e-mails that inform them of their position on a particular judicial nomination is an extremely low-cost mobilization tool. Not only do such e-mails keep members apprised of political events, but they also provide the group with a way to maintain its presence at the forefront of their donors' minds. For liberal and conservative interest groups, the current polarized political environment and the controversial nature of President George W. Bush's nominations to the Supreme Court have provided an opportunity to attempt to mobilize their respective bases into action electronically.

Immediately following Justice O'Connor's resignation, for example, NARAL Pro-Choice America used a mass e-mail to introduce its Supreme Court action plan, Choose Justice. This plan positioned NARAL as a "critical educational, lobbying, organizing and strategic" player in the fight over the upcoming nominations. It committed NARAL to the goals of (1) exposing the anti-choice records of Bush nominees and continuing to publicize their hostility to a woman's right to choose; (2) mobilizing millions of pro-choice allies to flood the Senate with calls, e-mails, and letters demanding moderate, pro-choice nominees; and (3) empowering the Choice Action Network (CAN) with more than 800,000 grassroots activists, including 30,000 Rapid Responders, to take the campaign to their communities using online and on-the-ground tactics.[65] NARAL continued to use e-mails to urge its members to help accomplish these goals by attending rallies and demonstrations, making donations, contacting senators, and volunteering at the group's home office in Washington, D.C.

NARAL's flurry of e-mails were not particularly effective, however, as the group continued to suffer ramifications from the anti-Roberts television ad discussed earlier. Thus, NARAL, which had attempted to become the key player in opposition to the new nominees, never got enough traction to energize its members. Neither did NOW, another liberal group that relied heavily on e-mails to mobilize its members.

NOW did not begin sending out anti-Roberts e-mails until the middle of September 2005. After its meager efforts failed and Roberts was confirmed, NOW encouraged its members to express their thanks to the twenty-two senators who voted no on the nomination. This was followed by several other—largely ineffective—e-mails asking supporters to contact Justice O'Connor and ask her to remain on the bench, to join a rally on the steps of the Supreme Court to protest attacks on women's reproductive rights, and to demand that senators filibuster the Alito nomination.[66]

Much more successfully, on the conservative side, the American Center for Law and Justice (ACLJ) sent almost one million e-mails to its supporters on the evening of the Roberts nomination.[67] The ACLJ also sent nearly daily e-mails to supporters during the confirmation process, asking them to donate to the group. Late in August 2005, the ACLJ e-mailed its supporters to inform them that it had responded to a report by PFAW. PFAW's report, which attacked John Roberts, was refuted point-by-point by the ACLJ, which attempted to show the weaknesses of PFAW's claims and labeled Roberts "one of the best qualified nominees in the history of Supreme Court nominations."[68]

After Bush nominated Alito and Democrats were attempting to delay a vote, the ACLJ e-mailed its members that the Senate Judiciary Committee hearings on Judge Alito's nomination should proceed immediately. "It's time for the Senate to put aside the political posturing and move swiftly and without delay in confirmation hearings for Judge Samuel Alito," wrote Jay Sekulow, ACLJ's chief counsel.[69] PFA topped this effort by sending more than ten million e-mails to individuals on its own lists as well as on the lists of the Republican National Committee and other prominent conservative organizations.

Blogs.   Blogs, or Web journals, which exist on topics from politics to pets to sports, are updated regularly and can be both information sources and political platforms. During the 2004 election, for example, many news organizations even had blogs that collected and analyzed relevant stories about each of the campaigns; sites such as the Supreme Court blog sponsored by the *Washington Post* extended this idea to the judicial nomination process. But the work of independent bloggers and bloggers employed by interest groups was most important in spreading groups' messages about the three judicial nominees.

The coordination and organization of bloggers was particularly apparent among liberal groups, which were slow to respond on nearly every other front. Borrowing a tactic from Howard Dean's failed presidential campaign and MoveOn.org, NARAL Pro-Choice America, for example, updated its blog within hours of the initial nomination with talking points questioning Roberts's position on abortion.

In addition, BlogPAC, a group founded by several prominent liberal bloggers including the founder of the visible and influential Daily Kos, helped to organize a forty-five-minute conference call of bloggers the day after the Roberts nomination. The purpose of this call was to instruct liberal bloggers to continue to discuss Roberts so that the nomination remained in the forefront of readers' minds and on the public agenda. Although the call succeeded in reaching a number of bloggers, it did not lead to a unified message. Some bloggers chose to oppose Roberts vehemently while others chose to take a more moderate wait-and-see stance.[70] Still, liberal bloggers gave it their all, even going so far as to create a blog—AlitosAmerica.org—specifically to convince young people of the danger associated with an Alito appointment.

Conservative bloggers were also quick to learn from the use of blogs in the 2004 presidential campaign. Groups such as the ACLJ had online blog petitions, and a group called Blogs for Bush was especially active in mobilizing grassroots support for Roberts and Alito. New groups also turned to blogs to muster support for the nominees. The Confirm Alito Coalition blog, for example, was created on October 31, 2005, to give a voice to those supporting the judge.

Groups were not the only special interests to enter the blogosphere.[71] Nomination Nation, a blog run by lawyers at Goldstein & Howe, was just one example of myriad sites hosted by law firms and law schools. Blogs were so influential, in fact, that Harriet Miers told supporters at a post-nomination luncheon, "I think I needed you out in the blog world."[72]

Does Interest Group Activity Make a Difference?

By all accounts, conservative groups were quicker than their liberal counterparts to react and take strong positions on all three nominees. But were these quick reactions a major part of why the conservatives got what they wanted in all three cases? Probably not.

At the time of the nominations, Republicans held not only the presidency but also both houses of Congress. These majorities were almost certainly more important in determining the ultimate outcome of the recent nominations than any of the activity undertaken by interest groups on either side of the aisle. The Republican majorities may also go a long way toward explaining why liberal groups were less active during the recent nominations than many analysts expected.

Furthermore, many liberal interest groups suffer from outsider fatigue and find it increasingly difficult to muster the resources and grassroots support necessary to oppose judicial nominees, who often are not at the forefront of the public agenda in a time of war and concerns over domestic security. Moreover, without constituent pressure, members of the Senate are freer to follow their political party. One political expert, Charlie Cook, offered the following analysis of the Alito and Roberts nominations: "What you see is activists on each side posturing, but the American people aren't engaged in this debate." Cook asserted that the American public was instead more engaged in issues that affect their daily lives more directly, including the war in Iraq and the economy.[73]

The power of external political variables does not mean that interest groups have no place in the judicial nomination process. Their role is, however, greater in the case of a nominee who has true shortcomings, be they political, ideological, or ethical.[74] In the cases of Bork and Thomas, for example, interest groups played an important role in determining the outcome of the nomination process. By successfully raising public awareness about the ideological, intellectual, and constitutional philosophies of these nominees, liberal interest groups got the public—the constituents of the men and women who serve in the Senate—to pay attention and make their opinions heard. Still, without good targets and an attuned public, it is difficult for any interest groups opposing a nomination to be successful. Thus, in the interest group world it makes little sense to waste scarce resources on unwinnable wars.

Notes

1. Nathan Hakman, "Lobbying the Supreme Court: An Appraisal of the Political Science Folklore," *Fordham Law Review* 36 (1966): 15–50.
2. Lauren M. Cohen, "Missing in Action: Interest Groups and Federal Judicial Appointments," *Judicature* 82 (1998): 119–123.
3. In 2006, the ABA had 400,000 members.
4. The ABA, nevertheless, has continued to provide evaluation of the professional qualifications of nominees for the administration, the Senate, and the public.
5. A filibuster is a procedural tactic allowed by Senate rules that permits an individual senator or group of senators to prevent voting on a bill or on a nominee. A senator launching a filibuster must talk without stopping. The only way that senator can then be cut off is by a three-fifths vote of the Senate. If this occurs, a vote can then be taken on the bill or on the nominee. Filibusters are quite rare and are most often used as a threat rather than as an actual action to stall a vote.
6. In 2005, fourteen members of the Senate joined in a bipartisan coalition to agree not to filibuster any well-qualified candidates for any federal judgeships, including nominees to the U.S. Supreme Court. Without this action, the fourteen feared that Republicans would resort to what was being termed the "nuclear option." The nuclear option is a parliamentary procedure that would allow the filibuster to be ended with a simple majority of fifty-one votes rather than the supermajority of sixty votes that is traditionally required.
7. Henry J. Abraham, "Nominees, Rejection of," in *The Oxford Companion to the Supreme Court of the United States*, 2d ed., ed. Kermit L. Hall (New York: Oxford University Press, 2005), 692.
8. Paul A. Freund, "Essays on the Supreme Court Appointment Process: Appointment of Justices: Some Historical Perspectives," *Harvard Law Review* 101 (1988): 1146–1163.
9. Karen O'Connor, *Women's Organizations' Use of the Courts* (Lexington, Mass.: Lexington Books, 1980); and Clement E. Vose, "The National Consumers League and the Brandeis Brief," *Midwest Journal of Political Science* 1 (1957): 267–290.
10. O'Connor, *Women's Organizations' Use of the Courts.*
11. Freund, "Essays on the Supreme Court Appointment Process."
12. Ibid.
13. John Anthony Maltese, "The Selling of Clement Haynsworth: Politics and the Confirmation of Supreme Court Justices," *Judicature* 72 (1989): 339–347.
14. Quoted in Norman Viera and Leonard Gross, *Supreme Court Appointments: Judge Bork and the Politicization of Senate Confirmations* (Carbondale: Southern Illinois University Press, 1998).
15. Viera and Gross, *Supreme Court Appointments.*
16. Steven J. Rosenstone and John Mark Hansen, *Mobilization, Participation, and Democracy in America* (New York: Macmillan, 1993), 109–110.
17. David O'Brien, *Storm Center: The Supreme Court in American Politics* (New York: Norton, 2003).

18. Jeffrey M. Berry, *Interest Group Society*, 3d ed. (New York: Longman, 1997).
19. Viera and Gross, *Supreme Court Appointments*, 33.
20. Ibid.
21. O'Brien, *Storm Center*.
22. Berry, *Interest Group Society*.
23. Coalitions for America was an umbrella organization of conservative interest groups founded by Paul M. Weyrich, an architect of the successful conservative movement that began in the 1980s. As early as 1973, he worked with other conservatives to found the Heritage Foundation, a conservative think tank, to counter the more liberal Brookings Institution.
24. Christine DeGregorio and Jack E. Rossotti, "Campaigning for the Court: Interest Group Participation in the Bork and Thomas Confirmation Processes," in *Interest Group Politics*, 4th ed., ed. Allan J. Cigler and Burdett A. Loomis (Washington, D.C.: CQ Press: 1995).
25. O'Brien, *Storm Center*.
26. Berry, *Interest Group Society*.
27. O'Brien, *Storm Center*, 81.
28. Martin Shapiro, "Interest Groups and Supreme Court Appointments," *Northwestern University Law Review* 84 (1990): 935.
29. Shapiro, "Interest Groups and Supreme Court Appointments"; and Robert H. Salisbury, "An Exchange Theory of Interest Groups," *Midwest Journal of Political Science* 12 (1969): 1–32.
30. Donald R. Matthews and James A. Stimson, *Yeas and Nays: Normal Decision-Making in the U.S. House of Representatives* (New York: Wiley, 1975).
31. Gregory A. Caldeira and John R. Wright, "Lobbying for Justice: Organized Interest Supreme Court Nominations, and United States Senate," *American Journal of Political Science* 42 (1998): 499–523; see also Gregory A. Caldeira, Marie Hojnacki, and John R. Wright, "Lobbying Activities of Organized Interests in Federal Judicial Nominations," *Journal of Politics* 62 (2000): 51–69; Arthur T. Denazu and Michael C. Munger, "Legislators and Interest Groups: How Unorganized Interests Get Represented," *American Political Science Review* 80 (1986): 89–106; and John Mark Hansen, *Gaining Access: Congress and the Farm Lobby, 1919–1981* (Chicago: University of Chicago Press, 1981).
32. Caldeira and Wright, "Lobbying for Justice," 509.
33. Souter was nominated to the Court by President George H.W. Bush in 1990 and ultimately was confirmed by the Senate by a 90–9 vote after thirteen liberal and eight conservative groups appeared before the Senate Judiciary Committee.
34. Caldeira and Wright, "Lobbying for Justice."
35. Cohen, "Missing in Action."
36. Ibid., 120.
37. Seth Stern and Keith Perine, "Beyond the Roberts Confirmation," *CQ Weekly*, September 30, 2005, 2650.
38. Seth Stern, "Roberts Questionnaire Shows White House Was Vetting Candidates Months Ago," *CQ Weekly*, August 5, 2005, 2192.
39. "NY Times Reported That Miers Withdrew 'Because of Criticism of her Credentials, Not Her Views'—But Her Views Generated Strong Conservative Opposition," Media Matters for America, November 4, 2005, http://www.mediamatters.org/items/200511040013, April 15, 2005.
40. Christopher G. Anderson, "Conservative Opposition to Miers Heats Up," *Jurist* 25 (October 2005): 1.
41. Quoted in Anderson, "Conservative Opposition to Miers Heats Up," 1.
42. Quoted in Mel Seesholtz, "'Sincerely Yours': Samuel Alito's Letter to James Dobson," Counterbias.com, March 9, 2006, http://www.counterbias.com/586.html, March 9, 2006.

43. Kate Michelman, who served as president of NARAL Pro-Choice America for eighteen years, was called to testify. Her replacement, Nancy Keenan, was not. Thus, Michelman was testifying as a private citizen.

44. During 2005 and 2006, subcommittees of the House and Senate Judiciary Committees that were dealing with constitutional issues such as the right to privacy and *Roe v. Wade* held hearings on these controversial issues and intentionally excluded liberal interest groups from testifying. Instead, subcommittee staff worked with lawyers at large Washington, D.C.-based law firms that often do pro bono work for liberal interest groups to secure pro-choice legal academics not affiliated with any groups to testify in support of continued privacy rights.

45. Michael A. Fletcher and Thomas B. Edsall, "Campaign Is on for Roberts: Liberals Are Wary as Conservatives Gear Up," *Washington Post*, August 7, 2005, sec. D.

46. Quoted in Fletcher and Edsall, "Campaign Is on for Roberts."

47. Quoted in Michael McGough, "First Liberal Group States Stance against Roberts," *Pittsburgh Post-Gazette*, August 25, 2005, sec. A.

48. McGough, "First Liberal Group."

49. Natalia Kennedy, "Interest Group Showdown over Alito Likely to Trigger Major Ad War," Justice at Stake Campaign, November 3, 2005, http://www.justiceatstake. org/contentViewer.asp?breadcrumb=7,55,718, April 17, 2006.

50. "Conservative Women Unite to Support Alito," *Christian Post*, January 6, 2006, 1.

51. Marcia Davis, "And the Nominee Is: a) All Right b) Not Quite: The Supreme Court Succession Campaign Turns Shockingly Sedate," *Washington Post*, August 7, 2005, sec. D.

52. Sheryl Gay Stohlberg, "Abortion Rights Group Plans to Pull Ad on Roberts," *New York Times*, August 12, 2005, sec. A.

53. Quoted in Stohlberg, "Abortion Rights Group."

54. Natalia Kennedy, "In Run-Up to Alito Confirmation Hearings, Experts Predict Biggest Ad War since Bork: After Holiday Reprieve, Sides Gird for Battle," Brennan Center for Justice, press release, January 5, 2006.

55. Jamie Wilson, "Abortion Rights Group Launches Campaign against Bush Nominee," *Guardian*, August 12, 2005, 11.

56. Jan LaRue, "A Litmus Test for Judges?" *Family Voice*, July–August 2005, 8–9.

57. "CWA's Amos Project Wins with Chief Justice Roberts," *Family Voice*, November–December 2005, 4–5.

58. Pamela P. Wong, "A+ for Alito: CWA Played Big Role in New Justice's Confirmation," *Family Voice*, March–April 2006, 8–9.

59. Nancy Keenan, "Dear Dr. O'Connor," letter, July 1, 2005.

60. James A. Thurber and Colton Campbell, *Congress and the Internet* (Upper Saddle River, N.J.: Prentice Hall, 2002).

61. Glen Justice, "Set for Alito Battle, with Dollars at the Ready," *New York Times*, November 14, 2005, sec. A.

62. "Progress for America Announces 20 State Coalitions, Websites," Progress for America, August 8, 2005, http://www.prnewswire.com/cgi-bin/stories.pl?ACCT =104&STORY=/www/story/08-08-2005/0004084430&EDATE=, April 17, 2006.

63. Justice, "Set for Alito Battle."

64. Progress for America, "Progress for America Announces 20 State Coalitions, Websites."

65. NARAL Pro Choice America, "Supreme Court Action Plan: Choose Justice," e-mail, July 15, 2005, from can@ProChoiceAmerica.org.

66. NOW National Action Center, "NOW Goes to Court," e-mail, November 29, 2005, from now@now.org.

67. Mark Memmot, "Interest Groups Immediately Line Up Forces in Debate," *USA Today*, July 20, 2005, sec. A.

68. "ACLJ Responds to People for the American Way's Attack against Supreme Court Nominee John Roberts," American Center for Law and Justice, n.d., http://www. aclj.org/media/pdf/PFAW_Rebuttal_MemoF.pdf, May 9, 2006.

69. "ACLJ: Don't Play Political Games With Confirmation Hearings for Supreme Court Nominee Judge Samuel Alito," American Center for Law and Justice, January 9, 2006, http://www.aclj.org/news/Read.aspx?ID=2067, May 9, 2006.

70. Howard Kurtz, "Court Nominee in the Eye of the Blogger Swarm," *Washington Post*, July 21, 2005, sec. C.

71. Harriet Miers was the latest in a line of famous—or infamous—individuals, including Kim Jong-il and Hulk Hogan, to have a spoof blog established by creative users of blogspot.com. On harrietmiers.blogspot.com, the writers, pretending to be the nominee, engage in a number of creative campaign tactics, including posting a series of graphics promoting Miers's nomination and gushing about the nominees' favorite color—pink, of course!

72. Quoted in Colleen McCain Nelson, "White House Counsel Speaks in Dallas," *Dallas Morning News*, April 29, 2006.

73. Quoted in Jo Becker, "Television Ad War on Alito Begins: Liberals Try to Paint Court Pick as Tool of the Right Wing," *Washington Post*, November 18, 2005, sec. A.

74. Lee Epstein et al., "The Changing Dynamics of Senate Voting on Supreme Court Nominees," *Journal of Politics* 68 (2006): 296–307; Jeffrey A. Segal and Harold J. Spaeth, *The Supreme Court and the Attitudinal Model Revisited* (Cambridge: Cambridge University Press, 2002), ch. 5.

16

Emerging Issues, New Organizations
Interest Groups and the Making
of Nanotechnology Policy

Christopher J. Bosso and Ruben Rodrigues

Where do interest groups come from? That question has drawn the attention of scholars for more than fifty years. Especially in the wake of economist Mancur Olson's analysis in the 1960s, political scientists could no longer assume that groups would spring up in some organic way when the political system somehow required such organization. As Robert Salisbury observed, groups need entrepreneurs to build them, often in a context of affluence, as much as they need issues that will motivate members to join. Organized interests proliferated in the second half of the twentieth century, yet it remains unclear why groups organize when and how they do.

In this chapter, Christopher J. Bosso and Ruben Rodrigues take advantage of the emergence of a new technology and its related industry to track the rise of group representation within an economic sector—nanotechnology—that is almost certain to grow rapidly in the decades to come. Indeed, the authors observe that organized interests have grown directly in response to national government policies that have created, within the nanotechnology policy community, a new set of stakeholders. Although we often think of individual members or companies as forming groups, organized interests frequently receive substantial assistance from patrons such as wealthy individuals, foundations, or the government itself. Bosso and Rodrigues point to the federal government as the key patron in encouraging the growth of nanotechnology groups; such organizations are useful for the government in that they can represent various parts of an important emerging economic sector.

Although this chapter addresses a relatively small (if expanding) number of groups, it offers a way to understand the roles organized interests play in the give-and-take of American politics. The interests certainly find it useful to organize, but so too does the government, which relies on groups to formulate and implement policies within a complex and changing policy arena.

This chapter examines the emergence of a new policy advocacy community, so new that its dimensions remain a bit embryonic. The community in question is emerging around research, development, and, sooner than many realize, commercialization of products, substances, and devices based on nanotechnology—"the ability to work at the molecular level, atom by atom, to create large structures of fundamentally new molecular organization."[1] In its simplest form, nanotechnology combines advances in the sciences and engineering to manipulate substances at the scale of one billionth of a meter. A human hair, to offer contrast, is approximately 10,000 nanometers in diameter—so we're talking really small.[2]

The promise of nanotechnology lies in taking advantage of unique, and still as yet incompletely understood, nanoscale properties of substances like carbon to create revolutionary new products and devices. New types of computer circuits based on self-assembled carbon nanowires, for example, may eliminate the problem of excess heat that currently limits miniaturization in silicon-based microelectronics, leading to dramatic leaps in computing power and memory to the point that, as President Bill Clinton exuberantly exclaimed in a December 2000 speech, it will be possible to shrink "all of the information housed at the Library of Congress into the device the size of a sugar cube."[3]

Other nanoscale innovations hold promise for a wide range of medical applications (for example, destroying individual cancer cells, alleviating Parkinson's disease), defense uses (nearly impenetrable body armor, sensing devices for detecting biological and nuclear threats), in energy (solar power generation, storage, and transmission), and, in between, everything serious and silly (carbon nanotube-enhanced golf clubs, for example). Some even see nanotechnology, paired with parallel revolutions in genetic engineering and artificial intelligence, one day producing profoundly new forms of human-machine consciousness.[4] Considered as a distinct sector, nanotechnology has in a very short period of time become a really big deal in the popular imagination—ominously in Michael Crichton's technothriller, *Prey*,[5] and prosaically in what its most ardent proponents predict will be the "Next Industrial Revolution."[6]

Based on such prognoses, the field is awash with optimistic predictions about nanotechnology's commercial potential, with estimates of a global market in the $1 trillion–$3 trillion range within a decade. Not surprisingly, both the public and private sectors are expending significant resources to promote the rapid development and effective commercialization of nanoscale applications. The U.S. government alone is now spending over $1 billion annually in targeted nanoscale research and development (R&D), private sector expenditures are estimated to equal if not exceed that figure, and many state governments are funding their own (often rather loosely defined) nanotechnology initiatives to ensure their future economic competitiveness.[7] Similar initiatives are evident in any number of other nations, notably South Korea, Japan, Germany, the United Kingdom, and, of course, China.

This next industrial revolution isn't happening on its own. As so often is the case in economic sectors requiring substantial and sometimes speculative investments in basic scientific research and technological development, the federal government is leading the way, in this instance with a vast R&D effort that, in turn, is laying the foundations for a potentially broad and internally variegated nanotechnology policy domain.[8]

The story of how the federal government, in the guise of the interagency National Nanotechnology Initiative (NNI), is fostering the emergence of a broad-spectrum nanotechnology advocacy sector is worth telling from the perspective of interest group scholarship. A lot of our literature focuses on how advocacy groups seek to shape issue politics and public policy, and under what circumstances.[9] In this instance, one question is whether groups as commonly understood had any role in originally shaping what has become the major federal science and technology effort of the current era, one nearly equal in scale and breadth to the space program of the 1960s.

The short answer to that question is "not much" because the nanotechnology policy domain is so new that there were relatively few organized actors positioned to advocate for or against particular dimensions of what emerged. Instead, federal policy developed largely through the efforts of a network of scientists within the federal establishment, supported by an array of like-minded university researchers and industries interested in an expansive federal R&D role focused on the physical sciences. In some ways, federal nanotechnology R&D policy fits our classic understanding of clientele politics, with federal science elites serving as the patrons.[10]

If interest groups as classically understood played little role in the development of current federal nanotechnology policy, the more interesting question is how government action designed to promote a set of national goals has very quickly led to the formation of a clutch of economic and advocacy interests that in many ways have come together into a loose but identifiable policy advocacy community, one that already displays discernible internal divisions. The emergence of a nanotechnology policy community is a notable example of government actions in the form of programs and budget allocations spawning a broad array of stakeholders who then organize themselves into an array of conventional advocacy organizations. In short, new policy precedes and produces new interest groups as well as provokes established groups to reposition themselves in response to perceived new opportunities or threats.

This chapter offers a broad description of the formation of the NNI, its immediate impacts on the array of actors with a vested interest in a strong federal fiscal commitment to nanotechnology R&D, and the emergence of an array of organized interests that are forming an embryonic nanotechnology policy domain. The chapter concludes by speculating on the eventual evolution of this domain and its attendant interests as public awareness about nanotechnology grows and as the nature of relevant policy questions moves in tandem with nanotechnology's own transition from an R&D effort to real applications, with real impacts on people's lives.

Government as Patron

Where do organized interests come from? At first glance this seems like an odd question. They exist because someone created them to do something. Yet the question isn't as simple, or simplistic, as it appears; and any assessment about any type of organized interest, be it a business association or a public interest advocacy group, must go back to origins: Why does it exist at all? How did it emerge, and what do the contexts of its origins tell us about the eventual composition of entire communities of organized interests?[11]

The political science literature on group formation is especially rich.[12] For our purposes, the most relevant line of inquiry sees advocacy organizations as intentional creations, designed to promote specific goals. The classic imagery here is of the policy entrepreneur who creates an advocacy group, attracts adherents to the cause, and through it pursues some political or policy end.[13] An important variation on this emphasis on the individual as entrepreneur is the patron who provides a new organization with critical seed capital and acts as its sponsor until it can walk on its own.[14] Scholars working out of this perspective tend to focus on the range of incentives that entrepreneurs extend to potential and current members in order to mobilize their support, maintain the organization, and wield influence in government.

But government itself is a patron, in many instances the most important one. Most often this dynamic of advocacy organization formation is a by-product of new policies or programs. As scholars like Jack Walker and James Q. Wilson observed, new policies create new stakeholders who then organize themselves (or who are represented by altruistic others) to maintain and even extend that policy, especially when economic self-interest is involved. Walker in particular believed that "intense, spontaneous political activities were the exception in our political system, and that highly organized and effective political activities required institutional and, particularly, governmental patrons except in extraordinary periods of social or political upheaval."[15]

Indeed, the story of American interest group formation over time reflects the expanded role of government itself. A telling early example of this dynamic is the American Farm Bureau Federation (AFBF), which emerged following passage in 1914 of the Smith-Lever Act establishing the Agricultural Extension Service in the U.S. Department of Agriculture. The service created and relied on a vast network of county extension agents to bring modern information and techniques to the farm, act as conduits for federal agricultural support, and, perhaps most important, organize farmers on their own behalf. Through the act the Agricultural Extension Service nurtured the development of county and state farm bureaus, the proliferation of which quickly led to the formation of a national federation of farm bureaus, the AFBF. Thus, the Smith-Lever Act was a charter for an advocacy and constituency service organization that continues to dominate U.S. agricultural politics and policymaking.[16]

In a smaller but informative subset of instances, individual government officials directly created external advocacy organizations to strengthen their own hands in intramural battles over policy and funding. A notable example here is the formation of the Wilderness Society, which traces its origins to an October 1934 roadside discussion among four advocates for wilderness preservation concerned that an aggressive New Deal road-building program, designed to make national parks and forests more accessible to automobiles while also providing thousands of sorely needed jobs, threatened what was left of "pure" wilderness, especially roadless tracts managed by the U.S. Forest Service.[17] Two of these men were sitting federal officials: Benton MacKaye, regional planner with the Tennessee Valley Authority (and "Father of the Appalachian Trail"), and Robert Marshall, head forester for the Bureau of Indian Affairs in the Department of the Interior. They founded the Wilderness Society to mobilize public support for wilderness preservation, thus creating an external ally in their own battles within the federal establishment. Marshall, as a result of inherited wealth, even acted as the organization's financial benefactor, enabling the Wilderness Society to pursue an uncompromising stance on wilderness preservation without fear of alienating potential contributors.[18] In some ways, as wilderness advocate David Brower later observed, the Wilderness Society "intentionally tied itself too closely to the Forest Service, to be its non-governmental supporter and watchdog."[19] Such examples of direct and visible government patronage—the formation of the National Wildlife Federation in 1936 also comes to mind—were remarkably common during the interwar era, probably the time that the United States most resembled a corporatist state.[20]

But these instances are the exceptions, and the emergence of the AFBF reflects the more typical narrative in interest group formation in the United States over time. In this story line, federal policy, initiated by governing elites, sooner or later begets organized interests whose existence is dedicated to defending that policy and any attendant spending. Whether this inevitable dynamic is seen as a good thing for public policy, the budget, or democratic government is a matter of debate and often breaks down along ideological lines on the size and scope of government.[21] The story of the NNI and its impacts on group formation may well be a more high-tech version of an old theme—think of university scientists instead of farmers—but it is nonetheless worth examination if only because it is important to study the dynamic of interest group creation as it unfolds.

Constructing the NNI

> If I were asked for an area of science and engineering that will most likely produce the breakthroughs of tomorrow, I would point to nanoscale science and engineering.
>
> *Neal Lane, Assistant to the President*
> *for Science and Technology, April 1998*[22]

For our purposes, the federal government's focus on nanotechnology begins in 1996, when an unofficial group of staff members and scientists representing an array of federal agencies including the National Science Foundation (NSF), the National Institutes of Health (NIH), the Department of Defense, and the Department of Energy and coordinated by the White House Office of Science and Technology Policy (OSTP) began to meet informally to discuss respective research plans in an emerging area of basic science and technological development.[23] Two years later this group was formalized as the Interagency Working Group on Nanoscience Engineering and Technology (IWGN) under the president's National Science and Technology Council (NSTC), and it was given the mandate to devise a coordinated plan for federal support for nanotechnology R&D built on extensive collaboration among researchers in federal agencies, universities, and affected industries.[24]

The IWGN convened a series of workshops and studies to assess the state of scientific knowledge and to forecast the potential applications for nanotechnology, and in 1999 it issued two reports. The first, "Nanostructure Science and Technology," compared U.S. nanoscale research within the international context and proposed ways to enhance American competitiveness in a field of technological development whose national security implications seemed to parallel its commercial potential.[25] The second, "Nanotechnology Research Directions," drew on the results of a workshop organized by the IWGN that brought together over 150 participants from federal agencies, government laboratories, universities, and interested companies like DuPont and Monsanto.[26] "Nanotechnology Research Directions" first described how advances in nanotechnology could have immense benefits for national economic growth, health care, and national security; second, it identified challenges and opportunities regarding nanotechnology development in the United States.

Soon thereafter, the IWGN was reconstituted as the Subcommittee on Nanoscale Science, Engineering and Technology of the National Science and Technology Council and, in that guise, drafted plans for an overarching national initiative to promote nanoscale R&D across the federal establishment and in myriad applications. Working with the OSTP, the White House, and the President's Council of Advisors on Science and Technology (PCAST), the committee laid out a detailed vision for the future in the *National Nanotechnology Initiative: The Initiative and Its Implementation Plan*, released in February 2000. Funding for the NNI, starting at over \$200 million a year, was included in the president's budget request to Congress for fiscal year 2001.[27]

At the same time, and not at all coincidentally, support for an expansive and coordinated federal nanotechnology program was becoming part of the elite-level discourse. In an opinion piece, "We Must Fund the Scientific Revolution," in the *Washington Post* on October 18, 1999, former Speaker of the House Newt Gingrich (a Republican) called for ramping up government investment in scientific research, and he explicitly mentioned nanotechnology as a priority. In January 2000, President Clinton (a Democrat) echoed that call in a speech at the California Institute of Technology, where Clinton proposed a major increase in overall federal R&D spending but with specific mention of nanotechnology.[28] With flush budgets as far as the eye could then see, and with no apparent partisan discord on the matter, Congress cleared the necessary appropriations bills in December 2000, leading to the creation of a National Nanotechnology Coordination Office charged with the task of implementing and overseeing the NNI.

Early on, the NNI emphasized targeted investments in basic nanoscale R&D. In 2003, Congress broadened the focus to include the initiative's capacity to translate government-sponsored research into commercial products and to serve homeland security needs after September 11, 2001. A bipartisan coalition of congressional supporters of sustained federal investments in nanotechnology R&D, led by members of the House Committee on Science, proposed legislation to boost spending in directions that best gave the United States a competitive advantage in the global marketplace. Subcommittee meetings were held in both the House Committee on Science and in the Senate Committee on Commerce, Science, and Transportation; attendees were almost exclusively federal science officials, university researchers, and corporate representatives. Support for the initiative generated little opposition, and on December 3, 2003, President Bush signed the 21st Century Nanotechnology Research and Development Act into law at an Oval Office signing ceremony attended by relevant members of Congress, agency officials, and industry representatives.

A Downsian Mobilization?

In their 1994 book, *Agendas and Instabilities in American Politics*, Baumgartner and Jones coined the term *Downsian mobilization*—after Anthony Downs's influential article, "Up and Down with Ecology: The Issue-Attention Cycle"[29]—to describe periods during which the dominant strain of interest mobilization typically reflected unconstrained enthusiasm for a new policy, program, or technology.[30] Based on evidence to date, one can argue that in part nanotechnology policy advocacy reflects broad and rather uniform enthusiasm for the potential benefits of the research under way. In some respects this is because current nanotechnology policy is mostly defined by federal research funding—a lot of it—and by generally positive media coverage of the potential benefits of this research. Any contrary voices, to date, are minority views.

A great deal of this enthusiasm may reflect basic economic self-interest, whether indirect (increased support for basic research in the physical sciences and engineering) or direct (expected profits from nanotechnologies). There are already dozens of public and private institutions and firms, representing thousands of employees, with some type of economic stake in the future of nanotechnology. These firms, along with their kindred spirits situated in relevant congressional committees and federal agencies, could provide the basis for a future nanotechnology subgovernment to promote future direct spending for and policy decisions in support of the sector.[31]

The 21st Century Nanotechnology Research and Development Act increased overall federal funding for nanotechnology-specific research to $3.7 billion over four years, established guidelines for ensuring effective technology transfer from the laboratory to commercial production, and created the National Nanotechnology Advisory Panel (NNAP) to set and oversee short-, medium-, and long-term goals for the NNI. As Figure 16.1

Figure 16.1.   Direct Federal Spending on the National
Nanotechnology Initiative, 2000–2007

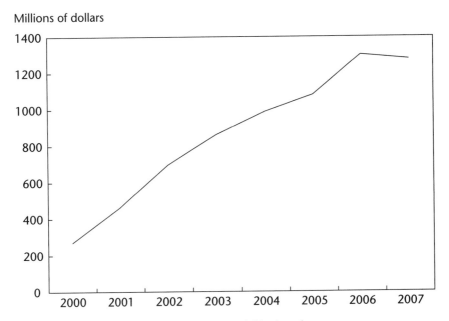

Millions of dollars

Source: National Nanotechnology Initiative data compiled by the authors.

Note: Data are shown according to fiscal year; FY 2006 is estimated, FY 2007 is the administration's request.

shows, annual federal spending for nanotechnology R&D through the NNI alone rose quickly thereafter, to over $1 billion annually.

The impacts of such federal largesse can be measured in several ways, starting with the sheer number of academic institutions that have garnered federal funding for nanoscale research (see Box 16.1). As of May 2006,

---

Box 16.1. Universities with One or More Major National Nanotechnology Initiative (NNI) Centers or Institutes, June 2006

Arizona State University
Baylor University
Brown University
California Institute of Technology
Central Michigan University
Columbia University
Cornell University
Emory University
Georgia Institute of Technology
Harvard University
Howard University
Johns Hopkins University
Massachusetts Institute of Technology
Michigan State University
Northeastern University
Northwestern University
Pennsylvania State University
Princeton University
Purdue University
Rensselaer Polytechnic Institute
Rice University
Stanford University
Texas A&M
University of Alabama
University of Arkansas
University of California, Los Angeles
University of California, San Diego
University of California, San Francisco
University of California, Santa Barbara
University of Illinois, Urbana-Champaign
University of Maryland

(continued)

Box 16.1.   *(continued)*

University of Massachusetts, Amherst
University of Minnesota
University of Nebraska, Lincoln
University of New Mexico
University of North Carolina
University of Oklahoma
University of Pennsylvania
University of Texas at Austin
University of Virginia
University of Washington
University of Wisconsin, Madison
Washington University
Yale University

---

the NNI alone supported coordinated funding for twenty-two major NSF university-based centers and networks (each at $1–$3 million annually), fourteen NIH centers, three major Department of Defense centers (for example, the Institute for Soldier Nanotechnologies at the Massachusetts Institute of Technology), five Department of Energy centers, four National Aeronautics and Space Administration centers, and centers at the National Institute of Standards and Technology and the National Institute for Occupational Safety and Health. That's a lot of federal money spread out among an array of government centers and university laboratories. Indeed, the distribution of federal spending for nanotechnology throughout the country might bring to mind the wry observation that the ideal weapons program is that which has a subcontractor in each of 435 House districts, were it not for rigorous peer review of grant proposals (the occasional legislative earmark notwithstanding).

The typical NNI research center involves a web of collaborating universities, companies, and outreach partners (for example, a local science museum), so the impact of each center goes far beyond the core institution. For example, the Center for High-rate Nanomanufacturing at Northeastern University, with which the authors are affiliated, extends to a team of research faculty and student assistants at four universities in three states, has connections with scholars in at least seven other universities around the world, and works with any number of private sector firms, state economic development officials, and educators.[32] This pattern is repeated throughout the NNI, thereby amplifying the impacts of any single grant.

Figure 16.2 shows the trend in the number of U.S. universities getting direct NSF support for nanotechnology research of some type over the

Figure 16.2.   Universities with Direct National Science
Foundation Support for Nanotechnology
Research, 2001–2006

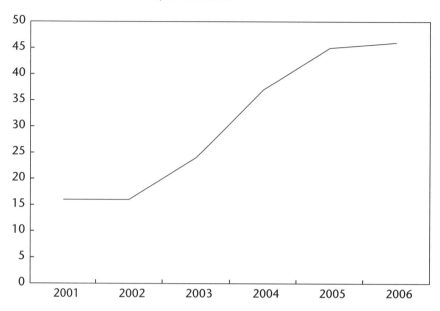

Source: National Science Foundation data compiled by the authors.

life of the NNI. Such figures do not reflect the significant additional funding by the NIH and federal agencies like the Department of Defense and
the Department of Energy, among others. Although NNI funding for
nanotechnology research does not automatically make recipients mindless
advocates for continued funding or outright enthusiasts for the technology
in question, the centrality of soft money to basic science research does
argue for a keen and not always selfless interest in continuing support.
Indeed, a few observers, usually reflecting libertarian views about the role
of government, have aired concerns that the NNI undermines the discipline imposed by markets and that it is little more than a massive pork
barrel science project.[33]

As expected, and as desired by Congress, robust federal spending on
nanoscale R&D has begun to stimulate the formation of private sector
nanotechnology companies, some of them spin-offs founded by university researchers whose basic research was funded by the federal government. Figure 16.3 shows the trend in the founding of new nanotechnology
companies, broadly (if imprecisely) defined. These totals do not reflect
significant investments in nanoscale R&D by established companies
like DuPont, IBM, Sherwin-Williams, Monsanto, and Intel, to name just
a few, nor does it include the innumerable law firms that have already

Figure 16.3. Nanotechnology Company Startups in the United States, by Year, 1980–2004

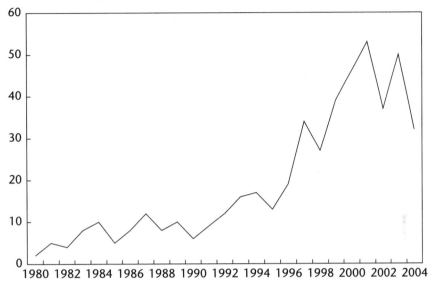

Number of startups

Source: International Nanotechnology Business directory data compiled by the authors; http://www.nanovip.com/.

Note: Data for 2004 may be incomplete.

started up nanotechnology practices and hired additional patent experts to handle the expected deluge of new patents and related intellectual property fights. Moreover, there is already in place a "nano-media" of sorts, ranging from specialized journals like *Nanotechnology Law and Business* to more broad-based outlets like the puckishly named *Small Times*. Anyone who types the term *nanotechnology* into Google or Yahoo! will certainly get the point.

An Emerging Nanotechnology Advocacy Community

Tonight I announce an American Competitiveness Initiative, to encourage innovation throughout our economy, and to give our nation's children a firm grounding in math and science. First, I propose to double the federal commitment to the most critical basic research programs in the physical sciences over the next 10 years. This funding will support the work of America's most creative minds as they explore promising areas such as nanotechnology, supercomputing, and alternative energy sources.

President George W. Bush, State of the Union Address,
January 31, 2006[34]

A few years after the inception of the NNI, we already see the out-lines of a constellation of institutions and actors with a shared stake in the future of nanotechnology R&D. Not surprisingly, we are beginning to see the outlines of a definable nanotechnology policy community, with already discernible camps within.

To further our understanding of the emergence of organized interests, it is useful here to delineate among nanotechnology enthusiasts, hopefuls, skeptics, and opponents.[35] These four rough categories are derived from two axes in a conceptual typology: along one axis, stronger versus weaker belief in the potential of a technology—any technology—to solve myriad societal problems; along the other axis, stronger versus weaker belief in the responsiveness of the political system to act on behalf of the broad public good. As with any such typology, the respective axes are more continua than absolutes, but the effort to categorize is useful to thinking about respective niches in any advocacy community, particularly one as nascent as this. The discussion of each category in Figure 16.4 focuses a modal type, but many (if not most) organizations in fact straddle categories, depending on particular applications or issues.

Figure 16.4.   Typology of Nanotechnology Interests and Examples of Groups Adhering to Niche Positions

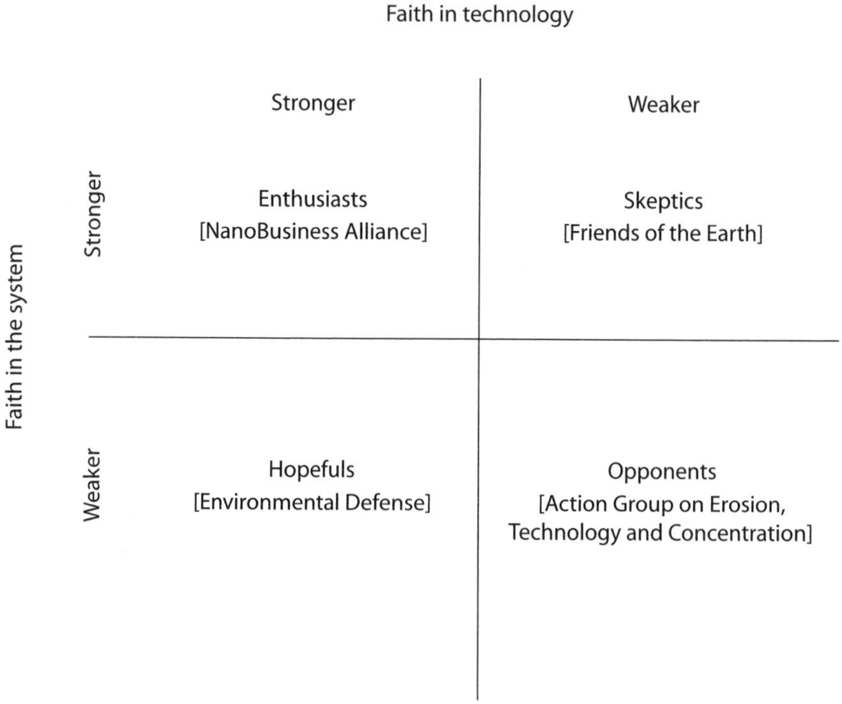

Faith in technology

	Stronger	Weaker
Stronger	Enthusiasts [NanoBusiness Alliance]	Skeptics [Friends of the Earth]
Weaker	Hopefuls [Environmental Defense]	Opponents [Action Group on Erosion, Technology and Concentration]

Faith in the system

Enthusiasts

The formation of new self-described business, professional, and trade associations that claim to relate in one way or another to the promotion of nanotechnology seems to track the general growth—and hype—in nanotechnology R&D. As one might expect in any emerging economic sector, most of these new organizations are rather small, modestly funded, and have few if any members in the traditional sense of the term. In some respects they serve as niche complements to already existing broad-spectrum professional associations and business groups.[36] Some self-professed industry associations also seem to be little more than vehicles to enable adept entrepreneurs to profit from the current enthusiasm for nanoscale R&D.

With these caveats firmly in mind, we recognize two organizations that seem to jockey for the role of the lead nanotechnology professional association. One, the Nano Science and Technology Institute (NSTI), was founded in 1997 in the merger of a number of scientific societies and "is chartered with the promotion and integration of nano and other advanced technologies through education, technology and business development." The NSTI hosts an annual nanotechnology conference and trade show and produces an array of scientific and business publications.[37] The other, the International Association of Nanotechnology (IANT), is a "non-profit professional association, managed by a group of members who volunteer their time and resources to create a global network of nanotechnologists and business executives to foster research collaboration worldwide for the benefit of society." Like NSTI, the IANT sponsors an annual conference to bring "clarity and focus to the scientific research, product development, intellectual property and technology transfer, research collaboration, venture capital investment, safety, regulation, ethics, environmental and societal aspects of Nanotechnology."[38] The degree to which the two organizations complement or compete with each other is as yet unclear because to date they have managed to avoid direct competition by holding their respective national meetings at different times of the year, almost guaranteeing an overlapping participant base.

The NanoBusiness Alliance, formed in 2001 by three young nanotechnology enthusiasts, is the purported (or at least self-described) industry association of the moment. Its founders claim that its biweekly newsletter, *NanoBusiness News*, "is the most read publication in the nanotech field," and that the alliance played a critical role in the development and passage of the 21st Century Nanotechnology Research and Development Act, although such claims are difficult to verify.[39] Tax returns filed by the NanoBusiness Alliance (Internal Revenue Service Form 990, which is a public record) show that more than one-third of the group's revenue in FY 2004 came from government grants, probably to organize a nanotechnology trade show.

More important over the long term, however, are already established and politically potent business and trade associations that focus less on specific technologies than on general policy outcomes that affect economic development, including tax incentives, patent law, liability standards, and regulatory requirements. Indeed, President Bush's announcement in his 2006 State of the Union address of an American Competitiveness Initiative, which proposed to double the federal commitment to research in the physical sciences, probably owed more to concerted lobbying by Fortune 500 companies like Intel and Lockheed Martin and to representatives of the nation's scientific establishment such as the American Association for the Advancement of Science than to any sector-specific advocacy organization.[40]

Hopefuls

The promises of nanotechnology also come with acknowledged environmental, health, and ethical uncertainties, along with concerns that existing federal and state regulatory institutions and laws may lack the capacity to address those challenges.[41] Such concerns are buttressed by experiences with other technologies, in particular biotechnology, and especially its agricultural variant, genetically modified organisms.[42] Still, the organizations in this category are generally hopeful about the potential of nanotechnology, but they want its development and commercialization to benefit the public good as much as they enrich private shareholders.

The leading self-identified nanotechnology advocacy group in this category is arguably the Foresight Nanotech Institute, founded in 1986 and "the first organization to educate society about the benefits and risks of nanotechnology." Foresight today claims over 14,000 dues-paying members drawn from an array of sectors, and it promotes an agenda that focuses on "ensuring the beneficial implementation of nanotechnology."[43] A much smaller organization, the Center for Responsible Nanotechnology (CRN), was founded in 2002 and focuses on publishing white papers directed at educating the public about nanotechnology, its benefits, and its risks.[44]

Niche actors like Foresight and CRN notwithstanding, the real players in this category are likely to be established environmental organizations like Environmental Defense and the Natural Resources Defense Council (NRDC), experienced science-and-law groups that can bring to the table notable institutional capacity, budgets, scientific and legal expertise, and experience in the political realm with prior technologies (pesticides, for example) and their resultant problems.[45] Taking the lead in this regard is Environmental Defense, which proclaimed its goal, "Getting Nanotechnology Right the First Time," in a widely circulated article and newspaper opinion essay.[46] In its authors' view, "There is a real opportunity to advance nanotechnology in a responsible manner that acknowledges risks, takes the steps necessary to address them, and meaningfully engages the full array of stakeholders to help shape this technology's trajectory—in short, the opportunity to 'get it right the first time.'"[47] Befitting its long-standing orientation toward developing collaborative working relationships with corporations, Environmental Defense in October 2005 announced a joint project with chemical giant DuPont to develop "a framework for the responsible development, production, use and disposal of nanoscale materials...."[48]

Reflecting their somewhat greater skepticism—at least compared with Environmental Defense—in the efficacy or desirability of market solutions in addressing environmental problems, the staff at the NRDC typically express concern about the adequacy of federal and state regulations governing nanotechnology development or use. "The federal government, state regulators, and industry have an opportunity to develop this exciting new technology openly, with public participation and government oversight," they note. "Otherwise we will be allowing the nanotechnology industry to conduct an uncontrolled experiment on the American people."[49]

Similar views on the promise and potential peril of nanotechnology are expressed by established law and policy centers like the Environmental Law Institute and Resources for the Future, which, along with Environmental Defense and NRDC, can be said to occupy the mainstream center of the broader national environmental community.[50] Intellectual and financial support for this moderate view on nanotechnology is offered by the Pew Charitable Trusts, which has played a patronage role of its own in funding the Woodrow Wilson International Center's Project on Emerging Nanotechnology, with a research and outreach center "dedicated to helping ensure that as nanotechnologies advance, possible risks are minimized, public and consumer engagement remains strong, and the potential benefits of these new technologies are realized."[51]

Skeptics

If those at the Foresight Nanotech Institute and Environmental Defense are generally hopeful about the promise of nanotechnology but simultaneously cautious about the need to get it right, leaders of other established environmental and consumer safety organizations express more skepticism about claims of nanotechnology's benefits; they have less faith in the capacity of any technology to solve deep-rooted societal problems, and they have greater concerns about corporate dominance, elite decision making, and an absence of stewardship in the public good. If, as one observer noted, advocates of nanotechnology want to avoid "a replay of the debacle over genetically engineered food, widely viewed as a classic case of an emerging science that squandered an opportunity to gain public trust," they already confront an array of advocacy organizations deeply skeptical about compromise.[52] Most of these organizations aren't opposed to technology as such, but their leaders and members are much more jaded about the capacity or willingness of political and economic elites to serve the public good. Included in this camp are long-established public interest advocacy organizations like the Center for Science in the Public Interest, on issues like consumer safety; and the Federation of American Scientists, on issues relating to military applications and privacy. In most instances their attention to nanotechnology is fairly new and is an outgrowth of current concerns.

The modal type in this category is arguably Friends of the Earth, which, along with Greenpeace, stands out among the major national environmental organizations as most likely to express a strong critique of free market capitalism and corporate power in American politics. The organization's focus on nanotechnology is for the most part an extension of its long-standing concerns about toxic chemicals and cancer-causing agents—nanoparticles in cosmetics, for example. In May 2006, Friends of the Earth was part of a coalition of organizations that petitioned the U.S. Food and Drug Administration (FDA) to impose a moratorium on "further commercial release of personal care products that contain engineered nanomaterials, and the withdrawal of such products currently on the market until adequate, publicly available, independent peer-reviewed safety studies have been completed." Friends of the Earth also called on the federal government to revise existing environmental, health, and worker safety regulations to bring them more in line with the potential effects of the new technology.[53]

Opponents

A decided minority of organizations expresses even greater opposition to both the technology and the capacity of the political system to act on behalf of the public good. Activists in these organizations typically believe that the technology in and of itself has great potential to cause harm unless proved otherwise—a more absolutist reading of the precautionary principle than is expressed by mainstream environmental and public health groups. Indeed, groups in this category are more likely to call for moratoria on R&D—not just on commercial production—until such concerns are fully addressed.[54]

A notable representative of this view is the International Center for Technology Assessment (known as CTA), founded in 1994 to promote a "full exploration of the economic, ethical, social, environmental and political impacts that can result from the applications of technology or technological systems."[55] CTA led the coalition that petitioned the FDA to impose the moratorium on personal care products and, even when compared with Friends of the Earth, expresses a more stringent view that all nanotechnology commercialization should cease until products containing nanoparticles are proved safe.[56]

The most oppositional of all groups is probably the Action Group on Erosion, Technology and Concentration (ETC Group), based in Ottawa,

Ontario. Once known as the Rural Advancement Foundation International, the group established itself as a leading opponent of agricultural biotechnology and of corporations like Monsanto. Relabeled the ETC Group, the organization broadened its concerns to include nanotechnology after becoming concerned at both the acceleration of nanoscale R&D sponsored by the NNI and the role of major corporations in the initiative.[57] Unlike skeptics like Friends of the Earth, which tend to see technological development as inevitable even as they criticize the actions of government and corporate elites, those in groups like ETC argue for legal moratoria, if not outright bans, on nanoscale R&D because they think it too dangerous for the public good.

Mandating Conflict

If, echoing Baumgartner and Jones, nanotechnology enthusiasts and even nanotechnology hopefuls are part of a Downsian mobilization that promotes the promise of nanotechnology, the skeptics and opponents already in place are part of a ready-made countermobilization of critics prepared to influence public debate and shape future government policy as nanotechnologies move from the laboratory to the marketplace.[58] To Baumgartner and Jones, these skeptics and opponents comprise a "Schattschneider mobilization"—after E. E. Schattschneider's insight that those opposing the status quo are most likely to raise alarms in order to expand issue conflict, attract the attentive public, and, in the end, foment policy change.[59] But, unlike the cases of pesticide regulation and nuclear power at the core of the Baumgartner and Jones study, where a Schattschneider mobilization took years to emerge, in some respects we see both types of mobilization occurring simultaneously and in a much more condensed span of time. Even if the promoters of nanotechnology are in the clear majority, minority voices will have policy influence from the start. Conflict is apparent, even while the technology itself is more potential than real.

More interesting, from an interest representation perspective, is that much of this debate is being supported by the NNI itself, especially with the passage of the 21st Century Nanotechnology Research and Development Act. Section 2 of the act explicitly provided for funded research into the "ethical, legal, environmental, and other appropriate societal concerns" about nanotechnology; it also mandated "public input and outreach to be integrated into the Program by the convening of regular and ongoing public discussions, through mechanisms such as citizens' panels, consensus conferences, and educational events, as appropriate."[60] Thus, the NNI requires and even funds public education and participation, notably through major NSF centers at Arizona State University (at $6 million initially), the University of California at Santa Barbara ($5 million), and the University of South Carolina ($1.5 million) as well as through a $20 million NSF-funded Nanoscale Informal Science Education Network (NISE Network) administered through a partnership of the Boston Museum of Science, the Science Museum of Minnesota, and the Exploratorium in San Francisco. NISE Network citizen forums have covered the range of viewpoints about nanotechnology and offered informed citizens opportunities to express their views about technology, corporate dominance, and the role for government.

Moreover, a quick glance at many of the workshops and conferences funded though the NSF shows an impressive range of participating organizations, from enthusiasts like the NanoBusiness Alliance to opponents like the Center for Technology Assessment, and everyone in between. Unlike previous instances where contrary voices emerged only after the unwelcome side effects of a technology were apparent to all, in this instance the debate has begun beforehand, and with intent. As a result, it is unlikely that any eventual nanotechnology-related environmental and health policy is going to proceed absent those critical voices. The Downsian mobilization of nanotechnology boosterism may well be short-lived and modulated from the start.

The Future of Nanotechnology Advocacy: From Noun to Adjective

At this early stage what passes for a nanotechnology policy domain is largely populated by a broad collection of generally enthusiastic academic, government, and industry supporters of nanotech R&D, positioned against a smaller but undeniably legitimate cadre of long-established public interest organizations with varying degrees of concerns about the environmental, health, and safety effects of emerging technologies and their applications.

Prognostications about the future of any advocacy sector are fraught with peril, but a few observations are worth venturing. In many ways the relative unanimity among enthusiasts for nanotechnology is an artifact of the embryonic nature of the sector itself. Like nuclear power's long forgotten promise of "electricity too cheap to meter," in many ways nanotechnology today is pure potential, with little real downside.[61] More to the point, right now—largely owing to the NNI—nanotechnology is a noun, an entity in and of itself, so most of the debates are more theoretical and prospective.[62]

Once we move past the R&D phase, however, we are likely to witness an inevitable fragmentation of nanotechnology issues and interest coalitions into communities defined by specific uses (consumer products and medical applications, for example), side effects (nanoparticles, toxics), or affected populations (the poor, the sick, developing countries). In some respects, this reflects the reality that nanotechnology is simply a technology, not an end in itself. Nanotechnology will eventually become an adjective— nanomedical, nanoagricultural, nanoelectronic, and so on—with each area of application and innovation in its own sector, with attendant intellectual property disputes, legal implications, side effects, and, of course, arrays of perceived winners and losers.

In some respects, then, the heyday of the nanotechnology advocacy sector may be right now, during the R&D gold rush, its duration as short-lived as nanoparticles are small. After all, once a medical device based on nanoscale technologies begins to go through FDA approval, in some respects it's simply another medical device, and its inventor is simply another medical device company.[63] Once this happens, multisector business organizations like the NanoBusiness Alliance may not make practical sense, so its founders may as well enjoy the ride while it lasts.

If nano becomes an adjective, we are also unlikely to see the emergence of many new nano-related public interest groups. After all, one will not need a nano-specific environmental group when one already can choose from among Environmental Defense, NRDC, and Friends of the Earth, for starters. Indeed, the public interest advocacy landscape is already dense with well-established environmental, consumer protection, and ethical technology groups. These organizations already have the institutional capacity and clout to be taken seriously by the industry and by government regulators.[64] They will simply add nano—as an adjective—to their current policy agendas.

Notes

This research is partially supported by National Science Foundation award EEC #0425826, the Nanoscale Science and Engineering Center for High-rate Nanomanu-facturing, Northeastern University, http://www.nano.neu.edu.

1. Committee on Technology, National Science and Technology Council, "National Nanotechnology Initiative: Leading to the Next Industrial Revolution," report by the Interagency Working Group on Nanoscience, Engineering and Technology, Washington, D.C., February 2000, 15, http://www.ostp.gov/NSTC/html/iwgn/iwgn.fy01budsuppl/nni.pdf.
2. For a good layperson's guide to nanotechnology, see Mark Ratner and Daniel Ratner, *Nanotechnology: A Gentle Introduction to the Next Big Idea* (Upper Saddle River, N.J.: Prentice Hall, 2003).
3. Ibid., 11.
4. Ray Kurzweil, *The Singularity Is Near: When Humans Transcend Biology* (New York: Viking, 2005).
5. Michael Crichton, *Prey* (New York: HarperCollins, 2003).
6. Committee on Technology, "National Nanotechnology Initiative."
7. Nanoscale Science, Engineering and Technology Subcommittee, *The National Nanotechnology Initiative: Strategic Plan* (Arlington, Va.: National Nanotechnology Coordination Office, 2004): iii, http://www.nano.gov/NNI_Strategic_Plan_2004.pdf.
8. On the concept of policy domain, see Paul Burstein, "Policy Domains: Organization, Culture, and Policy Outcomes," *Annual Review of Sociology* 17 (1991): 327–350.
9. See, for example, Christopher J. Bosso, *Pesticides and Politics: The Life Cycle of a Public Issue* (Pittsburgh: University of Pittsburgh Press, 1987); and Robert Duffy, *Nuclear Politics in America: A History and Theory of Government Regulation* (Lawrence: University Press of Kansas, 1997).

10. See Theodore Lowi, *The End of Liberalism*, 2d ed. (New York: Norton, 1979).
11. For a lengthier consideration see Christopher J. Bosso, *Environment Inc.: From Grassroots to Beltway* (Lawrence: University Press of Kansas, 2005), chap. 2.
12. Frank R. Baumgartner and Beth L. Leech, *Basic Interests: The Importance of Groups in Politics and in Political Science* (Princeton: Princeton University Press, 1998).
13. Robert Salisbury, "An Exchange Theory of Interest Groups," *Midwest Journal of Political Science* 13, no. 1 (February 1969): 1–32.
14. Jack L. Walker Jr., *Mobilizing Interest Groups in America: Patrons, Professions, and Social Movements* (Ann Arbor: University of Michigan Press, 1991); James Q. Wilson, *Political Organizations* (New York: Basic Books, 1973).
15. Walker, *Mobilizing Interest Groups in America*, ix.
16. See Bosso, *Pesticides and Politics*, 35–37; William P. Browne, *Private Interests, Public Policy, and American Agriculture* (Lawrence: University Press of Kansas, 1988); Graham K. Wilson, *Interest Groups in America* (New York: Oxford University Press, 1981); Christiana M. Campbell, *The Farm Bureau and the New Deal* (Urbana: University of Illinois Press, 1962).
17. Paul S. Sutter, *Driven Wild: How the Fight against Automobiles Launched the Modern Wilderness Movement* (Seattle: University of Washington Press, 2002); Stephen Fox, *John Muir and His Legacy: The American Conservation Movement* (Boston: Little, Brown, 1981), 181–217.
18. Fox, *John Muir and His Legacy*, 212.
19. David R. Brower, *For Earth's Sake: the Life and Times of David Brower* (Salt Lake City, Utah: Peregrine Smith Books, 1990), 229.
20. On the New Deal, see George Hoberg, *Pluralism by Design: Environmental Policy and the American Regulatory State* (Westport, Conn.: Praeger, 1992).
21. See Lowi, *The End of Liberalism;* Mancur Olson, *The Rise and Decline of Nations: Economic Growth, Stagflation, and Social Rigidities* (New Haven: Yale University Press, 1984).
22. Committee on Technology, "National Nanotechnology Initiative," 12.
23. R.W. Siegel, Evelyn L. Hu, and M.C. Roco, eds., *R&D Status and Trends in Nanoparticles, Nanostructured Materials, and Nanodevices in the United States*, National Science Foundation, World Technology Evaluation Center, January 1998, http://www.wtec.org/loyola/pdf/nanousws.pdf.
24. For the history of the NNI, see "History," National Nanotechnology Initiative, http://www.nano.gov/html/about/history.html; for the National Science and Technology Council, see http://www.ostp.gov/nstc/index.html.
25. R.W. Siegel, Evelyn L. Hu, and Mihail C. Roco, eds., "Nanostructure Science and Technology: A Worldwide Study," National Science and Technology Council (NSTC), Committee on Technology, Interagency Working Group on NanoScience, Engineering and Technology (IWGN), August 1999, http://www.wtec.org/loyola/nano/IWGN.Worldwide.Study/.
26. M.C. Roco, S. Williams, and P. Alivisatos, eds., "Nanotechnology Research Directions: IWGN Workshop Report," National Science and Technology Council (NSTC), Committee on Technology, Interagency Working Group on NanoScience, Engineering and Technology (IWGN), September 1999, http://www.wtec.org/loyola/nano/IWGN.Research.Directions/.
27. National Science and Technology Council, Committee on Technology, Subcommittee on Nanoscale Science, Engineering and Technology, *National Nanotechnology Initiative: The Initiative and Its Implementation Plan* (Washington, D.C.: Office of Science and Technology Policy, July 2000), http://www.wtec.org/loyola/nano/IWGN.Implementation.Plan/nni.implementation.plan.pdf.
28. Rene Sanchez, "Clinton Proposes More Spending for Research; Nearly $3 Billion in Extra Funding Planned For Science, Technology," *Washington Post*, January 22, 2000, sec. A.

29. Anthony Downs, "Up and Down with Ecology: The Issue-Attention Cycle," *Public Interest* 28 (Summer 1972): 38–50.
30. Frank R. Baumgartner and Bryan D. Jones, *Agendas and Instabilities in American Politics* (Chicago: University of Chicago Press, 1994), 83–102.
31. On this notion of subgovernments, see Bosso, *Pesticides and Politics*, chap. 2; Douglass Cater, *Power in Washington* (New York: Random House, 1964); A. Grant McConnell, *Private Power and American Democracy* (New York: Knopf, 1966); Emmette S. Redford, *Democracy in the Administrative State* (New York: Oxford University Press, 1969); Hugh Heclo, "Issue Networks and the Executive Establishment," in *The New American Political System*, ed. Anthony King (Washington, D.C.: American Enterprise Institute, 1979), 87–124.
32. See the Web site of the Center for High-rate Nanomanufacturing, http://www.nano.neu.edu/team.html.
33. Wayne Crews, "End Subsidies for Nanotechnology," *Washington Post*, February 12, 2004, sec. A.
34. "State of the Union Address by the President," January 31, 2006, http://www.whitehouse.gov/stateoftheunion/2006/.
35. See Michael Bennett, "Does Existing Law Fail to Address Nanotechnoscience?" *IEEE Technology and Society* 23, no. 4 (Winter 2004): 27–32.
36. On this notion of niche organizations, see Bosso, *Environment, Inc.*
37. For additional information about NSTI, see http://www.nsti.org/about/.
38. For additional information about IANT, see http://www.ianano.org/aboutus.htm.
39. For additional information about the NanoBusiness Alliance, see http://nanobusiness.org/.
40. John Markoff, "Behind Bush's New Stress on Science, Lobbying by Republican Executives," *New York Times*, February 2, 2006, http://www.nytimes.com/2006/02/02/business/02research.html?pagewanted=print.
41. Ahson Wardak, *Nanotechnology & Regulation: A Case Study Using the Toxic Substance Control Act (TSCA)*, Foresight and Governance Project (Washington, D.C.: Woodrow Wilson International Center for Scholars, 2003), http://www.foresightandgovernance.org/images/nanotsca_final2.pdf.
42. See Ronald Sandler and W. D. Kay, "The GMO-Nanotech (Dis)Analogy?" *Bulletin of Science, Technology, and Society* 26, no. 1 (2006): 57–62; Julia Moore, "Lessons from the GMO and Frankenfood Debate: Building Public Trust in New Technology and Science" (paper presented at the Woodrow Wilson International Center for Scholars, Washington, D.C., November 19, 2002), http://www.environmentalfutures.org/nanotech.htm.
43. For additional information about the Foresight Nanotech Institute, see http://www.foresight.org/.
44. For additional information about the Center for Responsible Nanotechnology, see http://www.crnano.org/index.html.
45. On Environmental Defense and the Natural Resources Defense Council as organizations, see Bosso, *Environment, Inc.*
46. John Balbus et al., "Getting Nanotechnology Right the First Time," *Issues in Science and Technology* (Summer 2005): 65–71, http://www.environmentaldefense.org/documents/4816_nanotechstatementNA.pdf; Fred Krupp and Chad Holliday, "Let's Get Nanotech Right," *Wall Street Journal*, June 15, 2005, sec. B.
47. Balbus et al., "Getting Nanotechnology Right the First Time," 65–66.
48. "Environmental Defense and DuPont: Global Nanotechnology Standards of Care Partnership," October 11, 2005, http://www.environmentaldefense.org/article.cfm?contentID=4821.
49. "Nanotechnologies: Tiny Particles Promise Much, But Could Pose Big Risk," Natural Resources Defense Council, March 2005, http://www.nrdc.org/health/science/nano.asp.

50. See Bosso, *Environment, Inc.*, chap. 3.

51. Project on Emerging Nanotechnologies, Woodrow Wilson International Center for Scholars, http://www.wilsoncenter.org/index.cfm?fuseaction=topics.home&topic_id=166192.

52. Rick Weiss, "Nanotech Group's Invitations Declined: Critics Say Effort Glosses Over Risks," *Washington Post,* October 28, 2004, sec. A.

53. Rick Weiss, "FDA Asked to Better Regulate Nanotechnology," *Washington Post,* May 17, 2006, sec. A; Georgia Miller et al., *Nanomaterials, Sunscreens and Cosmetics: Small Ingredients, Big Risks* (Washington, D.C.: Friends of the Earth, May 2006), http://www.foe.org/camps/comm/nanotech/nanocosmetics.pdf.

54. Bennett, "Does Existing Law Fail to Address Nanotechnoscience?" 28.

55. For an evaluation of the CTA, see http://www.fas.org/pub/gen/cta/.

56. "Tiny Technology, Significant Risk," International Center for Technology Assessment, 2004, http://www.icta.org/nanotech/index.cfm.

57. Barnaby J. Feder, "New Economy: Nanotechnology Has Arrived; A Serious Opposition Is Forming," *New York Times,* August 19, 2002, sec. C; for additional information about the ETC Group, see http://www.etcgroup.org/about.asp.

58. Baumgartner and Jones, *Agendas and Instabilities in American Politics,* 83–102.

59. Ibid. See also E.E. Schattschneider, *The Semisovereign People: A Realist's View of Democracy in America* (New York: Holt, Rinehart and Winston, 1960).

60. *The 21st Century Nanotechnology Research and Development Act,* Public Law 108-153, section 2b.

61. See Duffy, *Nuclear Politics in America;* Baumgartner and Jones, *Agendas and Instabilities in American Politics.*

62. Credit for this distinction goes to Jim Hurd of the NanoScience Exchange, who offered it as an observation during his talk, "Nanotechnology 2006: The Realities of Commercialization," at the fourth New England International Nanomanufacturing Workshop, Northeastern University, Boston, Mass., June 27–28, 2006.

63. On the other hand, if manufactured nanoparticles and applications are fundamentally different, all bets are off.

64. See Bosso, *Environment, Inc.,* on the evolution of the major environmental organizations.

17

The Well-Informed Lobbyist
Information and Interest Group Lobbying
Rogan Kersh

When most Americans think of interest groups and lobbying, they think of political action committees, high-dollar fund-raisers, and lavish trips provided to legislators. And while contributions and social functions have long been part of how groups win access to lawmakers, money in itself plays a secondary role in most successful lobbying. Rather, as Rogan Kersh observes, the coin of the realm in lobbying is information. Members of Congress, legislative staff, executive branch officials, and regulators all value high quality information—on policies, politics, and procedures.

In this chapter, Kersh draws on his intensive study of Washington lobbying to offer a sophisticated understanding of how providing information affects the policy-making process. Experienced lobbyists, who understand the nature of Washington politics, serve as the brokers for information, paying particular attention to targets (for example, congressional staff) and types (for example, favorable printed studies). Interest group scholars have long considered information a crucial weapon in lobbyists' arsenals, but Kersh draws upon his excellent access to make sharp observations about the subtleties in the use of information that may have value only in context—such as a vote count on a key amendment—but whose short-term value may be overwhelming. In sum, Kersh offers us a systematic look at the intersection of lobbying and decision making, where the best possible information is worth more than any trip or campaign contribution.

"Money is the root of all evil ... and all lobbying." "You can't talk about lobbying without talking about money." "Money is the mother's milk of politics."[1] These and a host of similar adages suggest that to really understand interest group politics, one must pay attention to the movement of resources. Or, in another well-worn phrase, "follow the money."

Yet if you ask a Washington lobbyist about the main determinants of professional success, financial matters—campaign contributions, legislative earmarks or other monetary benefits sought by lobbyists, even client payments—will be well down the list. Ask most members of Congress and their staff, administration officials, or other Beltway insiders, and their answers likely will be similar: not money but *information* is the coin of the realm in interest group lobbying. The most sought-after lobbyists are hired not because of their ability to control, raise, or disperse funds, but primarily on the basis of their strategic capacity to deploy information in the service of their clients and policy makers as well as advance their own desired ends.

Why this is so, and how information is obtained, organized, and presented by lobbyists, are the subjects of this chapter. Four main lines of argument are explored. First, information is central to lobbying. Searching for, analyzing, and presenting information compose the central activity in most lobbyists' daily work. Second, interest groups' information is vitally important to government officials and, by extension, to the millions of people they serve. Like other sometimes overlooked organisms in complex systems (think pilot fish, worker bees, and so forth), lobbyists are essential to maintaining the flow of ideas, arguments, and findings that fuels policy making in the United States. Whether their central place in the Washington information economy[2] is desirable from a democratic standpoint is taken up in this chapter's conclusion.

Third, not all information is created equal. Knowing what qualifies as valuable—to policy makers and also to clients and fellow lobbyists—is critical to successful lobbying, as is the ability to obtain and communicate that useful information. Fourth, although lobbyists are commonly viewed as masters of manipulation, selectively applying information to serve particular (and, in the popular imagination, usually nefarious) purposes, most of the information they present is relatively *un*biased. It is also remarkably consistent: legislative allies and foes and Democratic and Republican decision makers alike receive similar briefing papers and talking points. Spin is certainly present, but much more often in the oral presentations that accompany printed or broadcast information. The substantive messages that lobbyists communicate to policy makers are little changed across different congressional or executive branch offices.

Learning about Lobbying and Information

The primary method employed in this chapter is participant observation of lobbyists and the public officials they seek to influence.[3] Since

January 1999, I have periodically followed a group of eleven Washington, D.C., health care lobbyists as they carry out their regular professional activities. Over this period I have also interviewed many other interest group representatives and their clients; executive branch officials, both career and political appointees; and members of Congress (MCs) and their staff members. Those interviews supplement my direct observations of lobbyists: of their discussions with clients; meetings with congressional staff and MCs as well as with George W. Bush administration and Clinton administration officials; interest group coalition meetings to strategize and exchange information; and in-house lobbyist strategy meetings.

Most of the lobbyists I follow chiefly represent private (usually industry and corporate) interests. Although this fact may skew my findings somewhat, corporate representatives are by far the least-studied interest group actors compared with lobbyists for consumer groups, unions, state and local governments, and other membership organizations. Otherwise, the eleven lobbyists make up a diverse group with respect to type of firm, age, gender, experience, and health policy expertise. A condition of this ethnographic research was anonymity; lobbyists are therefore referred to in this chapter by number (Lobbyist no. 1, Lobbyist no. 2, and so forth).

This analysis of interest groups and information is supplemented by an original database of lobbying documents. Of a collection of health-lobbying documents prepared by lobbyists for consumption by the public (who are usually policy makers), I randomly chose 550 separate items—all used during two specified three-month periods during 2000 and 2002—ranging from full-fledged research reports to one-page talking points. These were analyzed and coded for certain features, as described at points in this chapter.

Information as Coin of the Realm

Definitions of lobbying typically center on organized interests' efforts to influence government officials. Specifying the direct effects of lobbying on policy outcomes (or on legislators' votes or on bill language) is notoriously difficult, leading scholars and reporters to focus on lobbyists' access to policy makers. Usually access is treated as a proxy for money: as a recent overview of interest group research summarizes, "one common view has a lobbyist buy access through campaign contributions." After spending a year tracking interest group involvement in congressional policy making, journalist Mary Clay Berry concluded, "Money has everything to do with lobbying.... It is all very well to insist, as most politicians do, that the campaign contributions guarantee the donor no more than access. In lobbying, access is everything."[4] But without persuasive information, at least in a developed liberal democracy like the United States, attempts at influence rarely get far. Thus, along with viewing lobbyists as influence-peddlers, we should also see them as political information seekers, processors, translators, and deployers.

The typical interest group representative spends far more time analyzing and obtaining information than on any other activity, including persuading public officials, attending fund-raisers or other campaign-related activities, and seeking new clients. And lobbyists themselves, as do virtually all other actors in the political system, attribute success in their work to being well informed. "Getting in [a policy maker's office] is fine, as far as that goes, but if you don't have something to say—something that matters to the congressman or whoever you're lobbying—then your access just doesn't mean much, and in fact will dry up pretty quickly," comments prominent lobbyist Tony Podesta. Another well-respected Washington hand concurs, "access and influence are very, very different things."[5]

Figures 17.1 and 17.2 provide empirical support for the claim that information is central to lobbying. Figure 17.1 shows the time the eleven lobbyists I studied spend on various activities, with information gathering, research and analysis, and dissemination together making up the vast bulk of the total. Figure 17.2 reports lobbyists' own assessment of the most important tools or factors involved in their professional success; "providing information" outranks all other items except "solo/direct lobbying," an activity that intrinsically involves direct transmission of information.

Academic studies increasingly acknowledge the value of information to the legislative (and, less extensively, administrative) process. Keith Krehbiel's *Information and Legislative Organization* launched a subliterature on asymmetric information and signaling models. David Whiteman's *Communication in Congress* provides a wealth of detail on how Congress obtains policy information, affirming along the way interest groups' important role. And Kevin Esterling's *Political Economy of Expertise* untangles the complex mechanisms linking policy expertise, often supplied by lobbying groups, to legislative activity.[6] Apart from Whiteman's, most relevant studies treat information as a generic strategic tool: the real research questions concern which legislators are targeted by lobbyists, when and why groups choose to share information with one another, and so forth.[7] Information itself, in other words, is rarely a subject of investigation. Given its importance to policy making, it seems worth undertaking a sustained investigation of political information and lobbying: what counts as valuable information, where lobbyists obtain it, how they analyze material and deploy the results, what purposes such efforts serve, and the implications for democratic governance.

Lobbyists and Politically Valuable Information

As the volume of potentially informative material continues to increase in Washington—U.S. House and Senate chaplains now offer prayers for divine assistance in the face of "information overkill" and a "glut of information"[8]—sifting worthwhile (reliable, timely, accurate) from irrelevant or misleading information is ever more important ... and more difficult. Interest groups have become vital to the work of locating and presenting useful

Figure 17.1.   Lobbyists' Rankings of Their Activities

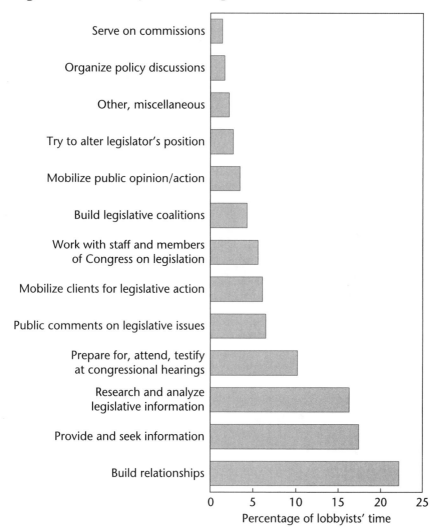

Source: Author's data.

arguments, data, and anecdotes, so much so that it is hard to imagine the policy process functioning without them.

Singling out ExxonMobil lobbyist J. O. Mitchell as among the best in her field in 2006, a colleague enthused: "She knows when to knock on a door, what information is important and what is not, and when to leave someone alone."[9] Identifying information as important or useful is a complicated business, although some examples appear straightforward: research

Figure 17.2.   Importance of Various Lobbying Tools

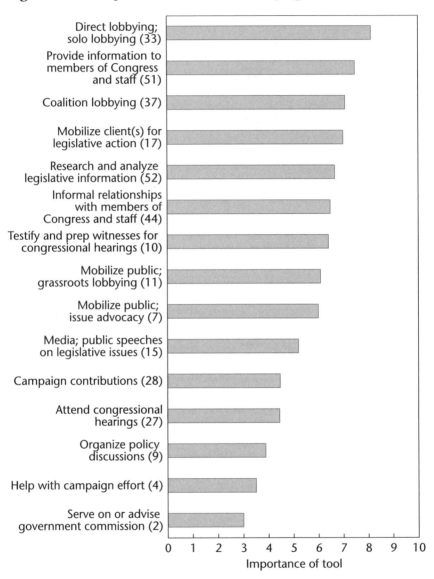

Source: Author's data.

Notes: Data taken from a sample of fifty-four issues, as ranked by eleven lobbyists. Numbers in parentheses show the number of issues on which this tool was employed. The bars on the figure show the average importance; 1 shows lowest importance, and 10 shows highest importance.

that aids an MC's reelection campaign via district-specific analysis; innovative arguments that help advance a bill through the labyrinthine legislative process; findings that attract media attention, boosting an issue's salience. Clear instances of these are rare. Determining information's utility may be evident only after a vote or other definitive decision, and even retrospective judgments are contestable in Washington's ambiguous policy environment. Which of the hundreds or even thousands of ideas, studies, talking points, and data analyses advanced during the tobacco debates, to take one prominent issue, proved significant?

Thus, lobbyists often use a simple index of information's value. "The highest-priority material I work on," explained Lobbyist no. 10 in a comment repeated in various forms by all the group representatives I follow, "is whatever a [congressional] staffer asks me for, or what I'm pretty certain they'll find valuable." I tracked the primary research efforts undertaken by my eleven lobbyists over a nine-week period in 2000; of this list of forty-eight separate items, nearly half were suggested or informally requested by policy makers.

This symbiotic connection is manifested in different ways. Interest groups are publicly asked by legislators for information, usually while testifying before a congressional committee. "Would you give us something in writing, positive things you think we can do?" requested Representative Nathan Deal, R-Ga., chairman of the Subcommittee on Health, at a 2005 session of the House Committee of Energy and Commerce on the subject of Medicare.[10] The official transcript of most congressional hearings includes an appendix featuring witnesses' responses to members' requests for follow-up details and studies. In what Jeffrey Berry terms our "interest group society,"[11] prominent lobbyists' views on legislative proposals are sought by reporters and policy makers; they are also expected to supply informative data and other background in support.

Information requests are often made through back channels, as when a senior House of Representatives staff member privately asked Lobbyist no. 5 to "pull together a study" supporting the lobbyist's assertion that state regulations on insurance companies had slowed the growth of health care premiums in certain states. Once the document was prepared, the staff member suggested several other congressional offices to circulate it to. "I can't be too obvious in promoting this," she told the lobbyist. "Better if it comes from you." Staff members regularly advise lobbyists on how to improve or supplement the information they provide, including how to make it more palatable to their own Senate or House bosses. "You're not going to convince him with this [set of] arguments," a House legislative director confided of his boss to Lobbyist no. 10, as the patients' rights debate heated up on Capitol Hill. "Do a letter that sets out the alternatives you guys want to see [enacted] ... and he'll pay attention."

The Washington policy community also favors another measure of worthy information: novelty. New information takes two main forms: exclusive and original. *Exclusive information*, a constantly produced government commodity, comprises just-published (or, even better, not-yet-released) material like the draft of a bill or administrative rule as well as political exclusives—which way an MC's vote is leaning, in-house poll data from a closely watched campaign, an official's impending resignation. The mostly friendly rivalry among lobbyists to garner these tidbits before their colleagues resembles journalists' efforts to secure a scoop.

In contrast, *original information* involves new ideas (or data, arguments, and so forth), often produced by lobbyists for consumption in the wider policy community. Novelty is no guarantor of quality, of course, but in this observer's experience original or otherwise innovative views receive close, even eager, attention from policy makers. In part, this is a self-interested calculation: MCs' chances of winning reelection increase if they are seen as promoting path-breaking legislative ideas.[12] Policy makers' interest in the new also likely owes to the seemingly eternal recurrence of so many national issues.

Medical malpractice reform, for example, was first a high Washington policy priority—attracting presidential comments, congressional hearings, and legislation—in 1968–1969, and then again in the mid-1970s, mid-1980s, 1998–1999, and again in 2002–2005. Across nearly forty years of debate, most stakeholders (the American Medical Association, Association of Trial Lawyers of America, and groups representing hospitals and insurance companies) have remained constant, advancing arguments that have all but calcified from repeated use. When a new position is mooted—during the most recent malpractice crisis, the idea that increasingly costly malpractice insurance might be provided through the Medicare program was perceived as an innovation—participants readily turn to debating this novel perspective.[13]

Lobbyists as Vital Information Providers

Lobbyists are merely one source of original ideas, to be sure. Members of congressional staffs, like many members themselves, are policy experts in their own right—as are executive branch analysts in the White House and executive agencies and departments. Legislators can also draw on a wide range of specialized expertise, most notably from support agencies like the Congressional Research Service (CRS), Congressional Budget Office (CBO), and Government Accountability Office (GAO) as well as the extensive community of political consultants, think-tank analysts, and academic researchers. Still, for at least three reasons, lobbyists play a central role in the drama of policy innovation.

First, private firms and public interest groups alike devote substantial resources to researching issues and publicizing their findings. More than $2 billion is spent annually on lobbying activities, dwarfing political action committee campaign funds.[14] Expenditures are devoted to such efforts as data analysis, grass-roots programs designed to mobilize citizens around an issue, and polling in congressional districts—the last of which supplies interest groups with another information gold standard: constituency opinion.

A second basis for interest groups' pivotal place in the political-information economy is lobbyists' tendency to work within a particular issue area, developing expertise on a well-defined handful of topics. This is a level of focus that most policy makers, especially in Congress, are hard-pressed to match, given the dizzying range of political topics they constantly face.

Third, lobbyists and the interest groups housing them are important repositories of institutional memory on many policy issues. As many MCs lament, Capitol Hill staff members' terms of employment are measured in months, not years.[15] (When staff members leave, they overwhelmingly opt for positions as public or private lobbyists, taking with them their knowledge and contacts.) Along similar lines, lobbyists are invariably pack rats, storing file cabinets and boxes full of material on a wide range of issues. This enhances their value as custodians of policy history, as even high-ranking committee aides or senior White House officials usually have offices too small to permit much in the way of paper storage.

In an attempt to better specify lobbyists' role in transmitting valuable information, I identified and tracked twenty-four new ideas in the health care arena over the life of the 106th Congress (1999–2000). I defined "new" on the basis of media reports and assessments by legislative staff and lobbyists themselves: these were novel, at least in recent memory, concepts or arguments introduced into ongoing debates. Some, like reimportation of prescription drugs, were large-scale innovations; many were more focused niche ideas.[16] Exactly half of the twenty-four were primarily attributed (in a combination of media reports and interviews with staff members and lobbyists) to lobbyists. And in all twenty-four examples, various networks of health care lobbyists proved essential to communicating the ideas across Capitol Hill. (One—a compromise on reusing medical devices—was eventually enacted; most of the others continue to rattle around in legislative proposals today.)

Further empirical confirmation of lobbyists' importance in information analysis, at least among congressional staff, comes in Whiteman's *Communication in Congress*. Surveying Capitol Hill staff members working on a range of issues, Whiteman found that interest groups were the second-most-often-consulted sources of information, after committee staff—and more frequently contacted than personal staff (those staff members serving in allied MCs' offices), executive branch agencies, constituents, support agencies like CRS or GAO, and think tanks or other policy research organizations. Moreover, staff members who were most engaged on an issue consulted lobbyists as often as they did committee staff.[17] Whether this finding is disturbing is taken up at this chapter's end; for now, it affirms lobbyists' vital place in Washington's information-saturated policy process.

Managing Information

Discerning the difference between more and less valuable material is only a preliminary step to effective information lobbying. Armed with that knowledge, interest groups must obtain, analyze, and make use of the information so essential to their work.

Gathering Information

The informative materials lobbyists use come from a wide range of sources. Think of lobbyists as magpies, picking up valuable bits of information in various places and weaving them into reports for clients and legislators. Much of this material exists in the evanescent realm of speech: claims and counterclaims, gossip and innuendo, promises kept and broken (or forgotten). But written information—"paper," in the argot of Washington—is especially valuable. "If it's written down somewhere," Lobbyist no. 9 told me, "that's golden: I can pull it up later, quote it back to the congressman or whoever, and reuse it in a million ways." Thus, in a ceaseless effort to obtain prized paper, lobbyists line up outside hearing rooms and committee offices where reports, testimony, press releases, and the like are printed. Experienced lobbyists often enjoy access to a photocopier in an office of a friendly House or Senate staff member, permitting them to share and swiftly circulate printed information among fellow lobbyists and policy makers.

This information falls into two broad categories: material *from* public officials—a copy of an amendment to be introduced; a draft administrative rule prepared by an executive agency; a "Dear Colleague" letter indicating a member's viewpoint on an issue, which lobbyists utilize in their regular reports to clients—and information lobbyists prepare for delivery *to* policy makers, deployed in efforts to reshape or block legislative items. Let us look at each of these in turn.

Information from Public Officials.   Interest group lobbyists' efforts for their clients only occasionally involve action items—helping draft legislation, securing an earmark in an appropriations bill, delivering testimony, and the like. Far more common in lobbyists' routine work of writing reports to and conversing with clients is providing informative nuggets: this senator supports that bill, this issue is heating up in that subcommittee, and so forth. Monitor, observe, question, report: these are the verbs that describe a lobbyist's professional life. Much of this activity involves obtaining information from (or about) public officials not readily available otherwise.

Consider a lobbyist's typical working day. At home or upon arriving at the office, most spend a half hour or more absorbing the morning news. Sources comprise a combination of Web sites (favorites include ABC's The Note, *National Journal's* Earlybird, and, among conservative lobbyists, FOX News or RealClearPolitics) and at least two of the big-three daily newspapers (*New York Times, Washington Post, Wall Street Journal*). Lobbyists also scan subscription-only publications specific to the industry they represent or issues they work on, most of which provide daily updates along with longer weekly newsletters and journals. A sampling of titles read regularly by my lobbyists includes: *Health Care Policy Report* published by the Bureau of National Affairs; *CQ HealthBeat*, published by Congressional Quarterly; daily reports from the Health Policy Tracking Service; and California Healthline.

During—or, more often, after—their workday, lobbyists also closely monitor the enormous stream of information published by the government itself. The daily *Federal Register* provides a wealth of executive branch details; but individual agencies and departments constantly issue reports, decisions, advisories, press releases, and the like, and they frequently revise their method of notification. Web postings are increasingly common, but URL locations for these can change in seemingly random (and, to lobbyists, maddening) fashion. Offices of congressional committees and members of Congress also produce rafts of information, usually easier to locate and obtain than material from the executive branch. Lobbyists most prize hard-to-get items, though, like working drafts of legislation. Especially valuable are the "chairman's mark" of bills or amendments, usually representing a near-final draft of the version considered by a committee, and the "clean bill" assembled by the committee staff after major revisions in committee.

All this reading and monitoring is usually interspersed with several daily rounds of phone calls, as a lobbyist checks in with fellow interest group representatives and friendly legislative staff or, less often, executive branch administrators. "What's going on?" Lobbyist no. 2 asked a dozen or more colleagues every morning during the time that I watched her in action. "What's happening?" And then, in subsequent calls: "Did you hear...."

Along with office-based information searches, lobbyists constantly circulate in person. More than twice a week, on average, the lobbyists I follow attend coalition meetings with fellow interest group representatives (and sometimes policy makers), exchanging views and determining what colleagues are planning, have learned, and need to know. Lobbyists also venture to Capitol Hill for an hour or two on most weekdays and longer when Congress is in session. These trips are sometimes to hold a planned meeting with legislators or staff but are often simply to, as Lobbyist no. 9 put it, "be on the scene—I'm my clients' eyes and ears, so I go up there [to the Hill] to see and hear as much as I can." Early-rising lobbyists can be found scattered through House and Senate cafeterias, greeting MCs and staff members as they pass through with a bagel or the day's first cup of coffee.

Lobbyists also congregate around any official activity relevant to their issue area—which, on Capitol Hill, usually means legislative hearings. Rarely is any dramatic news made at committee hearings, leading some observers to wonder why high-priced lobbyists bother to show up at all, much less sit through hours of predictable (and preprinted) testimony and a handful of questions from members. They do so partly to collect any paper available and partly to gather information barely discernable to the untrained eye: a stray comment here, whispered consultation with a staff member there, and a valuable item is registered for subsequent reporting to colleagues across town in Washington or to clients in San Francisco or Chicago (or Brussels, Tokyo, Nairobi, and everywhere else that keen interest is taken in the doings of U.S. officials).

Finally, lobbyists collect information from each other. One lobbyist I follow is an in-house representative for a pharmaceutical company; several times a day she checks in individually or in a group meeting with her fellow lobbyists for the firm, quite literally comparing notes. Following is a verbatim sample of one conversation, from summer 2003, repeated with minor variants in hundreds of lobbying offices across Washington every day:

> PHARMACEUTICAL LOBBYIST A (PLA): "Tracked down [a Republican senator's chief of staff] today.... Is he [angry]."

> PHARMACEUTICAL LOBBYIST B (PLB): "What now?"

> PHARMACEUTICAL LOBBYIST C (PLC) (WHO IS ALSO MY LOBBYIST NO. 4): "About Part D?"

> PLA: "What else?"

> PLC: "He [the senator]'s off the reservation on this."

> PHARMACEUTICAL LOBBYIST D (PLD) (ENTERING ROOM): "You talking [the senator]? He's on the rez, believe me ... even if they go higher than 450."

> PLA: "Not what [the senator's chief of staff] told me about an hour ago."

> PLD: "You talked to him?"

> PLC: "Yeah, he did. He told [a Finance Committee staff member] that if they're not stopping at four, he's gonna have a real problem."

> PLB: "This is looking more and more like a train wreck."

> PLC: "Which could mean a special...."

Thus was the pharmaceutical company's vice president for government relations, based far from the Capitol, able to alert colleagues that, based on expert Washington-office assessment, no prescription drug benefit (Part D of Medicare) would pass until late in the year. Indeed, an extra (or special) congressional session might be required—thanks to certain senior Republicans balking at the anticipated cost of the bill, now over $450 billion.

Information for Public Officials.   Obtaining information for clients is "not exactly heavy lifting, most of the time," Lobbyist no. 4 remarked after my first observation of a lobbyist-client conversation. Most clients' distance from and relative unfamiliarity with national policy making permits a reasonably well-informed lobbyist to provide engaging reports without plumbing the depths of officialdom. Analysis intended for consumption by public officials is a different story. In the information-suffused Washington policy realm, lobbyists must work hard to sift items of value from the glut of material. Agency bureaucrats and congressional staff are well-informed in their own right; most policy makers receive a collection of daily reports culled by staff members from the same Web sites and big-three newspapers that lobbyists consult, plus home state organs.

Whence, then, comes lobbyists' comparative advantage? As noted earlier, lobbyists are able to develop deeper expertise, given their concentration on one or a handful of issues. Lobbyists are also able to take a synthetic approach to a policy topic. Decision makers' attention is episodic; spend a half hour in any Member's office while Congress is in session and the crush of time pressure is immediately apparent, severely limiting opportunities to read widely and deeply into a topic. Lobbyists' ability to pull together disparate reports into a coherent document is deeply valued by public officials. Moreover, health care lobbyists like those in other fields are embedded in a vast network of colleagues. Comparing notes, sharing information, trading ideas: this constant exchange helps form a consensus around a proposed policy or issue area. Congressional staff members are typically avid consumers of the collective lobbying-community perspectives (usually at least one from lobbying partisans on each side) that result. When, for example, the top aides from all House and Senate offices gather weekly—separated by party—to discuss policy items currently before Congress, the group is frequently briefed by knowledgeable lobbyists.

Analyzing Information

Few lobbyists engage in extensive primary research; instead, most are skilled synthesizers. The bulk of lobbying firms and some individual lobbyists employ research assistants (or contract out the work) to create in-house documents. Even these feature little in the way of original analysis: of the 550 lobbying items examined in detail for this information study, only a small number (around 13 percent) were based chiefly on lobbyist-generated research.[18] More often a lobbyist draws on existing studies by think-tank analysts, academics, or government officials and then repackages the results (usually with at least partial attribution) for policy makers, reporters, and clients' consumption.

One contribution lobbyists regularly make in their information syntheses is to combine substantive and political information. Academic researchers' empirical policy analyses often supply substance in the form of data and factual details; thus many health care lobbyists at least skim journals like *JAMA*, *Health Affairs*, or the *New England Journal of Medicine*, and they receive summaries of relevant findings in their specialized trade publications. Political analysis—such as how a policy proposal will affect industries (or be received by constituents) in a congressional district—is more familiar terrain for lobbyists; consultants and pollsters are useful sources of this political information as well. Talented lobbyists combine the two, simultaneously reporting the likely scientific impact of a policy proposal as well as its political feasibility.

Deploying Information: Lobbyists' Three Audiences

Once information is gathered, analyzed, and organized, it must be disseminated. This is a critical step for lobbyists, and most are extremely effective at getting the word out. They do so to three major audiences: their clients, as noted above; policy makers of each party, in both Congress and the administration (and, at times, in selected state capitals); and each other, in coalition meetings and informal exchanges.

Informing Clients.   Most of the official information lobbyists gather is transformed rapidly into client reports. Lobbyists who serve multiple clients check in on a regular, and usually rotating, basis with each client; this necessitates several daily client phone calls, usually in late afternoon. Trade association lobbyists, some of whom have dozens of member companies to keep informed consistently, maintain a similar reporting schedule. In-house lobbyists (those representing a single firm) usually prepare weekly or bimonthly reports on pending legislative and regulatory issues, but even these lobbyists are in daily contact with the home office.

Thus, lobbyists devote a substantial portion of their professional lives to client reporting. No elaborate policy studies, or even bulleted lists of talking points, are involved here; instead, lobbyists survey the political landscape and offer informed advice, along with qualified predictions. In principle, lobbyists' communication with clients is the culmination of their immense efforts at information harvesting and presenting. In practice, the substantive content of lobbyist-client exchanges is usually far lower than lobbyist-legislator (or lobbyist-lobbyist) interactions. Only the rare client who manifests a real interest in and grasp of a policy matter or whose key issue faces an imminent decision by Congress or an administrative agency merits detailed lobbyist attention. Much more often, lobbyists provide a form of reassurance: your flanks are protected from government regulation or tax hikes or a reversal of all you've fought for; go back to doing what you do best and leave Washington concerns to me.

For their part, clients are generally aware that the information their lobbyists provide is a combination of speculation and substance.[19] The benefit of hiring interest group representatives, as they see it, is not that their lobbyist will derail harmful legislation single-handedly, but that their firm (or nonprofit organization) will be better able to estimate the likelihood of regulation or other government action and either engage in advocacy or make other corrective moves as needed.

Informing Policy Makers. "The key word here," Lobbyist no. 6 told me after I asked about delivering information to public officials, "is *pressure.* Like in a boiler room where the gauge is off the charts and beginning to blow." This dramatic description echoes many others in the interest group community: as the advocacy explosion continues to advance, lobbyists face constant and growing competition for policy makers' attention. The interest group scholar James Thurber has boosted his estimate of lobbyists active in Washington from 75,000 to "well over 100,000" over the past few years.[20] Anecdotally, even experienced lobbyists have more difficulty securing meetings with MCs and top committee or personal staff members, owing to the sheer number of advocates striving for what most call face time. And as MCs spend a larger proportion of their workweek at home in the state or district—a trend visible over the past few years[21]—opportunities for direct contact shrink further.

How to compensate? Lobbyists seeking official audiences resort to a variety of means: eye-catching information packaging; devoted attention to staff, including (where legal) sponsoring welcoming lunches or other informal get-to-know-you events; and, most recently, a relaxation of once-strict norms against discussing policy matters, including current legislation, at fund-raising events. Some MCs still cast a withering pall over any lobbyist's attempt to talk policy at fund-raisers but many do not, and some even initiate conversations. "Hey, [first name]," a Republican House member cheerily greeted Lobbyist no. 3 at a fund-raiser held in his behalf. "Anything you got going on that I should know about?" I was stunned—this was early in my lobbyist-following tenure—but when I talked privately later to the lobbyist, he shrugged. "Happens every so often, not every [fund-raiser], but not never," he said. "It's not like sensitive decisions are being made.... Members just want to let you know they're glad you're there and appreciate your contribution."

As I watched lobbyists, a few informal rules about strategically utilizing information became clear:

- **Never spend all your capital in the same place.** "I make sure to spread out tidbits to different [congressional] offices," Lobbyist no. 11 told me. "Then they're more willing to see you the next time you come around."
- **Offer exclusives to a single MC where possible.** "We would never pitch a new idea to a big group of members or staffers," Lobbyist no. 4 told me as we trudged between fund-raisers one early evening. "[None of them] will be interested because they can't claim credit for the idea as their own."

- **Make constituency connections where possible, but don't stretch it.**
  "I want my [information] to stand on its own, without saying 'so here's how your Peoria constituents will all benefit from this program.' That's for grass-roots types and amateurs," said Lobbyist no. 11.

Informing Each Other.   Almost unheard of in Washington is the lobbyist who is a lone wolf. The making of health policy, like any other issue realm, is flooded by so much information that an informal version of Adam Smith's divided-labor principle is necessary to survival. Interest groups therefore form elaborate networks to exchange information. Hundreds of lobbying coalitions have been established around various policy concerns, as researchers have extensively detailed.[22] Less well chronicled is that lobbyists often form small teams of three or four, sharing paper and other information they gather, splitting up to cover committee hearings occurring simultaneously, and even occasionally comparing notes about client reports, despite the fact that competition for clients is a fact of lobbying life. The natural analogy is to pool reports, wherein one reporter attends an executive briefing and reports details to other journalists. Yes, the results are utilized in the competition's broadcasts or print stories, but such mutually beneficial exchanges are the rule among members of the media—and among lobbyists.

Seven of the eleven lobbyists I follow routinely work in informal teams, at least in a primary issue area, sharing information as described above. The other four join numerous coalitions—on average just over nine coalitions each, although none is especially active in more than two or three coalition groups at a given time. (Three of the four work with other lobbyists in their firm or trade association, so the need for professional partners is less pressing.)

The information lobbyists provide each other is often in raw, unrefined form. It is also largely free of ornamentation or other elaboration. "I can cut through the [garbage] pretty quick, and so can the next [lobbyist], and the next guy," Lobbyist no. 5 explained. "That's what we do for a living. So I'm not wasting time listening to it from my colleagues, and I'm not about to try and spin them. Straightforward, direct, 'what you need to know.' That's it." Such no-nonsense statements aside, lobbyists do engage in strategic disclosure. I listened to Lobbyist no. 2 explain a provision on health privacy in eight separate conversations with fellow lobbyists one June morning; each of the eight heard a slightly different portion of the whole. "No sense in showing all my hand," she said with a wink at morning's end.

Lobbyists' constant work of information gathering, analysis, and dissemination includes plentiful rumor, innuendo, spinning of expectations, and the like. Ultimately, however, much of the information lobbyists traffic in is cold, hard (and often dull, data-driven) fact. Table 17.1 provides a

Table 17.1.   Typology of Information, 2000 (percent)

Type of information	Written information[a]	Personal information[b]
Policy-factual	88	53
Political-strategic: electoral	17	21
Political-strategic: legislative	31	24
Normative-ideological	13	18

Source: Author's data.

[a]Column represents 550 randomly selected items that lobbyists prepare for policy makers and other audiences.
[b]Column represents 1,772 randomly selected items that lobbyists conveyed through informal e-mails and conversation, either on the telephone or face-to-face, over a three-week period.

summary view of my sample of lobbyist information, contrasted with information provided orally (either in face-to-face meetings or over the telephone). The basis for the column labeled "written information" is, again, the 550 randomly selected items that lobbyists prepare for policy makers and other audiences. The column labeled "personal information" represents items that lobbyists conveyed through informal e-mails and conversation, either on the telephone or face-to-face, over a three-week period, again randomly selected, during 2000. I recorded observations during 1,772 separate communications during that time, including at least 20 from each of my eleven lobbyists (one, Lobbyist no. 2, was particularly active during this period, supplying just over 400 of the observed communications). For each set of exchanges, written and personal, I noted the type of information communicated; several documents and most conversations included multiple types. I omitted passing mentions in both cases; in written materials, at least a paragraph (or a visual aid, such as a graphical table) had to be included before an item was coded. Similarly, I recorded only the conversational mentions that lasted more than a few seconds or were clearly important, given the context.

As Table 17.1 displays, fully 88 percent of the 550 documents conveyed factual information about public policy. A smaller percentage (17 percent) discussed strategic political information related to electoral issues, and approximately one-third of the documents (31 percent) included references to legislative strategy (for example, "insurance market changes ['poison pills'] have been added to the managed care legislation. These newly added provisions would have such a detrimental effect on the people covered by state regulated health plans that the President has vowed to veto any legislation that includes them."). Finally, a small proportion of the written documents included normative or ideological information, meaning either strongly partisan arguments or those urging action of the it's-the-right-thing-to-do variety. Personal communications also most often conveyed factual information, compared with other types. Table 17.1 leads to a central discussion about information lobbying and those who carry it out.

Information Bias: It's All About the Spin ... or Is It?

A widely held view of interest groups holds that lobbyists provide information that is subtly—or blatantly—repackaged, depending on the audience. "Information is tailored narrowly to spin the target," runs one characteristic claim. "Democratic information for Democrats, Republican information for Republicans." The notion also makes sense in rational-actor terms: as "cheap speech," lobbyist information is presumably sculpted for maximum appeal to the policy maker–recipient.[23]

After observing lobbyists for years and reading hundreds of the information packets they prepare for legislators, executive branch officials, and reporters, I have concluded that this claim seems dubious at best. To test it empirically, I conducted an experiment to investigate the extent to which information was altered or repackaged. For eight of the lobbyists I follow regularly, during a three-month period in 2000 I collected all the lobbying documents that each used on three primary issues (the issues differed from lobbyist to lobbyist, but all were high-priority to medium-high-priority topics for each). I simultaneously tried to track every usage of each document—for example, a two-page patients' bill of rights issues-and-answers brief prepared by Lobbyist no. 4 was personally delivered to at least twenty-one MCs or staff, left in or sent to another sixteen congressional offices, and circulated to at least forty-four fellow lobbyists and other members of the Beltway policy community.

The result yielded a relatively small number of documents—itself an indication that lobbyists alter their presentations far less than one might expect. Each document was used an average of just over sixteen times. Separately, I analyzed the 550 lobbying documents collected during 2000–2003 (none was included among the set described just above), looking for multiple versions of a single lobbying item. I also asked lobbyists in interviews, formal and informal, about their practice in this regard. "I'll tell you why I usually don't do different [versions of a] document," explained Lobbyist no. 8. "Partly because I'm not always organized enough to figure out what I've already given to who.... But mainly it's because these guys [congressional staff] talk to each other, and sometimes share paper, and the last thing I want is two different graphics floating around. That means ten different angry phone calls about [mimics irate caller] 'How could you give that version to somebody else?'" Lobbyist no. 4 concisely reinforced the point: "I double-deal one time, and my credibility in this town is gone."

My observational evidence supported these anecdotes. Groups almost never altered their printed information in significant—or even minor—ways to influence their audience. Republican legislators received the same set of facts and figures as did Democratic staff members and their members of Congress. Occasionally groups plugged in different information based on an MC's district, but in only 8 percent of the matched pairings (information provided by a lobbyist to Democratic and Republican lawmakers) did I see arguments shaded toward perceived party affiliation. Rather than make an effort to conform to partisan positions, lobbyists usually worked to ensure the information remained constant. I attended more than ninety meetings between lobbyists and staff members or legislators on these fifteen issues during the selected time period, and differences of emphasis were certainly present in discussion. But information leave-behinds—the printed research and analysis designed to shift arguments in the lobbyist's preferred direction—remained the same from office to office, audience to audience.

I also tested additional claims. Joseph White argues bluntly in his study of the appropriations process that "members of Congress are far more likely to get one-sided information" from interest groups than are their staff members.[24] Possibly this holds true for appropriators, but among the health policy lobbyists I follow, none prepared special or otherwise different briefing materials for members. But do they perhaps treat senators or House members and staff members differently in conversation? "In our direct pitch [to MCs] we'll be a little more general [than to staff members]," said Lobbyist no. 4. "That's because they rarely know the issue as well [in as much detail as do staff members]. But we certainly won't tell them something new and different—that's a recipe for disaster with the staffers." After attending dozens of lobbyist meetings in congressional offices, I can affirm that this verity seemed to be upheld. And the handful of policy-related conversations I witnessed between lobbyists and MCs or staff at fund-raisers and other informal events were carried out in the most general of terms; so little substance was exchanged that scant opportunity arose to present misinformation.

What might explain this unexpected constancy? One is the mundane matter of time: although lobbyists may have more temporal and financial resources to research an issue than do congressional staff or executive administrators, they still must work swiftly to put together persuasive material. "Peddling different papers to every office?" Lobbyist no. 11 said with a laugh when I asked about this possibility. "I barely have time to figure out how to explain what's written on *this* sheet [indicates a lobbying document], much less put together a new dog-and-pony show every time I come up here [to Capitol Hill]."

Even lobbyists who work on an issue for months prepare a single set of talking points, which they alter only slightly—and then in conversation, not on printed materials—for Democratic or Republican lawmakers. Reputation is the key here. Every lobbyist I asked about information provision had a story about a predecessor who "tried to pull a fast one," in Lobbyist no. 2's description. "Put one set of numbers together for the steel caucus and another set for the [health care] crowd. Like those two don't overlap, ever ... he's selling life-term policies for Nationwide [Insurance] now." (Variations on the tale had the spin-besotted ex-lobbyist working as a "teacher, last I heard—isn't that a laugh?" [Lobbyist no. 4], as a "tour guide" [Lobbyist no. 8], and as "some kind of consultant, but not in Washington" [Lobbyist no. 7].)

With a sincerity that eventually persuaded this observer, actors throughout the policy sphere—legislative staff, administration officials, and lobbyists themselves—insisted that a lobbyist's standing in the Washington health policy community would be damaged or ruined by promoting false information and diminished considerably by shoddy or oft-altered research. Certainly oversimplification was a common crime among the hundreds of documents I examined, and errors of omission—citing the sections of a study most favorable to a lobbyist's own position while ignoring those that might damage the case—were plentiful as well. But I found almost no examples of lobbyists' pitches changing as they worked their way across the Capitol or executive agencies. This reputational rationale was succinctly summed up to me by a senior Senate aide: the best lobbyists "provide really good information, ideally very quickly, and capitalize on what you already want to do—not something that's bad for you or your [MC]. If they try to spin you, as opposed to giving good, straightforward information, that's not good ... and their reputation will decline, fast."

Along with limited time and a concern to protect their reputation, most lobbyists also believe the viewpoints they promote, or they genuinely appear to, and they insist that the facts they have amassed in support will sway any decision maker who grants them a hearing. "I know these guys [House members, or perhaps staff members—the antecedent was unclear] like my own family," Lobbyist no. 5 stated during one of our early interactions. "Sure, I try to pick my time and place to make my case. But when I do, believe me, it's the same case day in and day out.... Usually I have a stronger case than the other side [the competing lobbyist, for example], and I know I can win on the merits." Watching him in subsequent weeks and months, that claim about constancy was repeatedly upheld.

Democratic Deficit?

Lobbyists' information matters. Their ideas, arguments, and factual details turn up in policy makers' speeches, legislation, and administrative rules. Recognizing this importance leads us to ask about its desirability. Should lobbyists—unelected, self-interested, often highly paid—be a source or even the principal contributor of the information that drives public policy making?

From an efficiency standpoint, lobbyists seem a desirable option. Legislators and executive administrators receive what essentially amounts to a large public subsidy in the form of interest groups' elaborate information searches and analyses. On virtually any policy issue, several or even dozens of groups swiftly supply a raft of carefully researched findings. A savvy staff member or public official can obtain detailed studies from multiple lobbying groups across the ideological spectrum (along with other sources such as CRS and GAO, noted earlier) and perform their own comparative study. If lobbyists were somehow banned tomorrow from informing public officials, a vast increase in government spending would be required to replace their work.

Similarly, lobbyists' information provision appears to enhance government expertise. As Esterling notes, interest groups' policy analysis "often is the best thinking about how to solve persistent social and economic problems.... Because lobbyists intend to persuade members of Congress on complex policy questions, they must concern themselves with and make investments in gathering high-quality research."[25] Much of lobbyists' work is accurate and relatively unbiased, as we have seen. And, at least anecdotally, policy makers are able to detect and punish peddlers of misinformation.

In liberal democracies, efficiency and expertise must be balanced against the necessity for broad representation of public views, values, and interests. Lobbyists' central place in Washington policy making arguably violates democratic norms. For one, lobbyists' information—though not blatantly one-sided—can be subtly biased in various ways. A set of established interests, while differing over technical details, can essentially omit alternative perspectives. Interest groups can also become filters, blocking potentially important findings from legislators' views.

A more common concern among democratic theorists arises from lobbyists' position, so significant in a policy realm in which, in Graham Allison's famous phrase, "where you stand depends on where you sit."[26] Lobbyists are unelected, interested professionals who supply materials on which the people's representatives make decisions. Even if those materials are relatively unbiased, lobbyists' intervention disturbs the democratic process by which legislators hear directly from those they represent. Only if the interest group system is made more representative do we approach James Madison's memorable admonition that only a people armed with knowledge are capable of self-government.

For the present, most stakeholders in U.S. government—policy makers, the American people they represent, media and opinion experts, lobbyists themselves—seem content with, or at least resigned to, the existing state of affairs. In the swirl of lobbying-reform proposals emerging in the immediate wake of the Jack Abramoff scandal of 2005–2006, most were concerned with financial matters—lobbyists' campaign contributions, gifts and meals to policy makers, privately funded travel. Not a single significant proposal targeted the web of information exchanges between lobbyists and decision makers, each group profoundly reliant on the facts, figures, positions, and conclusions they mutually supply.

Notes

1. District Attorney Ronnie Earle, quoted in the documentary film *The Big Buy* (released May 19, 2006); Richard Palmer, "On Point: Decoding the Secret World of Lobbying," *The Report* (newsletter of the College of Business Administration and Public Policy, California State University, Dominguez Hills) 2 (February 2006), 1, http://som.csudh.edu/newsletter/022006/on_point.htm; attributed to Jesse Unruh, as originally reported in Allan L. Otten, "California Clash," *Wall Street Journal*, June 5, 1963, 20.

2. Although much of the discussion in this chapter could also apply to state politics, the focus here is on lobbying the federal government.

3. On this underutilized methodology in political science, see Richard Fenno, *Watching Politicians: Essays on Participant Observation* (Lanham, Md.: University Press of America, 1992). Further details on this project's method are in Rogan Kersh, "Corporate Lobbyists as Political Actors," in *Interest Group Politics*, 6th ed., ed. Allan J. Cigler and Burdett A. Loomis (Washington, D.C.: CQ Press, 2002), 228–231.

4. Amihai Glazer, "Rewarding Political Supporters," *Public Choice* 126 (2006), 454; Mary Clay Berry, "The Case for Public Financing," *APF Reporter* 9 (1977), 2.

5. Tony Podesta, interview with author, August 9, 2000; Drew Littman, communication with author, April 19, 2006.

6. Keith Krehbiel, *Information and Legislative Organization* (Ann Arbor: University of Michigan Press, 1992); David Whiteman, *Communication in Congress: Members, Staff, and the Search for Information* (Lawrence: University Press of Kansas, 1995); Kevin M. Esterling, *The Political Economy of Expertise: Information and Efficiency in American National Politics* (Ann Arbor: University of Michigan Press, 2004).

7. Two recent examples are Eric S. Heberlig, "Getting to Know You and Getting Your Vote: Lobbyists' Uncertainty and the Contacting of Legislators," *Political Research Quarterly* 58, no. 3 (2005), on how lobbyists seek information on legislators' preferences; and Daniel P. Carpenter, Kevin M. Esterling, and David M. J. Lazer, "Friends, Brokers, and Transitivity: Who Informs Whom in Washington Politics?" *Journal of Politics* 66, no. 1 (2004): 224–246 (on information sharing among interest groups).

8. Whiteman, *Communication in Congress*, 39.

9. "The Lobby League: Oil Refining," *The Hill*, May 24, 2006, 18.

10. "Long-Term Care and Medicaid: Spiraling Costs and the Need for Reform," House Energy and Commerce Committee, Subcommittee on Health, April 27, 2005, 167, http://energycommerce.house.gov/108/Hearings/04272005hearing1487/hearing.htm.

11. Jeffrey M. Berry, *The Interest Group Society*, 3d ed. (New York: Longman, 1997).

12. Richard L. Hall, *Participation in Congress* (New Haven: Yale University Press, 1996).

13. On malpractice politics more generally, see Rogan Kersh, "Medical Malpractice and the New Politics of Health Care," in *Medical Malpractice and the U.S. Health Care System*, ed. William M. Sage and Rogan Kersh (New York: Cambridge University Press, 2006).

14. Lobbyist spending, unlike campaign expenditures, is difficult to track; Open Secrets (www.opensecrets.org) and PoliticalMoneyLine (http://www.fecinfo.com/) are useful sources.

15. The typical House of Representatives staff member remains on the job for approximately 1.5 years; Senate staff members stay for 2.2 years. The overall time House staff members remain in Congress is just over 4 years; Senate staff remain an average of 5 years. See "Senate Salary, Tenure & Demographic Data, 1991–2001" (Washington, D.C.: Congressional Management Foundation, 2002); and "2004 House Staff Employment Study" (Washington, D.C.: Congressional Management Foundation, 2005).

16. For a list and more detailed treatment, see Rogan Kersh, *Unhealthy Influence? Watching Lobbyists in American Government* (forthcoming), chap. 4.

17. Whiteman, *Communication in Congress*, 133, Table 6.1; 106–108; 132–154.
18. In 61 cases no source information was discernable; of the other 489, 65 (13.3 percent) were primarily lobbyist-generated research.
19. For an extended account of clients' views of lobbyists, see Kersh, *Unhealthy Influence?* chap. 2.
20. Thurber quoted in Bara Vaida, Eliza Newlin Carney, and Lisa Caruso, "Potholes on K Street," *National Journal*, March 25, 2006, 18.
21. Thomas E. Mann and Norman J. Ornstein, *The Broken Branch: How Congress Is Failing America and How to Get It Back on Track* (New York: Oxford University Press, 2006).
22. See especially Kevin W. Hula, *Lobbying Together: Interest Group Coalitions in Legislative Politics* (Washington: Georgetown University Press, 1999).
23. Roger Larocca, "Strategic Diversion in Political Communication," *Journal of Politics* 66, no. 2 (2004); Lars Frisell and Johan N. M. Lagerlöf, "Lobbying, Information Transmission and Unequal Representation," DP 4313 (London: Centre for Economic Policy Research, March 2004).
24. Joseph White, "Making Connections to the Appropriations Process," in *The Interest Group Connection*, 2d ed., ed. Paul S. Herrnson, Ronald G. Shaiko, and Clyde Wilcox (Washington, D.C.: CQ Press, 2005), 174.
25. Esterling, *Political Economy of Expertise*, 44, 245.
26. Graham Allison, "Conceptual Models and the Cuban Missile Crisis," *American Political Science Review* 63, no. 4 (1969): 711.

18

Does K Street Run Through Capitol Hill?
Lobbying Congress in the Republican Era
Burdett A. Loomis

In 1994, congressional Republicans won a historic electoral victory that placed them in control of both the Senate and the House of Representatives. Almost immediately, Speaker of the House Newt Gingrich, R-Ga., and fellow leaders sought to enact an extensive agenda of conservative policies. With a slim majority in the House, Gingrich and his lieutenants worked hard—with both carrots and sticks—to produce a high level of Republican support for their agenda items. Much of the heavy lifting fell to Representative Tom DeLay, R-Texas, first as majority whip, then as majority leader. Part of DeLay's strategy to increase Republican strength in the House has been to enlist Washington lobbyists to his cause. Through the so-called K Street Project, DeLay and other congressional Republicans have sought to place their own loyalists in key lobbying positions, to use these individuals to help pass the party's policies, and to encourage them to raise funds that will help the party retain control of Congress.

DeLay's attempt to incorporate members of the extensive Washington lobbying community into his legislative empire is truly ambitious because lobbyists and organized interests have usually been unwilling to give their unwavering loyalty to a single party. In this chapter, Burdett Loomis examines the K Street Project from the perspectives of both the congressional and interest group literatures. He argues that the attempt to dominate the lobbying community is bound to fail, given the fragmentation of American politics and the difficulty faced by legislative leaders, even in a highly partisan era, in guaranteeing sufficient payoffs for groups to risk the chance that Democrats might shut them out in future years. Although there has been a lot of credit claiming as lobbying firms do recruit more Republicans, much of this trend can be explained by the natural, and short-term, desire of lobbying firms to work with a unified Republican government.

As Republicans control more and more K Street jobs, they will reap more and more K Street money, which will help them win larger majorities on the Hill. The larger the Republican majority, the less reason K Street has to hire Democratic lobbyists or contribute to the campaigns of Democratic politicians, slowly starving them of the means by which to challenge GOP rule.

Nicholas Confessore, "Welcome to the Machine"

The congressional Republicans' K Street Project, which has sought for more than a decade to extend the reach of party influence into the Washington lobbying community, presents an unusual opportunity to examine an attempt to change what has long seemed the natural order of political life in the nation's capital. That is, could lobbyists and interest groups, who have historically focused on what benefited them on relatively narrow and specific grounds, be induced to operate in more partisan ways that would benefit the majority Republican Party? If so, such a change would mark a major shift in how organized interests approach the Congress, to say nothing of the executive branch and myriad regulatory bodies that make policy in the nation's capital.

In 2003, journalist Nicholas Confessore concluded that the congressional Republicans had indeed succeeded in creating a new version of the political machine, where GOP loyalists were placed in lobbying positions from which they would provide extensive support—both logistical and financial—to the Republican Party.[1] In return, the lobbyists would be well paid, and Republican congressional majorities would help them win victories for their clients, whose interests (oil and pharmaceuticals, for example) generally meshed with the party's probusiness perspective.

Both the GOP's intent and Confessore's conclusions run up against scholars' conventional wisdom as to the relationships between lobbyists and legislators, which have generally been depicted as tangentially related to partisan considerations.[2] Even as the K Street Project has proceeded, with no attempts to mask its intent of creating strong partisan ties between lawmakers and lobbyists, students of both Congress and interest groups have paid little attention to its machinery, implications, and potential impact. Indeed, searches of scholarly databases like JSTOR and Google Scholar produced no matches for the term, K Street Project. This seems more than strange, given the project's essential openness, continuing notoriety,[3] and alleged successes.[4] Moreover, during the past thirty years, both legislative and interest group scholars have been quick to identify and analyze other emerging trends, such as the strengthening of political parties on Capitol Hill and the roles played by political action committees (PACs).

Although this chapter's central thrust will be to flesh out the nature of the K Street Project, its secondary purpose will be to examine why scholars have exhibited almost no interest in a development that might well profoundly affect the actions of both organized interests and members of Congress. Still, the insights of congressional and interest group scholars are important in understanding the K Street Project and will provide our jumping-off point in addressing the extension of legislative partisanship into the domain of organized interests and lobbyists.

Legislatures and Organized Interests: Two Perspectives

Comparing the scholarly work on legislatures and organized interests demonstrates the value of having a well-organized subfield, where knowledge accumulates so as to incorporate and address changes in context and behavior and draw upon historical insights for illuminating contemporary issues. So it has been with the study of legislatures, and especially of the U.S. Congress over the past fifty-plus years, from Don Matthews's earliest work on the Senate to the recent substantial contributions of many excellent young scholars.[5] As political scientist Morris Fiorina put it more than a decade ago, "The legislative subfield illustrates the progress made by a genuine research *community*."[6]

Having a well-developed subfield means that changes in structure and behavior receive timely attention. The growth of partisanship in Congress represents a particularly apt case. As partisanship rose during the 1980s, scholars like such as David Rohde, Barbara Sinclair, and Ken Shepsle (among many others) wrote a series of papers and books that both chronicled and analyzed this trend.[7] Shepsle, for example, placed the 1980s' nascent increase in congressional partisanship in the historical context of the "textbook Congress" of mid-century and the transitional, fragmented body of the 1970s. His anticipation was more than warranted, and, by the early 1990s, congressional scholars had a raft of books and articles that brought intellectual rigor to both the particulars of the growing partisanship on Capitol Hill and the theoretical-conceptual bases for strong legislative parties with relatively powerful leaders.[8]

In a brief paper, Cox and McCubbins summarize the "post-reform" (circa 1980) study of leadership, with its emphasis the principal-agent metaphor:[9]

> In a field dominated by two extreme theories of leadership (one where leadership was distributed amongst many, if not all, office holders, and one where leaders were viewed as generals marching the troops to battle), Sinclair [in her 1983 *Majority Leadership in the U.S. House*] presented what would become the new consensus view—a view of legislative leadership in which leaders not only exercise real power and influence, but also act as *agents of their parties*. To Sinclair, party leaders are responsible for building winning coalitions and maintaining intra-party peace, and her work has provided a foundation for contemporary theories of legislative leadership and legislative organization.[10]

From this core insight, Rohde and Aldrich developed their conditional party government (CPG) model, and Cox and McCubbins produced their cartel approach to party leadership.[11] Though somewhat different in emphasis and implication, both models rely on the principal-agent perspective.[12] Party actions on Capitol Hill have generally offered strong, steady evidence to support the accuracy and usefulness of these models as well, especially given the consistent ability of House Republicans to maintain their majority, to provide their leaders with substantial authority, to rein them in on occasion, and even to fire them (for example, Representatives Newt Gingrich, R-Ga.; Bob Livingston, R-La.; and Tom DeLay, R-Texas) when they lacked adequate support within the House Republican Conference (the caucus of all GOP members).

Sinclair thus concludes, "extreme partisan polarization characterizes… the contemporary House of Representatives," but the question is: Does such polarization flow from the ideological makeup of members (and indirectly their constituencies), or does it depend on the internal organization of the Congress?[13] This question is important (if unanswered here) because its answer—probably "some of each"—directly addresses the extent to which Republican leaders in the House and, to a lesser extent the Senate, have incorporated lobbyists into the principal-agent nexus that has produced effective, highly partisan approaches to agenda setting and decision making on Capitol Hill.

Even though congressional scholars have not systematically examined the K Street Project, the overall thrust of their literature offers them a well-developed, empirically sound framework in which the Republicans' experiment can be assessed. As we shall see, students of Congress, while somewhat surprised by the 1994 election results and the continuing GOP electoral and policy successes over the following twelve years, could offer relatively straightforward explanations of these successes, especially in the House, based on the subfield's cumulative research on parties during the fifteen years prior to the Republican takeover.[14]

In contrast, the interest group subfield, as of the mid-1990s, was far less prepared to deal with the changing context of lobbying produced by the GOP takeover of Congress. But that scarcely comes as a surprise, given the status of interest group scholarship in the contemporary era.[15] As one recent article on lobbying noted, "Empirical research on interest group influence has accumulated for decades, but this literature is noteworthy for the noncumulative, frequently inconsistent nature of its findings."[16] For example, various analyses of lobbying, published well after the GOP takeover of Congress, make no serious mention of parties as important contextual elements.[17] Indeed, Charls Walker, an astute lobbyist and veteran observer of the profession, noted "The 'Republican Revolution' of November 1994 did not change what constitutes effective lobbying. Effective lobbying is keyed to the democratic system. The Republican majority in Congress will do basically what their constituents want or that majority will again become a minority."[18] In one sense, this is a truism, but to assert that the Republican majority had not changed things simply ignored major shifts in the structure and actions of the Washington lobbying community.[19]

Jacob Hacker and Paul Pierson's recent partisan analysis of the post-1994 era, *Off Center: The Republican Revolution and the Erosion of American Democracy*, does pay some heed to the K Street Project, but without coming to any conclusion as to its effectiveness.[20] Still, they conclude, "the Republican leadership [in Congress, and especially the House] has built an unprecedented apparatus to monitor lobbyist activities," which can range from fund raising to hiring to solicitation of grassroots support.[21] It's striking that Hacker and Pierson's work relies much more heavily on journalistic sources than academic ones, and it certainly does not develop any kind of interest group explanation for changes within the lobbying community's partisan activities.

Contemporary students of lobbying have depicted lobbyists as largely independent of parties, even as they often engage in partisan activities.[22] In other words, lobbyists have long identified themselves with one party or the other, and many helped organize political conventions, raise funds, and recruit individuals on both sides of the government–private sector revolving door. But in pursuing their livelihoods, lobbyists are generally seen as providing informational services or subsidies to legislators as individuals, rather than as members of partisan teams.[23] Traditionally, lobbying firms have recruited both nominal Republican and Democratic lobbyists, so as to serve all legislators on Capitol Hill. In short, lobbyists were usually labeled as partisans, but their partisanship was rarely central to their daily activities, especially given the bipartisan nature of most firms. In 2005, political scientists Paul Herrnson, Ron Shaiko, and Clyde Wilcox summarized the situation:

> The relationship between members of Congress and lobbyists relies on an exchange: lobbyists provide members with valuable technical and political information on specific issues, and members may fulfill interest groups' objectives by enacting preferred policies.[24]

To their credit, these authors do briefly note the implications of strong Republican leadership on Capitol Hill (and the White House), but their overall approach remains wedded to a long-term perspective on organized interests and lobbying that emphasizes the broad diversity of groups and their representation within the political process, regardless of the power of congressional parties.[25]

In a similar vein, Rick Hall and Alan Deardorff have recently presented a sophisticated case for regarding lobbying as a legislative subsidy.[26] Their argument builds upon and extends the understanding of lobbying activities as "servicing front-line soldiers—... mainly the senators and representatives who were waging the battle within Congress," as articulated by Bauer, Pool, and Dexter in their path-breaking study of trade lobbying, published more than forty years ago.[27] Whether exchange or subsidy, or some of each, both the Hall-Deardorff and the Bauer-Pool-Dexter formulations address the relationships between lobbyists and individual legislators; there is no reason, to be sure, that legislative parties could not be the agents of exchange or the recipients of subsidies, but that would require a set of calculations different from those focusing on linkages between the lobbyists and interest groups and the individual lawmakers.

In the end, the well-organized subfield of legislative politics (and especially the study of Congress) has produced party-based theories of CPG and legislative party cartels, which can be plausibly extended to address relationships with lobbyists, while the interest group literature appears less well equipped to assess the significance of the K Street Project's intertwining of congressional parties with organized interests. At the same time, the scholarship on Congress offers the possibility that party leaders on Capitol Hill can ride herd not only on their members but also on an extensive team of lobbyists that represents specific (and often competing) interests.

K Street Project

The K Street Project is a term that gets kicked around with great frequency but relatively little precision. Virtually everyone agrees that, in essence, it is a personnel screening and tracking project made up of the Republican leadership on Capitol Hill as well as key lobbyists such as Grover Norquist; it is designed to place Republicans in Washington, D.C., lobbying jobs for major corporations, trade associations, and major contract lobbying firms (including law firms that lobby extensively). In practice, Norquist and Sen. Rick Santorum, R-Pa., held weekly meetings[28] to work on placement of Republicans to lobbying jobs:

> Santorum's Tuesday meetings are a crucial part of [the effort to break down the bipartisan complexion of K Street]. Every week, the lobbyists present pass around a list of jobs available and discuss whom to support. Santorum's job is to make sure each one is filled with a loyal Republican.... After Santorum settles on a candidate, the lobbyists present make sure it is known whom the Republican leadership favors. "The underlying theme was [to] place Republicans in key positions on K Street. Everybody taking part was a Republican and understood that that was the purpose of what we were doing," says Rod Chandler, a retired congressman and lobbyist who has participated in the Santorum meetings.[29]

What the K Street Project promised Republican legislators who were retiring (or defeated) and upwardly mobile staff members was that they could do well financially, continue to act in partisan and ideological ways, and remain active in the arena of national politics.[30] Such multiple goals have long attracted former members and staff to the lobbying trade, but the Republican leadership was in a position to guarantee great financial success as well as offer the possibility of continuing to contribute to the ideological crusade of the party and provide the enjoyable opportunity to participate in high-level politics.

Especially after the 2000 elections and in the wake of the federal government's reaction to the attacks of September 11, 2001, conditions were propitious on both the supply and demand sides of the lobbying business. The demand for Republican lobbyists rose with the onset of unified government in 2001 and was reinforced after both the 2002 and 2004 elections. One lobbyist noted, "Having the White House [allowed Republican congressional leaders] to enforce the K Street Project." Enforcement could come in many ways that ranged from denying access to lobbyists to rejecting their policy requests or to requiring that lobbyists, firms, and interest groups make large campaign contributions to Republican candidates and committees.

In addition, increased domestic security spending in the wake of the 9/11 attacks meant that the federal pie grew much larger, very quickly, which opened the door to intense lobbying over new spoils.[31] Moreover, by 2001 the Republican members' official congressional enterprises had produced a large supply of relatively young, reasonably experienced, and generally ideological staff who had worked with the majority and who were eager to make the traditional move to the private sector.[32] With their rise to majority status in 1995, Republicans had added hundreds of key staff jobs on committees and within the party leadership; like all those who preceded them in these positions, these staff members became valuable, viable candidates for the best lobbying openings, and the K Street Project offered a ready vehicle to move them into those jobs.

Although the most visible and prestigious lobbying slots received the most attention from the Santorum-Norquist-DeLay groups, the systematic growth of the Washington lobbying community meant that many mid-level lobbying positions also opened up, offering lucrative opportunities for younger staff members who wished to vacate their rabbit-warren Hill cubicles and move downtown to more luxurious office space and far higher salaries. Whether for top-level jobs or middle-range ones, the K Street Project has been remarkably open, to the point that it operates in part through a Web site, http://www.kstreetproject.com/[33] and does not shy away from publicity. In fact, the very openness of the project has been central to its strategy; that is, it publicizes widely the core idea that only loyal Republicans should be considered for key corporate and trade association lobbying jobs. Grover Norquist observed in 2005 that "there should be as many Democrats working on K Street representing corporate America as there are Republicans working in organized labor—and that number is close to zero," and to Norquist that meant in every position: "all of them—including secretaries."[34] If the GOP majorities on Capitol Hill could in fact enforce their will, then Norquist's wishful desire might not be far-fetched.

Assessing the overall effectiveness of the K Street Project in achieving its recruitment goals is imprecise at best, but most indications point to substantial success in altering the hiring patterns of many corporations, trade associations, law firms, and lobbying shops, even if some major plums have gone to prominent and well-qualified Democrats such as former representative David McCurdy, who became president of the Electronic Industries Alliance in 1998, and former representative Dan Glickman, President Clinton's agriculture secretary, who became president of the Motion Picture Association of America six years later. As one Capitol Hill journalist summarized in 2004, "Retiring House Democrats are feeling a cold draft from K Street as they seek post-congressional employment at lobbying firms, trade groups and corporations. By contrast, K Street is aggressively courting GOP lawmakers who have announced their retirements...."[35]

Still, even if the Santorum-DeLay-Norquist-based organization of the K Street Project has resulted in jobs for particular Republicans, and higher salaries for GOP lobbyists,[36] the impact of the organized effort is difficult to judge.[37] For one thing, Democratic staff members and former legislators do find positions within the Washington lobbying community (broadly defined to include top law firms and rainmaker positions, such as former Senate Democratic leader Tom Daschle's role at Alston & Bird, where he was recruited by former Senate Republican leader Bob Dole). As David Rehr, president of the National Association of Broadcasters and perhaps the archetypal lobbyist of the past twenty years in his previous role as head of the National Beer Wholesalers Association, put it, "Despite what Grover Norquist thinks, or I think, you can't just expect to get a top job because you are a Republican."[38] Rather, Republican lobbyists must provide added value, which can, of course, derive from their continuing ties to congressional leaders.[39] Thus, former DeLay staff member Tony Rudy could demonstrate such ties—and his accordingly elevated fees—by literally conducting business out of the majority leader's office. "It was known within leadership circles that Rudy was running the CAFE [mileage standards] vote operation out of the whip's office," said a former leadership staff member, adding: "Rudy was not shy in selling his access to DeLay."[40]

Moreover, as might be drawn from the CPG approach to strong congressional parties, Republican lobbyists should be favored within the unified context of national government, regardless of whether there is an active K Street Project or not. Given the GOP control of the White House and both houses of Congress, it makes good sense for those in search of lobbyists to search aggressively among Republican allies.

The overlapping partisan voting patterns for both president and Congress produce a condition in which the party base for Republican control of the agenda and the process has grown stronger, especially in the wake of the 2002 and 2004 elections. For example, only 59 House districts (less than 14 percent) produced different partisan results in their votes for president and representative in 2004, down from 190 such splits (almost 44 percent) in the 1980s.[41] As one House Republican leadership aide noted, referring to Grover Norquist's claiming credit for increased hiring of lobbyists with Republican ties, "It's [him] taking credit for market forces.... It doesn't take a rocket scientist to figure out that Washington is polarized, and it's smart to hire Republicans right now."[42] A former senior White House aide concurred: "Grover's smart, and a good organizer, but he claims way too much credit."[43] As if to confirm such observations, Norquist has sought to trademark the "K Street" label:

> Conservative activist Grover Norquist is seeking a trademark on "K Street Project," saying Democrats and Majority Leader John Boehner (R-Ohio) have wrongfully acquired the term to describe unethical practices that have nothing to do with his organization. Far from running away from the term, as most other Republicans have since January, when lobbyist Jack Abramoff agreed to plead guilty to corruption charges, Norquist is embracing it.... His group distributes weekly jobs bulletins by e-mail to 250 subscribers.... Norquist's trademark application [for a logo of a "K Street" street sign] could take up to a year and a half to be processed.[44]

Without question Republicans have gravitated to top lobbying jobs in disproportionate numbers since 1994, and especially since 2000, with various lists circulating via Senator Santorum, the GOP House leadership, and Grover Norquist, among others. But the importance of the K Street Project remains questionable at best; one lobbyist, formerly a House GOP leadership staff member said:

> The K Street Project has taken on a bigger-than-life perspective, particularly in the media.... Lobbying firms don't need Grover or Santorum, either one, to help them [decide whom to hire].... We are fully capable of figuring out "Oh, the Democrats [*sic*] are in control, so we need to shift who we have on staff in order to reflect that."[45]

The question does remain, however, of how much hiring grew out of the Republicans' control of the levers of power and how much came from strong, even intense, pressures from Capitol Hill to ensure that as many positions as possible, and especially the most visible ones, were placed in the hands of party loyalists.

It is still unclear how much the K Street Project did systematically affect lobbyist hiring between late 1994 and 2006. Certainly, Grover Norquist has taken credit for helping place GOP loyalists in lobbying positions, and party leaders in both the House (through Rep. Tom DeLay and members of his staff like Ed Buckham) and the Senate (through Sen. Rick Santorum) compiled lists of jobs that should go to their Republican allies.[46] At the same time, corporations, lobbying firms, and trade associations made the natural choice to employ more well-connected Republicans to deal with, at first, a GOP Congress and, later on, a unified GOP regime. Nor was the strength and discipline among congressional Republicans, especially in the House, a mystery to prospective employers. Thus, a highly partisan model of lobbyist hiring does make sense whether or not the K Street Project was instrumental; what's apparent is that partisanship was taken into account and often acted upon in hiring decisions.

At the same time, the long-term, bipartisan approach to lobbying Congress retains a powerful hold on K Street, in large part because the federal government does so much, and many decisions occur beyond the glare of partisan scrutiny and rely heavily on substantive expertise rather than ideology or partisan clout. Larry Noble, of the Center for Responsive Politics, concludes: "... the K Street Project ran counter to what was naturally happening in Washington, which was Republicans and Democrats getting together to lobby."[47] Another Washington observer sees the extreme partisanship of Capitol Hill as "contributing to this [bipartisan] trend," because issues other than top agenda items for congressional leaders and the president "have needed Republican and Democratic support to advance or risk being trapped in the partisan crossfire of the closely divided chambers."[48] Thus, even after three full years of unified Republican government and almost twelve years of GOP congressional control, major lobbying and law firms—the very ones that would have a lot to lose—have remained self-consciously bipartisan.

For all the apparent centralization and discipline on Capitol Hill, there are centrifugal forces of personal relationships, distributive politics, regionalism, and interindustry squabbles that require approaches to influence that transcend partisanship. Still, the past decade has proved kinder to Republicans than Democrats as they enter the lobbying community, owing in part to the K Street Project. Let us now turn to assessing the project from the perspectives of legislative studies and interest group politics.

Conditional Party Government and the K Street Project

Lucidly summarizing the CPG model, Aldrich and Rohde note the importance of "how much the members of a party agree on their preferences (preference homogeneity), especially among members of the majority party."[49] A second key element is the differences in preferences between the memberships of the majority and the minority:

> These two conditions—preference homogeneity and preference conflict—together form the "condition" in the theory of conditional party government. As they increase, the theory predicts that party members will be progressively more willing to create strong powers for leaders and to support the exercise of those powers in specific instances. But when diversity grows within parties, or the differences between parties are reduced, members will be reluctant to grant greater powers to leaders. This is the central prediction of CPG.[50]

Even though legislators have long enjoyed one-on-one relationships with individual lobbyists, who provided them with either general subsidies or exchanges with specific benefits, Republican legislators appeared sanguine in their willingness to go along with the hiring practices for the K Street Project as coordinated by the chambers' leadership offices, sometimes in conjunction with Norquist and a band of ideological lobbyists. With many staff members and some former members coming from Republican congressional ranks, the GOP senators and (especially) representatives surrendered some of their individual connections to lobbyists so that the leaders could enhance the party's overall chances of (a) staying in power (via the funneling of campaign contributions to competitive districts) and (b) winning beneficial policy victories through an extra layer of party-orchestrated lobbying. To an extent, subsidies from organized interests (for example, information) and campaign contributions went to the collective (the congressional party), and because of similar preferences among party lawmakers, Republican legislators generally benefited.

Crucial here for both legislators and lobbyists was the ability of the Republican leadership to produce a solid string of victories. This surely proved the case in the 108th Congress (2003–2004), as congressional scholar John Owens concluded:

> Republicans had enacted much of their program, as a strongly cohesive party. At different times centrists and hard-line conservatives had swallowed their lumps in the interests of their party. Fully-fledged American style party government was clearly in place as the House (and Senate) patterns on party unity votes demonstrated, ... matching levels commonly found in the British House of Commons.[51]

Lobbyists could see the benefits of lining up with this effective Republican leadership, which—at least in the House—could claim to have prevailed on all major votes. If the Republican leaders were seeking to place their staff members and former colleagues in lobbying jobs, organized interests should listen—and they apparently did. In fact, the hub of the K Street Project ran directly from House majority leader Tom DeLay's office, out of which at least eleven of his former staff members became high-paid lobbyists and seven more took on important corporate or trade group roles.[52] In 2003–2004, DeLay's eleven lobbyist alumni brought in $45.1 million for their firms, in sharp contrast with the alumni of the office of Speaker of the House J. Dennis Hastert, R-Ill., whose billings came to only $2.1 million.[53] It is no wonder that former DeLay chief of staff Susan Hirschmann set off a bidding war when she moved to the private sector, and that Ed Buckham could command record fees in his salad days with Alexander Strategy Group (before he was named as an unindicted co-conspirator in fellow DeLay alumnus Tony Rudy's guilty plea).[54] In many ways, DeLay—more than the Republican leadership as a whole—stood at the center of the K Street Project. In 2003, veteran Republican lobbyist Mark Isakowitz observed, "You can't find anyone who ignores the DeLay factor today. It's pervasive and part of the K Street culture."[55]

To the extent that the K Street Project was truly effective in linking the Washington lobbying establishment to the Republican leadership, DeLay and his extended enterprise (well into the lobbying community) may have been the most important element. With DeLay now gone from Congress, does the linchpin disappear for connecting the homogeneous majority to a more ideological lobbying core? More importantly, Republicans have become minorities in both House and Senate for the 110th Congress (2007–2008). To the extent that the hiring project had legs beyond the ordinary need for interests to work with the majority party within a unified government, DeLay provided both the ideological perspective and the organizational clout to make it work.

As luck would have it, Tom DeLay's indictment in 2005, his stepping down as majority leader, and his eventual resignation from the House of Representatives offer two opportunities to examine his personal role within the House GOP–K Street nexus. First, House Republicans chose among three candidates to replace DeLay: the sitting whip, Roy Blunt, R-Mo., a DeLay loyalist and lieutenant; the Education Committee chair, John Boehner, R-Ohio, a veteran conservative leader and friend to the lobbying community but not a DeLay confidante; and backbencher John Shadegg, R-Ariz., who campaigned as a conservative reformer and who would have backed the most sweeping changes to Congress's linkages to the lobbying community.[56] The House Republican Conference first eliminated Shadegg, who received 40 votes, while Blunt got 110 and Boehner 79. The members of the conference then voted 122–109 in favor of Boehner, as House Republicans weighed in against the current regime (Blunt) and for at least the veneer of reform.

Boehner campaigned for modest changes (for example, more reporting), rather than abolishing valuable perquisites such as private funding of legislators' travel. At the same time, Boehner had long enjoyed excellent connections to Washington lobbyists; indeed, he was a crucial figure in bringing legislators and lobbyists together in weekly meetings during the mid-1990s.[57] Whether Boehner can exercise the centralizing power that DeLay did as majority leader remains in doubt.

The second natural experiment that flows from Boehner's victory involves his ability to raise funds for the party from his lobbyist constituents. Here the evidence is strong that Boehner can make this part of the relationship work: in the February–July period of 2006, Boehner raised campaign contributions a the rate of $10,000 per day, with much of his fund-raising facilitated by the use of lobbyists' venues and resources (for example, private jets).[58] His totals surpassed DeLay's during the initial months of his service as majority leader.

Does CPG help us to understand the K Street Project? It may in at least two ways. First, given the success of the GOP within Congress, especially the House, and the level of confidence placed in DeLay as ideologue cum organizer and fund raiser, one can understand the ambitions of extending the reach of CPG beyond the confines of the chamber. In the end, although DeLay became the majority leader, he never stopped being the de facto chief whip who could reach almost any majority member.[59]

The question remains how much of this power was invested in DeLay and how much in the office of the majority leader (and the Republican leadership generally).

Second, within the American legislative party system, the *condition* in CPG—the roughly homogeneous preferences of the majority, and its distance from the minority—requires substantial discipline for lobbyists to work solely (or even largely) through the majority party leadership. In the end, despite hiring practices and personal ties, there are too many lobbyists, too many issues, and too many venues for a party-based lobbying strategy to dominate. Ironically, one result has been that 72 percent of lobbyists in a *National Journal* survey see the intense "partisanship [as making] it *more* difficult to achieve their objectives, which, in the end almost always differ from those of the party leaders."[60]

K Street Project and Organized Interests

> Unfortunately, the accumulated mass of quantitative and qualitative studies of lobbying behavior has generated a great number of contradictions, with few consistent findings.... While each of the studies may have its merits, collectively the literature has generated more confusion than clarity.[61]

So conclude Frank Baumgartner and Beth Leech after their exhaustive cataloguing of legislative lobbying in 1998; nothing has changed in the intervening years to provide more coherence, even as organized interests have grown more numerous and lobbying more expansive across numbers of activities and venues.[62] Expecting the lobbying literature to offer substantial insight into the K Street Project would seem unrealistic, yet it does provide some paths to understanding.

Hall and Deardorff examine and discard the theories of lobbyist-legislator exchange and lobbyist persuasion before they build a case for their notion of lobbying as subsidy.[63] Nothing in the K Street Project suggests that persuasion is relevant to lobbying success because policy information is not especially relevant, at least on major issues. But the exchange model may have some virtue in that the centralization of the exchange process at the party leadership level (or within Majority Leader DeLay's office specifically) provides an opportunity for (1) an exchange of lobbying support for particularized benefits to take place and for (2) the agreement to be enforced owing to the leaders' control of the legislative process, both substantively and procedurally. Moreover, to the extent that loyalist lobbyists direct campaign contributions to the GOP, the leadership has been well positioned to direct those resources to needy districts, with relatively little slippage.

If Republicans could deliver, there were great incentives for substantial exchanges in which the rewards—of earmarks, tax policies, reduced enforcement, and the like—were large and concrete (sometimes literally).

This so-called pay-for-play approach to policy making required enforcement, and DeLay was the one legislator who could provide predictable guarantees that deals would hold together.[64] The centralization of the Republicans' control of the House allowed the possibility of enforceable exchanges, carried out on a large scale; but DeLay's fall, along with the GOP's loss of control of the House, virtually eliminates the possibility of enforcement.

What, then, of the subsidy model? For one thing, Hall and Deardorff offer no clues as to how lobbyists' subsidies might operate within a strong-party legislature. In a sense, they place their audience back in the retail politics era of the 1970s, when every vote needed to be wooed, given the relatively weak party leadership (although it grew stronger) and the strongly entrepreneurial predispositions of most legislators. When the GOP controls the agenda and the floor, do legislators require subsidies? Regardless, they might well receive subsidies from savvy, anticipatory lobbyists who know which way the wind is blowing, especially if they have been part of the leadership organization in the past.[65]

At the same time, for those lobbyists who operate their boats full of influence outside the main channels of partisanship, the subsidy model may well have value, even if the overall partisan context may make the subsidies of public interest groups less valuable than during a less-partisan era.

K Street Project: Beyond Jobs and Ideology

The K Street Project—after twelve years of existence—has entered the American political lexicon, yet it has received little attention from either legislative or interest group scholars. Such academics may have good reason to doubt the import of this relatively ill-defined enterprise, given the exaggerated credit claiming of Grover Norquist, the variety of lobbyist-legislator contacts that can and do take place outside the congressional party organization framework, and the lingering questions of whether characterizations of the project as a political machine were even generally accurate.

In the end, there is probably enough smoke to suggest some real fire, in both hiring practices and, perhaps, the broader existence of substantial exchanges between legislative leaders and lobbyists. Without question, the CPG model helps to think through what it would take for either version of the K Street Project to succeed; indeed, the idea of the Republican leadership trying to enhance its power by engaging the K Street community to serve partisan purposes is truly ambitious. Likewise, the very existence of a strong, unified GOP congressional party with a leader capable of enforcing deals might resurrect the exchange model of interest group relations with Congress. Still, as Tom DeLay departs for an unknown future and as the Republican majority has disappeared in the wake of the 2006 elections, the centrifugal (and often bipartisan or nonpartisan) forces of interest group politics appear likely to reassert themselves. In fact, there is another way to view the K Street Project, one presented by journalists Confessore and Drew and adopted informally by many Washington insiders: as a kind of shorthand for current linkages between the Republican-led Congress and the lobbying community.[66] And the hiring of GOP lobbyists is merely one cog in a machine that processes a number of exchanges:

1. GOP leadership assists in placing lobbyists in return for future help on legislation unrelated to these jobs;
2. GOP leadership assists in obtaining positions for prospective lobbyists in return for future contributions from the lobbyists, their firms, and their clients, directed back to the leaders' campaign entities (including leadership PACs) or to specific, designated congressional campaigns;
3. Future contributions from lobbyists will be solicited in return for future favorable policy actions—the so-called pay-for-play arrangement that stands at the heart of many broad-gauged arguments over the alleged corruption of the lobbyist-legislator relationship.[67]

In many ways, various Republican lobbyists note, this resembles the tactics pursued by Democrats in the late 1980s and early 1990s, as Rep. Tony Coelho, D-Calif., played a similar role, first as Democratic Congressional Campaign Committee chair and then as House majority whip.[68] Coelho's program was surely innovative and brought millions of business contributions into Democratic coffers, but the partisan power of the Democratic leadership was far less than that of their Republican successors.

In the post-1995 Republican era, Democratic legislators, liberal publications (and bloggers), and even the mainstream media, on occasion, employ the expression "K Street Project" to describe imputed relationships that go far beyond the relatively straightforward hiring aims of the Santorum-Norquist-House GOP endeavor; in the end, examining the kinds of relationships that begin with the hiring of GOP lobbyists may represent the most important payoff for assessing the K Street Project. But exploring those possible linkages must reflect the aims of subsequent, more extensive research.

At first glance, scholars would be well advised not to write off the exchange model of influence, because the web of relationships that starts with staff members and former members finding lucrative lobbying jobs does appear to constitute a series of exchanges, encompassing both influence and financial gains that create powerful bonds. The Jack Abramoff scandal, while atypical, does cast light on various practices that represent one way of doing business within a disciplined, highly partisan House of Representatives.[69] The Senate remains messier and less ordered, even in a more partisan era. Still, a set of legislative leaders must be able to enforce exchanges (or threats), as is implied in models of strong congressional parties. Thus, the ability to maintain a political machine of any sort relies on staying in power with a working majority—hence the desire to make House districts as safe as possible for a narrow but solid Republican majority.[70] And lobbyists continue to be ready to contribute to campaigns, and bring their clients along, in order to maintain as well as overthrow the current majority.[71]

Notes

1. Nicholas Confessore, "Welcome to the Machine," *Washington Monthly*, July/August 2003, http://www.washingtonmonthly.com/features/2003/0307.confessore.html.
2. See, among others, Jeffrey Berry, *The Interest Group Society*, 3d ed. (New York: Longman, 1997).
3. Elizabeth Drew, "Selling Washington," *New York Review of Books*, June 23, 2005, http://www.nybooks.com/articles/18075.
4. Aside from Confessore and Drew, see, for example, Gail Russell Craddock, "Republicans Take Over K Street," *Christian Science Monitor*, April 23, 2003.
5. Donald Matthews, *U.S. Senators and Their World* (New York: Vintage, 1960); noting even a few younger scholars would be arbitrary and unnecessary. It is of some interest that Matthews, in his pioneering work argues that lobbyists essentially lobby those who are their allies and seek to "activate" their supporters, which addresses a contemporary debate over lobbying tactics (191–192).
6. Morris Fiorina, "Afterword (but Undoubtedly not the Last Word)," in *Positive Theories of Congressional Institutions*, ed. Kenneth Shepsle and Barry Weingast (Ann Arbor: University of Michigan Press, 1995), 303–312.
7. David Rohde, *Parties and Leaders in the Postreform House* (Chicago: University of Chicago Press, 1991); Barbara Sinclair, *Majority Leadership in the U.S. House* (Baltimore: Johns Hopkins University Press, 1983); Kenneth Shepsle, "The Changing Textbook Congress," in *American Political Institutions and the Problems of Our Time*, ed. John Chubb and Paul Peterson (Washington, D.C.: Brookings Institution Press, 1987).
8. In addition to Rohde, *Parties and Leaders in the Postreform House;* and Sinclair, *Majority Leadership in the U.S. House;* see Gary W. Cox and Mathew D. McCubbins, *Legislative Leviathan: Party Government in the House* (Berkeley: University of California Press, 1993); John H. Aldrich and David W. Rohde, "The Logic of Conditional Party Government: Revisiting the Electoral Connection," in *Congress Reconsidered*, 7th ed., ed. Lawrence Dodd and Bruce I. Oppenheimer (Washington: CQ Press, 2001); and John H. Aldrich, *Why Parties? The Origin and Transformation of Political Parties in America* (Chicago: University of Chicago Press, 1995), among many others.
9. Gary W. Cox and Mathew D. McCubbins, "A Précis on Legislative Leadership," n.d., http://mccubbins.ucsd.edu/precis.pdf.
10. Ibid., 1. Emphasis added.
11. David Rohde, *Parties and Leaders in the Post Reform House* (Chicago: University of Chicago Press, 1991); and Cox and McCubbins, *Legislative Leviathan*.
12. Barbara Sinclair, "Transformational Leader or Faithful Agent: Principal-Agent Theory and Majority Party Leadership," *Legislative Studies Quarterly* 24 (November 1999).
13. Barbara Sinclair, "Parties and Leadership in the House," in *The Legislative Branch*, ed. Paul J. Quirk and Sara A. Binder (New York: Oxford University Press, 2004), 224–254.
14. Barbara Sinclair, *Legislators, Leaders and Lawmaking* (Baltimore: Johns Hopkins University Press, 1995) provides a detailed snapshot of the status of research at the end of the Democratic era in 1994. For a mirror image, see William Connelly and Jack Pitney's (unintentionally) ironically titled book, *Congress's Permanent Minority?* (Lanham, Md.: Rowman and Littlefield, 1994) about the Republicans.

15. Allan J. Cigler, "Interest Groups: A Subfield in Search of an Identity," in *Political Science: Looking to the Future*, ed. William Crotty (Evanston, Ill.: Northwestern University Press, 1991); Frank R. Baumgartner and Beth L. Leech, *Basic Interests: The Importance of Groups in Politics and Political Science* (Princeton: Princeton University Press, 1998); Scott Ainsworth, *Analyzing Interest Groups: Group Influence on People and Policies* (New York: Norton, 2002).

16. Richard L. Hall and Alan V. Deardorff, "Lobbying as Legislative Subsidy," *American Political Science Review* 100, no. 1 (February 2006): 69.

17. See Darrell M. West and Burdett A. Loomis, *The Sound of Money* (New York: Norton, 1998); also Rogan Kersh, "Corporate Lobbyists as Political Actors: A View from the Field," in *Interest Group Politics*, 6th ed., ed. Allan J. Cigler and Burdett A. Loomis (Washington, D.C.: CQ Press, 2002), 225–248.

18. Charls Walker, "A Four-Decade Perspective on Lobbying in Washington," in *The Interest Group Connection: Electioneering, Lobbying, and Policymaking in Washington*, ed. Paul S. Herrnson, Ronald G. Shaiko, and Clyde Wilcox (Chatham, N.J.: Chatham House, 1998), 33–34.

19. Colin Campbell and Roger Davidson, "Coalition Building in Congress: The Consequences of Partisan Change," in *The Interest Group Connection*, 116–136, do begin to explore the impact of the Republican takeover and note Speaker Newt Gingrich's exclusion of some groups from the negotiation process on a partisan basis.

20. Jacob S. Hacker and Paul Pierson, *Off Center: The Republican Revolution and the Erosion of American Democracy* (New Haven: Yale University Press, 2005), 143.

21. Hacker and Pierson, *Off Center*.

22. Kersh, "Corporate Lobbyists as Political Actors." See also Burdett Loomis, "Doing Well, Doing Good, and—Shhhhh—Having Fun" (paper presented at the American Political Science Association meeting, 2003).

23. Raymond Bauer, Ithiel de Sola Pool, and Lewis Dexter, *American Business and Public Policy* (New York: Atherton Press, 1963); Hall and Deardorff, "Lobbying as Legislative Subsidy."

24. Paul S. Herrnson, Ronald G. Shaiko, and Clyde Wilcox, "Interest Group Connections in Changing Political Environments," in *The Interest Group Connection: Electioneering, Lobbying, and Policymaking in Washington*, 2d ed., ed. Paul S. Herrnson, Ronald G. Shaiko, and Clyde Wilcox (Washington, D.C.: CQ Press, 2005), 387.

25. Ibid., 392–393.

26. Hall and Deardorff, "Lobbying as Legislative Subsidy."

27. Bauer, Pool, and Dexter, *American Business and Public Policy*, 398.

28. In the wake of the Jack Abramoff scandal, in early 2006, Santorum announced that he would no longer hold these meetings; within a few weeks, however, he resumed the practice, moving the gatherings of staff and Republican lobbyists off Capitol Hill. See "Santorum Breaks Promise to End K Street Project Meetings," Keystone Politics, March 9, 2006, http://www.keystonepolitics.com/Article2714.html.

29. Confessore, "Welcome to the Machine."

30. Loomis, "Doing Well, Doing Good, and—Shhhhh—Having Fun."

31. For one example among legions, see Sarah Posner, "Security for Sale," *American Prospect*, January 5, 2006, http://www.prospect.org/web/page.ww?section=root&name =ViewPrint&articleId=10750.

32. On enterprises, see Robert Salisbury and Kenneth Shepsle, "The Congressman as Enterprise," *Legislative Studies* 6 (November 1981), 559–576; Burdett A. Loomis, *The New American Politician* (New York: Basic Books, 1988).

33. The Web site claims the project is bipartisan and has been in operation since the 1980s, but the Web site itself has been up only since 2005. Much of the Web site's content reflects a conservative and Republican perspective. See "The Mysterious K Street Project," The Hotline, January 18, 2006, http://hotlineblog.nationaljournal. com/archives/2006/01/that_mysterious.html.

34. Quoted in Drew, "Selling Washington."

35. Hans Nichols, "K Street Freezes Out Dems," *The Hill*, September 15, 2004.

36. Lisa Caruso, "Hard Times for K Street Democrats?" *National Journal*, January 22, 2005.

37. See Jeffrey Birnbaum, "GOP Freezes Jobs List, Vestige of K Street Project," *Washington Post*, January 26, 2006, sec. A.

38. Quoted in Caruso, "Hard Times for K Street Democrats?" I interviewed Rehr for another project, and he sent a bunch of beer wholesalers' goodies, including the wrist-rest for my office computer; I reveal this in the interest of full disclosure.

39. See Bara Vaida, Eliza Newlin Carney, and Lisa Caruso, "Potholes on K Street," *National Journal*, March 24, 2006.

40. Peter H. Stone, "Did a Lobbyist Use DeLay's Office?" *National Journal*, January 14, 2006, http://nationaljournal.com/pubs/nj/.

41. Gary Jacobson, "Polarized Politics and the 2004 Congressional and Presidential Elections," *Political Science Quarterly* 120 (Summer 2005): 199–218.

42. Caruso, "Hard Times for K Street Democrats?"

43. Personal communication, anonymity guaranteed.

44. Carrie Sheffield, "Norquist Seeks Trademark on 'K Street Project' Name," *The Hill*, April 11, 2005. Subsequently, it appears that he is attempting to trademark a K Street logo of a D.C. street sign.

45. Sheffield, "Norquist Seeks Trademark on 'K Street Project' Name."

46. Drew, "Selling Washington"; Jeremy Scahill, "Exile on K Street," *The Nation*, February 20, 2006.

47. Quoted in James A. Barnes, "Not the K Street Project," *National Journal*, March 24, 2006.

48. Ibid., emphasis added.

49. Aldrich and Rohde, "The Logic of Conditional Party Government," in *Congress Reconsidered*, 7th ed., 275.

50. Ibid., 275–276.

51. John E. Owens, "American-Style Party Government: Delivering the Bush Agenda, Delivering the Congress' Agenda," in *Right On? Political Change and Continuity in George Bush's America*, ed. Iwan Morgan and Philip John Davies (London and Washington: Institute for the Americas/Brookings Institution Press, forthcoming).

52. Kristin Jensen, Mike Forsythe, and Jonathon Salant, "DeLay's Former Aides Building Lobbying Empires in Washington," Bloomberg News Service, April 5, 2005, http://quote.bloomberg.com/apps/news?pid=nifea&&sid=at9zpiR3e9vo#.

53. Ibid.; see also Kate Ackley, "Business Booms for DeLay's Disciples," *Influence*, September 1, 2004, www.influence.biz.

54. Jeffery Smith, "Federal Probe Edges Closer to Texan," *Washington Post*, April 4, 2006, sec. A.

55. Quoted in Louis Jacobson, "Lobbying: The DeLay Factor on K Street," *National Journal*, January 4, 2003.

56. Jonathon Weisman, "In an Upset, Boehner Is Elected House GOP Leader," *Washington Post*, February 3, 2006, sec. A.

57. Sam Rosenfield, "Meet the New Boss," *American Prospect*, http://www.prospect.org/web/printfriendly-view.ww?id=11172.

58. Mike McIntire, "New House Majority Leader Keeps Old Ties to Lobbyists," *New York Times*, July 15, 2006, sec. A.

59. See Ackley, "Business Booms for DeLay's Disciples."

60. See Vaida, Carney, and Caruso, "Potholes on K Street." Emphasis added.

61. Baumgartner and Leech, *Basic Interests*, 140.

62. See, for example, Lisa Caruso, "What's in a Number?" *National Journal*, March 24, 2006.

63. Hall and Deardorff, "Lobbying as Legislative Subsidy," 70–71.

64. A nice summary of DeLay's tactics by a home-state newspaper can be found in Scott Shepard, "DeLay Leaves Legacy of Partisanship in Congress," *Austin American-Statesman*, April 5, 2006.

65. Ackley, "Business Booms for DeLay's Disciples."

66. Confessore, "Welcome to the Machine"; Drew, "Selling Washington"; see also Bill Moyers, "A Culture of Corruption," *Washington Spectator*, April 1, 2006, http://www.washingtonspectator.com/articles/20060401cleanmoney_1.cfm.

67. See, among many others, John Nichols, "What DeLay Left Behind," *The Nation*, April 6, 2006, http://www.thenation.com/doc/20060424/nichols.

68. See Brooks Jackson, *Honest Graft* (New York: Basic Books, 1988).

69. Assessing the practices is a different matter, from Timothy Noah's relative lack of concern ("Who Cares If DeLay Bullies Lobbyists?" *Slate*, July 11, 2003, http://www.slate.com/id/2085521/) to the alarms sounded by Hans Nichols ("K Street Freezes Out Dems") or Craddock ("Republicans Take Over K Street").

70. See, for example, Juliet Eilperin, *Fight Club Politics: How Partisanship Is Poisoning the House of Representatives* (Lanham, Md.: Rowman and Littlefield, 2006), chap. 2.

71. Brody Mullins, "Corporate Contributions Shift to the Left," *Wall Street Journal*, June 19, 2006, sec. A.

IV. CONCLUSION

19

Organized Interests, Political Parties, and Representation

James Madison, Tom DeLay, and the Soul of American Politics

Allan J. Cigler and Burdett A. Loomis

From the original calls for American independence, to the crafting of the Constitution, to the broadening and equalizing of the franchise in the twentieth century, politics in the United States has largely revolved around representation. Operating through the formal institutions of regular elections and the Congress, political parties and organized interests have served as the most important vehicles for representation in the American political context. Modern parties and interest groups, both established in the nineteenth century, have proven both resilient and adaptable as vehicles for representation over the course of the twentieth century. But it is U.S. politics at the dawn of the twenty-first century that commands our attention here, in that the Republican Party's unified, if tenuous, control of the national government has offered an approximation of representation through responsible party government, American style.[1] With President George W. Bush's polarizing leadership style[2] and House majority whip Tom DeLay's powerful mix of political incentives, cash, and sanctions, national Republicans have sought to govern through a tight-knit majority that leaves little room for the representation of minority party views.[3]

The Bush-DeLay[4] emphasis on a Republican agenda, passed with Republican votes, offers an excellent opportunity to think through the nature of representation in contemporary American politics and to assess the experiment in strong party government that the GOP leadership in Congress, in concert with the president, has sought to put in place. Indeed, the representational assumptions of this party government model differ profoundly from those that have ordinarily prevailed over the past 200 years.

American politics is quintessentially the politics of representation, through multiple layers of government; the separation of powers; a powerful, independent, bicameral legislature (elected by single-member districts); the development of modern political parties; and organization of legions of interest groups whose rights are protected by the First Amendment. Over time, American politics has grown more inclusive, with women, African Americans, and other groups being guaranteed the right to vote— and more generally participate actively in political life.

Political scientists have approached national-level issues of representation through three major political institutions: Congress, political parties, and organized interests. Over the years, these institutions, while overlapping, have generally represented their constituencies in distinct—and well-documented—ways.

- Organized interests and their agents represent relatively narrow interests (hence the term, special interests) within a Madisonian array of factions that produce real, if imperfect, competition across a wide, and growing, universe of all interests.[5]
- Political parties represent broad coalitions of interests that form to contest elections. Historically, these coalitions have often incorporated multiple, overlapping interests within a fragmented set of governing institutions, which makes it difficult for parties to push a systematic policy agenda that represents their coalitions' interests. Still, responsible party government scholars have articulated the idea that issue-oriented, well-disciplined parties could indeed impose a collective representation in which the governing party would set and enact its agenda and subsequently be held responsible for its actions.[6]
- Members of Congress represent interests through 435 separate House constituencies, as well as the dual Senate representation of the fifty state constituencies.[7] With two-year House terms, legislators must, it is argued, remain attuned to their voters' preferences; high reelection rates indicate that legislators are responsive, just as occasional national landslides demonstrate that the Congress, as a whole, can respond to broad, societal forces. In the end, the local nature of congressional constituencies makes building coalitions a difficult task, and one that often requires granting specific material benefits to pass broad policy initiatives.[8]

Since the early 1980s, the shape of representation by organized interests, political parties, and the Congress has changed substantially, largely because of two related trends: the strengthening of political parties as fundraisers and as legislative forces and the increasing polarization of American politics.[9] On occasion, such as at the turn of the twentieth century, for a few New Deal years, and in the 89th Congress (1965–1966), parties, groups, and Congress have coalesced to provide broad-gauged, programmatic representation. These interludes have been the exception although some recent scholarship has sought to cast midcentury politics—at least in terms of controlling the legislative agenda—in a much more partisan light.[10]

Congressional scholars have focused largely on legislators' relationships with their constituencies, interest group scholars on specific groups' successes or the composition of the interest group universe, and parties scholars on the decline and rebuilding of party organizations (within the context of broad partisan alignments among voters). Moreover, there is little general attention paid to policy representation in American politics—focusing on the overall content of policies produced by our representative institutions.[11]

Ironically, it is an exterminator, not a scholar, who has generated the most important recent questions about representation in the United States. As House Republican whip and majority leader, Representative Tom DeLay, R-Texas, in concert with many other GOP legislators, sought over the 1995–2006 period to combine party, Congress, and interests into an integrated entity that would coordinate a large number of exchanges among groups and lobbyists, party organizations (especially as fund-raisers), and members of Congress. Central here has been the unified party government in the 108th and 109th Congresses (2003–2006) and the ability of the Republican majorities in the House and, to a lesser extent, the Senate to enforce exchanges between those who supported the party and its candidates and those who were elected to office. Some of this party-group-Congress linkage derives from the pressure placed on Washington lobbyists to support Republican initiatives and candidates. Journalist Nicholas Confessore painted this picture in 2003:

> Like the urban Democratic machines of yore, this one is built upon patronage, contracts, and one-party rule. But unlike legendary Chicago mayor Richard J. Daley, who rewarded party functionaries with jobs in the municipal bureaucracy, *the GOP is building its machine outside government*, among Washington's thousands of trade associations and corporate offices, their tens of thousands of employees, and the hundreds of millions of dollars in political money at their disposal.[12]

Like Confessore, congressional scholar Barbara Sinclair sees the Republicans in Congress, especially in the House, as succeeding in extending their influence throughout much of the interest community, often to pass Bush administration agenda items. Writing in 2006, she states:

> As the parties have polarized, so to a large extent have interest groups active in the Washington policy process …; interest groups are increasingly being forced to align with one party or the other, to become part of one of two durable coalitions, and this is true of even groups that would prefer to play both sides of the fence. Staying neutral has become a progressively more untenable strategy for major interest groups.[13]

Such a conclusion may well be premature, despite some reasonably strong short-term evidence.[14] Moreover, an explicit emphasis on representation may not be at the heart of the Bush-DeLay approach to governing; Sinclair, for example, argues explicitly that the administration's "purpose of its interactions with groups is programmatic—to pass its program, rather than representational" in that its outreach is exclusive, to longtime supporting interests, not inclusive, so as to bring together the broad majorities typically required to pass major legislation.[15]

What exactly are the questions that address representation in the Republican era? Many emphasize money and exchanges between various actors within the overlapping members of the group-party-Congress community (for example, fund-raising bundlers and party leaders; lobbyists as brokers between their clients and legislative party leaders). In addition, a programmatic party surely makes representational decisions, regardless of whether it actively includes new groups or relies on historic ties. One central question is whether political parties, which ordinarily do need to reach out to new interests, can provide adequate glue to dominate the policy-making process over time by controlling enough of the myriad exchanges that take place, day to day, between organized interests, political parties in their various manifestations, and legislative leaders and their members.

From the perspective of Capitol Hill majority-party leaders, long periods of such control may well be possible, but from the vantage points of tens of thousands of individual interests, exchanges to maintain party dominance look less likely. This chapter will address the substance of mechanics of representation at the intersection of parties and interest groups. In particular, we will focus on the flow of campaign money within this nexus, as well as the ability of party leaders to enlist lobbyists and Washington representatives for organized interests as both their troops and their agents in enacting partisan policy decisions that represent their supportive groups.

Electoral Relations Between Organized Interests and Parties: The Blurring of Roles

Until the early 1970s, organized interests' involvement in elections was not typically characterized by extensive participation. The relatively few groups that did become involved, with the notable exception of organized labor, were ordinarily content simply to endorse candidates, encourage their members to vote and get involved in campaigns, and, less frequently, contribute to parties and candidates. Organized interests historically have been subservient to parties and candidate organizations—broadly supportive but normally not engaged in electioneering independently directed at the broader electorate. Party and interest group roles were functionally distinct.

The pattern has changed markedly in the contemporary era for a number of reasons.[16] Most important has been the expansion of government lawmaking and regulatory activity that raised the stakes of politics, creating incentives for groups and institutions of all kinds to become involved in elections. The electoral process itself became more permeable, which reduced barriers to group participation. By 2000, the breadth and intensity of groups' involvement in elections had increased substantially, even for those representing narrow interests. Accompanying this escalation of activity was an extensive rise in electoral spending, often independent of party and candidate campaign efforts.

Political parties had changed as well; they developed some of the policy-advocating characteristics typically associated with organized interests rather than focusing upon broad aggregation strategies, as in the past. At the same time parties have become less important in directly mobilizing voters and running campaigns, although they still play a key role in funding such activities.

As a result, the separate consideration of parties and interest groups as mediating institutions in the electoral process is less appropriate now, given the complexity of party-group-candidate linkages. Roles of parties and interest groups have grown less precise and bounded; at times they cooperate with one another, on other occasions they confront and compete. Often the relationship is mutually beneficial yet filled with tension. Just who represents whom is often unclear, unstated, and subject to change.

Initial Tensions

Since the early 1970s, various party and campaign finance reforms have altered the electoral roles played by parties and organized interests. Early on, Democratic Party reforms grew out of the McGovern-Fraser Commission deliberations after the raucous (and politically disastrous) 1968 Democratic convention and most profoundly affected the presidential nomination process.[17] In an effort to open up the party organization, the reforms mandated that delegates be selected either in primaries or open meetings (caucuses) and not by state central committees; in addition, racial groupings and women were to be represented as delegates in increasing numbers. Although the Republican Party did not formally follow suit, it addressed similar delegate selection issues because state party organizations frequently found themselves operating under the same laws mandating primaries or open caucus systems. In both parties, the hegemony of local and state party leaders over party affairs was essentially broken, resulting in expanded opportunities for organized interests, especially those who represented causes of different stripes.

The new Democratic Party rules altered the nomination strategies of presidential aspirants, in that candidates seeking to build a winning coalition needed to construct a coalition of issue-based groups and leaders rather than simply court state and local party officials. The new strategy, according to parties scholar Byron Shafer, "produced a political arena crowded with interest groups and issue organizations, seeking and being sought, demanding rewards and offering support, while both presidential aspirants and interested partisans tried to secure the maximum benefit from these negotiations."[18] The new system involved direct candidate negotiation with group leaders, "compelling them to court group supporters with a promiscuity that often appears excessive."[19] Party professionals played a relatively minor role, and issue activists emerged as the dominant players in internal party business.

The campaign finance reforms of the early 1970s also advantaged organized interests at the expense of political parties. The rapid growth of political action committees (PACs) after the enactment of the 1974 amendments to the 1971 Federal Election Campaign Act (FECA), the ceiling imposed by the act on party contributions to candidates, and the requirement that individual campaign organizations be the legal agent of the candidate all had the effect of decreasing an already diminished party role in providing campaign resources to candidates, and a wide range of organized interests quickly filled the vacuum.

For example, the number of federally registered PACs went from 608 in 1974 to nearly 4,200 a decade and a half later.[20] Incumbents became increasingly dependent on PAC money, to the point that in 1988 sitting House members received nearly one-half of their campaign funds from PACs, up from less than one-third in 1978, all while the absolute costs of electioneering were rising sharply. In the same ten years, Senate incumbents increased the proportion of their funding from PACs from 15 percent to 29 percent.[21] During the same period, the proportion of House candidates' total receipts from party committees declined from 7 percent to 4 percent, and only modestly increased for senatorial candidates (from 6 percent to 9 percent).[22]

The competition between PACs and parties went beyond merely fund raising from a limited pool of givers and providing alternative sources of funding and support for candidates. By the early 1980s, PACs were already exceeding parties in terms of direct efforts to influence voter choice, and they competed with parties in such traditional campaign activities as voter registration and get-out-the-vote drives.[23] Especially problematic for elected officials were the nonconnected, independent PACs, which were not tied to a particular group like a union or to an institution such as a corporation. Some of the PACs were aggressively anti-party and ideologically oriented. Most notorious was the behavior of the National Conservative Political Action Committee (NCPAC), led by Terry Dolan, who generally supported Republican candidates but had disdain for both parties.[24] In 1982, NCPAC even considered becoming a political party; it contributed large amounts of money to candidates who agreed with its agenda, but it also ran negative campaigns against candidates from both major parties. The defeat of a number of prominent Senate incumbents in 1978 and 1980 reinforced the perception that powerful, well-funded organized interests, especially the independent PACs, posed an increasing electoral risk for officeholders.[25]

Both the open party organization dominated by the new breed of issue activists and a PAC system that made politicians increasingly dependent on organized interests suggested to some that the system of candidate-centered campaigns was at risk. The extraordinary role played by New Right elements in the nomination of Ronald Reagan as the Republican standard-bearer in 1980, the influence of organized labor in the nomination of Democrat Walter Mondale in 1984, and an apparent deal with the National Organization for Women in the selection of Geraldine Ferraro as the vice presidential nominee indicated the power of organized interests within the nomination process. In congressional elections, PAC funding was especially worrisome, given the attempts by some PACs to "usurp functions of the two parties and establish themselves as substitutes by recruiting and creating pseudo-party organizations of their own."[26]

The challenges posed by organized interests to electoral security and incumbent independence created incentives for risk-averse officials to revamp the parties to counter the threat. Some efforts were made to influence the party-in-the-electorate dominated by the issue activists, but the primary thrust focused on strengthening the party-in-government wing of the national parties, particularly the Senate and House party campaign committees. By the mid-1980s the parties were increasingly becoming incumbent safety organizations—less the traditional voter-mobilizing agencies and coalition-building vehicles in the traditional party sense and more the service vendor organizations dedicated to the reelection of candidates of their party, largely unrelated to how they vote on issues.[27] Procuring campaign funds was the key to adapting to the realities of modern, candidate-centered campaigns. The PAC threat never materialized; both parties embraced their emerging financial brokers by forming loose fundraising alliances with many PACs and offering them assistance in targeting their funds to particular candidates as well as aiding candidates in soliciting funds from potential donor PACs. Once again, American political parties proved resilient in the face of challenges to their dominance of electoral politics.

Money, Expansion of Interests, and Blurring of Representation

A major purpose of the 1971 FECA and its later amendments was to curb the excessive influence of moneyed interests in elections, not just by limiting campaign contributions by law, but also by instituting a system that would disclose to voters whose interests were being represented in the process. By the late 1980s, however, two loopholes in federal campaign finance laws encouraged a tremendous increase in the amount of electoral spending by both organized interests and parties. Moreover, this spending often fell outside of the imposed limits and scrutiny of the Federal Election Commission (FEC).

One loophole involved the use of soft money—that is, funds contributed to the national parties by individuals or organized interests for supposed party-building purposes and designed to curb the growing PAC influence in campaigns. Although soft-money contributions were minimal in the immediate postreform era, by the late 1980s they had created a means for organized interests such as unions and corporations, which were prohibited from making direct hard-money contributions in federal elections, to funnel unlimited amounts to these alleged party-building accounts.[28] Contributions often ran to six and sometimes seven figures, notably from individual corporations or a single union, and they went undisclosed until the 1992 elections. In 1980 soft money contributions to the national parties stood at about $20 million; by the 1999–2000 election cycle, $495 million was raised and spent by the two major parties, largely from soft-money sources, an amount that dwarfed the total PAC contributions to federal candidates.[29]

Such an influx of soft money was a double-edged sword for the parties, especially for the Democrats who had a harder time raising funds from individual donors than the Republicans. While the abundance of soft money gave Democrats an enhanced role in helping their candidates, the party became highly dependent on large contributions from affluent interests, potentially in conflict with representing the party's social activists and traditional working class base.

The second loophole, issue advocacy electioneering, had a different source.[30] In its 1976 decision, *Buckley v. Valeo*, the Supreme Court spelled out its "express advocacy" guidelines. That is, any legal limitation on spending to influence elections would apply only to communications *expressly advocating* the election or defeat of a candidate, such as "vote for," "elect," "support," and "cast your ballot for." These so-called magic words came to mean that communication with voters (such as a television ad) that does not use these or similar words remains beyond the reach of government regulation and that no disclosure of donors or amounts expended is required. By the 1996 elections, both political parties and a variety of organized interests were active sponsors of issue ads in electioneering; the parties were legally permitted to use a substantial portion of their soft money for issue advocacy advertising.

In practice, organized interest issue advocacy ads have proven virtually indistinguishable from ads by the parties or candidates through television or radio commercials or by phone messages or flyer. This proliferation of ads and messages confuses voters and makes accountability, one key element of representation, difficult to achieve.[31] Such ads typically provide a picture of one or both of the candidates, usually mentioning their names, often in a negative way, while carefully avoiding any of the magic words. The identity of the organized interest sponsoring the ad is often unclear or misleading. With no disclosure requirements, groups could raise money for hard-hitting and often untraceable negative ads. Rather than encouraging voters to vote for a particular candidate, ads usually asked viewers to call or write a candidate to register their opposition or support for the candidate's positions and pronouncements. The intent of the issue advocacy ads to affect elections was clear, but organized interests were not limited in any way by existing campaign finance law.

With new tools at hand, the amount spent on federal election campaigns skyrocketed during the 1990s.[32] Parties and organized interests both came to play more prominent roles, largely at the expense of candidate-controlled agendas. Parties continued to extend their roles as service vendors to the candidates, not just with an expanded presence in campaign advertising but also by contracting out their traditional role of mobilizing voters to various groups by using their soft money to fund group electoral activity such as registration drives and telephone banks.[33] Republicans contributed to a number of anti-tax and pro-life groups, while Democrats channeled some of their funds to minority group organizations. Both parties, but Republicans in particular, "created a dazzling galaxy of policy institutes, foundations and think tanks, each of which can raise money from private interests and which can aid the party and party candidates in a variety of ways."[34]

The 1990s also saw a proliferation of groups becoming involved for the first time in electoral politics, as well as expanded efforts by organized interests with long-standing involvement. Groups like the venerable, nonprofit American Cancer Society made an initial foray into the electoral arena, contributing to party conferences and dinners. The American Cancer Society's spokesperson noted that the organization wanted to gain "the same access as others" and "to look like players and be players."[35] Groups like the National Rifle Association (see chapter 2), the AFL-CIO, and the Christian Coalition (see chapter 7) emerged as semi-permanent, full-service electoral organizations, at times operating on their own without the collaboration of either parties or candidates. It was not unusual to see members of such groups recruiting and training candidates to run for public office, serving as advisers to their campaigns in primary as well as general elections (typically in an unofficial capacity), as well as communicating with voters; their involvement was effectively indistinguishable from that of the candidate's own campaign or that of party electioneering.

While issue advocacy electioneering by organized interests was exploding, the increasing domination of grassroots electioneering and voter mobilization by groups was having perhaps even more impact on electoral outcomes. Such activities were extensive. For example, the religious forces that constituted the Christian right, energized by their role in the Republican takeover of Congress in 1994, distributed more than 54 million voter guides using church-based networks in 1996; one estimate counted roughly 200,000 movement activists as being involved in the 1996 elections at various levels.[36] By the early to middle 1990s, in a number of states, Christian right adherents had essentially captured the Republican Party organization, and the distinction between the party and the movement was problematic.[37]

With the rise of televised issue advocacy advertising by organized interests and the national parties, which drew the ire of both the media and a number of senators and representatives, campaign reform returned to the congressional agenda in the mid-1990s. The excessive impact of a few big-money spenders drew a lot of attention. For example, in the 1999–2000 election cycle, the biggest issue advocacy spender was an organization called Citizens for Better Medicare (CBM), a name designed to evoke the image of a group of senior citizens who sought to improve this important government program.[38] But whom exactly did CBM represent? Early on, it was difficult to tell, but it later became apparent that the group represented a coalition created in 1999 by a drug industry trade group, the Pharmaceutical Research and Manufacturers of America (PhRMA) and the HealthCare Leadership Council, which speaks for fifty drug companies, hospitals, and health care providers. These interests opposed the Clinton administration's plan to expand Medicare coverage, and no information ever revealed the group's specific financial supporters. CBM ran negative ads nationally, in most cases against competitive-seat Democrats who supported President Clinton, or positive ads on behalf of Republicans who opposed him. The group spent a figure roughly equivalent to 20 percent of the total soft money contributed to either the Republican or Democratic national committee during the 1999–2000 election cycle. In the first eight months of 2000, this single organized interest spent an estimated $34 million on issue ads, topped only by the Democratic National Committee ($35 million) and the Republican National Committee ($51 million).[39]

By the 2000 political season, existing campaign finance laws had little meaning. There had been a huge escalation of interest group fund raising and spending, which was not regulated by the FEC and was shielded from public scrutiny. Groups were becoming more brazen and sophisticated in their activities, while they depended less on parties and candidate organizations for advice concerning electoral strategies. Most legislators were generally uneasy about revisiting the campaign finance issue—Republicans because they felt they were advantaged by the overall current system of private funding and Democrats because they believed Republicans would try to eliminate their party's soft-money advantage. But many did realize that the evolving system was a potential threat to their control of campaign agendas and their electoral safety. In the end, incumbent politicians' fears would lead to new campaign finance legislation; the provisions of the new legislation have sought to rebalance the campaign influences of parties, organized interests, and candidates in elections, largely in the direction of more candidate control.

BCRA and Electoral Representation in the Contemporary Era: More Blurring

The Bipartisan Campaign Reform Act (BCRA) of 2002 was a controversial piece of legislation that was touted by its proponents as an effort, once again, to gain control over the impact of so-called fat cats in elections. Although publicly opposed by the Republican leadership in Congress and by President George W. Bush (and privately by many Democrats) and not a high priority on the public's agenda despite its cynicism about money and politics, passage was aided by a set of favorable circumstances. Especially influential was the Enron scandal, which heightened outrage over the nexus of campaign money and public policy and created a window of opportunity for reformers to pass legislation that looked hopeless at the beginning of the Bush presidency.[40]

In the continuing quest for electoral influence among organized interests, political parties (especially the activist wings), and candidate campaigns, BCRA clearly advantaged incumbents.[41] Incumbents' campaign coffers generally grew larger because the legislation did not change the limits on hard-money contributions from PACs and actually increased the amount from $1,000 to $2,000 in both the primary and general elections that individuals could give to candidates. Soft money contributed to national party committees was no longer permissible.

The legislation affected organized interests in various ways. BCRA provisions eliminated the Supreme Court's issue advocacy guidelines, which had come to dominate organized-interest campaign advertising, and replaced them with a new standard that addressed the *content* of electioneering communications with the public and *when* organized interests could engage in issue advocacy that related to a given election. "Electioneering communication" was defined as any broadcast, cable, or satellite communication that referred to a clearly identified federal candidate within thirty days of a primary or sixty days prior to the general election. BCRA essentially outlawed interest groups from using soft money for advocacy electioneering within these preelection windows. In addition, electioneering communication expenditures must be reported in a timely way, and corporations and unions must still abide with the original FECA clause that forbids them from using general funds for any type of campaign expenditures. For incumbents, uneasy about losing control over the campaign agenda to organized interests, these developments represented a clear plus.

Although a small group of reformist public interest groups applauded the new law, opposition, particularly to the provision limiting broadcast advertisements near an election, came from groups across the political spectrum. During congressional deliberations, the American Civil Liberties Union, the AFL-CIO, the National Rifle Association, the Christian Coalition, National Right to Life, and the U.S. Chamber of Commerce all opposed the provision to limit broadcast ads, and they also sought to have such limitations overturned by the courts.[42] One of the groups' main message tools was no longer an option, pending the Supreme Court's ruling.

The Court upheld virtually all of BCRA in a 5–4 decision, and its provisions were first applied in the 2004 federal elections, resulting in some major changes from previous election cycles. Individual donors rose in importance for party and candidate fund raising compared with earlier elections, and organized interests altered their campaign strategies. Their issue advocacy on the airwaves by groups continued to grow, but given the sixty-day blackout period for these ads before the general election, "St. Patrick's Day [seemed] to have replaced Labor Day as the start of the general election campaign."[43] Group and party attention outside of the presidential race still focused on the relatively few competitive House and Senate races. Organized interest activity during the general election most often emphasized ground-war tactics designed to increase the turnout of likely supporters and not covered by BCRA.

More important, organized interests found new ways to bring big money into the 2004 election campaigns. A new organization came to the fore: the 527 committee, which often reflected a hybrid grouping of party activists and interest group supporters (see chapter 9).[44] Even though the federal tax code provision for 527 committees had existed since 1974, organized interests began to use it extensively only after soft-money rules were changed. A 527 committee represents an independent political organization established to influence elections; as long as the committee does not engage in any hard-money activity and refrains from express advocacy, it remains exempt from federal taxation. Donations to such committees are unlimited, and before August 2000 the donors were undisclosed. A number of groups, including the Sierra Club and the NAACP, had been sponsoring active 527 committees since the mid-1990s, but the 2004 election cycle saw an explosion in the number and impact of such groups.

Even before BCRA's passage, Democratic National Committee chairman Terry McAuliffe named a task force to find ways to return soft money to the system, given the law's ban on such direct contributions to the parties.[45] The task force included party officials and consultants as well as prominent representatives of Democratic Party–allied interest groups like the Sierra Club, the AFL-CIO, and EMILY's List. Subsequently, a number of 527 organizations were created, tied closely to the Democratic Party through personnel and providers of campaign services; but they would operate independently, as anti-Bush organizations, rather than as formal parts of the Democratic Party. Such groups as America Coming Together, Joint Victory Campaign 2004, and the Media Fund collectively spent more than $200 million on both air-war and ground-war efforts to defeat Bush, largely in swing states.[46]

Without a primary contest, the Bush campaign was awash in money, and having strong grassroots support from Christian right elements, Republican allies had far less need for pro-Bush 527s. Several did play prominent roles in the campaign, especially Progress for America and the Swift Boat Veterans and POWs for Truth. The anti–John Kerry ads run in 2004 by the swift boat veterans after the Democratic convention, to which Kerry did not initially respond, may have been the turning point in the election, given their success in altering the Democrats' campaign agenda and putting Kerry on the defensive.[47] Although some 527s played major roles in a number of contested congressional and senatorial races, in 2004 the emphasis was clearly on the presidential race.

But what kind of interests exactly did the 527s represent? In the swift boat veterans' situation it was clear: a group of veterans who served in Vietnam were upset that Kerry's campaign would make the candidate's war record a focus of his presidential run. On another level, however, the swift boat veterans' ads reflected the backing of longtime Republican supporter Bob R. Perry, who provided most of the early funds for the ad campaign and who sought to attack the Democratic nominee, perhaps regardless of the issue.[48] With other 527s there were even fewer clear linkages back to the actual sponsors, even for those seemingly closely connected to the parties. The 527s raised and spent over $424 million overall, and $146 million came from just twenty-five very wealthy individuals, often in six- or seven-figure chunks.[49] George Soros alone contributed nearly $24 million to the anti-Bush 527s, while Peter Lewis, chairman of insurance giant Progressive, contributed over $22 million. The one exception to groups' depending on large contributors was MoveOn.org's 527, whose funds came from two million small contributors.

Overall, the most prominent 527s were neither party organizations nor traditional organized interests that sought to gain access to elected officials. Rather, contributions reflected ideological commitments. For example, Soros, while motivated by a fierce desire to defeat Bush, aspired to remake the Democratic Party in line with his own preferences and principles. As Grover Norquist, a conservative Republican activist and founder of a 527 named American Resolve, said: "It's not access money, it's movement money. They are not writing checks to sit down with congressmen."[50]

If the 2004 election is any indication, conflict in the electoral arena among party, candidates, and organized interests will likely continue. Many organized interests, though generally allied with parties, are more independent than first meets the eye. Thus, in 2004 the Democratic ally MoveOn.org often acted in ways detrimental to the party's cause with its extreme rhetoric; in 2006 the group eagerly backed Ned Lamont, a Democratic primary challenger to Senator Joe Lieberman, D-Conn., despite the wishes of national party operatives. On the Republican side, the Club for Growth, an anti-tax, free market group, has often challenged Republican incumbents in the party primaries. Parties themselves are often divided between their activist wings (which tend to control the presidential nomination process) and their congressional wings (largely oriented to protecting incumbents).

In short, no single entity controls the contemporary electoral process. Parties, candidate campaign organizations, and many organized interests are formidable players. The implications for representation are mixed and unclear, but straightforward, predictable principal-agent relationships and easily identified constituent-officeholder relationships are in short supply. Within the electoral process, candidates and elected officials must continually reassess the nature and intent of support that comes from individuals, groups, and parties—whose interests often differ substantially from those of their constituents. Indeed, American politics may have more representational clarity in the policy-making process, especially within the U.S. House, than it does in the traditional realm of campaigns and elections.

Parties and Interests (and the President): Can the Center Hold?

If electoral politics has tended to blur political lines, the legislative (and legislative-executive) politics of policy making has sought to bring parties and organized interests together. The evidence is clear that legislative parties—and especially the post-1994 Republicans—have stood at the center of a polarized, partisan politics that has dominated much of national policy making. Political scientist Barbara Sinclair's recent *Party Wars* offers a powerful twenty-five-year perspective on the growing strength of legislative parties on the ground and of the "conditional party government" model within the congressional literature.[51] Taking this partisanship as a given,[52] the more important focus here is the extent to which Republican congressional leadership can extend its reach by bringing parts of the Washington community, and especially lobbyists, into its orbit.

As Loomis points out (chapter 18), reaching out to the so-called K Street lobbying community was central to the strategy developed by Republican leaders like Senator Rick Santorum (Pa.), Representative John Boehner (Ohio), and, above all, the Republican whip and, later, majority leader Tom DeLay (Texas). Even though the members of the House Republican Conference had long enjoyed typical one-on-one relationships with individual lobbyists who provided them with either subsidies or exchanges that included particularistic benefits, Republican legislators appeared sanguine in their willingness to go along with the centralizing practices of their leaders. This meant that the recruitment and hiring practices for many top jobs in lobbying firms and trade associations were coordinated by the House and Senate leadership offices, sometimes in conjunction with Grover Norquist and a band of ideological lobbyists.[53] The GOP senators and (especially) representatives surrendered some of their individual prerogatives vis-à-vis lobbyists so that the leaders could enhance the party's overall chances of (a) staying in power (via the funneling of campaign contributions to competitive districts) and (b) winning beneficial policy victories through an extra layer of party-orchestrated lobbying. If legislators do benefit through subsidies from lobbyists and organized interests, as Hall and Deardorff argue,[54] these benefits increasingly went to the collective. And, because of the Republicans' general agreement on policy preferences, the lawmakers benefited both as individuals and as a group.

But separating out the overall impact of Republican majorities, especially after 2002, and the strength of the GOP leadership is difficult, in that lobbyists scarcely needed to put their fingers up to understand which way the wind was blowing. Crucial here for both legislators and lobbyists was the ability of the Republican leadership to produce a solid string of victories. This surely proved the case in the 108th Congress (2003–2004), as congressional scholar John Owens concluded:

> Republicans had enacted much of their program, as a strongly cohesive party. At different times centrists and hard-line conservatives had swallowed their lumps in the interests of their party. Fully fledged American style party government was clearly in place as the House (and Senate) patterns on party unity votes demonstrated, ... matching levels commonly found in the British House of Commons.[55]

Lobbyists could see the benefits of lining up with this effective Republican leadership, which—at least in the House—could claim to have prevailed on all major votes. If the Republican leaders were seeking to place their staff members and former colleagues in lobbying jobs, organized interests should listen—and they apparently did. In fact, the hub of the K Street Project ran directly out of Majority Leader Tom DeLay's office, where at least eleven of his former staff members became high-paid lobbyists and seven more took on important corporate or trade group roles.[56] In many ways, DeLay—not the Republican leadership as a whole—stood at the center of the K Street Project. In 2003, veteran Republican lobbyist Mark Isakowitz observed, "You can't find anyone who ignores the DeLay factor today. It's pervasive and part of the K Street culture."[57]

In less than three years, DeLay would be gone, replaced not by his deputy, the GOP whip, Roy Blunt (Mo.), but by John Boehner, whose relationships with lobbyists, while close, have been much more conventional. A party-dominated lobbying approach needs a rugged enforcer in a Congress where margins are thin, especially as electoral losses appear likely in 2006; and many GOP legislators have edged away from their leaders.[58] Without question, as Barbara Sinclair, journalist Jeffrey H. Birnbaum, and others note, there is a "team" approach to passing most important legislation such as tax cuts and Medicare D.[59] But there are real doubts as to the overall effectiveness of these strategies across all major issues (for example, Social Security), where party-oriented coalitions may well splinter. Likewise, as the possibility of losing their majorities in one or both houses (and certainly facing narrower majorities) increases, the Republicans' hold on organized interests has grown more tenuous. In June 2006, for example, James Blanchard, a Democrat who served formerly as both a House member and governor of Michigan, became head of the government affairs division of DLA Piper Rudnick Gray Cary US LLP and replaced a Republican in the process.[60] Moreover, some all-Republican firms, such as the highly successful Federalist Group, have begun to hire Democrats (three for this firm) and have argued that prospective Democratic gains in the 2006 elections were not the reason.[61] Indeed, assessing causality in many of the trends in political party–organized interest relations over the years is very difficult, especially when so many legislators (like Tom DeLay) and lobbyists (like Grover Norquist) seek to claim credit for cementing the party–interest group bonds and the policy outcomes that these linkages have produced.[62]

Structural Advantages: Organized Interests and Political Parties

During the past fifteen years, Gray and Lowery (see chapter 6), along with various others working along the same lines, have argued that the structure of representation provided by interest groups relates to the ecology of those organizations within particular political contexts (mostly states).[63] The growth and density of interest group populations thus influence the policy-making capacity of government and will directly affect the nature of representation by groups (and indirectly by the political system as a whole). The broad brushstrokes of the Gray-Lowery argument have been filled in a bit by others who have sought to explain how structural dimensions of American politics affect the representation provided by organized interests.

Michael T. Heaney (chapter 12), for example, has analyzed groups' conscious construction of their own identities, so that they can protect themselves as once-predictable political currents begin to change. Building on Browne's issue niche notion, Heaney concludes:

> Identity serves as a flexible mechanism to pull together myriad aspects of interest group activities, from grassroots organizing to elite lobbying to coalition building. A group's identity affects its ability to win sympathy from the public, dues from members, loyalty from staff, and favors from legislators. Thus, anything a group does to affect how it is viewed by one of these audiences also matters to the others. If a group's membership grows or shrinks considerably, for example, legislators have incentives to give it more or fewer favors. Likewise, if legislators regard the group with higher or lower esteem, members have greater or lesser incentives to contribute to the work of the organization. These responses from varied audiences do not operate seamlessly or automatically, and from time to time they will be significantly out of alignment with each other. When these identity crises surface, interest groups can and do turn to issue niches, representation, and branding as strategies to affect a realignment consistent with their goals.[64]

In large part, groups can construct their particular identities because, as separate organized interests, individual organizations have adequate space to emphasize their distinctive pattern of issue concerns, constituencies, and brands. In developing his idea of "institutionalized pluralism," Matt Grossman argues that "advocacy organizations succeed in Washington by becoming taken-for-granted position advocates in public debates as representatives of public constituencies."[65]

In short, the American constitutional structure, with its nooks and crannies of potential influence that are reinforced by the carrying limits of the political system, encourages groups to position themselves in niches or with particular identities so that they are taken into account within the policy-making process. Working with political parties may reflect a part of a group's strategies, but rarely do party contacts make up the sole (or even the major) element. Indeed, given the complexities of American politics, political parties are irrelevant to many decisions that are made in obscure regulatory, bureaucratic, or congressional committee venues. If groups define themselves effectively, they can seek to achieve their goals without the compromise (and added costs) of party politics. To be sure, political parties do structure competition and attempt to build winning coalitions; but for many groups, the institutional-structural context of American politics allows them to remain outside the fray.

Whose Game Do We Play?
(Apologies to E. E. Schattschneider[66])

E. E. Schattschneider, perhaps the father of analysis of relations between organized interests and political parties, argued in 1960 that the relationship between groups and parties would inevitably favor the latter because political parties organized the electorate:[67]

> It is not easy to manage the political interests of the business community because there is a perpetual stream of losers in intrabusiness conflicts who go to the government for relief and protection.... The fact that business has not become hopelessly divided and that it has retained great influence in American politics has been due chiefly to the over-all mediating role played by the Republican party.[68]

While James Madison worried extensively about the mischiefs of majority faction, Representative Tom DeLay—in both electoral and legislative politics—sought to exploit the full power of the majority-faction Republican Party. Moving far beyond Schattschneider's notion that Republicans could structure the conflict to the benefit of the business community (at least in the 1950s), DeLay and the rest of the GOP leadership, at least in the House, sought to both reward and pressure business allies in raising campaign cash and in lobbying for Republican initiatives. Such a policy-driven process, in concord with a similar approach from President George W. Bush, potentially reduced the representative capacity of the House and ultimately the Congress as a whole.

Through both electoral politics, with its emphasis on fund raising, and legislative politics, organized interests have offered representation to many constituencies, large and small, that have been excluded by the majority's willingness to govern (and even seek election victories) through polarizing mobilization strategies rather than by moving toward the center of a closely divided electorate and similarly divided legislative chambers. As Sinclair concludes in her assessment of a contemporary House of Representatives that makes compromise almost impossible:

> The most moderate and mild-mannered of Democrats perceive Republican rule as not just heavy-handed but dictatorial and fundamentally undemocratic. In fact, the perspectives and interests of minority party members and those they represent do not get a real hearing in the House.[69]

Polarization may well allow parties the chance to dominate organized interests, but for only a few years of the modern, post–Franklin D. Roosevelt era of American politics has a party been able to dominate and deliver. Schattschneider's moneyed-class interests surely retain advantages, but in large part because the party system and the interest group system, both reliant on immense funding from the private sector, serve these interests in complementary ways. Given the growth of organized interests, the extensive expansion of public programs and decision-making venues, and the rising stakes of policy choices, businesses and other advantaged groups would be foolish to put all their eggs in a single basket. Rather, group and party strategies are intertwined, with many advantaged interests investing in both political parties over time as well as maintaining their own lobbying capacity within the world of well-structured, institutional pluralism.

Polarization favors political parties overall, but the ordinary state of American politics has been to represent specific interests; unless a party can enforce not just the creation of an agenda but also its passage, the partisan model is wanting. Likewise, in electoral politics, because of the flow of money, organized interests will ally with parties but will work independently as well—often trying to move the parties to adapt their perspectives rather than responding to the parties' lead. And while Tom DeLay has retreated from electoral and legislative politics, James Madison's system, though bruised and buffeted, remains in place.

Notes

1. See, for example, John Owens, "American-Style Party Government: Delivering Bush's Agenda, Delivering the Congress' Agenda," in *Right On? Political Change and Continuity in George Bush's America*, ed. I. Morgan and P. John Davies (London: Institute for the Americas; Washington, D.C.: Brookings Institution Press, 2006); Gary W. Cox and Mathew D. McCubbins, *Setting the Agenda: Responsible Party Government in the U.S. House of Representatives* (New York: Cambridge University Press, 2005).
2. Gary Jacobson, *A Divider, Not a Uniter* (New York: Pearson Longman, 2007).
3. Among others, see Barbara Sinclair, *Party Wars: Polarization and the Politics of National Policy Making* (Norman: University of Oklahoma Press, 2006).
4. This label is clearly shorthand in that Majority Leader Bill Frist in the Senate and Speaker of the House J. Dennis Hastert, as well as many other legislators, have

endorsed such a party-based strategy, which has dominated GOP strategy from the outset of the party's post-1994 control of the Congress.

5. Among many others, James Madison, "Federalist 10," *The Federalist Papers;* David Truman, *The Governmental Process*, 2d ed. (New York: Knopf, 1971); E. E. Schattschneider, *The Semisovereign People: A Realist's View of Democracy in America* (New York: Holt, Rinehart and Winston, 1960).

6. E. E. Schattschneider, *Party Government* (New York: Farrar and Rinehart, 1942) and the American Political Science Association report on responsible party government, "Toward a More Responsible Two-Party System: A Report of the Committee on Political Parties," *American Political Science Review* 44, no. 3 (1950): supplement, http://www.apsanet.org/~pop/APSA_Report.htm#REPORT, among many others.

7. See Wendy Schiller, *Partners and Rivals: Representation in U.S. Senate Delegations* (Princeton: Princeton University Press, 2000).

8. David Mayhew, *Congress: The Electoral Connection* (New Haven: Yale University Press, 1974); Richard Fenno, *Home Style* (Boston: Little Brown, 1978); Bruce Cain, John Ferejohn, and Morris Fiorina, *The Personal Vote* (Cambridge: Harvard University Press, 1987), among many others.

9. Sinclair's recent narrative of these trends, *Party Wars*, offers a coherent summary of the politics of this era, largely, but not exclusively, from a legislative point of view.

10. Cox and McCubbins, *Setting the Agenda*.

11. See E. Scott Adler and John S. Lapinksi, eds., *The Macropolitics of Congress* (Princeton: Princeton University Press, 2006), for a selection of articles that examine representation writ large in the context of overall congressional performance.

12. Nicholas Confessore, "Welcome to the Machine," *Washington Monthly*, July/August 2003, http://www.washingtonmonthly.com/features/2003/0307.confessore.html. Emphasis added.

13. Sinclair, *Party Wars*, 308–309.

14. See Confessore, "Welcome to the Machine"; Sinclair, *Party Wars*, 312ff.; Jeffrey H. Birnbaum, "A Quiet Revolution in Business Lobbying," *Washington Post*, February 5, 2005, sec. A.

15. Sinclair, *Party Wars*, 321.

16. See, for example, Burdett A. Loomis and Allan J. Cigler, "The Changing Nature of Interest Group Politics," in *Interest Group Politics*, 6th ed., ed. Allan J. Cigler and Burdett A. Loomis (Washington, D.C.: CQ Press, 2002), 1–33; Mark J. Rozell and Clyde Wilcox, *Interest Groups in American Campaigns: The New Face of Electioneering* (Washington, D.C.: CQ Press, 1999).

17. Byron Shafer, *Quiet Revolution* (New York: Russell Sage Foundation, 1983).

18. Byron Shafer, *Bifurcated Politics* (Cambridge: Harvard University Press, 1989), 110.

19. James W. Caesar, "Political Parties—Declining, Stabilizing or Resurging?" in *The New American Political System*, 2d ed., ed. Anthony King (Washington, D.C.: American Enterprise Institute, 1990), 110.

20. Harold W. Stanley and Richard J. Niemi, *Vital Statistics on American Politics, 2005–2006* (Washington, D.C.: CQ Press, October 2005).

21. David B. Magleby and Candice Nelson, *The Money Chase* (Washington, D.C.: Brookings Institution Press, 1990), 91.

22. Ibid., 102.

23. Larry Sabato, *PAC Power* (New York: Norton, 1995), 150–151.

24. Ibid., 151.

25. To be fair, NCPAC did go out of business in the 1980s owing to its inability to raise sufficient funds to meets its high costs of operation.

26. Sabato, *PAC Power*, 151.

27. See, for example, Paul Herrnson, *Party Campaigning in the 1980s* (Cambridge: Harvard University Press, 1998); Xandra Kayden, "Alive and Well and Living in Washington,

D.C.: The American Political Parties," in *Manipulating Public Opinion*, ed. Michael Margolis and Gary Mauser (Pacific Grove, Calif.: Brooks/Cole, 1989), 114–136.

28. Marianne Holt, "The Surge in Party Money in Competitive 1998 Congressional Elections," in *Outside Money*, ed. David B. Magleby (Lanham, Md.: Rowman and Littlefield), 19.

29. Diana Dwyre and Robin Kolodny, "Throwing Out the Rule Book: Party Financing in the 2000 Election," in *Financing the 2000 Election*, ed. David B. Magleby (Washington, D.C.: Brookings Institution Press, 2002), 133–162.

30. Allan J. Cigler, "Issue Advocacy Electioneering: The Role of Money and Organized Interests," in *Law and Election Politics*, ed. Mathew J. Streb (Boulder: Lynne Rienner Publishers, 2005), 59–76.

31. David B. Magleby, *Dictum without Data: The Myth of Issue Advocacy and Party Building* (Provo, Utah: Brigham Young University, Center for the Study of Elections and Democracy, n.d.). For television ads in particular, see Craig B. Holman and Luke P. McLouglin, *Buying Time: Television Advertising in the 2000 Federal Election* (New York: Brennan Center for Justice at the New York University School of Law, 2001).

32. Candice Nelson, "Spending in the 2000 Elections," in Magleby, *Financing the 2000 Election*, 27.

33. Paul S. Herrnson, "Parties and Interest Groups in Postreform Congressional Elections," in *Interest Group Politics*, 5th ed., ed. Allan J. Cigler and Burdett A. Loomis (Washington, D.C.: CQ Press, 1998), 145–168.

34. Clyde Wilcox and Wesley Joe, "Dead Law: The Federal Election Finance Regulations, 1974–1996," *PS: Political Science and Politics* 31 (March 1998), 15.

35. Jonathan D. Salant, "Cancer Group Gave to GOP, Democrats," *Kansas City Star*, March 30, 1998, sec. A.

36. James L. Guth et al., "Thunder on the Right? Religious Mobilization in the 1996 Election," in *Interest Group Politics*, 5th ed., ed. Cigler and Loomis, 169–192.

37. John Persinos, "Has the Christian Right Taken Over the Republican Party?" *Campaigns and Elections* (September 1994): 20–24.

38. Allan J. Cigler, "Interest Groups and Financing the 2000 Election," in *Financing the 2000 Election*, ed. Magleby, 180–181; David B. Magleby, "Election Advocacy: Soft Money and Issue Advocacy in the 2000 Election," in *Election Advocacy: Soft Money and Issue Advocacy in the 2000 Congressional Election*, ed. David B. Magleby (Provo, Utah: Brigham Young University, Center for the Study of Elections and Democracy, 2000), 39.

39. Erika Falk, "Issue Advocacy Advertising through the Presidential Primary and 1999–2000 Election Cycle," Annenberg Public Policy Center of the University of Pennsylvania, press release, Sept. 20, 2000.

40. Allan J. Cigler, "Enron, a Perceived Crisis in Public Confidence, and the Bipartisan Campaign Reform Act of 2002," *Review of Policy Research* 21 (March 2004): 233–252.

41. For a review of the major provisions of BCRA, see Michael J. Malbin, "Thinking About Reform," in *Life After Reform*, ed. Michael J. Malbin (Lanham, Md.: Rowman and Littlefield, 2003), 3–20.

42. Ibid., 249.

43. Michael M. Franz, Joel Rivlin, and Kenneth Goldstein, "Much More of the Same: Television Advertising Pre- and Post-BCRA," in *The Election After Reform*, ed. Michael Malbin (Lanham, Md.: Rowman and Littlefield, 2006), 13.

44. Allan J. Cigler, "Interest Groups and Financing the 2004 Election," in *Financing the 2004 Election*, ed. David Magleby, Anthony Corrado, and Kelly D. Patterson (Washington, D.C.: Brookings Institution Press, 2006), especially 222–234.

45. See Harvard University, Institute of Politics, *Campaign for President: The Managers Look at 2004* (Lanham, Md.: Rowman and Littlefield , 2006), 212.

46. Cigler, "Interest Groups and Financing the 2004 Election," 229.

47. Harvard University, *Campaign for President*, 213.
48. "Republican-Funded Group Attacks Kerry's War Record," August 6, 2004, http://www.factcheck.org/article231.html.
49. David Broder, "Partisan Clout," *Kansas City Star*, March 15, 2005, sec. B; and Cigler, "Interest Groups and Financing the 2004 Election," 226.
50. Michael Janofsky, "Advocacy Groups Spent Record Amount on 2004 Election," *New York Times*, December 17, 2004, sec. A.
51. Perhaps most concisely articulated in John H. Aldrich and David W. Rohde, "The Logic of Conditional Party Government: Revisiting the Electoral Connection," in *Congress Reconsidered*, 7th ed., Lawrence Dodd and Bruce I. Oppenheimer (Washington, D.C.: CQ Press, 2001).
52. Owens, "American-Style Party Government."
53. Confessore, "Welcome to the Machine"; Hans Nichols, "K Street Freezes Out Dems," *The Hill*, September 15, 2004.
54. Richard L. Hall and Alan V. Deardorff, "Lobbying as Legislative Subsidy," *American Political Science Review* 100, no. 1 (February 2006): 69.
55. Owens, "American-Style Party Government."
56. Kristin Jensen, Mike Forsythe, and Jonathan Salant, "DeLay's Former Aides Building Lobbying Empires in Washington," Bloomberg News Service, April 6, 2005, accessed at http://quote.bloomberg.com/apps/news?pid=nifea&&sid=at9zpiR3e9vo#.
57. Quoted in Louis Jacobson, "Lobbying: The DeLay Factor on K Street," *National Journal*, January 4, 2003.
58. See Bara Vaida, Eliza Newlin Carney, and Lisa Caruso, "Potholes on K Street," *National Journal*, March 24, 2006.
59. Sinclair, *Party Wars*, chap. 9, calls the polarized coalitions "armed camps"; see also Birnbaum, " Quiet Revolution in Business Lobbying."
60. Jeffrey H. Birnbaum, "Democrats' Stock Is Rising on K Street," *Washington Post*, August 17, 2006, sec. A.
61. Ibid.
62. See Burdett Loomis, "Does K Street Run through Capitol Hill?" (paper presented at the meetings of the Midwest Political Science Association, Chicago, April 19–22, 2006).
63. See Virginia Gray and David Lowery, *The Population Ecology of Interest Representation* (Ann Arbor: University of Michigan Press, 1996).
64. Michael T. Heaney, "Identity Crisis: How Interest Groups Struggle to Define Themselves in Washington," in chap. 12 of this volume.
65. Matt Grossman, "Institutionalized Pluralism: Advocacy Organization Involvement in National Policymaking," University of California–Berkeley, unpublished manuscript.
66. In *The Semisovereign People: A Realist's View of Democracy in America*, rev. ed. (Hinsdale, Ill.: Dryden Press, 1975), E. E. Schattschneider entitles his third chapter, "Whose Game Do We Play?" arguing that parties will structure the political game more than organized interests (even in the weak-party era of the 1950s and 1960s).
67. Schattschneider, *The Semisovereign People*.
68. Ibid., 42.
69. Sinclair, *Party Wars*, 184.

Index

Note: page numbers followed by *f, t, b,* or n refer to
figures, tables, boxes, and endnotes, respectively.

H

I